McGraw-Hill's
HOMEWORK MANAGER **PLUS**™  onli

THE COMPLETE SOLUTION

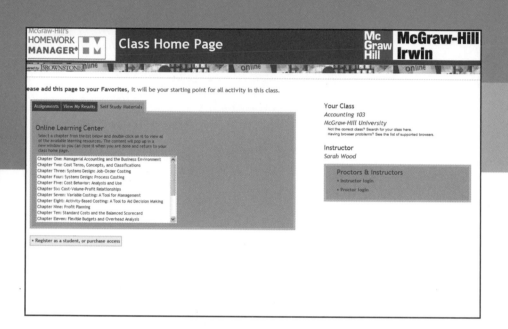

McGraw-Hill's
Homework Manager®

This online homework management solution contains the textbook's end-of-chapter material. Now you have the option to build assignments from static and algorithmic versions of the text problems and exercises or to build self-graded quizzes from the additional questions provided in the online test bank.

Features:

- Assigns book-specific problems/exercises to students

- Provides integrated test bank questions for quizzes and tests

- Automatically grades assignments and quizzes, storing results in one grade book

- Dispenses immediate feedback to students regarding their work

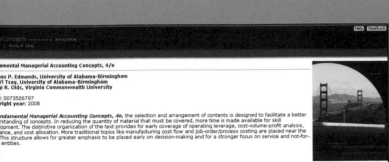

Fundamental Managerial Accounting Concepts, 4/e

Thomas P. Edmonds, University of Alabama-Birmingham
Bor-Yi Tsay, University of Alabama-Birmingham
Philip R. Olds, Virginia Commonwealth University

ISBN: 0073526797
Copyright year: 2008

Fundamental Managerial Accounting Concepts, 4e, the selection and arrangement of contents is designed to facilitate a better understanding of concepts. In reducing the quantity of material that must be covered, more time is made available for skill development. The distinctive organization of the text provides for early coverage of operating leverage, cost-volume-profit analysis, relevance, and cost allocation. More traditional topics like manufacturing cost flow and job-order/process costing are placed near the end. This structure allows for greater emphasis to be placed early on decision-making and for a stronger focus on service and not-for-profit entities.

To obtain an instructor login for this Online Learning Center, ask your local sales representative. If you're an instructor thinking about adopting this textbook, request a free copy for review.

Interactive Online Version
of the Textbook

In addition to the textbook, students can rely on this online version of the text for a convenient way to study. The interactive content is fully integrated with McGraw-Hill's Homework Manager® to give students quick access to relevant content as they work through problems, exercises, and practice quizzes.

Features:
- Online version of the text integrated with McGraw-Hill's Homework Manager

- Students referred to appropriate sections of the online book as they complete an assignment or take a practice quiz

- Direct link to related material that corresponds with the learning objective within the text

Edmonds
Fundamental Managerial
Accounting Concepts, 4e
978-0-07-322090-1

1 TERM

McGraw-Hill's Homework Manager Plus™ combines the power of McGraw-Hill's Homework Manager® with the latest interactive learning technology to create a comprehensive, fully integrated online study package. Students working on assignments in McGraw-Hill's Homework Manager can click a simple hotlink and instantly review the appropriate material in the Interactive Online Textbook.

By including McGraw-Hill's Homework Manager Plus with your textbook adoption, you're giving your students a vital edge as they progress through the course and ensuring that the help they need is never more than a mouse click away. Contact your McGraw-Hill representative or visit the book's Web site to learn how to add McGraw-Hill's Homework Manager Plus to your adoption.

McGraw-Hill's
HOMEWORK MANAGER®

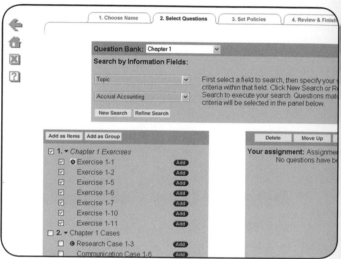

MANAGE YOUR CLASS.

Control how content is presented.

McGraw-Hill's Homework Manager® gives you a flexible and easy way to present course work to students. You determine which questions to ask and how much help students will receive as they work through assignments. You can determine the number of attempts a student can make with each problem or provide hints and feedback with each question. The questions can also be linked to an online version of the text for quick and simple reference while students complete an assignment.

Track student progress.

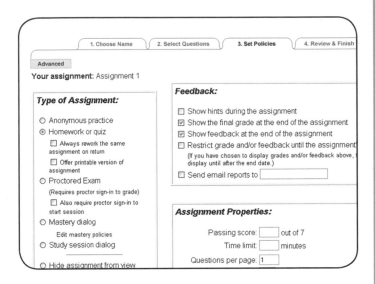

Assignments are graded automatically, with the results stored in your private grade book. Detailed results let you see at a glance how each student does on an assignment or an individual problem. You can even see how many attempts it took them to solve it. You can monitor how the whole class does on each problem and even determine where individual students might need extra help.

Immediately after finishing an assignment, students can compare their answers side-by-side with the detailed solutions. Students can try again with new numbers to see if they have mastered the concept.

Selected Chapters from

Fundamental
Managerial Accounting Concepts
4TH EDITION

Thomas P. Edmonds
University of Alabama–Birmingham

Bor-Yi Tsay
University of Alabama–Birmingham

Philip R. Olds
Virginia Commonwealth University

Managerial Accounting
ACC U301

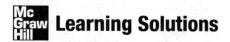
Learning Solutions

Boston   Burr Ridge, IL   Dubuque, IA   New York   San Francisco   St. Louis
Bangkok   Bogotá   Caracas   Lisbon   London   Madrid
Mexico City   Milan   New Delhi   Seoul   Singapore   Sydney   Taipei   Toronto

The McGraw·Hill Companies

Selected Chapters from
Fundamental Managerial Accounting Concepts, 4TH EDITION
Managerial Accounting ACC U301

This book is a McGraw-Hill Learning Solutions textbook and contains select material from *Fundamental Managerial Accounting Concepts*, Fourth Edition by Thomas P. Edmonds, Bor-Yi Tsay, and Philip R. Olds. Copyright © 2008 by The McGraw-Hill Companies, Inc. Reprinted with permission of the publisher. Many custom published texts are modified versions or adaptations of our best-selling textbooks. Some adaptations are printed in black and white to keep prices at a minimum, while others are in color.

567890 DIG DIG 09876

ISBN-13: 978-0-07-335261-9
ISBN-10: 0-07-335261-6

Editor: Bridget Iverson
Production Editor: Susan Culbertson
Printer/Binder: Digital Impressions

This book is dedicated to our students whose questions have so frequently caused us to reevaluate our method of presentation that they have, in fact, become major contributors to the development of this text.

NOTE FROM THE AUTHORS

Our goal in writing this text is to teach students managerial accounting concepts that will improve their ability to make sound business decisions. The text differs from traditional managerial accounting books in the following respects.

We emphasize the development of decision making skills.

Notice that the table of contents places decision making up front. Procedural topics like manufacturing cost flow, job-order, and process costing are placed at the end of our text while traditional books discuss these topics early. We put decision making front and center because we believe it is important. Beyond placement we introduce topics within a decision-making context. For example, in Chapter 2 we introduce "cost behavior" within the context of operating leverage. We focus on how cost behavior affects decisions such as "am I sure enough that volume will be high that I want to employ a fixed cost structure or do I want to reduce operating leverage risk by building a variable cost structure?" Further, notice that Chapter 3 is written around a realistic business scenario where a management team is using CVP data to evaluate decision alternatives. Indeed, all chapters are written in a narrative style with content focused on decision-making scenarios. This makes the text easy to read and interesting as well as informative.

We employ a step-wise learning model.

We believe students learn better if concepts are isolated and introduced progressively in a step-wise fashion. For example, understanding cost behavior is essential to comprehending the need for allocation and an understanding of allocation is essential for comprehending the concept of relevance. Likewise, understanding cost behavior and allocation is critical to comprehending the purpose and function of the manufacturing overhead account. This step-wise learning approach also explains the way chapters are arranged in the text. We provide thorough coverage of basic concepts before students are expected to use those concepts. Traditional texts fail to recognize the importance of this learning principle.

We place greater emphasis on service companies.

For example, our budgeting chapter uses a merchandising business while most traditional texts use a manufacturing company. Using a service company is not only more relevant but also simplifies the learning environment thereby making it easier for students to focus on budgeting concepts rather than procedural details. This is only one example of our efforts to place greater emphasis on service companies.

We provide extensive coverage of corporate governance.

The accounting scandals of Enron, MCI WorldCom, HealthSouth, and others led to the enactment of the Sarbanes-Oxley Act (SOX). SOX places significant pressure on managerial accountants to identify and eliminate fraudulent reporting. This text not only provides coverage of appropriate content but also provides a framework for emphasizing ethics throughout the text. We encourage you to review the content on pages 19 through 23 in Chapter 1. Further, look at Exercises 16 and 17, and Problem 26 to see how students are challenged to apply the new content. Also, notice that a corporate governance case is included in the Analyze, Think, and Communicate (ATC) section of end-of-chapter materials for every chapter in the text. Specifically, look at ATC Problem 5 in each chapter.

Tom Edmonds • Bor-Yi Tsay • Phil Olds

ATC 1-5 Ethical Dilemma *Product cost versus selling and administrative expense*

Eddie Emerson is a proud woman with a problem. Her daughter has been accepted into a prestigious law school. While Ms. Emerson beams with pride, she is worried sick about how to pay for the school; she is a single parent who has worked hard to support herself and her three children. She had to go heavily into debt to finance her own education. Even though she now has a good job, family needs have continued to outpace her income and her debt burden is staggering. She knows she will be unable to borrow the money needed for her daughter's law school.

Ms. Emerson is the Chief Financial Officer (CFO) of a small manufacturing company. She has just accepted a new job offer. Indeed, she has not yet told her employer that she will be leaving in a month. She is concerned that her year-end incentive bonus may be affected if her boss learns of her plans to

---

Thomas P. Edmonds

Thomas P. Edmonds, Ph.D., holds the Friends and Alumni Professorship in the Department of Accounting at the University of Alabama at Birmingham (UAB). He has been actively involved in teaching accounting principles throughout his academic career. Dr. Edmonds has coordinated the accounting principles courses at the University of Houston and UAB. He currently teaches introductory accounting in mass sections and in UAB's distance learning program. He has received five prestigious teaching awards including the Alabama Society of CPAs Outstanding Educator Award, the UAB President's Excellence in Teaching Award, and the distinguished Ellen Gregg Ingalls Award for excellence in classroom teaching. He has written numerous articles that have appeared in many publications including *Issues in Accounting*, the *Journal of Accounting Education*, *Advances in Accounting Education*, *Accounting Education: A Journal of Theory, Practice and Research,* the *Accounting Review*, *Advances in Accounting,* the *Journal of Accountancy*, *Management Accounting*, the *Journal of Commercial Bank Lending*, the *Banker's Magazine*, and the *Journal of Accounting, Auditing, and Finance.* Dr. Edmonds is a member of the editorial board for *Advances in Accounting: Teaching and Curriculum Innovations* and *Issues in Accounting Education.* He has published four textbooks, five practice problems (including two computerized problems), and a variety of supplemental materials including study guides, work papers, and solutions manuals. Dr. Edmonds's writing is influenced by a wide range of business experience. He is a successful entrepreneur. He has worked as a management accountant for Refrigerated Transport, a trucking company. Dr. Edmonds also worked in the not-for-profit sector as a commercial lending officer for the Federal Home Loan Bank. In addition, he has acted as a consultant to major corporations including First City Bank of Houston, AmSouth Bank in Birmingham, Texaco, and Cortland Chemicals. Dr. Edmonds began his academic training at Young Harris Community College in Young Harris, Georgia. He received a B.B.A. degree with a major in finance from Georgia State University in Atlanta, Georgia. He obtained an M.B.A. degree with a concentration in finance from St. Mary's University in San Antonio, Texas. His Ph.D. degree with a major in accounting was awarded by Georgia State University. Dr. Edmonds's work experience and academic training have enabled him to bring a unique user perspective to this textbook.

AUTHORS

Bor-Yi Tsay

Bor-Yi Tsay, Ph.D., CPA is Professor of Accounting at the University of Alabama at Birmingham (UAB) where he has taught since 1986. He has taught principles of accounting courses at the University of Houston and UAB. Currently, he teaches an undergraduate cost accounting course and an MBA accounting analysis course. Dr. Tsay received the 1996 Loudell Ellis Robinson Excellence in Teaching Award. He has also received numerous awards for his writing and publications including John L. Rhoads Manuscripts Award, John Pugsley Manuscripts Award, Van Pelt Manuscripts Award, and three certificates of merits from the Institute of Management Accountants. His articles appeared in *Journal of Accounting Education, Management Accounting, Journal of Managerial Issues, CPA Journal, CMA Magazine, Journal of Systems Management,* and *Journal of Medical Systems.* He currently serves as a member of the board of the Birmingham Chapter, Institute of Management Accountants. He is also a member of the American Institute of Certified Public Accountants and Alabama Society of Certified Public Accountants. Dr. Tsay received a B.S. in agricultural economics from National Taiwan University, an M.B.A. with a concentration in accounting from Eastern Washington University, and a Ph.D. in accounting from the University of Houston.

Philip R. Olds

Professor Olds is Associate Professor of Accounting at Virginia Commonwealth University (VCU). He serves as the coordinator of the introduction to accounting courses at VCU. Professor Olds received his A.S. degree from Brunswick Junior College in Brunswick, Georgia (now Costal Georgia Community College). He received a B.B.A. in accounting from Georgia Southern College (now Georgia Southern University) and his M.P.A. and Ph.D. degrees are from Georgia State University. After graduating from Georgia Southern, he worked as an auditor with the U.S. Department of Labor in Atlanta, Georgia. A CPA in Virginia, Professor Olds has published articles in various professional journals and presented papers at national and regional conferences. He also served as the faculty adviser to the VCU chapter of Beta Alpha Psi for five years. In 1989, he was recognized with an Outstanding Faculty Vice-President Award by the national Beta Alpha Psi organization.

HOW DOES THE BOOK HELP

STUDENTS SEE THE BIG PICTURE?

"I think Edmonds' approach to introducing concepts, and his flow of topics is the best of any accounting textbook I have used. His approach allows me to emphasis a piece of the puzzle at a time building to the whole picture."
**Gary Reynolds,
Ozark Technical
Community College**

"This is a balanced text, with concise topics that can all be covered in a single semester."
**Charles Russo,
Bloomsburg College of
Pennsyvania**

PRINCIPAL FEATURES

Isolating Concepts

How do you promote student understanding of concepts? We believe new concepts should be isolated and introduced individually in decision-making contexts. For example, we do not include a chapter covering cost terminology (usually Chapter 2 in traditional approaches). We believe introducing a plethora of detached cost terms in a single chapter is ineffective. Students have no conceptual framework for the new vocabulary.

Interrelationships between Concepts

Although introducing concepts in isolation enhances student comprehension of them, students must ultimately understand how business concepts interrelate. The text is designed to build knowledge progressively, leading students to integrate the concepts they have learned independently. For example, see how the concept of relevance is compared on page 195 of Chapter 5 to the concept of cost behavior (which is explained in Chapter 2) and how the definitions of direct costs are contrasted on page 148 of Chapter 4 with the earlier introduced concepts of cost behavior. Also, Chapters 1 through 12 include a comprehensive problem designed to integrate concepts across chapters. The problem builds in each successive chapter with the same company experiencing new conditions that require the application of concepts across chapter.

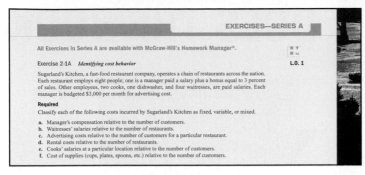

Context-Sensitive Nature of Terminology

Students can be confused when they discover the exact same cost can be classified as fixed, variable, direct, indirect, relevant, or not relevant. For example, the cost of a store manager's salary is fixed regardless of the number of customers that shop in the store. The cost of store manager salaries, however, is variable relative to the number of stores a company operates. The salary costs are directly traceable to particular stores but not to particular sales made in a store. The salary cost is relevant when deciding whether to eliminate a given store but not relevant to deciding whether to eliminate a department within a store. Students must learn to identify the circumstances that determine the classification of costs. The chapter material, exercises, and problems in this text are designed to encourage students to analyze the decision-making context rather than to memorize definitions. Exercise 2-1A in Chapter 2 illustrates how the text teaches students to interpret different decision-making environments.

Corporate Governance

Accountants have always recognized the importance of ethical conduct. However, the enactment of Sarbanes-Oxley (SOX) has signaled the need for educators to expand the subject of ethics to a broader concept of corporate governance. We focus our expanded coverage on four specific areas including:

- Quality of Earnings—We explain how financial statements can be manipulated.
- Standards of Ethical Conduct for Management Accountants—Our coverage focuses on the policies and practices promulgated by the Institute of Management Accountants.
- The Fraud Triangle—We discuss the three common features of criminal and ethical misconduct including opportunity, pressure, and rationalization.
- Specified Features of Sarbanes-Oxley (SOX)—We cover four key provisions of SOX that that are applicable to managerial accountants.

Corporate governance is introduced in Chapter 1. This chapter includes four exercises, two problems, and one case that relate to the subject. Thereafter a corporate governance case is included in every chapter, thereby enabling continuing coverage of this critically important topic.

"I believe the Excel templates are a very strong asset for the text as they introduce the students to the skills needed to design spreadsheets to solve business problems."
John Sneed, Jacksonville State University

Information Overload

The table of contents reflects our efforts to address the information overload problem. We believe existing managerial textbooks include significantly more material than can be digested by the typical managerial accounting student. In contrast with traditional texts that normally have between 18 and 20 chapters, we have limited this text to 14 chapters.

Excel Spreadsheets

Spreadsheet applications are essential to contemporary accounting practice. Students must recognize the power of spreadsheet software and know how accounting data are presented in spreadsheets. We discuss Microsoft Excel spreadsheet applications where appropriate throughout the text. In most instances, the text illustrates actual spreadsheets. End-of-chapter materials include problems students can complete using spreadsheet software. A sample of the logo used to identify problems suitable for Excel spreadsheet solutions is shown here.

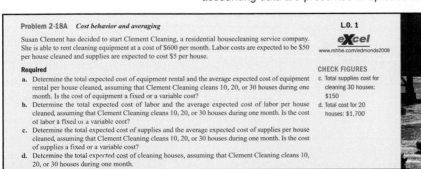

Real World Examples

The Edmonds' text provides a variety of thought-provoking, real-world examples of managerial accounting as an essential part of the management process.

The Curious Accountant

Each chapter opens with a short vignette that sets the stage and helps pique student interest. These vignettes pose a question about a real-world accounting issue related to the topic of the chapter. The answer to the question appears in a separate sidebar a few pages further into the chapter.

Focus on International Issues

These boxed inserts expose students to international issues in accounting.

Check Yourself

These short question/answer features occur at the end of each main topic and ask students to stop and think about the material just covered. The answer follows to provide immediate feedback before students go on to a new topic.

The Curious Accountant

News flash! On January 31, 2006, Google announced that its fourth-quarter earnings would be up 82 percent over the same quarter of 2005, yet its revenues were up only 23 percent.

On February 10, 2006, Volkswagen reported that while its 2005 revenues were 7.1 percent higher than in 2004, its earnings increased 61 percent. Also in February 2006, Tommy Hilfiger reported that for the quarter ending on December 1, 2005, its revenue fell 7.9 percent, compared to the same period in 2004, but its earnings fell 23 percent.

Can you explain why such relatively small changes in these companies' revenues resulted in such relatively large changes in their earnings or losses? In other words, if a company's sales increase 10 percent, why do its earnings not also increase 10 percent? (Answer on page …)

---

60   Chapter 2

Answers to The Curious Accountant

The explanation for how a company's earnings can rise faster, as a percentage, than its revenue rises is operating leverage, and operating leverage is due entirely to fixed costs. As the chapter explained, when a company's output goes up, its fixed cost per unit goes down. As long as it can keep prices about the same, this lower unit cost will result in higher profit per unit sold. In real world companies, the relationship between changing sales levels and changing earnings levels can be very complex, but the existence of fixed costs helps to explain why a 7 percent rise in revenue can cause a 61 percent rise in net earnings. Chapter 3 will investigate the relationships among an entity's cost structure, output level, pricing strategy, and profits earned in more depth.

FOCUS ON   INTERNATIONAL ISSUES

FINANCIAL ACCOUNTING VERSUS MANAGERIAL ACCOUNTING—AN INTERNATIONAL PERSPECTIVE

This chapter has already explained some of the conceptual differences between financial and managerial accounting, but these differences have implications for international businesses as well. With respect to financial accounting, publicly traded companies in most countries must follow the generally accepted accounting principles (GAAP) for their country, but these rules can vary from country to country. Only companies that are audited under the auditing standards of the United States have to follow the standards established by the Financial Accounting Standards Board. European companies follow the standards established by the International Accounting Standards Board. For example, the United States is one of very few countries whose GAAP allow the use of the LIFO inventory flow assumption.

Conversely, most of the managerial accounting concepts introduced in this course can be used by businesses in any country. For example, *activity-based costing (ABC)* in a topic addressed in Chapter 6, and it is used by many companies in the United States. Meanwhile, a study published in *Accountancy Ireland** found that approximately one-third of the companies surveyed in Ireland, the United Kingdom, and New Zealand are also either currently using ABC, or are considering adopting it.

he Irish Experience: True Innovation or Passing Fad?" *Accountancy Ireland*, October 2004, pp. 28-31.

CHECK YOURSELF 1.3

The cost of making a Burger King hamburger includes the cost of materials, labor, and overhead. Does this mean that Burger King is a manufacturing company?

Answer

No, Burger King is not a manufacturing company. It is a service company because its products are consumed immediately. In contrast, there may be a considerable delay between the time the product of a manufacturing company is made and the time it is consumed. For example, it could be several months between the time Ford Motor Company makes an Explorer and the time the Explorer is ultimately sold to a customer. The primary difference between service and manufacturing companies is that manufacturing companies have inventories of products and service companies do not.

"(Check Yourself) not only gives the student a chance to check his/her understanding of the topic, but it highlights and identifies the important concepts in each chapter."
Mark Kaiser, SUNY at Plattsburg

MOTIVATE STUDENTS?

Name and Type of Company Used as Main Chapter Example

Chapter Title	Company Used as Main Chapter Example	Company Logo	Type of Company
1. Management Accounting: A Value-Added Discipline	Patillo Manufacturing Company	PATILLO	Manufactures wooden tables
2. Cost Behavior, Operating Leverage, and Profitability Analysis	Star Productions, Inc. (SPI)	★	Promotes rock concerts
3. Analysis of Cost, Volume, and Pricing to Increase Profitability	Bright Day Distributors		Sells nonprescription health food supplements
4. Relevant Information for Special Decisions	Premier Office Products		Manufactures printers
5. Cost Accumulation, Tracing, and Allocation	In Style, Inc. (ISI)	STYLE	Retail clothing store
6. Cost Management in an Automated Business Environment: ABC, ABM, and TQM	Carver Soup Company (CSP)		Produces vegetable and tomato soup

Reality Bytes

Real-world applications related to specific chapter topics are introduced through *Reality Bytes*. Reality Bytes may offer survey results, graphics, quotations from business leaders, and other supplemental topics that enhance opportunities for students to connect the text material to actual accounting practice.

Chapter Focus Company

Each chapter introduces important managerial accounting topics within the context of a realistic company. Students see the impact of managerial accounting decisions on the company as they work through the chapter. When the Focus Company is presented in the chapter, its logo is shown so the students see its application to the text topics.

◀◀ A Look Back

Managers need to know the costs of products, processes, departments, activities, and so on. The target for which accountants attempt to determine cost is a *cost object.* Knowing the cost of specific objects enables management to control costs, evaluate performance, and price products. *Direct costs* can be cost-effectively traced to a cost object. *Indirect costs* cannot be easily traced to designated cost objects.

The same cost can be direct or indirect, depending on the cost object to which it is traced. For example, the salary of a Burger King restaurant manager can be directly traced to a particular store but cannot be traced to particular food items made and sold in the store. Classifying a cost as direct or indirect is independent of whether the cost behaves as fixed or variable; it is also independent of whether the cost is relevant to a given decision. A direct cost could be either fixed or variable or either relevant or irrelevant, depending on the context and the designated cost object.

A Look Forward ▶▶

The next chapter introduces the concept of *cost relevance.* Applying the concepts you have learned to real-world business problems can be challenging. Frequently, so much data is available that it is difficult to distinguish important from useless information. The next chapter will help you learn to identify information that is relevant in a variety of short-term decision-making scenarios including special offers, outsourcing, segment elimination, and asset replacement.

A Look Back/A Look Forward

Students need a roadmap to make sense of where the chapter topics fit into the "whole" picture. A Look Back reviews the chapter material and a Look Forward introduces students to what is to come.

"I like the book a great deal. I especially like how the text opens with an interesting 'big picture' question, covers more detailed information in the middle, then goes back to the 'big picture' (in more detail) at the end."
Steve Buccheit, Texas Tech University

"By following one company through several situations as the chapter progresses, more of a 'real world' decision-making process is obtained."
Aleecia Hibbets, University of Louisiana at Monroe

Regardless of the instructional approach, there is no shortcut to learning accounting. Students must practice to master basic accounting concepts. The text includes a prodigious supply of practice materials and exercises and problems.

Self-Study Review Problem

These representative example problems include a detailed, worked-out solution and provide another level of support for students before they work problems on their own. These review problems are included on the Topic Tackler Plus in an **animated audio presentation.**

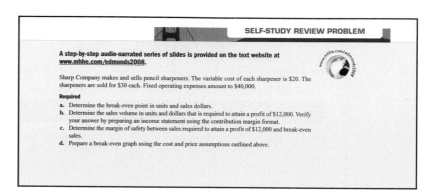

Exercise Series A & B and Problem Series A & B

There are two sets of problems and exercises, Series A and B. Instructors can assign one set for homework and another set for class work.

• Check figures

The figures provide a quick reference for students to check on their progress in solving the problem. These are included for all problems in Series A.

• Excel

Many exercises and problems can be solved using the Excel™ spreadsheet templates contained on the text's Online Learning Center. A logo appears in the margins next to these exercises and problems for easy identification.

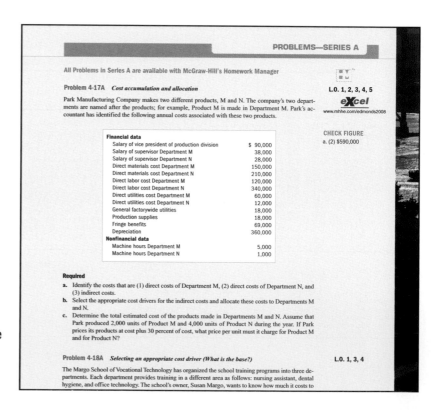

CONCEPTS REINFORCED?

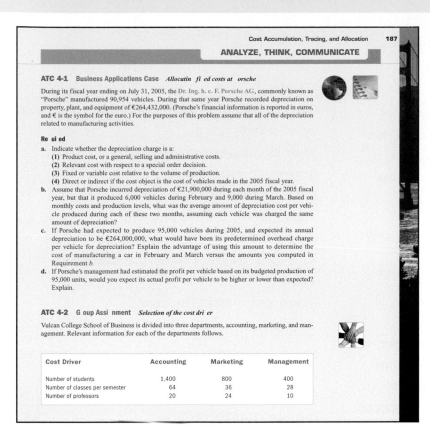

ANALYZE, THINK, COMMUNICATE

ATC 4-1   Business Applications Case   *Allocating fixed costs at Porsche*

During its fiscal year ending on July 31, 2005, the Dr. Ing. h. c. F. Porsche AG, commonly known as "Porsche" manufactured 90,954 vehicles. During that same year Porsche recorded depreciation on property, plant, and equipment of €264,432,000. (Porsche's financial information is reported in euros, and € is the symbol for the euro.) For the purposes of this problem assume that all of the depreciation related to manufacturing activities.

Required

a. Indicate whether the depreciation charge is a:
   (1) Product cost, or a general, selling and administrative costs.
   (2) Relevant cost with respect to a special order decision.
   (3) Fixed or variable cost relative to the volume of production.
   (4) Direct or indirect if the cost object is the cost of vehicles made in the 2005 fiscal year.
b. Assume that Porsche incurred depreciation of €21,900,000 during each month of the 2005 fiscal year, but that it produced 6,000 vehicles during February and 9,000 during March. Based on monthly costs and production levels, what was the average amount of depreciation cost per vehicle produced during each of these two months, assuming each vehicle was charged the same amount of depreciation?
c. If Porsche had expected to produce 95,000 vehicles during 2005, and expected its annual depreciation to be €264,000,000, what would have been its predetermined overhead charge per vehicle for depreciation? Explain the advantage of using this amount to determine the cost of manufacturing a car in February and March versus the amounts you computed in Requirement b.
d. If Porsche's management had estimated the profit per vehicle based on its budgeted production of 95,000 units, would you expect its actual profit per vehicle to be higher or lower than expected? Explain.

ATC 4-2   Group Assignment   *Selection of the cost driver*

Vulcan College School of Business is divided into three departments, accounting, marketing, and management. Relevant information for each of the departments follows.

Cost Driver	Accounting	Marketing	Management
Number of students	1,400	800	400
Number of classes per semester	64	36	28
Number of professors	20	24	10

Analyze, Think, Communicate (ATC)

Each chapter includes an innovative section entitled Analyze, Think, Communicate (ATC). This section contains:

- Writing assignments

- Group exercises   • Ethics cases

- Internet assignments   • Real Company Examples

ATC 3-6   Spreadsheet Assignment   *Using Excel*

Bishop Company has provided the estimated data that appear in rows 4 to 8 of the following spreadsheet.

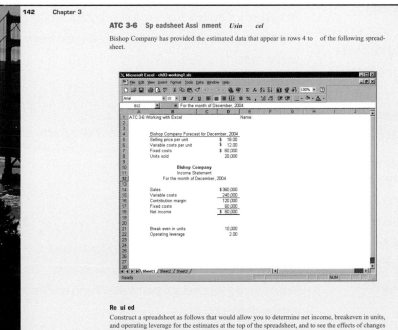

Required

Construct a spreadsheet as follows that would allow you to determine net income, breakeven in units, and operating leverage for the estimates at the top of the spreadsheet, and to see the effects of changes to the estimates. Set up this spreadsheet so that any change in the estimates will automatically be reflected in the calculation of net income, breakeven, and operating leverage.

Spreadsheet Tip

1. To center a heading across several columns, such as the Income Statement title, highlight the area to be centered (Columns B, C, and D), choose Format, then choose Cells, and click on the tab ti-

Mastering Excel and Using Excel

The Excel applications are used to make students comfortable with this analytical tool and to show its use in accounting.

"The innovative end-of-chapter materials are especially on target as an aid to improving student critical thinking and writing skills. The Excel spreadsheet applications are also excellent real-world activities."
Dan R. Ward,
University of Louisiana,
Lafayette

WHAT WE DID TO MAKE IT BETTER!

Accuracy

Accuracy is one of the most important aspects in writing a text because it impacts both instructors and students. Our goal this edition was to be precise and avoid errors wherever possible. To assure accuracy we employed a new error double-blind review process using top notch, professional error checkers.

What's New This Edition?

We thank our reviewers and focus group participants for their suggestions. Many of these suggestions motivated the changes described below:

Corporate Governance

Accountants have always recognized the importance of ethical conduct. However, the enactment of Sarbanes-Oxley (SOX) has signaled the need for educators to expand the subject of ethics to a broader concept of corporate governance. We focus our expanded coverage on four specific areas including:

- Quality of Earnings—We explain how financial statements can be manipulated.
- Standards of Ethical Conduct for Management Accountants—Our coverage focuses on the policies and practices promulgated by the Institute of Management Accountants.
- The Fraud Triangle—We discuss the three common features of criminal and ethical misconduct including opportunity, pressure, and rationalization.
- Specified Features of Sarbanes-Oxley (SOX)—We cover four key provisions of SOX that are applicable to managerial accountants. Corporate governance is introduced in Chapter 1. This chapter includes four exercises, two problems, and one case that relate to the subject. Thereafter a corporate governance case is included in every chapter, thereby enabling continuing coverage of this critically important topic.

Chapter 1

Revised learning objectives and strengthened their connection to text and end-of-chapter materials.

Revised the Curious Accountant opening with new high-profile companies and products (iPods).

Added a major section covering corporate governance. Related exercises, problems, and cases are provided.

Moved content related to emerging trends in accounting (TQM, activity-based management, and value chain analysis) to an appendix.

Updated exercises, problems, and cases.

Chapter 2

Revised learning objectives and strengthened their connection to text and end-of-chapter materials.

Revised the Curious Accountant opening with new high-profile companies and products (Google, Inc.).

Removed Exhibit 2-8 Cost Behavior and Revenue Relationships.

Reorganized text material to develop a more logical flow of content.

Added coverage of the regression method of estimating fixed and variable costs.

Updated exercises, problems, and cases.

Chapter 3

Revised learning objectives and strengthened their connection to text and end-of-chapter materials.

Centralized coverage of pricing strategy.

Updated exercises, problems, and cases.

Chapter 4

Reversed sequence of Chapters 4 and 5 to allow coverage of allocation before it is used in the discussion of relevance.

Revised learning objectives and strengthened their connection to text and end-of-chapter materials.

Revised the Curious Accountant opening with new high-profile companies.

Removed coverage of cost pools.

Updated exercises, problems, and cases.

Chapter 5

Reversed sequence of Chapters 4 and 5 to allow coverage of allocation before it is used in the discussion of relevance.

Revised learning objectives and strengthened their connection to text and end-of-chapter materials.

Reorganized text material to develop a more logical flow of content.

Replaced Focus on International Issues box with new scenario.

Updated exercises, problems, and cases.

Chapter 6

Revised learning objectives and strengthened their connection to text and end-of-chapter materials.

Updated exercises, problems, and cases.

Chapter 7

Updated exercises, problems, and cases.

Chapter 8

Revised learning objectives and strengthened their connection to text and end-of-chapter materials.

Revised the Curious Accountant opening with new high-profile companies and products.

Reorganized text material to develop a more logical flow of content.

Replaced Reality Bytes sidebar with new scenario.

Updated exercises, problems, and cases.

Chapter 9

Revised learning objectives and strengthened their connection to text and end-of-chapter materials.

Replaced Focus on International Issues box with new scenario.

Added content demonstrating that multiple ROIs and RIs are normally computed for different divisions and investment opportunities within the same company.

Updated exercises, problems, and cases and added new problems related to the calculation of multiple ROIs and RIs within the same company.

Chapter 10

Revised learning objectives and strengthened their connection to text and end-of-chapter materials.

Revised the Curious Accountant opening with new high-profile companies and products.

Updated Reality Bytes sidebar.

Updated exercises, problems, and cases.

Chapter 11

Revised learning objectives and strengthened their connection to text and end-of-chapter materials.

Updated exercises, problems, and cases.

Chapter 12

Revised learning objectives and strengthened their connection to text and end-of-chapter materials.

Revised the Curious Accountant opening with new high-profile companies and products.

Updated Reality Bytes sidebar.

Updated exercises, problems, and cases.

Chapter 13

Removed content related to the different graphical forms of displaying analytical data.

Updated exercises, problems, and cases.

Chapter 14

Revised the Curious Accountant opening with new high-profile companies and products.

HOW CAN TECHNOLOGY

Our technology resources help students and instructors focus on learning success. By using the Internet and multimedia students get book-specific help at their convenience. Compare our technology to that of any other books and we're confident you'll agree that **Fundamental Managerial Accounting Concepts** has the best in the market. Teaching aids make in-class presentations easy and stimulating. These aids give you more power than ever to teach your class the way you want.

McGraw-Hill's Homework Manager®

is a Web-based homework management system that gives you unparalleled power and flexibility in creating homework assignments, tests, and quizzes. McGraw-Hill's Homework Manager duplicates problem structures directly from the end-of-chapter material in your McGraw-Hill textbook, using algorithms to provide limitless variations of textbook problems. Use McGraw-Hill's Homework Manager to supply online self-graded practice for students, or create assignments and tests with unique versions of every problem: McGraw-Hill's Homework Manager can grade assignments automatically, provide instant feedback to students, and store all results in your private gradebook. Detailed results let you see at a glance how each student does and easily track the progress of every student in your course.

McGraw-Hill's Homework Manager Plus™

combines the power of McGraw-Hill's Homework Manager with the latest interactive learning technology to create a comprehensive, fully integrated online study package.

Students using McGraw-Hill's Homework Manager Plus can access not only McGraw-Hill's Homework Manager™ itself, but the Interactive Online Textbook as well. Far more than a textbook on a screen, this resource is completely integrated into McGraw-Hill's Homework Manager, allowing students working on assignments to click a hotlink and instantly review the appropriate material in the textbook.

By including McGraw-Hill's Homework Manager Plus with your textbook adoption, you're giving your students a vital edge as they progress through the course and ensuring that the help they need is never more than a mouse click away

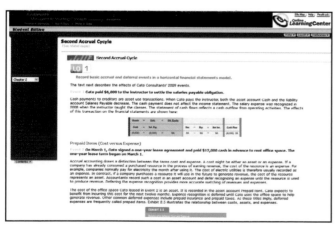

Interactive Online Version of the Textbook

In addition to the textbook, students can rely on this online version of the text for a convenient way to study. While other publishers offer a simple PDF, this interactive Web-based textbook contains hotlinks to key definitions and is integrated with McGraw-Hill's Homework Manager to give students quick access to relevant content as they work through problems, exercises, and practice quizzes.

HELP STUDENT SUCCESS?

iPod Content

Harness the power of one of the most popular technology tools students use today—the Apple iPod. Our innovative approach allows students to download audio and video presentations and quizzes for each chapter of this book right into their iPod and take learning materials with them wherever they go. It makes review and study time as easy as putting in headphones. Visit the Fundamental Managerial Accounting Concepts Online Learning Center to learn more details on available iPod content—and enhance your learning experience today.

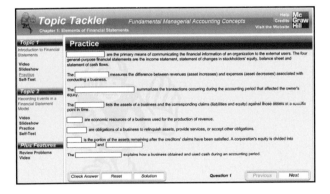

Topic Tackler Plus

Found on the text Online Learning Center, this software is a complete tutorial focusing on areas in the course that give students the most trouble. It provides help on two key topics for each chapter by use of

- Video clips
- PowerPoint slide shows
- Interactive exercises
- Self-grading quizzes

A logo in the text marks the topic given further coverage in Topic Tackler Plus. Topic Tackler Plus also includes the Self-Study Review Problem presented in an audio-narrated slide presentation, as well as a short video.

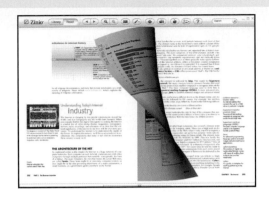

Zinio Digital Edition

A leader in digital media, Zinio offers students using Fundamental Managerial Accounting concepts the full benefit of its powerful, flexible digital reading system. Using the Zinio reader, you can search your digital textbook, highlight important passages, or jot down electronic notes. Navigating a textbook has never been easier. You can even print pages to study from off line. To order your Zinio Digital Edition visit www.textbooks.zinio.com

ALEKS

ALEKS for the Accounting Cycle
ALEKS for Financial Accounting

ALEKS (Assessment and Learning in Knowledge Spaces) provides precise assessment and individualized instruction in the fundamental skills your students need to succeed in accounting. ALEKS motivates your students because it can tell what a student knows, doesn't know, and is most ready to learn next. ALEKS uses an artificial intelligence engine to exactly identify a student's knowledge of accounting. To learn more about adding ALEKS to your accounting course, visit *www.business.aleks.com*.

> "We so often are asked by students what they can do to improve their performance in the course. Given all the support provided in Topic Tackler Plus, there is no excuse for a student who is willing to put the time into mastering the material."
> **Elliott Levy, Bentley College**

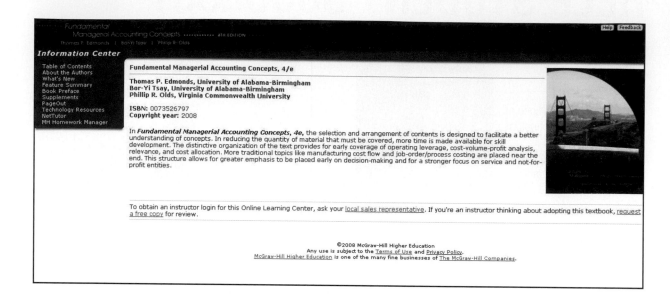

Online Learning Center (OLC)

www.mhhe.com/edmonds2008

More and more students are studying online. That's why we offer an Online Learning Center (OLC) that follows **Fundamental Managerial Accounting Concepts** chapter by chapter. The OLC includes the following:

- Excel Spreadsheets
- Spreadsheet Tips
- Text Updates
- Glossary
- Key Term Flashcards
- Chapter Learning Objectives
- Interactive Quizzes
- Electronic Lecture Slides
- Additional Check Figures
- Mobile Resources
- Topic Tackler Plus Tutorial

For instructors, the book's secured OLC contains essential course materials. You can pull all of this material into your PageOut course syllabus or use it as part of another online course management system. It doesn't require any building or maintenance on your part. It's ready to go the moment you type in the URL. You get all the resources available to students plus:

- Instructor's Manual
- Solutions Manual
- Solutions to Excel Template Assignments
- Sample Syllabi
- All Text Exhibits
- Text Updates
- Annual Report and Financial Statement Analysis Projects
- PowerPoint Slides

Instructor's Resource CD

This is your all-in-one resource. It allows you to create custom presentations from your own materials or from the following text-specific materials provided in the CD's asset library:

- Instructor's Manual
- Solutions Manual
- Test Bank
- Computerized Test Bank
- PowerPoint Presentations
- Excel Template Assignments and Solutions
- Video Clips
- Text Exhibits

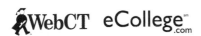

Online Course Management
WebCT, eCollege, and Blackboard

We offer **Fundamental Managerial Accounting Concepts** content for complete online courses. You can customize the Online Learning Center content and author your own course materials. No matter which online course solution you choose, you can count on the highest level of support.

CPS Classroom Performance System

This is a revolutionary system that brings ultimate interactivity to the classroom. CPS is a wireless response system that gives you immediate feedback from every student in the class. CPS units include easy-to-use software for creating and delivering questions and assessments to your class. With CPS you can ask subjective and objective questions. Then every student simply responds with their individual, wireless response pad, providing instant results. New features include a PowerPoint Plug-in, an improved data-sorting capability, a comprehensive grade book complement, web-based access to all McGraw-Hill CPS Content, and other powerful classroom learning functions.

ALEKS

ALEKS for the Accounting Cycle

ALEKS (Assessment and Learning in Knowledge Spaces) provides precise assessment and individualized instruction in the fundamental skills your students need to succeed in accounting. ALEKS uses an artificial intelligence engine to exactly identify a student's knowledge of accounting.

PageOut

McGraw-Hill's Course Management System
Pageout is the easiest way to create a Website for your accounting course. Just fill in a series of boxes and click on one of our professional designs. In no time your course is online with a Website that contains your syllabus. If you need help, our team of specialists is ready to take your course materials and build a custom website to your specifications. To learn more visit *www.pageout.net.*

SUPPLEMENTS for Instructors

Instructor's Manual
(Available on the password-protected Instructor
Online Learning Center (OLC) and Instructor's
Resource CD.)
This comprehensive manual includes step-by-step, explicit
instructions on how the text can be used to implement alternative
teaching methods. It also provides guidance for instructors who
use the traditional lecture method. The guide includes lesson plans
and demonstration problems with student work papers, as well as
solutions. It was prepared by Sue Cullers.

Solutions Manual
(Available on the password-protected Instructor
Online Learning Center (OLC) and Instructor's
Resource CD.)
Prepared by the authors, the manual contains complete solu-
tions-to all the text's end-of-chapter exercises, problems, and
cases.

**"This is the book you would like to adopt because it
helps your students to succeed in your course."
Nashwa George, Montclair State University**

Test Bank
(Available on the Instructor's Resource CD.)
This test bank in Word™ format contains multiple-choice
questions, essay, and short problems. Each test item is coded
for level of difficulty and learning objective. In addition to an
expansive array of traditional test questions, the test bank
includes new types of questions that focus exclusively on how
business events affect financial statements.

Algorithmic-Diploma Test Bank
ISBN-10:0073220957   ISBN-13:9780073220956
This test bank utilizes testing software to quickly create
customized exams. It can be used to make different versions of
the same test, change the answer order, edit and add questions,
and conduct online testing.

Instructor's Resource CD-ROM
ISBN-10: 007322085X   ISBN-13:9780073220857
This CD includes electronic versions of the Instructor's
Manual, Solutions Manual, Test Bank, computerized Test
Bank, as well as PowerPoint slides, video clips, all exhibits in
the text in PowerPoint, and spreadsheet templates with solu-
tions. This CD-ROM makes it easy for instructors to create multi-
media presentations.

Managerial Accounting Video Library
ISBN-10: 0072376171   ISBN-13:9780072376173
These short videos, developed by Dallas County Community
College, provide an impetus for class discussion. These provide a
focus on the preparation, analysis, and use of accounting informa-
tion for business decision making.

PowerPoint Presentation
(Available on the Online Learning Center (OLC) and
Instructor's Resource CD.)
These slides can serve as interactive class discussions and cover
key concepts in each chapter.

SUPPLEMENTS for Students

McGraw-Hill's Homework Manager Plus™

This integrates all of the text's multimedia resources. With just one access code, students can obtain state-of-the-art study aids, including McGraw-Hill's Homework Manager® and an online version of the text.

McGraw-Hill's Homework Manager®

This web-based software duplicates problem structures directly from the end-of-chapter material in the textbook. It uses algorithms to provide a limitless supply of self-graded practice for students. It shows students where they made errors. All Exercises and Problems in Series A are available with McGraw-Hill's Homework Manager.

Study Guide

ISBN-10: 0073220876   ISBN-13: 9780073220871
This proactive guide incorporates many of the accounting skills essential to student success. Each chapter contains a review and explanation of the chapter's learning objectives, as well as multiple-choice problems and short exercises. Unique to this Study Guide is a series of articulation problems that require students to indicate how accounting events affect the elements of financial statements.

Working Papers

This study aid contains forms that help students organize their solutions to homework exercises and problems and is available through Primis. Ask your sales representative for more information.

Topic Tackler Plus

(Available on the Online Learning Center (OLC))
This tutorial offers a virtual helping hand in understanding the most challenging topics in the managerial accounting course. Through a step-by-step sequence of video clips, PowerPoint slides, interactive practice exercises, and self tests, Topic Tackler Plus offers help on two key topics for each chapter. These topics are indicated by a logo in the text. Another component takes the Self-Study Review Problem in the book and demonstrates how to solve it in an animated audio presentation.

www.mhhe.com/edmonds2008

Excel Templates

(Available on the Online Learning Center (OLC))
These templates allow students to develop spreadsheet skills to solve selected assignments identified by an icon in the end-of-chapter material.

Electronic Lecture Slides

(Available on the Online Learning Center (OLC))
These PowerPoint slides cover key chapter topics in an audio-narrated presentation sure to help students learn.

ALEKS for the Accounting Cycle

ISBN-10: 0072975326
ISBN-13: 9780072975321

Or check the ALEKS website at *www.business.aleks.com*

Online Learning Center (OLC)

www.mhhe.com/edmonds2008

See page xviii for details.

ACKNOWLEDGEMENTS

Special thanks to the talented people who prepared the supplements. These take a great deal of time and effort to write and we appreciate their efforts. Sue Cullers of Tarleton State University prepared the Test Bank and Instructor's Manual. Tim Nygaard of Madisonville Community College developed the Self-Review Problem PowerPoint slides and wrote the online quizzes. Linda Schain of Hofstra University developed Topic Tackler Plus. Jack Terry of ComSource Associates prepared the Excel templates. Jon Booker and Charles W. Caldwell both of Tennessee Technological University, and Susan C. Galbreath of David Lipscomb University did the PowerPoint presentation. We also thank our accuracy checkers for checking the text manuscript and solutions manual. They include Beth Woods and Barbara Schnathorst. A special thanks to Linda Bell of William Jewell College for her contribution to the Financial Statement Analysis material that appears on the book's website.

We are deeply indebted to our sponsoring editor, Steve Schuetz. His direction and guidance have added clarity and quality to the text. We especially appreciate the efforts of our developmental editor, Gail Korosa. Gail has coordinated the exchange of ideas among our class testers, reviewers, copy editor, and error checkers; she has done far more than simply pass along ideas. She has contributed numerous original suggestions that have enhanced the quality of the text. Our editors have certainly facilitated our efforts to prepare a book that will facilitate a meaningful understanding of accounting. Even so, their contributions are to no avail unless the text reaches its intended audience. We are most grateful to Krista Bettino and Liz Farina and the sales staff for providing the informative advertising that has so accurately communicated the unique features of the concepts approach to accounting educators. Many others at McGraw-Hill/Irwin at a moment's notice redirected their attention to focus their efforts on the development of this text. We extend our sincere appreciation to Pat Frederickson, Elizabeth Mavetz, Michael McCormick, Artemio Ortiz, Matt Perry, and Lori Kramer. We deeply appreciate the long hours that you committed to the formation of a high-quality text.

Thomas P. Edmonds • Bor-Yi Tsay • Philip R. Olds

We express our sincere thanks to the following individuals who provided extensive reviews for the fourth edition:

Reviewers

Steve Buccheit, *Texas Tech University*

Chiaho Chang, *Montclair State University*

James Emig, *Villanova University*

Nashwa George, *Montclair State University*

Judith Harris, *Nova Southeastern University*

Aleecia Hibbets, *University of Louisiana at Monroe*

Jay Holmen, *University of Wisconsin at Eau Claire*

Shondra Johnson, *Bradley University*

Marrk Kaiser, *SUNY at Plattsburg*

Thomas Klammer, *University of North Texas*

Mehmet Kocakulah, *University of Southern Indiana*

Chor Lau, *California State University at Los Angeles*

Minwoo Lee, *Western Kentucky University*

Elliott Levy, *Bentley College*

Bruce Lindsey, *Genesee Community College*

Cathy Lumbattis, *Southern Illinois University*

Suneel Maheshwari, *Marshall University*

Pam Meyer, *Univeristy of Louisiana at Lafayette*

Michael Meyer, *Ohio University*

Michelle Moshier, *SUNY at Albany*

Roy Regel, *University of Montana at Missoula*

Luther Ross, *Central Piedmont Community College*

Harold Royer, *Miami-Dade College*

Charles Russo, *Bloomsburg University of Pennsylvania*

Angela Sandberg, *Jacksonville State University*

John Sneed, *Jacksonville State University*

John Stancil, *Florida Southern College*

Scott Stroher, *Glendale Community College*

Bill Talbot, *Montgomery College*

Our appreciation to those who reviewed previous editions

Daniel Benco, *Southeastern Oklahoma University*

Dennis Caplan, *Iowa State University*

Julie Chenier, *Louisiana State University*

Robert Fahnestock, *University of West Florida*

John Goetz, *University of Texas Arlington*

Judith Harris, *Nova Southeastern University*

Sheila Johnston, *University of Louisville, Louisville*

Julie Lockhart, *Western Washington University*

Lois Mahoney, *University of Central Florida*

David McIntyre, *Clemson University*

John Moore, *Virginia State University*

Chei Paik, *George Washington University*

Emil Radosevich, *Albuquerque TVI Community College*

Celia Renner, *Boise State University*

Gary Reynolds, *Ozark Technical Community College*

Nancy Ruhe, *West Virginia University, Morgantown*

Marilyn Salter, *University of Central Florida*

Angela Sandberg, *Jacksonville State University*

John Shaver, *Louisiana Tech University*

Scott Steinkamp, *College of Lake County*

Michael VanBreda, *Southern Methodist University*

Dan Ward, *University of Louisiana, Lafayette*

Jed Ashley, *Grossmont College*

James Bates, *Mountain Empire Community College*

Frank Beigbeder, *Rancho Santiago College*

Dorcas Berg, *Wingate College*

Ashton Bishop, *James Madison University*

Amy Bourne, *Tarrant County College*

Eric Carlsen, *Kean University*

Sue Counte, *Jefferson College*

Jill D'Aquila, *Iona College*

Walt Doehring, *Genesee Community College*

Patricia Douglas, *Loyola Marymount University*

Dean Edmiston, *Emporia State University*

Robert Elmore, *Tennessee Technological University*

Jeffrey Galbreath, *Greenfield Community College*

William Geary, *College of William and Mary*

Dinah Gottschalk, *James Madison University*

Donald Gribbin, *Southern Illinois University*

Larry Hegstad, *Pacific Lutheran University*

Fred Jex, *Macomb Community College*

Robert Landry, *Massassoit Community College*

Mark Lawrence, *University of Alabama at Birmingham*

Philip Little, *Western Carolina University*

Pat McMahon, *Palm Beach Community College*

Irvin Nelson, *Utah State University*

Bruce Neumann, *University of Colorado*

Hossein Nouri, *College of New Jersey*

Ashton Oravetz, *Tyler Junior College*

Thomas Phillips, *Louisiana Tech University*

Marjorie Platt, *Northeastern University*

Jane Reimers, *Florida State University*

Diane Riordan, *James Madison University*

Tom Robinson, *University of Alaska*

Kathryn Savage, *Northern Arizona University*

Bob Smith, *Florida State University*

Suneel Udpa, *St. Mary's College*

Sean Wright, *DeVry Institute of Technology, Phoenix*

Allan Young, *DeVry Institute of Technology, Atlanta*

Many others have contributed directly or indirectly to the development of the text. Participants in workshops and focus groups have provided useful feedback. Colleagues and friends have extended encouragement and support. Among these individuals our sincere appreciation is extended to Lowell Broom, University of Alabama at Birmingham; Bill Schwartz and Ed Spede of Virginia Commonwealth University; Doug Cloud, Pepperdine University—Malibu; Charles Bailey, University of Central Florida; Bob Holtfreter, Central Washington University; Kimberly Temme, Maryville University; Beth Vogel, Mount Mary College; Robert Minnear, Emory University; Shirish Seth, California State University at Fullerton; Richard Emery, Linfield College; Gail Hoover, Rockhurst; Bruce Robertson, Lock Haven University; Jeannie Folk, College of Dupage; Marvelyn Burnette, Wichita State University; Ron Mannino, University of Massachusetts; John Reisch, Florida Atlantic University; Rosalie Hallbauer, Florida International University; Lynne H. Shoaf, Belmont Abbey College; Jayne Maas, Towson University; Ahmed Goma, Manhattan College; John Rude, Bloomsburg University; Jack Paul, Lehigh University; Terri Gutierrez, University of Northern Colorado; Khondkar Karim, Monmouth University; Carol Lawrence, University of Richmond; Jeffrey Power, Saint Mary's University; Joanne Sheridan, Montana State University; and George Dow, Valencia Community College.

Brief Contents

Contents

Chapter 3   Analysis of Cost, Volume, and Pricing to Increase Profitability   104

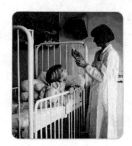

Chapter 6   Cost Management in an Automated Business Environment: ABC, ABM, and TQM   244

Chapter 9   Responsibility Accounting   386

CHAPTER 1

Management Accounting and Corporate Governance

LEARNING OBJECTIVES

After you have mastered the material in this chapter, you will be able to:

1. Distinguish between managerial and financial accounting.

2. Identify the cost components of a product made by a manufacturing company: the cost of materials, labor, and overhead.

3. Explain the effects on financial statements of product costs versus general, selling, and administrative costs.

4. Distinguish product costs from upstream and downstream costs.

5. Explain how product costing differs in service, merchandising, and manufacturing companies.

6. Show how just-in-time inventory can increase profitability.

7. Explain how cost classification can be used to manipulate financial statements.

8. Identify the standards of ethical conduct and the features that motivate misconduct.

9. Explain how the Sarbanes-Oxley Act affects management accountants.

10. Identify emerging trends in accounting (Appendix B).

The Curious Accountant

In the first course of accounting, you learned how retailers, such as **Best Buy Co.**, account for the cost of equipment that lasts more than one year. Recall that the equipment was recorded as an asset when purchased, and then it was depreciated over its expected useful life. The depreciation charge reduced the company's assets and increased its expenses. This approach was justified under the matching principle, which seeks to recognize costs as expenses in the same period that the cost (resource) is used to generate revenue.

In this course, the focus will often be on manufacturing entities, so consider the following scenario. **Apple Computer** manufactures iPod MP3 players that it sells to Best Buy. In order to produce the iPods, Apple had to purchase a robotic machine that it expects can be used to produce 1 million iPods.

Do you think Apple should account for depreciation on its manufacturing equipment the same way Best Buy accounts for depreciation on its registers at the checkout counters? If not, how should Apple account for its depreciation? Remember the matching principle when thinking of your answer. (Answer on page 13.)

CHAPTER OPENING

*Andy Grove, Senior Advisor to Executive Management of **Intel Corporation**, is credited with the motto "Only the paranoid survive." Mr. Grove describes a wide variety of concerns that make him paranoid. Specifically, he declares:*

> *I worry about products getting screwed up, and I worry about products getting introduced prematurely. I worry about factories not performing well, and I worry about having too many factories. I worry about hiring the right people, and I worry about morale slacking off. And, of course, I worry about competitors. I worry about other people figuring out how to do what we do better or cheaper, and displacing us with our customers.*

chapter 1

Do Intel's historical-based financial statements contain the information Mr. Grove needs? No.
Financial accounting *is not designed to satisfy all the information needs of business managers. Its
scope is limited to the needs of external users such as investors and creditors. The field of accounting designed to meet the needs of internal users is called* **managerial accounting.** ■

Differences between Managerial and Financial Accounting

LO 1

Distinguish between managerial
and financial accounting.

While the information needs of internal and external users overlap, the needs of managers
generally differ from those of investors or creditors. Some distinguishing characteristics are
discussed in the following section.

Users and Types of Information

Financial accounting provides information used primarily by investors, creditors, and others
outside a business. In contrast, managerial accounting focuses on information used by executives, managers, and employees who work *inside* the business. These two user groups need
different types of information.

Internal users need information to *plan, direct,* and *control* business operations. The nature of information needed is related to an employee's job level. Lower level employees use
nonfinancial information such as work schedules, store hours, and customer service policies. Moving up the organizational ladder, financial information becomes increasingly important. Middle managers use a blend of financial and nonfinancial information, while
senior executives concentrate on financial data. To a lesser degree, senior executives also
use general economic data and nonfinancial operating information. For example, an executive may consider the growth rate of the economy before deciding to expand the company's
workforce.

External users (investors and creditors) have greater needs for general economic information than do internal users. For example, an investor debating whether to purchase stock
versus bond securities might be more interested in government tax policy than financial
statement data. Exhibit 1.1 summarizes the information needs of different user groups.

Level of Aggregation

External users generally desire *global information* that reflects the performance of a company as a whole. For example, an investor is not so much interested in the performance of a
particular Sears store as she is in the performance of Sears Roebuck Company versus that
of JC Penney Company. In contrast, internal users focus on detailed information about
specific subunits of the company. To meet the needs of the different user groups financial
accounting data are more aggregated than managerial
accounting data.

Regulation

Financial accounting is designed to generate information for
the general public. In an effort to protect the public interest,
Congress established the **Securities and Exchange Commission (SEC)** and gave it authority to regulate public financial reporting practices. The SEC has delegated much of
its authority for developing accounting rules to the private
sector **Financial Accounting Standards Board (FASB),**
thereby allowing the accounting profession considerable
influence over financial accounting reports. The FASB supports a broad base of pronouncements and practices known
as **generally accepted accounting principles (GAAP).**
GAAP severely restricts the accounting procedures and
practices permitted in published financial statements.

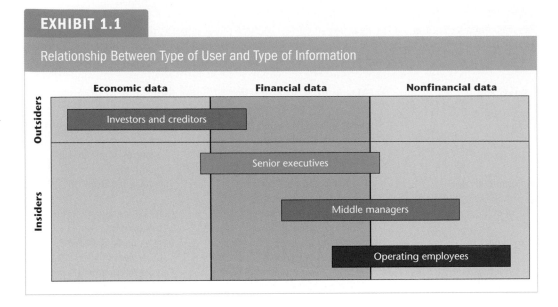

EXHIBIT 1.1

Relationship Between Type of User and Type of Information

Beyond financial statement data, much of the information generated by management accounting systems is proprietary information not available to the public. Since this information is not distributed to the public, it need not be regulated to protect the public interest. Management accounting is restricted only by the **value-added principle.** Management accountants are free to engage in any information gathering and reporting activity so long as the activity adds value in excess of its cost. For example, management accountants are free to provide forecasted information to internal users. In contrast, financial accounting as prescribed by GAAP does not permit forecasting.

Information Characteristics

While financial accounting is characterized by its objectivity, reliability, consistency, and historical nature, managerial accounting is more concerned with relevance and timeliness. Managerial accounting uses more estimates and fewer facts than financial accounting. Financial accounting reports what happened yesterday; managerial accounting reports what is expected to happen tomorrow.

Time Horizon and Reporting Frequency

Financial accounting information is reported periodically, normally at the end of a year. Management cannot wait until the end of the year to discover problems. Planning, controlling, and directing require immediate attention. Managerial accounting information is delivered on a continual basis.

Exhibit 1.2 summarizes significant differences between financial and managerial accounting.

Product Costing in Manufacturing Companies

A major focus for managerial accountants is determining **product cost.**[1] Managers need to know the cost of their products for a variety of reasons. For example, **cost-plus pricing** is a common business practice.[2] **Product costing** is also used to control business operations.

LO 2

Identify the cost components of a product made by a manufacturing company: the cost of materials, labor, and overhead.

---

[1]This text uses the term *product* in a generic sense to mean both goods and services.

[2]Other pricing strategies will be introduced in subsequent chapters.

EXHIBIT 1.2

Comparative Features of Managerial versus Financial Accounting Information

Features	Managerial Accounting	Financial Accounting
Users	Insiders including executives, managers, and operators	Outsiders including investors, creditors, government agencies, analysts, and reporters
Information type	Economic and physical data as well as financial data	Financial data
Level of aggregation	Local information on subunits of the organization	Global information on the company as a whole
Regulation	No regulation, limited only by the value-added principle	Regulation by SEC, FASB, and other determinors of GAAP
Information characteristics	Estimates that promote relevance and enable timeliness	Factual information that is characterized by objectivity, reliability, consistency, and accuracy
Time horizon	Past, present, and future	Past only, historically based
Reporting frequency	Continuous reporting	Delayed with emphasis on annual reports

Topic Tackler
PLUS

1-1

It is useful in answering questions such as: Are costs higher or lower than expected? Who is responsible for the variances between expected and actual costs? What action can be taken to control the variances?

The cost of making products includes the cost of materials, labor, and other resources (usually called **overhead**). To understand how these costs affect financial statements, consider the example of Tabor Manufacturing Company.

Tabor Manufacturing Company

Tabor Manufacturing Company makes wooden tables. The company spent $1,000 cash to build four tables: $390 for materials, $470 for a carpenter's labor, and $140 for tools used in making the tables. How much is Tabor's expense? The answer is zero. The $1,000 cash has been converted into products (four tables). The cash payments for materials, labor, and tools were *asset exchange* transactions. One asset (cash) decreased while another asset (tables) increased. Tabor will not recognize any expense until the tables are sold; in the meantime, the cost of the tables is held in an asset account called **Finished Goods** Inventory. Exhibit 1.3 illustrates how cash is transformed into inventory.

Average Cost per Unit

How much did each table made by Tabor cost? The *actual* cost of each of the four tables likely differs. The carpenter probably spent a little more time on some of the tables than others. Material and tool usage probably varied from table to table. Determining the exact cost of each table is virtually impossible. Minute details such as a second of labor time cannot be effectively measured. Even if Tabor could determine the exact cost of each table, the information would be of little use. Minor differences in the cost per table would make no difference in pricing or other decisions management needs to make. Accountants therefore normally calculate cost per unit as an *average*. In the case of Tabor Manufacturing, the **average cost** per table is $250 ($1,000 ÷ 4 units). Unless otherwise stated, assume *cost per unit* means *average cost per unit*.

EXHIBIT 1.3

Transforming the Asset Cash Into the Asset Finished Goods Inventory

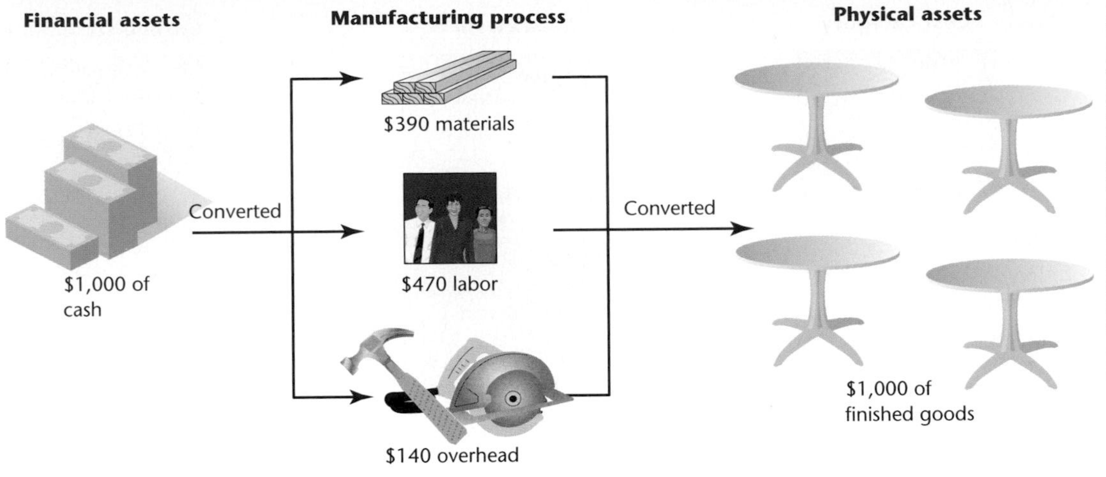

Financial assets **Manufacturing process** **Physical assets**

$390 materials

Converted

Converted

$1,000 of
cash

$470 labor

$1,000 of
finished goods

$140 overhead

All boxes of **General Mills'** Total Raisin Bran cereal are priced at exactly the same amount in your local grocery store. Does this mean that the actual cost of making each box of cereal was exactly the same price?

Answer

No, making each box would not cost exactly the same amount. For example, some boxes contain slightly more or less cereal than other boxes. Accordingly, some boxes cost slightly more or less to make than others do. General Mills uses average cost rather than actual cost to develop its pricing strategy.

Costs Can Be Assets or Expenses

It might seem odd that wages earned by production workers are recorded as inventory instead of being expensed. Remember, however, that expenses are assets used in the process of *earning revenue*. The cash paid to production workers is not used to produce revenue. Instead, the cash is used to produce inventory. Revenue will be earned when the inventory is used (sold). So long as the inventory remains on hand, all product costs (materials, labor, and overhead) remain in an inventory account.

When a table is sold, the average cost of the table is transferred from the Inventory account to the Cost of Goods Sold (expense) account. If some tables remain unsold at the end of the accounting period, part of the *product costs* is reported as an asset (inventory) on the balance sheet while the other part is reported as an expense (cost of goods sold) on the income statement.

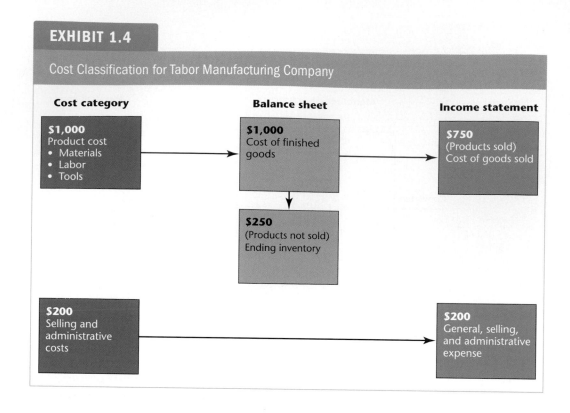

EXHIBIT 1.4

Cost Classification for Tabor Manufacturing Company

Costs that are not classified as product costs are normally expensed in the period in which they are incurred. These costs include *general operating costs, selling and administrative costs, interest costs,* and the *cost of income taxes.*

To illustrate, return to the Tabor Manufacturing example. Recall that Tabor made four tables at an average cost per unit of $250. Assume Tabor pays an employee who sells three of the tables a $200 sales commission. The sales commission is expensed immediately. The total product cost for the three tables (3 tables × $250 each = $750) is expensed on the income statement as cost of goods sold. The portion of the total product cost remaining in inventory is $250 (1 table × $250). Exhibit 1.4 shows the relationship between the costs incurred and the expenses recognized for Tabor Manufacturing Company.

Effect of Product Costs on Financial Statements

We illustrate accounting for product costs in manufacturing companies with Patillo Manufacturing Company, a producer of ceramic pottery. Patillo, started on January 1, 2008, experienced the following accounting events during its first year of operations.[3] *Assume that all transactions except 6, 8, and 10 are cash transactions.*

1. Acquired $15,000 cash by issuing common stock.
2. Paid $2,000 for materials that were used to make products. All products started were completed during the period.
3. Paid $1,200 for salaries of selling and administrative employees.
4. Paid $3,000 for wages of production workers.
5. Paid $2,800 for furniture used in selling and administrative offices.

LO 3

Explain the effects on financial statements of product costs versus general, selling, and administrative costs.

---

[3]This illustration assumes that all inventory started during the period was completed during the period. Patillo therefore uses only one inventory account, Finished Goods Inventory. Many manufacturing companies normally have three categories of inventory on hand at the end of an accounting period: Raw Materials Inventory, Work in Process Inventory (inventory of partially completed units), and Finished Goods Inventory. Chapter 11 discusses these inventories in greater detail.

EXHIBIT 1.5

Effect of Product versus Selling and Administrative Costs on Financial Statements

Event No.	Cash	+	Inventory	+	Office Furn.*	+	Manuf. Equip.*	=	Com. Stk.	+	Ret. Earn.	Rev.	−	Exp.	=	Net Inc.	Cash Flow
1	15,000							=	15,000								15,000 FA
2	(2,000)	+	2,000														(2,000) OA
3	(1,200)							=			(1,200)		− 1,200	=	(1,200)		(1,200) OA
4	(3,000)	+	3,000														(3,000) OA
5	(2,800)	+			2,800												(2,800) IA
6					(600)			=			(600)		− 600	=	(600)		
7	(4,500)	+					4,500										(4,500) IA
8			1,000	+			(1,000)										
9	7,500							=			7,500	7,500			=	7,500	7,500 OA
10			(4,000)					=			(4,000)		− 4,000	=	(4,000)		
Totals	9,000	+	2,000	+	2,200	+	3,500	=	15,000	+	1,700	7,500	− 5,800	=	1,700		9,000 NC

*Negative amounts in these columns represent accumulated depreciation.

6. Recognized depreciation on the office furniture purchased in Event 5. The furniture was acquired on January 1, had a $400 estimated salvage value, and a four-year useful life. The annual depreciation charge is $600 [($2,800 − $400) ÷ 4].

7. Paid $4,500 for manufacturing equipment.

8. Recognized depreciation on the equipment purchased in Event 7. The equipment was acquired on January 1, had a $1,500 estimated salvage value, and a three-year useful life. The annual depreciation charge is $1,000 [($4,500 − $1,500) ÷ 3].

9. Sold inventory to customers for $7,500 cash.

10. The inventory sold in Event 9 cost $4,000 to make.

The effects of these transactions on the balance sheet, income statement, and statement of cash flows are shown in Exhibit 1.5. Study each row in this exhibit, paying particular attention to how similar costs such as salaries for selling and administrative personnel and wages for production workers have radically different effects on the financial statements. The example illustrates the three elements of product costs, materials (Event 2), labor (Event 4), and overhead (Event 8). These events are discussed in more detail below.

Materials Costs (Event 2)

Materials used to make products are usually called **raw materials.** The cost of raw materials is first recorded in an asset account (Inventory). The cost is then transferred from the Inventory account to the Cost of Goods Sold account at the time the goods are sold. Remember that materials cost is only one component of total manufacturing costs. When inventory is sold, the combined cost of materials, labor, and overhead is expensed as *cost of goods sold.* The costs of materials that can be easily and conveniently traced to products are called **direct raw materials** costs.

Labor Costs (Event 4)

The salaries paid to selling and administrative employees (Event 3) and the wages paid to production workers (Event 4) are accounted for differently. Salaries paid to selling and

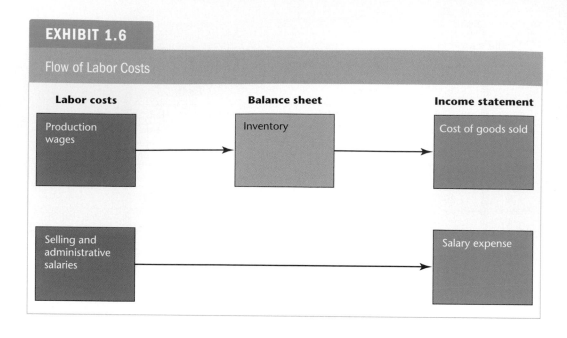

EXHIBIT 1.6

Flow of Labor Costs

Labor costs	Balance sheet	Income statement
Production wages	Inventory	Cost of goods sold
Selling and administrative salaries		Salary expense

administrative employees are expensed immediately, but the cost of production wages is added to inventory. Production wages are expensed as part of cost of goods sold at the time the inventory is sold. Labor costs that can be easily and conveniently traced to products are called **direct labor** costs. The cost flow of wages for production employees versus salaries for selling and administrative personnel is shown in Exhibit 1.6.

Overhead Costs (Event 8)

Although depreciation cost totaled $1,600 ($600 on office furniture and $1,000 on manufacturing equipment), only the $600 of depreciation on the office furniture is expensed directly on the income statement. The depreciation on the manufacturing equipment is split between the income statement (cost of goods sold) and the balance sheet (inventory). The depreciation cost flow for the manufacturing equipment versus the office furniture is shown in Exhibit 1.7.

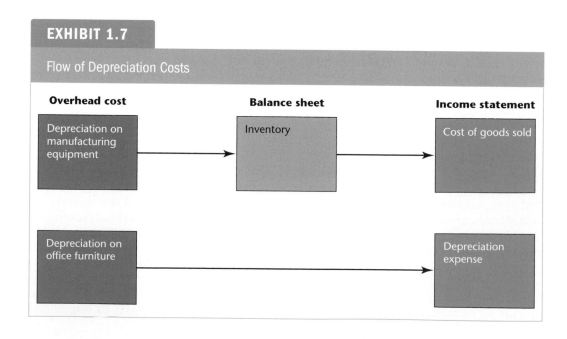

EXHIBIT 1.7

Flow of Depreciation Costs

Overhead cost	Balance sheet	Income statement
Depreciation on manufacturing equipment	Inventory	Cost of goods sold
Depreciation on office furniture		Depreciation expense

Total Product Cost. A summary of Patillo Manufacturing's total product cost is shown in Exhibit 1.8.

Financial Statements

The income statement, balance sheet, and statement of cash flows for Patillo Manufacturing are displayed in Exhibit 1.9.

Product Costs. The $4,000 cost of goods sold reported on the income statement includes a portion of the materials, labor, and overhead costs incurred by Patillo during the year. Similarly, the $2,000 of finished goods inventory on the balance sheet includes materials, labor, and overhead costs. These product costs will be recognized as expense in the next accounting period when the goods are sold. Initially classifying a cost as a product cost delays, but does not eliminate, its recognition as an expense. All product costs are ultimately recognized as expense (cost of goods sold). Cost classification does not affect cash flow. Cash inflows and outflows are recognized in the period that cash is collected or paid regardless of whether the cost is recorded as an asset or expensed on the income statement.

General, Selling, and Administrative Costs. **General, selling, and administrative costs** (GS&A) are normally expensed *in the period* in which they are incurred. Because of this recognition pattern, nonproduct expenses are sometimes called **period costs.** In Patillo's case, the salary expense for selling and administrative employees and the depreciation on office furniture are period costs reported directly on the income statement.

Overhead Costs: A Closer Look

Costs such as depreciation on manufacturing equipment cannot be easily traced to products. Suppose that Patillo Manufacturing makes both tables and chairs. What part of the depreciation is caused by manufacturing tables versus manufacturing chairs? Similarly, suppose a production supervisor oversees employees who work on both tables and chairs. How much of the supervisor's salary relates to tables and how much to chairs? Likewise, the cost of glue used in the production department would be difficult to trace to tables versus chairs. You could count the drops of glue used on each product, but the information would not be useful enough to merit the time and money spent collecting the data.

Costs that cannot be traced to products and services in a *cost-effective* manner are called **indirect costs.** The indirect costs incurred to make products are called **manufacturing overhead.** Some of the items commonly included in manufacturing overhead are indirect materials, indirect labor, factory utilities, rent of manufacturing facilities, and depreciation on manufacturing assets.

CHECK YOURSELF 1.2

Lawson Manufacturing Company paid production workers wages of $100,000. It incurred materials costs of $120,000 and manufacturing overhead costs of $160,000. Selling and administrative salaries were $80,000. Lawson started and completed 1,000 units of product and sold 800 of these units. The company sets sales prices at $220 above the average per unit production cost. Based on this information alone, determine the amount of gross margin and net income. What is Lawson's pricing strategy called?

Answer

Total product cost is $380,000 ($100,000 labor + $120,000 materials + $160,000 overhead). Cost per unit is $380 ($380,000 ÷ 1,000 units). The sales price per unit is $600 ($380 + $220). Cost of goods sold is $304,000 ($380 × 800 units). Sales revenue is $480,000 ($600 × 800 units). Gross margin is $176,000 ($480,000 revenue − $304,000 cost of goods sold). Net income is $96,000 ($176,000 gross margin − $80,000 selling and administrative salaries). Lawson's pricing strategy is called *cost-plus* pricing.

Since indirect costs cannot be effectively traced to products, they are normally assigned to products using **cost allocation,** a process of dividing a total cost into parts and assigning the parts to relevant cost objects. To illustrate, suppose that production workers spend an eight-hour day making a chair and a table. The chair requires two hours to complete and the table requires six hours. Now suppose that $120 of utilities cost is consumed during the day. How much of the $120 should be assigned to each piece of furniture? The utility cost cannot be directly traced to each specific piece of furniture, but the piece of furniture that required more labor also likely consumed more of the utility cost. Using this line of reasoning, it is rational to allocate the utility cost to the two pieces of furniture based on *direct labor hours* at a rate of $15 per hour ($120 ÷ 8 hours). The chair would be assigned $30 ($15 per hour × 2 hours) of the utility cost and the table would be assigned the remaining $90 ($15 × 6 hours) of utility cost. The allocation of the utility cost is shown in Exhibit 1.10.

We discuss the details of cost allocation in a later chapter. For now, recognize that overhead costs are normally allocated to products rather than traced directly to them.

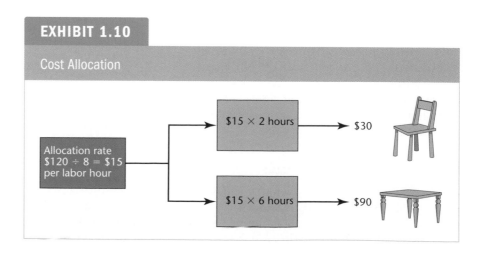

EXHIBIT 1.10

Cost Allocation

Allocation rate
$120 ÷ 8 = $15 per labor hour

$15 × 2 hours → $30

$15 × 6 hours → $90

Manufacturing Product Cost Summary

As explained, the cost of a product made by a manufacturing company is normally composed of three categories: direct materials, direct labor, and manufacturing overhead. Relevant information about these three cost components is summarized in Exhibit 1.11.

EXHIBIT 1.11

Components of Manufacturing Product Cost

Component 1—Direct Materials
Sometimes called *raw materials*. In addition to basic resources such as wood or metals, it can include manufactured parts. For example, engines, glass, and car tires can be considered as raw materials for an automotive manufacturer. If the amount of a material in a product is known, it can usually be classified as a direct material. The cost of direct materials can be easily traced to specific products.

Component 2—Direct Labor
The cost of wages paid to factory workers involved in hands-on contact with the products being manufactured. If the amount of time employees worked on a product can be determined, this cost can usually be classified as direct labor. Like direct materials, labor costs must be easily traced to a specific product in order to be classified as a direct cost.

Component 3—Manufacturing Overhead
Costs that cannot be easily traced to specific products. Accordingly, these costs are called indirect costs. They can include but are not limited to the following:

1. Indirect materials such as glue, nails, paper, and oil. Indeed, note that indirect materials used in the production process may not appear in the finished product. An example is a chemical solvent used to clean products during the production process but not a component material found in the final product.
2. Indirect labor such as the cost of salaries paid to production supervisors, inspectors, and maintenance personnel.
3. Rental cost for manufacturing facilities and equipment.
4. Utility costs.
5. Depreciation.
6. Security.
7. The cost of preparing equipment for the manufacturing process (i.e., setup costs).
8. Maintenance cost for the manufacturing facility and equipment.

Answers to The Curious Accountant

As you have seen, accounting for depreciation related to manufacturing assets is different from accounting for depreciation for nonmanufacturing assets. Depreciation on the checkout equipment at **Best Buy** is recorded as depreciation expense. Depreciation on manufacturing equipment at **Apple Computer** is considered a product cost. It is included first as a part of the cost of inventory and eventually as a part of the expense, cost of goods sold. Recording depreciation on manufacturing equipment as an inventory cost is simply another example of the matching principle, because the cost does not become an expense until revenue from the product sale is recognized.

Upstream and Downstream Costs

Most companies incur product-related costs before and after, as well as during, the manufacturing process. For example, **Ford Motor Company** incurs significant research and development costs prior to mass producing a new car model. These **upstream costs** occur before the

Distinguish product costs from upstream and downstream costs.

manufacturing process begins. Similarly, companies normally incur significant costs after the manufacturing process is complete. Examples of **downstream costs** include transportation, advertising, sales commissions, and bad debts. While upstream and downstream costs are not considered to be product costs for financial reporting purposes, profitability analysis requires that they be considered in cost-plus pricing decisions. To be profitable, a company must recover the total cost of developing, producing, and delivering its products to customers.

Product Costing in Service and Merchandising Companies

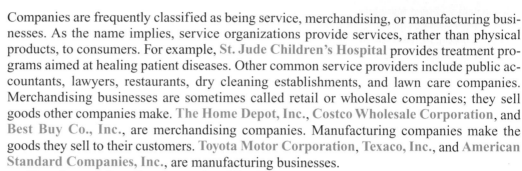

LO 5

Explain how product costing differs in service, merchandising, and manufacturing companies.

Companies are frequently classified as being service, merchandising, or manufacturing businesses. As the name implies, service organizations provide services, rather than physical products, to consumers. For example, St. Jude Children's Hospital provides treatment programs aimed at healing patient diseases. Other common service providers include public accountants, lawyers, restaurants, dry cleaning establishments, and lawn care companies. Merchandising businesses are sometimes called retail or wholesale companies; they sell goods other companies make. The Home Depot, Inc., Costco Wholesale Corporation, and Best Buy Co., Inc., are merchandising companies. Manufacturing companies make the goods they sell to their customers. Toyota Motor Corporation, Texaco, Inc., and American Standard Companies, Inc., are manufacturing businesses.

How do manufacturing companies differ from service and merchandising businesses? Do service and merchandising companies incur materials, labor, and overhead costs? Yes. For example, Ernst & Young, a large accounting firm, must pay employees (labor costs), use office supplies (material costs), and incur utilities, depreciation, and so on (overhead costs) in the process of conducting audits. *The primary difference between manufacturing entities and service companies is that the products provided by service companies are consumed immediately.* In contrast, products made by manufacturing companies can be held in the form of inventory until they are sold to consumers. Similarly, most labor and overhead costs incurred by merchandising companies result from providing assistance to customers. These costs are normally treated as general, selling, and administrative expenses rather than accumulated in inventory accounts. Indeed, merchandising companies are often viewed as service companies rather than considered a separate business category.

The important point to remember is that all business managers are expected to control costs, improve quality, and increase productivity. Like managers of manufacturing companies, managers of service and merchandising businesses can benefit from the analysis of the cost of satisfying their customers. For example, Wendy's, a service company, can benefit from knowing how much a hamburger costs in the same manner that Bayer Corporation, a manufacturing company, benefits from knowing the cost of a bottle of aspirin.

CHECK YOURSELF 1.3

The cost of making a Burger King hamburger includes the cost of materials, labor, and overhead. Does this mean that Burger King is a manufacturing company?

Answer

No, Burger King is not a manufacturing company. It is a service company because its products are consumed immediately. In contrast, there may be a considerable delay between the time the product of a manufacturing company is made and the time it is consumed. For example, it could be several months between the time Ford Motor Company makes an Explorer and the time the Explorer is ultimately sold to a customer. The primary difference between service and manufacturing companies is that manufacturing companies have inventories of products and service companies do not.

Just-in-Time Inventory

Companies attempt to minimize the amount of inventory they maintain because of the high cost of holding it. Many **inventory holding costs** are obvious: financing, warehouse space, supervision, theft, damage, and obsolescence. Other costs are hidden: diminished motivation, sloppy work, inattentive attitudes, and increased production time.

Many businesses have been able to simultaneously reduce their inventory holding costs and increase customer satisfaction by making products available **just in time** (**JIT**) for customer consumption. For example, hamburgers that are cooked to order are fresher and more individualized than those that are prepared in advance and stored until a customer orders one. Many fast-food restaurants have discovered that JIT systems lead not only to greater customer satisfaction but also to lower costs through reduced waste.

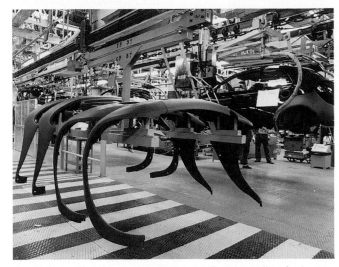

At **Ford Motor Company**'s plant in Valencia, Spain, suppliers feed parts such as these bumpers just in time and in the right order directly to the assembly line.

Just-in-Time Illustration

To illustrate the benefits of a JIT system, consider Paula Elliot, a student at a large urban university. She helps support herself by selling flowers. Three days each week, Paula drives to a florist, purchases 25 single stem roses, returns to the school, and sells the flowers to individuals from a location on a local street corner. She pays $2 per rose and sells each one for $3. Some days she does not have enough flowers to meet customer demand. Other days, she must discard one or two unsold flowers; she believes quality is important and refuses to sell flowers that are not fresh. During May, she purchased 300 roses and sold 280. She calculated her driving cost to be $45. Exhibit 1.12 displays Paula's May income statement.

Show how just-in-time inventory can increase profitability.

After studying just-in-time inventory systems in her managerial accounting class, Paula decided to apply the concepts to her small business. She *reengineered* her distribution system by purchasing her flowers from a florist within walking distance of her sales location. She had considered purchasing from this florist earlier but had rejected the idea because the florist's regular selling price of $2.25 per rose was too high. After learning about *most-favored customer status,* she developed a strategy to get a price reduction. By guaranteeing that she would buy at least 30 roses per week, she was able to convince the local florist to match her current cost of $2.00 per rose. The local florist agreed that she could make purchases in batches of any size so long as the total amounted to at least 30 per week. Under this arrangement, Paula was able to buy roses *just in time* to meet customer demand. Each day she purchased a small number of flowers. When she ran out, she simply returned to the florist for additional ones.

The JIT system also enabled Paula to eliminate the cost of the *nonvalue-added activity* of driving to her former florist. Customer satisfaction actually improved because no one was ever turned away because of the lack of inventory. In June, Paula was able to buy and sell 310 roses with no waste and no driving expense. The June income statement is shown in Exhibit 1.13.

Paula was ecstatic about her $115 increase in profitability ($310 in June − $195 in May = $115 increase), but

EXHIBIT 1.12

Income Statement

Sales Revenue (280 units × $3 per unit)	$840
Cost of Goods Sold (300 units × $2 per unit)	(600)
Gross Margin	240
Driving Expense	(45)
Net Income	$195

EXHIBIT 1.13

Income Statement

Sales Revenue (310 units × $3 per unit)	$930
Cost of Goods Sold (310 units × $2 per unit)	(620)
Gross Margin	310
Driving Expense	0
Net Income	$310

she was puzzled about the exact reasons for the change. She had saved $40 (20 flowers × $2 each) by avoiding waste and eliminated $45 of driving expenses. These two factors explained only $85 ($40 waste + $45 driving expense) of the $115 increase. What had caused the remaining $30 ($115 − $85) increase in profitability? Paula asked her accounting professor to help her identify the remaining $30 difference.

The professor explained that May sales had suffered from *lost opportunities*. Recall that under the earlier inventory system, Paula had to turn away some prospective customers because she sold out of flowers before all customers were served. Sales increased from 280 roses in May to 310 roses in June. A likely explanation for the 30 unit difference (310 − 280) is that customers who would have purchased flowers in May were unable to do so because of a lack of availability. May's sales suffered from the lost opportunity to earn a gross margin of $1 per flower on 30 roses, a $30 **opportunity cost.** This opportunity cost is the missing link in explaining the profitability difference between May and June. The total $115 difference consists of (1) $40 savings from waste elimination, (2) $45 savings from eliminating driving expense, and (3) opportunity cost of $30. The subject of opportunity cost has widespread application and is discussed in more depth in subsequent chapters of the text.

CHECK YOURSELF 1.4

A strike at a General Motors brake plant caused an almost immediate shutdown of many of the company's assembly plants. What could have caused such a rapid and widespread shutdown?

Answer

A rapid and widespread shutdown could have occurred because General Motors uses a just-in-time inventory system. With a just-in-time inventory system, there is no stockpile of inventory to draw on when strikes or other forces disrupt inventory deliveries. This illustrates a potential negative effect of using a just-in-time inventory system.

Corporate Governance

Corporate governance is the set of relationships between the board of directors, management, shareholders, auditors, and other stakeholders that determine how a company is operated. Until recently, corporations were generally free to govern themselves. However, several high-profile scandals have motivated governmental authorities to enact legislation designed to influence corporate governance. This section of the chapter examines the factors affecting corporate governance. We examine the motives and means of management corruption. Further, we introduce the mechanisms for self control including codes of ethics and internal controls. Finally, we discuss recent legislation designed to influence managerial responsibility for financial reporting.

Management accountants are at the forefront of corporate governance. They are the guardians of the information used to report on the financial condition of their companies. The information they prepare and analyze is used by the board of directors and company executives to formulate the company's operating strategy. Indeed, management accountants constitute the intelligence function of corporate governance. Scandals usually begin with schemes to manipulate a company's financial reports and end when the falsification is so great it becomes obvious the reports no longer represent reality. The appropriate management of the information function is a highly effective force against corrupt governance. It is little wonder why recent legislation requires the chief financial officer along with the chief executive officer to personally certify that the company's annual report does not contain false statements nor omit significant facts.

The Motive to Manipulate

Many managers are judged on their companies' financial statements or the companies' stock price which is determined, in part, by the financial statements. Managers are rewarded for strong financial statements with promotions, pay raises, bonuses, and stock options. Weak financials can result in a manager being passed over for promotions, demoted, or even fired. It is little wonder that some executives are tempted to manipulate financial statements.

Explain how cost classification can be used to manipulate financial statements.

Marion Manufacturing Company

To illustrate implications of statement manipulation, consider the events experienced by Marion Manufacturing Company (MMC) during its first year of operations. All transactions are cash transactions.

1. MMC was started when it acquired $12,000 from issuing common stock.
2. MMC incurred $4,000 of costs to design its product and plan the manufacturing process.
3. MMC incurred specifically identifiable product costs (materials, labor, and overhead) of $8,000.
4. MMC made 1,000 units of product and sold 700 of the units for $18 each.

Exhibit 1.14 displays a set of financial statements that are prepared under the following two scenarios.

EXHIBIT 1.14

Financial Statements Under Alternative Cost Classification Scenarios

Income Statements	Scenario 1	Scenario 2
Sales Revenue (700 × $18)	$12,600	$12,600
Cost of Goods Sold	(5,600)	(8,400)
Gross Margin	7,000	4,200
Selling and Administrative Expense	(4,000)	0
Net Income	$ 3,000	$ 4,200

Balance Sheets		
Assets		
Cash	$12,600	$12,600
Inventory	2,400	3,600
Total Assets	$15,000	$16,200
Stockholders' Equity		
Common Stock	$12,000	$12,000
Retained Earnings	3,000	4,200
Total Stockholders' Equity	$15,000	$16,200

Statement of Cash Flows		
Operating Activities		
Inflow from Customers	$12,600	$12,600
Outflow for Inventory	(8,000)	(12,000)
Outflow for S&A	(4,000)	0
Net Inflow from Operating Activities	600	600
Investing Activities	0	0
Financing Activities		
Acquisition of Capital	12,000	12,000
Net Change in Cash	12,600	12,600
Beginning Cash Balance	0	0
Ending Cash Balance	$12,600	$12,600

Scenario 1: The $4,000 of design and planning costs are classified as selling and administrative expenses.

Scenario 2: The $4,000 of design and planning costs are classified as product costs, meaning they are first accumulated in the Inventory account and then expensed when the goods are sold. Given that MMC made 1,000 units and sold 700 units of inventory, 70% (700 ÷ 1,000) of the design cost has passed through the Inventory account into the Cost of Goods Sold account, leaving 30% (300 ÷ 1,000) remaining in the Inventory account.

Statement Differences

Comparing the financial statements prepared under Scenario 1 with those prepared under Scenario 2 reveals the following.

1. There are no selling and administrative expenses under Scenario 2. The design cost was treated as a product cost and placed into the Inventory account rather than being expensed.
2. Cost of goods sold is $2,800 ($4,000 design cost × .70) higher under Scenario 2.
3. Net income is $1,200 higher under Scenario 2 ($4,000 understated expense − $2,800 overstated cost of goods sold).
4. Ending inventory is $1,200 ($4,000 design cost × .30) higher under Scenario 2.

While the Scenario 2 income statement and balance sheet are overstated, cash flow is not affected by the alternative cost classifications. Regardless of how the design cost is classified, the same amount of cash was collected and paid. This explains why financial analysts consider the statement of cash flows to be a critical source of information.

Practical Implications

The financial statement differences shown in Exhibit 1.14 are *timing differences*. When MMC sells the remaining 300 units of inventory, the $1,200 of design and planning costs included in inventory under Scenario 2 will be expensed through cost of goods sold. In other words, once the entire inventory is sold, total expenses and retained earnings will be the same under both scenarios. Initially recording cost in an inventory account only delays eventual expense recognition. However, the temporary effects on the financial statements can influence the (1) availability of financing, (2) motivations of management, and (3) timing of income tax payments.

Availability of Financing

The willingness of creditors and investors to provide capital to a business is influenced by their expectations of the business's future financial performance. In general, more favorable financial statements enhance a company's ability to obtain financing from creditors or investors.

Management Motivation

Financial statement results might affect executive compensation. For example, assume that Marion Manufacturing adopted a management incentive plan that provides a bonus pool equal to 10 percent of net income. In Scenario 1, managers would receive $300 ($3,000 × 0.10). In Scenario 2, however, managers would receive $420 ($4,200 × 0.10). Do not be deceived by the small numbers used for convenience in the example. We could illustrate with millions of dollars just as well as with hundreds of dollars. Managers would clearly favor Scenario 2. In fact, managers might be tempted to misclassify costs to manipulate the content of financial statements.

Income Tax Considerations

Since income tax expense is calculated as a designated percentage of taxable income, managers seek to minimize taxes by reporting the minimum amount of taxable income. Scenario 1 in Exhibit 1.14 depicts the most favorable tax condition. In other words, with respect to taxes, managers prefer to classify costs as expenses rather than assets. The Internal Revenue Service is responsible for enforcing the proper classification of costs. Disagreements between the Internal Revenue Service and taxpayers are ultimately settled in federal courts.

Ethical Considerations

The preceding discussion provides some insight into conflicts of interest management accountants might face. It is tempting to misclassify a cost if doing so will significantly increase a manager's bonus. Management accountants must be prepared not only to make difficult choices between legitimate alternatives but also to face conflicts of a more troubling nature, such as pressure to:

Identify the standards of ethical conduct and the features that motivate misconduct.

1. Undertake duties they have not been trained to perform competently.
2. Disclose confidential information.
3. Compromise their integrity through falsification, embezzlement, bribery, and so on.
4. Issue biased, misleading, or incomplete reports.

To provide management accountants with guidance for ethical conduct the Institute of Management Accountants (IMA) issued a *Statement of Ethical Professional Practice*, which is shown in Exhibit 1.15. Management accountants are also frequently required to abide by organizational codes of ethics. Failure to adhere to professional and organizational ethical standards can lead to personal disgrace, loss of employment, or imprisonment.

EXHIBIT 1.15

Statement of Ethical Professional Practice

Members of IMA shall behave ethically. A commitment to ethical professional practice includes overarching principles that express our values, and standards that guide our conduct. IMA's overarching ethical principles include: Honesty, Fairness, Objectivity, and Responsibility. Members shall act in accordance with these principles and shall encourage others within their organizations to adhere to them. A member's failure to comply with the following standards may result in disciplinary action.

Competence Each member has a responsibility to
- Maintain an appropriate level of professional expertise by continually developing knowledge and skills.
- Perform professional duties in accordance with relevant laws, regulations, and technical standards.
- Provide decision support information and recommendations that are accurate, clear, concise, and timely.
- Recognize and communicate professional limitations or other constraints that would preclude responsible judgment or successful performance of an activity.

Confidentiality Each member has a responsibility to
- Keep information confidential except when disclosure is authorized or legally required.
- Inform all relevant parties regarding appropriate use of confidential information. Monitor subordinates' activities to ensure compliance.
- Refrain from using confidential information for unethical or illegal advantage.

Integrity Each member has a responsibility to
- Mitigate actual conflicts of interest and avoid apparent conflicts of interest. Advise all parties of any potential conflicts.
- Refrain from engaging in any conduct that would prejudice carrying out duties ethically.
- Abstain from engaging in or supporting any activity that might discredit the profession.

Credibility Each member has a responsibility to
- Communicate information fairly and objectively.
- Disclose all relevant information that could reasonably be expected to influence an intended user's understanding of the reports, analyses, or recommendations.
- Disclose delays or deficiencies in information, timeliness, processing, or internal controls in conformance with organization policy and/or applicable law.

Resolution of Ethical Conflict In applying these standards, you may encounter problems identifying unethical behavior or resolving an ethical conflict. When faced with ethical issues, follow your organization's established policies on the resolution of such conflict. If these policies do not resolve the ethical conflict, consider the following courses of action:
- Discuss the issue with your immediate supervisor except when it appears that the supervisor is involved. In that case, present the issue to the next level. If you cannot achieve a satisfactory resolution, submit the issue to the next management level. Communication of such problems to authorities or individuals not employed or engaged by the organization is not considered appropriate, unless you believe there is a clear violation of the law.
- Clarify relevant ethical issues by initiating a confidential discussion with an IMA Ethics Counselor or other impartial advisor to obtain a better understanding of possible courses of action.
- Consult your own attorney as to legal obligations and rights concerning the ethical conflict.

REALITY BYTES

In March 2002, Gene Morse, an accountant employed by WorldCom, discovered accounting fraud at the company. He relayed his findings to his boss, Cynthia Cooper, the company's vice president of internal audit. After further investigation, Ms. Cooper reported her findings to WorldCom's board of directors in June 2002, and the chief financial officer, Scott Sullivan, was fired.

If company management had refused to let Ms. Cooper address the board, would it have been appropriate for her and Mr. Morse to tell the press about the fraud? If they were members of the Institute of Management Accountants (IMA) it would probably have been unethical for them to be "whistleblowers." IMA standards (*SMA Number 1C,* 1983) require a management accountant who is unable to satisfactorily resolve an ethical conflict between himself and his employer to resign from the organization and to submit an informative memorandum to an appropriate representative of the organization. Disclosing such conflicts outside the organization is an inappropriate breach of confidentiality unless required by law. The audit committee of the company's board of directors is an "appropriate representative." In a matter as significant as the WorldCom fraud, the employee would be well advised to seek legal counsel.

For more details on this story, see: "How Three Unlikely Sleuths Discovered Fraud at WorldCom," by Susan Pullman and Deborah Solomon, *The Wall Street Journal,* October 30, 2002, pp. 1 and 16.

Common Features of Criminal and Ethical Misconduct

Unfortunately, it takes more than a code of conduct to stop fraud. People frequently engage in activities that they know are unethical or even criminal. The auditing profession has determined that the following three elements are typically present when fraud occurs:

1. The availability of an *opportunity.*
2. The existence of some form of *pressure* leading to an incentive.
3. The capacity to *rationalize.*

The three elements are frequently arranged in the shape of a triangle as shown in Exhibit 1.16.

Opportunity is shown at the head to the triangle because without opportunity fraud could not exist. The most effective way to reduce opportunities for ethical or criminal misconduct is to implement an effective set of internal controls. *Internal controls* are policies and procedures that a business implements to reduce opportunities for fraud and to ensure that its objectives will be accomplished. Specific controls are tailored to meet the individual needs of particular businesses. For example, banks use elaborate vaults to protect cash and safety deposit boxes, but universities have little use for this type of equipment. Even so, many of the same procedures are used by a wide variety of businesses. Exhibit 1.17 contains a summary of many of the internal control policies and procedures that have gained widespread acceptance.

Only a few employees turn to the dark side even when internal control is weak and opportunities abound. So, what causes one person to commit fraud and another to remain honest? The second element of the fraud triangle

EXHIBIT 1.16

Opportunity

Pressure   Rationalization

EXHIBIT 1.17

Common Internal Control Practices

Internal Control Practice	Explanation
Separating duties	Separating the duties necessary to complete a task and assigning the separated duties to two or more employees reduces the opportunity for either employee to defraud the company. It would require collusion between the two employees in order to make payment for a fabricated expense.
Hiring competent personnel	Cheap labor is not a bargain if the employees are incompetent. Employees should be properly trained and have a record that attests to personal integrity.
Bonding employees	Employees in positions of trust should be bonded through insurance policies that protect a company from losses caused by employee dishonesty.
Requiring extended absences	Forcing extended absences (such a vacations) creates an opportunity for the temporary replacement employee to check the work of the absent employees. Fraud is difficult to cover up if you are not present to do so.
Establishing clear lines of authority and responsibility	Employees tend to be more zealous in supporting company policies when they have clear authority to exercise enforcement. Further, they take their work more seriously when they realize that they cannot shirk responsibility.
Using prenumbered documents	Missing documents become apparent when there are gaps in a recorded sequence of numbers. For example, a stolen check would become apparent if a check register omits a check number.
Establishing physical controls	Keeping money in a safe; holding inventory in locked warehouses; and bolting computers to a desk are examples of using physical controls designed to protect assets.
Performing evaluations at regular intervals	Knowing that inventory will be counted on a regular basis encourages the inventory control manager to maintain documents that support the actual balance of inventory on hand. Similarly verifying the mileage on a car will encourage employees to use company-owned vehicles for legitimate business purposes. Regular evaluations and examinations are strong deterrents to the inappropriate utilization of company-owned assets.

recognizes *pressure* as a key ingredient of misconduct. A manager who is told to either make the numbers or be fired is more likely to cheat than one who is told to tell it like it is. Pressure can come from a variety of sources, including:

- Personal vices such as drug addition, gambling, and promiscuity.
- Intimidation from superiors.
- Personal debt from credit cards, consumer loans, mortgage loans or poor investments.
- Family expectations to provide a standard of living that is beyond one's capabilities.
- Business failure caused by poor decision making or temporary factors such as a poor economy.
- Loyalty or trying to be agreeable.

The third and final element of the fraud triangle is *rationalization*. Few individuals think of themselves as evil. They develop rationalizations to justify their misconduct. Common rationalizations include the following:

- Everybody does it.
- They are not paying me enough. I'm only taking what I deserve.

- I'm only borrowing the money. I'll pay it back.
- The company can afford it. Look what they are paying the officers.
- I'm taking what my family needs to live like everyone else.

Most people are able to resist pressure and the tendency to rationalize ethical or legal misconduct. However, some people will yield to temptation. What can companies do to protect themselves from unscrupulous characters? The answer lies in personal integrity. The best indicator of personal integrity is past performance. Accordingly companies must exercise due care in performing appropriate background investigations before hiring people to fill positions of trust.

Sarbanes-Oxley Act of 2002

Explain how the Sarbanes-Oxley Act affects management accountants.

In spite of ethics training and accounting controls, fraud and its devastating consequences persist. **Enron**, **WorldCom**, and **HealthSouth** are examples of massive scandals that destroyed or crippled major U.S. corporations in recent years. These high-profile cases led government officials to conclude that the force of law would be necessary to restore and maintain confidence in the capital markets. The **Sarbanes-Oxley (SOX) Act,** which became effective July 30, 2002, provides the muscle that Congress hopes will deter future fiascos. SOX affects four groups including: management, boards of directors, external auditors, and the Public Company Accounting Oversight Board (PCAOB). In this text, we focus on how SOX affects corporate management. While extensive coverage of SOX is beyond the scope of this text, all management accountants should be aware of the following:

- SOX holds the chief executive officer (CEO) and the chief financial officer (CFO) responsible for the establishment and enforcement of a strong set of internal controls.

FOCUS ON INTERNATIONAL ISSUES

FINANCIAL ACCOUNTING VERSUS MANAGERIAL ACCOUNTING—AN INTERNATIONAL PERSPECTIVE

This chapter has already explained some of the conceptual differences between financial and managerial accounting, but these differences have implications for international businesses as well. With respect to financial accounting, publicly traded companies in most countries must follow the generally accepted accounting principles (GAAP) for their country, but these rules can vary from country to country. Only companies that are audited under the auditing standards of the United States have to follow the standards established by the Financial Accounting Standards Board. European companies follow the standards established by the International Accounting Standards Board. For example, the United States is one of very few countries whose GAAP allow the use of the LIFO inventory flow assumption.

Conversely, most of the managerial accounting concepts introduced in this course can be used by businesses in any country. For example, *activity-based costing (ABC)* in a topic addressed in Chapter 6, and it is used by many companies in the United States. Meanwhile, a study published in *Accountancy Ireland** found that approximately one-third of the companies surveyed in Ireland, the United Kingdom, and New Zealand are also either currently using ABC, or are considering adopting it.

*Bernard Pierce, "Activity-Based Costing; the Irish Experience: True Innovation or Passing Fad?" *Accountancy Ireland,* October 2004, pp. 28–31.

Along with its annual report, companies are required to report on the effectiveness of their internal controls. Also, the company's external auditors are required to attest to the accuracy of the internal controls report.

■ SOX charges the CEO and the CFO with the ultimate responsibility for the accuracy of the company's financial statements and the accompanying footnotes. Even though lower level managers will likely prepare the annual report, the CEO and CFO are required to certify that they have reviewed the report and that, to their knowledge, the report does not contain false statements or significant omissions. An intentional misrepresentation is punishable by a fine of up to $5 million and imprisonment of up to 20 years.

■ ○ SOX requires management to establish a code of ethics and to file reports on the code in the company's annual 10K report filed with the Securities and Exchange Commission.

■ SOX demands that management establish a hotline and other mechanisms for the anonymous reporting of fraudulent activities. Further, SOX prohibits companies from punishing whistleblowers, employees who legally report corporate misconduct.

The accounting profession and government authorities are becoming increasingly intolerant of unethical conduct and illegal activity. A single mistake can jeopardize an accountant's career. A person guilty of white-collar crime loses the opportunity for white-collar employment. Second chances are rarely granted.

A Look Back

Managerial accounting focuses on the information needs of *internal* users, while *financial accounting* focuses on the information needs of *external* users. Managerial accounting uses economic, operating, and nonfinancial, as well as financial, data. Managerial accounting information is local (pertains to the company's subunits), is limited by cost/benefit considerations, is more concerned with relevance and timeliness, and is future oriented. Financial accounting information, on the other hand, is more global than managerial accounting information. It supplies information that applies to the whole company. Financial accounting is regulated by numerous authorities, is characterized by objectivity, is focused on reliability and accuracy, and is historical in nature.

Both managerial and financial accounting are concerned with product costing. Financial accountants need product cost information to determine the amount of inventory reported on the balance sheet and the amount of cost of goods sold reported on the income statement. Managerial accountants need to know the cost of products for pricing decisions and for control and evaluation purposes. When determining unit product costs, managers use the average cost per unit. Determining the actual cost of each product requires an unreasonable amount of time and record keeping and it makes no difference in product pricing and product cost control decisions.

Product costs are the costs incurred to make products: the costs of direct materials, direct labor, and overhead. *Overhead costs* are product costs that cannot be cost effectively traced to a product; therefore, they are assigned to products using *cost allocation*. Overhead costs include indirect materials, indirect labor, depreciation, rent, and utilities for manufacturing facilities. Product costs are first accumulated in an asset account (Inventory). They are expensed as cost of goods sold in the period the inventory is sold. The difference between sales revenue and cost of goods sold is called *gross margin.*

General, selling, and administrative costs are classified separately from product costs. They are subtracted from gross margin to determine net income. General, selling, and administrative costs can be divided into two categories. Costs incurred before the manufacturing process begins (research and development costs) are *upstream costs*. Costs incurred after manufacturing is complete (transportation) are *downstream costs*. Service companies, like manufacturing companies, incur materials, labor, and overhead costs, but the products provided by service companies are consumed immediately. Therefore, service company product costs are not accumulated in an Inventory account. A *code of ethical conduct* is needed in the accounting profession because accountants hold positions of trust and face conflicts of interest. In recognition of the temptations that accountants face, the IMA has issued *Standards of Ethical Conduct for Management Accountants,* which provides accountants guidance in resisting temptations and in making difficult decisions.

Emerging trends such as *just-in-time inventory* and *activity-based management* are methods that many companies have used to reengineer their production and delivery systems to eliminate waste, reduce errors, and minimize costs. Activity-based management seeks to eliminate or reduce *nonvalue-added activities* and to create new *value-added activities*. Just-in-time inventory seeks to reduce inventory holding costs and to lower prices for customers by making inventory available just in time for customer consumption.

>> A Look Forward

In addition to distinguishing costs by product versus G, S, & A classification, other classifications can be used to facilitate managerial decision making. In the next chapter, costs are classified according to the *behavior* they exhibit when the number of units of product increases or decreases (volume of activity changes). You will learn to distinguish between costs that vary with activity volume changes versus costs that remain fixed with activity volume changes. You will learn not only to recognize *cost behavior* but also how to use such recognition to evaluate business risk and opportunity.

APPENDIX A

Understanding Cash Flow

The **statement of cash flows** explains how a company obtained and used *cash* during the accounting period (usually one year). The sources of cash are called *cash inflows,* and the uses are known as *cash outflows*. The statement classifies cash receipts (inflows) and payments (outflows) into three categories: operating activities, investing activities, and financing activities. The **operating activities** section of the statement of cash flows reports the cash received from revenue and the cash paid for expenses.

The **investing activities** section of the statement of cash flows includes cash received from the sales of or the amount paid for productive assets. **Productive assets** are assets used to operate the business. They are sometimes called *long-term* assets because they are normally used for more than one accounting period. For example, cash outflows for the purchase of land or cash inflows from the sale of a building would be reported in the investing activities section of the statement of cash flows. In contrast, cash spent for the purchase of supplies would be reported in the operating activities section because supplies represent short-term assets that would generally be consumed within a single accounting period.

The **financing activities** section of the statement of cash flows reports the cash transactions associated with the resource providers (owners and creditors). More specifically, financing activities include cash obtained from or paid to owners, including dividends. Also, cash borrowed from or principal repaid to creditors would be reported in the financing activities section. However, note that interest paid to creditors is treated as an expense and is reported in the operating activities section of the statement of cash flows. The primary cash inflows and outflows associated with each type of business activity are shown in Exhibit 1.18; the list of items in the exhibit is not comprehensive. More detailed coverage of the statement of cash flows is presented in Chapter 14.

EXHIBIT 1.18

Classification Scheme: Statement of Cash Flows

Cash flows from operating activities:
Cash receipts (inflows) from revenue
Cash payments (outflows) for expenses (including interest)

Cash flows from investing activities:
Cash receipts (inflows) from the sale of long-term assets
Cash payments (outflows) for the purchase of long-term assets

Cash flows from financing activities:
Cash receipts (inflows) from borrowed funds
Cash receipts (inflows) from issuing common stock
Cash payments (outflows) to repay borrowed funds
Cash payments (outflows) for dividends

Emerging Trends in Managerial Accounting

Global competition has forced many companies to reengineer their production and delivery systems to eliminate waste, reduce errors, and minimize costs. A key ingredient of successful **reengineering** is benchmarking. **Benchmarking** involves identifying the **best practices** used by world-class competitors. By studying and mimicking these practices, a company uses benchmarking to implement highly effective and efficient operating methods. Best practices employed by world-class companies include total quality management (TQM), activity-based management (ABM), and value-added assessment.

LO 10

Identify emerging trends in accounting.

Total Quality Management

To promote effective and efficient operations, many companies practice **total quality management (TQM).** TQM is a two-dimensional management philosophy using (1) a systematic problem-solving philosophy that encourages front-line workers to achieve *zero defects* and (2) an organizational commitment to achieving *customer satisfaction.* A key component of TQM is **continuous improvement,** an ongoing process through which employees strive to eliminate waste, reduce response time, minimize defects, and simplify the design and delivery of products and services to customers.

Activity-Based Management

Simple changes in perspective can have dramatic results. For example, imagine how realizing the world is round instead of flat changed the nature of travel. A recent change in perspective developing in management accounting is the realization that an organization cannot manage *costs.* Instead, it manages the *activities* that cause costs to be incurred. **Activities** represent the measures an organization takes to accomplish its goals.

The primary goal of all organizations is to provide products (goods and services) their customers *value.* The sequence of activities used to provide products is called a **value chain. Activity-based management** assesses the value chain to create new or refine existing **value-added activities** and to eliminate or reduce *nonvalue-added activities.* A value-added activity is any unit of work that contributes to a product's ability to satisfy customer needs. For example, cooking is an activity that adds value to food served to a hungry customer. **Nonvalue-added** activities are tasks undertaken that do not contribute to a product's ability to satisfy customer needs. Waiting for the oven to preheat so that food can be cooked does not add value. Most customers value cooked food, but they do not value waiting for it.

To illustrate, consider the value-added activities undertaken by a pizza restaurant. Begin with a customer who is hungry for pizza; certain activities must occur to satisfy that hunger. These activities are pictured in Exhibit 1.19. At a minimum, the restaurant must conduct research and development (devise a recipe), obtain raw materials (acquire the ingredients), manufacture the product (combine and bake the ingredients), market the product (advertise its availability), and deliver the product (transfer the pizza to the customer).

Businesses gain competitive advantages by adding activities that satisfy customer needs. For example, **Domino's Pizza** grew briskly by recognizing the value customers placed on the convenience of home pizza delivery. Alternatively, **Little Caesar's** has been highly successful by satisfying customers

EXHIBIT 1.19

Value Chain

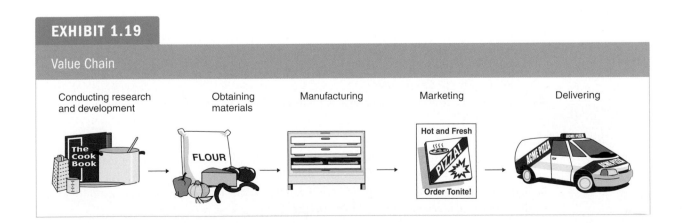

| Conducting research and development | Obtaining materials | Manufacturing | Marketing | Delivering |

who value low prices. Other restaurants capitalize on customer values pertaining to taste, ambience, or location. Businesses can also gain competitive advantages by identifying and eliminating nonvalue-added activities, providing products of comparable quality at lower cost than competitors.

Value Chain Analysis Across Companies

Comprehensive value chain analysis extends from obtaining raw materials to the ultimate disposition of finished products. It encompasses the activities performed not only by a particular organization but also by that organization's suppliers and those who service its finished products. For example, **PepsiCo** must be concerned with the activities of the company that supplies the containers for its soft drinks as well as the retail companies that sell its products. If cans of Pepsi fail to open properly, the customer is more likely to blame PepsiCo than the supplier of the cans. Comprehensive value chain analysis can lead to identifying and eliminating nonvalue-added activities that occur between companies. For example, container producers could be encouraged to build manufacturing facilities near Pepsi's bottling factories, eliminating the nonvalue-added activity of transporting empty containers from the manufacturer to the bottling facility. The resulting cost savings benefits customers by reducing costs without affecting quality.

SELF-STUDY REVIEW PROBLEM

A step-by-step audio-narrated series of slides is provided on the text website at www.mhhe.com/edmonds2008.

Tuscan Manufacturing Company makes a unique headset for use with mobile phones. During 2008, its first year of operations, Tuscan experienced the following accounting events. Other than the adjusting entries for depreciation, assume that all transactions are cash transactions.

1. Acquired $850,000 cash from the issue of common stock.
2. Paid $50,000 of research and development costs to develop the headset.
3. Paid $140,000 for the materials used to make headsets, all of which were started and completed during the year.
4. Paid salaries of $82,200 to selling and administrative employees.
5. Paid wages of $224,000 to production workers.
6. Paid $48,000 to purchase furniture used in selling and administrative offices.
7. Recognized depreciation on the office furniture. The furniture, acquired January 1, had an $8,000 estimated salvage value and a four-year useful life. The amount of depreciation is computed as [(cost − salvage) ÷ useful life]. Specifically, [($48,000 − $8,000) ÷ 4 = $10,000].
8. Paid $65,000 to purchase manufacturing equipment.
9. Recognized depreciation on the manufacturing equipment. The equipment, acquired January 1, had a $5,000 estimated salvage value and a three-year useful life. The amount of depreciation is computed as [(cost − salvage) ÷ useful life]. Specifically, [($65,000 − $5,000) ÷ 3 = $20,000].
10. Paid $136,000 for rent and utility costs on the manufacturing facility.
11. Paid $41,000 for inventory holding expenses for completed headsets (rental of warehouse space, salaries of warehouse personnel, and other general storage costs).
12. Tuscan started and completed 20,000 headset units during 2008. The company sold 18,400 headsets at a price of $38 per unit.
13. Compute the average product cost per unit and recognize the appropriate amount of cost of goods sold.

Required

a. Show how these events affect the balance sheet, income statement, and statement of cash flows by recording them in a horizontal financial statements model.

b. Explain why Tuscan's recognition of cost of goods sold expense had no impact on cash flow.

c. Prepare a formal income statement for the year.

d. Distinguish between the product costs and the upstream and downstream costs that Tuscan incurred.

e. The company president believes that Tuscan could save money by buying the inventory that it currently makes. The warehouse supervisor said that would not be possible because the purchase price of $27 per unit was above the $26 average cost per unit of making the product. Assuming that the purchased inventory would be available on demand, explain how the company president could be correct and why the warehouse supervisor could be biased in his assessment of the option to buy the inventory.

Solution to Requirement a

Event No.	Cash	Inventory +	Office Furn.* +	Manuf. Equip.* =	Com. Stk. +	Ret. Ear.	Rev. −	Exp. =	Net Inc.	Cash Flow	
			Assets		**=**	**Equity**					
1	850,000				850,000					850,000	FA
2	(50,000)					(50,000)	−	50,000	(50,000)	(50,000)	OA
3	(140,000)	140,000								(140,000)	OA
4	(82,200)					(82,200)	−	82,200	(82,200)	(82,200)	OA
5	(224,000)	224,000								(224,000)	OA
6	(48,000)		48,000							(48,000)	IA
7			(10,000)			(10,000)	−	10,000	(10,000)		
8	(65,000)			65,000						(65,000)	IA
9		20,000		(20,000)							
10	(136,000)	136,000								(136,000)	OA
11	(41,000)					(41,000)	−	41,000	(41,000)	(41,000)	OA
12	699,200					699,200	699,200		699,200	699,200	OA
13		(478,400)				(478,400)	−	478,400	(478,400)		
Totals	763,000 +	41,600 +	38,000 +	45,000 =	850,000 +	37,600	699,200 −	661,600 =	37,600	763,000	NC

*Negative amounts in these columns represent accumulated depreciation.

The average cost per unit of product is determined by dividing the total product cost by the number of headsets produced. Specifically, ($140,000 + $224,000 + $20,000 + $136,000) ÷ 20,000 = $26. Cost of goods sold is $478,400 ($26 × 18,400).

Solution to Requirement b

The impact on cash flow occurs when Tuscan pays for various product costs. In this case, cash outflows occurred when Tuscan paid for materials, labor, and overhead. The cash flow consequences of these transactions were recognized before the cost of goods sold expense was recognized.

Solution to Requirement c

TUSCAN MANUFACTURING COMPANY	
Income Statement	
For the Year Ended December 31, 2008	
Sales Revenue (18,400 units × $38)	$699,200
Cost of Goods Sold (18,400 × $26)	(478,400)
Gross Margin	220,800
R & D Expenses	(50,000)
Selling and Admin. Salary Expense	(82,200)
Admin. Depreciation Expense	(10,000)
Inventory Holding Expense	(41,000)
Net Income	$ 37,600

Solution to Requirement d

Inventory product costs for manufacturing companies focus on the costs necessary to make the product. The cost of research and development (Event 2) occurs before the inventory is made and is therefore an upstream cost, not an inventory (product) cost. The inventory holding costs (Event 11) are incurred after the inventory has been made and are therefore downstream costs, not product costs. Selling costs (included in Events 4 and 7) are normally incurred after products have been made and are therefore usually classified as downstream costs. Administrative costs (also included in Events 4 and 7) are not related to making products and are therefore not classified as product costs. Administrative costs may be incurred before, during, or after products are made, so they may be classified as either upstream or downstream costs. Only the costs of materials, labor, and overhead that are actually incurred for the purpose of making goods (Events 3, 5, 9, and 10) are classified as product costs.

Solution to Requirement e

Since the merchandise would be available on demand, Tuscan could operate a just-in-time inventory system thereby eliminating the inventory holding expense. Since the additional cost to purchase is $1 per unit ($27 − $26), it would cost Tuscan an additional $20,000 ($1 × 20,000 units) to purchase its product. However, the company would save $41,000 of inventory holding expense. The warehouse supervisor could be biased by the fact that his job would be lost if the company purchased its products and thereby could eliminate the need for warehousing inventory. If Tuscan does not maintain inventory, it would not need a warehouse supervisor.

KEY TERMS

Activities 25	Financial Accounting	Just in time (JIT) 15	Reengineering 25
Activity-based management	Standards Board	Managerial accounting 4	Sarbanes-Oxley Act
(ABM) 25	(FASB) 4	Manufacturing overhead 12	of 2002 22
Average cost 6	Financing activities 24	Nonvalue-added	Securities and Exchange
Benchmarking 25	Finished goods 6	activities 25	Commission (SEC) 4
Best practices 25	General, selling, and	Operating activities 24	Statement of cash flows 24
Continuous improvement 25	administrative costs 11	Opportunity cost 16	Total quality management
Cost allocation 12	Generally accepted	Overhead 6	(TQM) 25
Cost-plus pricing 5	accounting principles	Period costs 11	Upstream costs 13
Direct labor 10	(GAAP) 4	Product costs 5	Value-added activity 25
Direct raw materials 9	Indirect costs 12	Product costing 5	Value-added principle 5
Downstream costs 14	Inventory holding costs 15	Productive assets 24	Value chain 25
Financial accounting 4	Investing activities 24	Raw materials 9	

QUESTIONS

1. What are some differences between financial and managerial accounting?

2. What does the value-added principle mean as it applies to managerial accounting information? Give an example of value-added information that may be included in managerial accounting reports but is not shown in publicly reported financial statements.

3. What are the two dimensions of a total quality management (TQM) program? Why is TQM being used in business practice? (Appendix B)

4. How does product costing used in financial accounting differ from product costing used in managerial accounting?

5. What does the statement "costs can be assets or expenses" mean?

6. Why are the salaries of production workers accumulated in an inventory account instead of being expensed on the income statement?

7. How do product costs affect the financial statements? How does the classification of product cost (as an asset vs. an expense) affect net income?

8. What is an indirect cost? Provide examples of product costs that would be classified as indirect.

9. How does a product cost differ from a general, selling, and administrative cost? Give examples of each.

10. Why is cost classification important to managers?

11. What is cost allocation? Give an example of a cost that needs to be allocated.

12. How has the Institute of Management Accountants responded to the need for high standards of ethical conduct in the accounting profession?

13. What are some of the common ethical conflicts that accountants encounter?

14. What costs should be considered in determining the sales price of a product?

15. What is a just-in-time (JIT) inventory system? Name some inventory costs that can be eliminated or reduced by its use.

16. What does the term *reengineering* mean? Name some reengineering practices. (Appendix B)

17. What does the term *activity-based management* mean? (Appendix B)

18. What is a value chain? (Appendix B)

19. What do the terms *value-added activity* and *nonvalue-added activity* mean? Provide an example of each type of activity. (Appendix B)

MULTIPLE-CHOICE QUESTIONS

Multiple-choice questions are provided on the text website at www.mhhe.com/edmonds2008.

EXERCISES—SERIES A

All Exercises in Series A are available with McGraw-Hill's Homework Manager®.

Exercise 1-1A *Identifying financial versus managerial accounting items*   L.O. 1

Required

Indicate whether each of the following items is representative of managerial or of financial accounting.

a. Information includes economic and nonfinancial data as well as financial data.
b. Information is global and pertains to the company as a whole.
c. Information is provided to insiders including executives, managers, and operators.
d. Information is factual and is characterized by objectivity, reliability, consistency, and accuracy.
e. Information is reported continuously and has a current or future orientation.
f. Information is provided to outsiders including investors, creditors, government agencies, analysts, and reporters.
g. Information is regulated by the SEC, FASB, and other sources of GAAP.
h. Information is based on estimates that are bounded by relevance and timeliness.
i. Information is historically based and usually reported annually.
j. Information is local and pertains to subunits of the organization.

Exercise 1-2A *Identifying product versus general, selling, and administrative costs*   L.O. 3

Required

Indicate whether each of the following costs should be classified as a product cost or as a general, selling, and administrative cost.

a. Research and development costs incurred to create new drugs for a pharmaceutical company.
b. The cost of secretarial supplies used in a doctor's office.
c. Depreciation on the office furniture of the company president.
d. Direct materials used in a manufacturing company.
e. Indirect materials used in a manufacturing company.

f. Salaries of employees working in the accounting department.
g. Commissions paid to sales staff.
h. Interest on the mortgage for the company's corporate headquarters.
i. Indirect labor used to manufacture inventory.
j. Attorney's fees paid to protect the company from frivolous lawsuits.

L.O. 3

Exercise 1-3A   *Classifying Costs: Product or GS&A/Asset or Expense*

Required

Use the following format to classify each cost as a product cost or a general, selling, and administrative (GS&A) cost. Also indicate whether the cost would be recorded as an asset or an expense. The first item is shown as an example.

Cost Category	Product/ GS&A	Asset/ Expense
Promotion costs	GS&A	Expense
Production supplies		
Depreciation on administration building		
Depreciation on manufacturing equipment		
Research and development costs		
Cost to set up manufacturing equipment		
Utilities used in factory		
Cars for sales staff		
Distributions to stockholders		
General office supplies		
Raw materials used in the manufacturing process		
Cost to rent office equipment		
Wages of production workers		
Advertising costs		

L.O. 3

Exercise 1-4A   *Identifying effect of product versus general, selling, and administrative costs on financial statements*

Required

Highfield Corporation recognized accrued compensation cost. Use the following model to show how this event would affect the company's financial statement under the following two assumptions: (1) the compensation is for office personnel and (2) the compensation is for production workers. Use pluses or minuses to show the effect on each element. If an element is not affected, indicate so by placing the letters NA under the appropriate heading.

	Assets	=	Liab.	+	Equity	Rev.	−	Exp.	=	Net Inc.	Cash Flow
1.											
2.											

L.O. 3

Exercise 1-5A   *Identify effect of product versus general, selling, and administrative costs on financial statements*

Required

Lowder Industries recognized the annual cost of depreciation on December 31, 2008. Using the following horizontal financial statements model, indicate how this event affected the company's financial statements under the following two assumptions: (1) the depreciation was on office furniture and (2) the depreciation was on manufacturing equipment. Indicate whether the event increases (I), decreases (D), or has no affect (NA) on each element of the financial statements. Also, in the Cash Flow column, indicate whether the cash flow is associated with operating activities (OA), investing activities (IA), or financing activities (FA). (Note: Show accumulated depreciation as a decrease in the book value of the appropriate asset account.)

Event No.		Assets				Equity							Cash Flow
	Cash	+ Inventory	+ Manuf. Equip.	+ Office Furn.	=	Com. Stk.	+	Ret. Ear.		Rev.	− Exp.	= Net Inc.	
1.													
2.													

Exercise 1-6A *Identifying product costs in a manufacturing company*   L.O. 2

Jill Rogers was talking to another accounting student, Frank Vinson. Upon discovering that the accounting department offered an upper-level course in cost measurement, Jill remarked to Frank, "How difficult can it be? My parents own a toy store. All you have to do to figure out how much something costs is look at the invoice. Surely you don't need an entire course to teach you how to read an invoice."

Required

a. Identify the three main components of product cost for a manufacturing entity.
b. Explain why measuring product cost for a manufacturing entity is more complex than measuring product cost for a retail toy store.
c. Assume that Jill's parents rent a store for $8,000 per month. Different types of toys use different amounts of store space. For example, displaying a bicycle requires more store space than displaying a deck of cards. Also, some toys remain on the shelf longer than others. Fad toys sell rapidly, but traditional toys sell more slowly. Under these circumstances, how would you determine the amount of rental cost required to display each type of toy? Identify two other costs incurred by a toy store that may be difficult to allocate to individual toys.

Exercise 1-7A *Identifying product versus general, selling, and administrative costs*   L.O. 3

A review of the accounting records of Borland Manufacturing indicated that the company incurred the following payroll costs during the month of September.

1. Salary of the company president—$128,000.
2. Salary of the vice president of manufacturing—$64,000.
3. Salary of the chief financial officer—$75,200.
4. Salary of the vice president of marketing—$62,400.
5. Salaries of middle managers (department heads, production supervisors) in manufacturing plant—$784,000.
6. Wages of production workers—$3,752,000.
7. Salaries of administrative secretaries—$448,000.
8. Salaries of engineers and other personnel responsible for maintaining production equipment—$712,000.
9. Commissions paid to sales staff—$1,008,000.

Required

a. What amount of payroll cost would be classified as general, selling, and administrative expense?
b. Assuming that Borland made 4,000 units of product and sold 3,600 of them during the month of September, determine the amount of payroll cost that would be included in cost of goods sold.

Exercise 1-8A *Recording product versus general, selling, and administrative costs in a*   L.O. 2, 3
financial statements model

Guyton Manufacturing experienced the following events during its first accounting period.

1. Recognized depreciation on manufacturing equipment.
2. Recognized depreciation on office furniture.

3. Recognized revenue from cash sale of products.
4. Recognized cost of goods sold from sale referenced in Event 3.
5. Acquired cash by issuing common stock.
6. Paid cash to purchase raw materials that were used to make products.
7. Paid wages to production workers.
8. Paid salaries to administrative staff.

Required

Use the following horizontal financial statements model to show how each event affects the balance sheet, income statement, and statement of cash flows. Indicate whether the event increases (I), decreases (D), or has no effect (NA) on each element of the financial statements. In the Cash Flow column, indicate whether the cash flow is associated with operating activities (OA), investing activities (IA), or financing activities (FA). The first transaction has been recorded as an example. (*Note:* Show accumulated depreciation as a decrease in the book value of the appropriate asset account.)

Event No.	Assets				Equity						
	Cash	+ Inventory	+ Manuf. Equip.* +	Office Furn. =	Com. Stk. +	Ret. Ear.	Rev. −	Exp. =	Net Inc.	Cash Flow
1.	NA	I	D	NA	NA	NA	NA	NA	NA	NA

L.O. 2

Exercise 1-9A *Allocating product costs between ending inventory and cost of goods sold*

Lyon Manufacturing Company began operations on January 1. During the year, it started and completed 4,000 units of product. The company incurred the following costs.

1. Raw materials purchased and used—$4,000.
2. Wages of production workers—$6,000.
3. Salaries of administrative and sales personnel—$2,400.
4. Depreciation on manufacturing equipment—$7,200.
5. Depreciation on administrative equipment—$2,800.

Lyon sold 3,000 units of product.

Required

a. Determine the total product cost for the year.
b. Determine the total cost of the ending inventory.
c. Determine the total of cost of goods sold.

L.O. 3

Exercise 1-10A *Financial statement effects for manufacturing versus service organizations*

The following financial statements model shows the effects of recognizing depreciation in two different circumstances. One circumstance represents recognizing depreciation on a machine used in a factory. The other circumstance recognizes depreciation on computers used in a consulting firm. The effects of each event have been recorded using the letter (I) to represent increase, (D) for decrease, and (NA) for no effect.

Event No.	Assets				Equity						
	Cash	+ Inventory	+ Equip. =	Com. Stk. +	Ret. Ear.	Rev. −	Exp. =	Net Inc.	Cash Flow
1	NA	NA	D	NA	D	NA	I	D	NA
2	NA	I	D	NA	NA	NA	NA	NA	NA

Required

a. Identify the event that represents depreciation on the computers.
b. Explain why recognizing depreciation on equipment used in a manufacturing company affects financial statements differently from recognizing depreciation on equipment used in a service organization.

Exercise 1-11A *Identifying the effect of product versus general, selling, and administrative cost on the income statement and statement of cash flows*

L.O. 3

Required

Each of the following events describes acquiring an asset that requires a year-end adjusting entry. Explain how acquiring the asset and making the adjusting entry affect the amount of net income and the cash flow shown on the year-end financial statements. Also, in the Cash Flow column, indicate whether the cash flow is associated with operating activities (OA), investing activities (IA), or financing activities (FA). Use (NA) for no effect. Assume a December 31 annual closing date. The first event has been recorded as an example. Assume that any products that have been made have not been sold.

Event No.	Net Income Amount of Change	Cash Flow Amount of Change
1. Purchase of computer equipment	NA	(7,000)
1. Make adjusting entry	$(1,500)	NA

1. Paid $7,000 cash on January 1 to purchase computer equipment to be used for administrative purposes. The equipment had an estimated expected useful life of four years and a $1,000 salvage value.
2. Paid $7,000 cash on January 1 to purchase manufacturing equipment. The equipment had an estimated expected useful life of four years and a $1,000 salvage value.
3. Paid $6,000 cash in advance on May 1 for a one-year rental contract on administrative offices.
4. Paid $6,000 cash in advance on May 1 for a one-year rental contract on manufacturing facilities.
5. Paid $1,000 cash to purchase supplies to be used by the marketing department. At the end of the year, $200 of supplies was still on hand.
6. Paid $1,000 cash to purchase supplies to be used in the manufacturing process. At the end of the year, $200 of supplies was still on hand.

Exercise 1-12A *Upstream and downstream costs*

L.O. 4

During 2008, Adair Manufacturing Company incurred $9,000,000 of research and development (R&D) costs to create a long-life battery to use in computers. In accordance with FASB standards, the entire R&D cost was recognized as an expense in 2008. Manufacturing costs (direct materials, direct labor, and overhead) are expected to be $26 per unit. Packaging, shipping, and sales commissions are expected to be $5 per unit. Adair expects to sell 200,000 batteries before new research renders the battery design technologically obsolete. During 2008, Adair made 22,000 batteries and sold 20,000 of them.

Required

a. Identify the upstream and downstream costs.
b. Determine the 2008 amount of cost of goods sold and the ending inventory balance.
c. Determine the sales price assuming that Adair desires to earn a profit margin that is equal to 25 percent of the *total cost* of developing, making, and distributing the batteries.
d. Prepare an income statement for 2008. Use the sales price developed in Requirement *c*.
e. Why would Adair price the batteries at a level that would generate a loss for the 2008 accounting period?

Exercise 1-13A *Identify the effect of a just-in-time inventory system on financial statements*

L.O. 6

After reviewing the financial statements of Martina Company, Joe Santana concluded that the company was a service company. Mr. Santana based his conclusion on the fact that Martina's financial statements displayed no inventory accounts.

Required

Explain how Martina's implementation of a 100 percent effective just-in-time inventory system could have led Mr. Santana to a false conclusion regarding the nature of Martina's business.

L.O. 6

Exercise 1-14A   *Using JIT to minimize waste and lost opportunity*

Kim Weston, a teacher at Reid Middle School, is in charge of ordering the T-shirts to be sold for the school's annual fund-raising project. The T-shirts are printed with a special Reid School logo. In some years, the supply of T-shirts has been insufficient to satisfy the number of sales orders. In other years, T-shirts have been left over. Excess T-shirts are normally donated to some charitable organization. T-shirts cost the school $4 each and are normally sold for $6 each. Ms. Weston has decided to order 500 shirts.

Required

a. If the school receives actual sales orders for 450 shirts, what amount of profit will the school earn? What is the cost of waste due to excess inventory?

b. If the school receives actual sales orders for 550 shirts, what amount of profit will the school earn? What amount of opportunity cost will the school incur?

c. Explain how a JIT inventory system could maximize profitability by eliminating waste and opportunity cost.

L.O. 6

Exercise 1-15A   *Using JIT to minimize holding costs*

Cedric Pet Supplies purchases its inventory from a variety of suppliers, some of which require a six-week lead time before delivering the goods. To ensure that she has a sufficient supply of goods on hand, Ms. Keiser, the owner, must maintain a large supply of inventory. The cost of this inventory averages $40,000. She usually finances the purchase of inventory and pays a 10 percent annual finance charge. Ms. Keiser's accountant has suggested that she establish a relationship with a single large distributor who can satisfy all of her orders within a two-week time period. Given this quick turnaround time, she will be able to reduce her average inventory balance to $10,000. Ms. Keiser also believes that she could save $6,000 per year by reducing phone bills, insurance, and warehouse rental space costs associated with ordering and maintaining the larger level of inventory.

Required

a. Is the new inventory system available to Ms. Keiser a pure or approximate just-in-time system?

b. Based on the information provided, how much of Ms. Keiser's inventory holding cost could be eliminated by taking the accountant's advice?

L.O. 9

Exercise 1-16A   *Applications of the Sarbanes-Oxley Act*

The CFO of the Bancor Microscope Corporation intentionally misclassified a downstream transportation expense in the amount of $50,000,000 as a product cost in an accounting period when the company made 10,000 microscopes and sold 8,000 microscopes. Bancor rewards its officers with bonuses that are based on net earnings.

Required

a. Indicate whether the elements on the financial statements (i.e., assets, liabilities, equity, revenue, expense, net income, and cash flow) would be overstated or understated as a result of the misclassification of the upstream research and development expense. Determine the amount of the overstatement or understatement for each element.

b. Based on the provisions of the Sarbanes-Oxley Act, what is the maximum penalty that the CFO could face for deliberately missrepresenting the financial statements?

L.O. 9

Exercise 1-17A   *Professional conduct and code of ethics*

In February 2006 former senator Warren Rudman of New Hampshire completed a 17-month investigation of an $11 billion accounting scandal at Fannie Mae (a major enterprise involved in home-mortgage financing), The Rudman investigation concluded that Fannie Mae's CFO and controller used an accounting gimmick to manipulate financial statements in order to meet earnings-per-share (EPS) targets. Meeting the EPS targets triggered bonus payments for the executives.

Required

Review the standards of professional conduct shown in Exhibit 1.15. Identify and comment on which of the standards the CFO and controller violated.

Appendix

Exercise 1-18A   *Value chain analysis*

L.O. 10

SoundWave Company manufactures and sells high-quality audio speakers. The speakers are encased in solid walnut cabinets supplied by Herrin Cabinet, Inc. Herrin packages the speakers in durable moisture-proof boxes and ships them by truck to SoundWave's manufacturing facility, which is located 50 miles from the cabinet factory.

Required

Identify the nonvalue-added activities that occur between the companies described in the preceding scenario. Provide a logical explanation as to how these nonvalue-added activities could be eliminated.

PROBLEMS—SERIES A

All Problems in Series A are available with McGraw-Hill's Homework Manager®.

Problem 1-19A   *Product versus general, selling, and administrative costs*

L.O. 2, 3

Rousey Manufacturing Company was started on January 1, 2008, when it acquired $90,000 cash by issuing common stock. Rousey immediately purchased office furniture and manufacturing equipment costing $10,000 and $28,000, respectively. The office furniture had a five-year useful life and a zero salvage value. The manufacturing equipment had a $4,000 salvage value and an expected useful life of three years. The company paid $12,000 for salaries of administrative personnel and $16,000 for wages to production personnel. Finally, the company paid $18,000 for raw materials that were used to make inventory. All inventory was started and completed during the year. Rousey completed production on 5,000 units of product and sold 4,000 units at a price of $12 each in 2008. (Assume that all transactions are cash transactions.)

CHECK FIGURES
a. Average Cost per Unit:
   $8.40
f. $90,400

Required

a. Determine the total product cost and the average cost per unit of the inventory produced in 2008.
b. Determine the amount of cost of goods sold that would appear on the 2008 income statement.
c. Determine the amount of the ending inventory balance that would appear on the December 31, 2008, balance sheet.
d. Determine the amount of net income that would appear on the 2008 income statement.
e. Determine the amount of retained earnings that would appear on the December 31, 2008, balance sheet.
f. Determine the amount of total assets that would appear on the December 31, 2008, balance sheet.
g. Determine the amount of net cash flow from operating activities that would appear on the 2008 statement of cash flows.
h. Determine the amount of net cash flow from investing activities that would appear on the 2008 statement of cash flows.

Problem 1-20A   *Effect of product versus period costs on financial statements*

L.O. 2, 3
eXcel
www.mhhe.com/edmonds2008
CHECK FIGURES
Cash balance: $47,400
Net income: $10,700

Giovanni Manufacturing Company experienced the following accounting events during its first year of operation. With the exception of the adjusting entries for depreciation, assume that all transactions are cash transactions.

1. Acquired $67,000 cash by issuing common stock.
2. Paid $9,500 for the materials used to make its products, all of which were started and completed during the year.
3. Paid salaries of $5,300 to selling and administrative employees.
4. Paid wages of $6,200 to production workers.
5. Paid $9,600 for furniture used in selling and administrative offices. The furniture was acquired on January 1. It had a $1,600 estimated salvage value and a four-year useful life.
6. Paid $27,000 for manufacturing equipment. The equipment was acquired on January 1. It had a $3,000 estimated salvage value and a three-year useful life.
7. Sold inventory to customers for $38,000 that had cost $20,000 to make.

Required

Explain how these events would affect the balance sheet, income statement, and statement of cash flows by recording them in a horizontal financial statements model as indicated here. The first event is recorded as an example. In the Cash Flow column, indicate whether the amounts represent financing activities (FA), investing activities (IA), or operating activities (OA).

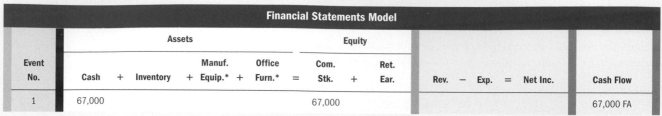

Financial Statements Model

Event No.	Assets					Equity							
	Cash	+ Inventory	+ Manuf. Equip.*	+ Office Furn.*	=	Com. Stk.	+	Ret. Ear.	Rev.	− Exp.	= Net Inc.	Cash Flow
1	67,000					67,000						67,000 FA

*Record accumulated depreciation as negative amounts in these columns.

L.O. 2, 3

Problem 1-21A   *Product versus general, selling, and administrative costs*

The following transactions pertain to 2007, the first-year operations of Kirby Company. All inventory was started and completed during 2007. Assume that all transactions are cash transactions.

1. Acquired $2,000 cash by issuing common stock.
2. Paid $400 for materials used to produce inventory.
3. Paid $600 to production workers.
4. Paid $200 rental fee for production equipment.
5. Paid $160 to administrative employees.
6. Paid $80 rental fee for administrative office equipment.
7. Produced 300 units of inventory of which 200 units were sold at a price of $7.00 each.

Required

Prepare an income statement, balance sheet, and statement of cash flows.

L.O. 2, 3, 5

www.mhhe.com/edmonds2008

Problem 1-22A   *Service versus manufacturing companies*

Chekwa Company began operations on January 1, 2008, by issuing common stock for $36,000 cash. During 2008, Chekwa received $48,000 cash from revenue and incurred costs that required $72,000 of cash payments.

Required

Prepare an income statement, balance sheet, and statement of cash flows for Chekwa Company for 2008, under each of the following independent scenarios.

a. Chekwa is a promoter of rock concerts. The $72,000 was paid to provide a rock concert that produced the revenue.

b. Chekwa is in the car rental business. The $72,000 was paid to purchase automobiles. The automobiles were purchased on January 1, 2008, have four-year useful lives, with no expected salvage value. Chekwa uses straight-line depreciation. The revenue was generated by leasing the automobiles.

c. Chekwa is a manufacturing company. The $72,000 was paid to purchase the following items:
    (1) Paid $9,600 cash to purchase materials that were used to make products during the year.
    (2) Paid $24,000 cash for wages of factory workers who made products during the year.
    (3) Paid $2,400 cash for salaries of sales and administrative employees.
    (4) Paid $36,000 cash to purchase manufacturing equipment. The equipment was used solely to make products. It had a three-year life and a $7,200 salvage value. The company uses straight-line depreciation.
    (5) During 2007, Chekwa started and completed 2,000 units of product. The revenue was earned when Chekwa sold 1,500 units of product to its customers.

d. Refer to Requirement *c*. Could Chekwa determine the actual cost of making the 500th unit of product? How likely is it that the actual cost of the 500th unit of product was exactly the same as the cost of producing the 501st unit of product? Explain why management may be more interested in average cost than in actual cost.

Problem 1-23A   *Importance of cost classification*

Bailey Manufacturing Company (BMC) was started when it acquired $40,000 by issuing common stock. During the first year of operations, the company incurred specifically identifiable product costs (materials, labor, and overhead) amounting to $24,000. BMC also incurred $16,000 of engineering design and planning costs. There was a debate regarding how the design and planning costs should be classified. Advocates of Option 1 believe that the costs should be classified as general, selling, and administrative costs. Advocates of Option 2 believe it is more appropriate to classify the design and planning costs as product costs. During the year, BMC made 4,000 units of product and sold 3,000 units at a price of $14 each. All transactions were cash transactions.

L.O. 2, 3, 7, 8

CHECK FIGURE
a. Option 1: NI = $8,000
    Option 2: Total
    Assets = $52,000

Required

a. Prepare an income statement, balance sheet, and statement of cash flows under each of the two options.

b. Identify the option that results in financial statements that are more likely to leave a favorable impression on investors and creditors.

c. Assume that BMC provides an incentive bonus to the company president equal to 10 percent of net income. Compute the amount of the bonus under each of the two options. Identify the option that provides the president with the higher bonus.

d. Assume a 35 percent income tax rate. Determine the amount of income tax expense under each of the two options. Identify the option that minimizes the amount of the company's income tax expense.

e. Comment on the conflict of interest between the company president as determined in Requirement *c* and the owners of the company as indicated in Requirement *d*. Describe an incentive compensation plan that would avoid a conflict of interest between the president and the owners.

Problem 1-24A   *Using JIT to reduce inventory holding costs*

DiChara Manufacturing Company obtains its raw materials from a variety of suppliers. DiChara's strategy is to obtain the best price by letting the suppliers know that it buys from the lowest bidder. Approximately four years ago, unexpected increased demand resulted in materials shortages. DiChara was unable to find the materials it needed even though it was willing to pay premium prices. Because of the lack of raw materials, DiChara was forced to close its manufacturing facility for two weeks. Its president vowed that her company would never again be at the mercy of its suppliers. She immediately ordered her purchasing agent to perpetually maintain a one-month supply of raw materials. Compliance with the president's orders resulted in a raw materials inventory amounting to approximately $2,000,000. Warehouse rental and personnel costs to maintain the inventory amounted to $10,000 per month. DiChara has a line of credit with a local bank that calls for a 12 percent annual rate of interest. Assume that DiChara finances the raw materials inventory with the line of credit.

L.O. 6

CHECK FIGURE
a. $360,000

Required

a. Based on the information provided, determine the annual holding cost of the raw materials inventory.

b. Explain how a JIT system could reduce DiChara's inventory holding cost.

c. Explain how most-favored customer status could enable DiChara to establish a JIT inventory system without risking the raw materials shortages experienced in the past.

Problem 1-25A   *Using JIT to minimize waste and lost opportunity*

Pass CPA, Inc., provides review courses twice each year for students studying to take the CPA exam. The cost of textbooks is included in the registration fee. Text material requires constant updating and is useful for only one course. To minimize printing costs and ensure availability of books on the first day of class, Pass CPA has books printed and delivered to its offices two weeks in advance of the first class. To ensure that enough books are available, Pass CPA normally orders 10 percent more than expected enrollment. Usually there is an oversupply and books are thrown away. However, demand occasionally exceeds expectations by more than 10 percent and there are too few books available for student use. Pass CPA has been forced to turn away students because of a lack of textbooks. Pass CPA expects to enroll approximately 100 students per course. The tuition fee is $800 per student. The cost of teachers is $25,000 per course, textbooks cost $60 each, and other operating expenses are estimated to be $35,000 per course.

L.O. 6

www.mhhe.com/edmonds2008

CHECK FIGURES
a. $900
b. $3,700

Required

a. Prepare an income statement, assuming that 95 students enroll in a course. Determine the cost of waste associated with unused books.

b. Prepare an income statement, assuming that 115 students attempt to enroll in the course. Note that five students are turned away because of too few textbooks. Determine the amount of lost profit resulting from the inability to serve the five additional students.

c. Suppose that textbooks can be produced through a high-speed copying process that permits delivery *just in time* for class to start. The cost of books made using this process, however, is $65 each. Assume that all books must be made using the same production process. In other words, Pass CPA cannot order some of the books using the regular copy process and the rest using the high-speed process. Prepare an income statement under the JIT system assuming that 95 students enroll in a course. Compare the income statement under JIT with the income statement prepared in Requirement *a*. Comment on how the JIT system would affect profitability.

d. Assume the same facts as in Requirement *c* with respect to a JIT system that enables immediate delivery of books at a cost of $65 each. Prepare an income statement under the JIT system, assuming that 115 students enroll in a course. Compare the income statement under JIT with the income statement prepared in Requirement *b*. Comment on how the JIT system would affect profitability.

e. Discuss the possible effect of the JIT system on the level of customer satisfaction.

L.O. 9

Problem 1-26A   *Internal control procedures*

James Blunt is a model employee. He has not missed a day of work in the last five years. He even forfeits his vacation time to make sure that things run smoothly. James literally does the work of two people. He started out working as the purchasing agent in charge of buying raw materials for a small manufacturing company. Approximately five years ago the inventory control agent in the receiving department resigned. James agreed to assume the duties of the control agent until a replacement could be hired. After all, James said that he knew what was supposed to be delivered to the company because as the purchasing agent he had been the person who placed orders for the inventory purchases. James did such a good job that the company never got around to hiring a replacement. James received the employee of the year award five out of the last six years. James is also very active in his community. He works with underprivileged children. His weekends are always filled with community service. Indeed, his commitment to social consciousness is described by some people as bordering on fanatical.

James recently had a serious heart attack. People said that he had overworked himself. His hospital room was filled with flowers and a steady stream of friends visited him. So, people were in shock when James was charged with embezzlement. Ultimately, it was revealed that while James was in the hospital his replacement discovered that James had been purchasing excess quantities of raw materials. He then sold the extra materials and kept the money for himself. This became apparent when the companies to whom James had been selling the excess materials called to place new orders. It was difficult to determine the extent of the embezzlement. After the accounting department paid for James's excess purchases, he would remove the paid voucher forms from the accounting files and destroy them. Since the forms were not numbered, it was impossible to determine how many of the paid forms were missing. At his trial, James's only explanation was: "I did it for the children. They needed the money far more than the company needed it."

Required

a. If the internal control procedures shown in Exhibit 1.17 had been followed, this embezzlement could have been avoided. Name the internal control procedures that were violated in this case.

b. Identify the specific components of the fraud triangle that were present in this case.

Appendix

Problem 1-27A   *Value chain analysis*

Palmer Company invented a new process for manufacturing ice cream. The ingredients are mixed in high-tech machinery that forms the product into small round beads. Like a bag of balls, the ice cream beads are surrounded by air pockets in packages. This design has numerous advantages. First, each bite of ice cream melts rapidly when placed in a person's mouth, creating a more flavorful sensation when compared to ordinary ice cream. Also, the air pockets mean that a typical serving includes a smaller amount of ice cream. This not only reduces materials cost but also provides the consumer with a low-calorie snack. A cup appears full of ice cream, but it is really half full of air. The consumer eats only half the ingredients that are contained in a typical cup of blended ice cream. Finally, the texture of the ice cream makes scooping it out of a large container a very easy task. The frustration of trying to get a spoon into a rock-solid package of blended ice cream has been eliminated. Palmer Company named the new product Sonic Cream.

Like many other ice cream producers, Palmer Company purchases its raw materials from a food wholesaler. The ingredients are mixed in Palmer's manufacturing plant. The packages of finished product are distributed to privately owned franchise ice cream shops that sell Sonic Cream directly to the public.

Palmer provides national advertising and is responsible for all research and development costs associated with making new flavors of Sonic Cream.

Required

a. Based on the information provided, draw a comprehensive value chain for Palmer Company that includes its suppliers and customers.
b. Identify the place in the chain where Palmer Company is exercising its opportunity to create added value beyond that currently being provided by its competitors.

EXERCISES—SERIES B

Exercise 1-1B   *Financial versus managerial accounting items*

L.O. 1

Required

Indicate whether each of the following items is representative of financial or managerial accounting.

a. Financial results used by stockbrokers to evaluate a company's profitability.
b. Quarterly budgets used by management to determine future borrowing needs.
c. Financial statements prepared in accordance with generally accepted accounting principles.
d. Annual financial reports submitted to the SEC in compliance with federal securities laws.
e. Projected budget information used to make logistical decisions.
f. Condensed financial information sent to current investors at the end of each quarter.
g. Audited financial statements submitted to bankers when applying for a line of credit.
h. A weekly cash budget used by the treasurer to determine whether cash on hand is excessive.
i. Monthly sales reports used by the vice president of marketing to help allocate funds.
j. Divisional profit reports used by the company president to determine bonuses for divisional vice presidents.

Exercise 1-2B   *Identifying product versus general, selling, and administrative costs*

L.O. 3

Required

Indicate whether each of the following costs should be classified as a product cost or as a general, selling, and administrative cost.

a. Wages paid to workers in a manufacturing plant.
b. The salary of the receptionist working in the sales department.
c. Supplies used in the sales department.
d. Wages of janitors who clean the factory floor.
e. The salary of the company president.
f. The salary of the cell phone manufacturing plant manager.
g. The depreciation on administrative buildings.
h. The depreciation on the company treasurer's computer.
i. The fabric used in making a customized sofa for a customer.
j. The salary of an engineer who maintains all manufacturing plant equipment.

Exercise 1-3B   *Classifying costs: product or period/asset or expense*

L.O. 3

Required

Use the following format to classify each cost as a product cost or a general, selling, and administrative (GS&A) cost. Also indicate whether the cost would be recorded as an asset or an expense. The first cost item is shown as an example.

Cost Category	Product/ G, S, & A	Asset/ Expense
Cost of a delivery truck	G, S, & A	Asset
Cash dividend to stockholders		
Cost of merchandise shipped to customers		
Depreciation on vehicles used by salespeople		
Wages of administrative building security guards		
Supplies used in the plant manager's office		
Computers for the accounting department		
Depreciation on computers used in factory		
Natural gas used in the factory		
Cost of television commercials		
Wages of factory workers		
Paper and ink cartridges used in the cashier's office		
Raw material used to make products		
Lubricant used to maintain factory equipment		

L.O. 3

Exercise 1-4B *Effect of product versus general, selling, and administrative costs on financial statements*

Required

Dunn Plastics Company accrued a tax liability for $2,500. Use the following horizontal financial statements model to show the effect of this accrual under the following two assumptions: (1) the tax is on administrative buildings or (2) the tax is on production equipment. Use plus signs and/or minus signs to show the effect on each element. If an element is not affected, indicate so by placing the letters NA under the appropriate heading.

	Assets	=	Liab.	+	Equity	Rev.	−	Exp.	=	Net Inc.	Cash Flow
1.											
2.											

L.O. 3

Exercise 1-5B *Effect of product versus general, selling, and administrative cost on financial statements*

Required

Fletcher Corporation recognized the annual expiration of insurance on December 31, 2008. Using the following horizontal financial statements model shown, indicate how this event affected the company's financial statements under the following two assumptions: (1) the insurance was for office equipment or (2) the insurance was for manufacturing equipment. Indicate whether the event increases (I), decreases (D), or does not affect (NA) each element of the financial statements. In the Cash Flow column, indicate whether the cash flow is associated with operating activities (OA), investing activities (IA), or financing activities (FA).

	Assets				Equity					
Event No.	Cash	+ Prepaid Insurance	+ Inventory	=	Com. Stk.	+ Ret. Ear.	Rev.	− Exp.	= Net Inc.	Cash Flow
1.										
2.										

Exercise 1-6B *Product costs in a manufacturing company*

L.O. 2

Because friends and neighbors frequently praise her baking skills, Susan Spann plans to start a new business baking cakes for customers. She wonders how to determine the cost of her cakes.

Required

a. Identify and give examples of the three components of product cost incurred in producing cakes.

b. Explain why measuring product cost for a bakery is more complex than measuring product cost for a retail store.

c. Assume that Susan decides to bake cakes for her customers at her home. Consequently, she will avoid the cost of renting a bakery. However, her home utility bills will increase. She also plans to offer different types of cakes for which baking time will vary. Cakes mixed with ice cream will require freezing, and other cakes will need refrigeration. Some can cool at room temperature. Under these circumstances, how can Susan estimate the amount of utility cost required to produce a given cake? Identify two costs other than utility cost that she will incur that could be difficult to measure.

Exercise 1-7B *Product versus general, selling, and administrative costs*

L.O. 3

In reviewing Quartey Company's September accounting records, Ken Helm, the chief accountant, noted the following depreciation costs.

1. Factory buildings—$25,000.
2. Computers used in manufacturing—$4,000.
3. A building used to display finished products—$8,000.
4. Trucks used to deliver merchandise to customers—$14,000.
5. Forklifts used in the factory—$22,000.
6. Furniture used in the president's office—$9,000.
7. Elevators in administrative buildings—$6,000.
8. Factory machinery—$9,000.

Required

a. What amount of depreciation cost would be classified as general, selling, and administrative expense?

b. Assume that Quartey manufactured 3,000 units of product and sold 2,000 units of product during the month of September. Determine the amount of depreciation cost that would be included in cost of goods sold.

Exercise 1-8B *Recording product versus general, selling, and administrative costs in a financial statements model*

L.O. 2, 3

Long Electronics Company experienced the following events during its first accounting period.

1. Received $200,000 cash by issuing common stock.
2. Paid $30,000 cash for wages to production workers.
3. Paid $20,000 for salaries to administrative staff.
4. Purchased for cash and used $18,000 of raw materials.
5. Recognized $2,000 of depreciation on administrative offices.
6. Recognized $3,000 of depreciation on manufacturing equipment.
7. Recognized $96,000 of sales revenue from cash sales of products.
8. Recognized $60,000 of cost of goods sold from the sale referenced in Event 7.

Required

Use a horizontal financial statements model to show how each event affects the balance sheet, income statement, and statement of cash flows. Indicate whether the event increases (I), decreases (D), or does not affect (NA) each element of the financial statements. In the Cash Flow column, indicate whether the cash flow is associated with operating activities (OA), investing activities (IA), or financing activities (FA). The first transaction is shown as an example. (*Note:* Show accumulated depreciation as a decrease in the book value of the appropriate asset account.)

Event No.	Assets				Equity						
	Cash	+ Inventory	+ Manuf. Equip.	+ Adm. Offices	= Com. Stk.	+ Ret. Ear.	Rev.	− Exp.	= Net Inc.	Cash Flow	
1	I	NA	NA	NA	I	NA	NA	NA	NA	I	FA

L.O. 2, 3 **Exercise 1-9B** *Allocating product costs between ending inventory and cost of goods sold*

Kawa Manufacturing Company began operations on January 1. During January, it started and completed 2,000 units of product. The company incurred the following costs:

1. Raw materials purchased and used—$2,500.
2. Wages of production workers—$2,000.
3. Salaries of administrative and sales personnel—$1,000.
4. Depreciation on manufacturing equipment—$1,500.
5. Depreciation on administrative equipment—$1,200.

Kawa sold 1,600 units of product.

Required

a. Determine the total product cost.
b. Determine the total cost of the ending inventory.
c. Determine the total of cost of goods sold.

L.O. 3 **Exercise 1-10B** *Financial statement effects for manufacturing versus service organizations*

The following horizontal financial statements model shows the effects of recording the expiration of insurance in two different circumstances. One circumstance represents the expiration of insurance on a factory building. The other circumstance represents the expiration of insurance on an administrative building. The cash flow effects are shown using (I) for increase, (D) for decrease, and (NA) for no effect.

Event No.	Assets			Equity						
	Cash	+ Prepaid Insurance	+ Inventory	= Com. Stk.	+ Ret. Ear.	Rev.	− Exp.	= Net Inc.	Cash Flow	
1.	NA	D	I	NA	NA	NA	NA	NA	NA	
2.	NA	D	NA	NA	D	NA	I	D	NA	

Required

a. Identify the event that represents the expiration of insurance on the factory building.
b. Explain why recognizing the expiration of insurance on a factory building affects financial statements differently than recognizing the expiration of insurance on an administrative building.

L.O. 3 **Exercise 1-11B** *Effect of product versus general, selling, and administrative cost on the income statement and statement of cash flows*

Each of the following asset acquisitions requires a year-end adjusting entry.

Event No.	Net Income Amount of Change	Cash Flow Amount of Change
1. Purchased franchise	NA	(50,000) IA
1. Adjusting Entry	(5,000)	NA

1. Paid $50,000 cash on January 1 to purchase a hamburger franchise that had an estimated expected useful life of 10 years and no salvage value.
2. Paid $50,000 cash on January 1 to purchase a patent to manufacture a special product. The patent had an estimated expected useful life of 10 years.
3. Paid $3,600 cash on April 1 for a one-year insurance policy on the administrative building.
4. Paid $3,600 cash on April 1 for a one-year insurance policy on the manufacturing building.

5. Paid $1,200 cash to purchase office supplies for the accounting department. At the end of the year, $300 of office supplies was still on hand.

6. Paid $1,200 cash to purchase factory supplies. At the end of the year, $300 of factory supplies was still on hand.

Required

Explain how both acquiring the asset and recording the adjusting entry affect the amount of net income and the cash flow reported in the annual financial statements. In the Cash Flow Column, indicate whether the cash flow is associated with operating activities (OA), investing activities (IA), or financing activities (FA). Assume a December 31 annual closing date. The first event is shown as an example. Assume that any products that have been made have not been sold.

Exercise 1-12B   *Upstream and downstream costs*

L.O. 4

During 2007 Moseley Pharmaceutical Company incurred $10,000,000 of research and development (R&D) costs to develop a new hay fever drug called Allergone. In accordance with FASB standards, the entire R&D cost was recognized as expense in 2007. Manufacturing costs (direct materials, direct labor, and overhead) to produce Allergone are expected to be $40 per unit. Packaging, shipping, and sales commissions are expected to be $5 per unit. Moseley expects to sell 1,000,000 units of Allergone before developing a new drug to replace it in the market. During 2007, Moseley produced 160,000 units of Allergone and sold 100,000 of them.

Required

a. Identify the upstream and downstream costs.

b. Determine the 2007 amount of cost of goods sold and the December 31, 2007, ending inventory balance.

c. Determine the unit sales price Moseley should establish assuming it desires to earn a profit margin equal to 40 percent of the *total cost* of developing, manufacturing, and distributing Allergone.

d. Prepare an income statement for 2007 using the sales price from Requirement *c*.

e. Why would Moseley price Allergone at a level that would generate a loss for 2007?

Exercise 1-13B   *Effect of a just-in-time inventory system on financial statements*

L.O. 6

In reviewing Crocker Company's financial statements for the past two years, Rita King, a bank loan officer, noticed that the company's inventory level had increased significantly while sales revenue had remained constant. Such a trend typically indicates increasing inventory carrying costs and slowing cash inflows. Ms. King concluded that the bank should deny Crocker's credit line application.

Required

Explain how implementing an effective just-in-time inventory system would affect Crocker's financial statements and possibly reverse Ms. King's decision about its credit line application.

Exercise 1-14B   *Using JIT to minimize waste and lost opportunity*

L.O. 6

Daisy Tang is the editor-in-chief of her school's yearbook. The school has 750 students and 50 faculty and staff members. The firm engaged to print copies of the yearbook charges the school $10 per book and requires a 10-day lead time for delivery. Daisy and her editors plan to order 600 copies to sell at the school fair for $15 each.

Required

a. If the school sells 550 yearbooks, what amount of profit will it earn? What is the cost of waste due to excess inventory?

b. If 150 buyers are turned away after all yearbooks have been sold, what amount of profit will the school earn? What amount of opportunity cost will the school incur?

c. How could Daisy use a JIT inventory system to maximize profits by eliminating waste and opportunity cost?

Exercise 1-15B   *Using JIT to minimize holding costs*

L.O. 6

Cathy's Beauty Salon purchases inventory supplies from a variety of vendors, some of which require a four-week lead time before delivering inventory purchases. To ensure that she will not run out of supplies, Cathy Jetter, the owner, maintains a large inventory. The average cost of inventory on hand is $9,000. Ms. Jetter usually finances inventory purchases with a line of credit that has a 12 percent annual interest charge. Her accountant has suggested that she purchase all inventory from a single large distributor that can satisfy all of her orders within a three-day period. With such prompt delivery,

Ms. Jetter would be able to reduce her average inventory balance to $2,000. She also believes that she could save $1,000 per year through reduced phone bills, insurance costs, and warehouse rental costs associated with ordering and maintaining the higher level of inventory.

Required

a. Is the inventory system the accountant suggested to Ms. Jetter a pure or approximate just-in-time system?
b. Based on the information provided, how much inventory holding cost could Ms. Jetter eliminate by taking the accountant's advice?

L.O. 9

Exercise 1-16B   *The fraud triangle*

The accounting records of Masterson Manufacturing Company (MMC) revealed that the company incurred $3 million of materials, $5 million of production labor, $4 million of manufacturing overhead, and $6 million of general, selling, and administrative expense during 2008. It was discovered that MMC's chief financial officer (CFO) included $2.6 million dollars of upstream research and development expense in the manufacturing overhead account when it should have been classified as general, selling, and administrative expense. MMC made 5,000 units of product and sold 4,000 units of product in 2008.

Required

a. Indicate whether the elements on the 2008 financial statements (i.e., assets, liabilities, equity, revenue, expense, net income, and cash flow) would be overstated or understated as a result of the misclassification of the upstream research and development expense. Determine the amount of the overstatement or understatement for each element.
b. Speculate as to what would cause the CFO to intentionally misclassify the research and development expense. (Hint: Review the chapter material regarding the fraud triangle.)

L.O. 9

Exercise 1-17B   *Applications of the Sarbanes-Oxley Act*

Greg Madrid, a HealthSouth billing clerk filed a suit under the False Claims Act charging that Health-South purchased computer equipment from a company owned by Richard Scrushy's parents at prices two and three times the normal price. At the time, Richard Scrushy was the CEO of HealthSouth. The overcharges inflated HealthSouth's expense ratios that the government used when calculating a Medicare reimbursement rate. As a result, the government was overcharged for services provided by HealthSouth. While refusing to recognize any wrongdoing, HealthSouth agreed to pay an $8 million settlement related to the lawsuit brought by the whistleblower.

Required

Explain how the provisions of Sarbanes-Oxley would provide protection to a whistleblower such as Greg Madrid.

Appendix

L.O. 10

Exercise 1-18B   *Value chain analysis*

Fastidious Vincent washed his hair at home and then went to a barbershop for a haircut. The barber explained that shop policy is to shampoo each customer's hair before cutting, regardless of how recently it had been washed. Somewhat annoyed, Vincent submitted to the shampoo, after which the barber cut his hair with great skill. After the haircut, the barber dried his hair and complimented Vincent on his appearance. He added, "That will be $18, $3 for the shampoo and $15 for the cut and dry." Vincent did not tip the barber.

Required

Identify the nonvalue-added activity described. How could the barber modify this nonvalue-added activity?

PROBLEMS—SERIES B

L.O. 2, 3

Problem 1-19B   *Product versus general, selling, and administrative costs*

Qazi Manufacturing Company was started on January 1, 2007, when it acquired $134,000 cash by issuing common stock. Qazi immediately purchased office furniture and manufacturing equipment costing $20,000 and $38,000, respectively. The office furniture had a four-year useful life and a zero salvage value. The manufacturing equipment had a $2,000 salvage value and an expected useful life of six years. The company paid $14,000 for salaries of administrative personnel and $18,000 for wages of production personnel. Finally, the company paid $24,000 for raw materials that were used to make inventory. All inventory was started and completed during the year. Qazi completed production on 8,000 units of product and sold 6,000 units at a price of $14 each in 2007. (Assume that all transactions are cash transactions.)

Required

a. Determine the total product cost and the average cost per unit of the inventory produced in 2007.
b. Determine the amount of cost of goods sold that would appear on the 2007 income statement.
c. Determine the amount of the ending inventory balance that would appear on the December 31, 2007, balance sheet.
d. Determine the amount of net income that would appear on the 2007 income statement.
e. Determine the amount of retained earnings that would appear on the December 31, 2007, balance sheet.
f. Determine the amount of total assets that would appear on the December 31, 2007, balance sheet.
g. Determine the amount of net cash flow from operating activities that would appear on the 2007 statement of cash flows.
h. Determine the amount of net cash flow from investing activities that would appear on the 2007 statement of cash flows.

Problem 1-20B *Effect of product versus general, selling, and administrative costs on financial statements*   **L.O. 2, 3**

Tyndal Company experienced the following accounting events during its first year of operation. With the exception of the adjusting entries for depreciation, all transactions were cash transactions.

1. Acquired $99,000 cash by issuing common stock.
2. Paid $18,750 for the materials used to make its products. All products started were completed during the period.
3. Paid salaries of $7,500 to selling and administrative employees.
4. Paid wages of $11,250 to production workers.
5. Paid $15,000 for furniture used in selling and administrative offices. The furniture was acquired on January 1. It had a $1,875 estimated salvage value and a seven-year useful life.
6. Paid $27,500 for manufacturing equipment. The equipment was acquired on January 1. It had a $2,500 estimated salvage value and a five-year useful life.
7. Sold inventory to customers for $53,750 that had cost $31,250 to make.

Required

Explain how these events would affect the balance sheet, income statement, and statement of cash flows by recording them in a horizontal financial statements model as indicated here. The first event is recorded as an example. In the Cash Flow column, indicate whether the amounts represent financing activities (FA), investing activities (IA), or operating activities (OA).

Financial Statements Model												
	Assets					Equity						
Event No.	Cash	+ Inventory	Manuf. + Equip.*	Office + Furn.*	=	Com. Stk.	+	Ret. Ear.	Rev.	− Exp.	= Net Inc.	Cash Flow
1	99,000					99,000						99,000 FA

*Record accumulated depreciation as negative amounts in these columns.

Problem 1-21B *Product versus general, selling, and administrative costs*   **L.O. 2, 3**

The following transactions pertain to 2008, the first year of operations of Pinion Company. All inventory was started and completed during the accounting period. All transactions were cash transactions.

1. Acquired $56,000 of contributed capital from its owners.
2. Paid $9,600 for materials used to produce inventory.
3. Paid $4,400 to production workers.
4. Paid $5,000 rental fee for production equipment.

5. Paid $1,500 to administrative employees.
6. Paid $3,200 rental fee for administrative office equipment.
7. Produced 1,900 units of inventory of which 1,500 units were sold at a price of $17.40 each.

Required

Prepare an income statement, balance sheet, and statement of cash flows.

L.O. 2, 3, 5

Problem 1-22B *Service versus manufacturing companies*

Voger Company began operations on January 1, 2007, by issuing common stock for $75,200 cash. During 2007, Voger received $61,600 cash from revenue and incurred costs that required $72,000 of cash payments.

Required

Prepare an income statement, balance sheet, and statement of cash flows for Voger Company for 2007, under each of the following independent scenarios.

a. Voger is an employment agency. The $72,000 was paid for employee salaries and advertising.
b. Voger is a trucking company. The $72,000 was paid to purchase two trucks. The trucks were purchased on January 1, 2007, had five-year useful lives and no expected salvage value. Voger uses straight-line depreciation.
c. Voger is a manufacturing company. The $72,000 was paid to purchase the following items:
   (1) Paid $14,400 cash to purchase materials used to make products during the year.
   (2) Paid $22,400 cash for wages to production workers who make products during the year.
   (3) Paid $3,200 cash for salaries of sales and administrative employees.
   (4) Paid $32,000 cash to purchase manufacturing equipment. The equipment was used solely for the purpose of making products. It had a six-year life and a $3,200 salvage value. The company uses straight-line depreciation.
   (5) During 2007, Voger started and completed 2,600 units of product. The revenue was earned when Voger sold 2,200 units of product to its customers.
d. Refer to Requirement *c*. Could Voger determine the actual cost of making the 500th unit of product? How likely is it that the actual cost of the 500th unit of product was exactly the same as the cost of producing the 501st unit of product? Explain why management may be more interested in average cost than in actual cost.

L.O. 2, 3, 7

Problem 1-23B *Importance of cost classification*

Russo Company was started when it acquired $70,000 by issuing common stock. During the first year of operations, the company incurred specifically identifiable product costs (materials, labor, and overhead) amounting to $40,000. Russo also incurred $20,000 of product development costs. There was a debate regarding how the product development costs should be classified. Advocates of Option 1 believed that the costs should be included in the general, selling, and administrative cost category. Advocates of Option 2 believed it would be more appropriate to classify the product development costs as product costs. During the first year, Russo made 10,000 units of product and sold 8,000 units at a price of $14 each. All transactions were cash transactions.

Required

a. Prepare an income statement, balance sheet, and statement of cash flows under each of the two options.
b. Identify the option that results in financial statements that are more likely to leave a favorable impression on investors and creditors.
c. Assume that Russo provides an incentive bonus to the company president that is equal to 8 percent of net income. Compute the amount of the bonus under each of the two options. Identify the option that provides the president with the higher bonus.
d. Assume a 35 percent income tax rate. Determine the amount of income tax expense under each of the two options. Identify the option that minimizes the amount of the company's income tax expense.
e. Comment on the conflict of interest between the company president as determined in Requirement *c* and the stockholders of the company as indicated in Requirement *d*. Describe an incentive compensation plan that would avoid conflicts between the interests of the president and the owners.

Problem 1-24B   *Using JIT to reduce inventory holding costs*

L.O. 6

Cole Automobile Dealership, Inc. (CAD), buys and sells a variety of cars made by Great Motor Corporation. CAD maintains about 30 new cars in its parking lot for customers' selection; the cost of this inventory is approximately $320,000. Additionally, CAD hires security guards to protect the inventory from theft and a maintenance crew to keep the facilities attractive. The total payroll cost for the guards and maintenance crew amounts to $80,000 per year. CAD has a line of credit with a local bank that calls for a 15 percent annual rate of interest. Recently, Ron Nader, the president of CAD, learned that a competitor in town, Smartt Dealership, has been attracting some of CAD's usual customers because Smartt could offer them lower prices. Mr. Nader also discovered that Smartt carries no inventory at all but shows customers a catalog of cars as well as pertinent information from online computer databases. Smartt promises to deliver any car that a customer identifies within three working days.

Required
a. Based on the information provided, determine CAD's annual inventory holding cost.
b. Name the inventory system that Smartt uses and explain how the system enables Smartt to sell at reduced prices.

Problem 1-25B   *Using JIT to minimize waste and lost opportunity*

L.O. 6

Laurie's Hamburger is a small fast-food shop in a busy shopping center that operates only during lunch hours. Laurie Kemp, the owner and manager of the shop, is confused. On some days, she does not have enough hamburgers to satisfy customer demand. On other days, she has more hamburgers than she can sell. When she has excess hamburgers, she has no choice but to dump them. Usually, Ms. Kemp prepares about 160 hamburgers before the busy lunch hour. The product cost per hamburger is approximately $0.75; the sales price is $2.50 each. Ms. Kemp pays general, selling, and administrative expenses that include daily rent of $50 and daily wages of $40.

Required
a. Prepare an income statement based on sales of 100 hamburgers per day. Determine the cost of wasted hamburgers if 160 hamburgers were prepared in advance.
b. Prepare an income statement assuming that 200 customers attempt to buy a hamburger. Since Ms. Kemp has prepared only 160 hamburgers, she must reject 40 customer orders because of insufficient supply. Determine the amount of lost profit.
c. Suppose that hamburgers can be prepared quickly after each customer orders. However, Ms. Kemp must hire an additional part-time employee at a cost of approximately $20 per day. The per unit cost of each hamburger remains at $0.75. Prepare an income statement under the JIT system assuming that 100 hamburgers are sold. Compare the income statement under JIT with the income statement prepared in Requirement *a*. Comment on how the JIT system would affect profitability.
d. Assume the same facts as in Requirement *c* with respect to a JIT system that requires additional labor costing $20 per day. Prepare an income statement under the JIT system, assuming that 200 hamburgers are sold. Compare the income statement under JIT with the income statement prepared in Requirement *b*. Comment on how the JIT system would affect profitability.
e. Explain how the JIT system might be able to improve customer satisfaction as well as profitability.

Problem 1-26B   *The fraud triangle, ethics, and the Sarbanes-Oxley Act*

L.O. 9

The CEO and the CFO of Automation Company were both aware that the company's controller was reporting fraudulent revenues. Upper level executives are paid very large bonuses when the company meets the earnings goals established in the company's budgets. While the CEO had pushed the CFO and controller to "make the numbers," he had not told him to "make up the numbers." Besides, he could plead ignorance if the fraud was ever discovered. The CFO knew he should prohibit the fraudulent reporting but also knew the importance of making the numbers established in the budget. He told himself that it wasn't just for his bonus but for the stockholders as well. If the actual earnings were below the budgeted target numbers, the stock price would drop and the shareholders would suffer. Besides, he believed that the actual revenues would increase dramatically in the near future and they could cover for the fraudulent revenue by underreporting these future revenues. He concluded that no one would get hurt and everything would be straightened out in the near future.

Required
a. Explain why the internal control practice of separation of duties failed to prevent the fraudulent reporting.

b. Identify and discuss the elements of the fraud triangle that motivated the fraud.
c. Explain how the provisions of the Sarbanes-Oxley Act would serve to deter this type of fraudulent reporting.
d. Review the standards of professional conduct shown in Exhibit 1.15. Identify and comment on which of the standards were violated by the CFO.

Appendix

L.O. 10

Problem 1-27B *Value chain analysis*

Julie Woodley visited her personal physician for treatment of flu symptoms. She was greeted by the receptionist, who gave her personal history and insurance forms to complete. She needed no instructions; she completed these same forms every time she visited the doctor. After completing the forms, Ms. Woodley waited for 30 minutes before being ushered into the patient room. After waiting there for an additional 15 minutes, Dr. Bohn entered the room. The doctor ushered Ms. Woodley into the hallway where he weighed her and called her weight out to the nurse for recording. Ms. Woodley had gained 10 pounds since her last visit, and the doctor suggested that she consider going on a diet. Dr. Bohn then took her temperature and asked her to return to the patient room. Ten minutes later, he returned to take a throat culture and draw blood. She waited another 15 minutes for the test results. Finally, the doctor returned and told Ms. Woodley that she had strep throat and bronchitis. Dr. Bohn prescribed an antibiotic and told her to get at least two days of bed rest. Ms. Woodley was then ushered to the accounting department to settle her bill. The accounting clerk asked her several questions; the answers to most of them were on the forms that she had completed when she first arrived at the office. Finally, Ms. Woodley paid her required copayment and left the office. Three weeks later, she received a bill indicating that she had not paid the copayment. She called the accounting department, and, after a search of the records, the clerk verified that the bill had, in fact, been paid. The clerk apologized for the inconvenience and inquired as to whether Ms. Woodley's health had improved.

Required

a. Identify at least three value-added and three nonvalue-added activities suggested in this scenario.
b. Provide logical suggestions for how to eliminate the nonvalue-added activities.

ANALYZE, THINK, COMMUNICATE

ATC 1-1   **Business Applications Case**   *Financial versus managerial accounting*

An article in the April 12, 2004, edition of *BusinessWeek,* "The Costco Way—Higher Wages Mean Higher Profits" compared **Costco Wholesale Corporation** data with **Wal-Mart's Sam's Club** data. The tables below present some of the data used to support this claim.

How Costco Spends More on Employees		
	Costco	Sam's Club
Average hourly wage rate	$15.97	$11.53
Employees covered by a health-care plan	82%	47%
Average annual health-care costs per employee	$5,735	$3,500
Employees covered by a retirement plan	91%	64%
Average annual retirement costs per employee	$1,330	$747

Benefits to Costco from Spending More on Emplyees		
	Costco	Sam's Club
Annual employee turnover	6%	21%
Labor and overhead cost as a percent of sales	9.8%	17%
Annual sales per square foot	$795	$516
Annual profit per employee	$13,647	$11,039

Required

a. Is the information in the tables above best described as primarily financial accounting data or managerial accounting data in nature? Explain.

b. Provide additional examples of managerial and financial accounting information that could apply to Costco.

c. Explain why a manager of an individual Costco store needs different kinds of information than someone who is considering lending the company money or investing in its common stock.

ATC 1-2 Group Assignment *Product versus upstream and downstream costs*

Victor Holt, the accounting manager of Sexton, Inc., gathered the following information for 2006. Some of it can be used to construct an income statement for 2006. Ignore items that do not appear on an income statement. Some computation may be required. For example, the cost of manufacturing equipment would not appear on the income statement. However, the cost of manufacturing equipment is needed to compute the amount of depreciation. All units of product were started and completed in 2006.

1. Issued $864,000 of common stock.
2. Paid engineers in the product design department $10,000 for salaries that were accrued at the end of the previous year.
3. Incurred advertising expenses of $70,000.
4. Paid $720,000 for materials used to manufacture the company's product.
5. Incurred utility costs of $160,000. These costs were allocated to different departments on the basis of square footage of floor space. Mr. Holt identified three departments and determined the square footage of floor space for each department to be as shown in the table below.

Department	Square Footage
Research and development	10,000
Manufacturing	60,000
Selling and administrative	30,000
Total	100,000

6. Paid $880,000 for wages of production workers.
7. Paid cash of $658,000 for salaries of administrative personnel. There was $16,000 of accrued salaries owed to administrative personnel at the end of 2006. There was no beginning balance in the Salaries Payable account for administrative personnel.
8. Purchased manufacturing equipment two years ago at a cost of $10,000,000. The equipment had an eight-year useful life and a $2,000,000 salvage value.
9. Paid $390,000 cash to engineers in the product design department.
10. Paid a $258,000 cash dividend to owners.
11. Paid $80,000 to set up manufacturing equipment for production.
12. Paid a one-time $186,000 restructuring cost to redesign the production process to implement a just-in-time inventory system.
13. Prepaid the premium on a new insurance policy covering nonmanufacturing employees. The policy cost $72,000 and had a one-year term with an effective starting date of May 1. Four employees work in the research and development department and eight employees in the selling and administrative department. Assume a December 31 closing date.
14. Made 69,400 units of product and sold 60,000 units at a price of $70 each.

Required

a. Divide the class into groups of four or five students per group, and then organize the groups into three sections. Assign Task 1 to the first section of groups, Task 2 to the second section of groups, and Task 3 to the third section of groups.

Group Tasks

(1) Identify the items that are classified as product costs and determine the amount of cost of goods sold reported on the 2006 income statement.

(2) Identify the items that are classified as upstream costs and determine the amount of upstream cost expensed on the 2006 income statement.

(3) Identify the items that are classified as downstream costs and determine the amount of downstream cost expensed on the 2006 income statement.

b. Have the class construct an income statement in the following manner. Select a member of one of the groups assigned the first group task identifying the product costs. Have that person go to the board and list the costs included in the determination of cost of goods sold. Anyone in the other groups who disagrees with one of the classifications provided by the person at the board should voice an objection and explain why the item should be classified differently. The instructor should lead the class to a consensus on the disputed items. After the amount of cost of goods sold is determined, the student at the board constructs the part of the income statement showing the determination of gross margin. The exercise continues in a similar fashion with representatives from the other sections explaining the composition of the upstream and downstream costs. These items are added to the income statement started by the first group representative. The final result is a completed income statement.

ATC 1-3   Research Assignment   *Skills needed by managerial accountants*

The September 1999 issue of *Strategic Finance* contains the article "Counting More, Counting Less: Transformations in the Management Accounting Profession," written by Keith Russell, Gary Siegel, and C. S. Kuleszo. It appears on pages 38 to 44. This article reviews findings from a survey of managerial accountants conducted by the Institute of Management Accountants (IMA). Read this article and complete the following requirements.

Required

a. What skills did the management accountants identify as being most important for their success?

b. Did the respondents see their work as being most closely associated with the accounting or finance function?

c. Like all business professionals, management accountants must continuously update their skills. What were the five most important skills the respondents said they had acquired in the five years prior to the survey?

d. Non-accountants often view accountants as persons who work alone sitting at a desk. What percentage of the respondents to the IMA survey said they work on cross-functional teams?

ATC 1-4   Writing Assignment   *Emerging practices in managerial accounting*

The 1998 annual report of the Maytag Corporation contained the following excerpt:

During the first quarter of 1996, the Company announced the restructuring of its major appliance operations in an effort to strengthen its position in the industry and to deliver improved performance to both customers and shareowners. This included the consolidation of two separate organizational units into a single operation responsible for all activities associated with the manufacture and distribution of the Company's brands of major appliances and the closing of a cooking products plant in Indianapolis, Indiana, with transfer of that production to an existing plant in Cleveland, Tennessee.

The restructuring cost Maytag $40 million and disrupted the lives of many of the company's employees.

Required

Assume that you are Maytag's vice president of human relations. Write a letter to the employees who are affected by the restructuring. The letter should explain why it was necessary for the company to undertake the restructuring. Your explanation should refer to the ideas discussed in the section "Emerging Trends in Managerial Accounting" of this chapter (see Appendix B).

ATC 1-5   Ethical Dilemma   *Product cost versus selling and administrative expense*

Eddie Emerson is a proud woman with a problem. Her daughter has been accepted into a prestigious law school. While Ms. Emerson beams with pride, she is worried sick about how to pay for the school; she is a single parent who has worked hard to support herself and her three children. She had to go heavily into debt to finance her own education. Even though she now has a good job, family needs have continued to outpace her income and her debt burden is staggering. She knows she will be unable to borrow the money needed for her daughter's law school.

Ms. Emerson is the Chief Financial Officer (CFO) of a small manufacturing company. She has just accepted a new job offer. Indeed, she has not yet told her employer that she will be leaving in a month. She is concerned that her year-end incentive bonus may be affected if her boss learns of her plans to leave. She plans to inform the company immediately after receiving the bonus. She knows her behavior is less than honorable, but she believes that she has been underpaid for a long time. Her boss, a relative of the company's owner, makes twice what she makes and does half the work. Why should she care about leaving with a little extra cash? Indeed, she is considering an opportunity to boost the bonus.

Ms. Emerson's bonus is based on a percentage of net income. Her company recently introduced a new product line that required substantial production start-up costs. Ms. Emerson is fully aware that GAAP requires these costs to be expensed in the current accounting period, but no one else in the company has the technical expertise to know exactly how the costs should be treated. She is considering misclassifying the start-up costs as product costs. If the costs are misclassified, net income will be significantly higher, resulting in a nice boost in her incentive bonus. By the time the auditors discover the misclassification, Ms. Emerson will have moved on to her new job. If the matter is brought to the attention of her new employer, she will simply plead ignorance. Considering her daughter's needs, Ms. Emerson decides to classify the start-up costs as product costs.

Required

a. Based on this information, indicate whether Ms. Emerson believes the number of units of product sold will be equal to, less than, or greater than, the number of units made. Write a brief paragraph explaining the logic that supports your answer.

b. Explain how the misclassification could mislead an investor or creditor regarding the company's financial condition.

c. Explain how the misclassification could affect income taxes.

d. Identify the specific components of the fraud triangle that were present in this case.

e. Review the standards of ethical conduct shown in Exhibit 1.15 and identify at least two standards that Ms. Emerson's misclassification of the start-up costs violated.

f. Describe the maximum penalty that could be imposed under the Sarbanes-Oxley Act for the actions Ms. Emerson has taken.

g. Comment on how proper internal controls could have prevented the fraudulent reporting in this case.

ATC 1-6 Spreadsheet Assignment *Using Excel*

The following transactions pertain to 2006, the first year of operations of the Barlett Company. All inventory was started and completed during 2006. Assume that all transactions are cash transactions.

1. Acquired $2,000 cash by issuing common stock.
2. Paid $400 for materials used to produce inventory.
3. Paid $600 to production workers.
4. Paid $200 rental fee for production equipment.
5. Paid $160 to administrative employees.
6. Paid $80 rental fee for administrative office equipment.
7. Produced 300 units of inventory of which 200 units were sold at a price of $7.00 each.

Required

Construct a spreadsheet that includes the income statement, balance sheet, and statement of cash flows.

ATC 1-7 Spreadsheet Assignment *Mastering Excel*

Mantooth Manufacturing Company experienced the following accounting events during its first year of operation. With the exception of the adjusting entries for depreciation, assume that all transactions are cash transactions.

1. Acquired $50,000 by issuing common stock.
2. Paid $8,000 for the materials used to make its products, all of which were started and completed during the year.
3. Paid salaries of $4,400 to selling and administrative employees.
4. Paid wages of $7,000 to production workers.
5. Paid $9,600 for furniture used in selling and administrative offices. The furniture was acquired on January 1. It had a $1,600 estimated salvage value and a four-year useful life.
6. Paid $13,000 for manufacturing equipment. The equipment was acquired on January 1. It had a $1,000 estimated salvage value and a three-year useful life.
7. Sold inventory to customers for $25,000 that had cost $14,000 to make.

Construct a spreadsheet of the financial statements model as shown here:

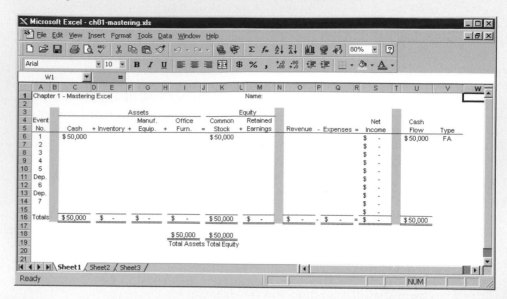

Required

Place formulas in row 16 to automatically add the columns. Also add formulas in column S to calculate net income after each event, and add formulas in row 18 to compute total assets and equity. Notice that you must enter the events since only the first one is shown as an example.

Spreadsheet Tips

1. The column widths are set by choosing Format, then Column, and then Width.
2. The shading in columns B, N, and T is added by highlighting a column and choosing Format, then Cells, and then clicking on the tab titled Patterns and choosing a color.
3. The sum function is an easy way to add a column or row. For example, the formula in cell C16 is =SUM(C6:C15).
4. As an example of the formulas in column S (net income), the formula in cell S7 is =O7−Q7.
5. If you find that some of the columns are too far to the right to appear on your screen, you can set the zoom level to show the entire spreadsheet. The zoom is set by choosing View, then Zoom, and then clicking on Custom and typing 100 percent in the box. The shortcut method to set the zoom is to click in the box on the right side of the top tool bar that appears immediately below the menu.

COMPREHENSIVE PROBLEM

Magnificent Modems, Inc., makes modem cards that are used in notebook computers. The company completed the following transactions during 2006. All purchases and sales were made with cash.

1. Acquired $750,000 of cash from the owners.
2. Purchased $270,000 of manufacturing equipment. The equipment has a $30,000 salvage value and a four-year useful life. Label the purchase of the equipment as **Event 2a** and the recognition of depreciation as **Event 2b.**
3. The company started and completed 5,000 modems. Direct materials purchased and used amounted to $40 per unit.
4. Direct labor costs amounted to $25 per unit.
5. The cost of manufacturing supplies used amounted to $4 per unit.
6. The company paid $50,000 to rent the manufacturing facility.
7. Magnificent sold all 5,000 units at a cash price of $120 per unit. Label the recognition of the sale as **Event 7a** and the cost of goods sold as **Event 7b.** (Hint: It will be necessary to determine the manufacturing costs in order to record the cost of goods sold.)

8. The sales staff was paid a $6 per unit sales commission.

9. Paid $39,000 to purchase equipment for administrative offices. The equipment was expected to have a $3,000 salvage value and a three-year useful life. Label the purchase of the equipment as **Event 9a** and the recognition of depreciation as **Event 9b.**

10. Administrative expenses consisting of office rental and salaries amounted to $71,950.

Required

a. Record the transaction data for Magnificent Modems, Inc., in the financial statements like the one shown below. In the cash flow column, use parentheses to indicate cash outflows. Indicate whether each cash flow item is a financing activity (FA), investing activity (IA), or operating activity (OA). The first transaction is recorded as an example.

Event No.	Assets				=	Equity						
	Cash	+ Inventory +	Manuf. Equip.* +	Office Equip.* =		C. Stock +	Ret. Ear.	Rev.	−	Exp.	= Net Inc.	Cash Flow
1.	750,000					750,000						750,000 FA
Ck. Fig.	544,050 +	0	+ 210,000 +	27,000 =		750,000 +	31,050	600,000	−	568,950	= 31,050	544,050 NC

*Negative amounts in these columns represent accumulated depreciation.

b. Use the following forms to prepare an income statement and balance sheet.

MAGNIFICENT MODEMS, INC.
Income Statement
For the Period Ended December 31, 2006

Sales	
Cost of Goods Sold	
Gross Margin	
Sales Commission	
Depreciation Expense	
Administrative Expense	
Net Income	$31,050

MAGNIFICENT MODEMS, INC.
Balance Sheet
As of December 31, 2006

Assets:	
Cash	
Manufacturing Equipment, Net of Acc. Depreciation	
Administrative Equipment, Net of Acc. Depreciation	
Finished Goods Inventory	
Total Assets	$781,050
Equity	
Common Stock	
Retained Earnings	
Total Stockholder's Equity	$781,050

CHAPTER 2

Cost Behavior, Operating Leverage, and Profitability Analysis

LEARNING OBJECTIVES

After you have mastered the material in this chapter, you will be able to:

1. Identify and describe fixed, variable, and mixed cost behavior.

2. Demonstrate the effects of operating leverage on profitability.

3. Prepare an income statement using the contribution margin approach.

4. Demonstrate how the magnitude of operating leverage affects profitability.

5. Demonstrate how the relevant range and decision context affect cost behavior.

6. Select an appropriate time period for calculating the average cost per unit.

7. Use the high-low method, scattergraphs, and regression analysis to estimate fixed and variable costs.

The Curious Accountant

News flash! On January 31, 2006, Google announced that its fourth-quarter earnings would be up 82 percent over the same quarter of 2005, yet its revenues were up only 23 percent.

On February 10, 2006, Volkswagen reported that while its 2005 revenues were 7.1 percent higher than in 2004, its earnings increased 61 percent. Also in February 2006, Tommy Hilfiger reported that for the quarter ending on December 1, 2005, its revenue fell 7.9 percent, compared to the same period in 2004, but its earnings fell 23 percent.

Can you explain why such relatively small changes in these companies' revenues resulted in such relatively large changes in their earnings or losses? In other words, if a company's sales increase 10 percent, why do its earnings not also increase 10 percent? (Answer on page 60.)

CHAPTER OPENING

Three college students are planning a vacation. One of them suggests inviting a fourth person along, remarking that four can travel for the same cost as three. Certainly, some costs will be the same whether three or four people go on the trip. For example, the hotel room costs $800 per week, regardless of whether three or four people stay in the room. In accounting terms the cost of the hotel room is a fixed cost. *The total amount of a fixed cost does not change when volume changes. The total hotel room cost is $800 whether 1, 2, 3, or 4 people use the room. In contrast, some costs vary in direct proportion with changes in volume. When volume increases, total variable cost increases; when volume decreases,* total *variable cost decreases. For example, the cost of tickets to a theme park is a **variable cost.** The total cost of tickets increases proportionately with each vacationer who goes to the theme park. Cost behavior (fixed versus variable) can significantly impact profitability. This chapter explains cost behavior and ways it can be used to increase profitability.* ■

Fixed Cost Behavior

Topic Tackler
PLUS
2-1

How much more will it cost to send one additional employee to a sales meeting? If more people buy our products, can we charge less? If sales increase by 10 percent, how will profits be affected? Managers seeking answers to such questions must consider **cost behavior.** Knowing how costs behave relative to the level of business activity enables managers to more effectively plan and control costs. To illustrate, consider the entertainment company Star Productions, Inc. (SPI).

SPI specializes in promoting rock concerts. It is considering paying a band $48,000 to play a concert. Obviously, SPI must sell enough tickets to cover this cost. In this example, the relevant activity base is the number of tickets sold. The cost of the band is a **fixed cost** because it does not change regardless of the number of tickets sold. Exhibit 2.1 illustrates the fixed cost behavior pattern, showing the *total cost* and the *cost per unit* at three different levels of activity.

Total versus *per unit* fixed costs behave differently. The total cost for the band remains constant (fixed) at $48,000. In contrast, fixed cost per unit decreases as volume (number of tickets sold) increases. The term *fixed cost* is consistent with the behavior of *total cost.* Total fixed cost remains constant (fixed) when activity changes. However, there is a contradiction between the term *fixed cost per unit* and the *per unit behavior pattern of a fixed cost.* Fixed cost per unit is *not* fixed. It changes with the number of tickets sold. This contradiction in terminology can cause untold confusion. Study carefully the fixed cost behavior patterns in Exhibit 2.2.

EXHIBIT 2.1

Fixed Cost Behavior

Number of tickets sold (a)	2,700	3,000	3,300
Total cost of band (b)	$48,000	$48,000	$48,000
Cost per ticket sold (b ÷ a)	$17.78	$16.00	$14.55

EXHIBIT 2.2

Fixed Cost Behavior

When Activity	Increases	Decreases
Total fixed cost	Remains constant	Remains constant
Fixed cost **per unit**	Decreases	Increases

The fixed cost data in Exhibit 2.1 help SPI's management decide whether to sponsor the concert. For example, the information influences potential pricing choices. The per unit costs represent the minimum ticket prices required to cover the fixed cost at various levels of activity. SPI could compare these per unit costs to the prices of competing entertainment events (such as the prices of movies, sporting events, or theater tickets). If the price is not competitive, tickets will not sell and the concert will lose money. Management must also consider the number of tickets to be sold. The volume data in Exhibit 2.1 can be compared to the band's track record of ticket sales at previous concerts. A proper analysis of these data can reduce the risk of undertaking an unprofitable venture.

Operating Leverage

Topic Tackler
PLUS
2-2

Heavy objects can be moved with little effort using *physical* leverage. Business managers apply **operating leverage** to magnify small changes in revenue into dramatic changes in profitability. The *lever* managers use to achieve disproportionate changes between revenue and profitability is fixed costs. The leverage relationships between revenue, fixed costs, and profitability are displayed in Exhibit 2.3.

When all costs are fixed, every sales dollar contributes one dollar toward the potential profitability of a project. Once sales dollars cover fixed costs, each additional sales dollar represents pure profit. As a result, a small change in sales volume can significantly affect profitability. To illustrate, assume SPI estimates it will sell 3,000 tickets for $18 each. A 10 percent difference in actual sales volume will produce a 90 percent difference in profitability. Examine the data in Exhibit 2.4 to verify this result.

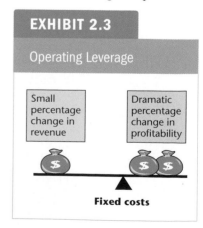

EXHIBIT 2.3

Operating Leverage

Small percentage change in revenue

Dramatic percentage change in profitability

Fixed costs

FOCUS ON INTERNATIONAL ISSUES

FIXED COSTS BRING INTERNATIONAL INTRIGUE INTO THE AUTOMOBILE INDUSTRY

In 2000, amidst great fanfare, **General Motors (GM)** and **Fiat S.p.A.** of Italy announced that GM had purchased a 20 percent equity stake in Fiat for $2.4 billion. The two automakers planned to combine some operations that had been separate, reducing the operating costs for both companies. In some cases these savings were achieved. A special clause in the contract, however, became problematic for GM in 2005.

As part of the financial agreement, Fiat insisted on the right to require GM to purchase all of Fiat between 2005 and 2010. This arrangement is called a *put option*. When the deal was struck neither company thought Fiat would ever exercise the option, but if it did, the two companies would have to negotiate a purchase price. By late 2004, circumstances had changed.

Fiat's CEO suggested he might force GM to purchase Fiat unless GM paid a significant price to void the put option. GM did not want to make such a payment, and the two sides entered difficult negotiations with legal action looking likely. What caused this drastic change in conditions? As *The Wall Street Journal* put it, "Fiat Auto ... is caught in a trap of high fixed costs and shrinking market share." The same could be said of GM and the automobile manufacturing business in general. Manufacturing vehicles requires high fixed costs. By 2005 automakers' worldwide *excess* capacity was 24 million units. In 2004, GM, the largest company in the auto industry, produced only 9.1 million vehicles worldwide. GM was already at risk of experiencing a downgrade in its debt rating and did not need the added burden of Fiat's unprofitable operations and high debt. Facing high fixed costs and the inability to raise prices due to the glut of cars on the market, Fiat was at risk of bankruptcy without a new source of cash.

Both companies faced difficult choices. The heavily fixed-cost structure of the auto industry, coupled with excess capacity, is a major source of their problems. If a company had only variable costs, it would have no excess capacity, but it would have no economies of scale either. When times are good and sales are expanding, fixed costs can cause profits to soar. In recent years, however, the auto industry has not experienced great sales growth, so its high fixed costs have created problems for many manufacturers.

In March of 2005, GM agreed to pay Fiat $2 billion to cancel the deal described above.

Source: Company data and "Separation Anxiety: For GM and Fiat, a Messy Breakup Could Be in the Works," *The Wall Street Journal,* January 24, 2005, pp. A-1 and A-13.

EXHIBIT 2.4

Effect of Operating Leverage on Profitability

Number of tickets sold	2,700	⇐−10%⇐	3,000	⇒+10%⇒	3,300	
Sales revenue ($18 per ticket)	$48,600		$54,000		$59,400	
Cost of band (fixed cost)	(48,000)		(48,000)		(48,000)	
Gross margin	$ 600	⇐−90%⇐	$ 6,000	⇒+90%⇒	$11,400	

Calculating Percentage Change

The percentages in Exhibit 2.4 are computed as follows:

$$[(\text{Alternative measure} - \text{Base measure}) \div \text{Base measure}] = \%\text{ change}$$

The base measure is the starting point. To illustrate, compute the percentage change in gross margin when moving from 3,000 units (base measure) to 3,300 units (the alternative measure).

$$[(\text{Alternative measure} - \text{Base measure}) \div \text{Base measure}] = \%\text{ change}$$
$$[(\$11,400 - \$6,000) \div \$6,000] = 90\%$$

The percentage *decline* in profitability is similarly computed:

$$[(\text{Alternative measure} - \text{Base measure}) \div \text{Base measure}] = \% \text{ change}$$
$$[(600 - \$6,000) \div \$6,000] = (90\%)$$

Risk and Reward Assessment

Risk refers to the possibility that sacrifices may exceed benefits. A fixed cost represents a commitment to an economic sacrifice. It represents the ultimate risk of undertaking a particular business project. If SPI pays the band but nobody buys a ticket, the company will lose $48,000. SPI can avoid this risk by substituting *variable costs* for the *fixed cost*.

Variable Cost Behavior

LO 1

Identify and describe fixed, variable, and mixed cost behavior.

To illustrate variable cost behavior, assume SPI arranges to pay the band $16 per ticket sold instead of a fixed $48,000. Exhibit 2.5 shows the total cost of the band and the cost per ticket sold at three different levels of activity.

EXHIBIT 2.5

Variable Cost Behavior

Number of tickets sold (a)	2,700	3,000	3,300
Total cost of band (b)	$43,200	$48,000	$52,800
Cost per ticket sold (b ÷ a)	$16	$16	$16

Since SPI will pay the band $16 for each ticket sold, the *total* variable cost increases in direct proportion to the number of tickets sold. If SPI sells one ticket, total band cost will be $16 (1 × $16); if SPI sells two tickets, total band cost will be $32 (2 × $16); and so on. The total cost of the band increases proportionately as ticket sales move from 2,700 to 3,000 to 3,300. The variable cost *per ticket* remains $16, however, regardless of whether the number of tickets sold is 1, 2, 3, or 3,000. The behavior of variable cost *per unit* is contradictory to the word *variable*. Variable cost per unit remains *constant* regardless of how many tickets are sold. Study carefully the variable cost behavior patterns in Exhibit 2.6.

EXHIBIT 2.6

Variable Cost Behavior

When Activity	Increases	Decreases
Total variable cost	Increases proportionately	Decreases proportionately
Variable cost **per unit**	Remains constant	Remains constant

Risk and Reward Assessment

LO 2

Demonstrate the effects of operating leverage on profitability.

Shifting the cost structure from fixed to variable enables SPI to avoid the fixed cost risk. If no one buys a ticket, SPI loses nothing because it incurs no cost. If only one person buys a ticket at an $18 ticket price, SPI earns a $2 profit ($18 sales revenue − $16 cost of band). Should managers therefore avoid fixed costs whenever possible? Not necessarily.

Shifting the cost structure from fixed to variable reduces not only the level of risk but also the potential for profits. Managers cannot avoid the risk of fixed costs without also sacrificing the benefits. Variable costs do not offer operating leverage. Exhibit 2.7 shows that a variable cost structure produces a proportional relationship between sales and profitability. A 10 percent increase or decrease in sales results in a corresponding 10 percent increase or decrease in profitability.

EXHIBIT 2.7

Variable Cost Eliminates Operating Leverage

Number of tickets sold	2,700	⇐−10%⇐	3,000	⇒+10%⇒	3,300
Sales revenue ($18 per ticket)	$48,600		$54,000		$59,400
Cost of band (variable cost)	(43,200)		(48,000)		(52,800)
Gross margin	$ 5,400	⇐−10%⇐	$ 6,000	⇒+10%⇒	$ 6,600

Suppose that you are sponsoring a political rally at which Ralph Nader will speak. You estimate that approximately 2,000 people will buy tickets to hear Mr. Nader's speech. The tickets are expected to be priced at $12 each. Would you prefer a contract that agrees to pay Mr. Nader $10,000 or one that agrees to pay him $5 per ticket purchased?

Answer

Your answer would depend on how certain you are that 2,000 people will purchase tickets. If it were likely that many more than 2,000 tickets would be sold, you would be better off with a fixed cost structure, agreeing to pay Mr. Nader a flat fee of $10,000. If attendance numbers are highly uncertain, you would be better off with a variable cost structure thereby guaranteeing a lower cost if fewer people buy tickets.

CHECK YOURSELF 2.1

Effect of Cost Structure on Profit Stability

The preceding discussion suggests that companies with higher levels of fixed costs are more likely to experience earnings volatility. To illustrate, suppose three companies produce and sell the same product. Each company sells 10 units for $10 each. Furthermore, each company incurs costs of $60 in the process of making and selling its products. However, the companies operate under radically different **cost structures.** The entire $60 of cost incurred by Company A is fixed. Company B incurs $30 of fixed cost and $30 of variable cost ($3 per unit). All $60 of cost incurred by Company C is variable ($6 per unit). Exhibit 2.8 displays income statements for the three companies.

When sales change, the amount of the corresponding change in net income is directly influenced by the company's cost structure. The more fixed cost, the greater the fluctuation in net income. To illustrate, assume sales increase by one unit; the resulting income statements are displayed in Exhibit 2.9.

Company A, with the highest level of fixed costs, experienced a $10 ($50 − $40) increase in profitability; Company C, with the lowest level of fixed cost (zero), had only a $4 ($44 − $40) increase in profitability. Company B, with a 50/50 mix of fixed and variable cost, had a mid-range $7 ($47 − $40) increase in net income. The effect of fixed cost on volatility applies to decreases as well as increases in sales volume. To illustrate, assume sales decrease by one unit (from 10 to 9 units). The resulting income statements are displayed in Exhibit 2.10.

LO 2

Demonstrate the effects of operating leverage on profitability.

EXHIBIT 2.8

Income Statements

	Company Name		
	A	**B**	**C**
Variable Cost per Unit (a)	$ 0	$ 3	$ 6
Sales Revenue (10 units × $10)	$100	$100	$100
Variable Cost (10 units × a)	0	(30)	(60)
Fixed Cost	(60)	(30)	0
Net Income	$ 40	$ 40	$ 40

Answers to The Curious Accountant

The explanation for how a company's earnings can rise faster, as a percentage, than its revenue rises is operating leverage, and operating leverage is due entirely to fixed costs. As the chapter explained, when a company's output goes up, its fixed cost per unit goes down. As long as it can keep prices about the same, this lower unit cost will result in higher profit per unit sold. In real-world companies, the relationship between changing sales levels and changing earnings levels can be very complex, but the existence of fixed costs helps to explain why a 7 percent rise in revenue can cause a 61 percent rise in net earnings. Chapter 3 will investigate the relationships among an entity's cost structure, output level, pricing strategy, and profits earned in more depth.

EXHIBIT 2.9

Income Statements

| | Company Name | | |
	A	B	C
Variable Cost per Unit (a)	$ 0	$ 3	$ 6
Sales Revenue (11 units × $10)	$110	$110	$110
Variable Cost (11 units × a)	0	(33)	(66)
Fixed Cost	(60)	(30)	0
Net Income	$ 50	$ 47	$ 44

EXHIBIT 2.10

Income Statements

| | Company Name | | |
	A	B	C
Variable Cost per Unit (a)	$ 0	$ 3	$ 6
Sales Revenue (9 units × $10)	$90	$90	$90
Variable Cost (9 units × a)	0	(27)	(54)
Fixed Cost	(60)	(30)	0
Net Income	$30	$33	$36

Company A again experiences the largest variance in earnings ($10 decrease). Company B had a moderate decline of $7, and Company C had the least volatility with only a $4 decline.

What cost structure is the best? Should a manager use fixed or variable costs? The answer depends on sales volume expectations. A manager who expects revenues to increase should use a fixed cost structure. On the other hand, if future sales growth is uncertain or if the manager believes revenue is likely to decline, a variable cost structure makes more sense.

CHECK YOURSELF 2.2

If both **Kroger Food Stores** and **Delta Airlines** were to experience a 5 percent increase in revenues, which company would be more likely to experience a higher percentage increase in net income?

Answer

Delta would be more likely to experience a higher percentage increase in net income because a large portion of its cost (e.g., employee salaries and depreciation) is fixed cost, while a large portion of Kroger's cost is variable (e.g., cost of goods sold).

An Income Statement under the Contribution Margin Approach

LO 3

Prepare an income statement using the contribution margin approach.

The impact of cost structure on profitability is so significant that managerial accountants frequently construct income statements that classify costs according to their behavior patterns. Such income statements first subtract variable costs from revenue; the resulting subtotal is called the **contribution margin.** The contribution margin represents the amount available to cover fixed expenses and thereafter to provide company profits. Net income is computed by subtracting the fixed costs from the contribution margin. A contribution margin style income statement cannot be used for public reporting (GAAP prohibits its use in external financial reports), but it is widely used for internal reporting purposes. Exhibit 2.11 illustrates income statements prepared using the contribution margin approach.

EXHIBIT 2.11

Income Statements

	Company Name	
	Bragg	**Biltmore**
Variable Cost per Unit (a)	$ 6	$ 12
Sales Revenue (10 units × $20)	$200	$200
Variable Cost (10 units × a)	(60)	(120)
Contribution Margin	140	80
Fixed Cost	(120)	(60)
Net Income	$ 20	$ 20

Using Fixed Cost to Provide a Competitive Operating Advantage

LO 2

Demonstrate the effects of operating leverage on profitability.

Mary MaHall and John Strike have established tutoring companies to support themselves while they attend college. Both Ms. MaHall and Mr. Strike function as owner/managers; they each hire other students to actually provide the tutoring services. Ms. MaHall pays her tutors salaries; her labor costs are fixed at $16,000 per year regardless of the number of hours of tutoring performed. Mr. Strike pays his employees $8 per hour; his labor is therefore a variable cost. Both businesses currently provide 2,000 hours of tutoring services at a price of $11 per hour. As shown in Exhibit 2.12, both companies currently produce the same profit.

Suppose Ms. MaHall adopts a strategy to win over Mr. Strike's customers by reducing the price of tutoring services from $11 per hour to $7 per hour. If Ms. MaHall succeeds, her

EXHIBIT 2.12

Comparative Profitability at 2,000 Hours of Tutoring

		MaHall		**Strike**
Number of hours of tutoring provided		2,000		2,000
Service revenue ($11 per hour)		$22,000		$22,000
Cost of tutors	Fixed	(16,000)	Variable ($8 × 2,000)	(16,000)
Net income		$ 6,000		$ 6,000

company's income will double as shown in Exhibit 2.13. Mr. Strike is in a vulnerable position because if he matches MaHall's price cut he will lose $1 ($7 new per hour price − $8 cost per hour for tutor) for each hour of tutoring service that his company provides.

EXHIBIT 2.13

MaHall's Profitability at 4,000 Hours of Tutoring		MaHall
Number of hours of tutoring provided		4,000
Service revenue ($7 per hour)		$28,000
Cost of tutors	Fixed	(16,000)
Net income (loss)		$12,000

Is Mr. Strike's business doomed? Not necessarily; Ms. MaHall's operating leverage strategy only works if volume increases. If Mr. Strike matches Ms. MaHall's price, thereby maintaining the existing sales volume levels between the two companies, both companies incur losses. Exhibit 2.14 verifies this conclusion. Under these circumstances, Ms. MaHall would be forced to raise her price or to face the same negative consequences that she is attempting to force on Mr. Strike.

EXHIBIT 2.14

Comparative Profitability at 2,000 Hours of Tutoring		MaHall		Strike
Number of hours of tutoring provided		2,000		2,000
Service revenue ($7 per hour)		$14,000		$14,000
Cost of tutors	Fixed	(16,000)	Variable ($8 × 2,000)	(16,000)
Net income (loss)		$ (2,000)		$ (2,000)

Measuring Operating Leverage Using Contribution Margin

LO 4

Demonstrate how the magnitude of operating leverage affects profitability.

A contribution margin income statement allows managers to easily measure operating leverage. The magnitude of operating leverage can be determined as follows:

$$\text{Magnitude of operating leverage} = \frac{\text{Contribution margin}}{\text{Net income}}$$

Applying this formula to the income statement data reported for Bragg Company and Biltmore Company in Exhibit 2.11 produces the following measures.

Bragg Company:

$$\text{Magnitude of operating leverage} = \frac{140}{20} = 7$$

Biltmore Company:

$$\text{Magnitude of operating leverage} = \frac{80}{20} = 4$$

EXHIBIT 2.15

Comparative Income Statements for Bragg Company

Units (a)	10		11
Sales Revenue ($20 × a)	$200	⇒+10%⇒	$220
Variable Cost ($6 × a)	(60)		(66)
Contribution Margin	140		154
Fixed Cost	(120)		(120)
Net Income	$ 20	⇒+70%⇒	$ 34

EXHIBIT 2.16

Comparative Income Statements for Biltmore Company

Units (a)	10		11
Sales Revenue ($20 × a)	$200	⇒+10%⇒	$220
Variable Cost ($12 × a)	(120)		(132)
Contribution Margin	80		88
Fixed Cost	(60)		(60)
Net Income	$ 20	⇒+40%⇒	$ 28

The computations show that Bragg is more highly leveraged than Biltmore. Bragg's change in profitability will be seven times greater than a given percentage change in revenue. In contrast, Biltmore's profits change by only four times the percentage change in revenue. For example, a 10 percent increase in revenue produces a 70 percent increase (10 percent × 7) in profitability for Bragg Company and a 40 percent increase (10 percent × 4) in profitability for Biltmore Company. The income statements in Exhibits 2.15 and 2.16 confirm these expectations.

Operating leverage itself is neither good nor bad; it represents a strategy that can work to a company's advantage or disadvantage, depending on how it is used. The next section explains how managers can use operating leverage to create a competitive business advantage.

Boeing Company's 2001 10K annual report filed with the Securities and Exchange Commission refers to "higher commercial airlines segment margins." Is Boeing referring to gross margins or contribution margins?

Answer

Since the data come from the company's external annual report, the reference must be to gross margins (revenue − cost of goods sold), a product cost measure. The contribution margin (revenue − variable cost) is a measure used in internal reporting.

Cost Behavior Summarized

The term *fixed* refers to the behavior of *total* fixed cost. The cost *per unit* of a fixed cost *varies inversely* with changes in the level of activity. As activity increases, fixed cost per unit decreases. As activity decreases, fixed cost per unit increases. These relationships are graphed in Exhibit 2.17.

The term *variable* refers to the behavior of *total* variable cost. Total variable cost increases or decreases proportionately with changes in the volume of activity. In contrast, variable cost *per unit* remains *fixed* at all levels of activity. These relationships are graphed in Exhibit 2.18.

The relationships between fixed and variable costs are summarized in the chart in Exhibit 2.19. Study these relationships thoroughly.

LO 1

Identify and describe fixed, variable, and mixed cost behavior.

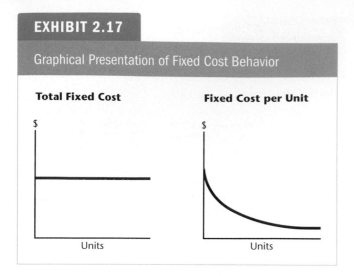

EXHIBIT 2.17

Graphical Presentation of Fixed Cost Behavior

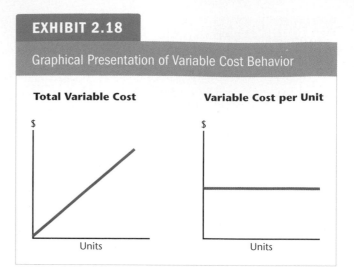

EXHIBIT 2.18

Graphical Presentation of Variable Cost Behavior

EXHIBIT 2.19

Fixed and Variable Cost Behavior

When Activity Level Changes	Total Cost	Cost per Unit
Fixed costs	Remains constant	Changes *inversely*
Variable costs	Changes in direct proportion	Remains constant

The Relevant Range

LO 5

Demonstrate how the relevant range and decision context affect cost behavior.

Suppose SPI, the rock concert promoter mentioned earlier, must pay $5,000 to rent a concert hall with a seating capacity of 4,000 people. Is the cost of the concert hall fixed or variable? Since total cost remains unchanged regardless of whether one ticket, 4,000 tickets, or any number in between is sold, the cost is fixed relative to ticket sales. However, what if demand for tickets is significantly more than 4,000? In that case, SPI might rent a larger concert hall at a higher cost. In other words, *the cost is fixed only for a designated range of activity (1 to 4,000).*

A similar circumstance affects many variable costs. For example, a supplier may offer a volume discount to buyers who purchase more than a specified number of products. The point is that descriptions of cost behavior pertain to a specified range of activity. The range of activity over which the definitions of fixed and variable costs are valid is commonly called the **relevant range.**

Context-Sensitive Definitions of Fixed and Variable

The behavior pattern of a particular cost may be either fixed or variable, depending on the context. For example, the cost of the band was fixed at $48,000 when SPI was considering hiring it to play a single concert. Regardless of how many tickets SPI sold, the total band cost was $48,000. However, the band cost becomes variable if SPI decides to hire it to perform at a series of concerts. The total cost and the cost per concert for one, two, three, four, or five concerts are shown in Exhibit 2.20.

In this context, the total cost of hiring the band increases proportionately with the number of concerts while cost per concert remains constant. The band cost is therefore variable. The same cost can behave as either a fixed cost or a variable cost, depending on the **activity base.** When identifying a cost as fixed or variable, first ask, fixed or variable *relative to what activity base?* The cost of the band is fixed relative to *the number of tickets sold for a specific concert;* it is variable relative to *the number of concerts produced.*

EXHIBIT 2.20

Cost Behavior Relative to Number of Concerts

Number of concerts (a)	1	2	3	4	5
Cost per concert (b)	$48,000	$48,000	$ 48,000	$ 48,000	$ 48,000
Total cost (a × b)	$48,000	$96,000	$144,000	$192,000	$240,000

Is the compensation cost for managers of **Pizza Hut Restaurants** a fixed cost or a variable cost?

Answer

The answer depends on the context. For example, since a store manager's salary remains unchanged regardless of how many customers enter a particular restaurant, it can be classified as a fixed cost relative to the number of customers at a particular restaurant. However, the more restaurants that Pizza Hut operates, the higher the total managers' compensation cost will be. Accordingly, managers' salary cost would be classified as a variable cost relative to the number of restaurants opened.

CHECK YOURSELF 2.4

Cost Averaging

Lake Resorts, Inc. (LRI), offers water skiing lessons for guests. Since the demand for lessons is seasonal (guests buy more lessons in July than in December), LRI has chosen to rent (rather than own) the necessary equipment (boats, skis, ropes, life jackets) only when it is needed. LRI's accountant has collected the following data pertaining to providing ski lessons:

LO 6

Select an appropriate time period for calculating the average cost per unit.

1. The daily fee to rent equipment is $80.
2. Instructors are paid $15 per lesson hour.
3. Fuel costs are $2 per lesson hour.
4. Lessons take one hour each.
5. LRI can provide up to 20 lessons in one day.

During a recent weekend, LRI provided 2 lessons on Friday, 10 on Saturday, and 20 on Sunday. Exhibit 2.21 shows the total cost per day and average cost per lesson for each of the three days. Since equipment rental cost is fixed relative to the number of lessons provided, the cost per lesson declines as the number of lessons increases. This explains why the cost per lesson is significantly lower on Sunday than Friday.

EXHIBIT 2.21

Analysis of Total and Unit Cost

Number of Lessons (a)	2	10	20
Cost of equipment rental	$ 80	$ 80	$ 80
Cost of instruction (a × $15)	30	150	300
Cost of fuel (a × $2)	4	20	40
Total cost (b)	$114	$250	$420
Cost per lesson (b ÷ a)	$ 57	$ 25	$ 21

Assume LRI uses a cost plus pricing strategy. The cost per lesson figures shown in Exhibit 2.21 are not useful in determining the price to charge customers. For example, it makes no sense to charge more for lessons on days like Friday when demand is low. Indeed, many businesses lower prices on days when demand is low in order to stimulate business.

Stella is a business student who works part time at **Costco Wholesale Corporation** to help pay for her college expenses. She is currently taking a managerial accounting course and has heard her instructor refer to depreciation as a fixed cost. However, as a requirement for her first accounting course, Stella reviewed Costco's financial statements for 2002, 2003, and 2004. The depreciation expense increased about 29 percent over these three years. She is not sure why depreciation expense would be considered a fixed cost.

Stella's accounting instructor reminded her that when an accountant says a cost is fixed, he or she means the cost is fixed in relation to one particular factor. A cost that is fixed in relation to one factor can be variable when compared to some other factor. For example, the depreciation for a retailer may be fixed relative to the number of customers who visit a particular store, but variable relative to the number of stores the company opens. In fact, Costco's depreciation increased from 2002 to 2004 mainly because the company built and opened additional stores.

Stella's instructor suggested that Costco's depreciation expense would be more stable if analyzed on a per store basis, rather than in total. Being curious, Stella prepared the following table, where costs are in thousands. Over the three years, she noted that total depreciation expense increased 28.9 percent, while depreciation per store increased only 15.6 percent. Although the costs on a per store basis were more stable than the total depreciation costs, they still were not fixed, so she asked her instructor for further explanation.

Fiscal year	Total Depreciation Expense	Average Depreciation Expense per Store
2002	$341,781	$ 913.9
2003	391,302	985.6
2004	440,721	1,056.9

The instructor suggested Costco's average per store depreciation costs were increasing because the equipment and buildings purchased for the new stores (opened from 2002 to 2004) probably cost more than those purchased for the older stores. This would raise the average depreciation expense per store. The instructor also reminded her that in the real world very few costs are perfectly fixed or perfectly variable.

The pricing problem can be solved by averaging the cost over a longer span of time. To illustrate, assume LRI provides 46 lessons during the entire week at a total cost of $2,760, resulting in an average cost per lesson of $60 ($2,760 ÷ 46). If LRI desires to earn a gross profit of $10 per lesson, the company would charge customers $70 ($60 cost + $10 profit margin) per lesson regardless of when the lesson is provided. On slow days like Friday when only two lessons are provided, the actual profit margin is less than $10. However, on busy days such as Sunday, the profit margin is more than $10 per lesson. By averaging the cost over the span of one week LRI is able to charge the same amount per lesson regardless of the level of demand and still earn an average gross profit of $10 per lesson.

The need for a weekly average occurs because the number of lessons per day fluctuates radically, thereby causing significant differences in the cost per lesson when calculated on a daily basis. A similar problem occurs if the number of lessons per week fluctuates radically from week to week. For example, the demand for skiing lessons may increase significantly during the week of July 4th or other holidays. Similarly, the demand for lessons may taper off toward the end of the summer. In this case, it will be necessary to expand the time frame for which the average is calculated, perhaps over the summer months or even several seasons.

Distortions can occur when the time period is too long as well as too short. For example, the price of fuel and equipment rental changes over time. If older costs are mixed with newer costs, the average does not represent current conditions. Choosing the best time frame for calculating the average cost of a product or service requires thoughtful analysis and judgment.

Use of Estimates in Real-World Problems

Imagine trying to classify as fixed or variable all the different costs incurred by a large company such as **Delta Airlines**. Record keeping would be horrendous. Further complications would arise because some costs have both fixed and variable components. Consider the cost Delta incurs to use airport facilities. An airport may charge Delta a flat annual rental fee for terminal space plus a charge each time a plane takes off or lands. The flat rental fee is a fixed cost while the charge per flight is variable. The total facilities cost is mixed. Such costs are called **mixed costs** or **semivariable costs.**

Identify and describe fixed, variable, and mixed cost behavior.

To minimize the record keeping difficulties involved in identifying actual fixed and variable costs, many companies make decisions using estimated rather than actual costs. Several techniques exist to divide total cost into estimated fixed and variable components.

High-Low Method of Estimating Fixed and Variable Costs

The management of Rainy Day Books (RDB) wants to expand operations. To help evaluate risks involved in opening an additional store, the company president wants to know the amount of fixed cost a new store will likely incur. Suppose RDB's accountant decides to use the **high-low method** to supply the president with the requested information. The estimated amount of fixed cost for the new store would be developed in the following four steps.

Use the high-low method, scattergraphs, and regression analysis to estimate fixed and variable costs.

Step 1 *Assemble sales volume and cost history for an existing store.* Assuming the new store would operate with roughly the same cost structure, the accountant can use the historical data to estimate the fixed cost likely to be incurred by the new store. To illustrate, assume the accounting data set for the existing store is displayed in Exhibit 2.22.

Step 2 *Select the high and low points in the data set.* In this example, the month with the lowest number of units sold does not correspond to the month with the lowest total cost. The lowest point in units sold occurred in May; the lowest total cost occurred in March. Because the total cost depends on the *number of units sold,* May should be classified as the low point. The high point in sales volume occurred in December. The units sold and cost data for the December and May high and low points follow:

	Units Sold	Total Cost
High (December)	34,000	$540,000
Low (May)	10,000	$180,000

EXHIBIT 2.22

Cost Data

Month	Units Sold	Total Cost
January	30,000	$450,000
February	14,000	300,000
March	12,000	150,000
April	25,000	440,000
May	10,000	180,000
June	11,000	240,000
July	20,000	350,000
August	18,000	400,000
September	17,000	360,000
October	16,000	320,000
November	27,000	490,000
December	34,000	540,000

Step 3 *Determine the estimated variable cost per unit.* The variable cost per unit is determined by dividing the difference in the total cost by the difference in the number of units sold. In this case, the variable cost per unit is as follows:

$$\frac{\text{Variable}}{\text{cost per unit}} = \frac{\text{Difference in total cost}}{\text{Difference in volume}} = \frac{(\$540,000 - \$180,000)}{(34,000 - 10,000)} = \frac{\$360,000}{24,000} = \$15$$

Step 4   ***Determine the estimated total fixed costs.*** The total fixed cost can now be determined by subtracting the variable cost from the total cost using either the high point or the low point. Either point yields the same result. Computations using the high point follow:

$$\text{Fixed cost} + \text{Variable Cost} = \text{Total Cost}$$
$$\text{Fixed Cost} = \text{Total Cost} - \text{Variable Cost}$$
$$\text{Fixed Cost} = \$540,000 - (\$15 \times 34,000 \text{ units})$$
$$\text{Fixed Cost} = \$30,000$$

Although 12 data points are available, the high-low method uses only 2 of them to estimate the amounts of fixed and variable costs. If either or both of these points is not representative of the true relationship between fixed and variable costs, the estimates produced by the high-low method will be inaccurate. *The chief advantage of the high-low method is its simplicity; the chief disadvantage is its vulnerability to inaccuracy.* RDB's accountant decides to test the accuracy of the high-low method results.

Scattergraph Method of Estimating Fixed and Variable Costs

Use the high-low method, scattergraphs, and regression analysis to estimate fixed and Variable costs.

Scattergraphs are sometimes used as an estimation technique for dividing total cost into fixed and variable cost components. To assess the accuracy of the high-low estimate of fixed cost, RDB's accountant constructs a **scattergraph.** The horizontal axis is labeled with the number of books sold and the vertical axis with total costs. The 12 data points are plotted on the graph, and a line is drawn through the high and low points in the data set. The result is shown in Exhibit 2.23.

After studying the scattergraph in Exhibit 2.23, the accountant is certain that the high and low points are not representative of the data set. Most of the data points are above the high-low line. As shown in the second scattergraph in Exhibit 2.24, the line should be shifted upward to reflect the influence of the other data points.

The graph in Exhibit 2.24 is identical to the graph in Exhibit 2.23 except the straight line is plotted through the center of the entire data set rather than just the high and low points. The new line, a **visual fit line,** is drawn to visually minimize the total distance between the data points and the line. Usually, half of the data points are above and half below a visual fit line. The estimated

EXHIBIT 2.23

Scattergraph Depicting High-Low Estimate

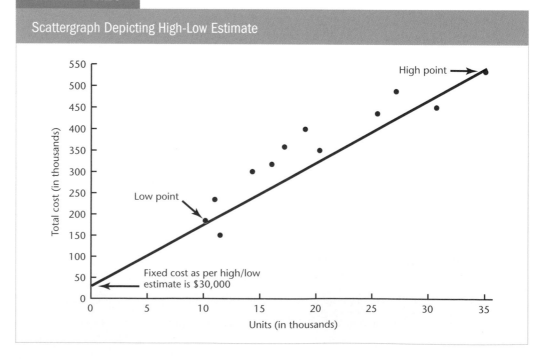

EXHIBIT 2.24

Scattergraph Depicting Line Drawn by Visual Inspection

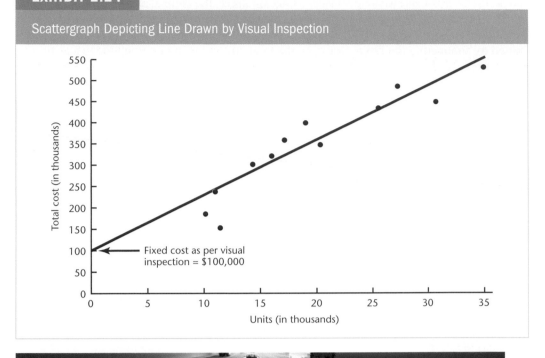

Fixed cost as per visual inspection = $100,000

FOCUS ON INTERNATIONAL ISSUES

ANOTHER REASON FIXED COSTS AREN'T ALWAYS FIXED

Suppose that a company is renting a facility at an annual rental rate that does not change for the next five years *no matter what.* Is this a fixed cost? By now, you are aware that the proper response is to ask fixed in relation to what? Is the rental cost of this facility fixed in relation to the activity at this facility? The answer seems to be yes, but it might be "not necessarily."

Consider the **Exxon Mobil Corporation**. If Exxon Mobil rents facilities in a country in the eastern hemisphere, Malaysia for example, the annual rental fee may be stated and paid in the local currency. In Malaysia, this is the ringgit. Even though Exxon Mobil may be paying the same number of ringgit in rent each year, Exxon Mobil's rental cost in U.S. dollars could vary greatly over time. Such potential foreign currency exchange fluctuations cause companies to enter very complex hedging arrangements to add stability to transactions that must be paid in foreign currencies.

Exxon Mobil was founded and has its headquarters in the United States. It does much business in the United States. Furthermore, it is listed on the New York Stock Exchange and prepares its financial statements in U.S. dollars. However, it does much more business and has many more assets in countries outside the United States. Consider the following table from Exxon Mobil's 2004 financial statements. Before a multinational company can determine whether a cost is fixed, it must determine the applicable currency.

Geographical Area	Earnings*	Percentage of Total	Total Assets*	Percentage of Total
United States	$ 8,154	32%	$ 42,117	25%
Non-United States	17,655	68	124,944	75
Totals	$25,809	100%	$167,061	100%

*Amounts in millions.

variable cost per unit is measured by the slope (steepness) of the visual fit line. The fixed cost is the point (the *intercept*) where the visual fit line intersects the vertical axis (the total cost line).

The intercept in Exhibit 2.24 provides a fixed cost estimate of $100,000. Although RDB's president had only asked for the amount of fixed cost, the variable cost can be easily determined by subtracting the fixed cost from the total cost at any point along the visual fit line. For example, at 15,000 units, total cost is $300,000. Variable cost is determined as follows:

$$\text{Fixed cost} + \text{Variable Cost} = \text{Total Cost}$$

$$\text{Variable Cost} = \text{Total Cost} - \text{Fixed Cost}$$

$$\text{Variable Cost} = \$300,000 - \$100,000$$

$$\text{Variable Cost} = \$200,000$$

Variable cost per unit is $13.33, calculated by dividing the total variable cost by the number of units ($200,000 ÷ 15,000 units = $13.33 per unit).

Regression Method of Cost Estimation

LO 7

Use the high-low method, scattergraphs, and regression analysis to estimate fixed and variable costs.

Since the scattergraph is drawn by simple visual inspection, it is subject to human error. A better fit can be obtained using a statistical procedure known as **least-squares regression.**[1] Many of today's spreadsheet programs include a regression procedure. For example, the regression estimates shown in Exhibit 2.25 were generated in an *Excel* spreadsheet by performing the following functions.

1. Enter the data in spreadsheet columns[2] (see columns B and C, rows 3 through 14 in Exhibit 2.25).
2. Click *Tools.*
3. Click *Data Analysis.*[3]
4. Click *Regression* and then *OK.*
5. Define data ranges and click *Line Fit Plot.*
6. Click *OK.*

The regression function returns an estimate of $72,848 for fixed cost and $14.30 per unit for variable costs. These estimates are highlighted in blue in the spreadsheet shown in Exhibit 2.25. The regression statistics and other information shown in the worksheet output are provided to enable the assessment of the quality of the estimates. A detailed discussion of this topic is beyond the scope of this text. For more in-depth discussion of the reliability issue, please refer to a statistics textbook.

---

[1]Although the least-squares regression is a more accurate method than the high-low method and the visual scattergraph method, the three methods follow the same logical reasoning. Basically, the procedure locates a straight line on a coordinate with the *Y* axis representing the cost in dollars and the *X* axis representing the cost driver. In the examples shown in this chapter, the measurement of production in units is used as the cost driver and appears on the *X* axis. The basic regression model can be explained in the following equation:

$$Y = a + bX$$

Where

a = total fixed cost, or the *Y* intercept of the regression line

b = variable cost per unit of *X,* or the slope of the regression line

X = independent variable

Y = dependent variable

[2]Statistical reliability requires an information set that includes more than 30 data points. The illustration shown here has been limited in size to simplify the demonstration.

[3]If the pull-down menu does not contain a data analysis option, it is likely that the statistical functions have not been activated in your program. You will need to consult the *Excel* user manual or help routine for instructions to activate the statistical functions.

EXHIBIT 2.25

Excel Spreadsheet Showing the Results of Least-Squares Regression

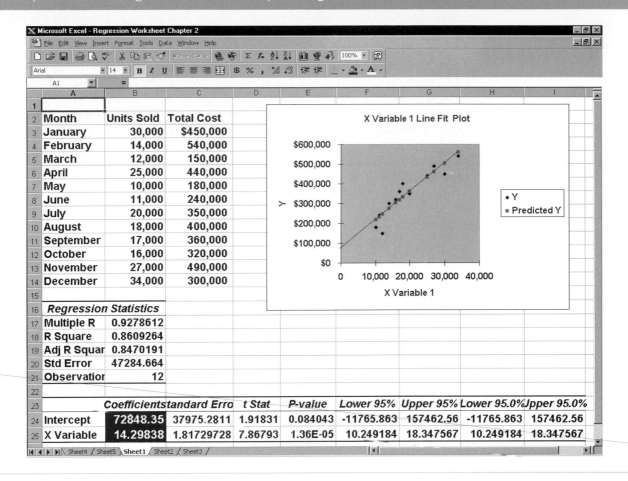

Month	Units Sold	Total Cost
January	30,000	$450,000
February	14,000	540,000
March	12,000	150,000
April	25,000	440,000
May	10,000	180,000
June	11,000	240,000
July	20,000	350,000
August	18,000	400,000
September	17,000	360,000
October	16,000	320,000
November	27,000	490,000
December	34,000	300,000

Regression Statistics

Multiple R	0.9278612
R Square	0.8609264
Adj R Square	0.8470191
Std Error	47284.664
Observations	12

	Coefficients	standard Error	t Stat	P-value	Lower 95%	Upper 95%	Lower 95.0%	Upper 95.0%
Intercept	72848.35	37975.2811	1.91831	0.084043	-11765.863	157462.56	-11765.863	157462.56
X Variable	14.29838	1.81729728	7.86793	1.36E-05	10.249184	18.347567	10.249184	18.347567

A Look Back

To plan and control business operations effectively, managers need to understand how different costs behave in relation to changes in the volume of activity. Total *fixed cost* remains constant when activity changes. Fixed cost per unit decreases with increases in activity and increases with decreases in activity. In contrast, total *variable cost* increases proportionately with increases in activity and decreases proportionately with decreases in activity. Variable cost per unit remains constant regardless of activity levels. The definitions of fixed and variable costs have meaning only within the context of a specified range of activity (the relevant range) for a defined period of time. In addition, cost behavior depends on the relevant volume measure (a store manager's salary is fixed relative to the number of customers visiting a particular store but is variable relative to the number of stores operated). A mixed cost has both fixed and variable cost components.

Fixed costs allow companies to take advantage of *operating leverage.* With operating leverage, each additional sale decreases the cost per unit. This principle allows a small percentage change in volume of revenue to cause a significantly larger percentage change in profits. The *magnitude of operating leverage* can be determined by dividing the contribution margin by net income. When all costs are fixed and revenues have covered fixed costs, each additional dollar of revenue represents pure profit. Having a fixed cost structure (employing operating leverage) offers a company both risks and rewards. If sales volume increases, costs do not increase, allowing profits to soar. Alternatively, if sales volume decreases, costs do not decrease and profits decline significantly more than revenues. Companies with high variable costs in relation to fixed costs do not experience as great a level of operating leverage. Their costs increase or decrease in proportion to changes in revenue. These companies face less risk but fail to reap disproportionately higher profits when volume soars.

Under the contribution margin approach, variable costs are subtracted from revenue to determine the *contribution margin*. Fixed costs are then subtracted from the contribution margin to determine net income. The contribution margin represents the amount available to pay fixed costs and provide a profit. Although not permitted by GAAP for external reporting, many companies use the contribution margin format for internal reporting purposes.

Cost per unit is an average cost that is easier to compute than the actual cost of each unit and is more relevant to decision making than actual cost. Accountants must use judgment when choosing the time span from which to draw data for computing the average cost per unit. Distortions can result from using either too long or too short a time span.

Fixed and variable costs can be estimated using such tools as the *high-low method, scattergraphs* and **regression analysis.** The high-low method and scattergraphs are easy to use. Regression analysis is more accurate.

>> A Look Forward

The next chapter will show you how changes in cost, volume, and pricing affect profitability. You will learn to determine the number of units of product that must be produced and sold in order to break even (the number of units that will produce an amount of revenue that is exactly equal to total cost). You will learn to establish the price of a product using a cost-plus pricing approach and to establish the cost of a product using a target-pricing approach. Finally, the chapter will show you how to use a break-even chart to examine potential profitability over a range of operating activity and how to use a technique known as *sensitivity analysis* to examine how simultaneous changes in sales price, volume, fixed costs, and variable costs affect profitability.

SELF-STUDY REVIEW PROBLEM

A step-by-step audio-narrated series of slides is provided on the text website at www.mhhe.com/edmonds2008.

Mensa Mountaineering Company (MMC) provides guided mountain climbing expeditions in the Rocky Mountains. Its only major expense is guide salaries; it pays each guide $4,800 per climbing expedition. MMC charges its customers $1,500 per expedition and expects to take five climbers on each expedition.

Part 1
Base your answers on the preceding information.

Required
a. Determine the total cost of guide salaries and the cost of guide salaries per climber assuming that four, five, or six climbers are included in a trip. Relative to the number of climbers in a single expedition, is the cost of guides a fixed or a variable cost?
b. Relative to the number of expeditions, is the cost of guides a fixed or a variable cost?
c. Determine the profit of an expedition assuming that five climbers are included in the trip.
d. Determine the profit assuming a 20 percent increase (six climbers total) in expedition revenue. What is the percentage change in profitability?
e. Determine the profit assuming a 20 percent decrease (four climbers total) in expedition revenue. What is the percentage change in profitability?
f. Explain why a 20 percent shift in revenue produces more than a 20 percent shift in profitability. What term describes this phenomenon?

Part 2
Assume that the guides offer to make the climbs for a percentage of expedition fees. Specifically, MMC will pay guides $960 per climber on the expedition. Assume also that the expedition fee charged to climbers remains at $1,500 per climber.

Required

g. Determine the total cost of guide salaries and the cost of guide salaries per climber assuming that four, five, or six climbers are included in a trip. Relative to the number of climbers in a single expedition, is the cost of guides a fixed or a variable cost?

h. Relative to the number of expeditions, is the cost of guides a fixed or a variable cost?

i. Determine the profit of an expedition assuming that five climbers are included in the trip.

j. Determine the profit assuming a 20 percent increase (six climbers total) in expedition revenue. What is the percentage change in profitability?

k. Determine the profit assuming a 20 percent decrease (four climbers total) in expedition revenue. What is the percentage change in profitability?

l. Explain why a 20 percent shift in revenue does not produce more than a 20 percent shift in profitability.

Solution to Part 1, Requirement a

Number of climbers (a)	4	5	6
Total cost of guide salaries (b)	$4,800	$4,800	$4,800
Cost per climber (b ÷ a)	1,200	960	800

Since the total cost remains constant (fixed) regardless of the number of climbers on a particular expedition, the cost is classified as fixed. Note that the cost per climber decreases as the number of climbers increases. This is the *per unit* behavior pattern of a fixed cost.

Solution to Part 1, Requirement b
Since the total cost of guide salaries changes proportionately each time the number of expeditions increases or decreases, the cost of salaries is variable relative to the number of expeditions.

Solution to Part 1, Requirements c, d, and e

Number of Climbers	4	Percentage Change	5	Percentage Change	6
Revenue ($1,500 per climber)	$6,000	⇐ (20%) ⇐	$7,500	⇒ +20% ⇒	$9,000
Cost of guide salaries (fixed)	4,800		4,800		4,800
Profit	$1,200	⇐ (55.6%) ⇐	$2,700	⇒ +55.6% ⇒	$4,200

Percentage change in revenue: ±$1,500 ÷ $7,500 = ±20%

Percentage change in profit: ±$1,500 ÷ $2,700 = ±55.6%

Solution to Part 1, Requirement f
Since the cost of guide salaries remains fixed while volume (number of climbers) changes, the change in net income, measured in absolute dollars, exactly matches the change in revenue. More specifically, each time MMC increases the number of climbers by one, revenue and net income increase by $1,500. Since the base figure for net income ($2,700) is lower than the base figure for revenue ($7,500), the percentage change in net income ($1,500 ÷ $2,700 = 55.6%) is higher than percentage change in revenue ($1,500 ÷ $7,500). This phenomenon is called *operating leverage.*

Solution for Part 2, Requirement g

Number of climbers (a)	4	5	6
Per climber cost of guide salaries (b)	$ 960	$ 960	$ 960
Cost per climber (b × a)	3,840	4,800	5,760

Since the total cost changes in proportion to changes in the number of climbers, the cost is classified as variable. Note that the cost per climber remains constant (stays the same) as the number of climbers increases or decreases. This is the *per unit* behavior pattern of a variable cost.

Solution for Part 2, Requirement h
Since the total cost of guide salaries changes proportionately with changes in the number of expeditions, the cost of salaries is also variable relative to the number of expeditions.

Solution for Part 2, Requirements i, j, and k

Number of Climbers	4	Percentage Change	5	Percentage Change	6
Revenue ($1,500 per climber)	$6,000	⇐ (20%) ⇐	$7,500	⇒ +20% ⇒	$9,000
Cost of guide salaries (variable)	3,840		4,800		5,760
Profit	$2,160	⇐ (20%) ⇐	$2,700	⇒ +20% ⇒	$3,240

Percentage change in revenue: ±$1,500 ÷ $7,500 = ±20%

Percentage change in profit: ±$540 ÷ $2,700 = ±20%

Solution for Part 2, Requirement l

Since the cost of guide salaries changes when volume (number of climbers) changes, the change in net income is proportionate to the change in revenue. More specifically, each time the number of climbers increases by one, revenue increases by $1,500 and net income increases by $540 ($1,500 − $960). Accordingly, the percentage change in net income will always equal the percentage change in revenue. This means that there is no operating leverage when all costs are variable.

KEY TERMS

Activity base 64
Contribution margin 61
Cost averaging 65
Cost behavior 56

Cost structure 59
Fixed cost 56
High-low method 67
Least-squares regression 70

Mixed costs (semivariable costs) 67
Operating leverage 56
Regression analysis 72

Relevant range 64
Scattergraph 68
Variable cost 55
Visual fit line 68

QUESTIONS

1. Define *fixed cost* and *variable cost* and give an example of each.
2. How can knowing cost behavior relative to volume fluctuations affect decision making?
3. Define the term *operating leverage* and explain how it affects profits.
4. How is operating leverage calculated?
5. Explain the limitations of using operating leverage to predict profitability.
6. If volume is increasing, would a company benefit more from a pure variable or a pure fixed cost structure? Which cost structure would be advantageous if volume is decreasing?
7. When are economies of scale possible? In what types of businesses would you most likely find economies of scale?
8. Explain the risk and rewards to a company that result from having fixed costs.
9. Are companies with predominately fixed cost structures likely to be more profitable?
10. How is the relevant range of activity related to fixed and variable cost? Give an example of how the definitions of these costs become invalid when volume is outside the relevant range.
11. Sam's Garage is trying to determine the cost of providing an oil change. Why would the average cost of this service be more relevant information than the actual cost for each customer?
12. When would the high-low method be appropriate for estimating variable and fixed costs? When would least-squares regression be the most desirable?
13. Which cost structure has the greater risk? Explain.
14. The president of Bright Corporation tells you that he sees a dim future for his company. He feels that his hands are tied because fixed costs are too high. He says that fixed costs do not change and therefore the situation is hopeless. Do you agree? Explain.
15. All costs are variable because if a business ceases operations, its costs fall to zero. Do you agree with the statement? Explain.
16. Because of seasonal fluctuations, Norel Corporation has a problem determining the unit cost of the products it produces. For example, high heating costs during the winter months causes per unit cost

to be higher than per unit cost in the summer months even when the same number of units of product is produced. Suggest several ways that Norel can improve the computation of per unit costs.

17. Verna Salsbury tells you that she thinks the terms fixed cost and variable cost are confusing. She notes that fixed cost per unit changes when the number of units changes. Furthermore, variable cost per unit remains fixed regardless of how many units are produced. She concludes that the terminology seems to be backward. Explain why the terminology appears to be contradictory.

MULTIPLE-CHOICE QUESTIONS

Multiple-choice questions are provided on the text website at www.mhhe.com/edmonds2008.

EXERCISES—SERIES A

All Exercises in Series A are available with McGraw-Hill's Homework Manager®.

Exercise 2-1A   *Identifying cost behavior*

L.O. 1

Sugarland's Kitchen, a fast-food restaurant company, operates a chain of restaurants across the nation. Each restaurant employs eight people; one is a manager paid a salary plus a bonus equal to 3 percent of sales. Other employees, two cooks, one dishwasher, and four waitresses, are paid salaries. Each manager is budgeted $3,000 per month for advertising cost.

Required

Classify each of the following costs incurred by Sugarland's Kitchen as fixed, variable, or mixed.

a. Manager's compensation relative to the number of customers.
b. Waitresses' salaries relative to the number of restaurants.
c. Advertising costs relative to the number of customers for a particular restaurant.
d. Rental costs relative to the number of restaurants.
e. Cooks' salaries at a particular location relative to the number of customers.
f. Cost of supplies (cups, plates, spoons, etc.) relative to the number of customers.

Exercise 2-2A   *Identifying cost behavior*

L.O. 1

At the various activity levels shown, Warren Company incurred the following costs.

	Units sold	20	40	60	80	100
a.	Total salary cost	$1,200.00	$1,600.00	$2,000.00	$2,400.00	$2,800.00
b.	Total cost of goods sold	1,800.00	3,600.00	5,400.00	7,200.00	9,000.00
c.	Depreciation cost per unit	240.00	120.00	80.00	60.00	48.00
d.	Total rent cost	3,200.00	3,200.00	3,200.00	3,200.00	3,200.00
e.	Total cost of shopping bags	2.00	4.00	6.00	8.00	10.00
f.	Cost per unit of merchandise sold	90.00	90.00	90.00	90.00	90.00
g.	Rental cost per unit of merchandise sold	36.00	18.00	12.00	9.00	7.20
h.	Total phone expense	80.00	100.00	120.00	140.00	160.00
i.	Cost per unit of supplies	1.00	1.00	1.00	1.00	1.00
j.	Total insurance cost	480.00	480.00	480.00	480.00	480.00

Required

Identify each of these costs as fixed, variable, or mixed.

L.O. 1

Exercise 2-3A *Determining fixed cost per unit*

Loehman Corporation incurs the following annual fixed costs:

Item	Cost
Depreciation	$110,000
Officers' salaries	240,000
Long-term lease	60,000
Property taxes	20,000

Required

Determine the total fixed cost per unit of production, assuming that Loehman produces 4,000, 4,500, or 5,000 units.

L.O. 1

Exercise 2-4A *Determining total variable cost*

The following variable production costs apply to goods made by Anchor Manufacturing Corporation.

Item	Cost per Unit
Materials	$5.00
Labor	2.80
Variable overhead	0.40
Total	$8.20

Required

Determine the total variable production cost, assuming that Anchor makes 10,000, 15,000, or 20,000 units.

L.O. 1

Exercise 2-5A *Fixed versus variable cost behavior*

Franklin Company's cost and production data for two recent months included the following:

	March	April
Production (units)	50	100
Rent	$2,000	$2,000
Utilities	$ 800	$1,600

Required

a. Separately calculate the rental cost per unit and the utilities cost per unit for both March and April.
b. Based on both total and per unit amounts, identify which cost is variable and which is fixed. Explain your answer.

L.O. 1

Exercise 2-6A *Fixed versus variable cost behavior*

Bradford Trophies makes and sells trophies it distributes to little league ballplayers. The company normally produces and sells between 10,000 and 13,000 trophies per year. The following cost data apply to various activity levels.

Number of trophies	10,000	11,000	12,000	13,000
Total costs incurred				
Fixed	$ 60,000			
Variable	50,000			
Total costs	$110,000			
Cost per unit				
Fixed	$ 6.00			
Variable	5.00			
Total cost per trophy	$11.00			

Required

a. Complete the preceding table by filling in the missing amounts for the levels of activity shown in the first row of the table. Round all cost per unit figures to the nearest whole penny.

b. Explain why the total cost per trophy decreases as the number of trophies increases.

Exercise 2-7A   *Fixed versus variable cost behavior*

L.O. 1

Joyner Entertainment sponsors rock concerts. The company is considering a contract to hire a band at a cost of $50,000 per concert.

Required

a. What are the total band cost and the cost per person if concert attendance is 2,000, 2,500, 3,000, 3,500, or 4,000?

b. Is the cost of hiring the band a fixed or a variable cost?

c. Draw a graph and plot total cost and cost per unit if attendance is 2,000, 2,500, 3,000, 3,500, or 4,000.

d. Identify Joyner's major business risks and explain how they can be minimized.

Exercise 2-8A   *Fixed versus variable cost behavior*

L.O. 1

Joyner Entertainment sells souvenir T-shirts at each rock concert that it sponsors. The shirts cost $8 each. Any excess shirts can be returned to the manufacturer for a full refund of the purchase price. The sales price is $12 per shirt.

Required

a. What are the total cost of shirts and cost per shirt if sales amount to 2,000, 2,500, 3,000, 3,500, or 4,000?

b. Is the cost of T-shirts a fixed or a variable cost?

c. Draw a graph and plot total cost and cost per shirt if sales amount to 2,000, 2,500, 3,000, 3,500, or 4,000.

d. Comment on Joyner's likelihood of incurring a loss due to its operating activities.

Exercise 2-9A   *Graphing fixed cost behavior*

L.O. 1

The following graphs depict the dollar amount of fixed cost on the vertical axes and the level of activity on the horizontal axes.

Total fixed cost

$

Units

Fixed cost per unit

$

Units

Required

a. Draw a line that depicts the relationship between total fixed cost and the level of activity.
b. Draw a line that depicts the relationship between fixed cost per unit and the level of activity.

L.O. 1

Exercise 2-10A   *Graphing variable cost behavior*

The following graphs depict the dollar amount of variable cost on the vertical axes and the level of activity on the horizontal axes.

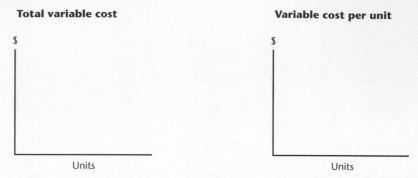

Total variable cost

Variable cost per unit

Required

a. Draw a line that depicts the relationship between total variable cost and the level of activity.
b. Draw a line that depicts the relationship between variable cost per unit and the level of activity.

L.O. 1

Exercise 2-11A   *Mixed cost at different levels of activity*

Pence Corporation paid one of its sales representatives $5,000 during the month of March. The rep is paid a base salary plus $15 per unit of product sold. During March, the rep sold 200 units.

Required

Calculate the total monthly cost of the sales representative's salary for each of the following months.

Month	April	May	June	July
Number of units sold	240	160	250	160
Total variable cost				
Total fixed cost				
Total salary cost				

L.O. 1, 2, 3

Exercise 2-12A   *Using fixed cost as a competitive business strategy*

The following income statements illustrate different cost structures for two competing companies.

Income Statements		
	Company Name	
	Sander	**Norland**
Number of Customers (a)	80	80
Sales Revenue (a × $250)	$20,000	$20,000
Variable Cost (a × $200)	N/A	(16,000)
Variable Cost (a × $0)	0	N/A
Contribution Margin	20,000	4,000
Fixed Cost	(16,000)	0
Net Income	$ 4,000	$ 4,000

Required

a. Reconstruct Sander's income statement, assuming that it serves 160 customers when it lures 80 customers away from Norland by lowering the sales price to $150 per customer.
b. Reconstruct Norland's income statement, assuming that it serves 160 customers when it lures 80 customers away from Sander by lowering the sales price to $150 per customer.
c. Explain why the price-cutting strategy increased Sander Company's profits but caused a net loss for Norland Company.

Exercise 2-13A *Using contribution margin format income statement to measure the magnitude of operating leverage*   **L.O. 3,4**

The following income statement was drawn from the records of Tucker Company, a merchandising firm.

TUCKER COMPANY
Income Statement
For the Year Ended December 31, 2007

Sales Revenue (4,000 units × $150)	$600,000
Cost of Goods Sold (4,000 units × $80)	(320,000)
Gross Margin	280,000
Sales Commissions (10% of sales)	(60,000)
Administrative Salaries Expense	(90,000)
Advertising Expense	(40,000)
Depreciation Expense	(50,000)
Shipping and Handling Expenses (4,000 units × $1)	(4,000)
Net Income	$ 36,000

Required

a. Reconstruct the income statement using the contribution margin format.
b. Calculate the magnitude of operating leverage.
c. Use the measure of operating leverage to determine the amount of net income Tucker will earn if sales increase by 10 percent.

Exercise 2-14A *Assessing the magnitude of operating leverage*   **L.O. 4**

The following income statement applies to Wong Company for the current year:

Income Statement

Sales Revenue (400 units × $25)	$10,000
Variable Cost (400 units × $10)	(4,000)
Contribution Margin	6,000
Fixed Costs	(3,500)
Net Income	$ 2,500

Required

a. Use the contribution margin approach to calculate the magnitude of operating leverage.
b. Use the operating leverage measure computed in Requirement *a* to determine the amount of net income that Wong Company will earn if it experiences a 20 percent increase in revenue. The sales price per unit is not affected.

c. Verify your answer to Requirement *b* by constructing an income statement based on a 20 percent increase in sales revenue. The sales price is not affected. Calculate the percentage change in net income for the two income statements.

L.O. 6

Exercise 2-15A   *Averaging costs*

Sparta Camps, Inc., leases the land on which it builds camp sites. Sparta is considering opening a new site on land that requires $2,000 of rental payment per month. The variable cost of providing service is expected to be $4 per camper. The following chart shows the number of campers Sparta expects for the first year of operation of the new site.

Jan.	Feb.	Mar.	Apr.	May	June	July	Aug.	Sept.	Oct.	Nov.	Dec.	Total
200	100	300	300	400	600	800	800	500	300	200	300	4,800

Required

Assuming that Sparta wants to earn $10 per camper, determine the price it should charge for a camp site in February and August.

L.O. 7

Exercise 2-16A   *Estimating fixed and variable costs using the high-low method*

Ahmed Boat Company makes inexpensive aluminum fishing boats. Production is seasonal, with considerable activity occurring in the spring and summer. Sales and production tend to decline in the fall and winter months. During 2007, the high point in activity occurred in June when it produced 300 boats at a total cost of $175,000. The low point in production occurred in January when it produced 140 boats at a total cost of $111,000.

Required

Use the high-low method to estimate the amount of fixed cost incurred each month by Ahmed Boat Company.

PROBLEMS—SERIES A

All Problems in Series A are available with McGraw-Hill's Homework Manager®.

L.O. 1

Problem 2-17A   *Identifying cost behavior*

Required

Identify the following costs as fixed or variable.

Costs related to plane trips between Portland, Oregon, and Charlotte, North Carolina, follow. Pilots are paid on a per trip basis.

a. Pilots' salaries relative to the number of trips flown.
b. Depreciation relative to the number of planes in service.
c. Cost of refreshments relative to the number of passengers.
d. Pilots' salaries relative to the number of passengers on a particular trip.
e. Cost of a maintenance check relative to the number of passengers on a particular trip.
f. Fuel costs relative to the number of trips.

Northwest Bank operates several branch offices in grocery stores. Each branch employs a supervisor and two tellers.

g. Tellers' salaries relative to the number of tellers in a particular district.
h. Supplies cost relative to the number of transactions processed in a particular branch.
i. Tellers' salaries relative to the number of customers served at a particular branch.
j. Supervisors' salaries relative to the number of branches operated.
k. Supervisors' salaries relative to the number of customers served in a particular branch.
l. Facility rental costs relative to the size of customer deposits.

Costs related to operating a fast-food restaurant follow.

m. Depreciation of equipment relative to the number of restaurants.
n. Building rental cost relative to the number of customers served in a particular restaurant.
o. Manager's salary of a particular store relative to the number of employees.
p. Food cost relative to the number of customers.
q. Utility cost relative to the number of restaurants in operation.
r. Company president's salary relative to the number of restaurants in operation.
s. Land costs relative to the number of hamburgers sold at a particular restaurant.
t. Depreciation of equipment relative to the number of customers served at a particular restaurant.

Problem 2-18A   *Cost behavior and averaging*

Susan Clement has decided to start Clement Cleaning, a residential housecleaning service company. She is able to rent cleaning equipment at a cost of $600 per month. Labor costs are expected to be $50 per house cleaned and supplies are expected to cost $5 per house.

Required

a. Determine the total expected cost of equipment rental and the average expected cost of equipment rental per house cleaned, assuming that Clement Cleaning cleans 10, 20, or 30 houses during one month. Is the cost of equipment a fixed or a variable cost?
b. Determine the total expected cost of labor and the average expected cost of labor per house cleaned, assuming that Clement Cleaning cleans 10, 20, or 30 houses during one month. Is the cost of labor a fixed or a variable cost?
c. Determine the total expected cost of supplies and the average expected cost of supplies per house cleaned, assuming that Clement Cleaning cleans 10, 20, or 30 houses during one month. Is the cost of supplies a fixed or a variable cost?
d. Determine the total expected cost of cleaning houses, assuming that Clement Cleaning cleans 10, 20, or 30 houses during one month.
e. Determine the average expected cost per house, assuming that Clement Cleaning cleans 10, 20, or 30 houses during one month. Why does the cost per unit decrease as the number of houses increases?
f. If Ms. Clement tells you that she prices her services at 25 percent above cost, would you assume that she means average or actual cost? Why?

Problem 2-19A   *Context-sensitive nature of cost behavior classifications*

Elliott Bank's start-up division establishes new branch banks. Each branch opens with three tellers. Total teller cost per branch is $90,000 per year. The three tellers combined can process up to 90,000 customer transactions per year. If a branch does not attain a volume of at least 60,000 transactions during its first year of operations, it is closed. If the demand for services exceeds 90,000 transactions, an additional teller is hired, and the branch is transferred from the start-up division to regular operations.

Required

a. What is the relevant range of activity for new branch banks?
b. Determine the amount of teller cost in total and the average teller cost per transaction for a branch that processes 60,000, 70,000, 80,000, or 90,000 transactions. In this case (the activity base is the number of transactions for a specific branch), is the teller cost a fixed or a variable cost?
c. Determine the amount of teller cost in total and the average teller cost per branch for Elliott Bank, assuming that the start-up division operates 10, 15, 20, or 25 branches. In this case (the activity base is the number of branches), is the teller cost a fixed or a variable cost?

Problem 2-20A   *Context-sensitive nature of cost behavior classifications*

Betty Holland operates a sales booth in computer software trade shows, selling an accounting software package, *Accountsoft*. She purchases the package from a software manufacturer for $200 each. Booth space at the convention hall costs $7,500 per show.

Required

a. Sales at past trade shows have ranged between 100 and 300 software packages per show. Determine the average cost of sales per unit if Ms. Holland sells 100, 150, 200, 250, or 300 units of *Accountsoft* at a trade show. Use the following chart to organize your answer. Is the cost of booth space fixed or variable?

	Sales Volume in Units (a)				
	100	150	200	250	300
Total cost of software (a × $200)	$20,000				
Total cost of booth rental	7,500				
Total cost of sales (b)	$27,500				
Average cost per unit (b ÷ a)	$275.00				

b. If Ms. Holland wants to earn a $60 profit on each package of software she sells at a trade show, what price must she charge at sales volumes of 100, 150, 200, 250, or 300 units?

c. Record the total cost of booth space if Ms. Holland attends one, two, three, four, or five trade shows. Record your answers in the following chart. Is the cost of booth space fixed or variable relative to the number of shows attended?

	Number of Trade Shows Attended				
	1	2	3	4	5
Total cost of booth rental	$7,500				

d. Ms. Holland provides decorative shopping bags to customers who purchase software packages. Some customers take the bags; others do not. Some customers stuff more than one software package into a single bag. The number of bags varies in relation to the number of units sold, but the relationship is not proportional. Assume that Ms. Holland uses $40 of bags for every 50 software packages sold. What is the additional cost per unit sold? Is the cost fixed or variable?

L.O. 2

Problem 2-21A   *Effects of operating leverage on profitability*

Kapp Training Services (KTS) provides instruction on the use of computer software for the employees of its corporate clients. It offers courses in the clients' offices on the clients' equipment. The only major expense KTS incurs is instructor salaries; it pays instructors $5,000 per course taught. KTS recently agreed to offer a course of instruction to the employees of Jenkins Incorporated at a price of $400 per student. Jenkins estimated that 20 students would attend the course.

Base your answer on the preceding information.

Part 1:

Required

a. Relative to the number of students in a single course, is the cost of instruction a fixed or a variable cost?

b. Determine the profit, assuming that 20 students attend the course.

c. Determine the profit, assuming a 10 percent increase in enrollment (i.e., enrollment increases to 22 students). What is the percentage change in profitability?

d. Determine the profit, assuming a 10 percent decrease in enrollment (i.e., enrollment decreases to 18 students). What is the percentage change in profitability?

e. Explain why a 10 percent shift in enrollment produces more than a 10 percent shift in profitability. Use the term that identifies this phenomenon.

Part 2:

The instructor has offered to teach the course for a percentage of tuition fees. Specifically, she wants $250 per person attending the class. Assume that the tuition fee remains at $400 per student.

Required

f. Is the cost of instruction a fixed or a variable cost?

g. Determine the profit, assuming that 20 students take the course.

h. Determine the profit, assuming a 10 percent increase in enrollment (i.e., enrollment increases to 22 students). What is the percentage change in profitability?

i. Determine the profit, assuming a 10 percent decrease in enrollment (i.e., enrollment decreases to 18 students). What is the percentage change in profitability?

j. Explain why a 10 percent shift in enrollment produces a proportional 10 percent shift in profitability.

Part 3:

KTS sells a workbook with printed material unique to each course to each student who attends the course. Any workbooks that are not sold must be destroyed. Prior to the first class, KTS printed 20 copies of the books based on the client's estimate of the number of people who would attend the course. Each workbook costs $25 and is sold to course participants for $40. This cost includes a royalty fee paid to the author and the cost of duplication.

Required

k. Calculate the workbook cost in total and per student, assuming that 18, 20, or 22 students attempt to attend the course.

l. Classify the cost of workbooks as fixed or variable relative to the number of students attending the course.

m. Discuss the risk of holding inventory as it applies to the workbooks.

n. Explain how a just-in-time inventory system can reduce the cost and risk of holding inventory.

Problem 2-22A *Effects of fixed and variable cost behavior on the risk and rewards of business opportunities*

L.O. 2

East and West Universities offer executive training courses to corporate clients. East pays its instructors $6,000 per course taught. West pays its instructors $300 per student enrolled in the class. Both universities charge executives a $360 tuition fee per course attended.

Required

a. Prepare income statements for East and West, assuming that 20 students attend a course.

b. East University embarks on a strategy to entice students from West University by lowering its tuition to $200 per course. Prepare an income statement for East assuming that the university is successful and enrolls 40 students in its course.

c. West University embarks on a strategy to entice students from East University by lowering its tuition to $200 per course. Prepare an income statement for West, assuming that the university is successful and enrolls 40 students in its course.

d. Explain why the strategy described in Requirement *b* produced a profit but the same strategy described in Requirement *c* produced a loss.

e. Prepare income statements for East and West Universities, assuming that 15 students attend a course, assuming that both universities charge executives a $360 tuition fee per course attended.

f. It is always better to have fixed rather than variable cost. Explain why this statement is false.

g. It is always better to have variable rather than fixed cost. Explain why this statement is false.

CHECK FIGURES
a. West NI: $1,200
b. NI: $2,000

Problem 2-23A *Analyzing operating leverage*

L.O. 4

www.mhhe.com/edmonds2008

Ken Ritch is a venture capitalist facing two alternative investment opportunities. He intends to invest $1 million in a start-up firm. He is nervous, however, about future economic volatility. He asks you to analyze the following financial data for the past year's operations of the two firms he is considering and give him some business advice.

	Company Name	
	Hayden	**Mauldin**
Variable Cost per Unit (a)	$12	$6
Sales Revenue (10,000 units × $16)	$160,000	$160,000
Variable Cost (10,000 units × a)	(120,000)	(60,000)
Contribution Margin	$40,000	$100,000
Fixed Cost	(20,000)	(80,000)
Net Income	$ 20,000	$ 20,000

Required

a. Use the contribution margin approach to compute the operating leverage for each firm.
b. If the economy expands in coming years, Hayden and Mauldin will both enjoy a 10 percent per year increase in sales, assuming that the selling price remains unchanged. Compute the change in net income for each firm in dollar amount and in percentage. (*Note:* Since the number of units increases, both revenue and variable cost will increase.)
c. If the economy contracts in coming years, Hayden and Mauldin will both suffer a 10 percent decrease in sales volume, assuming that the selling price remains unchanged. Compute the change in net income for each firm in dollar amount and in percentage. (*Note:* Since the number of units decreases, both total revenue and total variable cost will decrease.)
d. Write a memo to Ken Ritch with your analyses and advice.

L.O. 6

Problem 2-24A   *Selecting the appropriate time period for cost averaging*

Ryan Cinemas is considering a contract to rent a movie for $1,600 per day. The contract requires a minimum one-week rental period. Estimated attendance is as follows:

Monday	Tuesday	Wednesday	Thursday	Friday	Saturday	Sunday
500	400	100	500	900	1,000	600

Required

a. Determine the average cost per person of the movie rental contract separately for each day.
b. Suppose that Ryan chooses to price movie tickets at cost as computed in Requirement *a* plus $3.00. What price would it charge per ticket on each day of the week?
c. Use weekly averaging to determine a reasonable price to charge for movie tickets.
d. Comment on why weekly averaging may be more useful to business managers than daily averaging.

L.O. 6

Problem 2-25A   *Identifying relevant issues for cost averaging*

Cliff Corporation, offers mountain-climbing expeditions for its customers, providing food, equipment, and guides. Climbs normally require one week to complete. The company's accountant is reviewing historical cost data to establish a pricing strategy for the coming year. The accountant has prepared the following table showing cost data for the most recent climb, the company's average cost per year, and the five-year average cost.

	Span of Time		
	Recent Climb	One Year	Five Years
Total cost of climbs (a)	$8,000	$506,540	$1,550,000
Number of climbers (b)	10	620	2,500
Cost per climber (a ÷ b)	$800	$817	$620

Required

Write a memo that explains the potential advantages and disadvantages of using each of the per unit cost figures as a basis for establishing a price to charge climbers during the coming year. What other factors must be considered in developing a pricing strategy?

L.O. 7

Problem 2-26A   *Estimating fixed and variable cost*

Ubben Computer Services, Inc., has been in business for six months. The following are basic operating data for that period.

	Month					
	July	Aug.	Sept.	Oct.	Nov.	Dec.
Service hours	120	136	260	420	320	330
Revenue	$6,000	$6,800	$13,000	$21,000	$16,000	$16,500
Operating costs	$4,300	$5,300	$ 7,100	$11,200	$ 9,100	$10,600

Required:
a. What is the average service revenue per hour for the six-month time period?
b. Use the high-low method to estimate the total monthly fixed cost and the variable cost per hour.
c. Determine the average contribution margin per hour.
d. Use the scattergraph method to estimate the total monthly fixed cost and the variable cost per hour.
e. Compare the results of the two methods and comment on the difference.

Problem 2-27A   *Estimating fixed and variable cost*

L.O. 7

CHECK FIGURE
c. VC/unit: $5

Hind Woodcraft Company (HWC) manufactures "antique" wooden cabinets to house modern radio and CD players. HWC began operations in January of last year. James Hind, the owner, asks for your assistance. He believes that he needs to better understand the cost of the cabinets for pricing purposes. You have collected the following data concerning actual production over the past year:

Month	Number of Cabinets Produced	Total Cost
January	800	$21,000
February	3,600	32,500
March	1,960	29,500
April	600	18,600
May	1,600	29,000
June	1,300	27,000
July	1,100	25,600
August	1,800	31,000
September	2,280	32,000
October	2,940	31,500
November	3,280	32,000
December	400	16,500

Required
a. To understand the department's cost behavior, you decide to plot the points on graph paper and sketch a total cost line.
   (1) Enter the number of units and their costs in increasing order.
   (2) Plot the points on the graph.
   (3) Sketch a graph so the line "splits" all of the points (half of the points appear above and half below the line).
b. Using the line you just sketched, visually estimate the total cost to produce 2,000 units.
c. Using the high-low method, compute the total cost equation for the preceding data.
   (1) Compute the variable cost per unit.
   (2) Compute total fixed costs.
   (3) Assemble the total cost equation.
   (4) Sketch a line between the high and low points on your graph.
d. Using the high-low method, estimate the total cost to produce 2,000 units.
e. After discussing the results with your teammates, decide which method you believe is better.

Problem 2-28A *Estimating fixed and variable cost using the regression method*

Peters and Marvin Tax Services Company has 31 branch offices in the nation. Each office has about three to six professional accountants and one to two secretaries. In a busy season, the office manager, who is also a professional accountant, can hire temporary employees for support work such as document filing and typing. John Casey, the president, is wondering whether he should expand his business by opening more offices. One of the factors that he is considering is how to estimate office support costs. Josie Ander, the accountant, collected the following cost data for all 31 offices:

Branch	Professional Hours	Support Costs	Branch	Professional Hours	Support Costs
A1	225	$4,241	F2	165	$ 3,856
A2	113	3,435	G1	358	5,936
A3	387	6,398	G2	471	8,615
A4	412	6,502	G3	492	9,639
B1	258	4,140	G4	328	5,968
B2	146	3,368	G5	359	7,115
B3	275	3,820	G6	174	3,287
D1	364	6,396	H1	394	7,515
D2	190	3,946	H2	386	7,374
D3	484	8,189	I2	279	5,376
D4	251	4,506	I5	314	5,784
D5	377	6,744	J2	283	5,426
E1	264	4,645	J3	198	4,418
E2	169	6,073	J4	226	4,506
E3	338	6,290	J5	341	6,488
F1	437	9,113			

Required

a. The company uses the number of professional hours as the cost driver for office support costs. Use an algebraic equation to describe how total office support costs can be estimated.
b. Use a spreadsheet program to perform a regression analysis. Use office support costs as the dependent variable (Y) and the professional hours as the independent variable (X). Determine the total fixed cost per office and variable cost per professional hour.
c. Mr. Casey plans to open a new branch office in a Chicago suburb. He expects that the monthly professional hours will be 3,000. Estimate the total office support cost for Mr. Casey. What portion of the total cost is fixed and what portion is variable?

EXERCISES—SERIES B

Exercise 2-1B *Identifying cost behavior*

Perry Copies Company provides professional copying services to customers through the 20 copy stores it operates in the southwestern United States. Each store employs a manager and four assistants. The manager earns $3,500 per month plus a bonus of 3 percent of sales. The assistants earn hourly wages. Each copy store costs $3,000 per month to lease. The company spends $5,000 per month on corporate-level advertising and promotion.

Required

Classify each of the following costs incurred by Perry Copies as fixed, variable, or mixed.

a. Store manager's salary relative to the number of copies made for customers.
b. Cost of paper relative to the number of copies made for customers.
c. Lease cost relative to the number of stores.
d. Advertising and promotion costs relative to the number of copies a particular store makes.
e. Lease cost relative to the number of copies made for customers.
f. Assistants' wages relative to the number of copies made for customers.

Exercise 2-2B *Identifying cost behavior*

At the various sales levels shown, Hale Company incurred the following costs.

	Units sold	50	100	150	200	250
a.	Total shipping cost	$ 40.00	$ 80.00	$ 120.00	$ 160.00	$ 200.00
b.	Rent cost per unit of merchandise sold	12.00	6.00	4.00	3.00	2.40
c.	Total utility cost	200.00	300.00	400.00	500.00	600.00
d.	Supplies cost per unit	4.00	4.00	4.00	4.00	4.00
e.	Total insurance cost	500.00	500.00	500.00	500.00	500.00
f.	Total salary cost	1,500.00	2,000.00	2,500.00	3,000.00	3,500.00
g.	Cost per unit of merchandise sold	8.00	8.00	8.00	8.00	8.00
h.	Total cost of goods sold	4,000.00	8,000.00	12,000.00	16,000.00	20,000.00
i.	Depreciation cost per unit	30.00	15.00	10.00	7.50	6.00
j.	Total rent cost	600.00	600.00	600.00	600.00	600.00

Required
Identify each of these costs as fixed, variable, or mixed.

Exercise 2-3B *Determining fixed cost per unit*

Dinga Corporation incurs the following annual fixed production costs:

Item	Cost
Insurance cost	$ 75,000
Patent amortization cost	1,000,000
Depreciation cost	500,000
Property tax cost	60,000

Required
Determine the total fixed production cost per unit if Dinga produces 10,000, 20,000, or 50,000 units

Exercise 2-4B *Determining total variable cost*

The following variable manufacturing costs apply to goods produced by Garcia Manufacturing Corporation.

Item	Cost per Unit
Materials	$3.00
Labor	2.00
Variable overhead	1.00
Total	$6.00

Required
Determine the total variable manufacturing cost if Garcia produces 4,000, 6,000, or 8,000 units.

L.O. 1

Exercise 2-5B   *Fixed versus variable cost behavior*

Herrera Company's production and total cost data for two recent months follow.

	January	February
Units produced	500	1,000
Total depreciation cost	$4,000	$4,000
Total factory supplies cost	$2,000	$4,000

Required

a. Separately calculate the depreciation cost per unit and the factory supplies cost per unit for both January and February.
b. Based on total and per unit amounts, identify which cost is variable and which is fixed. Explain your answer.

L.O. 1

Exercise 2-6B   *Fixed versus variable cost behavior*

Vanity Chairs Corporation produces ergonomically designed chairs favored by architects. The company normally produces and sells from 5,000 to 8,000 chairs per year. The following cost data apply to various production activity levels.

Number of Chairs	5,000	6,000	7,000	8,000
Total costs incurred				
Fixed	$ 84,000			
Variable	60,000			
Total costs	$144,000			
Per unit chair cost				
Fixed	$ 16.80			
Variable	12.00			
Total cost per chair	$ 28.80			

Required

a. Complete the preceding table by filling in the missing amounts for the levels of activity shown in the first row of the table.
b. Explain why the total cost per chair decreases as the number of chairs increases.

L.O. 1

Exercise 2-7B   *Fixed versus variable cost behavior*

Lou Jordan needs extra money quickly because his mother's sudden hospitalization has resulted in unexpected medical bills. Mr. Jordan has learned fortune-telling skills through his long friendship with Jack Lovell, who tells fortunes during the day at the city market. Mr. Lovell has agreed to let Mr. Jordan use his booth to tell fortunes during the evening for a rent of $50 per night.

Required

a. What is the booth rental cost both in total and per customer if the number of customers is 5, 10, 15, 20, or 25?
b. Is the cost of renting the fortune-telling booth fixed or variable relative to the number of customers?
c. Draw two graphs. On one, plot total booth rental cost for 5, 10, 15, 20, and 25 customers; on the other, plot booth rental cost per customer for 5, 10, 15, 20, or 25 customers.
d. Mr. Jordan has little money. What major business risks would he take by renting the fortune-telling booth? How could he minimize those risks?

L.O. 1

Exercise 2-8B   *Fixed versus variable cost behavior*

In the evenings, Lou Jordan works telling fortunes using his friend Jack Lovell's booth at the city market. Mr. Lovell pays the booth rental, so Mr. Jordan has no rental cost. As a courtesy, Mr. Jordan provides each customer a soft drink. The drinks cost him $0.50 per customer.

Required

a. What is the soft drink cost both in total and per customer if the number of customers is 5, 10, 15, 20, or 25?
b. Is the soft drink cost fixed or variable?
c. Draw two graphs. On one, plot total soft drink cost for 5, 10, 15, 20, and 25 customers; on the other, plot soft drink cost per customer for 5, 10, 15, 20, and 25 customers.
d. Comment on the likelihood that Mr. Jordan will incur a loss on this business venture.

Exercise 2-9B   *Graphing fixed cost behavior*   L.O. 1

Merkle Computers leases space in a mall at a monthly rental cost of $3,000. The following graphs depict rental cost on the vertical axes and activity level on the horizontal axes.

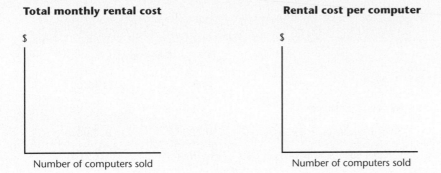

Total monthly rental cost

$

Number of computers sold

Rental cost per computer

$

Number of computers sold

Required

a. Draw a line that depicts the relationship between the total monthly rental cost and the number of computers sold.
b. Draw a line that depicts the relationship between rental cost per computer and the number of computers sold.

Exercise 2-10B   *Graphing variable cost behavior*   L.O. 1

Moore Computers purchases computers from a manufacturer for $500 per computer. The following graphs depict product cost on the vertical axes and activity level on the horizontal axes.

Total product cost

$

Number of computers sold

Product cost per computer

$

Number of computers sold

Required

a. Draw a line that depicts the relationship between total product cost and the number of computers sold.
b. Draw a line that depicts the relationship between cost per computer and the number of computers sold.

Exercise 2-11B   *Mixed cost at different levels of activity*   L.O. 1

Odom Hats Corporation uses workers in Indonesia to manually weave straw hats. The company pays the workers a daily base wage plus $0.10 per completed hat. On Monday, workers produced 100 hats for which the company paid wages of $60.

Required

Calculate the total cost of the workers' wages for each of the following days.

Day	Monday	Tuesday	Wednesday	Thursday
Number of hats woven	100	120	160	80
Total variable cost				
Total fixed cost				
Total wages cost				

L.O. 1, 2   **Exercise 2-12B**   *Effect of cost structure on projected profits*

Oak and Riggs compete in the same market. The following budgeted income statements illustrate their cost structures.

Income Statements		
	Company	
	Oak	Riggs
Number of Customers (a)	80	80
Sales Revenue (a × $125)	$10,000	$10,000
Variable Cost (a × $80)	NA	(6,400)
Contribution Margin	10,000	3,600
Fixed Costs	(6,400)	N/A
Net Income	$ 3,600	$ 3,600

Required

a. Assume that Oak can lure all 80 customers away from Riggs by lowering its sales price to $75 per customer. Reconstruct Oak's income statement based on 160 customers.

b. Assume that Riggs can lure all 80 customers away from Oak by lowering its sales price to $75 per customer. Reconstruct Rigg's income statement based on 160 customers.

c. Why does the price-cutting strategy increase Oak's profits but result in a net loss for Riggs?

L.O. 3, 4   **Exercise 2-13B**   *Using a contribution margin format income statement to measure the magnitude of operating leverage*

Peak Company, a merchandising firm, reported the following operating results.

Income Statements	
Sales Revenue (8,000 units × $100)	$ 800,000
Cost of Goods Sold (8,000 units × $60)	(480,000)
Gross Margin	320,000
Sales Commissions (10% of sales revenue)	(80,000)
Administrative Salaries Expense	(60,000)
Advertising Expense	(75,000)
Depreciation Expense	(68,000)
Shipping and Handling Expense (8,000 units × $1)	(8,000)
Net Income	$ 29,000

Required

a. Reconstruct the income statement using the contribution margin format.

b. Calculate the magnitude of operating leverage.

c. Use the measure of operating leverage to determine the amount of net income that Peak will earn if sales revenue increases by 10 percent.

Exercise 2-14B *Assessing the magnitude of operating leverage*

L.O. 4

The following budgeted income statement applies to Musso Company:

Income Statement	
Sales Revenue (600 units × $90)	$54,000
Variable Cost (600 units × $50)	(30,000)
Contribution Margin	24,000
Fixed Costs	(16,000)
Net Income	$ 8,000

Required

a. Use the contribution margin approach to calculate the magnitude of operating leverage.
b. Use the operating leverage measure computed in Requirement *a* to determine the amount of net income that Musso Company will earn if sales volume increases by 10 percent. Assume the sales price per unit remains unchanged at $90.
c. Verify your answer to Requirement *b* by constructing an alternative income statement based on a 10 percent increase in sales volume. The sales price per unit remains unchanged at $90. Calculate the percentage change in net income for the two income statements.

Exercise 2-15B *Averaging costs*

L.O. 6

Cooper Entertainment Company operates a movie theater that has monthly fixed expenses of $5,000. In addition, the company pays film distributors $2.00 per ticket sold. The following chart shows the number of tickets Cooper expects to sell in the coming year:

Jan.	Feb.	Mar.	Apr.	May	June	July	Aug.	Sept.	Oct.	Nov.	Dec.	Total
2,000	1,600	3,200	3,400	3,200	4,200	5,100	4,000	5,000	3,100	3,000	2,200	40,000

Required

Assume that Cooper wants to earn $3.00 per movie patron. What price should it charge for a ticket in January and in September?

Exercise 2-16B *Estimating fixed and variable costs using the high-low method*

L.O. 7

Payne Ice Cream Company produces various ice cream products for which demand is highly seasonal. The company sells more ice cream in warmer months and less in colder ones. Last year, the high point in production activity occurred in August when Payne produced 45,000 gallons of ice cream at a total cost of $36,000. The low point in production activity occurred in February when the company produced 21,000 gallons of ice cream at a total cost of $300.

Required

Use the high-low method to estimate the amount of fixed cost per month incurred by Payne Ice Cream Company.

PROBLEMS—SERIES B

L.O. 1

Problem 2-17B *Identifying cost behavior*

Required

Identify the following costs as fixed or variable.

Costs related to operating a retail gasoline company.

  a. The company's cost of national TV commercials relative to the number of stations in operation.
  b. Depreciation of equipment relative to the number of customers served at a station.
  c. Property and real estate taxes relative to the amount of gasoline sold at a particular station.
  d. Depreciation of equipment relative to the number of stations.
  e. Cashiers' wages relative to the number of customers served in a station.
  f. Salary of a manager of a particular station relative to the number of employees.
  g. Gasoline cost relative to the number of customers.
  h. Utility cost relative to the number of stations in operation.

Costs related to shuttle bus trips between Chicago's O'Hare International Airport and downtown Chicago. Each bus driver receives a specific salary per month. A manager schedules bus trips and supervises drivers, and a secretary receives phone calls.

  i. Fuel costs relative to the number of passengers on a particular trip.
  j. Drivers' salaries relative to the number of trips driven.
  k. Office staff salaries relative to the number of passengers on a particular trip.
  l. Depreciation relative to the number of buses in service.
  m. A driver's salary relative to the number of passengers on a particular trip.
  n. Fuel costs relative to the number of trips.

Janet's Barbershop operates several stores in shopping centers. Each store employs a supervisor and three barbers. Each barber receives a specific salary per month plus a 10 percent commission based on the service revenues he or she has generated.

  o. Store rental costs relative to the number of customers.
  p. Barbers' commissions relative to the number of customers.
  q. Supervisory salaries relative to the number of customers served in a particular store.
  r. Barbers' salaries relative to the number of barbers in a particular district.
  s. Supplies cost relative to the number of hair services provided in a particular store.
  t. Barbers' salaries relative to the number of customers served at a particular store.

L.O. 1

Problem 2-18B   *Cost behavior and averaging*

Paul Ditto asks you to analyze the operating cost of his lawn services business. He has bought the needed equipment with a cash payment of $27,000. Upon your recommendation, he agrees to adopt straight-line depreciation. The equipment has an expected life of three years and no salvage value. Mr. Ditto pays his workers $30 per lawn service. Material costs, including fertilizer, pesticide, and supplies, are expected to be $6 per lawn service.

Required

  a. Determine the total cost of equipment depreciation and the average cost of equipment depreciation per lawn service, assuming that Mr. Ditto provides 20, 25, or 30 lawn services during one month. Is the cost of equipment a fixed or a variable cost?
  b. Determine the total expected cost of labor and the average expected cost of labor per lawn service, assuming that Mr. Ditto provides 20, 25, or 30 lawn services during one month. Is the cost of labor a fixed or a variable cost?
  c. Determine the total expected cost of materials and the average expected cost of materials per lawn service, assuming that Mr. Ditto provides 20, 25, or 30 lawn services during one month. Is the cost of fertilizer, pesticide, and supplies a fixed or a variable cost?
  d. Determine the total expected cost per lawn service, assuming that Mr. Ditto provides 20, 25, or 30 lawn services during one month.
  e. Determine the average expected cost per lawn service, assuming that Mr. Ditto provides 20, 25, or 30 lawn services during one month. Why does the cost per unit decrease as the number of lawn services increases?
  f. If Mr. Ditto tells you that he prices his services at 30 percent above cost, would you assume that he means average or actual cost? Why?

L.O. 1

Problem 2-19B   *Context-sensitive nature of cost behavior classifications*

Richardo and Griffin Tax Services' Development Department is responsible for establishing new community branches. Each branch opens with two tax accountants. Total cost of payroll per branch is $80,000 per year. Together the two accountants can process up to 2,500 simple tax returns per year. The firm's policy requires closing branches that do not reach the quota of 1,500 tax returns per year.

On the other hand, the firm hires an additional accountant for a branch and elevates it to the status of a regular operation if the customer demand for services exceeds 2,500 tax returns.

Required

a. What is the relevant range of activity for a new branch established by the Development Department?

b. Determine the amount of payroll cost in total and the average payroll cost per transaction for a branch that processes 1,500, 2,000, or 2,500 tax returns. In this case (the activity base is the number of tax returns for a specific branch), is the payroll cost a fixed or a variable cost?

c. Determine the amount of payroll cost in total and the average payroll cost per branch for Richardo and Griffin Tax Services, assuming that the Development Department operates 20, 30, or 40 branches. In this case (the activity base is the number of branches), is the payroll cost a fixed or a variable cost?

Problem 2-20B   *Context-sensitive nature of cost behavior classifications*   L.O. 1

Leo White sells a newly developed camera, Superb Image. He purchases the cameras from the manufacturer for $150 each and rents a store in a shopping mall for $5,000 per month.

Required

a. Determine the average cost of sales per unit if Mr. White sells 100, 200, 300, 400, or 500 units of Superb Image per month. Use the following chart to organize your answer.

	Sales Volume in Units (a)				
	100	200	300	400	500
Total cost of cameras (a × $150)	$15,000				
Total cost of store rental	5,000				
Total cost of sales (b)	$20,000				
Average cost per unit (b ÷ a)	$200.00				

b. If Mr. White wants to make a gross profit of $20 on each camera he sells, what price should he charge at sales volumes of 100, 200, 300, 400, or 500 units?

c. Record the total cost of store rental if Mr. White opens a camera store at one, two, three, four, or five shopping malls. Record your answers in the following chart. Is the cost of store rental fixed or variable relative to the number of stores opened?

	Shopping Malls				
	1	2	3	4	5
Total cost of store rental	$5,000				

d. Mr. White provides decorative ornaments to customers who purchase cameras. Some customers take the ornaments, others do not, and some take more than one. The number of ornaments varies in relation to the number of cameras sold, but the relationship is not proportional. Assume that, on average, Mr. White gives away $150 worth of ornaments for every 100 cameras sold. What is the additional cost per camera sold? Is the cost fixed or variable?

Problem 2-21B   *Effects of operating leverage on profitability*   L.O. 2

CMAs R Us conducts CMA review courses. Public universities that permit free use of a classroom support the classes. The only major expense incurred by CMAs R Us is the salary of instructors, which is $7,500 per course taught. The company recently planned to offer a review course in Dallas for $400 per candidate; it estimated that 50 candidates would attend the course.
Complete these requirements based on the preceding information.

Part 1:

Required

a. Relative to the number of CMA candidates in a single course, is the cost of instruction a fixed or a variable cost?

b. Determine the profit, assuming that 50 candidates attend the course.

c. Determine the profit, assuming a 10 percent increase in enrollment (i.e., enrollment increases to 55 students). What is the percentage change in profitability?

d. Determine the profit, assuming a 10 percent decrease in enrollment (i.e., enrollment decreases to 45 students). What is the percentage change in profitability?

e. Explain why a 10 percent shift in enrollment produces more than a 10 percent shift in profitability. Use the term that identifies this phenomenon.

Part 2:

The instructor has offered to teach the course for a percentage of tuition fees. Specifically, he wants $150 per candidate attending the class. Assume that the tuition fee remains at $400 per candidate.

Required

f. Is the cost of instruction a fixed or a variable cost?

g. Determine the profit, assuming that 50 candidates take the course.

h. Determine the profit, assuming a 10 percent increase in enrollment (i.e., enrollment increases to 55 students). What is the percentage change in profitability?

i. Determine the profit, assuming a 10 percent decrease in enrollment (i.e., enrollment decreases to 45 students). What is the percentage change in profitability?

j. Explain why a 10 percent shift in enrollment produces a proportional 10 percent shift in profitability.

Part 3:

CMAs R Us sells a workbook to each student who attends the course. The workbook contains printed material unique to each course. Workbooks that are not sold must be destroyed. Prior to the first class, CMAs R Us printed 50 copies of the books based on the estimated number of people who would attend the course. Each workbook costs $40 and is sold for $50. This cost includes a royalty fee paid to the author and the cost of duplication.

Required

k. Calculate the total cost and the cost per candidate of the workbooks, assuming that 45, 50, or 55 candidates attempt to attend the course.

l. Classify the cost of workbooks as fixed or variable relative to the number of candidates attending the course.

m. Discuss the risk of holding inventory as it applies to the workbooks.

n. Explain how a just-in-time inventory system can reduce the cost and risk of holding inventory.

L.O. 2

Problem 2-22B *Effects of fixed and variable cost behavior on the risk and rewards of business opportunities*

Green Club and Wood Club are competing health and recreation clubs in Chicago. They both offer tennis training clinics to adults. Green pays its coaches $6,000 per season. Wood pays its coaches $200 per student enrolled in the clinic per season. Both clubs charge a tuition fee of $300 per season.

Required

a. Prepare income statements for Green and Wood, assuming that 30 students per season attend each clinic.

b. The ambitious new director of Green Club tries to increase his market share by reducing the club's tuition per student to $180 per clinic. Prepare an income statement for Green, assuming that the club attracts all of Wood's customers and therefore is able to enroll 60 students in its clinics.

c. Independent of Requirement *b*, Wood Club tries to lure Green's students by lowering its price to $180 per student. Prepare an income statement for Wood, assuming that the club succeeds in enrolling 60 students in its clinics.

d. Explain why the strategy described in Requirement *b* produced a profit while the same strategy described in Requirement *c* produced a loss.

e. Prepare an income statement for Green Club and Wood Club, assuming that 18 students attend a clinic at the original $300 tuition price.

f. It is always better to have fixed rather than variable cost. Explain why this statement is false.

g. It is always better to have variable rather than fixed cost. Explain why this statement is false.

Problem 2-23B   *Analysis of operating leverage*   L.O. 5, 6

Michelle Welch has invested in two start-up companies. At the end of the first year, she asks you to evaluate their operating performance. The following operating data apply to the first year.

	Company Name	
	Hardy	**Lavoy**
Variable cost per unit (a)	$24	$12
Sales revenue (25,000 units × $32)	$800,000	$800,000
Variable cost (25,000 units × a)	(600,000)	(300,000)
Contribution margin	200,000	500,000
Fixed cost	(100,000)	(400,000)
Net income	$100,000	$100,000

Required

a. Use the contribution margin approach to compute the operating leverage for each firm.

b. If the economy expands in the coming year, Hardy and Lavoy will both enjoy a 10 percent per year increase in sales volume, assuming that the selling price remains unchanged. (*Note:* Since the number of units increases, both revenue and variable cost will increase.) Compute the change in net income for each firm in dollar amount and in percentage.

c. If the economy contracts in the following year, Hardy and Lavoy will both suffer a 10 percent decrease in sales volume, assuming that the selling price remains unchanged. (*Note:* Since the number of units decreases, both revenue and variable cost decrease.) Compute the change in net income for each firm in both dollar amount and percentage.

d. Write a memo to Michelle Welch with your evaluation and recommendations.

Problem 2-24B   *Selecting the appropriate time period for cost averaging*   L.O. 6

The Bullion Amusement Park is considering signing a contract to hire a circus at a cost of $2,700 per day. The contract requires a minimum performance period of one week. Estimated circus attendance is as follows:

Monday	Tuesday	Wednesday	Thursday	Friday	Saturday	Sunday
600	500	450	700	960	1,450	1,340

Required

a. For each day, determine the average cost of the circus contract per person attending.

b. Suppose that the park prices circus tickets at cost as computed in Requirement *a* plus $1.80. What would be the price per ticket charged on each day of the week?

c. Use weekly averaging to determine a reasonable price to charge for the circus tickets.

d. Comment on why weekly averaging may be more useful to business managers than daily averaging.

Problem 2-25B   *Identifying relevant issues for cost averaging*   L.O 5

Southwest Tours, Inc., organizes adventure tours for people interested in visiting a desert environment. A desert tour generally lasts three days. Southwest provides food, equipment, and guides. Nick Boles, the president of Southwest Tours, needs to set prices for the coming year. He has available the company's past cost data in the following table.

	Span of Time		
	Recent Tour	**One Year**	**Ten Years**
Total cost of tours (a)	$9,600	$465,000	$2,880,000
Number of tourists (b)	32	1,500	12,000
Cost per tourist (a ÷ b)	$ 300	$ 310	$ 240

Required

Write a memo to Mr. Boles explaining the potential advantages and disadvantages of using each of the different per tourist cost figures as a basis for establishing a price to charge tourists during the coming year. What other factors must Mr. Boles consider in developing a pricing strategy?

L.O. 7

Problem 2-26B *Estimating fixed and variable costs*

Berger Legal Services provides legal advice to clients. The following data apply to the first six months of operation.

	Month					
	Jan.	**Feb.**	**Mar.**	**Apr.**	**May**	**June**
Service hours	50	80	125	140	170	195
Revenue	$4,000	$6,400	$10,000	$11,200	$13,600	$15,600
Operating costs	6,200	7,100	8,380	8,500	8,761	9,680

Required

a. What is the average service revenue per hour for the six-month time period?
b. Use the high-low method to estimate the total monthly fixed cost and the variable cost per hour.
c. Determine the average contribution margin per hour.
d. Use the scattergraph method to estimate the total monthly fixed cost and the variable cost per hour.
e. Compare the results of the two methods and comment on any differences.

L.O. 7

Problem 2-27B *Estimating fixed and variable cost*

Deluxe Frames Company (DFC), which manufactures ornate frames for original art work, began operations in January 2007. Ed McDowell, the owner, asks for your assistance. He believes that he needs to better understand the cost of the frames for pricing purposes. You have collected the following data concerning actual production over the past year:

Month	Number of Frames Produced	Total Cost
January	1,600	$42,000
February	7,200	65,000
March	3,920	59,000
April	1,200	37,200
May	3,200	58,000
June	2,600	54,000
July	2,200	51,200
August	3,600	62,000
September	4,560	64,000
October	5,880	63,000
November	6,560	64,000
December	800	33,000

Required

a. To understand the department's cost behavior, you decide to plot the points on graph paper and sketch a total cost line.
   (1) Enter the number of units and their costs in increasing order.
   (2) Plot the points on the graph.
   (3) Sketch a graph so the line "splits" all of the points (half of the points appear above and half appear below the line).
b. Using the line you just sketched, visually estimate the total cost to produce 4,000 units.
c. Using the high-low method, compute the total cost equation for the preceding data.
   (1) Compute the variable cost per unit.
   (2) Compute total fixed costs.
   (3) Assemble the total cost equation.
   (4) Sketch a line between the high and low points on your graph.
d. Using the high-low method, estimate the total cost to produce 4,000 units.
e. After discussing the results with your teammates, decide which method you believe is better.

Problem 2-28B *Estimating fixed and variable cost using the regression method*   L.O. 7

Kenny Loftin, the production manager of Newton Construction Components, is trying to figure out the cost behavior of his factory supplies cost. The company uses machine hours as the cost driver. Tony Serrano, the assistant manager, collected the following cost data for the last 32 weeks:

Week No.	Machine Hours	Supplies Costs	Week No.	Machine Hours	Supplies Costs
1	86	$3,819	17	64	$3,856
2	72	3,610	18	88	4,279
3	79	3,916	19	129	5,633
4	62	2,915	20	137	5,298
5	91	4,327	21	144	6,721
6	42	2,214	22	37	2,448
7	37	2,106	23	56	3,528
8	33	2,390	24	49	2,837
9	23	2,107	25	12	1,359
10	96	4,868	26	57	3,296
11	94	5,021	27	54	3,472
12	91	4,811	28	65	3,264
13	72	3,580	29	77	3,925
14	60	2,800	30	85	4,002
15	48	2,269	31	92	4,583
16	53	2,748	32	82	3,523

Required

a. The company uses the number of professional hours as the cost driver for factory supplies costs. Use an algebraic equation to describe how total office support costs can be estimated.
b. Use a spreadsheet program to perform a regression analysis. Use factory supplies costs as the dependent variable (Y) and the machine hours as the independent variable (X). Determine the total fixed cost per week and variable cost per professional hour.
c. Determine the estimated total cost of factory supplies, if machine hour usage amounts 100 hours for the next week. What portion of the total cost is fixed and what portion is variable?

ANALYZE, THINK, COMMUNICATE

ATC 2-1 **Business Applications** *Operating leverage*

The following information was taken from the Form 10-K SEC filings for CSX Corporation and Starbucks Corporation. It is from the 2004 fiscal year reports, and all dollar amounts are in millions.

Description of Business for CSX Corporation

CSX Corporation (CSX or the Company), operates one of the largest rail networks in the United States and also provides intermodal transportation services across the United States and key markets in Canada and Mexico. Its marine operations include an international terminal services company and a domestic container-shipping company.

CSX Corporation	2004	2003
Operating revenues	$8,020	$7,566
Operating earnings	418	137

Description of Business for Starbucks Corporation

Starbucks Corporation (together with its subsidiaries, Starbucks or the Company) purchases and roasts high-quality whole bean coffees and sells them, along with fresh, rich-brewed coffees, Italian-style espresso beverages, cold blended beverages, a variety of pastries and confections, coffee-related accessories and equipment, a selection of premium teas, and a line of compact discs primarily through Company-operated retail stores.

At fiscal year-end, Starbucks had 4,095 Company-operated stores in the United States and Canada as well as 373 stores in the United Kingdom, 40 stores in Australia, and 38 stores in Thailand.

Starbucks	2004	2003
Operating revenues	$5,294	$4,076
Operating earnings	392	268

Required

a. Determine which company appears to have the higher operating leverage.
b. Write a paragraph or two explaining why the company you identified in Requirement *a* might be expected to have the higher operating leverage.
c. If revenues for both companies declined, which company do you think would likely experience the greatest decline in operating earnings? Explain your answer.

ATC 2-2   Group Assignment   *Operating leverage*

The Parent Teacher Association (PTA) of Meadow High School is planning a fund-raising campaign. The PTA is considering the possibility of hiring Eric Logan, a world-renowned investment counselor, to address the public. Tickets would sell for $28 each. The school has agreed to let the PTA use Harville Auditorium at no cost. Mr. Logan is willing to accept one of two compensation arrangements. He will sign an agreement to receive a fixed fee of $10,000 regardless of the number of tickets sold. Alternatively, he will accept payment of $20 per ticket sold. In communities similar to that in which Meadow is located, Mr. Logan has drawn an audience of approximately 500 people.

Required

a. In front of the class, present a statement showing the expected net income assuming 500 people buy tickets.
b. The instructor will divide the class into groups and then organize the groups into four sections. The instructor will assign one of the following tasks to each section of groups.

Group Tasks

(1) Assume the PTA pays Mr. Logan a fixed fee of $10,000. Determine the amount of net income that the PTA will earn if ticket sales are 10 percent higher than expected. Calculate the percentage change in net income.
(2) Assume that the PTA pays Mr. Logan a fixed fee of $10,000. Determine the amount of net income that the PTA will earn if ticket sales are 10 percent lower than expected. Calculate the percentage change in net income.

(3) Assume that the PTA pays Mr. Logan $20 per ticket sold. Determine the amount of net income that the PTA will earn if ticket sales are 10 percent higher than expected. Calculate the percentage change in net income.

(4) Assume that the PTA pays Mr. Logan $20 per ticket sold. Determine the amount of net income that the PTA will earn if ticket sales are 10 percent lower than expected. Calculate the percentage change in net income.

c. Have each group select a spokesperson. Have one of the spokespersons in each section of groups go to the board and present the results of the analysis conducted in Requirement *b.* Resolve any discrepancies in the computations presented at the board and those developed by the other groups.

d. Draw conclusions regarding the risks and rewards associated with operating leverage. At a minimum, answer the following questions.

(1) Which type of cost structure (fixed or variable) produces the higher growth potential in profitability for a company?

(2) Which type of cost structure (fixed or variable) faces the higher risk of declining profitability for a company?

(3) Under what circumstances should a company seek to establish a fixed cost structure?

(4) Under what circumstances should a company seek to establish a variable cost structure?

ATC 2-3 Research Assignment *Fixed versus variable cost*

The March 8, 2004, edition of *BusinessWeek* contained an article titled "Courting the Mass Affluent" (see page 68). The article discusses the efforts of Charles Schwab Corp. to attract a bigger share of investors who have $100,000 to $1 million to invest. Read this article and complete the following requirements.

Required

a. Schwab increased its marketing budget during the first quarter of 2004. What was the amount of the increase? Is this cost fixed or variable relative to the number of new customers that the company attracts.

b. Assume that Schwab acquires a significant number of new customers. Name several costs that are likely to remain fixed as revenue increases.

c. Assume that Schwab acquires a significant number of new customers. Name several costs that are likely to vary with increasing revenue.

d. Consider the cost of establishing a new customer account. Describe a set of circumstances under which this would be a fixed cost and a different set of circumstances under which this would be a variable cost.

ATC 2-4 Writing Assignment *Cost averaging*

Candice Sterling is a veterinarian. She has always been concerned for the pets of low-income families. These families love their pets but frequently do not have the means to provide them proper veterinary care. Dr. Sterling decides to open a part-time veterinary practice in a low-income neighborhood. She plans to volunteer her services free of charge two days per week. Clients will be charged only for the actual costs of materials and overhead. Dr. Sterling leases a small space for $300 per month. Utilities and other miscellaneous costs are expected to be approximately $180 per month. She estimates the variable cost of materials to be approximately $10 per pet served. A friend of Dr. Sterling who runs a similar type of clinic in another area of town indicates that she should expect to treat the following number of pets during her first year of operation.

Jan.	Feb.	Mar.	Apr.	May	June	July	Aug.	Sept.	Oct.	Nov.	Dec.
18	26	28	36	42	54	63	82	42	24	20	15

Dr. Sterling's friend has noticed that visits increase significantly in the summer because children who are out of school tend to bring their pets to the vet more often. Business tapers off during the winter and reaches a low point in December when people spend what little money they have on Christmas presents for their children. After looking at the data, Dr. Sterling becomes concerned that the people in the neighborhood will not be able to afford pet care during some months of operation even if it is offered at cost. For example, the cost of providing services in December would be approximately $42 per pet treated ($480 overhead ÷ 15 pets = $32 per pet, plus $10 materials cost). She is willing to provide her services free of charge, but she realizes that she cannot afford to subsidize the practice further by personally paying for the costs of materials and overhead in the months of low activity. She decides to discuss the matter with her accountant to find a way to cut costs even more. Her accountant tells her that her problem is cost *measurement* rather than cost *cutting*.

Required

Assume that you are Dr. Sterling's accountant. Write a memo describing a pricing strategy that resolves the apparent problem of high costs during months of low volume. Recommend in your memo the price to charge per pet treated during the month of December.

ATC 2-5   Ethical Dilemma   *Profitability versus social conscience (effects of cost behavior)*

Advances in biological technology have enabled two research companies, Bio Labs, Inc., and Scientific Associates, to develop an insect-resistant corn seed. Neither company is financially strong enough to develop the distribution channels necessary to bring the product to world markets. World Agra Distributors, Inc., has negotiated contracts with both companies for the exclusive right to market their seed. Bio Labs signed an agreement to receive an annual royalty of $1,000,000. In contrast, Scientific Associates chose an agreement that provides for a royalty of $0.50 per pound of seed sold. Both agreements have a 10-year term. During 2004, World Agra sold approximately 1,600,000 pounds of the Bio Labs, Inc., seed and 2,400,000 pounds of the Scientific Associates seed. Both types of seed were sold for $1.25 per pound. By the end of 2004, it was apparent that the seed developed by Scientific Associates was superior. Although insect infestation was virtually nonexistent for both types of seed, the seed developed by Scientific Associates produced corn that was sweeter and had consistently higher yields.

World Agra Distributors' chief financial officer, Roger Weatherstone, recently retired. To the astonishment of the annual planning committee, Mr. Weatherstone's replacement, Ray Borrough, adamantly recommended that the marketing department develop a major advertising campaign to promote the seed developed by Bio Labs, Inc. The planning committee reluctantly approved the recommendation. A $100,000 ad campaign was launched; the ads emphasized the ability of the Bio Labs seed to avoid insect infestation. The campaign was silent with respect to taste or crop yield. It did not mention the seed developed by Scientific Associates. World Agra's sales staff was instructed to push the Bio Labs seed and to sell the Scientific Associates seed only on customer demand. Although total sales remained relatively constant during 2005, sales of the Scientific Associates seed fell to approximately 1,300,000 pounds while sales of the Bio Labs, Inc., seed rose to 2,700,000 pounds.

Required

a. Determine the amount of increase or decrease in profitability experienced by World Agra in 2005 as a result of promoting Bio Labs seed. Support your answer with appropriate commentary.

b. Did World Agra's customers in particular and society in general benefit or suffer from the decision to promote the Bio Labs seed?

c. Review the standards of ethical conduct in Exhibit 1.15 of Chapter 1 and comment on whether Mr. Borrough's recommendation violated any of the standards in the code of ethical conduct.

d. Comment on your belief regarding the adequacy of the Standards of Ethical Conduct for Managerial Accountants to direct the conduct of management accountants.

e. Are the actions of Ray Borrough in violation of the provisions of Sarbanes-Oxley that were described in Chapter 1? Explain your answer.

ATC 2-6   Spreadsheet Assignment   *Using Excel*

Charlie Stork rented a truck for his business on two previous occasions. Since he will soon be renting a truck again, he would like to analyze his bills and determine how the rental fee is calculated. His two bills for truck rental show that on September 1, he drove 1,000 miles and the bill was $1,500, and on December 5, he drove 600 miles and the bill was $1,380.

Required

Construct a spreadsheet to calculate the variable and fixed costs of this mixed cost that will allow Mr. Stork to predict his cost if he drives the truck 700 miles. The cells that show as numbers should all be formulas except C5, C6, E5, E6, and C18. Constructing the spreadsheet in this manner will allow you to change numbers in these five cells to recalculate variable cost, fixed cost, or predicted total cost.

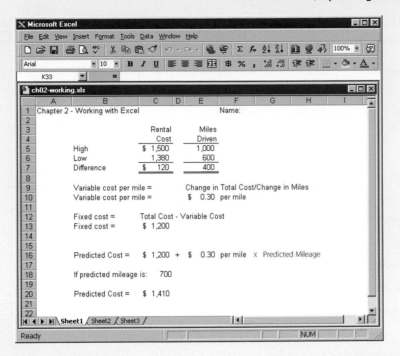

Spreadsheet Tip

1. To format cells to show dollar signs, commas, or both, choose Format, then Cells, then click on the tab titled Numbers, and choose Accounting.

ATC 2-7 Spreadsheet Assignment *Mastering Excel*

Siwa Company makes and sells a decorative ceramic statue. Each statue costs $50 to manufacture and sells for $75. Siwa spends $3 to ship the statue to customers and pays salespersons a $2 commission for each statue sold. The remaining annual expenses of operation are administrative salaries, $70,000; advertising, $20,000; and rent, $30,000. Siwa plans to sell 9,000 statues in the coming year.

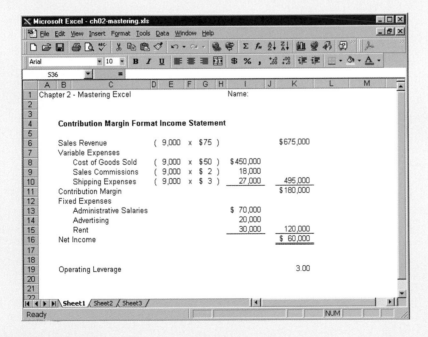

Required

Construct a spreadsheet that shows a contribution margin format income statement and that calculates operating leverage. Place formulas in the spreadsheet to allow changes to any of the preceding information to be automatically reflected in the income statement and operating leverage.

COMPREHENSIVE PROBLEM

Use the same transaction data for Magnificant Modems, Inc., as was used in Chapter 1 (see page 52).

Required

a. Based on these data, identify each cost incurred by the company as (1) fixed versus variable relative to the number of units produced and sold; and (2) product versus general, selling, and administrative (G, S, & A). The solution for the first item is shown as an example.

Cost Item	Fixed	Variable	Product	G,S,&A
Depreciation on manufacturing equipment	X		X	
Direct materials				
Direct labor				
Production supplies				
Rent on manufacturing facility				
Sales commissions				
Depreciation on administrative equipment				
Administrative costs (rent and salaries)				

b. Replace the question marks in the following table to indicate the product cost per unit assuming levels of production of 5,000, 6,000, 7,000, and 8,000.

Cost of Goods Sold	$455,000	?	?	?
Divided by Number of Units	5,000	6,000	7,000	8,000
Cost Per Unit	$ 91	?	?	?

CHAPTER 3

Analysis of Cost, Volume, and Pricing to Increase Profitability

LEARNING OBJECTIVES

After you have mastered the material in this chapter, you will be able to:

1. Use the contribution margin per unit approach to calculate the sales volume required to break even or earn a target profit.

2. Set selling prices by using cost-plus, prestige, and target pricing.

3. Use the contribution margin per unit to conduct cost-volume-profit analysis.

4. Draw and interpret a cost-volume-profit graph.

5. Calculate margin of safety.

6. Conduct sensitivity analysis for cost-volume-profit relationships.

7. Use the contribution margin ratio and the equation method to conduct cost-volume-profit analysis.

8. Perform multiple-product break-even analysis (Appendix).

The Curious Accountant

In August 2002, **American Airlines** announced several changes in its way of doing business. These changes included eliminating all of the first-class seats on some routes.

In February 2003, **Circuit City** laid off 3,900 sales personnel throughout its more than 600 stores in the United States. What makes this action unusual is that many of those fired were among the most productive salespeople in the company.

Why would American Airlines eliminate some of its highest priced seats at a time when airline traffic was already down around the globe? Why would Circuit City fire its best salespeople and replace them with less experienced, less proven employees? (Answers on page 111.)

CHAPTER OPENING

*The president of Bright Day Distributors recently completed a managerial accounting course. He was particularly struck by the operating leverage concept. His instructor had demonstrated how a small percentage increase in sales volume could produce a significantly higher percentage increase in profitability. Unfortunately, the discussion had been limited to the effects of changes in sales volume. In practice, changes in sales volume are often related to changes in sales price. For example, reducing selling prices often leads to increases in sales volume. Sales volume may also change in response to cost changes such as increasing the advertising budget. Furthermore, significant changes in sales volume could redefine the relevant range, changing the fixed and variable costs. Bright Day's president realized that understanding operating leverage was only one piece of understanding how to manage a business. He also needed to understand how changes in prices, costs, and volume affect profitability. Bright Day's president is interested in **cost-volume-profit (CVP) analysis.** ∎*

Chapter 3

Determining the Contribution Margin per Unit

Topic Tackler

PLUS

3-1

Use the contribution margin per unit approach to calculate the sales volume required to break even or earn a target profit.

Analyzing relationships among the CVP variables is simplified by using an income statement organized using the contribution margin format. Recall that the *contribution margin* is the difference between sales revenue and variable costs. It measures the amount available to cover fixed costs and thereafter to provide enterprise profits. Consider the following illustration.

Bright Day Distributors sells nonprescription health food supplements including vitamins, herbs, and natural hormones in the northwestern United States. Bright Day recently obtained the rights to distribute the new herb mixture Delatine. Recent scientific research found that Delatine delayed aging in laboratory animals. The researchers hypothesized that the substance would have a similar effect on humans. Their theory could not be confirmed because of the relatively long human life span. The news media reported the research findings; as stories turned up on television and radio news, talk shows, and in magazines, demand for Delatine increased.

Delatine costs $24 per bottle. Bright Day plans to sell the product at a price of $36 per bottle. The **contribution margin per unit** is:

Sales revenue per unit	$36
Variable cost per unit	24
Contribution margin per unit	$12

For every bottle of Delatine it sells, Bright Day earns a $12 contribution margin. Bright Day's first concern is whether it can sell enough units for total contribution margin to cover fixed costs. The president made this position clear when he said, "We don't want to lose money on this product. We have to sell enough units to pay our fixed costs." Bright Day can use the per unit contribution margin to determine the quantity of sales that is necessary to break even.

Determining the Break-Even Point

Use the contribution margin per unit approach to calculate the sales volume required to break even or earn a target profit.

Bright Day's management team suspects that enthusiasm for Delatine will abate quickly as the news media shift to other subjects. To attract customers immediately, the product managers consider television advertising. The marketing manager suggests running a campaign of several hundred cable channel ads at an estimated cost of $60,000. The company president asks, "How many bottles of Delatine would we have to sell to *break even?*"

The **break-even point** is the point where *total revenue equals total costs*. The cost of the advertising campaign is $60,000 regardless of the number of bottles of Delatine sold. It is a *fixed cost*. Given Bright Day's expected contribution margin of $12 per bottle, the break-even point measured in units is:

$$\text{Break-even volume in units} = \frac{\text{Fixed costs}}{\text{Contribution margin per unit}}$$

$$= \frac{\$60,000}{\$12} = 5,000 \text{ units}$$

The break-even point measured in *sales dollars* is the number of units that must be sold to break even multiplied by the sales price per unit. For Delatine, the break-even point in sales dollars is $180,000 (5,000 units × $36). The following income statement confirms these results.

Sales Revenue (5,000 units × $36)	$180,000
Total Variable Expenses (5,000 units × $24)	(120,000)
Total Contribution Margin (5,000 units × $12)	60,000
Fixed Expenses	(60,000)
Net Income	$ 0

Once fixed costs have been covered (5,000 units have been sold), net income will increase by $12 (*per unit contribution margin*) for each additional bottle sold. Similarly, profitability will decrease by $12 for each per unit decrease in sales volume. Study the effect of the per unit contribution margin on profitability by comparing the following income statements.

	Number of Units Sold (a)				
	4,998	**4,999**	**5,000**	**5,001**	**5,002**
Sales Revenue					
($36 per unit × a)	$179,928	$179,964	$180,000	$180,036	$180,072
Total Variable Expenses					
($24 per unit × a)	(119,952)	(119,976)	(120,000)	(120,024)	(120,048)
Total Contribution Margin					
($12 per unit × a)	59,976	59,988	60,000	60,012	60,024
Fixed Expenses	(60,000)	(60,000)	(60,000)	(60,000)	(60,000)
Net Income	$ (24)	$ (12)	$ 0	$ 12	$ 24

As sales increase from 5,000 to 5,001, net income increases from zero to $12. When sales increase by one additional unit, net income again rises by $12 (moves from $12 to $24). Income increases by the $12 per unit contribution margin with each additional unit sold. The effect of an increase or decrease in sales volume on net income can be computed by multiplying the amount of the change in sales volume by the contribution margin per unit. Suppose sales increase from 5,400 to 5,600 units. This increase will affect profitability by $2,400 [(5,600 − 5,400) × $12]. The following comparative income statements confirm this result.

	Number of Units Sold		200 Unit
	5,400	**5,600**	**Difference**
Sales Revenue ($36 per unit)	$194,400	$201,600	$7,200
Total Variable Expenses ($24 per unit)	(129,600)	(134,400)	(4,800)
Total Contribution Margin ($12 per unit)	64,800	67,200	2,400
Fixed Expenses	(60,000)	(60,000)	0
Net Income	$ 4,800	$ 7,200	$2,400

Determining the Sales Volume Necessary to Reach a Target Profit

Bright Day's president decides the ad campaign should produce a $40,000 profit. He asks the accountant to determine the sales volume that is required to achieve this level of profitability. For this result, the contribution margin must be sufficient to cover the fixed costs and to provide the desired profit. The required sales volume in units can be computed as shown here:

LO 1

Use the contribution margin per unit approach to calculate the sales volume required to break even or earn a target profit.

$$\text{Sales volume in units} = \frac{\text{Fixed costs} + \text{Desired profit}}{\text{Contribution margin per unit}}$$

$$= \frac{\$60,000 + \$40,000}{\$12} = 8,333.33 \text{ units}$$

The required volume in sales dollars is this number of units multiplied by the sales price per unit (8,333.33 units × $36 = $300,000). The following income statement confirms this result; all amounts are rounded to the nearest whole dollar.

Sales Revenue (8,333.33 units × $36)	$300,000
Total Variable Expenses (8,333.33 units × $24)	(200,000)
Total Contribution Margin (8,333.33 units × $12)	100,000
Fixed Expenses	(60,000)
Net Income	$ 40,000

In practice, the company will not sell partial bottles of Delatine. The accountant rounds 8,333.33 bottles to whole units. For planning and decision making, managers frequently make decisions using approximate data. Accuracy is desirable, but it is not as important as relevance. Do not be concerned when computations do not produce whole numbers. Rounding and approximation are common characteristics of managerial accounting data.

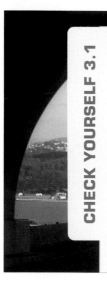

CHECK YOURSELF 3.1

VolTech Company manufactures small engines that it sells for $130 each. Variable costs are $70 per unit. Fixed costs are expected to be $100,000. The management team has established a target profit of $188,000. How many engines must VolTech sell to attain the target profit?

Answer

$$\text{Sales volume in units} = \frac{\text{Fixed costs} + \text{Desired profit}}{\text{Contribution margin per unit}} = \frac{\$100,000 + \$188,000}{\$130 - \$70} = 4,800 \text{ units}$$

Assessing the Pricing Strategy

LO 2

Set selling prices by using cost-plus, prestige, and target pricing.

After reviewing the accountant's computations, the president asked the marketing manager, "What are our chances of reaching a sales volume of 8,334 units?" The manager replied, "Slim to none." She observed that no Bright Day product has ever sold more than 4,000 bottles when initially offered. Further, she feels the $36 price is too high. She asked who set the $36 price and how it was established.

The accountant explained that the price was established using a **cost-plus pricing** strategy. The normal policy is to price products at variable cost plus 50 percent of the variable cost. In this case the variable cost was $24, resulting in a price of $36 [$24 + ($24 × .5)] The accountant knew the price was high but expected Delatine to sell anyway. Indeed, he supported his position by referencing a strategy known as **prestige pricing.** Many people will pay a premium to be the first to use a new product. Similarly, people will pay more for a product with a prestigious brand name. The accountant noted that the widespread news coverage coupled with Bright Day's brand identity makes Delatine a prime product for prestige pricing.

The marketing manager recognized the accountant's arguments, but contended that news coverage will fade rapidly, competitors will enter the market, and therefore, Delatine cannot support a $36 price for an extended period of time. As an alternative, she suggested they use a strategy known as target pricing. **Target pricing** begins by determining the market price at which a product will sell. This becomes the target price. The focus then shifts to developing the product at a cost that will enable the company to be profitable while selling the product at the target price. Since the target price leads to a target cost, this market-based pricing strategy is also called **target costing.**

Market research indicates that Delatine could sustain long-term sales at a price of $28 per bottle. At this price, the new contribution margin becomes a mere $4 ($28 − $24) per unit. As shown here, the significant drop in contribution margin per unit (from $12 to $4) will cause a dramatic increase in the sales volume necessary to attain the target profit:

$$\text{Sales volume in units} = \frac{\text{Fixed costs} + \text{Desired profit}}{\text{Contribution margin per unit}}$$

$$= \frac{\$60,000 + \$40,000}{\$4} = 25,000 \text{ units}$$

The required sales volume *in dollars* is $700,000 (25,000 units × $28 per bottle). The following income statement confirms these results.

Sales Revenue (25,000 units × $28)	$700,000
Total Variable Expenses (25,000 units × $24)	(600,000)
Total Contribution Margin (25,000 units × $4)	100,000
Fixed Expenses	(60,000)
Net Income	$ 40,000

The marketing manager recognized that it would be impossible to sell 25,000 bottles of Delatine. She noted that this is where target costing enters the picture. Delatine must be made at a cost that will enable the company to earn the desired profit of $40,000 while selling at a price of $28 per bottle. Clearly, the cost structure must change and the marketing manager has some suggestions for making the necessary changes.

Assessing the Effects of Changes in Variable Costs

The previously discussed $24 cost is for a bottle of 100 capsules, each containing 90 milligrams (mg) of pure Delatine. The manufacturer is willing to provide Delatine to Bright Day in two alternative package sizes: (1) a bottle costing $12 that contains 100 capsules of 30 mg strength pure Delatine and (2) a bottle costing $3 that contains 100 capsules containing 5 mg of Delatine mixed with a vitamin C compound. The 5 mg dosage is the minimum required to permit a package label to indicate the product contains Delatine. The marketing manager observes that either option would enable Bright Day to sell Delatine at a price customers would be willing to pay.

LO 3

Use the contribution margin per unit to conduct cost-volume-profit analysis.

The president vehemently rejected the second option, calling it a blatant attempt to deceive customers by suggesting they were buying Delatine when in fact they were getting vitamin C. *He considered the idea unethical and dangerous.* He vowed that he would not be seen on the six o'clock news trying to defend a fast buck scheme while his company's reputation went up in smoke. After calming down, he agreed that the first option had merit. The appropriate dosage for Delatine was uncertain; customers who wanted 90 mg per day could take three capsules instead of one. He asked the accountant, "What's the effect on the bottom line?"

The variable cost changes from $24 to $12 per bottle. The contribution margin per unit increases from $4 per bottle ($28 sales price − $24 variable cost per bottle) to $16 per bottle ($28 sales price − $12 variable cost per bottle). The significant increase in contribution margin per unit dramatically decreases the sales volume necessary to attain the target profit. The computations follow:

$$\text{Sales volume in units} = \frac{\text{Fixed costs} + \text{Desired profit}}{\text{Contribution margin per unit}}$$

$$= \frac{\$60,000 + \$40,000}{\$16} = 6,250 \text{ units}$$

FOCUS ON INTERNATIONAL ISSUES

COST-VOLUME-PROFIT ANALYSIS AT A GERMAN SOFTWARE COMPANY

The higher the percentage of a company's total costs that are fixed, the more sensitive the company's earnings are to changes in revenue or volume. Operating leverage, the relationship between changes in revenue and changes in earnings introduced earlier, applies to companies throughout the world, large or small.

Software development companies have high fixed costs relative to total costs. It costs a lot to develop a new computer program, but it costs little to produce additional copies. **SAP**, a German company founded in 1972, is a leading provider of enterprise resource planning (ERP) software. From 2001 through 2003 SAP's earnings *increased* by 31.4 percent although its revenue *decreased* by 4.3 percent. No doubt the high fixed cost of developing software is one of the reasons that SAP's three major competitors, **J.D. Edwards**, **PeopleSoft**, and **Oracle**, went from being three separate firms in 2003 to only one firm, Oracle, by 2005.

Studying SAP offers insight into the global company. Though headquartered in Germany, in its 2003 fiscal year 57 percent of its revenues came from European customers, 25 percent from customers in the United States, and 14 percent from Asian customers. SAP's decline in revenues in 2003 was not caused by lower unit sales, but by the rise of the value of the euro against the dollar, a risk of international business. SAP's financial statements are presented in accordance with U.S. GAAP, but they are audited using German audit standards. The statements are mostly presented in euros, but some data are duplicated in U.S. dollars. You can review SAP's annual report at www.sap.com, under "Investor Relations."

The required sales volume in sales dollars is $175,000 (6,250 units $\times$ $28 per bottle). The following income statement confirms these amounts.

Sales Revenue (6,250 units $\times$ $28)	$175,000
Total Variable Expenses (6,250 units $\times$ $12)	(75,000)
Total Contribution Margin (6,250 units $\times$ $16)	100,000
Fixed Expenses	(60,000)
Net Income	$ 40,000

Although the drop in required sales from 25,000 units to 6,250 was significant, the marketing manager was still uneasy about the company's ability to sell 6,250 bottles of Delatine. She observed again that no other Bright Day product had produced sales of that magnitude. The accountant suggested reducing projected fixed costs by advertising on radio rather than television. While gathering cost data for the potential television ad campaign, the accountant had consulted radio ad executives who had assured him radio ads could equal the TV audience exposure at about half the cost. Even though the TV ads would likely be more effective, he argued that since radio advertising costs would be half those of TV, the desired profit could be attained at a significantly lower volume of sales. The company president was impressed with the possibilities. He asked the accountant to determine the required sales volume if advertising costs were $30,000 instead of $60,000.

Answers to The Curious Accountant

American Airlines eliminated some first-class seats in order to increase its operating efficiency, even if it meant forgoing some revenue. To accomplish this, the company decided to reduce the number of flights it operated per day, and to reduce the number of different types of airplanes it uses. By reducing the number of flights, the occupancy level of each flight was increased. Since airlines have a significant amount of fixed costs for each flight operated, higher occupancy rates reduce the cost per passenger, and this should increase profits per flight. By reducing the number of different types of airplanes used, the company could reduce the costs of maintenance, since each type of plane requires its own inventory of replacement parts and special training for maintenance personnel.

Circuit City fired many of its most productive salespeople to reduce operating costs. These sales personnel were paid in part on a commission basis, so the more they sold,

the greater Circuit City's selling expenses were. The company's main rival, **Best Buy**, was paying its sales personnel an hourly wage only rather than commissions. Although sales commissions motivate employees to be more aggressive in selling the company's goods, the sales commission is paid on *all* sales made, and not just on the additional sales that result from motivation of the commission. Circuit City decided that the higher sales generated by the most successful members of the sales staff were not sufficient to justify their higher costs, so they were laid off.

Neither American Airlines nor Circuit City made their decisions by focusing only on revenues or only on costs. Rather, their decisions were based on an analysis of the interactions of costs, revenues, and the volume of sales that would be generated as cost and pricing strategies were altered.

Assessing the Effects of Changes in Fixed Costs

Since the contribution margin will cover a smaller amount of fixed costs, changing the fixed costs from $60,000 to $30,000 will dramatically reduce the sales level required to earn the target profit. The computations follow:

Use the contribution margin per unit to conduct cost-volume-profit analysis.

$$\text{Sales volume in units} = \frac{\text{Fixed costs} + \text{Desired profit}}{\text{Contribution margin per unit}}$$

$$= \frac{\$30,000 + \$40,000}{\$16} = 4,375 \text{ units}$$

The required sales volume in sales dollars is $122,500 (4,375 units × $28). The following income statement confirms these amounts.

Sales Revenue (4,375 units × $28)	$122,500
Total Variable Expenses (4,375 units × $12)	(52,500)
Total Contribution Margin (4,375 units × $16)	70,000
Fixed Expenses	(30,000)
Net Income	$ 40,000

The marketing manager supported using radio instead of television ads. Obviously, she could not guarantee any specific sales volume, but she felt confident that sales projections within a range of 4,000 to 5,000 units were reasonable.

Using the Cost-Volume Profit Graph

To visually analyze the revised projections, Bright Day's accountant prepared a cost-volume-profit (CVP) chart that pictured CVP relationships over a range of sales activity from zero to 6,000 units. The accountant followed the steps below to produce the CVP graph (sometimes

Draw and interpret a cost-volume-profit graph.

called a *break-even chart*) shown in Exhibit 3.1. The graph is drawn under the following assumptions:

- The contribution margin is $16 (sales price $28 − variable cost $12 per bottle).
- The fixed cost is $30,000.
- The desired profit is $40,000.

Procedures for Drawing the CVP Graph

1. *Draw and label the axes:* The horizontal axis represents activity (expressed in units) and the vertical axis represents dollars.

2. *Draw the fixed cost line:* Total fixed costs are constant for all levels of activity. Draw a horizontal line representing the amount of fixed costs across the graph at $30,000, the fixed-cost level.

3. *Draw the total cost line:* The total cost line representing the combination of fixed and variable costs is a diagonal line that rises as it moves from left to right. To draw the line, plot one point of the total cost line at the intersection of the fixed-cost line and the vertical axis. In this case, plot the first point at the zero level of activity and $30,000 (fixed cost). Next, select an arbitrary activity level. In this case we assume 6,000 units. At this volume, the total cost is $102,000 [(6,000 units × $12) + $30,000 fixed cost]. Plot a point at the coordinates of 6,000 units and $102,000. Draw a straight line through these two points.

4. *Draw the sales line:* Draw the revenue line using a procedure similar to that de-scribed for drawing the total cost line. Select some arbitrary level of activity and mul-tiply that volume by the sales price per unit. Plot the result on the graph and draw a line from the origin (zero units, zero revenue) through this point. For example, at a volume of 6,000 units, the revenue is $168,000 (6,000 units × $28). Plot a point at the coordinates of 6,000 units and $168,000. Draw a line from the origin through the plotted point.

Trace these steps to the graph in Exhibit 3.1.

EXHIBIT 3.1

Cost-Volume-Profit Graph

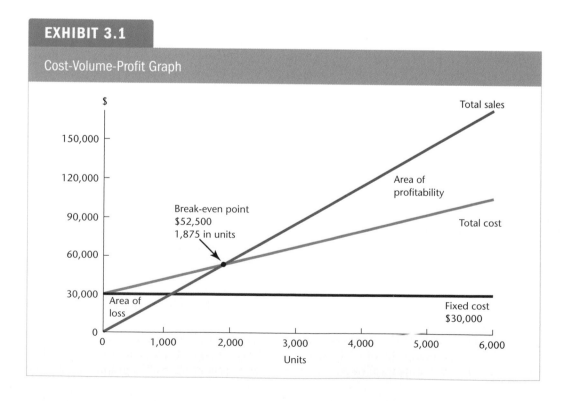

Calculating the Margin of Safety

The final meeting of Bright Day's management team focused on the reliability of the data used to construct the CVP chart. The accountant called attention to the sales volume figures in the area of profitability. Recall that Bright Day must sell 4,375 bottles of Delatine to earn the desired profit. In dollars, budgeted sales are $122,500 (4,375 bottles × $28 per bottle). The accountant highlighted the large gap between these budgeted sales and break-even sales. The amount of this gap, called the *margin of safety,* can be measured in units or in sales dollars as shown here:

LO 5

Calculate margin of safety.

	In Units	In Dollars
Budgeted sales	4,375	$122,500
Break-even sales	(1,875)	(52,500)
Margin of safety	2,500	$ 70,000

The **margin of safety** measures the cushion between budgeted sales and the break-even point. It quantifies the amount by which actual sales can fall short of expectations before the company will begin to incur losses.

Recap of Delatine Decision Process

Management considers a new product named Delatine. Delatine has a projected sales price of $36 and variable cost of $24 per bottle. Fixed cost is projected to be $60,000. The break-even point is 5,000 units [$60,000 ÷ ($36 − $24) = 5,000].

Management desires to earn a $40,000 profit on Delatine. The sales volume required to earn the desired profit is 8,334 units [($60,000 + $40,000) ÷ ($36 − $24) = 8,334].

The marketing manager advocates a target pricing approach that lowers the proposed selling price to $28 per bottle. The sales volume required to earn a $40,000 profit increases to 25,000 units [($60,000 + $40,000) ÷ ($28 − $24) = 25,000].

Target costing is employed to reengineer the product, thereby reducing variable cost to $12 per bottle. The sales volume required to earn a $40,000 profit decreases to 6,250 units [($60,000 + $40,000) ÷ ($28 − $12) = 6,250].

Target costing is applied further to reduce fixed cost to $30,000. The sales volume required to earn a $40,000 profit decreases to 4,375 units [($30,000 + $40,000) ÷ ($28 − $12) = 4,375]. The new break-even point is 1,875 units [$30,000 ÷ ($28 − $12) = 1,875].

In view of a 57.14% margin of safety [(4,375 − 1,875) ÷ 4,375 = .5714], management decides to add Delatine to its product line.

To help compare diverse products or companies of different sizes, the margin of safety can be expressed as a percentage. Divide the margin of safety by the budgeted sales volume[1] as shown here:

$$\text{Margin of safety} = \frac{\text{Budgeted sales} - \text{Break-even sales}}{\text{Budgeted sales}}$$

$$\text{Margin of safety} = \frac{\$122{,}500 - \$52{,}500}{\$122{,}500} = 57.14\%$$

This analysis suggests actual sales would have to fall short of expected sales by more than 57 percent before Bright Day would experience a loss on Delatine. The large margin of safety suggests the proposed radio advertising program to market bottles of 30mg Delatine capsules has minimal risk.

CHECK YOURSELF 3.2

Suppose that Bright Day is considering the possibility of selling a protein supplement that will cost Bright Day $5 per bottle. Bright Day believes that it can sell 4,000 bottles of the supplement for $25 per bottle. Fixed costs associated with selling the supplement are expected to be $42,000. Does the supplement have a wider margin of safety than Delatine?

Answer

Calculate the break-even point for the protein supplement.

$$\text{Break-even volume in units} = \frac{\text{Fixed costs}}{\text{Contribution margin per unit}} = \frac{\$42{,}000}{\$25 - \$5} = 2{,}100 \text{ units}$$

Calculate the margin of safety. Note that the margin of safety expressed as a percentage can be calculated using the number of units or sales dollars. Using either units or dollars yields the same percentage.

$$\text{Margin of safety} = \frac{\text{Budgeted sales} - \text{Break-even sales}}{\text{Budgeted sales}} = \frac{4{,}000 - 2{,}100}{4{,}000} = 47.5\%$$

The margin of safety for Delatine (57.14 percent) exceeds that for the protein supplement (47.5 percent). This suggests that Bright Day is less likely to incur losses selling Delatine than selling the supplement.

Performing Sensitivity Analysis Using Spreadsheet Software

LO 6

Conduct sensitivity analysis for cost-volume-profit relationships.

While useful, the margin of safety offers only a one dimensional measure of risk—change in sales volume. Profitability is affected by multidimensional forces. Fixed or variable costs, as well as sales volume, could differ from expectations. Exhibit 3.2 uses data pertaining to Bright Day's proposed project for marketing Delatine to illustrate an Excel spreadsheet showing the sensitivity of profits to simultaneous changes in fixed cost, variable cost, and sales volume. Recall the accountant estimated the radio ad campaign would cost $30,000. The spreadsheet projects profitability if advertising costs are as low as $20,000 or as high as $40,000. The effects of potential simultaneous changes in variable cost and sales volume are similarly projected.

The range of scenarios illustrated in the spreadsheet represents only a few of the many alternatives management can analyze with a few quick keystrokes. The spreadsheet program recalculates profitability figures instantly when one of the variables changes. If the president asks

---

[1]The margin of safety percentage can be based on actual as well as budgeted sales. For example, an analyst could compare the margins of safety of two companies under current operating conditions by substituting actual sales for budgeted sales in the computation, as follows: [(Actual sales − Break-even sales) ÷ Actual sales].

EXHIBIT 3.2

Spreadsheet Report to Facilitate "What-If" Analysis

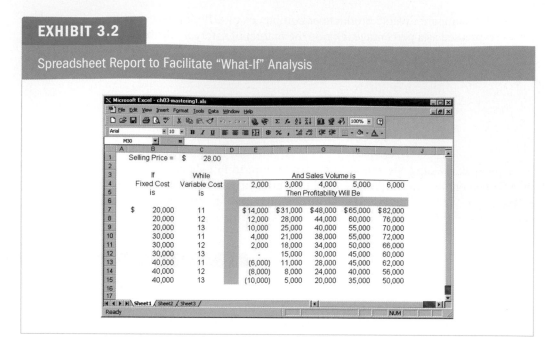

what would happen if Bright Day sold 10,000 units, the accountant merely substitutes the new number for one of the existing sales volume figures, and revised profitability numbers are instantly available. By changing the variables, management can get a real feel for the sensitivity of profits to changes in cost and volume. Investigating a multitude of what-if possibilities involving simultaneous changes in fixed cost, variable cost, and volume is called **sensitivity analysis.**

After reviewing the spreadsheet analysis, Bright Day's management team is convinced it should undertake radio advertising for Delatine. Only under the most dire circumstances (if actual sales are significantly below expectations while costs are well above expectations) will the company incur a loss.

Assessing the Effect of Simultaneous Changes in CVP Variables

Use the contribution margin per unit to conduct cost-volume-profit analysis.

The contribution approach previously illustrated to analyze one-dimensional CVP relationships easily adapts to studying the effects of simultaneous changes in CVP variables. To illustrate several possible scenarios, assume Bright Day has developed the budgeted income statement in Exhibit 3.3.

A Decrease in Sales Price Accompanied by an Increase in Sales Volume

The marketing manager believes reducing the sales price per bottle to $25 will increase sales volume by 625 units. The per unit contribution margin would drop to $13 ($25 sales price − $12 cost per bottle). The expected sales volume would become 5,000 (4,375 + 625). Should

EXHIBIT 3.3

Budgeted Income Statement

Sales Revenue (4,375 units × $28 sale price)	$122,500
Total Variable Expenses (4,375 units × $12 cost per bottle)	(52,500)
Total Contribution Margin (4,375 units × $16)	70,000
Fixed Expenses	(30,000)
Net Income	$ 40,000

Bright Day reduce the price? Compare the projected profit without these changes ($40,000) with the projected profit if the sales price is $25, computed as follows:

$$\text{Profit} = \text{Contribution margin} - \text{Fixed cost}$$

$$\text{Profit} = (5,000 \times \$13) - \$30,000 = \$35,000$$

Since budgeted income falls from $40,000 to $35,000, Bright Day should not reduce the sales price.

An Increase in Fixed Cost Accompanied by an Increase in Sales Volume

Return to the budgeted income statement in Exhibit 3.3. If the company buys an additional $12,000 of advertising, management believes sales can increase to 6,000 units. The contribution margin per unit will remain $16 ($28 − $12). Should Bright Day incur the additional advertising cost, increasing fixed costs to $42,000? The expected profit would be:

$$\text{Profit} = \text{Contribution margin} - \text{Fixed cost}$$

$$\text{Profit} = (6,000 \times \$16) - \$42,000 = \$54,000$$

Since budgeted income increases from $40,000 to $54,000, Bright Day should seek to increase sales through additional advertising.

A Simultaneous Reduction in Sales Price, Fixed Costs, Variable Costs, and Sales Volume

Return again to the budgeted income statement in Exhibit 3.3. Suppose Bright Day negotiates a $4 reduction in the cost of a bottle of Delatine. The management team considers passing some of the savings on to customers by reducing the sales price to $25 per bottle. Furthermore, the team believes it could reduce advertising costs by $8,000 and still achieve sales of 4,200 units. Should Bright Day adopt this plan to reduce prices and advertising costs?

The contribution margin would increase to $17 per bottle ($25 revised selling price − $8 revised variable cost per bottle) and fixed cost would fall to $22,000 ($30,000 − $8,000). Based on a sales volume of 4,200 units, the expected profit is:

$$\text{Profit} = \text{Contribution margin} - \text{Fixed cost}$$

$$\text{Profit} = (4,200 \times \$17) - \$22,000 = \$49,400$$

Because budgeted income increases from $40,000 to $49,400, Bright Day should proceed with the revised operating strategy.

Many other possible scenarios could be considered. The contribution approach can be used to analyze independent or simultaneous changes in the CVP variables.

Performing Cost-Volume-Profit (CVP) Analysis Using the Contribution Margin Ratio

The **contribution margin ratio** is the contribution margin divided by sales, computed using either total figures or per unit figures. The contribution margin *ratio* can be used in CVP analysis as an alternative to using the *per unit* contribution margin. To illustrate, assume Bright Day is considering selling a new product called Multi Minerals. The expected sales price, variable cost, and contribution margin per unit for Multi Minerals are:

LO 7

Use the contribution margin ratio and the equation method to conduct cost-volume-profit analysis.

Sales revenue per unit	$20
Variable cost per unit	12
Contribution margin per unit	$ 8

Based on these data, the *contribution margin ratio* for Multi Minerals is 40 percent ($8 ÷ $20). This ratio means every dollar of sales provides 40 cents ($1.00 × 0.40) to cover fixed costs. After fixed costs have been covered, each dollar of sales provides 40 cents of profit.

While the *per unit contribution margin* approach produces results measured in units, the *contribution margin ratio* approach produces results expressed in dollars. The two approaches merely represent different ways to reach the same conclusion. To illustrate, the two alternative approaches to calculate the break-even point are shown here, assuming Bright Day expects to incur $24,000 of fixed expenses to market Multi Minerals:

Per Unit Contribution Approach Break-even in Units	Contribution Ratio Approach Break-even in Dollars
$\dfrac{\text{Fixed costs}}{\text{Contribution margin per unit}} = \text{Units}$	$\dfrac{\text{Fixed costs}}{\text{Contribution margin ratio}} = \text{Dollars}$
$\dfrac{\$24,000}{\$8} = 3{,}000 \text{ units}$	$\dfrac{\$24,000}{40\%} = \$60{,}000$

Recall the break-even point in units can be converted to sales dollars by multiplying the number of units to break even by the sales price per unit (3,000 units × $20 per unit = $60,000). Alternatively, the break-even point in sales dollars can be converted to units by dividing ($60,000 ÷ $20 = 3,000). The two approaches represent different views of the same data. The relationship between the two approaches holds when other CVP variables are added or changed. For example, either approach can provide the sales volume necessary to reach a target profit of $8,000, as follows:

Per Unit Contribution Approach Sales Volume in Units	Contribution Ratio Approach Sales Volume in Dollars
$\dfrac{\text{Fixed costs} + \text{Desired profit}}{\text{Contribution margin per unit}} = \text{Units}$	$\dfrac{\text{Fixed costs} + \text{Desired profit}}{\text{Contribution margin ratio}} = \text{Dollars}$
$\dfrac{\$24,000 + \$8,000}{\$8} = 4{,}000 \text{ units}$	$\dfrac{\$24,000 + \$8,000}{40\%} = \$80{,}000$

Once again, multiplying the $20 sales price by the sales volume expressed in units equals the sales volume in dollars ($20 × 4,000 = $80,000).

Performing Cost-Volume-Profit Analysis Using the Equation Method

Use the contribution margin ratio and the equation method to conduct cost-volume-profit analysis.

Topic Tackler

PLUS

3-2

A third way to analyze CVP relationships uses the **equation method.** Begin with expressing the break-even point as an algebraic equation, as shown here.[2]

$$\text{Sales} = \text{Variable cost} + \text{Fixed cost}$$

[2]The equation method results in the same computation as the per unit contribution margin approach. Consider the following. Using the per unit contribution margin approach, the break-even point is determined as follows (X is the break-even point in units):

$$X = \text{Fixed cost} ÷ \text{Per unit contribution margin}$$

Using the equation method, the break-even point is determined as follows (X is the break-even point in units):

$$\text{Unit sales price } (X) = \text{Variable cost per unit } (X) + \text{Fixed cost}$$
$$(\text{Unit sales price} - \text{Variable cost per unit}) (X) = \text{Fixed cost}$$
$$\text{Per unit contribution margin } (X) = \text{Fixed cost}$$
$$X = \text{Fixed cost} ÷ \text{Per unit contribution margin}$$

Expanding the equation provides the basis for computing the break-even point in number of units, as shown here:

$$\begin{array}{c} \text{Selling price per unit} \\ \times \\ \text{Number of units sold} \end{array} = \begin{array}{c} \text{Variable cost per unit} \\ \times \\ \text{Number of units sold} \end{array} + \text{ Fixed cost}$$

Using the Multi Minerals $20 sales price, $12 variable cost, and $24,000 fixed cost, the *break-even point in units* is:

$$\$20 \times \text{Units} = \$12 \times \text{Units} + \$24,000$$

$$\$8 \times \text{Units} = \$24,000$$

$$\text{Units} = 3,000$$

As before, the break-even sales volume in *units* can be converted into break-even sales volume in *dollars* by multiplying the sales price per unit by the number of units sold. The *break-even point* for Multi Minerals expressed in *dollars* is:

$$\text{Selling price per unit} \times \text{Number of units sold } = \text{ Sales volume in dollars}$$

$$\$20 \qquad \times \qquad 3,000 \qquad = \qquad \$60,000$$

The equation method can also be used to analyze additional CVP relationships. For example, the equation to determine the sales volume necessary to attain a target profit of $8,000 is:

$$\begin{array}{c} \text{Selling price per unit} \\ \times \\ \text{Number of units sold} \end{array} = \begin{array}{c} \text{Variable cost per unit} \\ \times \\ \text{Number of units sold} \end{array} + \text{ Fixed cost } + \text{ Desired profit}$$

The computations are:

$$\$20 \times \text{Units} = \$12 \times \text{Units} + \$24,000 + \$8,000$$

$$\$8 \times \text{Units} = \$32,000$$

$$\text{Units} = 4,000$$

Comparing these results with those determined using the per unit contribution approach and the contribution margin ratio approach demonstrates that the equation method is simply another way to achieve the same result. The method to use depends on personal and management preferences.

Recall the information presented in Check Yourself 3-1. VolTech Company manufactures small engines that it sells for $130 each, with variable costs of $70 per unit, expected fixed costs of $100,000, and a target profit of $188,000. Use the equation method to calculate the number of engines VolTech must sell to attain the target profit.

Answer

$$\begin{array}{c} \text{Selling price per unit} \\ \times \\ \text{Number of units sold} \end{array} = \begin{array}{c} \text{Variable cost per unit} \\ \times \\ \text{Number of units sold} \end{array} + \text{ Fixed cost } + \text{ Desired profit}$$

$$\$130 \times \text{Units} = \$70 \times \text{Units} + \$100,000 + \$188,000$$
$$\$60 \times \text{Units} = \$288,000$$
$$\text{Units} = 4,800$$

This is the same result determined in the Check Yourself 3-1 exercise. The only difference is in the method used to make the computation.

CHECK YOURSELF 3.3

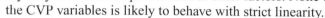

Cost-Volume-Profit Limitations

Because cost-volume-profit analysis presumes strictly linear behavior among the variables, its accuracy is limited. Actual CVP variables rarely behave with true linearity. Suppose, for example, a business receives volume discounts on materials purchases: the more material purchased, the lower the cost per unit. The total cost varies but not in direct proportion to the amount of material purchased. Similarly, fixed costs can change. A supervisor's fixed salary may change if the supervisor receives a raise. Likewise, the cost of telephone service, rent, insurance, taxes, and so on may increase or decrease. In practice, fixed costs frequently fluctuate. Furthermore, sales prices may vary as a result of promotions or other factors. None of the CVP variables is likely to behave with strict linearity.

Finally, CVP analysis presumes inventory levels remain constant during the period. In other words, sales and production are assumed to be equal. CVP formulas provide the estimated number of units that must be *produced and sold* to break even or to achieve some designated target profit. Manufacturing or acquiring, but not selling, inventory generates costs without producing corresponding revenue. Changes in inventory levels undoubtedly affect CVP relationships. The assumptions underlying CVP analysis are rarely entirely valid in business practice. Within the relevant range of activity, however, deviations from the basic assumptions are normally insignificant. A prudent business manager who exercises good judgment will find the projections generated by cost-volume-profit analysis useful regardless of these limitations.

<< A Look Back

Profitability is affected by changes in sales price, costs, and the volume of activity. The relationship among these variables is examined using *cost-volume-profit (CVP) analysis*. The *contribution margin,* determined by subtracting variable costs from the sales price, is a useful variable in CVP analysis. The *contribution margin per unit* is the amount each unit sold provides to cover fixed costs. Once fixed costs have been covered, each additional unit sold increases net income by the amount of the per unit contribution margin.

The *break-even point* (the point where total revenue equals total cost) in units can be determined by dividing fixed costs by the contribution margin per unit. The break-even point in sales dollars can be determined by multiplying the number of break-even units by the sales price per unit. To determine sales in units to obtain a designated profit, the sum of fixed costs and desired profit is divided by the contribution margin per unit. The contribution margin per unit can also be used to assess the effects on the company's profitability of changes in sales price, variable costs, and fixed costs.

Many methods are available to determine the prices at which products should sell. In *cost-plus pricing,* the sales price per unit is determined by adding a percentage markup to the cost per unit. In contrast, *target pricing* (*target costing*) begins with an estimated market price customers would be willing to pay for the product and then develops the product at a cost that will enable the company to earn its desired profit.

A *break-even graph* can depict cost-volume-profit relationships for a product over a range of sales activity. The horizontal axis represents volume of activity and the vertical axis represents dollars. Lines for fixed costs, total costs, and sales are drawn based on the sales price per unit, variable cost per unit, and fixed costs. The graph can be used to determine the break-even point in units and sales dollars.

The *margin of safety* is the number of units or the amount of sales dollars by which actual sales can fall below expected sales before a loss is incurred. The margin of safety can also be expressed as a percentage to permit comparing different size companies. The margin of safety can be computed as a percentage by dividing the difference between budgeted sales and break-even sales by the amount of budgeted sales.

Spreadsheet software as well as the contribution margin approach can be used to conduct sensitivity analysis of cost-volume-profit relationships. *Sensitivity analysis* predicts the effect on profitability of different scenarios of fixed costs, variable costs, and sales volumes. The effects of simultaneous changes in all three variables can be assessed. A *contribution margin ratio* can be used to determine the break-even point in sales dollars. The ratio is a percentage determined by dividing the contribution margin per unit by the sales price per unit. Using the contribution margin ratio, the break-even volume in dollars can be determined by dividing the total fixed costs by the ratio. Cost-volume-profit relationships can also be examined using this algebraic equation:

$$\text{Sales} = \text{Variable cost} + \text{Fixed cost}$$

Cost-volume-profit analysis is built upon certain simplifying assumptions. The analysis assumes true linearity among the CVP variables and a constant level of inventory. Although these assumptions are not literally valid in actual practice, CVP analysis nevertheless provides managers with helpful insights for decision making.

A Look Forward

The failure to accurately allocate indirect costs to cost objects can result in misinformation that impairs decision making. The next chapter explains how increased use of automation in production has caused allocations determined using traditional approaches to be distorted. The chapter introduces allocating indirect costs using more recently developed *activity-based costing* and explains how *activity-based management* can improve efficiency and productivity. Finally, the chapter introduces *total quality management,* a strategy that seeks to minimize the costs of conforming to a designated standard of quality.

APPENDIX

Multiple-Product Break-Even Analysis

When a company analyzes CVP relationships for multiple products that sell simultaneously, the break-even point can be affected by the relative number (sales mix) of the products sold. For example, suppose Bright Day decides to run a special sale on its two leading antioxidants, vitamins C and E. The income statements at the break-even point are presented in Exhibit 3.4.

Perform multiple-product break-even analysis.

EXHIBIT 3.4								
Budgeted Data for Antioxidant Special								
	Vitamin C			**Vitamin E**			**Total**	
	Budgeted Number	**Per Unit**	**Budgeted Amount**	**Budgeted Number**	**Per Unit**	**Budgeted Amount**	**Budgeted Number**	**Budgeted Amount**
Sales	2,000	@ $7.20 =	$14,400	700	@ $11.00 =	$7,700	2,700	$22,100
Variable cost	2,000	@ 6.00 =	(12,000)	700	@ 7.00 =	(4,900)	2,700	(16,900)
Contribution margin	2,000	@ 1.20 =	2,400	700	@ 4.00 =	2,800	2,700	5,200
Fixed cost			(2,400)			(2,800)		(5,200)
Net income			$ 0			$ 0		$ 0

Recall that the break-even point is the point where total sales equal total costs. Net income is zero at that point. The data in Exhibit 3.4 indicate that the budgeted break-even sales volume for the antioxidant special is 2,700 bottles of vitamins with a sales mix of 2,000 bottles of vitamin C and 700 bottles of vitamin E. What happens if the relative sales mix changes? Exhibit 3.5 depicts the expected condition if total sales remain at 2,700 units but the sales mix changes to 2,100 bottles of vitamin C and 600 bottles of vitamin E.

Although the total number of bottles sold remains at 2,700 units, profitability shifts from breaking even to a $280 loss because of the change in the sales mix of the two products, that is, selling more vitamin C than expected and less vitamin E. Because vitamin C has a lower contribution margin ($1.20 per bottle) than vitamin E ($4.00 per bottle), selling more of C and less of E reduces profitability. The opposite impact occurs if Bright Day sells more E and less C. Exhibit 3.6 depicts the expected condition if total sales remain at 2,700 units but the sales mix changes to 1,350 bottles each of vitamin C and vitamin E.

Companies must consider sales mix when conducting break-even analysis for multiproduct business ventures. The multiple product break-even point can be determined using the per unit contribution margin approach. However, it is necessary to use a weighted average to determine the per unit contribution margin. The contribution margin of each product must be weighted by its proportionate share of units sold. For example, in the preceding case, the relative sales mix between the two products is one half (1,350 units ÷ 2,700 units = 50 percent). What is the break-even point given a relative sales mix of one-half for each product? To answer this question, the companies must first determine

EXHIBIT 3.5

Budgeted Data for Antioxidant Special

	Vitamin C			Vitamin E			Total	
	Budgeted Number	Per Unit	Budgeted Amount	Budgeted Number	Per Unit	Budgeted Amount	Budgeted Number	Budgeted Amount
Sales	2,100	@ $7.20 =	$15,120	600	@ $11.00 =	$6,600	2,700	$21,720
Variable cost	2,100	@ 6.00 =	(12,600)	600	@ 7.00 =	(4,200)	2,700	(16,800)
Contribution margin	2,100	@ 1.20 =	2,520	600	@ 4.00 =	2,400	2,700	4,920
Fixed cost			(2,400)			(2,800)		(5,200)
Net income			$ 120			$ (400)		$ (280)

EXHIBIT 3.6

Budgeted Data for Antioxidant Special

	Vitamin C			Vitamin E			Total	
	Budgeted Number	Per Unit	Budgeted Amount	Budgeted Number	Per Unit	Budgeted Amount	Budgeted Number	Budgeted Amount
Sales	1,350	@ $7.20 =	$9,720	1,350	@ $11.00 =	$14,850	2,700	$24,570
Variable cost	1,350	@ 6.00 =	(8,100)	1,350	@ 7.00 =	(9,450)	2,700	(17,550)
Contribution margin	1,350	@ 1.20 =	1,620	1,350	@ 4.00 =	5,400	2,700	7,020
Fixed cost			(2,400)			(2,800)		(5,200)
Net income			$ (780)			$ 2,600		$ 1,820

the weighted average per unit contribution margin by multiplying the contribution margin of each product by 50 percent. The required computation is shown here.

Weighted Average Contribution Margin	
Vitamin C ($1.20 × 0.50)	$0.60
Vitamin E ($4.00 × 0.50)	2.00
Weighted average per unit contribution margin	$2.60

The break-even point in total units at a 50/50 sales mix is computed as follows.

Break-even point = Fixed costs ÷ Weighted average per unit contribution margin

Break-even point = $5,200 ÷ $2.60 = 2,000 total units

Next divide the total units to break even in proportion to the relative sales mix. In other words, the break-even point occurs at 1,000 bottles of Vitamin C (50 percent of 2,000) and 1,000 bottles of Vitamin E (50 percent of 2,000). The income statements presented in Exhibit 3.7 illustrate these results:

EXHIBIT 3.7

Budgeted Data for Antioxidant Special

	Vitamin C			Vitamin E			Total	
	Budgeted Number	**Per Unit**	**Budgeted Amount**	**Budgeted Number**	**Per Unit**	**Budgeted Amount**	**Budgeted Number**	**Budgeted Amount**
Sales	1,000	@ $7.20 =	$ 7,200	1,000	@ $11.00 =	$11,000	2,000	$18,200
Variable cost	1,000	@ 6.00 =	(6,000)	1,000	@ 7.00 =	(7,000)	2,000	(13,000)
Contribution margin	1,000	@ 1.20 =	1,200	1,000	@ 4.00 =	4,000	2,000	5,200
Fixed cost			(2,400)			(2,800)		(5,200)
Net income			$(1,200)			$ 1,200		$ 0

SELF-STUDY REVIEW PROBLEM

A step-by-step audio-narrated series of slides is provided on the text website at **www.mhhe.com/edmonds2008**.

Sharp Company makes and sells pencil sharpeners. The variable cost of each sharpener is $20. The sharpeners are sold for $30 each. Fixed operating expenses amount to $40,000.

Required

a. Determine the break-even point in units and sales dollars.

b. Determine the sales volume in units and dollars that is required to attain a profit of $12,000. Verify your answer by preparing an income statement using the contribution margin format.

c. Determine the margin of safety between sales required to attain a profit of $12,000 and break-even sales.

d. Prepare a break-even graph using the cost and price assumptions outlined above.

Solution to Requirement a

Formula for Computing Break-even Point in Units

$$\frac{\text{Fixed cost} + \text{Target profit}}{\text{Contribution margin per unit}} = \frac{\$40,000 + \$0}{\$30 - \$20} = 4,000 \text{ Units}$$

Break-even Point in Sales Dollars

Sales price	$ 30
Times number of units	4,000
Sales volume in dollars	$120,000

Solution to Requirement b

Formula for Computing Unit Sales Required to Attain Desired Profit

$$\frac{\text{Fixed cost} + \text{Target profit}}{\text{Contribution margin per unit}} = \frac{\$40,000 + \$12,000}{\$30 - \$20} = 5,200 \text{ units}$$

Sales Dollars Required to Attain Desired Profit

Sales price	$ 30
Times number of units	5,200
Sales volume in dollars	$156,000

Income Statement

Sales Volume in Units (a)	5,200
Sales Revenue (a × $30)	$156,000
Variable Costs (a × $20)	(104,000)
Contribution Margin	52,000
Fixed Costs	(40,000)
Net Income	$ 12,000

Solution to Requirement c

Margin of Safety Computations	Units	Dollars
Budgeted sales	5,200	$156,000
Break-even sales	(4,000)	(120,000)
Margin of safety	1,200	$ 36,000

Percentage Computation

$$\frac{\text{Margin of safety in \$}}{\text{Budgeted sales}} = \frac{\$36,000}{\$156,000} = 23.08\%$$

Solution to Requirement d

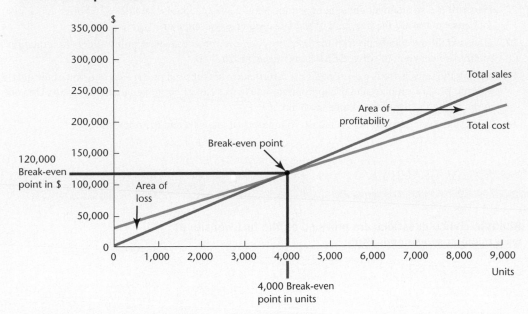

Break-even point 106
Contribution margin per
    unit 106
Contribution margin
    ratio 117

Cost-plus pricing 108
Cost-volume-profit (CVP)
    analysis 105

Equation method 118
Margin of safety 113
Prestige pricing 108

Sensitivity analysis 116
Target pricing (target
    costing) 108

1. What does the term *break-even point* mean? Name the two ways it can be measured.
2. How does a contribution margin income statement differ from the income statement used in financial reporting?
3. In what three ways can the contribution margin be useful in cost-volume-profit analysis?
4. If Company A has a projected margin of safety of 22 percent while Company B has a margin of safety of 52 percent, which company is at greater risk when actual sales are less than budgeted?
5. What variables affect profitability? Name two methods for determining profitability when simultaneous changes occur in these variables.
6. When would the customer be willing to pay a premium price for a product or service? What pricing strategy would be appropriate under these circumstances?
7. What are three alternative approaches to determine the break-even point? What do the results of these approaches show?
8. What is the equation method for determining the break-even point? Explain how the results of this method differ from those of the contribution margin approach.
9. If a company is trying to find the break-even point for multiple products that sell simultaneously, what consideration must be taken into account?
10. What assumptions are inherent in cost-volume-profit analysis? Since these assumptions are usually not wholly valid, why do managers still use the analysis in decision making?
11. Mary Hartwell and Jane Jamail, college roommates, are considering the joint purchase of a computer that they can share to prepare class assignments. Ms. Hartwell wants a particular model that costs $2,000; Ms. Jamail prefers a more economical model that costs $1,500. In fact, Ms. Jamail

is adamant about her position, refusing to contribute more than $750 toward the purchase. If Ms. Hartwell is also adamant about her position, should she accept Ms. Jamail's $750 offer and apply that amount toward the purchase of the more expensive computer?

12. How would the algebraic formula used to compute the break-even point under the equation method be changed to solve for a desired target profit?

13. Setting the sales price is easy: Enter cost information and desired profit data into one of the cost-volume-profit formulas, and the appropriate sales price can be computed mathematically. Do you agree with this line of reasoning? Explain.

14. What is the relationship between cost-volume-profit analysis and the relevant range?

MULTIPLE-CHOICE QUESTIONS

Multiple-choice questions are provided on the text website at www.mhhe.com/edmonds2008.

EXERCISES—SERIES A

All Exercises in Series A are available with McGraw-Hill's Homework Manager®.

L.O. 1

Exercise 3-1A   *Per unit contribution margin approach*

Coburn Corporation sells products for $12 each that have variable costs of $9 per unit. Coburn's annual fixed cost is $240,000.

Required

Use the per unit contribution margin approach to determine the break-even point in units and dollars.

L.O. 1

Exercise 3-2A   *Equation method*

Hamby Corporation produces products that it sells for $7 each. Variable costs per unit are $4, and annual fixed costs are $81,000.

Required

Use the equation method to determine the break-even point in units and dollars.

L.O. 7

Exercise 3-3A   *Contribution margin ratio*

Mozon Company incurs annual fixed costs of $90,000. Variable costs for Mozon's product are $6 per unit, and the sales price is $10 per unit. Mozon desires to earn an annual profit of $30,000.

Required

Use the contribution margin ratio approach to determine the sales volume in dollars and units required to earn the desired profit.

L.O. 7

Exercise 3-4A   *Equation method*

Robinson Company produces a product that sells for $21 per unit and has a variable cost of $15 per unit. Robinson incurs annual fixed costs of $230,000. It desires to earn a profit of $70,000.

Required

Use the equation method to determine the sales volume in units and dollars required to earn the desired profit.

L.O. 1

Exercise 3-5A   *Determining fixed and variable cost per unit*

Wolfe Corporation produced and sold 30,000 units of product during October. It earned a contribution margin of $90,000 on sales of $240,000 and determined that cost per unit of product was $7.

Required

Based on this information, determine the variable and fixed cost per unit of product.

Exercise 3-6A *Determining variable cost from incomplete cost data* **L.O. 1**

Bostany Corporation produced 150,000 watches that it sold for $24 each during 2006. The company determined that fixed manufacturing cost per unit was $6 per watch. The company reported a $600,000 gross margin on its 2006 financial statements.

Required

Determine the total variable cost, the variable cost per unit, and the total contribution margin.

Exercise 3-7A *Contribution margin per unit approach for break-even and desired profit* **L.O. 1**

Information concerning a product produced by Morris Company appears here.

Sales price per unit	$200
Variable cost per unit	$110
Total annual fixed manufacturing and operating costs	$630,000

Required

Determine the following:

a. Contribution margin per unit.
b. Number of units that Morris must sell to break even.
c. Sales level in units that Morris must reach to earn a profit of $270,000.

Exercise 3-8A *Changing sales price* **L.O. 3**

Smith Company produces a product that has a variable cost of $6 per unit; the product sells for $13 per unit. The company's annual fixed costs total $350,000; it had net income of $70,000 in the previous year. In an effort to increase the company's market share, management is considering lowering the selling price to $11.60 per unit.

Required

If Smith desires to maintain net income of $70,000, how many additional units must it sell to justify the price decline?

Exercise 3-9A *Simultaneous change in sales price and desired profit* **L.O. 3**

Use the cost data presented in Exercise 3-8A but assume that in addition to increasing its market share by lowering its selling price to $11.60, Smith desires to increase its net income by $14,000

Required

Determine the number of units the company must sell to earn the desired income.

Exercise 3-10A *Components of break-even graph* **L.O. 1, 4**

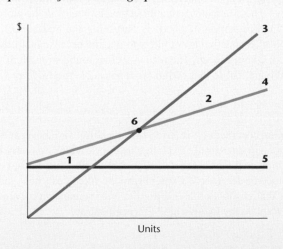

Required

Match the numbers shown in the graph with the following items.

a. Fixed cost line   d. Area of profit
b. Total cost line   e. Revenue line
c. Break-even point   f. Area of loss

L.O. 7

Exercise 3-11A   *Evaluating simultaneous changes in fixed and variable costs*

Kendall Company currently produces and sells 9,000 units annually of a product that has a variable cost of $15 per unit and annual fixed costs of $240,000. The company currently earns a $30,000 annual profit. Assume that Kendall has the opportunity to invest in new labor-saving production equipment that will enable the company to reduce variable costs to $13 per unit. The investment would cause fixed costs to increase by $12,000 because of additional depreciation cost.

Required

a. Use the equation method to determine the sales price per unit under existing conditions (current equipment is used).
b. Prepare a contribution margin income statement, assuming that Kendall invests in the new production equipment. Recommend whether Kendall should invest in the new equipment.

L.O. 5

Exercise 3-12A   *Margin of safety*

Roscoe Company makes a product that sells for $18 per unit. The company pays $8 per unit for the variable costs of the product and incurs annual fixed costs of $150,000. Roscoe expects to sell 24,000 units of product.

Required

Determine Roscoe's margin of safety expressed as a percentage.

L.O. 1, 3

Exercise 3-13A   *Cost-volume-profit relationship*

Tribble Corporation is a manufacturing company that makes small electric motors it sells for $30 per unit. The variable costs of production are $24 per motor, and annual fixed costs of production are $90,000.

Required

a. How many units of product must Tribble make and sell to break even?
b. How many units of product must Tribble make and sell to earn an $18,000 profit?
c. The marketing manager believes that sales would increase dramatically if the price were reduced to $29 per unit. How many units of product must Tribble make and sell to earn an $18,000 profit, if the sales price is set at $29 per unit?

L.O. 3

Exercise 3-14A   *Understanding of the global economy through CVP relationships*

An article published in the December 8, 1997, issue of *U.S. News & World Report* summarized several factors likely to support a continuing decline in the rate of inflation over the next decade. Specifically, the article stated that "global competition has . . . fostered an environment of cheap labor, cost cutting, and increased efficiency." The article notes that these developments in the global economy have led to a condition in which "the production of goods is outpacing the number of consumers able to buy them." Even so, the level of production is not likely to decline because factories have been built in developing countries where labor is cheap. The recent decline in the strength of the Asian economies is likely to have a snowballing effect so that within the foreseeable future, there will "be too many goods chasing too few buyers."

Required

a. Identify the production cost factor(s) referred to that exhibit variable cost behavior. Has (have) the cost factor(s) increased or decreased? Explain why the variable costs have increased or decreased.
b. Identify the production cost factor(s) referred to that exhibit fixed cost behavior. Has (have) the cost factor(s) increased or decreased? Explain why the fixed costs have increased or decreased.
c. The article implies that production levels are likely to remain high even though demand is expected to be weak. Explain the logic behind this implication.

d. The article suggests that manufacturers will continue to produce goods even though they may have to sell goods at a price that is below the total cost of production. Considering what you know about fixed and variable costs, speculate on how low manufacturers would permit prices to drop before they would stop production.

Exercise 3-15A   *Target costing*   L.O. 2

The marketing manager of Wei Corporation has determined that a market exists for a telephone with a sales price of $29 per unit. The production manager estimates the annual fixed costs of producing between 20,000 and 40,000 telephones would be $180,000.

Required

Assume that Wei desires to earn a $60,000 profit from the phone sales. How much can Wei afford to spend on variable cost per unit if production and sales equal 30,000 phones?

Appendix A

Exercise 3-16A   *Multiple product break-even analysis*   L.O. 8

O'Clair Company manufactures two products. The budgeted per unit contribution margin for each product follows.

	Panorama	Vista
Sales price	$85	$98
Variable cost per unit	(45)	(38)
Contribution margin per unit	$40	$60

O'Clair expects to incur annual fixed costs of $90,000. The relative sales mix of the products is 75 percent for Panorama and 25 percent for Vista.

Required

a. Determine the total number of products (units of Panorama and Vista combined) O'Clair must sell to break even.
b. How many units each of Panorama and Vista must O'Clair sell to break even?

PROBLEMS—SERIES A

All Problems in Series A are available with McGraw-Hill's Homework Manager®.

Problem 3-17A   *Determining the break-even point and preparing a contribution margin income statement*

L.O. 1, 7

e**X**cel

www.mhhe.com/edmonds2008

Latoma Manufacturing Company makes a product that it sells for $45 per unit. The company incurs variable manufacturing costs of $21 per unit. Variable selling expenses are $6 per unit, annual fixed manufacturing costs are $100,000, and fixed selling and administrative costs are $80,000 per year.

Required

Determine the break-even point in units and dollars using each of the following approaches.

a. Contribution margin per unit.
b. Equation method.
c. Contribution margin ratio.
d. Confirm your results by preparing a contribution margin income statement for the break-even sales volume.

CHECK FIGURE
a. 10,000 units

Problem 3-18A   *Determining the break-even point and preparing a break-even graph*

L.O. 1, 4, 7

Purcell Company is considering the production of a new product. The expected variable cost is $45 per unit. Annual fixed costs are expected to be $570,000. The anticipated sales price is $60 each.

CHECK FIGURE
a. $2,280,000

Required

Determine the break-even point in units and dollars using each of the following.

a. Contribution margin per unit approach.
b. Equation method.
c. Contribution margin ratio approach.
d. Prepare a break-even graph to illustrate the cost-volume-profit relationships.

L.O. 1, 3

CHECK FIGURE

b. 32,500 units

Problem 3-19A   *Effect of converting variable to fixed costs*

Hoskins Manufacturing Company reported the following data regarding a product it manufactures and sells. The sales price is $32.

Variable costs	
Manufacturing	$15 per unit
Selling	9 per unit
Fixed costs	
Manufacturing	$160,000 per year
Selling and administrative	40,000 per year

Required

a. Use the per unit contribution margin approach to determine the break-even point in units and dollars.
b. Use the per unit contribution margin approach to determine the level of sales in units and dollars required to obtain a profit of $60,000.
c. Suppose that variable selling costs could be eliminated by employing a salaried sales force. If the company could sell 32,000 units, how much could it pay in salaries for salespeople and still have a profit of $60,000? (*Hint:* Use the equation method.)

L.O. 7

CHECK FIGURE

c. 37,500 units

Problem 3-20A   *Analyzing change in sales price using the contribution margin ratio*

Bonin Company reported the following data regarding the product it sells.

Sales price	$32
Contribution margin ratio	20%
Fixed costs	$540,000

Required

Use the contribution margin ratio approach and consider each requirement separately.

a. What is the break-even point in dollars? In units?
b. To obtain a profit of $80,000, what must the sales be in dollars? In units?
c. If the sales price increases to $40 and variable costs do not change, what is the new break-even point in dollars? In units?

L.O. 7

e**X**cel

www.mhhe.com/edmonds2008

CHECK FIGURE

a. 8,000 units

Problem 3-21A   *Analyzing sales price and fixed cost using the equation method*

Abdur Company is considering adding a new product. The cost accountant has provided the following data.

Expected variable cost of manufacturing	$47 per unit
Expected annual fixed manufacturing costs	$78,000

The administrative vice president has provided the following estimates.

Expected sales commission	$3 per unit
Expected annual fixed administrative costs	$42,000

The manager has decided that any new product must at least break even in the first year.

Required

Use the equation method and consider each requirement separately.

a. If the sales price is set at $65, how many units must Abdur sell to break even?
b. Abdur estimates that sales will probably be 10,000 units. What sales price per unit will allow the company to break even?
c. Abdur has decided to advertise the product heavily and has set the sales price at $66. If sales are 9,000 units, how much can the company spend on advertising and still break even?

Problem 3-22A *Margin of safety and operating leverage*

Triozzl Company is considering the addition of a new product to its cosmetics line. The company has three distinctly different options: a skin cream, a bath oil, or a hair coloring gel. Relevant information and budgeted annual income statements for each of the products follow.

Relevant Information	Skin Cream	Bath Oil	Color Gel
Budgeted Sales in Units (a)	70,000	120,000	40,000
Expected Sales Price (b)	$8	$3	$12
Variable Costs Per Unit (c)	$5	$1	$ 7
Income Statements			
Sales Revenue (a × b)	$560,000	$360,000	$480,000
Variable Costs (a × c)	(350,000)	(120,000)	(280,000)
Contribution Margin	210,000	240,000	200,000
Fixed Costs	(150,000)	(200,000)	(150,000)
Net Income	$ 60,000	$ 40,000	$ 50,000

Required

a. Determine the margin of safety as a percentage for each product.
b. Prepare revised income statements for each product, assuming a 20 percent increase in the budgeted sales volume.
c. For each product, determine the percentage change in net income that results from the 20 percent increase in sales. Which product has the highest operating leverage?
d. Assuming that management is pessimistic and risk averse, which product should the company add to its cosmetic line? Explain your answer.
e. Assuming that management is optimistic and risk aggressive, which product should the company add to its cosmetics line? Explain your answer.

Problem 3-23A *Comprehensive CVP analysis*

Kersh Company makes and sells products with variable costs of $40 each. Kersh incurs annual fixed costs of $32,000. The current sales price is $60.

Required

The following requirements are interdependent. For example, the $8,000 desired profit introduced in Requirement *c* also applies to subsequent requirements. Likewise, the $50 sales price introduced in Requirement *d* applies to the subsequent requirements.

a. Determine the contribution margin per unit.
b. Determine the break-even point in units and in dollars. Confirm your answer by preparing an income statement using the contribution margin format.
c. Suppose that Kersh desires to earn an $8,000 profit. Determine the sales volume in units and dollars required to earn the desired profit. Confirm your answer by preparing an income statement using the contribution margin format.
d. If the sales price drops to $50 per unit, what level of sales is required to earn the desired profit? Express your answer in units and dollars. Confirm your answer by preparing an income statement using the contribution margin format.

e. If fixed costs drop to $24,000, what level of sales is required to earn the desired profit? Express your answer in units and dollars. Confirm your answer by preparing an income statement using the contribution margin format.

f. If variable cost drops to $30 per unit, what level of sales is required to earn the desired profit? Express your answer in units and dollars. Confirm your answer by preparing an income statement using the contribution margin format.

g. Assume that Kersh concludes that it can sell 1,600 units of product for $50 each. Recall that variable costs are $30 each and fixed costs are $24,000. Compute the margin of safety in units and dollars and as a percentage.

h. Draw a break-even graph using the cost and price assumptions described in Requirement g.

L.O. 1, 3, 4, 5

CHECK FIGURES
a. $750,000
c. 6,750 units

Problem 3-24A *Assessing simultaneous changes in CVP relationships*

Hinkle Corporation sells hammocks; variable costs are $75 each, and the hammocks are sold for $125 each. Hinkle incurs $250,000 of fixed operating expenses annually.

Required

a. Determine the sales volume in units and dollars required to attain a $50,000 profit. Verify your answer by preparing an income statement using the contribution margin format.

b. Hinkle is considering implementing a quality improvement program. The program will require a $10 increase in the variable cost per unit. To inform its customers of the quality improvements, the company plans to spend an additional $20,000 for advertising. Assuming that the improvement program will increase sales to a level that is 3,000 units above the amount computed in Requirement *a,* should Hinkle proceed with plans to improve product quality? Support your answer by preparing a budgeted income statement.

c. Determine the new break-even point in units and sales dollars as well as the margin of safety percentage, assuming that the quality improvement program is implemented.

d. Prepare a break-even graph using the cost and price assumptions outlined in Requirement *b.*

Appendix

L.O. 8

eXcel

www.mhhe.com/edmonds2008

Problem 3-25A *Determining the break-even point and margin of safety for a company with multiple products*

Mendoza Company produces two products. Budgeted annual income statements for the two products are provided here.

	Power			Lite			Total	
	Budgeted Number	Per Unit	Budgeted Amount	Budgeted Number	Per Unit	Budgeted Amount	Budgeted Number	Budgeted Amount
Sales	160	@ $500 =	$80,000	640	@ $450 =	$288,000	800	$368,000
Variable Cost	160	@ 320 =	(51,200)	640	@ 330 =	(211,200)	800	(262,400)
Contribution Margin	160	@ 180 =	28,800	640	@ 120 =	76,800	800	105,600
Fixed Cost			(12,000)			(54,000)		(66,000)
Net Income			$16,800			$ 22,800		$ 39,600

CHECK FIGURES
d. Power: 100 units
Lite: 400 units

Required

a. Based on budgeted sales, determine the relative sales mix between the two products.

b. Determine the weighted-average contribution margin per unit.

c. Calculate the break-even point in total number of units.

d. Determine the number of units of each product Mendoza must sell to break even.

e. Verify the break-even point by preparing an income statement for each product as well as an income statement for the combined products.

f. Determine the margin of safety based on the combined sales of the two products.

Exercise 3-1B   *Per unit contribution margin approach*   L.O. 1

Hunt Corporation manufactures products that have variable costs of $6 per unit. Its fixed cost amounts to $75,000. It sells the produce for $9 each.

Required

Use the per unit contribution margin approach to determine the break-even point in units and dollars.

Exercise 3-2B   *Equation method*   L.O. 7

Gann Corporation manufactures products that it sells for $29 each. Variable costs are $20 per unit, and annual fixed costs are $450,000.

Required

Use the equation method to determine the break-even point in units and dollars.

Exercise 3-3B   *Contribution margin ratio*   L.O. 7

Craw Company incurs annual fixed costs of $140,000. Variable costs for Craw's product are $12 per unit, and the sales price is $20 per unit. Craw desires to earn a profit of $40,000.

Required

Use the contribution margin ratio approach to determine the sales volume in dollars and units required to earn the desired profit.

Exercise 3-4B   *Equation method*   L.O. 7

Madden Company manufactures a product that sells for $71 per unit. It incurs fixed costs of $390,000. Variable cost for its product is $50 per unit. Madden desires to earn a target profit of $240,000.

Required

Use the equation method to determine the sales volume in units and dollars required to earn the desired profit.

Exercise 3-5B   *Fixed and variable cost per unit*   L.O. 1

Seibel Corporation broke even by producing and selling 20,000 units of product during 2007. It earned a contribution margin of $80,000 on sales of $480,000. The company determined that cost per unit of product was $27.

Required

Based on this information, determine the variable and fixed cost per unit of product.

Exercise 3-6B   *Determining variable cost from incomplete data*   L.O. 1

Talentino Corporation produced 75,000 tires and sold them for $60 each during 2007. The company determined that fixed manufacturing cost per unit was $16 per tire. The company reported gross profit of $900,000 on its 2007 financial statements.

Required

Determine the total variable cost, the variable cost per unit, and the total contribution margin.

Exercise 3-7B   *Contribution margin per unit approach for break-even and desired profit* L.O. 1

Information concerning a product produced by Willowby Company appears here:

Sales price per unit	$420
Variable cost per unit	$270
Total fixed manufacturing and operating costs	$750,000

Required

Determine the following:

a. Contribution margin per unit.
b. Number of units Willowby must sell to break even.
c. Sales level in units that Willowby must reach in order to earn a profit of $150,000.

L.O. 3   **Exercise 3-8B**   *Change in sales price*

Zucco Company manufactures a product that has a variable cost of $13 per unit. The company's fixed costs total $280,000. Zucco had net income of $80,000 in the previous year. Its product sells for $25 per unit. In an effort to increase the company's market share, management is considering lowering the product's selling price to $23 per unit.

Required

If Zucco desires to maintain net income of $80,000, how many additional units must it sell in order to justify the price decline?

L.O. 3   **Exercise 3-9B**   *Simultaneous change in sales price and desired profit*

Use the cost data presented in Exercise 3-8B, but assume that in addition to increasing its market share by lowering its selling price to $23, Zucco desires to increase its net income by $40,000.

Required

Determine the number of units that Zucco must sell to earn the desired income.

L.O. 1, 4   **Exercise 3-10B**   *Components of break-even graph*

Peter, a 10-year-old boy, wants to sell lemonade on a hot summer day. He hopes to make enough money to buy a new iPod. John, his elder brother, tries to help him compute his prospect of doing so. The following is the relevant information:

Variable costs	
Lemonade	$0.30 per cup
Paper cup	$0.10 per cup
Fixed costs	
Table and chair	$36.00
Price	$1.00 per cup

The following graph depicts the dollar amount of cost or revenue on the vertical axis and the number of lemonade cups sold on the horizontal axis.

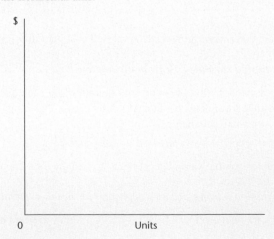

Required

a. Draw a line that depicts the total cost.
b. Draw a line that depicts the total revenue.
c. Identify the break-even point.
d. Identify the area representing profit.
e. Identify the area representing loss.

Exercise 3-11B   *Evaluating simultaneous changes in fixed and variable costs*   L.O. 7

Ramirez Company currently produces and sells 10,000 units of a telephone per year that has a variable cost of $13 per unit and a fixed cost of $380,000. The company currently earns a $120,000 annual profit. Assume that Ramirez has the opportunity to invest in a new machine that will enable the company to reduce variable costs to $10 per unit. The investment would cause fixed costs to increase by $15,000.

Required

a. Use the equation method to determine the sales price per unit under existing conditions (current machine is used).
b. Prepare a contribution margin income statement assuming Ramirez invests in the new technology. Recommend whether Ramirez should invest in the new technology.

Exercise 3-12B   *Margin of safety*   L.O. 5

Noel Company manufactures scanners that sell for $135 each. The company pays $55 per unit for the variable costs of the product and incurs fixed costs of $1,600,000. Noel expects to sell 36,000 scanners.

Required

Determine Noel's margin of safety expressed as a percentage.

Exercise 3-13B   *Cost-volume-profit relationship*   L.O. 1, 3

Larusso Corporation manufactures faucets. The variable costs of production are $7 per faucet. Fixed costs of production are $81,000. Larusso sells the faucets for a price of $25 per unit.

Required

a. How many faucets must Larusso make and sell to break even?
b. How many faucets must Larusso make and sell to earn a $27,000 profit?
c. The marketing manager believes that sales would increase dramatically if the price were reduced to $22 per unit. How many faucets must Larusso make and sell to earn a $27,000 profit, assuming the sales price is set at $22 per unit?

Exercise 3-14B   *Understanding the global economy through CVP relationships*   L.O. 3

An article published in the April 2, 2001, issue of *BusinessWeek* summarized several factors that had contributed to the economic slowdown that started in the fourth quarter of 2000. Specifically, the article stated, "When companies lowered their demand forecasts, they concluded that they didn't have just a little excess capacity—they had massive excessive capacity, . . ." The article continues to argue that companies with too much capacity have no desire to invest, no matter how low interest rates are.

Required

a. Identify the production cost factor(s) referred to that exhibit variable cost behavior. Has (have) the cost factor(s) increased or decreased? Explain why the variable costs have increased or decreased.
b. Identify the production cost factor(s) referred to that exhibit fixed cost behavior. Has (have) the cost factor(s) increased or decreased? Explain why the fixed costs have increased or decreased.
c. The article argues that new investments in production facilities will decrease. Explain the logic behind this argument.
d. In an economic downturn, manufacturers are pressured to sell their product at low prices. Comment on how low a manufacturer's prices can go before management decides to quit production.

Exercise 3-15B   *Target costing*   L.O. 2

After substantial marketing research, Ingram Corporation management believes that it can make and sell a new battery with a prolonged life for laptop computers. Management expects the market demand for its new battery to be 10,000 units per year if the battery is priced at $120 per unit. A team of engineers and accountants determines that the fixed costs of producing 8,000 units to 16,000 units is $450,000.

Required

Assume that Ingram desires to earn a $200,000 profit from the battery sales. How much can it afford to spend on variable cost per unit if production and sales equal 10,000 batteries?

Appendix

L.O. 8   **Exercise 3-16B**   *Multiple product break-even analysis*

Gardner Company makes two products. The budgeted per unit contribution margin for each product follows:

	Product M	Product N
Sales price	$48	$75
Variable cost per unit	33	40
Contribution margin per unit	$15	$35

Gardner expects to incur fixed costs of $115,000. The relative sales mix of the products is 60 percent for Product M and 40 percent for Product N.

Required

a. Determine the total number of products (units of M and N combined) Gardner must sell to break even.
b. How many units each of Product M and Product N must Gardner sell to break even?

PROBLEMS—SERIES B

L.O. 1, 7   **Problem 3-17B**   *Determining the break-even point and preparing a contribution margin income statement*

Dade Company manufactures radio and cassette players and sells them for $100 each. According to the company's records, the variable costs, including direct labor and direct materials, are $50. Factory depreciation and other fixed manufacturing costs are $192,000 per year. Dade pays its salespeople a commission of $18 per unit. Annual fixed selling and administrative costs are $128,000.

Required

Determine the break-even point in units and dollars, using each of the following.

a. Contribution margin per unit approach.
b. Equation method.
c. Contribution margin ratio approach.
d. Confirm your results by preparing a contribution margin income statement for the break-even point sales volume.

L.O. 1, 4, 7   **Problem 3-18B**   *Determining the break-even point and preparing a break-even graph*

Executive officers of Bozeman Company are assessing the profitability of a potential new product. They expect that the variable cost of making the product will be $36 per unit and fixed manufacturing cost will be $480,000. The executive officers plan to sell the product for $60 per unit.

Required

Determine the break-even point in units and dollars using each of the following approaches.

a. Contribution margin per unit.
b. Equation method.
c. Contribution margin ratio.
d. Prepare a break-even graph to illustrate the cost-volume-profit relationships.

L.O. 1, 3   **Problem 3-19B**   *Effect of converting variable to fixed costs*

Perdue Company manufactures and sells its own brand of cameras. It sells each camera for $42. The company's accountant prepared the following data:

Manufacturing costs	
Variable	$18 per unit
Fixed	$150,000 per year
Selling and administrative expenses	
Variable	$6 per unit
Fixed	$66,000 per year

Required

a. Use the per unit contribution margin approach to determine the break-even point in units and dollars.
b. Use the per unit contribution margin approach to determine the level of sales in units and dollars required to obtain a $126,000 profit.
c. Suppose that variable selling and administrative costs could be eliminated by employing a salaried sales force. If the company could sell 20,000 units, how much could it pay in salaries for the salespeople and still have a profit of $126,000? (*Hint:* Use the equation method.)

Problem 3-20B *Analyzing change in sales price using the contribution margin ratio*   **L.O. 7**

Kahn Company reported the following data regarding the one product it sells.

Sales price	$80
Contribution margin ratio	20%
Fixed costs	$160,000 per year

Required

Use the contribution margin ratio approach and consider each requirement separately.

a. What is the break-even point in dollars? In units?
b. To obtain a $80,000 profit, what must the sales be in dollars? In units?
c. If the sales price increases to $84 and variable costs do not change, what is the new break-even point in units? In dollars?

Problem 3-21B *Analyzing sales price and fixed cost using the equation method*   **L.O. 7**

Medlock Company is analyzing whether its new product will be profitable. The following data are provided for analysis.

Expected variable cost of manufacturing	$30 per unit
Expected fixed manufacturing costs	$48,000 per year
Expected sales commission	$6 per unit
Expected fixed administrative costs	$12,000 per year

The company has decided that any new product must at least break even in the first year.

Required

Use the equation method and consider each requirement separately.

a. If the sales price is set at $48, how many units must Medlock sell to break even?
b. Medlock estimates that sales will probably be 6,000 units. What sales price per unit will allow the company to break even?
c. Medlock has decided to advertise the product heavily and has set the sales price at $54. If sales are 9,000 units, how much can the company spend on advertising and still break even?

Problem 3-22B *Margin of safety and operating leverage*   **L.O. 5**

Powney Company has three distinctly different options available as it considers adding a new product to its automotive division: engine oil, coolant, or windshield washer. Relevant information and budgeted annual income statements for each product follow.

	Relevant Information		
	Engine Oil	**Coolant**	**Windshield Washer**
Budgeted Sales in Units (a)	20,000	30,000	125,000
Expected Sales Price (b)	$2.40	$2.85	$1.15
Variable Costs Per Unit (c)	$1.00	$1.25	$0.35
Income Statements			
Sales Revenue (a × b)	$48,000	$85,500	$143,750
Variable Costs (a × c)	(20,000)	(37,500)	(43,750)
Contribution Margin	28,000	48,000	100,000
Fixed Costs	(21,000)	(32,000)	(50,000)
Net Income	$ 7,000	$16,000	$ 50,000

Required

a. Determine the margin of safety as a percentage for each product.

b. Prepare revised income statements for each product, assuming 20 percent growth in the budgeted sales volume.

c. For each product, determine the percentage change in net income that results from the 20 percent increase in sales. Which product has the highest operating leverage?

d. Assuming that management is pessimistic and risk averse, which product should the company add? Explain your answer.

e. Assuming that management is optimistic and risk aggressive, which product should the company add? Explain your answer.

L.O. 1, 3, 4, 5 **Problem 3-23B** *Comprehensive CVP analysis*

Choate Company makes a product that it sells for $150. Choate incurs annual fixed costs of $160,000 and variable costs of $100 per unit.

Required

The following requirements are interdependent. For example, the $40,000 desired profit introduced in Requirement *c* also applies to subsequent requirements. Likewise, the $140 sales price introduced in Requirement *d* applies to the subsequent requirements.

a. Determine the contribution margin per unit.

b. Determine the break-even point in units and in dollars. Confirm your answer by preparing an income statement using the contribution margin format.

c. Suppose that Choate desires to earn a $40,000 profit. Determine the sales volume in units and dollars required to earn the desired profit. Confirm your answer by preparing an income statement using the contribution margin format.

d. If the sales price drops to $140 per unit, what level of sales is required to earn the desired profit? Express your answer in units and dollars. Confirm your answer by preparing an income statement using the contribution margin format.

e. If fixed costs drop to $140,000, what level of sales is required to earn the desired profit? Express your answer in units and dollars. Confirm your answer by preparing an income statement using the contribution margin format.

f. If variable costs drop to $80 per unit, what level of sales is required to earn the desired profit? Express your answer in units and dollars. Confirm your answer by preparing an income statement using the contribution margin format.

g. Assume that Choate concludes that it can sell 4,800 units of product for $136 each. Recall that variable costs are $80 each and fixed costs are $140,000. Compute the margin of safety in units and dollars and as a percentage.

h. Draw a break-even graph using the cost and price assumptions described in Requirement *g*.

Problem 3-24B *Assessing simultaneous changes in CVP relationships*   **L.O. 1, 3, 4, 5**

Vanhorn Company sells tennis racquets; variable costs for each are $75, and each is sold for $105. Vanhorn incurs $270,000 of fixed operating expenses annually.

Required

a. Determine the sales volume in units and dollars required to attain a $120,000 profit. Verify your answer by preparing an income statement using the contribution margin format.

b. Vanhorn is considering establishing a quality improvement program that will require a $10 increase in the variable cost per unit. To inform its customers of the quality improvements, the company plans to spend an additional $60,000 for advertising. Assuming that the improvement program will increase sales to a level that is 5,000 units above the amount computed in Requirement *a*, should Vanhorn proceed with plans to improve product quality? Support your answer by preparing a budgeted income statement.

c. Determine the new break-even point and the margin of safety percentage, assuming Vanhorn adopts the quality improvement program.

d. Prepare a break-even graph using the cost and price assumptions outlined in Requirement *b*.

Appendix

Problem 3-25B *Determining the break-even point and margin of safety for a company with*   **L.O. 8**
                  multiple products

Executive officers of Collier Company have prepared the annual budgets for its two products, Washer and Dryer, as follows.

	Washer			**Dryer**			**Total**	
	Budgeted Quantity	**Per Unit**	**Budgeted Amount**	**Budgeted Quantity**	**Per Unit**	**Budgeted Amount**	**Budgeted Quantity**	**Budgeted Amount**
Sales	400	@ $540 =	$216,000	1,200	@ $300 =	$360,000	1,600	$576,000
Variable Cost	400	@ 300 =	(120,000)	1,200	@ 180 =	(216,000)	1,600	(336,000)
Contribution Margin	400	@ 240 =	96,000	1,200	@ 120 =	144,000	1,600	240,000
Fixed Costs			(34,000)			(44,000)		(78,000)
Net Income			$ 62,000			$100,000		$162,000

Required

a. Based on the number of units budgeted to be sold, determine the relative sales mix between the two products.

b. Determine the weighted-average contribution margin per unit.

c. Calculate the break-even point in total number of units.

d. Determine the number of units of each product Collier must sell to break even.

e. Verify the break-even point by preparing an income statement for each product as well as an income statement for the combined products.

f. Determine the margin of safety based on the combined sales of the two products.

ANALYZE, THINK, COMMUNICATE

ATC 3-1 **Business Applications Case** *Cost-volume-profit behavior at Apple Computer, Inc.*

On April 14, 2004, Apple Computer announced that revenues for the second quarter of its 2004 fiscal year rose 29 percent, causing earnings to increase by 300 percent compared with the second quarter of the previous year. This increase was largely due to significantly higher sales of its iPod MP3 music players. Sales for this quarter were $1.91 billion.

On January 12, 2005, Apple announced that revenue for the first quarter of its 2005 fiscal year rose 74 percent causing earnings to increase by 468 percent compared with the second quarter of the previous year. Sales for this quarter were $3.49 billion. As in the previous year, sales of Apple's iPod continued to rise much faster than sales of its personal computers. By the end of 2004, revenue generated from iPod sales was considerably more than revenue from Apple's computer sales.

Required

a. What concept explains how Apple's net income could rise 300 percent when its revenue rose only 29 percent?

b. Does the concept identified in Requirement *a* result from fixed costs or variable costs?

c. Notice that in the second quarter of 2004 Apple's percentage increase in earnings was over 10 times more than the percentage increase in its revenue ($300 \div 29 = 10.3$). In the first quarter of 2005, however, Apple's percentage increase in earnings was only about six times that of revenue ($468 \div 74 = 6.3$). Explain why the ratio of increase in earnings to increase in revenue was lower in 2005 than in 2004. Assume Apple's general pricing policies and cost structure did not change.

ATC 3-2   **Group Assignment**   *Effect of changes in fixed and variable cost on profitability*

In a month when it sold 200 units of product, Queen Manufacturing Company (QMC) produced the following internal income statement.

Revenue	$8,000
Variable Costs	(4,800)
Contribution Margin	3,200
Fixed Costs	(2,400)
Net Income	$ 800

QMC has the opportunity to alter its operations in one of the following ways:

1. Increasing fixed advertising costs by $1,600, thereby increasing sales by 120 units.
2. Lowering commissions paid to the sales staff by $8 per unit, thereby reducing sales by 10 units.
3. Decreasing fixed inventory holding cost by $800, thereby decreasing sales by 20 units.

Required

a. The instructor will divide the class into groups and then organize the groups into two sections. For a large class (12 or more groups), four sections may be necessary. At least three groups in each section are needed. Having more groups in one section than another section is acceptable because offsetting advantages and disadvantages exist. Having more groups is advantageous because more people will work on the task but is disadvantageous because having more people complicates communication.

Group Task

The sections are to compete with each other to see which section can identify the most profitable alternative in the shortest period of time. No instruction is provided regarding how the sections are to proceed with the task. In other words, each section is required to organize itself with respect to how to accomplish the task of selecting the best alternative. A total quality management (TQM) constraint is imposed that requires zero defects. A section that turns in a wrong answer is disqualified. Once an answer has been submitted to the instructor, it cannot be changed. Sections continue to turn in answers until all sections have submitted a response. The first section to submit the correct answer wins the competition.

b. If any section submits a wrong answer, the instructor or a spokesperson from the winning group should explain how the right answer was determined.

c. Discuss the dynamics of group interaction. How was the work organized? How was leadership established?

ATC 3-3   **Research Assignment**   *Effect of costs changes*

An article in the January 26, 2004, issue of *BusinessWeek* explains how automobile manufacturers in the United States are beginning to adopt a practice already prevalent among Japanese manufacturers.

Specifically, rather than build each model of vehicle on its own unique chassis, or platform, the same basic platform is being used as the foundation for several very different models. For example, Honda uses the platform designed for the Civic as the platform for the CR-V, Element, and Acura R-SX.

Required

Read the article, "Detroit Tries It the Japanese Way," *BusinessWeek,* January 26, 2004, pp. 76–77. Based on the information in the article, prepare a memorandum that identifies as many reasons as you can think of to explain how using the same platform to produce several different models will reduce automobile manufacturers' costs. Be specific, and consider not only the concepts introduced in this chapter but also those from Chapters 1 and 2. For each reason you identify, provide a brief explanation about how this factor will help reduce the companies' costs. Also, explain which type of cost, fixed or variable, would be affected the most by the use of one platform to produce multiple models.

ATC 3-4 Writing Assignment *Operating leverage, margin of safety, and cost behavior*

The article "Up Front: More Condensing at the Digest?" in the October 19, 1998, issue of *BusinessWeek* reported that Thomas Ryder, CEO of Reader's Digest Association, was considering a spin-off of Reader's Digest's direct-marketing operations into a joint venture with Time Warner. The article's author, Robert McNatt, noted that the direct marketing of books, music, and videos is a far larger part of the Reader's Digest business than is its namesake magazine. Furthermore, the article stated that 1998 direct-marketing sales of $1.6 billion were down 11 percent from 1997. The decline in revenue caused the division's operating profits to decline 58 percent. The article stated that the contemplated alliance with Time Warner could provide some fast help. Gerald Levin, Time Warner chairman, has said that his company's operations provide customer service and product fulfillment far better than other Web sellers do because of Time Warner's established 250 Web sites.

Required

a. Write a memo explaining how an 11 percent decrease in sales could result in a 58 percent decline in operating profits.
b. Explain briefly how the decline in revenue will affect the company's margin of safety.
c. Explain why a joint venture between Reader's Digest's direct-marketing division and Time Warner could work to the advantage of both companies. (*Hint:* Consider the effects of fixed-cost behavior in formulating your response.)

ATC 3-5 Ethical Dilemma *Manipulating reported earnings*

The article "Garbage In, Garbage Out" (*Fortune,* May 25, 1998, pp. 130–38) describes a litany of questionable accounting practices that ultimately led to the demise of Waste Management, Inc. Under pressure to retain its reputation on Wall Street as a growth company, Waste Management extended its estimates of the lives of its garbage trucks two to four years beyond the standard used in the industry. It also began to use a $25,000 expected salvage value on each truck when the industry standard was to recognize a zero salvage value. Because Waste Management owned approximately 20,000 trucks, these moves had a significant impact on the company's earnings. Extended lives and exaggerated salvage values were also applied to the company's 1.5 million steel dumpsters and its landfill facilities. These accounting practices boosted reported earnings by approximately $110 million per year. The long-term effect on real earnings was disastrous, however; maintenance costs began to soar and the company was forced to spend millions to keep broken-down trucks on the road. Overvalued assets failed to generate expected revenues. The failure to maintain earnings growth ultimately led to the replacement of management. When the new managers discovered the misstated accounting numbers, the company was forced to recognize a pretax charge of $3.54 billion in its 1997 income statement. The stock price plummeted, and the company was ultimately merged out of existence.

Required

a. Did Waste Management manipulate the recognition of fixed or variable costs?
b. Explain how extending the life estimate of an asset increases earnings and the book value of assets.
c. Explain how inflating the salvage value of an asset increases earnings and the book value of assets.
d. Speculate as to what motive would cause executives to manipulate earnings.
e. Review the standards of ethical conduct shown in Exhibit 1.15 of Chapter 1 and comment on whether Waste Management's accounting practices violated any standards.
f. Comment on the provisions of the Sarbanes-Oxley Act that are designed to prevent the type of fraudulent reporting described in this case.

ATC 3-6 Spreadsheet Assignment *Using Excel*

Bishop Company has provided the estimated data that appear in rows 4 to 8 of the following spreadsheet.

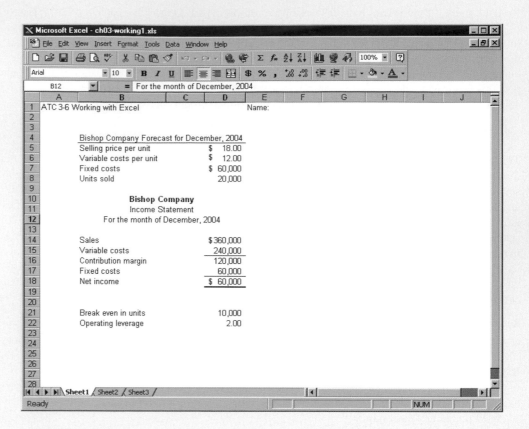

Required

Construct a spreadsheet as follows that would allow you to determine net income, breakeven in units, and operating leverage for the estimates at the top of the spreadsheet, and to see the effects of changes to the estimates. Set up this spreadsheet so that any change in the estimates will automatically be reflected in the calculation of net income, breakeven, and operating leverage.

Spreadsheet Tip

1. To center a heading across several columns, such as the Income Statement title, highlight the area to be centered (Columns B, C, and D), choose Format, then choose Cells, and click on the tab titled Alignment. Near the bottom of the alignment window, place a check mark in the box titled Merge cells. The shortcut method to merge cells is to click on the icon near the middle of the top icons that contains an *a* in a box.

ATC 3-7 Spreadsheet Assignment *Mastering Excel*

Required

Build the spreadsheet pictured in Exhibit 3.2. Be sure to use formulas that will automatically calculate profitability if fixed cost, variable cost, or sales volume is changed.

Spreadsheet Tip

1. The shading in column D and in row 6 can be inserted by first highlighting a section to be shaded, choosing Format from the main menu, then Cells, and then clicking on the tab titled Patterns, and then choosing a color for the shading. The shortcut method to accomplish the shading is to click on the fill color icon (it looks like a tipped bucket and is in the upper right area of the screen).

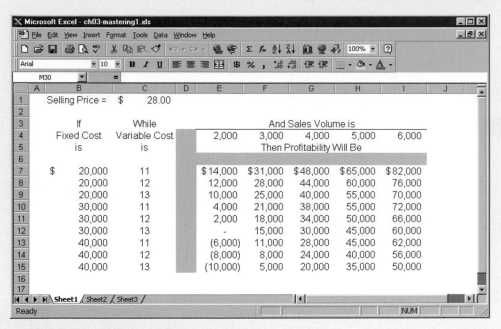

A	B	C	D	E	F	G	H	I	J
1	Selling Price =	$	28.00						
2									
3	If	While			And Sales Volume is				
4	Fixed Cost	Variable Cost		2,000	3,000	4,000	5,000	6,000	
5	is	is			Then Profitability Will Be				
6									
7	$ 20,000	11		$14,000	$31,000	$48,000	$65,000	$82,000	
8	20,000	12		12,000	28,000	44,000	60,000	76,000	
9	20,000	13		10,000	25,000	40,000	55,000	70,000	
10	30,000	11		4,000	21,000	38,000	55,000	72,000	
11	30,000	12		2,000	18,000	34,000	50,000	66,000	
12	30,000	13		-	15,000	30,000	45,000	60,000	
13	40,000	11		(6,000)	11,000	28,000	45,000	62,000	
14	40,000	12		(8,000)	8,000	24,000	40,000	56,000	
15	40,000	13		(10,000)	5,000	20,000	35,000	50,000	
16									
17									

2. Similar to basic math rules, the order of calculation within a formula is multiplication and division before addition and subtraction. Therefore, if you wish to subtract variable cost from selling price and multiply the difference by units sold, the formula must be = (28 − C8)*E5.

3. The quickest way to get the correct formulas in the area of E8 to I16 is to place the proper formula in cell E8 and then copy this formula to the entire block of E8:I16. However, the formulas must use the $ around the cell addresses to lock either the row or the column, or both. For example, the formula = 2*B8 can be copied to any other cell and the cell reference will remain B8 because the $ symbol locks the row and column. Likewise, $B8 indicates that only the column is locked, and B$8 indicates that only the row is locked.

COMPREHENSIVE PROBLEM

Use the same transaction data for Magnificent Modems, Inc., as was used in Chapter 1. (See page 52.)

Required

a. Use the following partially completed form to prepare an income statement using the contribution margin format.

Sales Revenue	$600,000
Variable Costs:	
Contribution Margin	225,000
Fixed costs	
Net Income	$31,050

b. Determine the break-even point in units and in dollars.

c. Assume that next year's sales are budgeted to be the same as the current year's sales. Determine the margin of safety expressed as a percentage.

CHAPTER 4

Cost Accumulation, Tracing, and Allocation

The Curious Accountant

A former patient of a California hospital complained about being charged $7 for a single aspirin tablet. After all, an entire bottle of 100 aspirins can be purchased at the local pharmacy store for around $2.

Can you think of any reasons, other than shameless profiteering, that a hospital would need to charge $7 for an aspirin? Remember that the hospital is not just selling the aspirin; it is also delivering it to the patient. (Answer on page 152.)

CHAPTER OPENING

What does it cost? This is one of the questions most frequently asked by business managers. Managers must have reliable cost estimates to price products, evaluate performance, control operations, and prepare financial statements. As this discussion implies, managers need to know the cost of many different things. The things we are trying to determine the cost of are commonly called **cost objects.** *For example, if we are trying to determine the cost of operating a department, that department is the cost object. Cost objects may be products, processes, departments, services, activities, and so on. This chapter explains techniques managerial accountants use to determine the cost of a variety of cost objects.* ■

Determine the Cost of Cost Objects

Identify cost objects and cost drivers.

Accountants use **cost accumulation** to determine the cost of a particular object. Suppose the Atlanta Braves advertising manager wants to promote a Tuesday night ball game by offering free baseball caps to all children who attend. What would be the promotion cost? The team's accountant must *accumulate* many individual costs and add them together. For simplicity consider only three cost components: (1) the cost of the caps, (2) the cost of advertising the promotion, and (3) the cost of an employee to work on the promotion.

Cost accumulation begins with identifying the cost objects. The primary cost object is the cost of the promotion. Three secondary cost objects are (1) the cost of caps, (2) the cost of advertising, and (3) the cost of labor. The costs of the secondary cost objects are combined to determine the cost of the primary cost object.

Determining the costs of the secondary cost objects requires identifying what *drives* those costs. A **cost driver** has a *cause-and-effect* relationship with a cost object. For example, the *number of caps* (cost driver) has an effect on the *cost of caps* (cost object). The *number of advertisements* is a cost driver for the *advertising cost* (cost object); the *number of labor hours* worked is a cost driver for the *labor cost* (cost object). Using the following assumptions about unit costs and cost drivers, the accumulated cost of the primary cost object (cost of the cap promotion) is:

Cost Object	Cost Per Unit	×	Cost Driver	=	Total Cost of Object
Cost of caps	$2.50	×	4,000 Caps	=	$10,000
Cost of advertising	$100.00	×	50 Advertisements	=	5,000
Cost of labor	$8.00	×	100 Hours	=	800
Cost of cap promotion					$15,800

The Atlanta Braves should run the promotion if management expects it to produce additional revenues exceeding $15,800.

Estimated Versus Actual Cost

The accumulated cost of the promotion—$15,800—is an *estimate.* Management cannot know *actual* costs and revenues until after running the promotion. While actual information is more accurate, it is not relevant for deciding whether to run the promotion because the decision must be made before the actual cost is known. Managers must accept a degree of inaccuracy in exchange for the relevance of timely information. Many business decisions are based on estimated rather than actual costs.

Managers use cost estimates to set prices, bid on contracts, evaluate proposals, distribute resources, plan production, and set goals. Certain circumstances, however, require actual cost data. For example, published financial reports and managerial performance evaluations use actual cost data. Managers frequently accumulate both estimated and actual cost data for the same cost object. For example, companies use cost estimates to establish goals and use actual costs to evaluate management performance in meeting those goals. The following discussion provides a number of business examples that use estimated data, actual data, or a combination of both.

Assignment of Costs to Objects in a Retail Business

Exhibit 4.1 displays the January income statement for In Style, Inc. (ISI), a retail clothing store. ISI subdivides its operations into women's, men's, and children's departments. To encourage the departmental managers to maximize sales, ISI began paying the manager of each department a bonus based on a percentage of departmental sales revenue.

Although the bonus incentive increased sales revenue, it also provoked negative consequences. The departmental managers began to argue over floor space; each manager wanted more space to display merchandise. The managers reduced prices; they increased sales commissions. In the drive to maximize sales, the managers ignored the need to control costs. To improve the situation, the store manager decided to base future bonuses on each department's contribution to profitability rather than its sales revenue.

Identifying Direct and Indirect Costs

The new bonus strategy requires determining the cost of operating each department. Each department is a separate *cost object*. Assigning costs to the departments (cost objects) requires **cost tracing** and **cost allocation**. *Direct costs* can be easily traced to a cost object. *Indirect costs* cannot be easily traced to a cost object. Whether or not a cost is easily traceable requires *cost/benefit analysis*.

Distinguish direct costs from indirect costs.

Some of ISI's costs can be easily traced to the cost objects (specific departments). The cost of goods sold is an example of an easily traced cost. Price tags on merchandise can be coded so cash register scanners capture the departmental code for each sale. The cost of goods sold is not only easily traceable but also very useful information. Companies need cost of goods sold information for financial reporting (income statement and balance sheet) and for management decisions (determining inventory reorder points, pricing strategies, and cost control). Because the cost of tracing *cost of goods sold* is small relative to the benefits obtained, cost of goods sold is a *direct cost.*

In contrast, the cost of supplies (shopping bags, sales slips, pens, staples, price tags) used by each department is much more difficult to trace. How could the number of staples used to seal shopping bags be traced to any particular department? The sales staff could count the number of staples used, but doing so would be silly for the benefits obtained. Although tracing the cost of supplies to each department may be possible, it is not worth the effort of doing so. The cost of supplies is therefore an *indirect cost.* Indirect costs are also called **overhead costs.**

EXHIBIT 4.1

Income Statement

IN STYLE, INC.
Income Statement
For the Month Ended January 31

Sales	$360,000
Cost of goods sold	(216,000)
Gross margin	144,000
Sales commissions	(18,000)
Dept. managers' salaries	(12,000)
Store manager's salary	(9,360)
Depreciation	(16,000)
Rental fee for store	(18,400)
Utilities	(2,300)
Advertising	(7,200)
Supplies	(900)
Net income	$ 59,840

Direct and indirect costs can be described as follows:

> **Direct costs** can be traced to cost objects in a *cost-effective* manner.
> **Indirect costs** cannot be traced to objects in a *cost-effective* manner.

By analyzing the accounting records, ISI's accountant classified the costs from the income statement in Exhibit 4.1 as direct or indirect, as shown in Exhibit 4.2. The next paragraph explains the classifications.

All figures represent January costs. Items 1 though 4 are direct costs, traceable to the cost objects in a cost-effective manner. Cost of goods sold is traced to departments at the point of sale using cash register scanners. Sales commissions are based on a percentage of departmental sales and are therefore easy to trace to the departments. Departmental managers' salaries are also easily traceable to the departments. Equipment, furniture, and fixtures are tagged with department codes that permit tracing depreciation charges directly to specific departments. Items 5 through 8 are incurred on behalf of the company as a whole and are therefore not directly traceable to a specific department. Although Item 9 could be traced to specific departments, the cost of doing so would exceed the benefits. The cost of supplies is therefore also classified as indirect.

EXHIBIT 4.2

Income Statement Classification of Costs

Cost Item	Direct Costs			Indirect Costs
	Women's	Men's	Children's	
1. Cost of goods sold—$216,000	$120,000	$58,000	$38,000	
2. Sales commissions—$18,000	9,500	5,500	3,000	
3. Dept. managers' salaries—$12,000	5,000	4,200	2,800	
4. Depreciation—$16,000	7,000	5,000	4,000	
5. Store manager's salary				$ 9,360
6. Rental fee for store				18,400
7. Utilities				2,300
8. Advertising				7,200
9. Supplies				900
Totals	$141,500	$72,700	$47,800	$38,160

Cost Classifications—Independent and Context Sensitive

Whether a cost is direct or indirect is independent of whether it is fixed or variable. In the ISI example, both cost of goods sold and the cost of supplies vary relative to sales volume (both are variable costs), but cost of goods sold is direct and the cost of supplies is indirect. Furthermore, the cost of rent and the cost of depreciation are both fixed relative to sales volume, but the cost of rent is indirect and the cost of depreciation is direct. In fact, the very same cost can be classified as direct or indirect, depending on the cost object. The store manager's salary is not directly traceable to a specific department, but it is traceable to a particular store.

Similarly, identifying costs as direct or indirect is independent of whether the costs are relevant to a given decision. ISI could avoid both cost of goods sold and the cost of supplies for a particular department if that department were eliminated. Both costs are relevant to a segment elimination decision, yet one is direct, and the other is indirect. You cannot memorize costs as direct or indirect, fixed or variable, relevant or not relevant. When trying to identify costs as to type or behavior, you must consider the context in which the costs occur.

Allocating Indirect Costs to Objects

LO 3

Allocate indirect costs to cost objects.

Topic Tackler PLUS

4-1

Cost **allocation** involves dividing a total cost into parts and assigning the parts to designated cost objects. How should ISI allocate the $38,160 of indirect costs to each of the three departments? First, identify a cost driver for each cost to be allocated. For example, there is a cause-and-effect relationship between store size and rent cost; the larger the building, the higher the rent cost. This relationship suggests that the more floor space a department occupies, the more rent cost that department should bear. To illustrate, assume ISI's store capacity is 23,000 square feet and the women's, men's, and children's departments occupy 12,000, 7,000, and 4,000 square feet, respectively. ISI can achieve a rational allocation of the rent cost using the following two-step process.[1]

Step 1. Compute the *allocation rate* by dividing the *total cost to be allocated* ($18,400 rental fee) by the *cost driver* (23,000 square feet of store space). *The cost driver is also called the* **allocation base.** This computation produces the **allocation rate,** as follows:

Total cost to be allocated ÷ Cost driver (allocation base) = Allocation rate

$18,400 rental fee ÷ 23,000 square feet = $0.80 per square foot

[1]Other mathematical approaches achieve the same result. This text consistently uses the two-step method described here. Specifically, the text determines allocations by (1) computing a *rate* and (2) multiplying the *rate* by the *weight of the base* (cost driver).

How does Southwest Airlines know the cost of flying a passenger from Houston, Texas, to Los Angeles, California? The fact is that Southwest does not know the actual cost of flying particular passengers anywhere. There are many indirect costs associated with flying passengers. Some of these include the cost of planes, fuel, pilots, office buildings, and ground personnel. Indeed, besides insignificant food and beverage costs, there are few costs that could be traced directly to customers. Southwest and other airlines are forced to use allocation and averaging to determine the estimated cost of providing transportation services to customers. Estimated rather than actual cost is used for decision-making purposes.

Consider that in its 2004 annual report Southwest reported the average operating expenses of flying one passenger one mile (called a *passenger mile*) were 7.77¢. However, this number was based on 76.9 million "available passenger miles." In 2004 Southwest operated at 69.5 percent of capacity, not 100 percent, so it was only able to charge passengers for 53.4 million passenger miles. Thus, its average operating expenses were closer to 11.2¢ for each mile for which they were able to charge. Had they operated at a higher capacity, their average costs would have been lower.

Step 2.   Multiply the *allocation rate* by the *weight of the cost driver* (weight of the base) to determine the allocation *per cost object,* as follows:

Cost Object	Allocation Rate	×	Number of Square Feet	=	Allocation per Cost Object
Women's department	$0.80	×	12,000	=	$ 9,600
Men's department	0.80	×	7,000	=	5,600
Children's department	0.80	×	4,000	=	3,200
Total			23,000		$18,400

It is also plausible to presume utilities cost is related to the amount of floor space a department occupies. Larger departments will consume more heating, lighting, air conditioning, and so on than smaller departments. Floor space is a reasonable cost driver for utility cost. Based on square footage, ISI can allocate utility cost to each department as follows:

Step 1.   Compute the allocation rate by dividing the total cost to be allocated ($2,300 utility cost) by the cost driver (23,000 square feet of store space):

$$\text{Total cost to be allocated} \div \text{Cost driver} = \text{Allocation rate}$$

$$\$2,300 \text{ utility cost} \div 23,000 \text{ square feet} = \$0.10 \text{ per square foot}$$

Step 2.   Multiply the *allocation rate* by the *weight of the cost driver* to determine the allocation *per cost object:*

Cost Object	Allocation Rate	×	Number of Square Feet	=	Allocation per Cost Object
Women's department	$0.10	×	12,000	=	$1,200
Men's department	0.10	×	7,000	=	700
Children's department	0.10	×	4,000	=	400
Total			23,000		$2,300

CHECK YOURSELF 4.1

HealthCare, Inc., wants to estimate the cost of operating the three departments (Dermatology, Gynecology, and Pediatrics) that serve patients in its Health Center. Each department performed the following number of patient treatments during the most recent year of operation: Dermatology, 2,600; Gynecology, 3,500; and Pediatrics, 6,200. The annual salary of the Health Center's program administrator is $172,200. How much of the salary cost should HealthCare allocate to the Pediatrics Department?

Answer

Step 1   Compute the *allocation rate*.

Total cost to be allocated ÷ Cost driver (patient treatments) =   Allocation rate

$172,200 salary cost ÷   (2,600 + 3,500 + 6,200) = $14 per patient treatment

Step 2   Multiply the *allocation rate* by the *weight of the cost driver* (weight of the base) to determine the allocation per *cost object*.

Cost Object	Allocation Rate	×	No. of Treatments	=	Allocation per Cost Object
Pediatrics department	$14	×	6,200	=	$86,800

Selecting a Cost Driver

LO 4

Select appropriate cost drivers for allocating indirect costs.

Topic Tackler

PLUS

4-2

Companies can frequently identify more than one cost driver for a particular indirect cost. For example, ISI's shopping bag cost is related to both the *number of sales transactions* and the *volume of sales dollars*. As either of these potential cost drivers increases, shopping bag usage also increases. The most useful cost driver is the one with the strongest cause-and-effect relationship.

Consider shopping bag usage for T-shirts sold in the children's department versus T-shirts sold in the men's department. Assume ISI studied T-shirt sales during the first week of June and found the following:

Department	Children's	Men's
Number of sales transactions	120	92
Volume of sales dollars	$1,440	$1,612

Given that every sales transaction uses a shopping bag, the children's department uses far more shopping bags than the men's department even though it has a lower volume of sales dollars. A reasonable explanation for this circumstance is that children's T-shirts sell for less than men's T-shirts. The number of sales transactions is the better cost driver because it has a stronger cause-and-effect relationship with shopping bag usage than does the volume of sales dollars. Should ISI therefore use the number of sales transactions to allocate supply cost to the departments? Not necessarily.

The *availability of information* also influences cost driver selection. While the number of sales transactions is the more accurate cost driver, ISI could not use this allocation base unless it maintains records of the number of sales transactions per department. If the store tracks the volume of sales dollars but not the number of transactions, it must use dollar volume even if the number of transactions is the better cost driver. For ISI, sales volume in dollars appears to be the best *available* cost driver for allocating supply cost.

Assuming that sales volume for the women's, men's, and children's departments was $190,000, $110,000, and $60,000, respectively, ISI can allocate the supplies cost as follows:

Step 1.   Compute the allocation rate by dividing the total cost to be allocated ($900 supplies cost) by the cost driver ($360,000 total sales volume):

Total cost to be allocated ÷   Cost driver   =   Allocation rate

$900 supplies cost   ÷ $360,000 sales volume = $0.0025 per sales dollar

Step 2.   Multiply the allocation rate by the weight of the cost driver to determine the allocation per cost object:

Cost Object	Allocation Rate	×	Sales Volume	=	Allocation per Cost Object
Women's department	$0.0025	×	$190,000	=	$475
Men's department	0.0025	×	110,000	=	275
Children's department	0.0025	×	60,000	=	150
Total			$360,000		$900

ISI believes sales volume is also the appropriate allocation base for advertising cost. The sales generated in each department were likely influenced by the general advertising campaign. ISI can allocate advertising cost as follows:

Step 1.   Compute the allocation rate by dividing the total cost to be allocated ($7,200 advertising cost) by the cost driver ($360,000 total sales volume):

Total cost to be allocated ÷   Cost driver   =   Allocation rate

$7,200 advertising cost ÷ $360,000 sales volume = $0.02 per sales dollar

Step 2.   Multiply the allocation rate by the weight of the cost driver to determine the allocation per cost object:

Cost Object	Allocation Rate	×	Sales Volume	=	Allocation per Cost Object
Women's department	$0.02	×	$190,000	=	$3,800
Men's department	0.02	×	110,000	=	2,200
Children's department	0.02	×	60,000	=	1,200
Total			$360,000		$7,200

There is no strong cause-and-effect relationship between the store manager's salary and the departments. ISI pays the store manager the same salary regardless of sales level, square footage of store space, number of labor hours, or any other identifiable variable. Because no plausible cost driver exists, ISI must allocate the store manager's salary arbitrarily. Here the manager's salary is simply divided equally among the departments as follows:

Step 1.   Compute the allocation rate by dividing the total cost to be allocated ($9,360 manager's monthly salary) by the allocation base (number of departments):

Total cost to be allocated   ÷   Cost driver   =   Allocation rate

$9,360 store manager's salary ÷ 3 departments = $3,120 per department

Answers to The Curious Accountant

When we compare the cost that a hospital charges for an aspirin to the price we pay for an aspirin, we are probably not considering the full cost that we incur to purchase aspirin. If someone asks you what you pay for an aspirin, you would probably take the price of a bottle, say $2, and divide it by the number of pills in the bottle, say 100. This would suggest their cost is $.02 each. Now, consider what it cost to buy the aspirins when all costs are considered. First, there is your time to drive to the store; what do you get paid per hour? Then, there is the cost of operating your automobile. You get the idea; in reality, the cost of an aspirin, from a business perspective, is much more than just the cost of the pills themselves.

Exhibit 4.3 shows the income statement of Hospital Corporation of America (HCA) for three recent years. HCA claims to be " . . . one of the leading health care services companies in the United States." In 2004 it operated 281 facilities in 23 states. As you can see, while it generated over $23 billion in revenue, it also incurred a lot of expenses. Look at its first two expense categories. Although it incurred $3.9 billion in supplies expenses, it incurred almost three times this amount in compensation expense. In other words, it cost a lot more to have someone deliver the aspirin to your bed than the aspirin itself costs.

In 2004 HCA earned $1.25 billion from its $23.5 billion in sales. This is a return on sales percentage of 5.3 percent ($1.25 ÷ $23.5). Therefore, on a $7 aspirin, HCA would earn 37 cents of profit, which is still not a bad profit for selling one aspirin. As a comparison, in 2005, Walgreens return on sales was 3.7 percent.

EXHIBIT 4.3

HCA INC.
Consolidated Income Statements
for the Years Ended December 31, 2004, 2003, and 2002
(Dollars in millions, except per share amounts)

	2004	2003	2002
Revenues	$23,502	$21,808	$19,729
Salaries and benefits	9,419	8,682	7,952
Supplies	3,901	3,522	3,158
Other operating expenses	3,797	3,676	3,341
Provision for doubtful accounts	2,669	2,207	1,581
(Gains) losses on investments	(56)	(1)	2
Equity in earnings of affiliates	(194)	(199)	(206)
Depreciation and amortization	1,250	1,112	1,010
Interest expense	563	491	446
Government settlement and investigation related costs	–	(33)	661
Gains on sales of facilities	–	(85)	(6)
Impairment of investment securities	–	–	168
Impairment of long-lived assets	12	130	19
Income before minority interests and income taxes	2,141	2,306	1,603
Minority interests in earnings of consolidated entities	168	150	148
Income before income taxes	1,973	2,156	1,455
Provision for income taxes	727	824	622
Net income	$ 1,246	$ 1,332	$ 833

Step 2. Multiply the allocation rate by the weight of the cost driver to determine the allocation per cost object:

Cost Object	Allocation Rate	×	Number of Departments	=	Allocation per Cost Object
Women's department	$3,120	×	1	=	$3,120
Men's department	3,120	×	1	=	3,120
Children's department	3,120	×	1	=	3,120
Total			3		$9,360

As the allocation of the store manager's salary demonstrates, many allocations are arbitrary or based on a weak relationship between the allocated cost and the allocation base (cost driver). Managers must use care when making decisions using allocated costs.

Behavioral Implications

Using the indirect cost allocations just discussed, Exhibit 4.4 shows the profit each department generated in January. ISI paid the three departmental managers bonuses based on each department's contribution to profitability. The store manager noticed an immediate change in the behavior of the departmental managers. For example, the manager of the women's department offered to give up 1,000 square feet of floor space because she believed reducing the selection of available products would not reduce sales significantly. Customers would simply buy different brands. Although sales would not decline dramatically, rent and utility cost allocations to the women's department would decline, increasing the profitability of the department.

In contrast, the manager of the children's department wanted the extra space. He believed the children's department was losing sales because it did not have enough floor space to display a competitive variety of merchandise. Customers came to the store to shop at the women's department, but they did not come specifically for children's wear. With additional space, the children's department could carry items that would draw customers to the store specifically to buy children's clothing. He believed the extra space would increase sales enough to cover the additional rent and utility cost allocations.

The store manager was pleased with the emphasis on profitability that resulted from tracing and assigning costs to specific departments.

EXHIBIT 4.4

Profit Analysis by Department

	Women's	Men's	Children's	Total
Sales	$190,000	$110,000	$60,000	$360,000
Cost of goods sold	(120,000)	(58,000)	(38,000)	(216,000)
Sales commissions	(9,500)	(5,500)	(3,000)	(18,000)
Dept. managers' salary	(5,000)	(4,200)	(2,800)	(12,000)
Depreciation	(7,000)	(5,000)	(4,000)	(16,000)
Store manager's salary	(3,120)	(3,120)	(3,120)	(9,360)
Rental fee for store	(9,600)	(5,600)	(3,200)	(18,400)
Utilities	(1,200)	(700)	(400)	(2,300)
Advertising	(3,800)	(2,200)	(1,200)	(7,200)
Supplies	(475)	(275)	(150)	(900)
Departmental profit	$ 30,305	$ 25,405	$ 4,130	$ 59,840

Effects of Cost Behavior on Selecting the Most Appropriate Cost Driver

Select appropriate cost drivers for allocating indirect costs.

As previously mentioned, indirect costs may exhibit variable or fixed cost behavior patterns. Failing to consider the effects of cost behavior when allocating indirect costs can lead to significant distortions in product cost measurement. We examine the critical relationships between cost behavior and cost allocation in the next section of the text.

Using Volume Measures to Allocate Variable Overhead Costs

A *causal relationship* exists between variable overhead product costs (indirect materials, indirect labor, inspection costs, utilities, etc.) and the volume of production. For example, the cost of indirect materials such as glue, staples, screws, nails, and varnish will increase or decrease in proportion to the number of desks a furniture manufacturing company makes. *Volume measures are good cost drivers* for allocating variable overhead costs.

Volume can be expressed by such measures as the number of units produced, the number of labor hours worked, or the amount of *direct* materials used in production. Given the variety of possible volume measures, how does management identify the most appropriate cost driver (allocation base) for assigning particular overhead costs? Consider the case of Filmier Furniture Company.

Using Units as the Cost Driver

During the most recent year, Filmier Furniture Company produced 4,000 chairs and 1,000 desks. It incurred $60,000 of *indirect materials* cost during the period. How much of this cost should Filmier allocate to chairs versus desks? Using number of units as the cost driver produces the following allocation.

Step 1. Compute the allocation rate.

Total cost to be allocated ÷ Cost driver = Allocation rate

$60,000 indirect materials cost ÷ 5,000 units = $12 per unit

Step 2. Multiply the allocation rate by the weight of the cost driver to determine the allocation per cost object.

Product	Allocation Rate	×	Number of Units Produced	=	Allocated Cost
Desks	$12	×	1,000	=	$12,000
Chairs	12	×	4,000	=	48,000
Total			5,000	=	$60,000

Using Direct Labor Hours as the Cost Driver

Using the number of units as the cost driver assigns an *equal amount* ($12) of indirect materials cost to each piece of furniture. However, if Filmier uses more indirect materials to make a desk than to make a chair, assigning the same amount of indirect materials cost to each is inaccurate. Assume Filmier incurs the following direct costs to make chairs and desks:

	Desks	Chairs	Total
Direct labor hours	3,500 hrs.	2,500 hrs.	6,000 hrs.
Direct materials cost	$1,000,000	$500,000	$1,500,000

Both direct labor hours and direct materials cost are volume measures that indicate Filmier uses more indirect materials to make a desk than a chair. It makes sense that the amount of direct labor used is related to the amount of indirect materials used. Because production workers use materials to make furniture, it is plausible to assume that the more hours they work, the more materials they use. Using this reasoning, Filmier could assign the indirect materials cost to the chairs and desks as follows:

Step 1.   Compute the allocation rate.

Total cost to be allocated   ÷ Cost driver = Allocation rate

$60,000 indirect materials cost ÷ 6,000 hours = $10 per hour

Step 2.   Multiply the allocation rate by the weight of the cost driver.

Product	Allocation Rate	×	Number of Labor Hours	=	Allocated Cost
Desks	$10.00	×	3,500	=	$35,000
Chairs	10.00	×	2,500	=	25,000
Total			6,000	=	$60,000

Basing the allocation on labor hours rather than number of units assigns a significantly larger portion of the indirect materials cost to desks ($35,000 versus $12,000). Is this allocation more accurate? Suppose the desks, but not the chairs, require elaborate, labor-intensive carvings. A significant portion of the labor is then not related to consuming indirect materials (glue, staples, screws, nails, and varnish). It would therefore be inappropriate to allocate the indirect materials cost based on direct labor hours.

Using Direct Material Dollars as the Cost Driver

If labor hours is an inappropriate allocation base, Filmier can consider direct material usage, measured in material dollars, as the allocation base. It is likely that the more lumber (direct material) Filmier uses, the more glue, nails, and so forth (indirect materials) it uses. It is reasonable to presume direct materials usage drives indirect materials usage. Using direct materials dollars as the cost driver for indirect materials produces the following allocation:

Step 1.   Compute the allocation rate.

Total cost to be allocated ÷ Cost driver = Allocation rate

$60,000 indirect materials cost ÷ $1,500,000 direct material dollars = $0.04 per direct material dollar

Step 2.   Multiply the allocation rate by the weight of the cost driver.

Product	Allocation Rate	×	Number of Direct Material Dollars	=	Allocated Cost
Desks	$0.04	×	$1,000,000	=	$40,000
Chairs	0.04	×	500,000	=	20,000
Total			$1,500,000	=	$60,000

Selecting the Best Cost Driver

Which of the three volume-based cost drivers (units, labor hours, or direct material dollars) results in the most accurate allocation of the overhead cost? Management must use judgment to decide. In this case, direct material dollars appears to have the most convincing relationship to indirect materials usage. If the cost Filmier was allocating were fringe benefits, however, direct labor hours would be a more appropriate cost driver. If the cost Filmier was allocating were machine maintenance cost, a different volume-based cost driver, machine hours, would be an appropriate base. The most accurate allocations of indirect costs may actually require using multiple cost drivers.

Boston Boat Company builds custom sailboats for customers. During the current accounting period, the company built five different size boats that ranged in cost from $35,000 to $185,000. The company's manufacturing overhead cost for the period was $118,000. Would you recommend using the number of units (boats) or direct labor hours as the base for allocating the overhead cost to the five boats? Why?

Answer

Using the number of units as the allocation base would assign the same amount of overhead cost to each boat. Since larger boats require more overhead cost (supplies, utilities, equipment, etc.) than smaller boats, there is no logical link between the number of boats and the amount of overhead cost required to build a particular boat. In contrast, there is a logical link between direct labor hours used and overhead cost incurred. The more labor used, the more supplies, utilities, equipment, and so on used. Since larger boats require more direct labor than smaller boats, using direct labor hours as the allocation base would allocate more overhead cost to larger boats and less overhead cost to smaller boats, producing a logical overhead allocation. Therefore, Boston should use direct labor hours as the allocation base.

Allocating Fixed Overhead Costs

Fixed costs present a different cost allocation problem. By definition, the volume of production does not drive fixed costs. Suppose Lednicky Bottling Company rents its manufacturing facility for $28,000 per year. The rental cost is fixed regardless of how much product Lednicky bottles. However, Lednicky may still use a volume-based cost driver as the allocation base. The object of allocating fixed costs to products is to distribute a *rational share* of the overhead cost to each product. Selecting an allocation base that spreads total overhead cost equally over total production often produces a rational distribution. For example, assume Lednicky produced 2,000,000 bottles of apple juice during 2006. If it sold 1,800,000 bottles of the juice during 2006, how much of the $28,000 of rental cost should Lednicky allocate to ending inventory and how much to cost of goods sold? A rational allocation follows:

Step 1. Compute the allocation rate.

Total cost to be allocated	÷	Allocation base (cost driver)	=	Allocation rate
$28,000 rental cost	÷	2,000,000 units	=	$0.014 per bottle of juice

Because the base (number of units) used to allocate the cost does not drive the cost, it is sometimes called an *allocation base* instead of a *cost driver*. However, many managers use the term cost driver in conjunction with fixed cost even though that usage is technically inaccurate. The terms allocation base and cost driver are frequently used interchangeably.

Step 2.   Multiply the allocation rate by the weight of the cost driver.

Financial Statement Item	Allocation Rate	×	Number of Bottles	=	Allocated Cost
Inventory	$0.014	×	200,000	=	$ 2,800
Cost of goods sold	0.014	×	1,800,000	=	25,200

Using number of units as the allocation base assigns equal amounts of the rental cost to each unit of product. Equal allocation is appropriate so long as the units are homogeneous. If the units are not identical, however, Lednicky may need to choose a different allocation base to rationally distribute the rental cost. For example, if some of the bottles are significantly larger than others, Lednicky may find using some physical measure, like liters of direct material used, to be a more appropriate allocation base. Whether an indirect cost is fixed or variable, selecting the most appropriate allocation base requires sound reasoning and judgment.

Allocating Costs to Solve Timing Problems

Monthly fluctuations in production volume complicate fixed cost allocations. To illustrate, assume Grave Manufacturing pays its production supervisor a monthly salary of $3,000. Furthermore, assume Grave makes 800 units of product in January and 1,875 in February. How much salary cost should Grave assign to the products made in January and February, respectively? The allocation seems simple. Just divide the $3,000 monthly salary cost by the number of units of product made each month as follows:

LO 5

Allocate costs to solve timing problems.

$$\text{January} \quad \$3,000 \div \quad 800 \text{ units} = \$3.75 \text{ cost per unit}$$

$$\text{February} \quad \$3,000 \div \ 1,875 \text{ units} = \$1.60 \text{ cost per unit}$$

If Grave Manufacturing based a cost-plus pricing decision on these results, it would price products made in January significantly higher than products made in February. It is likely such price fluctuations would puzzle and drive away customers. Grave needs an allocation base that will spread the annual salary cost evenly over annual production. A timing problem exists, however, because Grave must allocate the salary cost before the end of the year. In order to price its products, Grave needs to know the allocated amount before the actual cost information is available. Grave can manage the timing problem by using estimated rather than actual costs.

Grave Manufacturing can *estimate* the annual cost of the supervisor's salary (indirect labor) as $36,000 ($3,000 × 12 months). The *actual* cost of indirect labor may differ because the supervisor might receive a pay raise or be replaced with a person who earns less. Based on current information, however, $36,000 is a reasonable estimate of the annual indirect labor cost. Grave must also estimate total annual production volume. Suppose Grave produced 18,000 units last year and expects no significant change in the current year. It can allocate indirect labor cost for January and February as follows:

Step 1.   Compute the allocation rate.

$$\text{Total cost to be allocated} \div \text{Allocation base} = \text{Allocation rate}$$
$$\text{(cost driver)}$$

$$\$36,000 \qquad \div \quad 18,000 \text{ units} \ = \ \$2.00 \text{ per unit}$$

Step 2. Multiply the rate by the weight of the base (number of units per month) to determine how much of the salary cost to allocate to each month's production.

Month	Allocation Rate	×	Number of Units Produced	=	Allocation per Month
January	$2.00	×	800	=	$1,600
February	2.00	×	1,875	=	3,750

Grave Manufacturing will add these indirect cost allocations to other product costs to determine the total estimated product cost to use in cost-plus pricing or other managerial decisions.

Because the overhead allocation rate is determined *before* actual cost and volume data are available, it is called the **predetermined overhead rate.** Companies use predetermined overhead rates for product costing estimates and pricing decisions during a year, but they must use actual costs in published year-end financial statements. If necessary, companies adjust their accounting records at year-end when they have used estimated data on an interim basis. The procedures for making such adjustments are discussed in a later chapter.

Allocating Joint Costs

Allocate joint product costs.

Joint costs are common costs incurred in the process of making two or more **joint products.** The cost of raw milk is a joint cost of producing the joint products cream, whole milk, 2 percent milk, and skim milk. Joint costs include not only materials costs but also the labor and overhead costs of converting the materials into separate products. The point in the production process at which products become separate and identifiable is the **split-off point.** For financial reporting of inventory and cost of goods sold, companies must allocate the joint costs to the separate joint products. Some joint products require additional processing after the split-off point. Any additional materials, labor, or overhead costs incurred after the split-off point are assigned to the specific products to which they relate.

To illustrate, assume Westar Chemical Company produces from common raw materials the joint products Compound AK and Compound AL. Compound AL requires further processing before Westar can sell it. The diagram in Exhibit 4.5 illustrates the joint product costs.

EXHIBIT 4.5

Allocation of Joint Cost

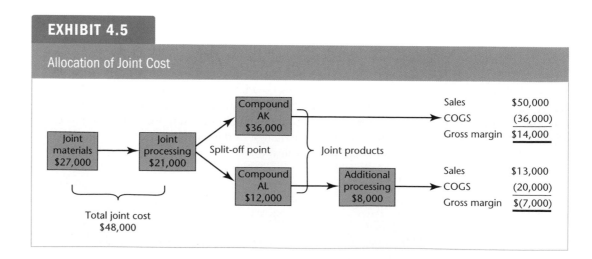

The joint cost of producing a batch of the two compounds is $48,000, representing $27,000 of materials cost and $21,000 of processing cost. A batch results in 3,000 gallons of Compound AK and 1,000 gallons of Compound AL. Westar allocates joint costs to the products based on the number of gallons produced, as follows:

Step 1.   Compute the allocation rate.

Total cost to be allocated $\div$ Allocation base $=$ Allocation rate

$48,000 joint cost $\div$ 4,000 gallons $=$ $12 per gallon

Step 2.   Multiply the allocation rate by the weight of the base.

Joint Product	Allocation Rate	×	Number of Gallons Produced	=	Allocated Cost
Compound AK	$12	×	3,000	=	$36,000
Compound AL	12	×	1,000	=	12,000

Westar sells 3,000 gallons of Compound AK for $50,000, and 1,000 gallons of Compound AL for $13,000. Exhibit 4.5 shows the gross margins for each product using the joint cost allocations computed above.

Relative Sales Value as the Allocation Base

Because Compound AL shows a $7,000 loss, a manager might mistakenly conclude that Westar should stop making and selling this product. If Westar stops making Compound AL, the total joint cost ($48,000) would be assigned to Compound AK and total gross margin would decline as shown below.

	With Compound AL		Without Compound AL
Sales	$63,000	($50,000 + $13,000)	$50,000
Cost of goods sold	(56,000)	($36,000 + $20,000)	(48,000)
Gross margin	$ 7,000		$ 2,000

To avoid the appearance that a product such as Compound AL is producing losses, many companies allocate joint cost to products based on the relative sales value of each product at the split-off point. Westar Chemical would allocate all of the joint cost to Compound AK because Compound AL has no market value at the split-off point. The resulting gross margins follow.

	Compound AK	Compound AL
Sales	$50,000	$13,000
Cost of goods sold	(48,000)	(8,000)
Gross margin	$ 2,000	$ 5,000

Westar's total profit on the joint products is $7,000 whether it allocates the joint costs using gallons or relative market value. However, using market value as the allocation base produces a positive gross margin for both products, reducing the likelihood that a manager will mistakenly eliminate a product that is contributing to profitability.

What are some logical split-off points for a meat processing company engaged in butchering beef?

Answer

The first logical split-off point occurs when processing separates the hide (used to produce leather) from the carcass. Other split-off points occur as further processing produces different cuts of meat (T-bone and New York strip steaks, various roasts, chops, ground chuck, etc.).

Cost Allocation: The Human Factor

LO 7

Recognize the effects of cost allocation on employee motivation.

Cost allocations significantly affect individuals. They may influence managers' performance evaluations and compensation. They may dictate the amount of resources various departments, divisions, and other organizational subunits receive. Control over resources usually offers managers prestige and influence over organization operations. The following scenario illustrates the emotional impact and perceptions of fairness of cost allocation decisions.

Using Cost Allocations in a Budgeting Decision

Sharon Southport, dean of the School of Business at a major state university, is in dire need of a budgeting plan. Because of cuts in state funding, the money available to the School of Business for copying costs next year will be reduced substantially. Dean Southport supervises four departments: management, marketing, finance, and accounting. The Dean knows the individual department chairpersons will be unhappy and frustrated with the deep cuts they face.

Using Cost Drivers to Make Allocations

To address the allocation of copying resources, Dean Southport decided to meet with the department chairs. She explained that the total budgeted for copying costs will be $36,000. Based on past usage, department allocations would be as follows: $12,000 for management, $10,000 for accounting, $8,000 for finance, and $6,000 for marketing.

Dr. Bill Thompson, the management department chair, immediately protested that his department could not operate on a $12,000 budget for copy costs. Management has more faculty members than any other department. Dr. Thompson argued that copy costs are directly related to the number of faculty members, so copy funds should be allocated based on the number of faculty members. Dr. Thompson suggested that number of faculty members rather than past usage should be used as the allocation base.

Since the School of Business has 72 faculty members (29 in management, 16 in accounting, 12 in finance, and 15 in marketing), the allocation should be as follows:

Step 1.   Compute the allocation rate.

Total cost to be allocated ÷ Cost driver =   Allocation rate

$36,000   ÷   72   = $500 per faculty member

Step 2.   Multiply the rate by the weight of the driver (the number of faculty per department) to determine the allocation per object (department).

Department	Allocation Rate	×	Number of Faculty	=	Allocation per Department	Allocation Based on Past Usage
Management	$500	×	29		$14,500	$12,000
Accounting	500	×	16		8,000	10,000
Finance	500	×	12		6,000	8,000
Marketing	500	×	15		7,500	6,000
Total					$36,000	$36,000

Seeing these figures, Dr. Bob Smethers, chair of the accounting department, questioned the accuracy of using the number of faculty members as the cost driver. Dr. Smethers suggested the number of *students* rather than the number of *faculty members* drives the cost of copying. He argued that most copying results from duplicating syllabi, exams, and handouts. The accounting department teaches mass sections of introductory accounting that have extremely high student/teacher ratios. Because his department teaches more students, it spends more on copying costs even though it has fewer faculty members. Dr. Smethers recomputed the copy cost allocation as follows.

Step 1.   Compute the allocation rate based on number of students. University records indicate that the School of Business taught 1,200 students during the most recent academic year. The allocation rate (copy cost per student) follows.

Total cost to be allocated ÷ Cost driver = Allocation rate

$36,000   ÷   1,200   = $30 per student

Step 2.   Multiply the rate by the weight of the driver (number of students taught by each department) to determine the allocation per object (department).

Department	Allocation Rate	×	Number of Students	=	Allocation per Department	Allocation Based on Past Usage
Management	$30	×	330		$ 9,900	$12,000
Accounting	30	×	360		10,800	10,000
Finance	30	×	290		8,700	8,000
Marketing	30	×	220		6,600	6,000
Total					$36,000	$36,000

Choosing the Best Cost Driver

Dr. Thompson objected vigorously to using the number of students as the cost driver. He continued to argue that the size of the faculty is a more appropriate allocation base. The chair of the finance department sided with Dr. Smethers, the chair of the marketing department kept quiet, and the dean had to settle the dispute.

Dean Southport recognized that the views of the chairpersons were influenced by self-interest. The allocation base affects the amount of resources available to each department. Furthermore, the dean recognized that the size of the faculty does drive some of the copying costs. For example, the cost of copying manuscripts that faculty submit for publication relates to faculty size. The more articles faculty submit, the higher the copying cost. Nevertheless, the dean decided the number of students has the most significant impact on copying costs. She also wanted to encourage faculty members to minimize the impact of funding cuts on student services. Dean Southport therefore decided to allocate copying costs based on the number of students taught by each department. Dr. Thompson stormed angrily out of the meeting. The dean developed a budget by assigning the available funds to each department using the number of students as the allocation base.

Controlling Emotions

Dr. Thompson's behavior may relieve his frustration but it doesn't indicate clear thinking. Dean Southport recognized that Dr. Thompson's contention that copy costs were related to faculty size had some merit. Had Dr. Thompson offered a compromise rather than an emotional outburst, he might have increased his department's share of the funds. Perhaps a portion of the allocation could have been based on the number of faculty members with the balance allocated based on the number of students. Had Dr. Thompson controlled his anger, the others might have agreed to compromise. Technical expertise in computing numbers is of little use without the interpersonal skills to persuade others. Accountants may provide numerical measurements, but they should never forget the impact of their reports on the people in the organization.

<< A Look Back

Managers need to know the costs of products, processes, departments, activities, and so on. The target for which accountants attempt to determine cost is a *cost object*. Knowing the cost of specific objects enables management to control costs, evaluate performance, and price products. *Direct costs* can be cost-effectively traced to a cost object. *Indirect costs* cannot be easily traced to designated cost objects.

The same cost can be direct or indirect, depending on the cost object to which it is traced. For example, the salary of a Burger King restaurant manager can be directly traced to a particular store but cannot be traced to particular food items made and sold in the store. Classifying a cost as direct or indirect is independent of whether the cost behaves as fixed or variable; it is also independent of whether the cost is relevant to a given decision. A direct cost could be either fixed or variable or either relevant or irrelevant, depending on the context and the designated cost object.

Indirect costs are assigned to cost objects using *cost allocation*. Allocation divides an indirect cost into parts and distributes the parts among the relevant cost objects. Companies frequently allocate costs to cost objects in proportion to the *cost drivers* that cause the cost to be incurred. The first step in allocating an indirect cost is to determine the allocation rate by dividing the total cost to be allocated by the chosen cost driver. The next step is to multiply the allocation rate by the amount of the cost driver for a particular object. The result is the amount of indirect cost to assign to the cost object.

A particular indirect cost may be related to more than one driver. The best cost driver is the one that most accurately reflects the amount of the resource used by the cost object. Objects that consume the most resources should be allocated a proportionately greater share of the costs. If no suitable cost driver exists, companies may use arbitrary allocations such as dividing a total cost equally among cost objects.

Cost allocations have behavioral implications. Using inappropriate cost drivers can distort allocations and lead managers to make choices that are detrimental to the company's profitability.

The joint costs incurred in the process of making two or more products are allocated among the products at the *split-off point,* the point at which products become separate and identifiable. The allocation base can be the products' relative sales values or some quantity measure of the amount of each product made. If one of the joint products requires additional processing costs to bring it to market, only these additional processing costs are relevant to a decision about whether to undertake further processing. The allocated joint costs are not relevant because they will be incurred whether or not the joint product is processed after the split-off point. By-products share common costs with other products but have an insignificant market value relative to their joint products.

A Look Forward

The next chapter introduces the concept of *cost relevance.* Applying the concepts you have learned to real-world business problems can be challenging. Frequently, so much data is available that it is difficult to distinguish important from useless information. The next chapter will help you learn to identify information that is relevant in a variety of short-term decision-making scenarios including special offers, outsourcing, segment elimination, and asset replacement.

APPENDIX

Allocating Service Center Costs

Most organizations establish departments responsible for accomplishing specific tasks. Departments that are assigned tasks leading to the accomplishment of the primary objectives of the organization are called **operating departments.** Those that provide support to operating departments are called **service departments.** For example, the department of accounting at a university is classified as an operating department because its faculty perform the university's primary functions of teaching, research, and service. In contrast, the maintenance department is classified as a service department because its employees provide janitorial services that support primary university functions. Professors are more likely to be motivated to perform university functions when facilities are clean, but the university's primary purpose is not to clean buildings. Similarly, the lending department in a bank is an operating department and the personnel department is a service department. The bank is in the business of making loans. Hiring employees is a secondary function that assists the lending activity.

Allocate service department costs to operating departments.

The costs to produce a product (or a service) include both operating and service department costs. Therefore, service department costs must somehow be allocated to the products produced (or services provided). Service department costs are frequently distributed to products through a two-stage allocation process. First-stage allocations involve the distribution of costs from service center cost pools to operating department cost pools. In the second stage, costs in the operating cost pools are allocated to products. Three different approaches can be used to allocate costs in the first stage of the two-stage costing process: the *direct method,* the *step method,* and the *reciprocal method.*

Direct Method

The **direct method** is the simplest allocation approach. It allocates service department costs directly to operating department cost pools. To illustrate, assume that Candler & Associates is a law firm that desires to determine the cost of handling each case. The firm has two operating departments, one that represents clients in civil suits and the other that defends clients in criminal cases. The two operating departments are supported by two service departments, personnel and secretarial support. Candler uses a two-stage allocation system to allocate the service centers' costs to the firm's legal cases. In the first stage, the costs to operate each service department are accumulated in separate cost pools. For example, the costs to operate the personnel department are $80,000 in salary, $18,000 in office rental, $12,000 in depreciation, $3,000 in supplies, and $4,000 in miscellaneous costs. These costs are added together in a single services department cost pool amounting to $117,000. Similarly, the costs incurred by the secretarial department are accumulated in a cost pool. We assume that this cost pool contains $156,800 of accumulated costs. The amounts in these cost pools are then allocated to the operating departments' cost pools. The appropriate allocations are described in the following paragraphs.

Assume that Candler's accountant decides that the number of attorneys working in the two operating departments constitutes a rational cost driver for the allocation of the personnel department cost pool and that the number of request forms submitted to the secretarial department constitutes a rational cost driver for the allocation of costs accumulated in the secretarial department cost pool. The total number of attorneys working in the two operating departments is 18, 11 in the civil department and 7 in the criminal department. The secretarial department received 980 work request forms with 380 from the civil department and 600 from the criminal department. Using these cost drivers as the allocation bases, the accountant made the following first-stage allocations.

Determination of Allocation Rates

$$\text{Allocation rate for personnel department cost pool} = \frac{\$117,000}{18} = \$6,500 \text{ per attorney}$$

$$\text{Allocation rate for secretarial department cost pool} = \frac{\$156,800}{980} = \$160 \text{ per request form}$$

The accountant then multiplied these rates by the weight of the base to determine the amount of each service cost pool to allocate to each operating department cost pool. The appropriate computations are shown in Exhibit 4.6.

As indicated, the allocated service department costs are pooled with other operating department overhead costs to form the operating department cost pools. In the second stage of the costing process, the costs in the operating department cost pools are allocated to the firm's products (cases). To illustrate second-stage allocations, assume that Candler allocates the operating department overhead cost pools on the basis of billable hours. Furthermore, assume that the civil department expects to bill 30,580 hours to its clients and the criminal department expects to bill 25,262 hours. Based on this information, the following predetermined overhead rates are used to allocate operating department cost pools to particular cases.

$$\text{Predetermined overhead rate for the civil department} = \frac{\$917,400}{30,580} = \$30 \text{ per billable hour}$$

$$\text{Predetermined overhead rate for the criminal department} = \frac{\$606,288}{25,262} = \$24 \text{ per billable hour}$$

EXHIBIT 4.6

First-Stage Allocations for Candler & Associates—Direct Method

Allocated Service Department Overhead	Allocation Rate	×	Weight of Base	=	Civil Department	Criminal Department	Total Service Department Cost Pool
Personnel	$6,500	×	11 attorneys	=	$ 71,500		
	6,500	×	7 attorneys	=		$ 45,500	
Total cost of personnel department							$117,000
Secretarial	160	×	380 requests	=	60,800		
	160	×	600 requests	=		96,000	
Total cost of secretarial department							156,800
Total of cost pools after allocation				=	132,300	141,500	$273,800
Other operating department overhead costs				=	785,100	464,788	
Total of operating department overhead cost pools				=	$917,400	$606,288	

These rates are used to calculate the amount of operating department cost pools to include in the determination of the cost to litigate specific cases. For example, a case in the civil department that required 300 billable hours of legal service is allocated $9,000 (300 hours × $30 predetermined overhead rate) of overhead cost. Assuming that the direct costs to litigate the case amounted to $25,000, the total cost of this particular case is $34,000 ($25,000 direct cost + $9,000 allocated overhead). This accumulated cost figure could be used as a guide to determine the charge to the client or the profitability of the case.

Step Method

The direct method of allocating service center costs fails to consider the fact that service departments render assistance to other service departments. A service that is performed by one service department for the benefit of another service department is called an **interdepartmental service.** To illustrate this, we return to the case of Candler & Associates. Suppose that Candler's personnel department works with the employees in the secretarial department as well as the attorneys in the civil and criminal operating departments. Under these circumstances, Candler needs a cost approach that recognizes the interdepartmental service activity. One such approach is known as the **step method.** The primary difference between the direct method and the step method is depicted graphically in Exhibit 4.7. Focus your attention on the first stage of the allocation process. Notice that the step method includes one additional allocation, specifically from the personnel department cost pool to the secretarial department cost pool. The direct method ignores this interdepartmental service cost allocation. Indeed, the direct method derives its name from the fact that it allocates costs only from service cost pools to operating cost pools.

The fact that the direct method ignores the effect of interdepartmental services may cause distortions in the measurement of cost objects. The primary purpose of the step method is to avoid such distortions, thereby improving the accuracy of product costing. To illustrate this point, consider Candler & Associates. First, note that the interdepartmental portion of the personnel department cost is, in fact, a cost of providing secretarial services. In other words, the personnel service costs could be reduced if the personnel department did not provide service to the secretarial staff. Accordingly, the cost of providing personnel support to the secretarial staff should be included in the secretarial cost pool. Under the direct method, however, the interdepartmental service cost is allocated between the civil and criminal operating departments. This is not a problem in and of itself because the cost of secretarial service is also allocated between the civil and criminal operating departments. Unfortunately, the base used to allocate personnel costs to the operating departments (i.e., number of attorneys) distributes more cost to the civil department than to the criminal department. This is unfortunate because the criminal department uses more secretarial service than the civil department does. In other words, more secretarial cost (i.e., interdepartmental personnel cost) is being allocated to the civil department although the criminal department uses more secretarial services. This means that ultimately the cost to litigate civil cases will be overstated and the cost to litigate criminal cases will be understated.

EXHIBIT 4.7

Comparison of Direct and Step Allocation Methods

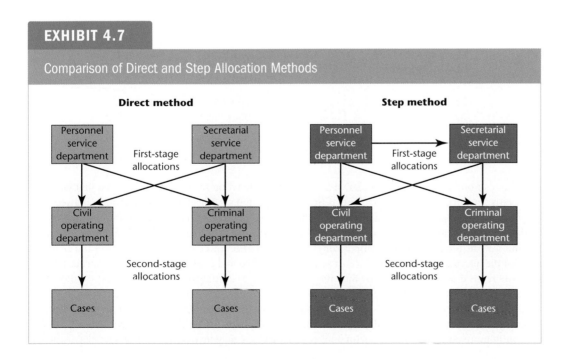

The step method corrects this distortion by distributing the interdepartmental personnel department cost to the secretarial department cost pool before it is allocated to the operating departments. Because the secretarial cost pool is allocated on the basis of requests for secretarial service, more of the interdepartmental cost will be allocated to the criminal operating deparment. To validate this result, assume that the personnel department cost pool is allocated to the secretarial department cost pool and the two operating department cost pools on the basis of the number of employees in each department. In addition to the 18 attorneys in the firm, assume that two employees work in the secretarial department. Accordingly, the allocation rate for the personnel cost pool is calculated as follows.

$$\text{Allocation rate for personnel department cost pool} = \frac{\$117,000}{20} = \$5,850 \text{ per employee}$$

Based on this rate, the first step in the allocation process distributes the personnel department cost pool as indicated here.

Personnel Cost Pool Allocated to	Allocation Rate		Weight of Base		Allocated Cost
Secretarial	$5,850	×	2 employees	=	$ 11,700
Civil	5,850	×	11 employees	=	64,350
Criminal	5,850	×	7 employees	=	40,950
Total			20 employees		$117,000

The result of the distribution of personnel department costs is shown as the Step 1 allocation in Exhibit 4.3A. The $11,700 interdepartmental personnel department cost allocated to the secretarial department cost pool is added to the $156,800 existing balance in that cost pool (See Exhibit 4.8). The result is the accumulation of secretarial cost of $168,500. The second step in the costing process allocates this cost pool to the operating departments. Recall that the secretarial cost pool is allocated on the basis of number of work request forms submitted. Furthermore, recall that 980 request forms were submitted to the secretarial department (380 from the civil department and 600 from the criminal department). Accordingly, the allocation rate for the secretarial department cost pool is computed as follows.

$$\text{Allocation rate for secretarial department cost pool} = \frac{\$168,500}{980} = \$171.93878 \text{ per request form}$$

Based on this rate, the second step in the allocation process distributes the secretarial cost pool as indicated here.

Secretarial Cost Pool Allocated to	Allocation Rate		Weight of Base		Allocated Cost
Civil	$171.93878	×	380 requests	=	$ 65,337
Criminal	171.93878	×	600 requests	=	103,163
Total		×	980 requests		$168,500

The result of this allocation is shown as the Step 2 allocation in Exhibit 4.8. Notice that the final cost pools for the operating departments reflect the expected shift in the cost distribution between the two departments. Specifically, the cost pool in the criminal department is higher and the cost pool in the civil department is lower than the comparable cost pool amounts computed under the direct method (see Exhibit 4.8 for the appropriate comparison). This distribution of cost is consistent with the fact that more of the interdepartmental service cost should be assigned to the criminal department because it uses more secretarial services than does the civil department. Accordingly, the step method of allocation more accurately reflects the manner in which the two operating departments consume resources.

The preceding illustration considered a simple two-stage allocation process with only two service departments and two operating departments. In large organizations, the costing process may be significantly more complex. Interdepartmental cost allocations may involve several service departments.

EXHIBIT 4.8

First-Stage Allocations for Candler & Associates—Step Method

	Personnel Cost Pool		Secretarial Cost Pool		Civil Department		Criminal Department
Cost to be allocated	$117,000		$156,800				
Step 1 allocation	(117,000)	=	11,700	+	$ 64,350	+	$ 40,950
Step 2 allocation			(168,500)	=	65,337	+	103,163
Total in cost pool after allocation	$ 0		$ 0		129,687		144,113
Other operating department overhead costs					785,100		464,788
Total of operating department overhead cost pool					$914,787		$608,901

For example, a personnel department may provide service to a secretarial department that provides service to an engineering department that provides service to the accounting department that provides service to several operating departments. In addition, general overhead costs may be allocated to both service and operating departments before costs are allocated from service to operating departments. For example, general utility costs may be pooled together and allocated to service and operating departments on the basis of square footage of floor space. These allocated utility costs are then redistributed to other service departments and to operating departments in a sequence of step-down allocations. The step-down process usually begins with the cost pool that represents resources used by the largest number of departments. This constitutes the first step in the costing process. The second step proceeds with allocations from the cost pool that represents resources used by the second largest number of departments and so on, until all overhead costs have been allocated to the operating departments. Accordingly, the first stage of a two-stage costing process may include many allocations (steps) before all costs have been distributed to the operating departments. Regardless of how many allocations are included in the first stage, the second stage begins when costs are allocated from the operating departments to the organizations' products.

Reciprocal Method

Note that the step method is limited to one-way interdepartmental relationships. In practice, many departments have two-way working relationships. For example, the personnel department may provide services to the secretarial department and receive services from it. Two-way associations in which departments provide and receive services from one another are called **reciprocal relationships.** Allocations that recognize reciprocal relationships require complex mathematical manipulation involving the use of simultaneous linear equations. The resultant cost distributions are difficult to interpret. Furthermore, the results attained with the **reciprocal method** are not significantly different from those attained through the step method. As a result, the reciprocal method is rarely used in practice.

SELF-STUDY REVIEW PROBLEM

A step-by-step audio-narrated series of slides is provided on the text website at www.mhhe.com/edmonds2008.

New budget constraints have pressured Body Perfect Gym to control costs. The owner of the gym has notified division managers that their job performance evaluations will be highly influenced by their ability to minimize costs. The gym has three divisions: weight lifting, aerobics, and spinning. The owner has formulated a report showing how much it costs to operate each of the three divisions last year. In preparing the report, Mr. Ripple identified several indirect costs that must be allocated among the divisions. These indirect costs are $4,200 of laundry expense, $48,000 of gym supplies, $350,000 of office rent, $50,000 of janitorial services, and $120,000 for administrative salaries. To provide a reasonably accurate cost allocation, Mr. Ripple has identified several potential cost drivers. These drivers and their association with each division follow.

Cost Driver	Weight Lifting	Aerobics	Spinning	Total
Number of participants	26	16	14	56
Number of instructors	10	8	6	24
Square feet of gym space	12,000	6,000	7,000	25,000
Number of staff	2	2	1	5

Required

a. Identify the appropriate cost objects.
b. Identify the most appropriate cost driver for each indirect cost, and compute the allocation rate for assigning each indirect cost to the cost objects.
c. Determine the amount of supplies expense that should be allocated to each of the three divisions.
d. The spinning manager wants to use the number of staff rather than the number of instructors as the allocation base for the supplies expense. Explain why the spinning manager would take this position.
e. Identify two cost drivers other than your choice for Requirement *b* that could be used to allocate the cost of the administrative salaries to the three divisions.

Solution to Requirement a

The objective is to determine the cost of operating each division. Therefore, the cost objects are the three divisions (weight lifting, aerobics, and spinning).

Solution to Requirement b

The costs, appropriate cost drivers, and allocation rates for assigning the costs to the departments follow:

Cost	Base	Computation	Allocation Rate
Laundry expense	Number of participants	$ 4,200 ÷ 56	$75 per participant
Supplies expense	Number of instructors	48,000 ÷ 24	$2,000 per instructor
Office rent	Square feet	350,000 ÷ 25,000	$14 per square foot
Janitorial service	Square feet	50,000 ÷ 25,000	$2 per square foot
Administrative salaries	Number of divisions	120,000 ÷ 3	$40,000 per division

There are other logical cost drivers. For example, supplies expense could be allocated based on the number of staff. It is also logical to use a combination of cost drivers. For example, the allocation of supplies expense could be based on the combined number of instructors and staff. For this problem, we assumed that Mr. Ripple chose the number of instructors as the base for allocating supplies expense.

Solution to Requirement c

Department	Cost to Be Allocated	Allocation Rate	×	Weight of Base	=	Amount Allocated
Weight lifting	Supplies expense	$2,000	×	10	=	$20,000
Aerobics	Supplies expense	2,000	×	8	=	16,000
Spinning	Supplies expense	2,000	×	6	=	12,000
Total						$48,000

Solution to Requirement d

If the number of staff were used as the allocation base, the allocation rate for supplies expense would be as follows:

$$\$48,000 \div 5 \text{ staff} = \$9,600 \text{ per staff member}$$

Using this rate, the total supplies expense would be allocated among the three divisions as follows:

Department	Cost to Be Allocated	Allocation Rate	×	Weight of Base	=	Amount Allocated
Weight lifting	Supplies expense	$9,600	×	2	=	$19,200
Aerobics	Supplies expense	9,600	×	2	=	19,200
Spinning	Supplies expense	9,600	×	1	=	9,600
Total						$48,000

By using the number of staff as the allocation base instead of the number of instructors, the amount of overhead cost allocated to the spinning division falls from $12,000 to $9,600. Since managers are evaluated based on minimizing costs, it is clearly in the spinning manager's self-interest to use the number of staff as the allocation base.

Solution to Requirement e
Among other possibilities, bases for allocating the administrative salaries include the number of participants, the number of lessons, or the number of instructors.

KEY TERMS

allocation 148
allocation base 148
allocation rate 148
cost accumulation 146
cost allocation 147
cost driver 146
cost objects 145
cost tracing 147
direct cost 147
direct method 163
indirect cost 147
interdepartmental service 165
joint costs 158
joint products 158
operating departments 163
overhead costs 147
predetermined overhead rate 158
reciprocal method 167
reciprocal relationships 167
service departments 163
split-off point 158
step method 165

QUESTIONS

1. What is a cost object? Identify four different cost objects in which an accountant would be interested.
2. Why is cost accumulation imprecise?
3. If the cost object is a manufactured product, what are the three major cost categories to accumulate?
4. What is a direct cost? What criteria are used to determine whether a cost is a direct cost?
5. Why are the terms *direct cost* and *indirect cost* independent of the terms *fixed cost* and *variable cost?* Give an example to illustrate.
6. Give an example of why the statement, "All direct costs are avoidable," is incorrect.
7. What are the important factors in determining the appropriate cost driver to use in allocating a cost?
8. How is an allocation rate determined? How is an allocation made?
9. In a manufacturing environment, which costs are direct and which are indirect in product costing?
10. Why are some manufacturing costs not directly traceable to products?
11. What is the objective of allocating indirect manufacturing overhead costs to the product?
12. On January 31, the managers of Integra, Inc., seek to determine the cost of producing their product during January for product pricing and control purposes. The company can easily determine the costs of direct materials and direct labor used in January production, but many fixed indirect costs are not affected by the level of production activity and have not yet been incurred. The managers can reasonably estimate the overhead costs for the year based on the fixed indirect costs

incurred in past periods. Assume the managers decide to allocate an equal amount of these estimated costs to the products produced each month. Explain why this practice may not provide a reasonable estimate of product costs in January.

13. Respond to the following statement: "The allocation base chosen is unimportant. What is important in product costing is that overhead costs be assigned to production in a specific period by an allocation process."

14. Larry Kwang insists that the costs of his school's fund-raising project should be determined after the project is complete. He argues that only after the project is complete can its costs be determined accurately and that it is a waste of time to try to estimate future costs. Georgia Sundum counters that waiting until the project is complete will not provide timely information for planning expenditures. How would you arbitrate this discussion? Explain the trade-offs between accuracy and timeliness.

15. What are the three methods used for allocating service center costs? How do the methods differ?

MULTIPLE-CHOICE QUESTIONS

Multiple-choice questions are provided on the text website at www.mhhe.com/edmonds2008.

EXERCISES—SERIES A

All Exercises in Series A are available with McGraw-Hill's Homework Manager®.

L.O. 1, 3

Exercise 4-1A *Allocating costs between divisions*

Drake Services Company (DSC) has 40 employees, 28 of whom are assigned to Division A and 12 to Division B. DSC incurred $240,000 of fringe benefits cost during 2006.

Required

Determine the amount of the fringe benefits cost to be allocated to Division A and to Division B.

L.O. 2

Exercise 4-2A *Direct versus indirect costs*

Oak Mountain Construction Company is composed of two divisions: (1) Home Construction and (2) Commercial Construction. The Home Construction Division is in the process of building 12 houses and the Commercial Construction Division is working on 3 projects. Cost items of the company follow:

Labor on a particular house
Salary of the supervisor of commercial construction projects
Supplies, such as glue and nails, used by the Home Construction Division
Cost of building permits
Materials used in commercial construction project
Depreciation on home building equipment (small tools such as hammers or saws)
Company president's salary
Depreciation on crane used in commercial construction
Depreciation on home office building
Salary of corporate office manager
Wages of workers assigned to a specific construction project
Supplies used by the Commercial Construction Division

Required

a. Identify each cost as being a direct or indirect cost assuming the cost objects are the individual products (houses or projects).
b. Identify each cost as being a direct or indirect cost, assuming the cost objects are the two divisions.
c. Identify each cost as being a direct or indirect cost assuming the cost object is Oak Mountain Construction Company as a whole.

Exercise 4-3A   *Allocating overhead cost among products*   L.O. 3, 4

Tawana Hats Corporation manufactures three different models of hats: Vogue, Beauty, and Deluxe. Donna expects to incur $750,000 of overhead cost during the next fiscal year. Other budget information follows.

	Vogue	**Beauty**	**Deluxe**	**Total**
Direct labor hours	3,000	5,000	4,500	12,500
Machine hours	1,000	1,000	1,000	3,000

Required

a. Use direct labor hours as the cost driver to compute the allocation rate and the budgeted overhead cost for each product.
b. Use machine hours as the cost driver to compute the allocation rate and the budgeted overhead cost for each product.
c. Describe a set of circumstances where it would be more appropriate to use direct labor hours as the allocation base.
d. Describe a set of circumstances where it would be more appropriate to use machine hours as the allocation base.

Exercise 4-4A   *Allocating overhead costs among products*   L.O. 3, 4

Flemming Company makes three products in its factory: plastic cups, plastic tablecloths, and plastic bottles. The expected overhead costs for the next fiscal year include the following.

Factory manager's salary	$150,000
Factory utility cost	70,000
Factory supplies	30,000
Total overhead costs	$250,000

Flemming uses machine hours as the cost driver to allocate overhead costs. Budgeted machine hours for the products are as follows.

Cups	500 Hours
Tablecloths	800
Bottles	1,200
Total machine hours	2,500

Required

a. Allocate the budgeted overhead costs to the products.
b. Provide a possible explanation as to why Flemming chose machine hours, instead of labor hours, as the allocation base.

Exercise 4-5A   *Allocating costs among products*   L.O. 3, 4

Calvin Construction Company expects to build three new homes during a specific accounting period. The estimated direct materials and labor costs are as follows.

Expected Costs	Home 1	Home 2	Home 3
Direct labor	$60,000	$ 90,000	$170,000
Direct materials	90,000	130,000	180,000

Assume Calvin needs to allocate two major overhead costs ($40,000 of employee fringe benefits and $20,000 of indirect materials costs) among the three jobs.

Required

Choose an appropriate cost driver for each of the overhead costs and determine the total cost of each house.

L.O. 3, 5

Exercise 4-6A   *Allocating to smooth cost over varying levels of production*

Production workers for Gomez Manufacturing Company provided 320 hours of labor in January and 480 hours in February. Gomez expects to use 4,000 hours of labor during the year. The rental fee for the manufacturing facility is $7,200 per month.

Required

Explain why allocation is needed. Based on this information, how much of the rental cost should be allocated to the products made in January and to those made in February?

L.O. 3, 5

Exercise 4-7A   *Allocating to solve a timing problem*

Production workers for Miller Manufacturing Company provided 3,200 hours of labor in January and 2,000 hours in February. The company, whose operation is labor intensive, expects to use 36,000 hours of labor during the year. Miller paid a $45,000 annual premium on July 1 of the prior year for an insurance policy that covers the manufacturing facility for the following 12 months.

Required

Explain why allocation is needed. Based on this information, how much of the insurance cost should be allocated to the products made in January and to those made in February?

L.O. 3, 5

Exercise 4-8A   *Allocating to solve a timing problem*

Pacific Air is a large airline company that pays a customer relations representative $4,000 per month. The representative, who processed 1,000 customer complaints in January and 1,300 complaints in February, is expected to process 16,000 customer complaints during 2007.

Required

a. Determine the total cost of processing customer complaints in January and in February.
b. Explain why allocating the cost of the customer relations representative would or would not be relevant to decision making.

L.O. 3, 5

Exercise 4-9A   *Allocating overhead cost to accomplish smoothing*

Mensah Corporation expects to incur indirect overhead costs of $50,000 per month and direct manufacturing costs of $7 per unit. The expected production activity for the first four months of 2007 is as follows.

	January	February	March	April
Estimated production in units	4,000	7,000	3,000	6,000

Required

a. Calculate a predetermined overhead rate based on the number of units of product expected to be made during the first four months of the year.
b. Allocate overhead costs to each month using the overhead rate computed in Requirement *a*.
c. Calculate the total cost per unit for each month using the overhead allocated in Requirement *b*.

Exercise 4-10A   *Allocating overhead for product costing*

Hinch Manufacturing Company produced 1,200 units of inventory in January 2007. It expects to produce an additional 8,400 units during the remaining 11 months of the year. In other words, total production for 2007 is estimated to be 9,600 units. Direct materials and direct labor costs are $64 and $52
per unit, respectively. Hinch Company expects to incur the following manufacturing overhead costs
during the 2007 accounting period.

Production supplies	$ 4,800
Supervisor salary	192,000
Depreciation on equipment	144,000
Utilities	36,000
Rental fee on manufacturing facilities	96,000
Total	$472,800

Required

a. Determine the cost of the 1,200 units of product made in January.
b. Is the cost computed in Requirement *a* actual or estimated? Could Hinch improve accuracy by
    waiting until December to determine the cost of products? Identify two reasons that a manager
    would want to know the cost of products in January. Discuss the relationship between accuracy and
    relevance as it pertains to this problem.

Exercise 4-11A   *How the allocation of fixed cost affects a pricing decision*

Kyle Manufacturing Co. expects to make 24,000 chairs during the 2008 accounting period. The company made 4,000 chairs in January. Materials and labor costs for January were $16,000 and $24,000,
respectively. Kyle produced 2,000 chairs in February. Material and labor costs for February were
$8,000 and $12,000, respectively. The company paid the $120,000 annual rental fee on its manufac-
turing facility on January 1, 2008.

Required

Assuming that Kyle desires to sell its chairs for cost plus 40 percent of cost, what price should be
charged for the chairs produced in January and February?

Exercise 4-12A   *Allocating joint product cost*

Terry Chemical Company makes three products, B217, K360, and X639, which are joint products
from the same materials. In a standard batch of 300,000 pounds of raw materials, the company generates 70,000 pounds of B217, 150,000 pounds of K360, and 80,000 pounds of X639. A standard batch
costs $1,800,000 to produce. The sales prices per pound are $4.00, $9.60, and $16.00 for B217, K360,
and X639, respectively.

Required

a. Allocate the joint product cost among the three final products using weight as the allocation base.
b. Allocate the joint product cost among the three final products using market value as the allocation
    base.

Appendix

Exercise 4-13A   *Human factor*

Jenkins Clinics provides medical care in three departments: internal medicine (IM), pediatrics (PD),
and obstetrics gynecology (OB). The estimated costs to run each department follow:

	IM	PD	OB
Physicians	$400,000	$300,000	$200,000
Nurses	80,000	120,000	160,000

Jenkins expects to incur $360,000 of indirect (overhead) costs in the next fiscal year.

Required

a. Name four allocation bases that could be used to assign the overhead cost to each department.
b. Assume the manager of each department is permitted to recommend how the overhead cost should be allocated to the departments. Which of the allocation bases named in Requirement *a* is the manager of OB most likely to recommend? Explain why. What argument may the manager of OB use to justify his choice of the allocation base?
c. Which of the allocation bases would result in the fairest allocation of the overhead cost from the perspective of the company president?
d. Explain how classifying overhead costs into separate pools could improve the fairness of the allocation of the overhead costs.

L.O. 3, 8

Exercise 4-14A   *Allocating a service center cost to operating departments*

York Corporation's computer services department assists two operating departments in using the company's information system effectively. The annual cost of computer services is $400,000. The production department employs 22 employees, and the sales department employs 18 employees. York uses the number of employees as the cost driver for allocating the cost of computer services to operating departments.

Required

Allocate the cost of computer services to operating departments.

L.O. 3, 8

Exercise 4-15A   *Allocating costs of service centers to operating departments—step method*

Wendel Health Care Center, Inc., has three clinics servicing the Birmingham metropolitan area. The company's legal services department supports the clinics. Moreover, its computer services department supports all of the clinics and the legal services department. The annual cost of operating the legal services department is $960,000. The annual cost of operating the computer services department is $480,000. The company uses the number of patients served as the cost driver for allocating the cost of legal services and the number of computer workstations as the cost driver for allocating the cost of computer services. Other relevant information follows.

	Number of Patients	Number of Workstations
Hoover clinic	6,000	15
Eastwood clinic	4,200	16
Gardendale clinic	5,800	12
Legal services		7
Computer services		10

Required

a. Allocate the cost of computer services to all of the clinics and the legal services department.
b. After allocating the cost of computer services, allocate the cost of legal services to the three clinics.
c. Compute the total allocated cost of service centers for each clinic.

L.O. 3, 8

Exercise 4-16A   *Allocating costs of service centers to operating departments—direct method*

Napper Trust Corporation has two service departments: actuary and economic analysis. Napper also has three operating departments: annuity, fund management, and employee benefit services. The annual costs of operating the service departments are $520,000 for actuary and $640,000 for economic analysis. Napper uses the direct method to allocate service center costs to operating departments. Other relevant data follow.

	Operating Costs*	Revenue
Annuity	$500,000	$ 840,000
Fund management	900,000	1,260,000
Employee benefit services	600,000	1,100,000

*The operating costs are measured before allocating service center costs.

Required

a. Use operating costs as the cost driver for allocating service center costs to operating departments.

b. Use revenue as the cost driver for allocating service center costs to operating departments.

PROBLEMS—SERIES A

All Problems in Series A are available with McGraw-Hill's Homework Manager®.

Problem 4-17A   *Cost accumulation and allocation*

Park Manufacturing Company makes two different products, M and N. The company's two departments are named after the products; for example, Product M is made in Department M. Park's accountant has identified the following annual costs associated with these two products.

L.O. 1, 2, 3, 4, 5

eXcel

www.mhhe.com/edmonds2008

CHECK FIGURE
a. (2) $590,000

Financial data	
Salary of vice president of production division	$ 90,000
Salary of supervisor Department M	38,000
Salary of supervisor Department N	28,000
Direct materials cost Department M	150,000
Direct materials cost Department N	210,000
Direct labor cost Department M	120,000
Direct labor cost Department N	340,000
Direct utilities cost Department M	60,000
Direct utilities cost Department N	12,000
General factorywide utilities	18,000
Production supplies	18,000
Fringe benefits	69,000
Depreciation	360,000
Nonfinancial data	
Machine hours Department M	5,000
Machine hours Department N	1,000

Required

a. Identify the costs that are (1) direct costs of Department M, (2) direct costs of Department N, and (3) indirect costs.

b. Select the appropriate cost drivers for the indirect costs and allocate these costs to Departments M and N.

c. Determine the total estimated cost of the products made in Departments M and N. Assume that Park produced 2,000 units of Product M and 4,000 units of Product N during the year. If Park prices its products at cost plus 30 percent of cost, what price per unit must it charge for Product M and for Product N?

Problem 4-18A   *Selecting an appropriate cost driver (What is the base?)*

L.O. 1, 3, 4

The Margo School of Vocational Technology has organized the school training programs into three departments. Each department provides training in a different area as follows: nursing assistant, dental hygiene, and office technology. The school's owner, Susan Margo, wants to know how much it costs to operate each of the three departments. To accumulate the total cost for each department, the accountant has identified several indirect costs that must be allocated to each. These costs are $8,400 of phone expense, $1,680 of office supplies, $864,000 of office rent, $96,000 of janitorial services, and $72,000 of salary paid to the dean of students. To provide a reasonably accurate allocation of costs, the accountant has identified several possible cost drivers. These drivers and their association with each department follow.

Cost Driver	Department 1	Department 2	Department 3
Number of telephones	28	32	52
Number of faculty members	20	16	12
Square footage of office space	24,000	14,000	10,000
Number of secretaries	2	2	2

Required

a. Identify the appropriate cost objects.
b. Identify the appropriate cost driver for each indirect cost and compute the allocation rate for assigning each indirect cost to the cost objects.
c. Determine the amount of telephone expense that should be allocated to each of the three departments.
d. Determine the amount of supplies expense that should be allocated to Department 3.
e. Determine the amount of office rent that should be allocated to Department 2.
f. Determine the amount of janitorial services cost that should be allocated to Department 1.
g. Identify two cost drivers not listed here that could be used to allocate the cost of the dean's salary to the three departments.

L.O. 1, 2

Problem 4-19A   *Cost allocation in a service industry*

Hallit Airlines is a small airline that occasionally carries overload shipments for the overnight delivery company Never-Fail, Inc. Never-Fail is a multimillion-dollar company started by Peter Never immediately after he failed to finish his first accounting course. The company's motto is "We Never-Fail to Deliver Your Package on Time." When Never-Fail has more freight than it can deliver, it pays Hallit to carry the excess. Hallit contracts with independent pilots to fly its planes on a per trip basis. Hallit recently purchased an airplane that cost the company $6,000,000. The plane has an estimated useful life of 100,000,000 miles and a zero salvage value. During the first week in January, Hallit flew two trips. The first trip was a round trip flight from Chicago to San Francisco, for which Hallit paid $500 for the pilot and $350 for fuel. The second flight was a round trip from Chicago to New York. For this trip, it paid $300 for the pilot and $150 for fuel. The round trip between Chicago and San Francisco is approximately 4,400 miles and the round trip between Chicago and New York is 1,600 miles.

Required

a. Identify the direct and indirect costs that Hallit incurs for each trip.
b. Determine the total cost of each trip.
c. In addition to depreciation, identify three other indirect costs that may need to be allocated to determine the cost of each trip.

L.O. 1, 3, 4

Problem 4-20A   *Cost allocation in a manufacturing company*

Elridge Manufacturing Company makes tents that it sells directly to camping enthusiasts through a mail-order marketing program. The company pays a quality control expert $72,000 per year to inspect completed tents before they are shipped to customers. Assume that the company completed 1,600 tents in January and 1,200 tents in February. For the entire year, the company expects to produce 12,000 tents.

Required

a. Explain how changes in the cost driver (number of tents inspected) affect the total amount of fixed inspection cost.
b. Explain how changes in the cost driver (number of tents inspected) affect the amount of fixed inspection cost per unit.
c. If the cost objective is to determine the cost per tent, is the expert's salary a direct or an indirect cost?
d. How much of the expert's salary should be allocated to tents produced in January and February?

L.O. 1, 4, 7

Problem 4-21A   *Fairness in the allocation process*

Kabila Manufacturing Company uses two departments to make its products. Department I is a cutting department that is machine intensive and uses very few employees. Machines cut and form parts and then place the finished parts on a conveyor belt that carries them to Department II where they are assembled into finished goods. The assembly department is labor intensive and requires many workers to assemble parts into finished goods. The company's manufacturing facility incurs two significant overhead costs: employee fringe benefits and utility costs. The annual costs of fringe benefits are $504,000 and utility costs are $360,000. The typical consumption patterns for the two departments are as follows.

	Department I	Department II	Total
Machine hours used	16,000	4,000	20,000
Direct labor hours used	5,000	13,000	18,000

The supervisor of each department receives a bonus based on how well the department controls costs. The company's current policy requires using a single allocation base (machine hours or labor hours) to allocate the total overhead cost of $864,000.

Required

a. Assume that you are the supervisor of Department I. Choose the allocation base that would minimize your department's share of the total overhead cost. Calculate the amount of overhead that would be allocated to both departments using the base that you selected.

b. Assume that you are the supervisor of Department II. Choose the allocation base that would minimize your department's share of the total overhead cost. Calculate the amount of overhead that would be allocated to both departments using the base that you selected.

c. Assume that you are the plant manager and have the authority to change the company's overhead allocation policy. Formulate an overhead allocation policy that would be fair to the supervisors of both Department I and Department II. Compute the overhead allocations for each department using your policy.

Problem 4-22A *Allocation to accomplish smoothing*

L.O. 1, 3, 5

CHECK FIGURES
a. $4
c. March: $62

Ginter Corporation estimated its overhead costs would be $24,000 per month except for January when it pays the $72,000 annual insurance premium on the manufacturing facility. Accordingly, the January overhead costs were expected to be $108,000 ($72,000 + $36,000). The company expected to use 7,000 direct labor hours per month except during July, August, and September when the company expected 9,000 hours of direct labor each month to build inventories for high demand that normally occurs during the Christmas season. The company's actual direct labor hours were the same as the estimated hours. The company made 3,500 units of product in each month except July, August, and September in which it produced 4,500 units each month. Direct labor costs were $24 per unit, and direct materials costs were $10 per unit.

Required

a. Calculate a predetermined overhead rate based on direct labor hours.
b. Determine the total allocated overhead cost for January, March, and August.
c. Determine the cost per unit of product for January, March, and August.
d. Determine the selling price for the product, assuming that the company desires to earn a gross margin of $20 per unit.

Problem 4-23A *Allocating indirect costs between products*

L.O. 1, 3, 5

CHECK FIGURES
a. Cost/unit for
EZRecords: $225
b. Cost/unit for
ProOffice: $230

June Pasara is considering expanding her business. She plans to hire a salesperson to cover trade shows. Because of compensation, travel expenses, and booth rental, fixed costs for a trade show are expected to be $15,000. The booth will be open 30 hours during the trade show. Ms. Pasara also plans to add a new product line, ProOffice, which will cost $180 per package. She will continue to sell the existing product, EZRecords, which costs $100 per package. Ms. Pasara believes that the salesperson will spend approximately 20 hours selling EZRecords and 10 hours marketing ProOffice.

Required

a. Determine the estimated total cost and cost per unit of each product, assuming that the salesperson is able to sell 80 units of EZRecords and 50 units of ProOffice.

b. Determine the estimated total cost and cost per unit of each product, assuming that the salesperson is able to sell 200 units of EZRecords and 100 units of ProOffice.

c. Explain why the cost per unit figures calculated in Requirement *a* are different from the amounts calculated in Requirement *b*. Also explain how the differences in estimated cost per unit will affect pricing decisions.

Problem 4-24A   *Allocating joint product cost*

Mahdi Chicken Corporation processes and packages chicken for grocery stores. It purchases chickens from farmers and processes them into two different products: chicken drumsticks and chicken steak. From a standard batch of 12,000 pounds of raw chicken that costs $7,000, the company produces two parts: 2,800 pounds of drumsticks and 4,200 pounds of breast for a processing cost of $2,450. The chicken breast is further processed into 3,200 pounds of steak for a processing cost of $2,000. The market price of drumsticks per pound is $1.00 and the market price per pound of chicken steak is $3.40. If Mahdi decided to sell chicken breast instead of chicken steak, the price per pound would be $2.00.

Required

a. Allocate the joint cost to the joint products, drumsticks and breasts, using weight as the allocation base. Calculate the net income for each product. Since the drumsticks are producing a net loss, should that product line be eliminated?

b. Reallocate the joint cost to the joint products, drumsticks and breasts, using relative market values as the allocation base. Calculate the net income for each product. Compare the total net income (drumsticks + breasts) computed in Requirement *b* with that computed in Requirement *a* above. Explain why the total amount is the same. Comment on which allocation base (weight or market value) is more appropriate.

c. Should you further process chicken breasts into chicken steak?

Appendix

Problem 4-25A   *Allocating service center costs—step method and direct method*

Gregory Information Services, Inc., has two service departments: human resources and billing. Gregory's operating departments, organized according to the special industry each department serves, are health care, retail, and legal services. The billing department supports only the three operating departments, but the human resources department supports all operating departments and the billing department. Other relevant information follows.

	Human Resources	Billing	Health Care	Retail	Legal Services
Number of employees	30	60	120	100	80
Annual cost*	$720,000	$1,710,000	$6,000,000	$4,800,000	$2,800,000
Annual revenue	—	—	$9,000,000	$6,200,000	$4,800,000

*This is the operating cost before allocating service department costs.

Required

a. Allocate service department costs to operating departments, assuming that Gregory adopts the step method. The company uses the number of employees as the base for allocating human resources department costs and department annual revenue as the base for allocating the billing department costs.

b. Allocate service department costs to operating departments, assuming that Gregory adopts the direct method. The company uses the number of employees as the base for allocating the human resources department costs and department annual revenue as the base for allocating the billing department costs.

c. Compute the total allocated cost of service centers for each operating department using each allocation method.

Exercise 4-1B *Allocating costs between divisions*

L.O. 1, 3

Siedman and Karr, LLP, has three departments: auditing, tax, and information systems. The departments occupy 2,500 square feet, 1,500 square feet, and 1,000 square feet of office space, respectively. The firm pays $7,500 per month to rent its offices.

Required

How much monthly rent cost should Siedman and Karr allocate to each department?

Exercise 4-2B *Direct versus indirect costs*

L.O. 2

Mullin and Associates, LLP, is an accounting firm that provides two major types of professional services: (1) tax services as provided by the tax department and (2) auditing services as provided by the audit department. Each department has numerous clients. Engagement with each individual client is a separate service (i.e., product) and each department has several engagements in each period. Cost items of the firm follow.

Salary of the partner in charge of the audit department
Salary of the managing partner of the firm
Cost of office supplies such as paper, pencils, erasers, etc.
Depreciation of computers used in the tax department
License fees of the firm
Professional labor for a tax engagement
Secretarial labor supporting both departments
Professional labor for an audit engagement
Depreciation of computers used in the audit department
Salary of the partner in charge of the tax department
Travel expenditures for an audit engagement

Required

a. Identify each cost as being a direct or indirect cost assuming the cost objects are the individual engagements (audit engagements or tax engagements).
b. Identify each cost as being a direct or indirect cost assuming the cost objects are the two departments.
c. Identify each cost as being a direct or indirect cost assuming the cost object is Mullin and Associates, LLP, as a whole.

Exercise 4-3B *Allocating overhead costs among products*

L.O. 3, 5

Jackson Company manufactures three different sizes of automobile sunscreens: large, medium, and small. Jackson expects to incur $900,000 of overhead costs during the next fiscal year. Other budget information for the coming year follows:

	Large	Medium	Small	Total
Direct labor hours	2,500	5,000	4,500	12,000
Machine hours	700	1,300	1,000	3,000

Required

a. Use direct labor hours as the cost driver to compute the allocation rate and the budgeted overhead cost for each product.
b. Use machine hours as the cost driver to compute the allocation rate and the budgeted overhead cost for each product.
c. Describe a set of circumstances where it would be more appropriate to use direct labor hours as the allocation base.
d. Describe a set of circumstances where it would be more appropriate to use machine hours as the allocation base.

L.O. 3, 4

Exercise 4-4B   *Allocating overhead costs among products*

Doddy Company makes three models of computer disks in its factory: Zip100, Zip250, and Zip40. The expected overhead costs for the next fiscal year are as follows:

Payroll for factory managers	$270,000
Factory maintenance costs	110,000
Factory insurance	40,000
Total overhead costs	$420,000

Doddy uses labor hours as the cost driver to allocate overhead cost. Budgeted labor hours for the products are as follows:

Zip100	2,000 hours
Zip250	1,300
Zip40	900
Total labor hours	4,200

Required

a. Allocate the budgeted overhead costs to the products.

b. Provide a possible explanation as to why Doddy chose labor hours, instead of machine hours, as the allocation base.

L.O. 3, 4

Exercise 4-5B   *Allocating costs among products*

Duong Company makes household plastic bags in three different sizes: Snack, Sandwich, and Storage. The estimated direct materials and direct labor costs are as follows.

Expected Costs	Snack	Sandwich	Storage
Direct materials	$140,000	$235,000	$375,000
Direct labor	75,000	145,000	280,000

Duong allocates two major overhead costs among the three products: $36,000 of indirect labor cost for workers who move various materials and products to different stations in the factory and $27,500 of employee pension costs.

Required

Determine the total cost of each product.

L.O. 3, 5

Exercise 4-6B   *Allocating indirect cost over varying levels of production*

Gatch Company's annual factory depreciation is $18,000. Gatch estimated it would operate the factory a total of 2,400 hours this year. The factory operated 200 hours in November and 150 hours in December.

Required

Why would Gatch need to allocate factory depreciation cost? How much depreciation cost should Gatch allocate to products made in November and those made in December?

L.O. 3, 5

Exercise 4-7B   *Allocating indirect cost over varying levels of production*

On January 1, Litton Corporation paid the annual royalty of $576,000 for rights to use patented technology to make batteries for laptop computers. Litton plans to use the patented technology to produce five different models of batteries. Litton uses machine hours as a common cost driver and plans to operate its machines 48,000 hours in the coming year. The company used 3,000 machine hours in June and 3,600 hours in July.

Required

Why would Litton need to allocate the annual royalty payment rather than simply assign it in total to January production? How much of the royalty cost should Litton allocate to products made in June and those made in July?

Exercise 4-8B   *Allocating a fixed cost*

L.O. 3, 5

Last year, Wes Lloyd bought an automobile for $29,000 to use in his taxi business. He expected to drive the vehicle for 150,000 miles before disposing of it for $2,000. Wes drove 3,200 miles this week and 2,800 miles last week.

Required

a. Determine the total cost of vehicle depreciation this week and last week.
b. Explain why allocating the vehicle cost would or would not be relevant to decision making.

Exercise 4-9B   *Allocating overhead cost to accomplish smoothing*

L.O. 3, 5

In 2007, Dupose Corporation incurred direct manufacturing costs of $20 per unit and manufacturing overhead costs of $135,000. The production activity for the four quarters of 2007 follows:

	1st Quarter	2nd Quarter	3rd Quarter	4th Quarter
Number of units produced	3,300	2,700	4,500	2,000

Required

a. Calculate a predetermined overhead rate based on the number of units produced during the year.
b. Allocate overhead costs to each quarter using the overhead rate computed in Requirement *a*.
c. Using the overhead allocation determined in Requirement *b*, calculate the total cost per unit for each quarter.

Exercise 4-10B   *Allocating overhead for product costing*

L.O. 3, 5

Abbott Manufacturing Company produced 500 units of inventory in January 2006. The company expects to produce an additional 5,900 units of inventory during the remaining 11 months of the year, for total estimated production of 6,400 units in 2006. Direct materials and direct labor costs are $74 and $84 per unit, respectively. Abbott expects to incur the following manufacturing overhead costs during the 2006 accounting period:

Indirect materials	$ 6,800
Depreciation on equipment	104,000
Utilities cost	29,200
Salaries of plant manager and staff	304,000
Rental fee on manufacturing facilities	84,000
Total	$528,000

Required

a. Determine the estimated cost of the 500 units of product made in January.
b. Is the cost computed in Requirement *a* actual or estimated? Could Abbott improve accuracy by waiting until December to determine the cost of products? Identify two reasons that a manager would want to know the cost of products in January. Discuss the relationship between accuracy and relevance as it pertains to this problem.

Exercise 4-11B   *How fixed cost allocation affects a pricing decision*

L.O. 3, 5

Eisner Manufacturing Company expects to make 30,000 travel sewing kits during 2007. In January, the company made 1,800 kits. Materials and labor costs for January were $7,200 and $9,000, respectively. In February, Eisner produced 2,200 kits. Material and labor costs for February were $8,800 and $11,000, respectively. The company paid $42,000 for annual factory insurance on January 10, 2007. Ignore other manufacturing overhead costs.

Required

Assuming that Eisner desires to sell its sewing kits for cost plus 25 percent of cost, what price should it charge for the kits produced in January and February?

L.O. 3, 6

Exercise 4-12B   *Allocating joint product cost*

Lofton Food Corporation makes two products from soybeans: cooking oil and cattle feed. From a standard batch of 100,000 pounds of soybeans, Lofton produces 20,000 pounds of cooking oil and 80,000 pounds of cattle feed. Producing a standard batch costs $10,000. The sales prices per pound are $1.00 for cooking oil and $0.75 for cattle feed.

Required

a. Allocate the joint product cost to the two products using weight as the allocation base.
b. Allocate the joint product cost to the two products using market value as the allocation base.

Appendix

L.O. 7

Exercise 4-13B   *Human factor*

McKay Company builds custom sailboats. McKay currently has three boats under construction. The estimated costs to complete each boat are shown below.

	Boat 1	Boat 2	Boat 3
Direct materials	$25,000	$32,000	$12,000
Direct labor	22,000	20,000	14,000

McKay expects to incur $36,000 of indirect (overhead) costs in the process of making the boats.

Required

a. Based on the information provided, name four allocation bases that could be used to assign the overhead costs to each boat.
b. Assume that the production manager of each boat is permitted to recommend how the overhead costs should be allocated to the boats. Which of the allocation bases named in Requirement *a* is the manager of Boat 2 most likely to recommend? Explain why. What argument may the manager of Boat 2 use to justify his choice of the allocation base?
c. Which of the allocation bases would result in the fairer allocation of the overhead costs from the perspective of the company president?
d. Explain how classifying overhead costs into separate pools could improve the fairness of the allocation of the overhead costs.

L.O. 3, 8

Exercise 4-14B   *Allocating a service center cost to operating departments*

The administrative department of Alford Consulting, LLC, provides office administration and professional support to its two operating departments. Annual administrative costs are $450,000. In 2008, the hours chargeable to clients generated by the information services department and the financial planning department were 24,000 and 36,000, respectively. Alford uses chargeable hours as the cost driver for allocating administrative costs to operating departments.

Required

Allocate the administrative costs to the two operating departments.

L.O. 3, 8

Exercise 4-15B   *Allocating service centers' costs to operating departments—step method*

Young Consulting, LLP, has three operating departments: tax, estate planning, and small business. The company's internal accounting and maintenance departments support the operating departments. Moreover, the maintenance department also supports the internal accounting department. Other relevant information follows:

	Annual Cost*	Square Feet	Operating Revenue
Tax	$4,800,000	8,000	$8,500,000
Estate planning	2,300,000	2,000	3,500,000
Small business	3,000,000	4,000	6,000,000
Internal accounting	690,000	1,000	0
Maintenance	450,000	1,000	0

*The annual cost figures do not include costs allocated from service departments.

Young allocates its maintenance cost based on the square footage of each department's office space. The firm allocates the internal accounting cost based on each department's operating revenue.

Required

a. Allocate the maintenance cost to the operating and internal accounting departments.
b. After allocating the maintenance cost, allocate the internal accounting cost to the three operating departments.
c. Compute the total allocated cost of the service departments for each operating department.

Exercise 4-16B *Allocating service centers' costs to operating departments—direct method*   **L.O. 3, 8**

Strait Corporation, a book publisher, has two service departments: editing and typesetting. Strait also has three operating departments: children's fiction, youth fiction, and adult fiction. The annual costs of operating the editing department are $240,000 and of operating the typesetting department are $420,000. Strait uses the direct method to allocate service center costs to operating departments. Other relevant data follow.

	Number of Pages	Number of Hours
Children	15,000	5,000
Youth	10,000	8,000
Adult	5,000	7,000

Required

a. Allocate the service center costs to the operating departments using the number of pages as the cost driver.
b. Allocate the service center costs to the operating departments using the number of hours as the cost driver.

PROBLEMS—SERIES B

Problem 4-17B *Cost accumulation and allocation*   **L.O. 1, 2, 3, 4, 5**

Peavy Tools Company has two production departments in its manufacturing facilities. Home tools specializes in hand tools for individual home users, and professional tools makes sophisticated tools for professional maintenance workers. Peavy's accountant has identified the following annual costs associated with these two products:

Financial data	
Salary of vice president of production	$180,000
Salary of manager, home tools	54,000
Salary of manager, professional tools	43,500
Direct materials cost, home tools	300,000
Direct materials cost, professional tools	375,000
Direct labor cost, home tools	336,000
Direct labor cost, professional tools	414,000
Direct utilities cost, home tools	75,000
Direct utilities cost, professional tools	30,000
General factorywide utilities	31,500
Production supplies	40,500
Fringe benefits	112,500
Depreciation	360,000
Nonfinancial data	
Machine hours, home tools	4,000
Machine hours, professional tools	2,000

Required

a. Identify the costs that are the (1) direct costs of home tools, (2) direct costs of professional tools, and (3) indirect costs.

b. Select the appropriate cost drivers and allocate the indirect costs to home tools and to professional tools.

c. Assume that each department makes only a single product. Home tools produces its Deluxe Drill for home use, and professional tools produces the Professional Drill. The company made 30,000 units of Deluxe Drill and 20,000 units of Professional Drill during the year. Determine the total estimated cost of the products made in each department. If Peavy prices its products at cost plus 30 percent of cost, what price per unit must it charge for the Deluxe Drill and the Professional Drill?

L.O. 1, 3, 4

Problem 4-18B   *Selecting an appropriate cost driver (What is the base?)*

Harbin Research Institute has three departments: biology, chemistry, and physics. The institute's controller wants to estimate the cost of operating each department. He has identified several indirect costs that must be allocated to each department including $11,200 of phone expense, $2,400 of office supplies, $1,120,000 of office rent, $140,000 of janitorial services, and $150,000 of salary paid to the director. To provide a reasonably accurate allocation of costs, the controller identified several possible cost drivers. These drivers and their association with each department follow.

Cost Driver	Biology	Chemistry	Physics
Number of telephones	10	14	16
Number of researchers	8	10	12
Square footage of office space	8,000	8,000	12,000
Number of secretaries	1	1	1

Required

a. Identify the appropriate cost objects.

b. Identify the appropriate cost driver for each indirect cost, and compute the allocation rate for assigning each indirect cost to the cost objects.

c. Determine the amount of telephone expense that should be allocated to each of the three departments.

d. Determine the amount of supplies expense that should be allocated to the physics department.

e. Determine the amount of office rent cost that should be allocated to the chemistry department.

f. Determine the amount of janitorial services cost that should be allocated to the biology department.

g. Identify two cost drivers not listed here that could be used to allocate the cost of the director's salary to the three departments.

L.O. 1, 2

Problem 4-19B   *Cost allocation in a service industry*

Dean, Ivy, and Associates provides legal services for its local community. In addition to its regular attorneys, the firm hires some part-time attorneys to handle small cases. Two secretaries assist all part-time attorneys exclusively. In 2009, the firm paid $48,000 for the two secretaries who worked a total of 3,200 hours. Moreover, the firm paid Vicky Landon $60 per hour and Dan Mosley $50 per hour for their part-time legal services.

In August 2009, Ms. Landon completed a case that took her 60 hours. Mr. Mosley finished a case on which he worked 20 hours. The firm also paid a private investigator to uncover relevant facts. The investigation fees cost $1,000 for Ms. Landon's case and $750 for Mr. Mosley's case. Ms. Landon used 30 hours of secretarial assistance, and Mr. Mosley used 40 hours.

Required

a. Identify the direct and indirect costs incurred in each case completed in August 2009.

b. Determine the total cost of each case.

c. In addition to secretaries' salaries, identify three other indirect costs that may need to be allocated to determine the cost of the cases.

L.O. 1, 3, 4

Problem 4-20B   *Cost allocation in a manufacturing company*

Gwin Door Corporation makes a particular type of door. The labor cost is $90 per door and the material cost is $160 per door. Gwin rents a factory building for $60,000 a month. Gwin plans to produce 24,000 doors annually. In March and April, it made 2,000 and 3,000 doors, respectively.

Required

a. Explain how changes in the cost driver (number of doors made) affect the total amount of fixed rental cost.
b. Explain how changes in the cost driver (number of doors made) affect the fixed rental cost per unit.
c. If the cost objective is to determine the cost per door, is the factory rent a direct or an indirect cost?
d. How much of the factory rent should be allocated to doors produced in March and April?

Problem 4-21B *Fairness in the allocation process*

Ponter Furniture Company has two production departments. The parts department uses automated machinery to make parts; as a result, it uses very few employees. The assembly department is labor intensive because workers manually assemble parts into finished furniture. Employee fringe benefits and utility costs are the two major overhead costs of the company's production division. The fringe benefits and utility costs for the year are $600,000 and $288,000, respectively. The typical consumption patterns for the two departments follow.

	Parts	Assembly	Total
Machine hours used	52,000	8,000	60,000
Direct labor hours used	3,500	20,500	24,000

The supervisor of each department receives a bonus based on how well the department controls costs. The company's current policy requires using a single activity base (machine hours or labor hours) to allocate the total overhead cost of $888,000.

Required

a. Assume that you are the parts department supervisor. Choose the allocation base that would minimize your department's share of the total overhead cost. Calculate the amount of overhead to allocate to both departments using the base that you selected.
b. Assume that you are the assembly department supervisor. Choose the allocation base that would minimize your department's share of the total overhead cost. Calculate the amount of overhead to allocate to both departments using the base that you selected.
c. Assume that you are the plant manager and that you have the authority to change the company's overhead allocation policy. Formulate an overhead allocation policy that would be fair to the supervisors of both the parts and assembly departments. Compute the overhead allocation for each department using your policy.

Problem 4-22B *Allocation to accomplish smoothing*

Lawson Corporation's overhead costs are usually $24,000 per month. However, the company pays $54,000 of real estate tax on the factory facility in March. Thus, the overhead costs for March increase to $78,000. The company normally uses 5,000 direct labor hours per month except for August, September, and October, in which the company requires 9,000 hours of direct labor per month to build inventories for high demand in the Christmas season. Last year, the company's actual direct labor hours were the same as usual. The company made 5,000 units of product in each month except August, September, and October in which it produced 9,000 units per month. Direct labor costs were $8 per unit; direct materials costs were $7 per unit.

Required

a. Calculate a predetermined overhead rate based on direct labor hours.
b. Determine the total allocated overhead cost for the months of March, August, and December.
c. Determine the cost per unit of product for the months of March, August, and December.
d. Determine the selling price for the product, assuming that the company desires to earn a gross margin of $7 per unit.

Problem 4-23B *Allocating indirect cost between products*

Bennett Corporation has hired a marketing representative to sell the company's two products: Marvelous and Wonderful. The representative's total salary and fringe benefits are $8,000 monthly. The product cost is $90 per unit for Marvelous and $144 per unit for Wonderful. Bennett expects the representative to spend 48 hours per month marketing Marvelous and 112 hours promoting Wonderful.

Required

a. Determine the estimated total cost and cost per unit, assuming that the representative is able to sell 100 units of Marvelous and 70 units of Wonderful in a month. Allocate indirect cost on the basis of labor hours.

b. Determine the estimated total cost and cost per unit, assuming that the representative is able to sell 250 units of Marvelous and 140 units of Wonderful. Allocate indirect cost on the basis of labor hours.

c. Explain why the cost per unit figures calculated in Requirement *a* differ from the amounts calculated in Requirement *b*. Also explain how the differences in estimated cost per unit will affect pricing decisions.

L.O. 3, 9

Problem 4-24B   *Allocating joint product cost*

Mountain Tea Co. makes two products: a high-grade tea branded Wulong and a low-grade tea branded San Tea for the Asian market. Mountain purchases tea leaves from tea firms in mountainous villages of Taiwan and processes the tea leaves into a high-quality product. The tea leaves are dried and baked in the manufacturing process. Mountain pays farmers $600 for 900 kilograms of tea leaves. For 900 kilograms of green leaves, the company can produce 100 kilograms of Wulong and 200 kilograms of tea fragments including dried leave stems and broken dried leaves. The cost of this process is $300 per batch. The tea fragments are packaged into San Tea. The market price for San Tea is $2.00 per kilogram. The market price is $20 per kilogram for Wulong. Mountain has an option of taking an additional process to refine the 100 kilograms of Wulong into 30 kilograms of Donding, a prestigious brand. The market price of Donding is $100 per kilogram. The cost of the additional process is $250 per batch.

Required

a. Allocate the joint cost to the joint products, Wulong and San Tea, using weight as the allocation base. Calculate the net income for each product. Since the San Tea is sold at a loss, should that product line be eliminated?

b. Allocate the joint cost to the joint products, Wulong and San Tea, using relative market value as the allocation base. Calculate the net income for each product. Compare the total net income (Wulong + San Tea) computed in Requirement *b* with that computed in Requirement *a* above. Explain why the total amount is the same. Comment on which allocation base (weight or relative market value) is more appropriate.

c. Should you further process Wulong into Donding?

Appendix

L.O. 3, 9

Problem 4-25B   *Allocating service center costs—step method and direct method*

Ryan Corporation has three production departments: forming, assembly, and packaging. The maintenance department supports only the production departments; the computer services department supports all departments including maintenance. Other relevant information follows.

	Forming	Assembly	Packaging	Maintenance	Computer Services
Machine hours	12,000	5,000	3,000	800	0
Number of computers	14	20	11	15	8
Annual cost*	$450,000	$800,000	$250,000	$100,000	$90,000

*This is the annual operating cost before allocating service department costs.

Required

a. Allocate service department costs to operating departments, assuming that Ryan adopts the step method. The company uses the number of computers as the base for allocating the computer services costs and machine hours as the base for allocating the maintenance costs.

b. Use machine hours as the base for allocating maintenance department costs and the number of computers as the base for allocating computer services cost. Allocate service department costs to operating departments, assuming that Ryan adopts the direct method.

c. Compute the total allocated cost of service centers for each operating department using each allocation method.

ATC 4-1 Business Applications Case *Allocating fixed costs at Porsche*

During its fiscal year ending on July 31, 2005, the Dr. Ing. h. c. F. Porsche AG, commonly known as "Porsche" manufactured 90,954 vehicles. During that same year Porsche recorded depreciation on property, plant, and equipment of €264,432,000. (Porsche's financial information is reported in euros, and € is the symbol for the euro.) For the purposes of this problem assume that all of the depreciation related to manufacturing activities.

Required

a. Indicate whether the depreciation charge is a:
   (1) Product cost, or a general, selling and administrative cost.
   (2) Relevant cost with respect to a special order decision.
   (3) Fixed or variable cost relative to the volume of production.
   (4) Direct or indirect if the cost object is the cost of vehicles made in the 2005 fiscal year.

b. Assume that Porsche incurred depreciation of €21,900,000 during each month of the 2005 fiscal year, but that it produced 6,000 vehicles during February and 9,000 during March. Based on monthly costs and production levels, what was the average amount of depreciation cost per vehicle produced during each of these two months, assuming each vehicle was charged the same amount of depreciation?

c. If Porsche had expected to produce 95,000 vehicles during 2005, and expected its annual depreciation to be €264,000,000, what would have been its predetermined overhead charge per vehicle for depreciation? Explain the advantage of using this amount to determine the cost of manufacturing a car in February and March versus the amounts you computed in Requirement *b*.

d. If Porsche's management had estimated the profit per vehicle based on its budgeted production of 95,000 units, would you expect its actual profit per vehicle to be higher or lower than expected? Explain.

ATC 4-2 Group Assignment *Selection of the cost driver*

Vulcan College School of Business is divided into three departments: accounting, marketing, and management. Relevant information for each of the departments follows.

Cost Driver	Accounting	Marketing	Management
Number of students	1,400	800	400
Number of classes per semester	64	36	28
Number of professors	20	24	10

Vulcan is a private school that expects each department to generate a profit. It rewards departments for profitability by assigning 20 percent of each department's profits back to that department. Departments have free rein as to how to use these funds. Some departments have used them to supply professors with computer technology. Others have expanded their travel budgets. The practice has been highly successful in motivating the faculty to control costs. The revenues and direct costs for the year 2004 follow.

	Accounting	Marketing	Management
Revenue	$29,600,000	$16,600,000	$8,300,000
Direct costs	24,600,000	13,800,000	6,600,000

Vulcan allocates to the School of Business $4,492,800 of indirect overhead costs such as administrative salaries and costs of operating the registrar's office and the bookstore.

Required

a. Divide the class into groups and organize the groups into three sections. Assign each section a department. For example, groups in Section 1 should represent the Accounting Department. Groups in Sections 2 and 3 should represent the Marketing Department and Management Department, respectively. Assume that the dean of the school is planning to assign an equal amount of the college overhead to each department. Have the students in each group prepare a response to the dean's plan. Each group should select a spokesperson who is prepared to answer the following questions.

(1) Is your group in favor of or opposed to the allocation plan suggested by the dean?

(2) Does the plan suggested by the dean provide a fair allocation? Why?

The instructor should lead a discussion designed to assess the appropriateness of the dean's proposed allocation plan.

b. Have each group select the cost driver (allocation base) that best serves the self-interest of the department it represents.

c. Consensus on Requirement *c* should be achieved before completing Requirement *d*. Each group should determine the amount of the indirect cost to be allocated to each department using the cost driver that best serves the self-interest of the department it represents. Have a spokesperson from each section go to the board and show the income statement that would result for each department.

d. Discuss the development of a cost driver(s) that would promote fairness rather than self-interest in allocating the indirect costs.

ATC 4-3   Research Assignment   *Cost accounting issues at real-world companies*

The July 2003 issue of *Strategic Finance* contains the article "Roles and Practices in Management Accounting Today: Results From the 2003 IMA-E&Y Survey" written by Ashish Garg, Debashis Ghosh, James Hudick, and Chwen Nowacki. This article reviews findings from a survey of managerial accountants conducted by the Institute of Management Accountants (IMA). Read this article and complete the following requirements.

Required

a. The article notes that cost management is an important element for strategic decision making. Why did respondents to the survey believe this was the case?

b. The authors noted that decision makers were most interested in "actionable" cost information. What are the attributes of actionable cost information?

c. Ninety-eight percent of respondents to the survey said that factors exist that cause distortions of cost information. What factors were identified that are responsible for these distortions?

d. Considering the proliferation of "off-the-shelf" software that is available, many people believe only a minority of companies develop their own cost management systems. According to the article, what percentage of companies actually do develop their systems "in house," and what do you think are the implications of the in-house development for managerial accountants?

ATC 4-4   Writing Assignment   *Selection of the appropriate cost driver*

Bullions Enterprises, Inc. (BEI), makes gold, silver, and bronze medals used to recognize outstanding athletic performance in regional and national sporting events. The per unit direct costs of producing the medals follow.

	Gold	Silver	Bronze
Direct materials	$300	$130	$ 35
Labor	120	120	120

During 2002, BEI made 1,200 units of each type of medal for a total of 3,600 (1,200 × 3) medals. All medals are created through the same production process, and they are packaged and shipped in identical containers. Indirect overhead costs amounted to $324,000. BEI currently uses the number of units as the cost driver for the allocation of overhead cost. As a result, BEI allocated $90 ($324,000 ÷ 3,600 units) of overhead cost to each medal produced.

Required

The president of the company has questioned the wisdom of assigning the same amount of overhead to each type of medal. He believes that overhead should be assigned on the basis of the cost to produce the medals. In other words, more overhead should be charged to expensive gold medals, less to silver, and even less to bronze. Assume that you are BEI's chief financial officer. Write a memo responding to the president's suggestion.

ATC 4-5   Ethical Dilemma   *Allocation to achieve fairness*

The American Acupuncture Association offers continuing professional education courses for its members at its annual meeting. Instructors are paid a fee for each student attending their courses but are charged a fee for overhead costs that is deducted from their compensation. Overhead costs include fees paid to rent instructional equipment such as overhead projectors, provide supplies to participants, and offer refreshments during coffee breaks. The number of courses offered is used as the allocation base for determining the overhead charge. For example, if overhead costs amount to $5,000 and 25 courses are offered, each course is allocated an overhead charge of $200 ($5,000 ÷ 25 courses). Heidi McCarl, who taught one of the courses, received the following statement with her check in payment for her instructional services.

Instructional fees (20 students × $50 per student)	$1,000
Less: Overhead charge	(200)
Less: Charge for sign language assistant	(240)
Amount due instructor	$ 560

Although Ms. McCarl was well aware that one of her students was deaf and required a sign language assistant, she was surprised to find that she was required to absorb the cost of this service.

Required

a. Given that the Americans with Disabilities Act stipulates that the deaf student cannot be charged for the cost of providing sign language, who should be required to pay the cost of sign language services?
b. Explain how allocation can be used to promote fairness in distributing service costs to the disabled. Describe two ways to treat the $240 cost of providing sign language services that improve fairness.

ATC 4-6   Spreadsheet Assignment   *Using Excel*

Brook Health Care Center, Inc., has three clinics servicing the Birmingham metropolitan area. The company's legal services department supports the clinics. Moreover, its computer services department supports all of the clinics and the legal services department. The company uses the number of computer workstations as the cost driver for allocating the cost of computer services and the number of patients as the cost driver for allocating the cost of legal services. The annual cost of the Department of Legal Services was $340,000, and the annual cost of the Department of Computer Services was $250,000. Other relevant information follows.

	Number of Patients	Number of Workstations
Hoover Clinic	3,100	17
Eastwood Clinic	2,300	13
Gardendale Clinic	2,800	6
Legal Services	0	14

Required

a. Construct a spreadsheet like the following one to allocate the service costs using the step method.

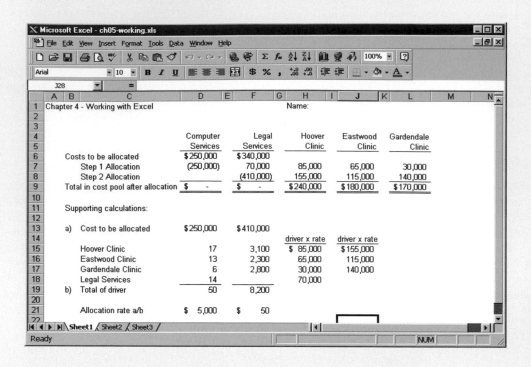

Spreadsheet Tips

1. The headings in rows 4 and 5 are right aligned. To right align text, choose Format, then Cells, and then click on the tab titled Alignment, and set the horizontal alignment to Right. The shortcut method to right align text is to click on the right align icon in the middle of the second tool bar.

2. The supporting calculation section must be completed simultaneously with the allocation table. However, most of the supporting calculations can be completed first. The exception is that the value in cell F13 refers to the sum of cells F6 and F7.

ATC 4-7   Spreadsheet Assignment   *Mastering Excel*

www.mhhe.com/edmonds2008

Phillips Paints manufactures three types of paint in a joint process: rubberized paint, rust-proofing paint, and aluminum paint. In a standard batch of 250,000 gallons of raw material, the outputs are 120,000 gallons of rubberized paint, 40,000 gallons of rust-proofing paint, and 90,000 gallons of aluminum paint. The production cost of a batch is $2,700,000. The sales prices per gallon are $15, $18, and $20 for rubberized, rust-proofing, and aluminum paint, respectively.

Required

a. Construct a spreadsheet to allocate joint costs to the three products using the number of gallons as the allocation base.

b. Include formulas in your spreadsheet to calculate the gross margin for each paint.

COMPREHENSIVE PROBLEM

Magnificent Modems has excess production capacity and is considering the possibility of making and selling paging equipment. The following estimates are based on a production and sales volume of 1,000 pagers.

Unit-level manufacturing costs are expected to be $20. Sales commissions will be established at $1 per unit. The current facility-level costs, including depreciation on manufacturing equipment ($60,000), rent on the manufacturing facility ($50,000), depreciation on the administrative equipment ($12,000), and other fixed administrative expenses ($71,950), will not be affected by the production of the pagers. The chief accountant has decided to allocate the facility-level costs to the existing product (modems) and to the new product (pagers) on the basis of the number of units of product made (i.e., 5,000 modems and 1,000 pagers).

Required

a. Determine the per-unit cost of making and selling 1,000 pagers.

b. Assuming the pagers could be sold at a price of $34 each, should Magnificent make the pagers?

c. Comment on the validity of using the number of units as an allocation base.

CHAPTER 5

Relevant Information for Special Decisions

After you have mastered the material in this chapter, you will be able to:

1. Identify the characteristics of relevant information.

2. Distinguish between unit-level, batch-level, product-level, and facility-level costs and understand how these costs affect decision making.

3. Make appropriate special order decisions.

4. Make appropriate outsourcing decisions.

5. Make appropriate segment elimination decisions.

6. Make appropriate asset replacement decisions.

7. Explain the conflict between short-term and long-term profitability (Appendix).

8. Make decisions about allocating scarce resources (Appendix).

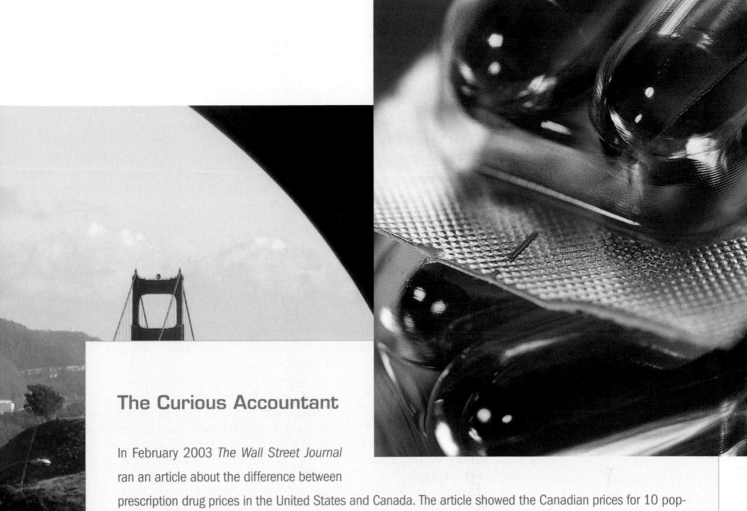

The Curious Accountant

In February 2003 *The Wall Street Journal* ran an article about the difference between prescription drug prices in the United States and Canada. The article showed the Canadian prices for 10 popular prescription drugs, such as **Celebrex** and **Zocor**, were only 38 percent of prices charged in the United States.

Major pharmaceutical companies have *earnings before tax* that average around 25 percent of sales, indicating that their costs average around 75 percent of the prices they charge. In other words, it cost approximately 75 cents to generate one dollar of revenue. Given that drugs are sold in Canada for 38 percent of the U.S. sales price, a drug that is sold in the U.S. for a dollar would be sold in Canada for only 38 cents.

How can drugs be sold in Canada for less (38 cents) than cost (75 cents)? (Answer on page 200.)

CHAPTER OPENING

Mary Daniels paid $25,000 cash to purchase a car that she rents to a relative. The car has a five-year useful life and a $5,000 salvage value. After renting the car for one year, the relative offered to buy the car from Ms. Daniels at a price of $18,000. While talking to her neighbor about the offer, the neighbor said the price was too low. Indeed, the neighbor showed her research data that proved the market value of the car was $19,000 and offered to pay her that amount for the car. Ms. Daniels really wanted to get rid of the car but

ultimately decided not to sell it because she did not want to take a loss on the car.[1] Did Ms. Daniels make the right decision?

Whether Ms. Daniels will be better off selling the car or keeping it is unknown. However, it is certain that she based her decision on irrelevant data. Ms. Daniels incurred a loss when the value of the car dropped. She cannot avoid a loss that already exists. Past mistakes should not affect current decisions. The current value of the car is $19,000. Ms. Daniels's decision is whether to take the money or keep the car. The book value of the car is not relevant. ∎

Relevant Information

Identify the characteristics of relevant information.

How can you avoid irrelevant information when making decisions? Two primary characteristics distinguish relevant from useless information. Specifically, **relevant information** (1) differs among the alternatives and (2) is future oriented.

The first characteristic recognizes that relevant information differs for one or more of the alternatives being considered. For example, in the Daniels case the offers to buy the car are relevant because the amounts of the offers are different. Ms. Daniels will receive $18,000 if she accepts the relative's offer or, alternatively, $19,000 if she accepts the neighbor's offer. In other words, the offering price makes a difference to the decision. In contrast, the $25,000 original cost is not relevant because it is the same regardless of whether the car is sold to the relative or the neighbor.

The second characteristic of relevant information is that it impacts the future. "Don't cry over spilt milk." "It's water over the dam." These aphorisms remind people they cannot change the past. With regard to business decisions, the principle means you cannot avoid a cost that has already been incurred. In the Daniels example, the historical cost ($25,000) of the car is not relevant to a decision regarding whether to sell the car today. The current market value of $19,000 is relevant to the decision regarding whether to sell the car today.

It is interesting to note that the two characteristics are merely different views of the same concept because historical information does not differ between the alternatives. In other words, we could say that historical costs are not relevant because they do not differ between alternatives associated with current decisions.

Sunk Cost

Historical costs are frequently called *sunk costs*. Since **sunk costs** have been incurred in past transactions, they cannot be changed and are not relevant for making current decisions. The $25,000 original cost of the car in the Daniels example is a sunk cost.

Why even bother to collect historical information if it is not relevant? Historical information may be useful in predicting the future. A company that earned $5 million last year is more likely to earn $5 million this year than a company that earned $5,000 last year. The predictive capacity is relevant because it provides insight into the future.

---

[1]Depreciation is $4,000 [($25,000 − $5,000) ÷ 5] per year. The book value of the car after one year is $21,000 ($25,000 cost − $4,000 accumulated depreciation). If Ms. Daniels accepts the neighbor's $19,000 offer, she will have to recognize a $2,000 loss ($21,000 book value − $19,000 selling price).

Opportunity Costs

An **opportunity cost** is the sacrifice that is incurred in order to obtain an alternative opportunity. For example, in the above case, Ms. Daniels must give up the opportunity to obtain $19,000 in order to keep the car. So, the opportunity cost of owning the car is $19,000. Since this cost differs between the alternatives of owning the car versus selling it and since it affects the present or future, it is relevant to the decision regarding whether to keep or sell the car.

Notice that Ms. Daniels has two offers to sell the car, the relative's $18,000 offer and the neighbor's $19,000. Does this mean that the opportunity cost of keeping the car is $37,000 ($18,000 + $19,000)? No. Opportunity costs are not cumulative. Ms. Daniels really has only one opportunity. If she accepts the neighbor's offer, she must reject the relative's offer or vice versa. Accountants normally measure opportunity cost as the highest value of the available alternatives. In this case, the opportunity cost of keeping the car is $19,000.

Aqua, Inc., makes statues for use in fountains. On January 1, 2003, the company paid $13,500 for a mold to make a particular type of statue. The mold had an expected useful life of four years and a salvage value of $1,500. On January 1, 2005, the mold had a market value of $3,000 and a salvage value of $1,200. The expected useful life did not change. What is the relevant cost of using the mold during 2005?

Answer

The relevant cost of using the mold in 2005 is the opportunity cost [(market value − salvage value) ÷ remaining useful life], in this case, ($3,000 − $1,200) ÷ 2 = $900. The book value of the asset and associated depreciation is based on a sunk cost that cannot be avoided because it has already been incurred and therefore is not relevant to current decisions. In contrast, Aqua could avoid the opportunity cost (market value) by selling the mold.

CHECK YOURSELF 5.1

Relevance Is an Independent Concept

The concept of relevance is independent from the concept of cost behavior. In a given circumstance, **relevant costs** could be either fixed or variable. Consider the following illustration. Executives of Better Bakery Products are debating whether to add a new product, either cakes or pies, to the company's line. Projected costs for the two options follow.

Cost of Cakes		Cost of Pies	
Materials (per unit)	$ 1.50	Materials (per unit)	$ 2.00
Direct labor (per unit)	1.00	Direct labor (per unit)	1.00
Supervisor's salary*	25,000.00	Supervisor's salary*	25,000.00
Franchise fee†	50,000.00	Advertising‡	40,000.00

*It will be necessary to hire a new production supervisor at a cost of $25,000 per year.

†Cakes will be distributed under a nationally advertised label. Better Bakery pays an annual franchise fee for the right to use the product label. Because of the established brand name, Better Bakery will not be required to advertise the product.

‡Better Bakery will market the pies under its own name and will advertise the product in the local market in which the product sells.

Which costs are relevant? Fifty cents per unit of the materials can be avoided by choosing cakes instead of pies. A portion of the materials cost is therefore relevant. Labor costs will be one dollar per unit whether Better Bakery makes cakes or pies. Labor cost is therefore not relevant. Although both materials and direct labor are variable costs, one is relevant but the other is not.

REALITY BYTES

Determining what price to charge for their company's goods or services is one of the most difficult decisions that business managers make. Charge too much and customers will go elsewhere. Charge less than customers are willing to pay and lose the opportunity to earn profits. This problem is especially difficult when managers are deciding if they should reduce (mark down) the price of aging inventory—for example, flowers that are beginning to wilt, fruit that is beginning to over-ripen, or clothing that is going out of season.

At first managers may be reluctant to mark down the inventory below its cost because this would cause the company to take a loss on the aging inventory. However, the concept of sunk cost applies here. Since the existing inventory has already been paid for, its cost is sunk. Since the cost is sunk it is not relevant to the decision. Does this mean the merchandise should be sold for any price? Not necessarily. The concept of opportunity cost must also be considered.

If the goods are marked down too far, too quickly, they may be sold for less than is possible. The lost potential revenue is an opportunity cost. To minimize the opportunity cost, the amount of a markdown must be the smallest amount necessary to sell the merchandise. The decision is further complicated by qualitative considerations. If a business develops a reputation for repeated markdowns, customers may hesitate to buy goods, thinking that the price will fall further if they only wait a while. The result is a dilemma as to when and how much to mark down aging inventories.

How do managers address this dilemma? Part of the answer has been the use of technology. For years airlines have used computerized mathematical models to help them decide how many seats on a particular flight should be sold at a discount. More recently, retailers began using this same type of modeling software. Such software allows retailers to take fewer markdowns at more appropriate times, thereby resulting in higher overall gross profit margins.

Since Better Bakery must hire a supervisor under either alternative, the supervisor's salary is not relevant. The franchise fee can be avoided if Better Bakery makes pies and advertising costs can be avoided if it makes cakes. All three of these costs are fixed, but only two are relevant. Finally, all the costs (whether fixed or variable) could be avoided if Better Bakery rejects both products. Whether a cost is fixed or variable has no bearing on its relevance.

Relevance Is Context-Sensitive

A particular cost that is relevant in one context may be irrelevant in another. Consider a store that carries men's, women's, and children's clothing. The store manager's salary could not be avoided by eliminating the children's department, but it could be avoided if the entire store were closed. The salary is not relevant to deciding whether to eliminate the children's department but is relevant with respect to deciding to close a store. In one context, the salary is not relevant. In the other context, it is relevant.

Relationship Between Relevance and Accuracy

Information need not be exact to be relevant. You may decide to delay purchasing a laptop computer you want if you know its price is going to drop even if you don't know exactly how much the price decrease will be. You know part of the cost can be avoided by waiting; you are just not sure of the amount.

The most useful information is both relevant and precise. Totally inaccurate information is useless. Likewise, irrelevant information is useless regardless of its accuracy.

Quantitative Versus Qualitative Characteristics of Decision Making

Relevant information can have both **quantitative** and **qualitative characteristics.** The previous examples focused on quantitative data. Now consider qualitative issues. Suppose you are deciding which of two laptop computers to purchase. Computer A costs $300 more than Computer B. Both computers satisfy your technical requirements; however, Computer A has a more attractive appearance. From a quantitative standpoint, you would select Computer B because you could avoid $300 of cost. However, if the laptop will be used in circumstances when clients need to be impressed, appearance—a qualitative characteristic—may be more important than minimizing cost. You might purchase Computer A even though quantitative factors favor Computer B. Both qualitative and quantitative data are relevant to decision making.

As with quantitative data, qualitative features must *differ* between the alternatives to be relevant. If the two computers were identical in appearance, attractiveness would not be relevant to making the decision.

Differential Revenue and Avoidable Cost

Since relevant revenue *differs* among the alternatives, it is sometimes called **differential revenue.** To illustrate, assume Pecks Department Stores sells men's, women's, and children's clothing and is considering eliminating the children's line. The revenue generated by the children's department is differential (relevant) revenue because Pecks' total revenue would be different if the children's department were eliminated.

Why would Pecks consider eliminating the children's department and thereby lose the differential (relevant) revenue? Pecks may be able to save more by eliminating the cost of operating the department than it loses in differential revenue. Some but not all of the costs associated with operating the children's department can be saved. For example, if Pecks Department Stores eliminates the children's department, the company can eliminate the cost of the department manager's salary but cannot get rid of the salary of the company president. The costs that stay the same are not relevant. The costs that can be *avoided* by closing the department are relevant. Indeed, relevant costs are frequently called *avoidable costs.*

Avoidable costs are the costs managers can eliminate by making specific choices. In the Pecks example, the cost of the department manager's salary is an avoidable (relevant) cost. The cost of the president's salary is not avoidable and is not relevant to the elimination decision.

Relationship of Cost Avoidance to a Cost Hierarchy

LO 2

Distinguish between unit-level, batch-level, product-level, and facility-level costs and understand how these costs affect decision making.

Topic Tackler

PLUS

5-1

Classifying costs into one of four hierarchical levels helps identify avoidable costs.[2]

1. *Unit-level costs.* Costs incurred each time a company generates one unit of product are **unit-level costs.**[3] Examples include the cost of direct materials, direct labor, inspections, packaging, shipping, and handling. Incremental (additional) unit-level costs increase *with each additional unit of product generated. Unit-level costs can be avoided by eliminating the production of a single unit of product.*

2. *Batch-level costs.* Many products are generated in batches rather than individual units. For example, a heating and air conditioning technician may service a batch of air conditioners in an apartment complex. Some of the job costs apply only to individual units, and other costs relate to the entire batch. For instance, the labor to service each air conditioner is a unit-level cost, but the cost of driving to the site is a **batch-level cost.**

   Classifying costs as unit- versus batch-level frequently depends on the context rather than the type of cost. For example, shipping and handling costs to send 200 computers to a university are batch-level costs. In contrast, the shipping and handling cost to deliver a single computer to each of a number of individual customers is a unit-level cost. Eliminating a batch of work avoids both batch-level and unit-level costs. Similarly, adding a batch of work increases batch-level and unit-level costs. Increasing the number of units in a particular batch increases unit-level but not batch-level costs. Decreasing the number of units in a batch reduces unit-level costs but not batch-level costs.

3. *Product-level costs.* Costs incurred to support specific products or services are called **product-level costs.** Product-level costs include quality inspection costs, engineering design costs, the costs of obtaining and defending patents, the costs of regulatory compliance, and inventory holding costs such as interest, insurance, maintenance, and storage. *Product-level costs can be avoided by discontinuing a product line.* For example, suppose the Snapper Company makes the engines used in its lawn mowers. Buying engines from an outside supplier instead of making them would allow Snapper to avoid the product-level costs such as legal fees for patents, manufacturing supervisory costs of producing the engines, and the maintenance and inventory costs of holding engine parts.

4. *Facility-level costs.* **Facility-level costs** are incurred to support the entire company. They are not related to any specific product, batch, or unit of product. Because these costs maintain the facility as a whole, they are frequently called *facility-sustaining costs.* Facility-level costs include building rent or depreciation, personnel administration and training, property and real estate taxes, insurance, maintenance, administrative salaries, general selling costs, landscaping, utilities, and security. Total facility-level costs cannot be avoided unless the entire company is dissolved. However, eliminating a business segment (such as a division, department, or office) may enable a company to avoid some facility-level

---

[2]R. Cooper and R. S. Kaplan, *The Design of Cost Management Systems* (Englewood Cliffs, NJ: Prentice-Hall, 1991). Our classifications are broader than those typically presented. They encompass service and merchandising companies as well as manufacturing businesses. The original cost hierarchy was developed as a platform for activity-based costing, a topic introduced later. These classifications are equally useful as a tool for identifying avoidable costs.

[3]Recall that we use the term *product* in a generic sense to represent producing goods or services.

costs. For example, if a bank eliminates one of its branches, it can avoid the costs of renting, maintaining, and insuring that particular branch building. In general, *segment-level* facility costs can be avoided when a segment is eliminated. In contrast, *corporate-level* facility costs cannot be avoided unless the corporation is eliminated.

Precise distinctions between the various categories are often difficult to draw. One company may incur sales staff salaries as a facility-level cost while another company may pay sales commissions traceable to product lines or even specific units of a product line. Cost classifications cannot be memorized. Classifying specific cost items into the appropriate categories requires thoughtful judgment.

Relevant Information and Special Decisions

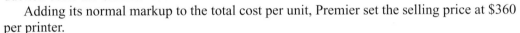

Five types of special decisions are frequently encountered in business practice: (1) special order, (2) outsourcing, (3) segment elimination, (4) asset replacement, and (5) scarce resource allocation. The following sections discuss using relevant information in making the first four types of special decisions. The Appendix to this chapter discusses scarce resource decisions.

LO 3

Make appropriate special order decisions.

Special Order Decisions

Occasionally, a company receives an offer to sell its goods at a price significantly below its normal selling price. The company must make a **special order decision** to accept or reject the offer.

Topic Tackler

PLUS

5-2

Quantitative Analysis

Assume Premier Office Products manufactures printers. Premier expects to make and sell 2,000 printers in 10 batches of 200 units per batch during the coming year. Expected production costs are summarized in Exhibit 5.1.

PREMIER OFFICE PRODUCTS

Adding its normal markup to the total cost per unit, Premier set the selling price at $360 per printer.

Suppose Premier receives a *special order* from a new customer for 200 printers. If Premier accepts the order, its expected sales would increase from 2,000 units to 2,200 units. But the special order customer is willing to pay only $250 per printer. This price is well below not only Premier's normal selling price of $360 but also the company's expected per unit cost of $329.25. Should Premier accept or reject the special order? At first glance, it seems Premier should reject the special order because the customer's offer is below the expected cost per unit. Analyzing relevant costs and revenue leads, however, to a different conclusion.

The quantitative analysis follows in three steps.

Step 1   Determine the amount of the relevant (differential) revenue Premier will earn by accepting the special order. Premier's alternatives are (1) to accept or (2) to reject the special order. If Premier accepts the special order, additional revenue will be $50,000 ($250 × 200 units). If Premier rejects the special order, additional revenue will be zero. Since the amount of revenue differs between the alternatives, the $50,000 is relevant.

EXHIBIT 5.1

Budgeted Cost for Expected Production of 2,000 Printers

Unit-level costs		
Materials costs (2,000 units × $90)	$180,000	
Labor costs (2,000 units × $82.50)	165,000	
Overhead (2,000 units × $7.50)	15,000	
Total unit-level costs (2,000 × $180)		$360,000
Batch-level costs		
Assembly setup (10 batches × $1,700)	17,000	
Materials handling (10 batches × $500)	5,000	
Total batch-level costs (10 batches × $2,200)		22,000
Product-level costs		
Engineering design	14,000	
Production manager salary	63,300	
Total product-level costs		77,300
Facility level costs		
Segment-level costs		
Division manager's salary	85,000	
Administrative costs	12,700	
Corporate-level costs		
Company president's salary	43,200	
Depreciation	27,300	
General expenses	31,000	
Total facility-level costs		199,200
Total expected cost		$658,500

Cost per unit: $658,500 ÷ 2,000 = $329.25

Answers to The Curious Accountant

There are several factors that enable drug companies to reduce their prices to certain customers. One significant factor is the issue of relevant cost. Pharmaceutical manufacturers have a substantial amount of fixed cost, such as research and development. For example, in 2004 **Pfizer Inc.** had research and development expenses that were 14.6 percent of sales, while its cost of goods sold expense was only 14.4 percent of sales. With respect to a special order decision, the research and development costs would not change and therefore would not be relevant. In contrast, the unit-level cost of goods sold would increase and therefore would be relevant. Clearly, relevant costs are significantly less than the total cost. If Canadian prices are based on relevant costs, that is, if drug companies view Canadian sales as a special order opportunity, the lower prices may provide a contribution to profitability even though they are significantly less than the prices charged in the United States.

Step 2 **Determine the amount of the relevant (differential) cost Premier will incur by accepting the special order.** Examine the costs in Exhibit 5.1. If Premier accepts the special order, it will incur additional unit-level costs (materials, labor, and overhead). It will also incur the cost of one additional 200-unit batch. The unit- and batch-level costs are relevant because Premier could avoid them by rejecting the special order. The other costs in Exhibit 5.1 are not relevant because Premier will incur them whether it accepts or rejects the special order.

Step 3 **Accept the special order if the relevant revenue exceeds the relevant (avoidable) cost. Reject the order if relevant cost exceeds relevant revenue.** Exhibit 5.2 summarizes the relevant figures. Since the relevant revenue exceeds the relevant cost, Premier should accept the special order because profitability will increase by $11,800.

EXHIBIT 5.2

Relevant Information for Special Order of 200 Printers

Differential revenue ($250 × 200 units)	$50,000
Avoidable unit-level costs ($180 × 200 units)	(36,000)
Avoidable batch-level costs ($2,200 × 1 batch)	(2,200)
Contribution to income	$11,800

Opportunity Costs

Premier can consider the special order because it has enough excess productive capacity to make the additional units. Suppose Premier has the opportunity to lease its excess capacity (currently unused building and equipment) for $15,000. If Premier uses the excess capacity to make the additional printers, it must forgo the opportunity to lease the excess capacity to a third party. Sacrificing the potential leasing income represents an opportunity cost of accepting the special order. Adding this opportunity cost to the other relevant costs increases the cost of accepting the special order to $53,200 ($38,200 unit-level and batch-level costs + $15,000 opportunity cost). The avoidable costs would then exceed the differential revenue, resulting in a projected loss of $3,200 ($50,000 differential revenue − $53,200 avoidable costs). Under these circumstances Premier would be better off rejecting the special order and leasing the excess capacity.

Relevance and the Decision Context

Assume Premier does not have the opportunity to lease its excess capacity. Recall the original analysis indicated the company could earn an $11,800 contribution to profit by accepting a special order to sell 200 printers at $250 per unit (see Exhibit 5.2). Because Premier can earn a contribution to profit by selling printers for $250 each, can the company reduce its normal selling price (price charged to existing customers) to $250? The answer is no, as illustrated in Exhibit 5.3.

EXHIBIT 5.3

Projections Based on 2,200 Printers at a Sales Price of $250 per Unit		
Revenue ($250 × 2,200 units)		$ 550,000
Unit-level supplies and inspection ($180 × 2,200 units)	$396,000	
Batch-level costs ($2,200 × 11 batches)	24,200	
Product-level costs	77,300	
Facility-level costs	199,200	
Total cost		(696,700)
Projected loss		$(146,700)

If a company is to be profitable, it must ultimately generate revenue in excess of total costs. Although the facility-level and product-level costs are not relevant to the special order decision, they are relevant to the operation of the business as a whole.

Qualitative Characteristics

Should a company ever reject a special order if the relevant revenues exceed the relevant costs? Qualitative characteristics may be even more important than quantitative ones. If Premier's regular customers learn the company sold printers to another buyer at $250 per unit, they may demand reduced prices on future purchases. Exhibit 5.3 shows Premier cannot reduce the price for all customers. Special order customers should therefore come from outside Premier's normal sales territory. In addition, special order customers should be advised that the special price does not apply to repeat business. Cutting off a special order customer who has been permitted to establish a continuing relationship is likely to lead to ill-feelings and harsh words. A business's reputation can depend on how management handles such relationships. Finally, at full capacity, Premier should reject any special orders at reduced prices because filling those orders reduces its ability to satisfy customers who pay full price.

Outsourcing Decisions

Companies can sometimes purchase products they need for less than it would cost to make them. This circumstance explains why automobile manufacturers purchase rather than make many of the parts in their cars or why a caterer might buy gourmet desserts from a specialty company. Buying goods and services from other companies rather than producing them internally is commonly called **outsourcing.**

Make appropriate outsourcing decisions.

Quantitative Analysis

Assume Premier Office Products is considering whether to outsource production of the printers it currently makes. A supplier has offered to sell an unlimited supply of printers to Premier for $240 each. The estimated cost of making the printers is $329.25 per unit (see Exhibit 5.1). The data suggest that Premier could save money by outsourcing. Analyzing relevant costs proves this presumption wrong.

A two-step quantitative analysis for the outsourcing decision follows:

Step 1   **Determine the production costs Premier can avoid if it outsources printer production.** A review of Exhibit 5.1 discloses the costs Premier could avoid by outsourcing. If Premier purchases the printers, it can avoid the unit-level costs (materials, labor, overhead), assembly setup costs, and materials handling costs. It can also avoid the product-level costs (engineering design costs and production manager salary). Deciding to outsource will not, however, affect the facility-level costs. Because Premier will incur them whether or not it outsources printer production, the facility-level costs are not relevant to the outsourcing decision. Exhibit 5.4 shows the avoidable (relevant) costs of outsourcing.

Step 2   **Compare the avoidable (relevant) production costs with the cost of buying the product and select the lower-cost option.** Because the relevant production

That test was so easy. Why is your score so bad?

I outsourced my homework.

Relevant Cost for Expected Production for Outsourcing 2,000 Printers

Unit-level costs ($180 × 2,000 units)	$360,000
Batch-level costs ($2,200 × 10 batches)	22,000
Product-level costs	77,300
Total relevant cost	$459,300

Cost per unit: $459,300 ÷ 2,000 = $229.65

cost is less than the purchase price of the printers ($229.65 per unit versus $240.00), the quantitative analysis suggests that Premier should continue to make the printers. Profitability would decline by $20,700 [$459,300 − ($240 × 2,000)] if printer production were outsourced.

Opportunity Costs

Suppose Premier's accountant determines that the space Premier currently uses to manufacture printers could be converted to warehouse space for storing finished goods. Using this space for warehouse storage would save Premier the $40,000 per year it currently spends to rent warehouse space. By using the space to manufacture printers, Premier is *forgoing the opportunity* to save $40,000 in warehouse costs. Because this *opportunity cost* can be avoided by purchasing the printers, it is relevant to the outsourcing decision. After adding the opportunity cost to the other relevant costs, the total relevant cost increases to $499,300 ($459,300 + $40,000) and the relevant cost per unit becomes $249.65 ($499,300 ÷ 2,000). Since Premier can purchase printers for $240, it should outsource printer production. It would be better off buying the printers and using the warehouse space to store finished goods than to continue producing the printers.

Evaluating the Effect of Growth on the Level of Production

The decision to outsource would change if expected production increased from 2,000 to 3,000 units. Because some of the avoidable costs are fixed relative to the level of production, cost per unit decreases as volume increases. For example, the product-level costs (engineering design, production manager's salary, and opportunity cost) are fixed relative to the level of production. Exhibit 5.5 shows the relevant cost per unit if Premier expects to produce 3,000 printers.

At 3,000 units of production, the relevant cost of making printers is less than the cost of outsourcing ($230.10 versus $240.00). If management believes the company is likely to experience growth in the near future, it should reject the outsourcing option. Managers must consider potential growth when making outsourcing decisions.

Qualitative Features

A company that uses **vertical integration** controls the full range of activities from acquiring raw materials to distributing goods and services. Outsourcing reduces the level of vertical integration, passing some of a company's control over its products to outside suppliers. The reliability of the supplier is critical to an outsourcing decision. An unscrupulous supplier may lure an unsuspecting manufacturer into an outsourcing decision using **low-ball pricing.** Once the manufacturer is dependent on the supplier, the supplier raises prices. If a price sounds too good to be true, it probably is too good to be true. Other potential problems include product quality and delivery commitments. If the printers do not work properly or are not delivered on time, Premier's customers will be dissatisfied with Premier, not the supplier. Outsourcing requires that Premier depend on the supplier to deliver quality products at designated prices according to a specified schedule. Any supplier failures will become Premier's failures.

To protect themselves from unscrupulous or incompetent suppliers, many companies establish a select list of reliable **certified suppliers.** These companies seek to become the preferred customers of the suppliers by offering incentives such as guaranteed volume purchases with prompt payments. These incentives motivate the suppliers to ship high-quality products on a timely basis. The purchasing companies recognize that prices ultimately depend on the suppliers' ability to control costs, so the buyers and suppliers work together to minimize costs. For example, buyers may share confidential information about

Relevant Cost for Expected Production for Outsourcing 3,000 Printers

Unit-level costs ($180 × 3,000 units)	$540,000
Batch-level costs ($2,200 × 15 batches)	33,000
Product-level costs	77,300
Opportunity cost	40,000
Total relevant cost	$690,300

Cost per unit: $690,300 ÷ 3,000 units = $230.10

FOCUS ON INTERNATIONAL ISSUES

ARE YOU SURE YOUR GERMAN CAR WAS MADE IN GERMANY?

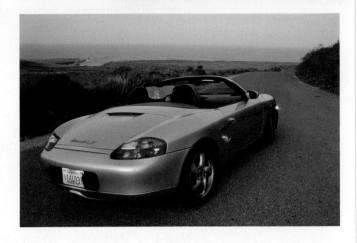

In recent years there has been much discussion about American companies outsourcing work to other workers in other countries. However, some activities that are seldom outsourced by American companies are routinely outsourced by companies in other countries. In fact, sometime the "foreign country" who provides the outsourcing is the United States.

Consider an example from the automotive industry. While American automobile companies may use parts that were manufactured in another country, the final assembly of cars they sell in the United States is usually performed in their own plants in the United States or Canada. Japanese auto companies also tend to perform the final assembly of their cars in their own plants, which may be located in another country. In contrast, European car makers are more willing to outsource the final assembly, as well as engineering and parts production, to independent companies. For example, most, if not all BMW X3s are not assembled at a **BMW** plant, but by the employees of **Magna Steyr** in Graz, Austria. This company, by the way, is a subsidiary of **Magna International**, which is a Canadian company. And that Porsche Boxster you are hoping to receive as a graduation gift— there is about a 2 to 1 chance it will be built by **Valumet Automotive** in Finland.

Source: For more details on outsourcing by European automakers, see "This Is Not a BMW Plant," *Fortune,* April 18, 2005.

their production plans with suppliers if such information would enable the suppliers to more effectively control costs.

Companies must approach outsourcing decisions cautiously even when relationships with reliable suppliers are ensured. Outsourcing has both internal and external effects. It usually displaces employees. If the supplier experiences difficulties, reestablishing internal production capacity is expensive once a trained workforce has been released. Loyalty and trust are difficult to build but easy to destroy. In fact, companies must consider not only the employees who will be discharged but also the morale of those who remain. Cost reductions achieved through outsourcing are of little benefit if they are acquired at the expense of low morale and reduced productivity.

In spite of potential pitfalls outsourcing entails, the vast majority of U.S. businesses engage in some form of it. Such widespread acceptance suggests that most companies believe the benefits achieved through outsourcing exceed the potential shortcomings.

Addison Manufacturing Company pays a production supervisor a salary of $48,000 per year. The supervisor manages the production of sprinkler heads that are used in water irrigation systems. Should the production supervisor's salary be considered a relevant cost to a special order decision? Should the production supervisor's salary be considered a relevant cost to an outsourcing decision?

Answer

The production supervisor's salary is not a relevant cost to a special order decision because Addison would pay the salary regardless of whether it accepts or rejects a special order. Since the cost does not differ for the alternatives, it is not relevant. In contrast, the supervisor's salary would be relevant to an outsourcing decision. Addison could dismiss the supervisor if it purchased the sprinkler heads instead of making them. Since the salary could be avoided by purchasing heads instead of making them, the salary is relevant to an outsourcing decision.

CHECK YOURSELF 5.2

Segment Elimination Decisions

Businesses frequently organize operating results into subcomponents called **segments.** Segment data are used to make comparisons among different products, departments, or divisions. For example, in addition to the companywide income statement provided for external users, **JCPenney** may prepare separate income statements for each retail store for internal users. Executives can then evaluate managerial performance by comparing profitability measures among stores. *Segment reports* can be prepared for products, services, departments, branches, centers, offices, or divisions. These reports normally show segment revenues and costs. The primary objective of segment analysis is to determine whether relevant revenues exceed relevant costs.

Quantitative Analysis

Assume Premier Office Products makes copy equipment and computers as well as printers. Each product line is made in a separate division of the company. Division (segment) operating results for the most recent year are shown in Exhibit 5.6. Initial review of the results suggests the copier division should be eliminated because it is operating at a loss. However, analyzing the relevant revenues and expenses leads to a different conclusion.

A three-step quantitative analysis for the segment elimination decision follows:

Step 1   **Determine the amount of relevant (differential) revenue that pertains to eliminating the copier division.** The alternatives are (1) to eliminate or (2) to continue to operate the copier division. If Premier eliminates the copier line it will lose the $550,000 of revenue the copier division currently produces. If the division continues to operate Premier will earn the revenue. Since the revenue differs between the alternatives, it is relevant.

Step 2   **Determine the amount of cost Premier can avoid if it eliminates the copier division.** If it eliminates copiers, Premier can avoid the unit-level, batch-level, product-level, and segment-level facility-sustaining costs. The relevant revenue and the avoidable costs are shown in Exhibit 5.7.

EXHIBIT 5.6

Projected Revenues and Costs by Segment

	Copiers	Computers	Printers	Total
Projected revenue	$550,000	$850,000	$780,000	$2,180,000
Projected costs				
Unit-level costs				
Materials costs	(120,000)	(178,000)	(180,000)	(478,000)
Labor costs	(160,000)	(202,000)	(165,000)	(527,000)
Overhead	(30,800)	(20,000)	(15,000)	(65,800)
Batch-level costs				
Assembly setup	(15,000)	(26,000)	(17,000)	(58,000)
Materials handling	(6,000)	(8,000)	(5,000)	(19,000)
Product-level costs				
Engineering design	(10,000)	(12,000)	(14,000)	(36,000)
Production manager salary	(52,000)	(55,800)	(63,300)	(171,100)
Facility-level costs				
Segment level				
Division manager salary	(82,000)	(92,000)	(85,000)	(259,000)
Administrative costs	(12,200)	(13,200)	(12,700)	(38,100)
Allocated—corporate level				
Company president salary	(34,000)	(46,000)	(43,200)	(123,200)
Building rental	(19,250)	(29,750)	(27,300)	(76,300)
General facility expenses	(31,000)	(31,000)	(31,000)	(93,000)
Projected profit (loss)	$ (22,250)	$136,250	$121,500	$ 235,500

Premier will incur the corporate-level facility-sustaining costs whether it eliminates the copier segment or continues to operate it. Since these costs do not differ between the alternatives, they are not relevant to the elimination decision.

Step 3 **If the relevant revenue is less than the avoidable cost, eliminate the segment (division). If not, continue to operate it.** Because operating the segment is contributing $62,000 per year to company profitability (see Exhibit 5.7), Premier should not eliminate the copiers division. Exhibit 5.8 shows Premier's estimated revenues and costs if the computers and printers divisions were operated without the copiers division. Projected company profit declines by $62,000 ($235,500 − $173,500) without the copiers segment, confirming that eliminating it would be detrimental to Premier's profitability.

Qualitative Considerations in Decisions to Eliminate Segments

As with other special decisions, management should consider qualitative factors when determining whether to eliminate segments. Employee lives will be disrupted; some employees may be reassigned elsewhere in the company, but others will be discharged. As with outsourcing decisions, reestablishing internal production capacity is difficult once a trained workforce has been released. Furthermore, employees in other

EXHIBIT 5.7

Relevant Revenue and Cost Data for Copier Segment

Projected revenue	$550,000
Projected costs	
Unit-level costs	
Materials costs	(120,000)
Labor costs	(160,000)
Overhead	(30,800)
Batch-level costs	
Assembly setup	(15,000)
Materials handling	(6,000)
Product-level costs	
Engineering design	(10,000)
Production manager salary	(52,000)
Facility-level costs	
Segment level	
Division manager salary	(82,000)
Administrative costs	(12,200)
Projected profit (loss)	$ 62,000

EXHIBIT 5.8

Projected Revenues and Costs Without Copier Division

	Computers	Printers	Total
Projected revenue	$850,000	$780,000	$1,630,000
Projected costs			
Unit-level costs			
Materials costs	(178,000)	(180,000)	(358,000)
Labor costs	(202,000)	(165,000)	(367,000)
Overhead	(20,000)	(15,000)	(35,000)
Batch-level costs			
Assembly setup	(26,000)	(17,000)	(43,000)
Materials handling	(8,000)	(5,000)	(13,000)
Product-level costs			
Engineering design	(12,000)	(14,000)	(26,000)
Production manager salary	(55,800)	(63,300)	(119,100)
Facility-level costs			
Segment level			
Division manager salary	(92,000)	(85,000)	(177,000)
Administrative costs	(13,200)	(12,700)	(25,900)
Allocated—corporate level*			
Company president salary	(63,000)	(60,200)	(123,200)
Depreciation	(39,375)	(36,925)	(76,300)
General facility expenses	(46,500)	(46,500)	(93,000)
Projected profit (loss)	$ 94,125	$ 79,375	$ 173,500

*The corporate-level facility costs that were previously *allocated* to the copier division have been reassigned on the basis of one-half to the computer division and one-half to the printer division.

segments, suppliers, customers, and investors may believe that the elimination of a segment implies the company as a whole is experiencing financial difficulty. These individuals may lose confidence in the company and seek business contacts with other companies they perceive to be more stable.

Management must also consider the fact that sales of different product lines are frequently interdependent. Some customers prefer one-stop shopping; they want to buy all their office equipment from one supplier. If Premier no longer sells copiers, customers may stop buying its computers and printers. Eliminating one segment may reduce sales of other segments.

What will happen to the space Premier used to make the copiers? Suppose Premier decides to make telephone systems in the space it previously used for copiers. The contribution to profit of the telephone business would be an *opportunity cost* of operating the copier segment. As demonstrated in previous examples, adding the opportunity cost to the avoidable costs of operating the copier segment could change the decision.

As with outsourcing, volume changes can affect elimination decisions. Because many costs of operating a segment are fixed, the cost per unit decreases as production increases. Growth can transform a segment that is currently producing real losses into a segment that produces real profits. Managers must consider growth potential when making elimination decisions.

CHECK YOURSELF 5.3

Capital Corporation is considering eliminating one of its operating segments. Capital employed a real estate broker to determine the marketability of the building that houses the segment. The broker obtained three bids for the building: $250,000, $262,000, and $264,000. The book value of the building is $275,000. Based on this information alone, what is the relevant cost of the building?

Answer

The book value of the building is a sunk cost that is not relevant. There are three bids for the building, but only one is relevant because Capital could sell the building only once. The relevant cost of the building is the highest opportunity cost, which in this case is $264,000.

Summary of Relationships Between Avoidable Costs and the Hierarchy of Business Activity

Distinguish between unit-level, batch-level, product-level, and facility-level costs and understand how these costs affect decision making.

A relationship exists between the cost hierarchy and the different types of special decisions just discussed. A special order involves making additional units of an existing product. Deciding to accept a special order affects unit-level and possibly batch-level costs. In contrast, outsourcing a product stops the production of that product. Outsourcing can avoid many product-level as well as unit- and batch-level costs. Finally, if a company eliminates an entire business segment, it can avoid some of the facility-level costs. The more complex the decision level, the more opportunities there are to avoid costs. Moving to a higher category does not mean, however, that all costs at the higher level of activity are avoidable. For example, all product-level costs may not be avoidable if a company chooses to outsource a product. The company may still incur inventory holding costs or advertising costs whether it makes or buys the product. Understanding the relationship between decision type and level of cost hierarchy helps when identifying avoidable costs. The relationships are summarized in Exhibit 5.9. For each type of decision, look for avoidable costs in the categories marked with an X. Remember also that sunk costs cannot be avoided.

EXHIBIT 5.9

Relationship Between Decision Type and Level of Cost Hierarchy

Decision Type	Unit level	Batch level	Product level	Facility level
Special order	X	X		
Outsourcing	X	X	X	
Elimination	X	X	X	X

Equipment Replacement Decisions

Equipment may become technologically obsolete long before it fails physically. Managers should base **equipment replacement decisions** on profitability analysis rather than physical deterioration. Assume Premier Office Products is considering replacing an existing machine with a new one. The following table summarizes pertinent information about the two machines:

LO 6

Make appropriate asset replacement decisions.

Old Machine		New Machine	
Original cost	$ 90,000	Cost of the new machine	$29,000
Accumulated depreciation	(33,000)	Salvage value (in 5 years)	4,000
Book value	$ 57,000	Operating expenses	
		($4,500 × 5 years)	22,500
Market value (now)	$ 14,000		
Salvage value (in 5 years)	2,000		
Annual depreciation expense	11,000		
Operating expenses			
($9,000 × 5 years)	45,000		

Quantitative Analysis

First determine what relevant costs Premier will incur if it keeps the *old machine.*

1. The *original cost* ($90,000), *current book value* ($57,000), *accumulated depreciation* ($33,000), and *annual depreciation expense* ($11,000) are different measures of a cost that was incurred in a prior period. They represent irrelevant sunk costs.

2. The $14,000 market value represents the current sacrifice Premier must make if it keeps using the existing machine. In other words, if Premier does not keep the machine, it can sell it for $14,000. In economic terms, *forgoing the opportunity* to sell the machine costs as much as buying it. The *opportunity cost* is therefore relevant to the replacement decision.

3. The salvage value of the old machine reduces the opportunity cost. Premier can sell the old machine now for $14,000 or use it for five more years and then sell it for $2,000. The opportunity cost of using the old machine for five more years is therefore $12,000 ($14,000 − $2,000).

4. Because the $45,000 ($9,000 × 5) of operating expenses will be incurred if the old machine is used but can be avoided if it is replaced, the operating expenses are relevant costs.

Next, determine what relevant costs will be incurred if Premier purchases and uses the *new machine.*

1. The cost of the new machine represents a future economic sacrifice Premier must incur if it buys the new machine. It is a relevant cost.

2. The salvage value reduces the cost of purchasing the new machine. Part ($4,000) of the $29,000 cost of the new machine will be recovered at the end of five years. The relevant cost of purchasing the new machine is $25,000 ($29,000 − $4,000).

3. The $22,500 ($4,500 $\times$ 5) of operating expenses will be incurred if the new machine is purchased; it can be avoided if the new machine is not purchased. The operating expenses are relevant costs.

The relevant costs for the two machines are summarized here:

Old Machine		New Machine	
Opportunity cost	$14,000	Cost of the new machine	$29,000
Salvage value	(2,000)	Salvage value	(4,000)
Operating expenses	45,000	Operating expenses	22,500
Total	$57,000	Total	$47,500

The analysis suggests that Premier should acquire the new machine because buying it produces the lower relevant cost. The $57,000 cost of using the old machine can be *avoided* by incurring the $47,500 cost of acquiring and using the new machine. Over the five-year period, Premier would save $9,500 ($57,000 − $47,500) by purchasing the new machine. One caution: this analysis ignores income tax effects and the time value of money, which are explained later. The discussion in this chapter focuses on identifying and using relevant costs in decision making.

‹‹ A Look Back

Decision making requires managers to choose from alternative courses of action. Successful decision making depends on a manager's ability to identify *relevant information*. Information that is relevant for decision making differs among the alternatives and is future oriented. Relevant revenues are sometimes called *differential revenues* because they differ among the alternatives. Relevant costs are sometimes called *avoidable costs* because they can be eliminated or avoided by choosing a specific course of action.

Costs that do not differ among the alternatives are not avoidable and therefore not relevant. *Sunk costs* are not relevant in decision making because they have been incurred in past transactions and therefore cannot be avoided. *Opportunity costs* are relevant because they represent potential benefits that may or may not be realized, depending on the decision maker's choice. In other words, future benefits that differ among the alternatives are relevant. Opportunity costs are not recorded in the financial accounting records.

Cost behavior (fixed or variable) is independent from the concept of relevance. Furthermore, a cost that is relevant in one decision context may be irrelevant in another context. Decision making depends on qualitative as well as quantitative information. *Quantitative information refers to information that can be measured using numbers. Qualitative information* is nonquantitative information such as personal preferences or opportunities.

Classifying costs into one of four hierarchical levels facilitates identifying relevant costs. *Unit-level costs* such as materials and labor are incurred each time a single unit of product is made. These costs can be avoided by eliminating the production of a single unit of product. *Batch-level costs* are associated with producing a group of products. Examples include setup costs and inspection costs related to a batch (group) of work rather than a single unit. Eliminating a batch would avoid both batch-level costs and unit-level costs. *Product-level costs* are incurred to support specific products or services (design and regulatory compliance costs). Product-level costs can be avoided by discontinuing a product line. *Facility-level costs,* like the president's salary, are incurred on behalf of the whole company or a segment of the company. In segment elimination decisions, the facility-level costs related to a particular segment being considered for elimination are relevant and avoidable. Those applying to the company as a whole are not avoidable.

Four types of special decisions that are frequently encountered in business are (1) *special orders,* (2) *outsourcing,* (3) *elimination decisions,* and (4) *asset replacement.* The relevant costs in a special order decision are the unit-level and batch-level costs that will be incurred if the special order is accepted. If the differential revenues from the special order exceed the relevant costs, the order should be accepted. Outsourcing decisions determine whether goods and services should be purchased from other companies. The relevant costs are the unit-level, batch-level, and product-level costs that could be avoided if the company outsources the product or service. If these costs are more than the cost to buy and the qualitative characteristics are satisfactory, the company should outsource. Segment-related unit-level, batch-level, product-level, and facility-level costs that can be avoided when a segment is eliminated are relevant. If the segment's avoidable costs exceed its differential revenues, it should be eliminated, assuming favorable qualitative factors. Asset replacement decisions compare the relevant costs of existing equipment with the relevant costs of new equipment to determine whether replacing the old equipment would be profitable.

A Look Forward

The failure to accurately allocate indirect costs to cost objects can result in misinformation that impairs decision making. The next chapter explains how increased use of automation in production has caused allocations determined using traditional approaches to be distorted. The chapter introduces allocating indirect costs using more recently developed *activity-based costing* and explain how *activity-based management* can improve efficiency and productivity. Finally, the chapter introduces *total quality management,* a strategy that seeks to minimize the costs of conforming to a designated standard of quality.

APPENDIX

Short-Term Versus Long-Term Goals

To examine conflicts between short-term versus long-term goals, we return to the equipment replacement decision made by the management team of Premier Office Products (see page 207 for details). Suppose that the final equipment replacement decision is made by a departmental supervisor who is under significant pressure to maximize profitability. She is told that if profitability declines, she will lose her job. Under these circumstances, the supervisor may choose to keep the old machine even though it is to the company's advantage to purchase the new one. This occurs because the beneficial impact of the new machine is realized in the second through fifth years. Indeed, replacing the equipment will result in more expense/loss recognition in the first year. To illustrate, study the following information.

Explain the conflict between short-term and long-term profitability.

Year	First	Second	Third	Fourth	Fifth	Totals
Keep old machine						
Depreciation expense*	$11,000	$11,000	$11,000	$11,000	$11,000	$ 55,000
Operating expense	9,000	9,000	9,000	9,000	9,000	45,000
Total	$20,000	$20,000	$20,000	$20,000	$20,000	$100,000
Replace old machine						
Loss on disposal†	$43,000	$ 0	$ 0	$ 0	$ 0	$ 43,000
Depreciation expense‡	5,000	5,000	5,000	5,000	5,000	25,000
Operating expense	4,500	4,500	4,500	4,500	4,500	22,500
Total	$52,500	$ 9,500	$ 9,500	$ 9,500	$ 9,500	$ 90,500

*($57,000 book value − $2,000 salvage) ÷ 5 years = $11,000

†($57,000 book value − $14,000 market value) = $43,000

‡($29,000 cost − $4,000 salvage) ÷ 5 years = $5,000

This analysis verifies that total cost at the end of the five-year period is $9,500 less if the equipment is replaced ($100,000 − $90,500). Notice, however, that total costs at the end of the first year are higher by $32,500 ($52,500 − $20,000) if the old machine is replaced. A decision maker under significant pressure to report higher profitability may be willing to sacrifice tomorrow's profits to look better today. By emphasizing short-term profitability, she may secure a promotion before the long-term effects of her decision become apparent. Even if she stays in the same position, her boss may be replaced by someone not so demanding in terms of reported profitability. The department supervisor's intent is to survive the moment and let the future take care of itself. Misguided reward systems can be as detrimental as threats of punishment. For example, a manager may choose short-term profitability to obtain a bonus that is based on reported profitability. It is the responsibility of upper-level management to establish policies and procedures that motivate subordinates to perform in ways that maximize the company's long-term profitability.

Decisions Regarding the Allocation of Scarce Resources

Make decisions about allocating scarce resources.

Suppose that Premier Office Products makes two types of computers: a high-end network server and an inexpensive personal computer. The relevant sales and variable cost data for each unit follow.

Network Server		Personal Computer	
Sales price	$4,000	Sales price	$1,500
Less: Variable cost	(3,760)	Less: Variable cost	(1,370)
Contribution margin	$ 240	Contribution margin	$ 130

In many circumstances, variable costs act as proxies for *avoidable costs.* For example, by definition, unit-level costs increase and decrease in direct proportion with the number of units of product made and sold. As previously indicated, unit-level costs are avoidable with respect to many special decision scenarios. To the extent that variable costs are proxies for avoidable costs, the contribution margin can be used as a measure of profitability. Other things being equal, higher contribution margins translate into more profitable products. If Premier could sell 1,000 computers, the company would certainly prefer that they be network servers. The contribution to profitability on those machines is almost double the contribution margin on the personal computer.

Even though the contribution margin is higher for network servers, selling personal computers may be more profitable. Why? If Premier can sell considerably more of the personal computers, the volume of activity will make up for the lower margin. In other words, selling three personal computers produces more total margin (3 × $130 = $390) than selling one network server (1 × $240). Many factors could limit the sales of one or both of the products. Factors that limit a business's ability to satisfy the demand for its product are called **constraints.** Suppose that warehouse space is limited (i.e., the warehouse is a scarce resource that constrains sales). Accordingly, Premier cannot warehouse all of the computers that it needs to satisfy its customer orders. If a network server requires considerably more warehouse space than a personal computer, stocking and selling personal computers may be more profitable than stocking and selling network servers. To illustrate, assume that it requires 5 square feet of warehouse space for a network server and 2 square feet for a personal computer. If only 2,100 square feet of warehouse space are available, which computer should Premier stock and sell?

In this case, the warehouse space is considered a scarce resource. The computer that produces the highest contribution margin per unit of scarce resource (i.e., per square foot) is the more profitable product. The per unit computations for each product are shown here.

	Network Server	Personal Computer
Contribution margin per unit (a)	$ 240	$ 130
Divide by warehouse space needed to store one unit (b)	5 sq. ft.	2 sq. ft.
Contribution margin per unit of scarce resource (a ÷ b)	$ 48	$ 65

The data suggest that Premier should focus on the personal computer. Even though the personal computer produces a lower contribution margin per product, its contribution margin per scarce resource is higher. The effect on total profitability is shown as follows.

	Network Server	Personal Computer
Amount of available warehouse space (a)	2,100	2,100
Divide by warehouse space needed to store one unit (b)	5 sq. ft.	2 sq. ft.
Warehouse capacity in number of units (a ÷ b) = (c)	420	1,050
Times contribution margin per unit (d)	$ 240	$ 130
Total profit potential (c × d)	$100,800	$136,500

Although the quantitative data suggest that Premier will maximize profitability by limiting its inventory to personal computers, qualitative considerations may force the company to maintain a reasonable sales mix between the two products. For example, a business that buys several personal computers may also need a network server. A customer who cannot obtain both products from Premier may choose to buy nothing at all. Instead, the customer will find a supplier who will satisfy all of his needs. In other words, Premier may still need to stock some servers to offer a competitive product line.

The chairman of the board of directors asked Premier's president why company sales had remained level while the company's chief competitor had experienced significant increases. The president replied, "You cannot sell what you do not have. Our warehouse is too small. We stop production when we fill up the warehouse. The products sell out rapidly, and then we have to wait around for the next batch of computers to be made. When we are out of stock, our customers turn to the competition. We are constrained by the size of the warehouse." In business terms, the warehouse is a **bottleneck.** Its size is limiting the company's ability to sell its products.

Many businesses use a management practice known as the **theory of constraints (TOC)** to increase profitability by managing bottlenecks or constrained resources. TOC's primary objective is to identify the bottlenecks restricting the operations of the business and then to open those bottlenecks through a practice known as **relaxing the constraints.** The effect of applying TOC to the Premier case is apparent via contribution margin analysis. According to the preceding computations, a new server and a new personal computer produce a contribution margin of $48 and $65 per square foot of storage space, respectively. So long as additional warehouse space can be purchased for less than these amounts, Premier can increase its profitability by acquiring the space.

SELF-STUDY REVIEW PROBLEM

A step-by-step audio-narrated series of slides is provided on the text website at www.mhhe.com/edmonds2008.

Flying High, Inc. (FHI), is a division of The Master Toy Company. FHI makes remote-controlled airplanes. During 2008, FHI incurred the following costs in the process of making 5,000 planes.

Unit-level materials costs (5,000 units @ $80)	$ 400,000
Unit-level labor costs (5,000 units @ $90)	450,000
Unit-level overhead costs (5,000 @ $70)	350,000
Depreciation cost on manufacturing equipment*	50,000
Other manufacturing overhead[†]	140,000
Inventory holding costs	240,000
Allocated portion of The Master Toy Company's facility-level costs	600,000
Total costs	$2,230,000

*The manufacturing equipment, which originally cost $250,000, has a book value of $200,000, a remaining useful life of four years, and a zero salvage value. If the equipment is not used in the production process, it can be leased for $30,000 per year.

[†]Includes supervisors' salaries and rent for the manufacturing building.

Required

a. FHI uses a cost-plus pricing strategy. FHI sets its price at product cost plus $100. Determine the price that FHI should charge for its remote-controlled airplanes.

b. Assume that a potential customer that operates a chain of high-end toy stores has approached FHI. A buyer for this chain has offered to purchase 1,000 planes from FHI at a price of $275 each. Ignoring qualitative considerations, should FHI accept or reject the order?

c. FHI has the opportunity to purchase the planes from Arland Manufacturing Company for $325 each. Arland maintains adequate inventories so that it can supply its customers with planes on demand. Should FHI accept the opportunity to outsource the making of its planes?

d. When completing this requirement use the sales price computed in Requirement *a*. Use the contribution margin format to prepare an income statement based on historical cost data. Prepare a second income statement that reflects the relevant cost data that Master Toy should consider in a segment elimination decision. Based on a comparison of these two statements, indicate whether Master Toy should eliminate the FHI division.

e. FHI is considering replacing the equipment it currently uses to manufacture its planes. It could purchase replacement equipment for $480,000 that has an expected useful life of four years and a salvage value of $40,000. The new equipment would increase productivity substantially, reducing unit-level labor costs by 20 percent. Assume that FHI would maintain its production and sales at 5,000 planes per year. Prepare a schedule that shows the relevant costs of operating the old equipment versus the costs of operating the new equipment. Should FHI replace the equipment?

Solution to Requirement a

Product Cost for Remote-Controlled Airplanes	
Unit-level materials costs (5,000 units × $80)	$ 400,000
Unit-level labor costs (5,000 units × $90)	450,000
Unit-level overhead costs (5,000 units × $70)	350,000
Depreciation cost on manufacturing equipment	50,000
Other manufacturing overhead	140,000
Total product cost	$1,390,000

The cost per unit is $278 ($1,390,000 ÷ 5,000 units). The sales price per unit is $378 ($278 + $100). Depreciation expense is included because cost-plus pricing is usually based on historical cost rather than relevant cost. To be profitable in the long run, a company must ultimately recover the amount it paid for the equipment (the historical cost of the equipment).

Solution to Requirement b

The incremental (relevant) cost of making 1,000 additional airplanes follows. The depreciation expense is not relevant because it represents a sunk cost. The other manufacturing overhead costs are not relevant because they will be incurred regardless of whether FHI makes the additional planes.

Per Unit Relevant Product Cost for Airplanes	
Unit-level materials costs	$ 80
Unit-level labor costs	90
Unit-level overhead costs	70
Total relevant product cost	$240

Since the relevant (incremental) cost of making the planes is less than the incremental revenue, FHI should accept the special order. Accepting the order will increase profits by $35,000 [($275 incremental revenue − $240 incremental cost) × 1,000 units].

Solution to Requirement c

Distinguish this decision from the special order opportunity discussed in Requirement *b*. That special order (Requirement *b*) decision hinged on the cost of making additional units with the existing production process. In contrast, a make-or-buy decision compares current production with the possibility of making zero units (closing down the entire manufacturing process). If the manufacturing process were shut down, FHI could avoid the unit-level costs, the cost of the lost opportunity to lease the equipment, the other manufacturing overhead costs, and the inventory holding costs. Since the planes can be purchased on demand, there is no need to maintain any inventory. The allocated portion of the facility-level costs is not relevant because it would be incurred regardless of whether FHI manufactured the planes. The relevant cost of making the planes follows.

Relevant Manufacturing Cost for Airplanes	
Unit-level materials costs (5,000 units × $80)	$ 400,000
Unit-level labor costs (5,000 units × $90)	450,000
Unit-level overhead costs (5,000 units × $70)	350,000
Opportunity cost of leasing the equipment	30,000
Other manufacturing overhead costs	140,000
Inventory holding cost	240,000
Total product cost	$1,610,000

The relevant cost per unit is $322 ($1,610,000 ÷ 5,000 units). Since the relevant cost of making the planes ($322) is less than the cost of purchasing them ($325), FHI should continue to make the planes.

Solution to Requirement d

Income Statements		
	Historical Cost Data	**Relevant Cost Data**
Revenue (5,000 units × $378)	$1,890,000	$1,890,000
Less variable costs:		
Unit-level materials costs (5,000 units × $80)	(400,000)	(400,000)
Unit-level labor costs (5,000 units × $90)	(450,000)	(450,000)
Unit-level overhead costs (5,000 units × $70)	(350,000)	(350,000)
Contribution margin	690,000	690,000
Depreciation cost on manufacturing equipment	(50,000)	
Opportunity cost of leasing manufacturing equipment		(30,000)
Other manufacturing overhead costs	(140,000)	(140,000)
Inventory holding costs	(240,000)	(240,000)
Allocated facility-level administrative costs	(600,000)	
Net loss	$ (340,000)	
Contribution to Master Toy's profitability		$ 280,000

Master Toy should not eliminate the segment (FHI). Although it appears to be incurring a loss, the allocated facility-level administrative costs are not relevant because Master Toy would incur these costs regardless of whether it eliminated FHI. Also, the depreciation cost on the manufacturing equipment is not relevant because it is a sunk cost. However, since the company could lease the equipment if the segment were eliminated, the $30,000 potential rental fee represents a relevant opportunity cost. The relevant revenue and cost data show that FHI is contributing $280,000 to the profitability of The Master Toy Company.

Solution to Requirement e

The relevant costs of using the old equipment versus the new equipment are the costs that differ for the two alternatives. In this case relevant costs include the purchase price of the new equipment, the opportunity cost of the old equipment, and the labor costs. These items are summarized in the following table. The data show the total cost over the four-year useful life of the replacement equipment.

Relevant Cost Comparison		
	Old Equipment	**New Equipment**
Opportunity to lease the old equipment ($30,000 × 4 years)	$ 120,000	
Cost of new equipment ($480,000 − $40,000)		$ 440,000
Unit-level labor costs (5,000 units × $90 × 4 years)	1,800,000	
Unit-level labor costs (5,000 units × $90 × 4 years × .80)		1,440,000
Total relevant costs	$1,920,000	$1,880,000

Since the relevant cost of operating the new equipment is less than the cost of operating the old equipment, FHI should replace the equipment.

KEY TERMS

Avoidable costs 197
Batch-level costs 198
Bottleneck 211
Certified suppliers 202
Constraints 210
Differential revenue 197
Equipment replacement
  decisions 207

Facility-level costs 198
Low-ball pricing 202
Opportunity cost 195
Outsourcing 201
Product-level costs 198
Qualitative
  characteristics 197

Quantitative
  characteristics 197
Relaxing the constraints 211
Relevant costs 195
Relevant information 194
Segment 204

Special order decisions 199
Sunk costs 194
Theory of constraints
  (TOC) 211
Unit-level costs 198
Vertical integration 202

QUESTIONS

1. Identify the primary qualities of revenues and costs that are relevant for decision making.
2. Are variable costs always relevant? Explain.
3. Identify the four hierarchical levels used to classify costs. When can each of these levels of costs be avoided?
4. Describe the relationship between relevance and accuracy.
5. "It all comes down to the bottom line. The numbers never lie." Do you agree with this conclusion? Explain your position.
6. Carmon Company invested $300,000 in the equity securities of Mann Corporation. The current market value of Carmon's investment in Mann is $250,000. Carmon currently needs funds for operating purposes. Although interest rates are high, Carmon's president has decided to borrow the needed funds instead of selling the investment in Mann. He explains that his company cannot afford to take a $50,000 loss on the Mann stock. Evaluate the president's decision based on this information.
7. What is an opportunity cost? How does it differ from a sunk cost?
8. A local bank advertises that it offers a free noninterest-bearing checking account if the depositor maintains a $500 minimum balance in the account. Is the checking account truly free?
9. A manager is faced with deciding whether to replace machine A or machine B. The original cost of machine A was $20,000 and that of machine B was $30,000. Because the two cost figures differ, they are relevant to the manager's decision. Do you agree? Explain your position.
10. Are all fixed costs unavoidable?
11. Identify two qualitative considerations that could be associated with special order decisions.
12. Which of the following would not be relevant to a make-or-buy decision?
    (a) Allocated portion of depreciation expense on existing facilities.
    (b) Variable cost of labor used to produce products currently purchased from suppliers.

(c) Warehousing costs for inventory of completed products (inventory levels will be constant regardless of whether products are purchased or produced).

(d) Cost of materials used to produce the items currently purchased from suppliers.

(e) Property taxes on the factory building.

13. What two factors should be considered in deciding how to allocate shelf space in a retail establishment?

14. What level(s) of costs is(are) relevant in special order decisions?

15. Why would a company consider outsourcing products or services?

16. Chris Sutter, the production manager of Satellite Computers, insists that the floppy drives used in the company's upper-end computers be outsourced since they can be purchased from a supplier at a lower cost per unit than the company is presently incurring to produce the drives. Jane Meyers, his assistant, insists that if sales growth continues at the current levels, the company will be able to produce the drives in the near future at a lower cost because of the company's predominately fixed cost structure. Does Ms. Meyers have a legitimate argument? Explain.

17. Identify some qualitative factors that should be considered in addition to quantitative costs in deciding whether to outsource.

18. The managers of Wilcox, Inc., are suggesting that the company president eliminate one of the company's segments that is operating at a loss. Why may this be a hasty decision?

19. Why would a supervisor choose to continue using a more costly old machine instead of replacing it with a less costly new machine?

20. Identify some of the constraints that limit a business's ability to satisfy the demand for its products or services.

MULTIPLE-CHOICE QUESTIONS

Multiple-choice questions are provided on the text website at www.mhhe.com/edmonds2008.

EXERCISES—SERIES A

All Exercises in Series A are available with McGraw-Hill's Homework Manager®.

Exercise 5-1A *Distinction between relevance and cost behavior*   **L.O. 1**

Tammy Bullock is trying to decide which of two different kinds of candy to sell in her retail candy store. One type is a name brand candy that will practically sell itself. The other candy is cheaper to purchase but does not carry an identifiable brand name. Ms. Bullock believes that she will have to incur significant advertising costs to sell this candy. Several cost items for the two types of candy are as follows:

Brandless Candy		Name Brand Candy	
Cost per box	$ 5.00	Cost per box	$ 6.50
Sales commissions per box	1.00	Sales commissions per box	1.00
Rent of display space	1,500.00	Rent of display space	1,500.00
Advertising	3,000.00	Advertising	2,000.00

Required

Identify each cost as being relevant or irrelevant to Ms. Bullock's decision and indicate whether it is fixed or variable relative to the number of boxes sold.

L.O. 1

Exercise 5-2A   *Distinction between relevance and cost behavior*

Hargrove Company makes and sells a single product. Hargrove incurred the following costs in its most recent fiscal year.

Cost Items Appearing on the Income Statement	
Materials Cost ($7 per unit)	Sales Commissions (2% of sales)
Company President's Salary	Salaries of Administrative Personnel
Depreciation on Manufacturing Equipment	Shipping and Handling ($0.25 per unit)
Customer Billing Costs (1% of sales)	Depreciation on Office Furniture
Rental Cost of Manufacturing Facility	Manufacturing Supplies ($0.25 per unit)
Advertising Costs ($250,000 per year)	Production Supervisor's Salary
Labor Cost ($5 per unit)	

Hargrove could purchase the products that it currently makes. If it purchased the items, the company would continue to sell them using its own logo, advertising program, and sales staff.

Required

Identify each cost as relevant or irrelevant to the outsourcing decision and indicate whether the cost is fixed or variable relative to the number of products manufactured and sold.

L.O. 1

Exercise 5-3A   *Distinction between avoidable costs and cost behavior*

Glamor Company makes fine jewelry that it sells to department stores throughout the United States. Glamor is trying to decide which of two bracelets to manufacture. Glamor has a labor contract that prohibits the company from laying off workers freely. Cost data pertaining to the two choices follow.

	Bracelet A	**Bracelet B**
Cost of materials per unit	$ 26	$ 45
Cost of labor per unit	40	40
Advertising cost per year	8,000	6,000
Annual depreciation on existing equip.	5,000	4,000

Required

a. Identify the fixed costs and determine the amount of fixed cost for each product.
b. Identify the variable costs and determine the amount of variable cost per unit for each product.
c. Identify the avoidable costs and determine the amount of avoidable cost for each product.

L.O. 2

Exercise 5-4A   *Cost hierarchy*

Costs can be classified into one of four categories including unit-level, batch-level, product-level, or facility-level costs.

Required

Classify each of the items listed below into one of the four categories listed above. The first item has been categorized as an example.

Cost Description	**Cost Classification**
Direct labor	Unit-level cost
Salary of company president	
Research and development cost	
Factory lawn care cost	
Cost of patent	
Startup cost to change color of a product	
Cost of resetting sewing machines to change shirt size	
Real estate tax for the factory	

Exercise 5-5A   *Special order decision*   L.O. 2, 3

Sturdy Concrete Company pours concrete slabs for single-family dwellings. Lynch Construction Company, which operates outside Sturdy's normal sales territory, asks Sturdy to pour 40 slabs for Lynch's new development of homes. Sturdy has the capacity to build 300 slabs and is presently working on 250 of them. Lynch is willing to pay only $3,000 per slab. Sturdy estimates the cost of a typical job to include unit-level materials, $1,500; unit-level labor, $1,000; and an allocated portion of facility-level overhead, $700.

Required

Should Sturdy accept or reject the special order to pour 40 slabs for $3,000 each? Support your answer with appropriate computations.

Exercise 5-6A   *Special order decision*   L.O. 2, 3

Mixon Company manufactures a personal computer designed for use in schools and markets it under its own label. Mixon has the capacity to produce 20,000 units a year but is currently producing and selling only 15,000 units a year. The computer's normal selling price is $1,600 per unit with no volume discounts. The unit-level costs of the computer's production are $600 for direct materials, $200 for direct labor, and $250 for indirect unit-level manufacturing costs. The total product- and facility-level costs incurred by Mixon during the year are expected to be $2,000,000 and $800,000, respectively. Assume that Mixon receives a special order to produce and sell 4,000 computers at $1,200 each.

Required

Should Mixon accept or reject the special order? Support your answer with appropriate computations.

Exercise 5-7A   *Identifying qualitative factors for a special order decision*   L.O. 3

Required

Describe the qualitative factors that Mixon should consider before accepting the special order described in Exercise 5-6A.

Exercise 5-8A   *Using the contribution margin approach for a special order decision*   L.O. 3

Griffin Company, which produces and sells a small digital clock, bases its pricing strategy on a 30 percent markup on total cost. Based on annual production costs for 25,000 units of product, computations for the sales price per clock follow.

Unit-level costs	$200,000
Fixed costs	75,000
Total cost (a)	275,000
Markup (a × 0.30)	82,500
Total sales (b)	$357,500
Sales price per unit (b ÷ 25,000)	$ 14.30

Required

a. Griffin has excess capacity and receives a special order for 6,000 clocks for $10 each. Calculate the contribution margin per unit; based on it, should Griffin accept the special order?
b. Support your answer by preparing a contribution margin income statement for the special order.

Exercise 5-9A   *Outsourcing decision*   L.O. 4

Fowler Bicycle Manufacturing Company currently produces the handlebars used in manufacturing its bicycles, which are high-quality racing bikes with limited sales. Fowler produces and sells only 5,000 bikes each year. Due to the low volume of activity, Fowler is unable to obtain the economies of scale that larger producers achieve. For example, Fowler could buy the handlebars for $30 each; they cost $34 each to make. The following is a detailed breakdown of current production costs.

Item	Unit Cost	Total
Unit-level costs		
Materials	$14	$ 70,000
Labor	11	55,000
Overhead	4	20,000
Allocated facility-level costs	5	25,000
Total	$34	$170,000

After seeing these figures, Fowler's president remarked that it would be foolish for the company to continue to produce the handlebars at $34 each when it can buy them for $30 each.

Required

Do you agree with the president's conclusion? Support your answer with appropriate computations.

L.O. 4

Exercise 5-10A *Establishing price for an outsourcing decision*

Pretty Lawn Company makes and sells lawn mowers for which it currently makes the engines. It has an opportunity to purchase the engines from a reliable manufacturer. The annual costs of making the engines are shown here.

Cost of materials (24,000 Units × $15)	$360,000
Labor (24,000 Units × $20)	480,000
Depreciation on manufacturing equipment*	12,000
Salary of supervisor of engine production	90,000
Rental cost of equipment used to make engines	24,000
Allocated portion of corporate-level facility-sustaining costs	30,000
Total cost to make 24,000 engines	$996,000

*The equipment has a book value of $56,000 but its market value is zero.

Required

a. Determine the maximum price per unit that Pretty Lawn would be willing to pay for the engines.
b. Would the price computed in Requirement *a* change if production increased to 30,000 units? Support your answer with appropriate computations.

L.O. 4

Exercise 5-11A *Outsourcing decision with qualitative factors*

Stein Corporation which makes and sells 80,000 radios annually, currently purchases the radio speakers it uses for $8 each. Each radio uses one speaker. The company has idle capacity and is considering the possibility of making the speakers that it needs. Stein estimates that the cost of materials and labor needed to make speakers would be a total of $7 for each speaker. In addition, the costs of supervisory salaries, rent, and other manufacturing costs would be $160,000. Allocated facility-level costs would be $96,000.

Required

a. Determine the change in net income Stein would experience if it decides to make the speakers.
b. Discuss the qualitative factors that Stein should consider.

L.O. 2, 4

Exercise 5-12A *Outsourcing decision affected by opportunity costs*

Foster Electronics currently produces the shipping containers it uses to deliver the electronics products it sells. The monthly cost of producing 9,000 containers follows.

Unit-level materials	$ 9,000
Unit-level labor	12,000
Unit-level overhead	7,800
Product-level costs*	18,000
Allocated facility-level costs	45,000

*One-third of these costs can be avoided by purchasing the containers.

Piazza Container Company has offered to sell comparable containers to Foster for $4.50 each.

Required

a. Should Foster continue to make the containers? Support your answer with appropriate computations.
b. Foster could lease the space it currently uses in the manufacturing process. If leasing would produce $18,000 per month, would your answer to Requirement *a* be different? Explain.

Exercise 5-13A   *Opportunity cost*

L.O. 6

Mann Freight Company owns a truck that cost $80,000. Currently, the truck's book value is $48,000, and its expected remaining useful life is four years. Mann has the opportunity to purchase for $60,000 a replacement truck that is extremely fuel efficient. Fuel cost for the old truck is expected to be $8,000 per year more than fuel cost for the new truck. The old truck is paid for but, in spite of being in good condition, can be sold for only $32,000.

Required

Should Mann replace the old truck with the new fuel-efficient model, or should it continue to use the old truck until it wears out? Explain.

Exercise 5-14A   *Opportunity costs*

L.O. 1

Andy Cotrand owns his own taxi, for which he bought an $18,000 permit to operate two years ago. Mr. Cotrand earns $33,000 a year operating as an independent but has the opportunity to sell the taxi and permit for $60,000 and take a position as dispatcher for Montgomery Taxi Co. The dispatcher position pays $30,000 a year for a 40-hour week. Driving his own taxi, Mr. Cotrand works approximately 55 hours per week. If he sells his business, he will invest the $60,000 and can earn a 10 percent return.

Required

a. Determine the opportunity cost of owning and operating the independent business.
b. Based solely on financial considerations, should Mr. Cotrand sell the taxi and accept the position as dispatcher?
c. Discuss the qualitative as well as quantitative factors that Mr. Cotrand should consider.

Exercise 5-15A   *Segment elimination decision*

L.O. 5

Newburg Company operates three segments. Income statements for the segments imply that profitability could be improved if Segment A were eliminated.

NEWBURG COMPANY			
Income Statements for the Year 2009			
Segment	A	B	C
Sales	$196,000	$260,000	$345,000
Cost of Goods Sold	(143,000)	(98,000)	(190,000)
Sales Commissions	(20,000)	(38,000)	(22,000)
Contribution Margin	33,000	124,000	133,000
General Fixed Oper. Exp. (allocation of president's salary)	(44,000)	(52,000)	(44,000)
Advertising Expense (specific to individual divisions)	(3,000)	(10,000)	0
Net Income	$ (14,000)	$ 62,000	$ 89,000

Required

a. Explain the effect on profitability if Segment A is eliminated.
b. Prepare comparative income statements for the company as a whole under two alternatives: (1) the retention of Segment A and (2) the elimination of Segment A.

Exercise 5-16A   *Segment elimination decision*

L.O. 5

Reese Transport Company divides its operations into four divisions. A recent income statement for Lombardo Division follows.

REESE TRANSPORT COMPANY
Lombardo Division
Income Statement for the Year 2006

Revenue	$ 500,000
Salaries for Drivers	(350,000)
Fuel Expenses	(50,000)
Insurance	(70,000)
Division-Level Facility-Sustaining Costs	(40,000)
Companywide Facility-Sustaining Costs	(80,000)
Net Loss	$ (90,000)

Required

a. Should Lombardo Division be eliminated? Support your answer by explaining how the division's elimination would affect the net income of the company as a whole. By how much would companywide income increase or decrease?

b. Assume that Lombardo Division is able to increase its revenue to $540,000 by raising its prices. Would this change the decision you made in Requirement *a?* Determine the amount of the increase or decrease that would occur in companywide net income if the segment were eliminated if revenue were $540,000.

c. What is the minimum amount of revenue required to justify continuing the operation of Lombardo Division?

L.O. 5

Exercise 5-17A   *Identifying avoidable cost of a segment*

Gerhardt Corporation is considering the elimination of one of its segments. The segment incurs the following fixed costs. If the segment is eliminated, the building it uses will be sold.

Advertising expense	$ 97,000
Supervisory salaries	159,000
Allocation of companywide facility-level costs	45,000
Original cost of building	100,000
Book value of building	60,000
Market value of building	70,000
Maintenance costs on equipment	50,000
Real estate taxes on building	7,000

Required

Based on this information, determine the amount of avoidable cost associated with the segment.

L.O. 6

Exercise 5-18A   *Asset replacement decision*

A machine purchased three years ago for $130,000 has a current book value using straight-line depreciation of $90,000; its operating expenses are $24,000 per year. A replacement machine would cost $200,000, have a useful life of nine years, and would require $8,000 per year in operating expenses. It has an expected salvage value of $16,000 after nine years. The current disposal value of the old machine is $60,000; if it is kept nine more years, its residual value would be $10,000.

Required

Based on this information, should the old machine be replaced? Support your answer.

L.O. 6

Exercise 5-19A   *Asset replacement decision*

Jeter Company is considering replacement of some of its manufacturing equipment. Information regarding the existing equipment and the potential replacement equipment follows.

Existing Equipment		Replacement Equipment	
Cost	$ 90,000	Cost	$95,000
Operating expenses*	105,000	Operating expenses*	20,000
Salvage value	10,000	Salvage value	14,000
Market value	60,000	Useful life	8 years
Book value	32,000		
Remaining useful life	8 years		

*The amounts shown for operating expenses are the cumulative total of all such expected expenses to be incurred over the useful life of the equipment.

Required

Based on this information, recommend whether to replace the equipment. Support your recommendation with appropriate computations.

Exercise 5-20A   *Asset replacement decision*

L.O. 6

Lange Company paid $60,000 to purchase a machine on January 1, 2007. During 2009, a technological breakthrough resulted in the development of a new machine that costs $112,500. The old machine costs $36,000 per year to operate, but the new machine could be operated for only $9,000 per year. The new machine, which will be available for delivery on January 1, 2010, has an expected useful life of four years. The old machine is more durable and is expected to have a remaining useful life of four years. The current market value of the old machine is $10,000. The expected salvage value of both machines is zero.

Required

Based on this information, recommend whether to replace the machine. Support your recommendation with appropriate computations.

Exercise 5-21A   *Annual versus cumulative data for replacement decision*

L.O. 6, 7

Because of rapidly advancing technology, Grayson Publications Corporation is considering replacing its existing typesetting machine with leased equipment. The old machine, purchased two years ago, has an expected useful life of six years and is in good condition. Apparently, it will continue to perform as expected for the remaining four years of its expected useful life. A four-year lease for equipment with comparable productivity can be obtained for $15,000 per year. The following data apply to the old machine.

Original cost	$180,000
Accumulated depreciation	60,000
Current market value	77,500
Estimated salvage value	7,500

Required

a. Determine the annual opportunity cost of using the old machine. Based on your computations, recommend whether to replace it.
b. Determine the total cost of the lease over the four-year contract. Based on your computations, recommend whether to replace the old machine.

Appendix

Exercise 5-22A   *Scarce resource decision*

L.O. 8

Colvin Funtime Novelties has the capacity to produce either 36,000 corncob pipes or 16,000 cornhusk dolls per year. The pipes cost $3 each to produce and sell for $6 each. The dolls sell for $10 each and cost $4 to produce.

Required

Assuming that Colvin Funtime Novelties can sell all it produces of either product, should it produce the corncob pipes or the cornhusk dolls? Show computations to support your answer.

PROBLEMS—SERIES A

All Problems in Series A are available with McGraw-Hill's Homework Manager®.

L.O. 1

Problem 5-23A *Context-sensitive relevance*

Required

Respond to each requirement independently.

a. Describe two decision-making contexts, one in which unit-level materials costs are avoidable, and the other in which they are unavoidable.

b. Describe two decision-making contexts, one in which batch-level setup costs are avoidable, and the other in which they are unavoidable.

c. Describe two decision-making contexts, one in which advertising costs are avoidable, and the other in which they are unavoidable.

d. Describe two decision-making contexts, one in which rent paid for a building is avoidable, and the other in which it is unavoidable.

e. Describe two decision-making contexts, one in which depreciation on manufacturing equipment is avoidable, and the other in which it is unavoidable.

L.O. 1

CHECK FIGURES
a. Contribution to profit
   for Job A: $115,800
b. Contribution to profit:
   $(8,200)

Problem 5-24A *Context-sensitive relevance*

Bisson Construction Company is a building contractor specializing in small commercial buildings. The company has the opportunity to accept one of two jobs; it cannot accept both because they must be performed at the same time and Bisson does not have the necessary labor force for both jobs. Indeed, it will be necessary to hire a new supervisor if either job is accepted. Furthermore, additional insurance will be required if either job is accepted. The revenue and costs associated with each job follow.

Cost Category	Job A	Job B
Contract price	$640,000	$580,000
Unit-level materials	246,000	216,000
Unit-level labor	237,000	242,400
Unit-level overhead	16,400	13,200
Supervisor's salary	72,400	72,400
Rental equipment costs	24,800	28,200
Depreciation on tools (zero market value)	20,000	20,000
Allocated portion of companywide facility-sustaining costs	6,400	5,800
Insurance cost for job	16,000	16,000

Required

a. Assume that Bisson has decided to accept one of the two jobs. Identify the information relevant to selecting one job versus the other. Recommend which job to accept and support your answer with appropriate computations.

b. Assume that Job A is no longer available. Bisson's choice is to accept or reject Job B alone. Identify the information relevant to this decision. Recommend whether to accept or reject Job B. Support your answer with appropriate computations.

L.O. 2, 3

CHECK FIGURE
a. Relevant cost per unit:
   $56

Problem 5-25A *Effect of order quantity on special order decision*

Karim Quilting Company makes blankets that it markets through a variety of department stores. It makes the blankets in batches of 1,000 units. Karim made 20,000 blankets during the prior accounting period. The cost of producing the blankets is summarized here.

Materials cost ($20 per unit × 20,000)	$ 400,000
Labor cost ($25 per unit × 20,000)	500,000
Manufacturing supplies ($3 × 20,000)	60,000
Batch-level costs (20 batches at $4,000 per batch)	80,000
Product-level costs	140,000
Facility-level costs	300,000
Total costs	$1,480,000
Cost per unit = $1,480,000 ÷ 20,000 = $74	

Required

a. Lucky Motels has offered to buy a batch of 500 blankets for $55 each. Karim's normal selling price is $90 per unit. Based on the preceding quantitative data, should Karim accept the special order? Support your answer with appropriate computations.

b. Would your answer to Requirement *a* change if Lucky offered to buy a batch of 1,000 blankets for $55 per unit? Support your answer with appropriate computations.

c. Describe the qualitative factors that Karim Quilting Company should consider before accepting a special order to sell blankets to Lucky Motels.

Problem 5-26A   *Effects of the level of production on an outsourcing decision*

L.O. 2, 4

Heacock Chemical Company makes a variety of cosmetic products, one of which is a skin cream designed to reduce the signs of aging. Heacock produces a relatively small amount (10,000 units) of the cream and is considering the purchase of the product from an outside supplier for $4.50 each. If Heacock purchases from the outside supplier, it would continue to sell and distribute the cream under its own brand name. Heacock's accountant constructed the following profitability analysis.

Revenue (10,000 units × $10)	$100,000
Unit-level materials costs (10,000 units × $1.40)	(14,000)
Unit-level labor costs (10,000 units × $0.50)	(5,000)
Unit-level overhead costs (10,000 × $0.10)	(1,000)
Unit-level selling expenses (10,000 × $0.25)	(2,500)
Contribution margin	77,500
Skin cream production supervisor's salary	(30,000)
Allocated portion of facility-level costs	(7,500)
Product-level advertising cost	(25,000)
Contribution to companywide income	$ 15,000

CHECK FIGURE
a. Total relevant cost: $50,000

Required

a. Identify the cost items relevant to the make-or-outsource decision.

b. Should Heacock continue to make the product or buy it from the supplier? Support your answer by determining the change in net income if Heacock buys the cream instead of making it.

c. Suppose that Heacock is able to increase sales by 5,000 units (sales will increase to 15,000 units). At this level of production, should Heacock make or buy the cream? Support your answer by explaining how the increase in production affects the cost per unit.

d. Discuss the qualitative factors that Heacock should consider before deciding to outsource the skin cream. How can Heacock minimize the risk of establishing a relationship with an unreliable supplier?

Problem 5-27A   *Outsourcing decision affected by equipment replacement*

L.O. 2, 4, 6

Taggart Bike Company (TBC) makes the frames used to build its bicycles. During 2006, TBC made 20,000 frames; the costs incurred follow.

Unit-level materials costs (20,000 units × $40)	$ 800,000
Unit-level labor costs (20,000 units × $50)	1,000,000
Unit-level overhead costs (20,000 × $10)	200,000
Depreciation on manufacturing equipment	100,000
Bike frame production supervisor's salary	80,000
Inventory holding costs	300,000
Allocated portion of facility-level costs	500,000
Total costs	$2,980,000

TBC has an opportunity to purchase frames for $102 each.

Additional Information

1. The manufacturing equipment, which originally cost $500,000, has a book value of $400,000, a remaining useful life of four years, and a zero salvage value. If the equipment is not used to produce bicycle frames, it can be leased for $60,000 per year.

2. TBC has the opportunity to purchase for $960,000 new manufacturing equipment that will have an expected useful life of four years and a salvage value of $80,000. This equipment will increase productivity substantially, reducing unit-level labor costs by 60 percent. Assume that TBC will continue to produce and sell 20,000 frames per year in the future.

3. If TBC outsources the frames, the company can eliminate 80 percent of the inventory holding costs.

Required

a. Determine the avoidable cost per unit of making the bike frames, assuming that TBC is considering the alternatives of making the product using the existing equipment or outsourcing the product to the independent contractor. Based on the quantitative data, should TBC outsource the bike frames? Support your answer with appropriate computations.

b. Assuming that TBC is considering whether to replace the old equipment with the new equipment, determine the avoidable cost per unit to produce the bike frames using the new equipment and the avoidable cost per unit to produce the bike frames using the old equipment. Calculate the impact on profitability if the bike frames were made using the old equipment versus the new equipment.

c. Assuming that TBC is considering whether to either purchase the new equipment or outsource the bike frame, calculate the impact on profitability between the two alternatives.

d. Discuss the qualitative factors that TBC should consider before making a decision to outsource the bike frame. How can TBC minimize the risk of establishing a relationship with an unreliable supplier?

Problem 5-28A *Eliminating a segment*

Mazzel Boot Co. sells men's, women's, and children's boots. For each type of boot sold, it operates a separate department that has its own manager. The manager of the men's department has a sales staff of nine employees, the manager of the women's department has six employees, and the manager of the children's department has three employees. All departments are housed in a single store. In recent years, the children's department has operated at a net loss and is expected to continue to do so. Last year's income statements follow.

	Men's Department	Women's Department	Children's Department
Sales	$ 800,000	$ 610,000	$ 268,000
Cost of Goods Sold	(332,000)	(267,000)	(160,000)
Gross Margin	468,000	343,000	108,000
Department Manager's Salary	(48,000)	(42,000)	(28,000)
Sales Commissions	(216,000)	(168,000)	(58,000)
Rent on Store Lease	(25,000)	(25,000)	(25,000)
Store Utilities	(5,000)	(5,000)	(5,000)
Net Income (loss)	$ 174,000	$ 103,000	$ (8,000)

Required

a. Determine whether to eliminate the children's department.

b. Confirm the conclusion you reached in Requirement *a* by preparing income statements for the company as a whole with and without the children's department.

c. Eliminating the children's department would increase space available to display men's and women's boots. Suppose management estimates that a wider selection of adult boots would increase the store's net earnings by $32,000. Would this information affect the decision that you made in Requirement *a*? Explain your answer.

Problem 5-29A *Effect of activity level and opportunity cost on segment elimination decision*

L.O. 5

CHECK FIGURE
a. Contribution to profit:
  $(40,000)

Monge Manufacturing Co. produces and sells specialized equipment used in the petroleum industry. The company is organized into three separate operating branches: Division A, which manufactures and sells heavy equipment; Division B, which manufactures and sells hand tools; and Division C, which makes and sells electric motors. Each division is housed in a separate manufacturing facility. Company headquarters is located in a separate building. In recent years, Division B has been operating at a net loss and is expected to continue to do so. Income statements for the three divisions for 2008 follow.

	Division A	Division B	Division C
Sales	$ 3,200,000	$ 750,000	$ 4,000,000
Less: Cost of Goods Sold			
Unit-Level Manufacturing Costs	(1,900,000)	(450,000)	(2,400,000)
Rent on Manufacturing Facility	(400,000)	(220,000)	(300,000)
Gross Margin	900,000	80,000	1,300,000
Less: Operating Expenses			
Unit-Level Selling and Admin. Expenses	(200,000)	(35,000)	(250,000)
Division-Level Fixed Selling and			
Admin. Expenses	(250,000)	(85,000)	(300,000)
Headquarters Facility-Level Costs	(150,000)	(150,000)	(150,000)
Net Income (loss)	$ 300,000	$(190,000)	$ 600,000

Required

a. Based on the preceding information, recommend whether to eliminate Division B. Support your answer by preparing companywide income statements before and after eliminating Division B.

b. During 2008, Division B produced and sold 20,000 units of hand tools. Would your recommendation in response to Requirement *a* change if sales and production increase to 30,000 units in 2009? Support your answer by comparing differential revenue and avoidable cost for Division B, assuming that it sells 30,000 units.

c. Suppose that Monge could sublease Division B's manufacturing facility for $320,000. Would you operate the division at a production and sales volume of 30,000 units, or would you close it? Support your answer with appropriate computations.

Problem 5-30A *Comprehensive problem including special order, outsourcing, and segment elimination decisions*

L.O. 3, 4, 5

*e**X**cel*

www.mhhe.com/edmonds2008

CHECK FIGURE
a. CM: $3,750

Shadeed Corporation makes and sells state-of-the-art electronics products. One of its segments produces The Math Machine, an inexpensive four-function calculator. The company's chief accountant recently prepared the following income statement showing annual revenues and expenses associated with the segment's operating activities. The relevant range for the production and sale of the calculators is between 30,000 and 60,000 units per year.

Revenue (40,000 units × $8)	$320,000
Unit-Level Variable Costs	
Materials Cost (40,000 × $2)	(80,000)
Labor Cost (40,000 × $1)	(40,000)
Manufacturing Overhead (40,000 × $0.50)	(20,000)
Shipping and Handling (40,000 × $0.25)	(10,000)
Sales Commissions (40,000 × $1)	(40,000)
Contribution Margin	130,000
Fixed Expenses	
Advertising Costs	(20,000)
Salary of Production Supervisor	(60,000)
Allocated Companywide Facility-Level Expenses	(80,000)
Net Loss	$ (30,000)

Required (Consider each of the requirements independently.)

a. A large discount store has approached the owner of Shadeed about buying 5,000 calculators. It would replace The Math Machine's label with its own logo to avoid affecting Shadeed's existing customers. Because the offer was made directly to the owner, no sales commissions on the transaction would be involved, but the discount store is willing to pay only $4.50 per calculator. Based on quantitative factors alone, should Shadeed accept the special order? Support your answer with appropriate computations. Specifically, by what amount would the special order increase or decrease profitability?

b. Shadeed has an opportunity to buy the 40,000 calculators it currently makes from a reliable competing manufacturer for $4.90 each. The product meets Shadeed's quality standards. Shadeed could continue to use its own logo, advertising program, and sales force to distribute the products. Should Shadeed buy the calculators or continue to make them? Support your answer with appropriate computations. Specifically, how much more or less would it cost to buy the calculators than to make them? Would your answer change if the volume of sales were increased to 60,000 units?

c. Because the calculator division is currently operating at a loss, should it be eliminated from the company's operations? Support your answer with appropriate computations. Specifically, by what amount would the segment's elimination increase or decrease profitability?

Appendix

L.O. 8

CHECK FIGURES
a. Contribution to margin
per hour:
$2 for A and
$1.50 for B

Problem 5-31A   *Allocating scarce resources*

The following information applies to the products of Zoghbi Company.

	Product A	Product B
Selling price per unit	$26	$24
Variable cost per unit	22	18

Required

Identify the product that should be produced or sold under each of the following constraints. Consider each constraint separately.

a. One unit of Product A requires 2 hours of labor to produce, and one unit of Product B requires 4 hours of labor to produce. Due to labor constraints, demand is higher than the company's capacity to make both products.

b. The products are sold to the public in retail stores. The company has limited floor space and cannot stock as many products as it would like. Display space is available for only one of the two products. Expected sales of Product A are 10,000 units and of Product B are 8,000 units.

c. The maximum number of machine hours available is 40,000. Product A uses 2 machine hours, and Product B uses 5 machine hours. The company can sell all the products it produces.

Problem 5-32A   *Conflict between short-term versus long-term performance*

L.O. 7

www.mhhe.com/edmonds2008

CHECK FIGURE
a. Relevant costs:
   $560,000 for keeping
   the old machine

Roy Notter manages the cutting department of Leng Timber Company. He purchased a tree-cutting machine on January 1, 2007, for $400,000. The machine had an estimated useful life of five years and zero salvage value, and the cost to operate it is $90,000 per year. Technological developments resulted in the development of a more advanced machine available for purchase on January 1, 2008, that would allow a 25 percent reduction in operating costs. The new machine would cost $240,000 and have a four-year useful life and zero salvage value. The current market value of the old machine on January 1, 2008, is $200,000, and its book value is $320,000 on that date. Straight-line depreciation is used for both machines. The company expects to generate $224,000 of revenue per year from the use of either machine.

Required

a. Recommend whether to replace the old machine on January 1, 2008. Support your answer with appropriate computations.
b. Prepare income statements for four years (2008 through 2011) assuming that the old machine is retained.
c. Prepare income statements for four years (2008 through 2011) assuming that the old machine is replaced.
d. Discuss the potential ethical conflicts that could result from the timing of the loss and expense recognition reported in the two income statements.

EXERCISES—SERIES B

Exercise 5-1B   *Distinction between relevance and cost behavior*

L.O. 1

Ted Mercer is planning to rent a small shop for a new business. He can sell either sandwiches or donuts. The following costs pertain to the two products.

Sandwiches		Donuts	
Cost per sandwich	$ 1.50	Cost per dozen donuts	$ 1.25
Sales commissions per sandwich	0.05	Sales commissions per dozen donuts	0.07
Monthly shop rental cost	1,000.00	Monthly shop rental cost	1,000.00
Monthly advertising cost	500.00	Monthly advertising cost	300.00

Required

Identify each cost as relevant or irrelevant to Mr. Mercer's product decision and indicate whether the cost is fixed or variable relative to the number of units sold.

Exercise 5-2B   *Distinction between relevance and cost behavior*

L.O. 1

Rox Company makes and sells a toy plane. Rox incurred the following costs in its most recent fiscal year:

Cost Items Reported on Income Statement
Costs of TV Commercials
Labor Costs ($3 per unit)
Sales Commissions (1% of sales)
Sales Manager's Salary
Shipping and Handling Costs ($0.75 per unit)
Cost of Renting the Administrative Building
Utility Costs for the Manufacturing Plant ($0.25 per unit produced)
Manufacturing Plant Manager's Salary
Materials Costs ($4 per unit produced)
Real Estate Taxes on the Manufacturing Plant
Depreciation on Manufacturing Equipment
Packaging Cost ($1 per unit produced)
Wages of the Plant Security Guard

Rox could purchase the toy planes from a supplier. If it did, the company would continue to sell them using its own logo, advertising program, and sales staff.

Required

Identify each cost as relevant or irrelevant to the outsourcing decision and indicate whether the cost is fixed or variable relative to the number of toy planes manufactured and sold.

L.O. 1   **Exercise 5-3B**   *Distinction between avoidable costs and cost behavior*

Treadaway Phones, Inc., makes telephones that it sells to department stores throughout the United States. Treadaway is trying to decide which of two telephone models to manufacture. The company could produce either telephone with its existing machinery. Cost data pertaining to the two choices follow:

	Model 90	Model 30
Materials cost per unit	$ 57	$ 57
Labor cost per unit	46	27
Product design cost	12,000	$7,000
Depreciation on existing manufacturing machinery	3,000	3,000

Required

a. Identify the fixed costs and determine the amount of fixed cost for each model.
b. Identify the variable costs and determine the amount of variable cost for each model.
c. Identify the avoidable costs.

L.O. 2   **Exercise 5-4B**   *Cost hierarchy*

Costs can be classified into one of four categories including unit-level, batch-level, product-level, or facility-level costs.

Required

Classify each of the items listed below into one of the four categories listed above. The first item has been categorized as an example.

Cost Description	Cost Classification
Product design	Product-level cost
Wages of factory janitors	
Machine setup cost for different production jobs	
Direct materials	
Salary of the manager in charge of making a product	
Tires used to assemble a car	
Payroll cost for assembly-line workers	
Electricity bill of the factory	

L.O. 2, 3   **Exercise 5-5B**   *Special order decision*

Varela Textile Company manufactures high-quality bed sheets and sells them in sets to a well-known retail company for $40 a set. Varela has sufficient capacity to produce 100,000 sets of sheets annually; the retail company currently purchases 80,000 sets each year. Varela's unit-level cost is $25 per set and its fixed cost is $800,000 per year. A motel chain has offered to purchase 10,000 sheet sets from Varela for $32 per set. If Varela accepts the order, the contract will prohibit the motel chain from reselling the bed sheets.

Required

Should Varela accept or reject the special order? Support your answer with appropriate computations.

Exercise 5-6B   *Special order decision*   **L.O. 2, 3**

Sago Automotive Company manufactures an engine designed for motorcycles and markets the product using its own brand name. Although Sago has the capacity to produce 28,000 engines annually, it currently produces and sells only 25,000 units per year. The engine normally sells for $400 per unit, with no quantity discounts. The unit-level costs to produce the engine are $150 for direct materials, $100 for direct labor, and $30 for indirect manufacturing costs. Sago expects total annual product- and facility-level costs to be $500,000 and $750,000, respectively. Assume Sago receives a special order from a new customer seeking to buy 1,000 engines for $300 each.

Required

Should Sago accept or reject the special order? Support your answer with appropriate computations.

Exercise 5-7B   *Identifying qualitative factors for a special order decision*   **L.O. 3**

Required

Describe the qualitative factors that Sago should consider before accepting the special order described in Exercise 5-6B.

Exercise 5-8B   *Using the contribution margin approach for a special order decision*   **L.O. 3**

Gonzalez Company produces and sells a food processor that it prices at a 25 percent markup on total cost. Based on data pertaining to producing and selling 40,000 food processors, Gonzalez computes the sales price per food processor as follows.

Unit-level costs	$ 800,000
Fixed costs	640,000
Total cost (a)	$1,440,000
Markup (a × .25)	360,000
Total sales revenue (b)	$1,800,000
Sales price per unit (b ÷ 40,000)	$45.00

Required

a. Gonzalez receives a special order for 7,000 food processors for $19 each. Gonzalez has excess capacity. Calculate the contribution margin per unit for the special order. Based on the contribution margin per unit, should Gonzalez accept the special order?

b. Support your answer by preparing a contribution margin income statement for the special order.

Exercise 5-9B   *Making an outsourcing decision*   **L.O. 4**

Rowe Boats Company currently produces a battery used in manufacturing its boats. The company annually manufactures and sells 2,000 units of a particular model of fishing boat. Because of the low volume of activity, Rowe is unable to obtain the economies of scale that larger producers achieve. For example, the costs associated with producing the batteries it uses are almost 30 percent more than the cost of purchasing comparable batteries. Rowe could buy batteries for $75 each; it costs $100 each to make them. A detailed breakdown of current production costs for the batteries follows:

Item	Unit Cost	Total
Unit-level costs:		
Materials	$ 30	$ 60,000
Labor	25	50,000
Overhead	5	10,000
Allocated facility-level costs	40	80,000
Total	$100	$200,000

Based on these figures, Rowe's president asserted that it would be foolish for the company to continue to produce the batteries at $100 each when it can buy them for $75 each.

Required

Do you agree with the president's conclusion? Support your answer with appropriate computations.

L.O. 4

Exercise 5-10B *Establishing a price for an outsourcing decision*

Pierce Corporation makes and sells skateboards. Pierce currently makes the 60,000 wheels used annually in its skateboards but has an opportunity to purchase the wheels from a reliable manufacturer. The costs of making the wheels follow.

Annual Costs Associated with Manufacturing Skateboard Wheels	
Materials (60,000 units × $5)	$300,000
Labor (60,000 units × $3)	180,000
Depreciation on manufacturing equipment*	24,000
Salary of wheel production supervisor	65,000
Rental cost of equipment used to make wheels	55,000
Allocated portion of corporate-level facility-sustaining costs	40,000
Total cost to make 60,000 wheels	$664,000

*The equipment has a book value of $74,000 but its market value is zero.

Required

a. Determine the maximum price per unit that Pierce would be willing to pay for the wheels.
b. Would the price computed in Requirement *a* change if production were increased to 80,000 units? Support your answer with appropriate computations.

L.O. 4

Exercise 5-11B *Making an outsourcing decision with qualitative factors considered*

Shipley Computers currently purchases for $15 each keyboard it uses in the 50,000 computers it makes and sells annually. Each computer uses one keyboard. The company has idle capacity and is considering whether to make the keyboards that it needs. Shipley estimates that materials and labor costs for making keyboards would be $9 each. In addition, supervisory salaries, rent, and other manufacturing costs would be $400,000. Allocated facility-level costs would amount to $70,000.

Required

a. Determine the change in net income that Shipley would experience if it decides to make the keyboards.
b. Discuss the qualitative factors that Shipley should consider.

L.O. 2, 4

Exercise 5-12B *Outsourcing decision affected by opportunity costs*

Taylor Doors Company currently produces the doorknobs for the doors it makes and sells. The monthly cost of producing 2,000 doorknobs is as follows:

Unit-level materials	$2,000
Unit-level labor	2,500
Unit-level overhead	1,600
Product-level costs*	4,000
Allocated facility-level costs	6,000

*Twenty percent of these costs can be avoided if the doorknobs are purchased.

Spivey Company has offered to sell comparable doorknobs to Taylor for $5 each.

Required

a. Should Taylor continue to make the doorknobs? Support you answer with appropriate computations.
b. For $5,000 per month, Taylor could lease the manufacturing space to another company. Would this potential cash inflow affect your response to Requirement *a*? Explain.

L.O. 6

Exercise 5-13B *Asset replacement decision*

Tidwell Fishing Tours, Inc., owns a boat that originally cost $98,000. Currently, the boat's net book value is $25,000, and its expected remaining useful life is four years. Tidwell has an opportunity to purchase for $72,000 a replacement boat that is extremely fuel efficient. Fuel costs for the old boat are expected to be $12,000 per year more than fuel costs would be for the replacement boat. Tidwell could sell the old boat, which is fully paid for and in good condition, for only $32,000.

Required

Should Tidwell replace the old boat with the new fuel-efficient model, or should it continue to use the old one until it wears out? Explain.

Exercise 5-14B   *Opportunity costs*   L.O. 1

Two years ago, Bob Walla bought a truck for $22,000 to offer delivery service. Bob earns $32,000 a year operating as an independent trucker. He has an opportunity to sell his truck for $15,000 and take a position as an instructor in a truck driving school. The instructor position pays $25,000 a year for working 40 hours per week. Driving his truck, Bob works approximately 60 hours per week. If Bob sells his truck, he will invest the proceeds of the sale in bonds that pay a 12 percent return.

Required

a. Determine the opportunity cost of owning and operating the independent delivery business.
b. Based solely on financial considerations, should Bob sell his truck and accept the instructor position?
c. Discuss the qualitative as well as quantitative characteristics that Bob should consider.

Exercise 5-15B   *Segment elimination decision*   L.O. 5

Willard Company operates three segments. Income statements for the segments imply that Willard could improve profitability if Segment X is eliminated.

THE WILLARD COMPANY Income Statement For the Year 2009			
Segment	**X**	**Y**	**Z**
Sales	$ 58,000	$140,000	$132,000
Cost of Goods Sold	(44,000)	(55,000)	(56,000)
Sales Commissions	(4,000)	(14,000)	(13,000)
Contribution Margin	10,000	71,000	63,000
General Fixed Oper. Exp. (allocation of president's salary)	(10,000)	(10,000)	(10,000)
Advertising Expense (specific to individual segments)	(6,000)	(7,000)	0
Net Income	$ (6,000)	$ 54,000	$ 53,000

Required

a. Explain the effect on Willard's profitability if Segment X is eliminated.
b. Prepare comparative income statements for the company as a whole under the two alternatives: (1) Segment X is retained or (2) Segment X is eliminated.

Exercise 5-16B   *Segment elimination decision*   L.O. 5

Yakovsky Company divides its operations into six divisions. A recent income statement for the Martin Division follows:

Income Statement	
Revenue	$ 750,000
Salaries for Employees	(500,000)
Operating Expenses	(169,000)
Insurance	(37,000)
Division-Level Facility-Sustaining Costs	(50,000)
Companywide Facility-Sustaining Costs	(58,000)
Net Loss	$ (64,000)

Required

a. Should Yakovsky eliminate the Martin Division? Support your answer by explaining how the division's elimination would affect the net income of the company as a whole. By how much would companywide income increase or decrease?

b. Assume that the Martin Division could increase its revenue to $770,000 by raising prices. Would this change the decision you made in response to Requirement *a*? Assuming Yakovsky's revenue becomes $770,000, determine the amount of the increase or decrease that would occur in companywide net income if the segment were eliminated.

c. What is the minimum amount of revenue the Martin Division must generate to justify its continued operation?

L.O. 5

Exercise 5-17B *Identifying avoidable cost of a segment*

Roberts Corporation is considering the elimination of one of its segments. The following fixed costs pertain to the segment. If the segment is eliminated, the building it uses will be sold.

Annual advertising expense	$169,000
Market value of the building	48,000
Annual depreciation on the building	18,000
Annual maintenance costs on equipment	26,000
Annual real estate taxes on the building	8,000
Annual supervisory salaries	72,000
Annual allocation of companywide facility-level costs	30,000
Original cost of the building	75,000
Current book value of the building	54,000

Required

Based on this information, determine the amount of avoidable cost associated with the segment.

L.O. 6

Exercise 5-18B *Asset replacement decision*

Weldon Electronics purchased a manufacturing plant four years ago for $7,500,000. The plant costs $2,000,000 per year to operate. Its current book value using straight-line depreciation is $5,500,000. Weldon could purchase a replacement plant for $12,000,000 that would have a useful life of 10 years. Because of new technology, the replacement plant would require only $500,000 per year in operating expenses. It would have an expected salvage value of $1,000,000 after 10 years. The current disposal value of the old plant is $1,400,000, and if Weldon keeps it 10 more years, its residual value would be $500,000.

Required

Based on this information, should Weldon replace the old plant? Support your answer with appropriate computations.

L.O. 6

Exercise 5-19B *Asset replacement decision*

Sorenson Company is considering whether to replace some of its manufacturing equipment. Information pertaining to the existing equipment and the potential replacement equipment follows:

Existing Equipment		Replacement Equipment	
Cost	$60,000	Cost	$45,000
Operating expenses*	50,000	Operating expenses*	10,000
Salvage value	12,000	Salvage value	10,000
Market value	20,000	Useful life	10 years
Book value	30,000		
Remaining useful life	10 years		

*The amounts shown for operating expenses are the cumulative total of all such expenses expected to be incurred over the useful life of the equipment.

Required

Based on this information, recommend whether to replace the equipment. Support your recommendation with appropriate computations.

Exercise 5-20B   *Asset replacement decision*

L.O. 6

Hulcher Company, a Texas-based corporation, paid $57,000 to purchase an air conditioner on January 1, 1997. During 2007, surging energy costs prompted management to consider replacing the air conditioner with a more energy-efficient model. The new air conditioner would cost $80,000. Electricity for the existing air conditioner costs the company $30,000 per year; the new model would cost only $20,000 per year. The new model, which has an expected useful life of 10 years, would be installed on January 1, 2008. Because the old air conditioner is more durable, Hulcher estimates it still has a remaining useful life of 10 years even though it has been used. The current market value of the old air conditioner is $27,000. The expected salvage value of both air conditioners is zero.

Required

Based on this information, recommend whether to replace the equipment. Support your recommendation with appropriate computations.

Exercise 5-21B   *Annual versus cumulative data for replacement decision*

L.O. 6, 7

Because their three adult children have all at last left home, Alex and Nancy Hough recently moved to a smaller house. Alex owns a riding lawnmower he bought three years ago to take care of the former house's huge yard; it should last another five years. With the new house's smaller yard, Alex thinks he could hire someone to cut his grass for $350 per year. He wonders if this option is financially sound. Relevant information follows.

Riding Lawn Mower	Amount
Original cost	$1,800
Accumulated depreciation	720
Current market value	1,000
Estimated salvage value	0

Required

a. What is the annual opportunity cost of using the riding mower? Based on your computations, recommend whether Alex should sell it and hire a lawn service.
b. Determine the total cost of hiring a lawn service for the next five years. Based on your computations, recommend whether Alex should sell the mower and hire a lawn service.

Appendix
Exercise 5-22B   *Scarce resource decision*

L.O. 8

Newtech has the capacity to annually produce either 50,000 desktop computers or 28,000 laptop computers. Relevant data for each product follow:

	Desktop	Laptop
Sales price	$1,000	$1,800
Variable costs	400	650

Required

Assuming that Newtech can sell all it produces of either product, should the company produce the desktop computers or the laptop computers? Provide computations to support your answer.

PROBLEMS–SERIES B

L.O. 1

Problem 5-23B *Context-sensitive relevance*

Required

Respond to each requirement independently.

a. Describe two decision-making contexts, one in which unit-level labor costs are avoidable, and the other in which they are unavoidable.
b. Describe two decision-making contexts, one in which batch-level shipping costs are avoidable, and the other in which they are unavoidable.
c. Describe two decision-making contexts, one in which administrative costs are avoidable, and the other in which they are unavoidable.
d. Describe two decision-making contexts, one in which the insurance premium paid on a building is avoidable, and the other in which it is unavoidable.
e. Describe two decision-making contexts, one in which amortization of a product patent is avoidable, and the other in which it is unavoidable.

L.O. 1

Problem 5-24B *Context-sensitive relevance*

Avery Machines Company is evaluating two customer orders from which it can accept only one because of capacity limitations. The data associated with each order follow.

Cost Category	Order A	Order B
Contract price	$960,000	$880,000
Unit-level materials	360,000	316,000
Unit-level labor	334,000	344,800
Unit-level overhead	106,000	98,000
Supervisor's salary	80,000	80,000
Rental equipment costs	20,000	24,000
Depreciation on tools (zero market value)	28,000	28,000
Allocated portion of companywide facility-sustaining costs	8,000	7,200
Insurance coverage	54,000	54,000

Required

a. Assume that Avery has decided to accept one of the two orders. Identify the information relevant to selecting one order versus the other. Recommend which job to accept, and support your answer with appropriate computations.
b. The customer presenting Order A has withdrawn it because of its financial hardship. Under this circumstance, Avery's choice is to accept or reject Order B alone. Identify the information relevant to this decision. Recommend whether to accept or reject Order B. Support your answer with appropriate computations.

L.O. 2, 3

Problem 5-25B *Effect of order quantity on special order decision*

Carroll Company made 100,000 electric drills in batches of 1,000 units each during the prior accounting period. Normally, Carroll markets its products through a variety of hardware stores. The following is the summarized cost to produce electric drills.

Materials cost ($5.00 per unit × 100,000)	$ 500,000
Labor cost ($4.00 per unit × 100,000)	400,000
Manufacturing supplies ($0.50 × 100,000)	50,000
Batch-level costs (100 batches at $2,000 per batch)	200,000
Product-level costs	150,000
Facility-level costs	180,000
Total costs	$1,480,000

Cost per unit = $1,480,000 ÷ 100,000 = $14.80

Required

a. Bypassing Carroll's regular distribution channel, Granado's Home Maintenance Company, has offered to buy a batch of 500 electric drills for $12.50 each directly from Carroll. Carroll's normal selling price is $20 per unit. Based on the preceding quantitative data, should Carroll accept the special order? Support your answer with appropriate computations.

b. Would your answer to Requirement *a* change if Granado's offered to buy a batch of 1,000 electric drills for $11.60 each? Support your answer with appropriate computations.

c. Describe the qualitative factors that Carroll should consider before accepting a special order to sell electric drills to Granado's.

Problem 5-26B   *Effects of the level of production on an outsourcing decision*   **L.O. 2, 4**

One of Eby Company's major products is a fuel additive designed to improve fuel efficiency and keep engines clean. Eby, a petrochemical firm, makes and sells 100,000 units of the fuel additive per year. Its management is evaluating the possibility of having an outside supplier manufacture the product for Eby for $2 each. Eby would continue to sell and distribute the fuel additive under its own brand name for either alternative. Eby's accountant constructed the following profitability analysis.

Revenue (100,000 units × $3.50)	$350,000
Unit-level materials costs (100,000 units × $0.80)	(80,000)
Unit-level labor costs (100,000 units × $0.12)	(12,000)
Unit-level overhead costs (100,000 × $0.38)	(38,000)
Unit-level selling expenses (100,000 × $0.20)	(20,000)
Contribution margin	200,000
Fuel additive production supervisor's salary	(80,000)
Allocated portion of facility-level costs	(20,000)
Product-level advertising cost	(40,000)
Contribution to companywide income	$ 60,000

Required

a. Identify the cost items relevant to the make-or-outsource decision.

b. Should Eby continue to make the fuel additive or buy it from the supplier? Support your answer by determining the change in net income if Eby buys the fuel additive instead of making it.

c. Suppose that Eby is able to increase sales by 60,000 units (sales will increase to 160,000 units). At this level of sales, should Eby make or buy the fuel additive? Support your answer by explaining how the increase in production affects the cost per unit.

d. Discuss the qualitative factors that Eby should consider before deciding to outsource the fuel additive. How can Eby minimize the risk of establishing a relationship with an unreliable supplier?

Problem 5-27B   *Outsourcing decision affected by equipment replacement*   **L.O. 2, 5, 6**

During 2007, Pleasant Toy Company made 15,000 units of Model K, the costs of which follow.

Unit-level materials costs (15,000 units × $6)	$ 90,000
Unit-level labor costs (15,000 units × $20)	300,000
Unit-level overhead costs (15,000 × $8)	120,000
Depreciation on manufacturing equipment	48,000
Model K production supervisor's salary	42,000
Inventory holding costs	108,000
Allocated portion of facility-level costs	72,000
Total costs	$780,000

An independent contractor has offered to make the same product for Pleasant for $42 each.

Additional Information:

1. The manufacturing equipment originally cost $420,000 and has a book value of $240,000, a remaining useful life of four years, and a zero salvage value. If the equipment is not used to produce Model K in the production process, it can be leased for $36,000 per year.

2. Pleasant has the opportunity to purchase for $200,000 new manufacturing equipment that will have an expected useful life of four years and a salvage value of $80,000. This equipment will increase productivity substantially, thereby reducing unit-level labor costs by 20 percent.

3. If Pleasant discontinues the production of Model K, the company can eliminate 50 percent of its inventory holding cost.

Required

a. Determine the avoidable cost per unit to produce Model K assuming that Pleasant is considering the alternatives between making the product using the existing equipment and outsourcing the product to the independent contractor. Based on the quantitative data, should Pleasant outsource Model K? Support your answer with appropriate computations.

b. Assuming that Pleasant is considering whether to replace the old equipment with the new equipment, determine the avoidable cost per unit to produce Model K using the new equipment and the avoidable cost per unit to produce Model K using the old equipment. Calculate the impact on profitability if Model K were made using the old equipment versus the new equipment.

c. Assuming that Pleasant is considering either to purchase the new equipment or to outsource Model K, calculate the impact on profitability between the two alternatives.

d. Discuss the qualitative factors that Pleasant should consider before making a decision to outsource Model K. How can Pleasant minimize the risk of establishing a relationship with an unreliable supplier?

L.O. 5

Problem 5-28B   *Eliminating a segment*

Chow's Grocery Store has three departments, meat, canned food, and produce, each of which has its own manager. All departments are housed in a single store. Recently, the produce department has been suffering a net loss and is expected to continue doing so. Last year's income statements follow.

	Meat Department	Canned Food Department	Produce Department
Sales	$670,000	$600,000	$440,000
Cost of Goods Sold	(270,000)	(330,000)	(260,000)
Gross Margin	400,000	270,000	180,000
Departmental Manager's Salary	(42,000)	(30,000)	(35,000)
Rent on Store Lease	(80,000)	(80,000)	(80,000)
Store Utilities	(20,000)	(20,000)	(20,000)
Other General Expenses	(98,000)	(98,000)	(98,000)
Net Income (loss)	$160,000	$ 42,000	$ (53,000)

Required

a. Determine whether to eliminate the produce department.

b. Confirm the conclusion you reached in Requirement *a* by preparing a before and an after income statement, assuming that the produce department is eliminated.

c. Eliminating the produce department would allow the meat department to expand. It could add seafood to its products. Suppose that management estimates that offering seafood would increase the store's net earnings by $160,000. Would this information affect the decision that you made in Requirement *a*? Explain your answer.

L.O. 2, 5

Problem 5-29B   *Effect of activity level and opportunity cost on segment elimination decision*

Gilder Company has three separate operating branches: Division X, which manufactures utensils; Division Y, which makes plates; and Division Z, which makes cooking pots. Each division operates its own facility. The company's administrative offices are located in a separate building. In recent years, Division Z has experienced a net loss and is expected to continue to do so. Income statements for 2008 follow.

	Division X	Division Y	Division Z
Sales	$2,000,000	$1,600,000	$1,710,000
Less: Cost of Goods Sold			
Unit-Level Manufacturing Costs	(1,100,000)	(580,000)	(900,000)
Rent on Manufacturing Facility	(240,000)	(220,000)	(450,000)
Gross Margin	660,000	800,000	360,000
Less: Operating Expenses			
Unit-Level Selling and Admin. Expenses	(60,000)	(45,000)	(150,000)
Division-Level Fixed Selling and Admin. Expenses	(140,000)	(125,000)	(240,000)
Administrative Facility-Level Costs	(80,000)	(80,000)	(80,000)
Net Income (loss)	$ 380,000	$ 550,000	$ (110,000)

Required

a. Based on the preceding information, recommend whether to eliminate Division Z. Support your answer by preparing companywide income statements before and after eliminating Division Z.

b. During 2008, Division Z produced and sold 30,000 units of product. Would your recommendation in Requirement *a* change if sales and production increase to 45,000 units in 2009? Support your answer by comparing differential revenue and avoidable cost for Division Z, assuming that 45,000 units are sold.

c. Suppose that Gilder could sublease Division Z's manufacturing facility for $910,000. Would you operate the division at a production and sales volume of 45,000 units, or would you close it? Support your answer with appropriate computations.

Problem 5-30B   *Comprehensive problem including special order, outsourcing, and segment elimination decisions*

L.O. 2, 3, 4, 5

Heth Company's electronics division produces a radio/cassette player. The vice president in charge of the division is evaluating the income statement showing annual revenues and expenses associated with the division's operating activities. The relevant range for the production and sale of the radio/cassette player is between 50,000 and 150,000 units per year.

Income Statement	
Revenue (60,000 units × $30)	$1,800,000
Unit-Level Variable Costs	
Materials Cost (60,000 × $15)	(900,000)
Labor Cost (60,000 × $8)	(480,000)
Manufacturing Overhead (60,000 × $1.50)	(90,000)
Shipping and Handling (60,000 × $0.50)	(30,000)
Sales Commissions (60,000 × $2)	(120,000)
Contribution Margin	180,000
Fixed Expenses	
Advertising Costs Related to the Division	(30,000)
Salary of Production Supervisor	(126,000)
Allocated Companywide Facility-Level Expenses	(120,000)
Net Loss	$ (96,000)

Required (Consider each of the requirements independently.)

a. An international trading firm has approached top management about buying 30,000 radio/cassette players for $26.50 each. It would sell the product in a foreign country, so that Heth's existing customers would not be affected. Because the offer was made directly to top management, no sales commissions on the transaction would be involved. Based on quantitative features alone, should Heth accept the special order? Support your answer with appropriate computations. Specifically, by what amount would profitability increase or decrease if the special order is accepted?

b. Heth has an opportunity to buy the 60,000 radio/cassette players it currently makes from a foreign manufacturer for $26 each. The manufacturer has a good reputation for reliability and quality, and

Heth could continue to use its own logo, advertising program, and sales force to distribute the products. Should Heth buy the radio/cassette players or continue to make them? Support your answer with appropriate computations. Specifically, how much more or less would it cost to buy the radio/cassette players than to make them? Would your answer change if the volume of sales were increased to 140,000 units?

c. Because the electronics division is currently operating at a loss, should it be eliminated from the company's operations? Support your answer with appropriate computations. Specifically, by what amount would the segment's elimination increase or decrease profitability?

Appendix

L.O. 8

Problem 5-31B   *Allocating scarce resources*

Hawn Company makes two products, M and N. Product information follows.

	Product M	Product N
Selling price per unit	$75	$90
Variable cost per unit	48	55

Required

Identify the product that should be produced or sold under each of the following constraints. Consider each constraint separately.

a. One unit of Product M requires 3 hours of labor to produce, and one unit of Product N requires 5 hours of labor to produce. Due to labor constraints, demand is higher than the company's capacity to make both products.

b. The products are sold to the public in retail stores. The company has limited floor space and cannot stock as many products as it would like. Display space is available for only one of the two products. Expected sales of Product M are 8,000 units, and expected sales of Product N are 7,000 units.

c. The maximum number of machine hours available is 36,000. Product M uses 6 machine hours, and Product N uses 10 machine hours. The company can sell all the products it produces.

L.O. 7

Problem 5-32B   *Conflict between short-term versus long-term performance*

Doyle Construction Components, Inc., purchased a machine on January 1, 2006, for $240,000. The chief engineer estimated the machine's useful life to be six years and its salvage value to be zero. The operating cost of this machine is $120,000 per year. By January 1, 2008, a new machine that requires 30 percent less operating cost than the existing machine has become available for $180,000; it would have a four-year useful life with zero salvage. The current market value of the old machine on January 1, 2008, is $100,000, and its book value is $160,000 on that date. Straight-line depreciation is used for both machines. The company expects to generate $320,000 of revenue per year from the use of either machine.

Required

a. Recommend whether to replace the old machine on January 1, 2008. Support your answer with appropriate computations.

b. Prepare income statements for four years (2008 through 2011) assuming that the old machine is retained.

c. Prepare income statements for four years (2008 through 2011) assuming that the old machine is replaced.

d. Discuss the potential ethical conflicts that could result from the timing of the loss and expense recognition reported in the two income statements.

ANALYZE, THINK, COMMUNICATE

ATC 5-1   Business Application Case   *Elimination of a product line*

The following excerpts were drawn from the article entitled "The Scottish Shogun," published in *U.S. News & World Report,* May 19, 1997, on pages 44 and 45.

The Japanese car maker [Mazda Motor Company] has accumulated nearly a billion dollars in operating losses in three years. Its market share in Japan fell from nearly 8 percent to below 5 percent in the first half of the decade, and its overall car production dropped by a stunning 46 percent. In fact, Mazda has been fighting for its life. To salvage the company, Ford Motor Co., Mazda's biggest shareholder, gambled $430 million [in 1996] and raised its equity stake in Mazda to 33.4 percent, which in practice gave it operating control. The U.S. car maker chose Henry Wallace, a Ford man for 25 years, to spearhead a turnaround. Mr. Wallace is the first foreigner to lead a big Japanese company. In this case, Mr. Wallace has been warmly embraced by the Japanese—both inside and outside Mazda. Wallace's first move was to retrench—cut product lines, consolidate sales channels, reduce inventory, and in the United States, halt unprofitable fleet and car-rental sales. Wallace also took action to instill a profit motive among the board of directors. Wallace observed, "I don't think previously there was a strong profit motive within the company." Instead, Mazda was a club of engineers who turned out wonderful niche cars—some with exotic styling, others with superb performance—that few consumers wanted to buy. When drivers developed a taste for sport utility vehicles, Mazda's beautiful sedans collected dust on the lots.

Required

a. The article indicated that one action Mr. Wallace took was to cut product lines. Explain which levels (unit, batch, product, and/or facility) of costs could be avoided by eliminating product lines. What sacrifices will Mazda likely have to make to obtain the cost savings associated with eliminating product lines?

b. Suppose that the cost data on the table below apply to three sales channels that were eliminated through the consolidation program.

Additional Information

(1) Sales are expected to drop by 20 percent because of the consolidation program. The remaining sales volume was absorbed by other sales channels.

(2) Forty percent of the sales staff accepted transfers that placed them in positions in other sales channels. The other 60 percent left the company.

(3) The supervisor of Channel 1 accepted a job transfer. The other two supervisors left the company.

Annual Costs of Operating Each Sales Channel	Channel 1	Channel 2	Channel 3
Unit-level selling costs:			
Selling supplies	$ 40,000	$ 32,000	$ 22,000
Sales commissions	425,000	355,000	225,000
Shipping and handling	49,000	40,000	24,000
Miscellaneous	29,000	20,000	17,000
Facility-level selling costs:			
Rent	240,000	245,000	236,000
Utilities	50,000	40,000	48,000
Staff salaries	1,088,000	900,000	855,000
Supervisors salaries	170,000	150,000	100,000
Depreciation on equipment	303,000	300,000	307,000
Allocated companywide expenses	100,000	100,000	100,000

(4) The combined equipment, with an expected remaining useful life of four years and a $450,000 projected salvage value, has a current market value of $650,000.

(5) The offices operated by the eliminated channels were closed.

Determine the amount of annual costs saved by consolidating the sales channels.

c. How will reducing inventory save costs?

d. Although the cost-cutting measures are impressive, Mr. Wallace was quoted as saying, "Obviously no one is going to succeed in our business just by reducing costs." Speculate as to some other measures that Mr. Wallace could take to improve Mazda's profitability.

ATC 5-2   Group Assignment   *Relevance and cost behavior*

Maccoa Soft, a division of Zayer Software Company, produces and distributes an automated payroll software system. A contribution margin format income statement for Maccoa Soft for the past year follows.

Revenue (12,000 units × $1,200)	$14,400,000
Unit-Level Variable Costs	
Product Materials Cost (12,000 × $60)	(720,000)
Installation Labor Cost (12,000 × $200)	(2,400,000)
Manufacturing Overhead (12,000 × $2)	(24,000)
Shipping and Handling (12,000 × $25)	(300,000)
Sales Commissions (12,000 × $300)	(3,600,000)
Nonmanufacturing Miscellaneous Costs (12,000 × $5)	(60,000)
Contribution Margin (12,000 × $608)	7,296,000
Fixed Costs	
Research and Development	(2,700,000)
Legal Fees to Ensure Product Protection	(780,000)
Advertising Costs	(1,200,000)
Rental Cost of Manufacturing Facility	(600,000)
Depreciation on Production Equipment (zero market value)	(300,000)
Other Manufacturing Costs (salaries, utilities, etc.)	(744,000)
Division-Level Facility Sustaining Costs	(1,730,000)
Allocated Companywide Facility-Level Costs	(1,650,000)
Net Loss	$ (2,408,000)

a. Divide the class into groups and then organize the groups into three sections. Assign Task 1 to the first section, Task 2 to the second section, and Task 3 to the third section. Each task should be considered independently of the others.

Group Tasks

(1) Assume that Maccoa has excess capacity. The sales staff has identified a large franchise company with 200 outlets that is interested in Maccoa's software system but is willing to pay only $800 for each system. Ignoring qualitative considerations, should Maccoa accept the special order?

(2) Maccoa has the opportunity to purchase a comparable payroll system from a competing vendor for $600 per system. Ignoring qualitative considerations, should Maccoa outsource producing the software? Maccoa would continue to sell and install the software if the manufacturing activities were outsourced.

(3) Given that Maccoa is generating a loss, should Zayer eliminate it? Would your answer change if Maccoa could increase sales by 1,000 units?

b. Have a representative from each section explain its respective conclusions. Discuss the following:

(1) Representatives from Section 1 should respond to the following: The analysis related to the special order (Task 1) suggests that all variable costs are always relevant. Is this conclusion valid? Explain your answer.

(2) Representatives from Section 2 should respond to the following: With respect to the outsourcing decision, identify a relevant fixed cost and a nonrelevant fixed cost. Discuss the criteria for determining whether a cost is or is not relevant.

(3) Representatives from Section 3 should respond to the following: Why did the segment elimination decision change when the volume of production and sales increased?

ATC 5-3   Research Assignment   *Systems replacement decision*

The April 2003 issue of *Strategic Finance* contains an article "Why Automate Payables and Receivables? Electronic Are More Accurate and Less Costly," written by Suzanne Hurt. It appears on pages 33 to 35. This article notes that while financial resource management (FRM) software is available to automate processing transactions such as receivables and payables, 86 percent of these transactions are still paper based. In the article, the author explains some of the reasons companies should consider switching to an Internet-based FRM system and gives some examples of the costs savings that companies such as General Electric have realized by adopting such software. Read this article and complete the following requirements.

Required

a. Identify the relevant costs a company should consider when considering the switch from a manual system to an Internet-based FRM system of accounting for receivables and payables. Think carefully. The article does not specifically identify all of these costs.

b. The article notes that one advantage of an Internet-based FRM system is that it allows companies to get money from receivables collected and deposited into the bank more quickly. What type of cost does this represent for a company that continues to use a manual system rather than adopt an automated system?

c. The author identifies what she thinks is the biggest challenge facing a company trying to switch to an Internet-based FRM system. What is this challenge?

ATC 5-4 Writing Assignment *Relevant versus full cost*

State law permits the State Department of Revenue to collect taxes for municipal governments that operate within the state's jurisdiction and allows private companies to collect taxes for municipalities. To promote fairness and to ensure the financial well-being of the state, the law dictates that the Department of Revenue must charge municipalities a fee for collection services that is above the cost of providing such services but does not define the term *cost*. Until recently, Department of Revenue officials have included a proportionate share of all departmental costs such as depreciation on buildings and equipment, supervisory salaries, and other facility-level overhead costs when determining the cost of providing collection services, a measurement approach known as *full costing*. The full costing approach has led to a pricing structure that places the Department of Revenue at a competitive disadvantage relative to private collection companies. Indeed, highly efficient private companies have been able to consistently underbid the Revenue Department for municipal customers. As a result, it has lost 30 percent of its municipal collection business over the last two years. The inability to be price competitive led the revenue commissioner to hire a consulting firm to evaluate the current practice of determining the cost to provide collection services.

The consulting firm concluded that the cost to provide collection services should be limited to the relevant costs associated with providing those services, defined as the difference between the costs that would be incurred if the services were provided and the costs that would be incurred if the services were not provided. According to this definition, the costs of depreciation, supervisory salaries, and other facility-level overhead costs are not included because they are the same regardless of whether the Department of Revenue provides collection services to municipalities. The Revenue Department adopted the relevant cost approach and immediately reduced the price it charges municipalities to collect their taxes and rapidly recovered the collection business it had lost. Indeed, several of the private collection companies were forced into bankruptcy. The private companies joined together and filed suit against the Revenue Department, charging that the new definition of cost violates the intent of the law.

Required

a. Assume that you are an accountant hired as a consultant for the private companies. Write a brief memo explaining why it is inappropriate to limit the definition of the costs of providing collection services to relevant costs.

b. Assume that you are an accountant hired as a consultant for the Department of Revenue. Write a brief memo explaining why it is appropriate to limit the definition of the costs of providing collection services to relevant costs.

c. Speculate on how the matter will be resolved.

ATC 5-5 Ethical Dilemma *Asset replacement clouded by self-interest*

John Dillworth is in charge of buying property used as building sites for branch offices of the National Bank of Commerce. Mr. Dillworth recently paid $110,000 for a site located in a growing section of the city. Shortly after purchasing this lot, Mr. Dillworth had the opportunity to purchase a more desirable lot at a significantly lower price. The traffic count at the new site is virtually twice that of the old site, but the price of the lot is only $80,000. It was immediately apparent that he had overpaid for the previous purchase. The current market value of the purchased property is only $75,000. Mr. Dillworth believes that it would be in the bank's best interest to buy the new lot, but he does not want to report a loss to his boss, Kelly Fullerton. He knows that Ms. Fullerton will severely reprimand him, even though she has made her share of mistakes. In fact, he is aware of a significant bad loan that Ms. Fullerton recently approved. When confronted with the bad debt by the senior vice president in charge of commercial lending, Ms. Fullerton blamed the decision on one of her former subordinates, Ira Sacks. Ms. Fullerton implied that Mr. Sacks had been dismissed for reckless lending decisions when, in fact, he had been an excellent loan officer with an uncanny ability to assess the creditworthiness of his customers. Indeed, Mr. Sacks had voluntarily resigned to accept a better position.

Required

a. Determine the amount of the loss that would be recognized on the sale of the existing branch site.
b. Identify the type of cost represented by the $110,000 original purchase price of the land. Also identify the type of cost represented by its current market value of $75,000. Indicate which cost is relevant to a decision as to whether the original site should be replaced with the new site.
c. Is Mr. Dillworth's conclusion that the old site should be replaced supported by quantitative analysis? If not, what facts do justify his conclusion?
d. Assuming that Mr. Dillworth is a certified management accountant (CMA), do you believe the failure to replace the land violates any of the standards of ethical conduct in Exhibit 1.15 in Chapter 1? If so, which standards would be violated?
e. Discuss the ethical dilemma that Mr. Dillworth faces within the context of the fraud triangle that was discussed in Chapter 1.
f. Would Mr. Dillworth be subject to criminal penalties under the Sarbanes-Oxley Act? Explain your answer.

ATC 5-6   Spreadsheet Assignment   *Using Excel*

Dorina Company makes cases of canned dog food in batches of 1,000 cases and sells each case for $15. The plant capacity is 50,000 cases; the company currently makes 40,000 cases. DoggieMart has offered to buy 1,500 cases for $12 per case. Because product-level and facility-level costs are unaffected by a special order, they are omitted.

Required

a. Prepare a spreadsheet like the following one to calculate the contribution to income if the special order is accepted. Construct formulas so that the number of cases or the price could be changed and the new contribution would be automatically calculated.
b. Try different order sizes (such as 2,000) or different prices to see the effect on contribution to profit.

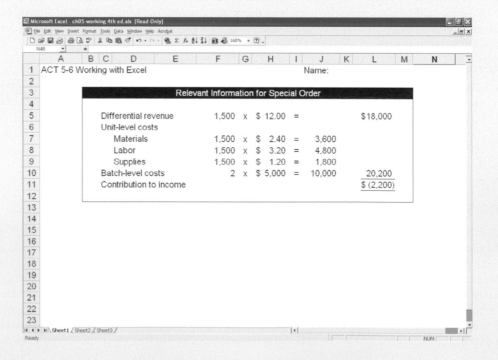

Spreadsheet Tips

1. The numbers in cells F7 to F9 should be formulas that refer to F5. This allows the number of cases to be changed in cell F5 with the other cells changing automatically.

2. The formula in cell F10 uses a function named ROUNDUP to calculate the even number of batches. The formula should be = ROUNDUP(F5/1000,0) where the zero refers to rounding up to the nearest whole number.

ATC 5-7   Spreadsheet Assignment   *Mastering Excel*

Refer to Problem 5-31A.

Required

a. Prepare a spreadsheet to solve Requirements *a, b,* and *c* in Problem 5-31A.
b. While constructing formulas for Requirement *a* of Problem 5-31A, include a formula to calculate contribution margin per labor hour.
c. While constructing formulas for Requirement *b* of Problem 5-31A, include formulas to calculate total contribution margin for each product.
d. While constructing formulas for Requirement *c* of Problem 5-31A, include formulas to calculate contribution margin per machine hour and total contribution margin for each product.

COMPREHENSIVE PROBLEM

Use the same transaction data for Magnificent Modems, Inc., as was used in Chapter 1. (See page 52.)

Required

a. One of Magnificent Modems' sales representatives receives a special offer to sell 1,000 modems at a price of $72 each. Should the offer be accepted?
b. Magnificent Modems has the opportunity to purchase the modems that it currently makes. The modems can be purchased at a price of $76 each. Assuming the manufacturing equipment has a zero market value, should Magnificent buy the modems?
c. Assume that Magnificent Modems expects production and sales to grow to 10,000. At this volume of production, should Magnificent buy the modems?

CHAPTER 6

Cost Management in an Automated Business Environment

ABC, ABM, and TQM

The Curious Accountant

A vendor's acceptance of credit and debit cards is expensive. Normally, the credit card company charges a fee by discounting the amount paid to the vendor for each charge. For example, suppose that the **U.S. Postal Service (USPS)** accepts a charge card as payment for $100 of stamps. When the USPS presents the credit card receipt to the credit card company for payment, the company pays USPS less than $100, perhaps $96. The actual discount rate depends on individual agreements between credit card companies and their customers. In this case, the USPS receives only $96 for $100 worth of stamps. Even so, the credit card customer must pay the bank $100. The $4 difference between the amount that the bank gave USPS and the amount that the customer paid the USPS is the fee that the bank charges for providing credit services. Incidentally, the credit card customer usually is required to pay the bank interest if the credit balance remains outstanding after the payment due date and may pay an annual fee. At a minimum, the USPS must pay a fee to enable its customers to pay for purchases with their charge cards.

Because the USPS has a virtual monopoly on regular delivery mail, why is it willing to pay fees to permit customers to use credit cards? Why doesn't the agency accept only cash or checks? (Answers on page 257.)

CHAPTER OPENING

Worldwide growth in capitalism has fostered an increasingly competitive global business environment. Companies have responded by using technology to increase productivity. Management accountants have worked with engineers to more accurately measure and control costs. They have eliminated many nonvalue-added activities and have employed quality control procedures that reduce costs and enhance customer satisfaction. These innovative business practices have enabled companies to eliminate unprofitable products and to promote products that maximize profitability. This chapter focuses on newer and emerging business practices employed by world-class companies. ■

Development of a Single Companywide Cost Driver

LO 1

Explain how activity-based costing improves accuracy in determining the cost of products and services.

When accountants first developed cost systems, manufacturing processes were labor intensive. Indirect manufacturing costs were relatively minor and highly correlated with labor use; products that used large amounts of labor consumed large amounts of overhead. This link made the number of labor hours a suitable cost driver for allocating overhead costs.

To illustrate, suppose during an eight-hour day Friedman Company production employees worked on two jobs, Job 1 for two hours and Job 2 for six hours. Friedman consumed utilities of $120 during the day. How much of the $120 should the company assign to each job? Friedman cannot trace the utility cost directly to a specific job, but the job that required more labor likely consumed more of the utility cost. The longer employees work the more heat, lights, and water they use. Allocating the utility cost to the two jobs based on *direct labor hours* produces rational results. Friedman could allocate the utility cost at $15 per hour ($120 ÷ 8 hours). It could assign Job 1 $30 of the utility cost ($15 per hour × 2 hours), and Job 2 the remaining $90 ($15 × 6 hours).

In addition to utilities, direct labor drives many other indirect costs. Consider the depreciation cost of tools employees use while working on production jobs. The more time employees work, the more they use the tools. Direct labor hours could be an effective cost driver (allocation base) for allocating tool depreciation costs. The same logic applies to supervisory salaries, production supplies, factory rent expense, and other overhead costs. Many companies applied this reasoning to justify using direct labor hours as the *sole base* for establishing a **companywide allocation rate.** These companies then allocated all overhead costs to their products or other cost objects using the single labor-based, companywide overhead rate. Even though using one base to allocate all overhead costs inaccurately measured some cost objects, in the labor intensive environment that spawned companywide allocation rates, overhead costs were relatively small compared to the costs of labor and materials. Allocation inaccuracies were relatively insignificant in amount.

Automation has changed the nature of manufacturing processes. The number of direct labor hours is no longer an effective allocation base in many modern manufacturing companies. Machines have replaced most human workers. Because they operate technically complex equipment, the remaining workers are highly skilled and not easily replaced. Companies resist laying off these trained workers when production declines. Neither do companies add employees when production increases. Adjusting production volume merely requires turning additional machines on or off. In such circumstances, direct labor is not related to production volume. Direct labor is therefore not an effective base for allocating overhead costs. Former labor-intensive companies that adopt automation usually must develop more sophisticated ways to allocate overhead costs.

When companies replace people with machines, overhead costs such as machinery depreciation and power usage become greater in proportion to total manufacturing costs. In highly automated companies, overhead costs may be greater than direct labor and direct materials costs combined. Although misallocating minor overhead amounts does little harm, misallocating major costs destroys the usefulness of accounting information and leads to poor decisions. Managers must consider how automation affects overhead cost allocation.

Effects of Automation on Selecting a Cost Driver

In an automated manufacturing environment, robots and sophisticated machinery, rather than human labor, transform raw materials into finished goods. To illustrate the effect of these changes on selecting a cost driver, return to the previous Friedman Company example. Suppose Friedman automates the production process for Job 2, replacing most labor with four hours of machine processing and reducing the number of direct labor hours required from six to one. Assume the new machinery acquired increases utility consumption and depreciation charges, raising daily overhead costs from $120 to $420. Because Job 1 requires two hours of direct labor and Job 2 now requires one hour of direct labor, Friedman's companywide allocation rate increases to $140 per direct labor hour ($420 ÷ 3 hours). The company would allocate $280 ($140 × 2 hours) of the total overhead cost to Job 1 and $140 ($140 × 1 hour) to Job 2. The pre- and postautomation allocations are compared here.

Product	Preautomation Cost Distribution	Postautomation Cost Distribution
Job 1	$ 30	$280
Job 2	90	140
Total	$120	$420

Using direct labor hours as the cost driver after automating production of Job 2 distorts the overhead cost allocation. Although Friedman did not change the production process for Job 1 at all, Job 1 received a $250 ($280 − $30) increase in its share of allocated overhead cost. This increase should have been assigned to Job 2 because automating production of Job 2 caused overhead costs to increase. The decrease in direct labor hours for Job 2 causes the distortion. Prior to automation, Job 2 used six of eight total direct labor hours and was therefore allocated 75 percent (6 ÷ 8) of the overhead cost. After automation, Job 2 consumed only one of three total direct labor hours, reducing its overhead allocation to only 33 percent of the total. These changes in the allocation base, coupled with the increase in total overhead cost, caused the postautomation overhead cost allocation for Job 1 to be significantly overstated and for Job 2 to be significantly understated.

One way to solve the misallocation problem is to find a more suitable volume-based cost driver. For example, Friedman could allocate utility costs using machine hours instead of direct labor hours. This text illustrated using different **volume-based cost drivers** (such as material dollars and direct labor hours) in Chapter 4. Unfortunately, automated production processes often generate costs which have no cause-and-effect relationship with volume-based cost drivers. Many companies have therefore adopted **activity-based cost drivers** to improve the accuracy of indirect cost allocations. To illustrate, consider the case of Carver Soup Company.

Activity-Based Cost Drivers

Carver Soup Company (CSC) produces batches of vegetable and tomato soup. Each time CSC switches production from vegetable soup to tomato soup or vice versa, it incurs certain costs. For example, production workers must clean the mixing, blending, and cooking equipment. They must change settings on the equipment to the specifications for the particular soup to be processed. CSC must test each batch for quality to ensure the recipe has been correctly followed. Because these costs are incurred for each new batch, they are called **start-up,** or **setup, costs.** CSC plans to make 180 batches of each type of soup during the coming year. The following table summarizes expected production information:

	Vegetable	Tomato	Total
Number of cans	954,000	234,000	1,188,000
Number of setups	180	180	360

CSC expects each setup will cost $264, for total expected setup costs of $95,040 ($264 × 360 setups). Using number of cans as the cost driver (volume-based driver) produces an allocation rate of $0.08 per can ($95,040 ÷ 1,188,000 cans). Multiplying the allocation rate by the weight of the base (number of cans) produces the following setup cost allocation:

Product	Allocation Rate	×	Number of Cans Produced	=	Allocated Product Cost
Vegetable	$0.08	×	954,000	=	$76,320
Tomato	0.08	×	234,000	=	18,720

As expected, the volume-based (number of cans) allocation rate assigns more cost to the high-volume vegetable soup product. However, assigning more setup cost to the vegetable soup makes little sense. Since both products require the *same number* of setups, the setup cost should be distributed equally between them. The volume-based cost driver *overcosts* the high-volume product (vegetable soup) and *undercosts* the low-volume product (tomato soup).

Setup costs are driven by the number of times CSC employees perform the setup activities. The more setups employees undertake, the greater the total setup cost. An *activity-based cost driver* (number of setups) provides a more accurate allocation base for setup costs. Using the allocation rate of $264 ($95,040 ÷ 360 setups) per setup assigns the same amount of setup cost to each product, as follows:

Product	Allocation Rate	×	Number of Setups	=	Allocated Product Cost
Vegetable	$264	×	180	=	$47,520
Tomato	264	×	180	=	47,520

Activity-Based Cost Drivers Enhance Relevance

The *activity-based cost driver* produces a better allocation because it distributes the *relevant* costs to the appropriate products. If CSC were to stop producing tomato soup, it could *avoid* spending $47,520 for 180 setups (assuming CSC could eliminate labor, supplies, and other resources used in the setup process). *Avoidable costs are relevant* to decision making. The inaccurate volume-based product cost data could mislead a manager into making a poor decision. Suppose a company specializing in setup activities offered to provide CSC 180 tomato soup setups for $40,000. A manager relying on the volume-based allocated cost of $18,720 would reject the $40,000 offer to outsource as too costly. In fact, CSC should accept the offer because it could avoid $47,520 of cost if the outside company performs the setup activity. In a highly automated environment in which companies produce many different products at varying volume levels, it is little wonder that many companies have turned to activity-based costing to improve the accuracy of cost allocations and the effectiveness of decisions.

CHECK YOURSELF 6.1

Professional Training Services, Inc. (PTSI), offers professional exam review courses for both the certified public accountant (CPA) and the certified management accountant (CMA) exams. Many more students take the CPA review courses than the CMA review courses. PTSI uses the same size and number of classrooms to teach both courses; its CMA courses simply have more empty seats. PTSI is trying to determine the cost of offering the two courses. The company's accountant has decided to allocate classroom rental cost based on the number of students enrolled in the courses. Explain why this allocation base will likely result in an inappropriate assignment of cost to the two cost objects. Identify a more appropriate allocation base.

Answer

Using the number of students as the allocation base will assign more of the rental cost to the CPA review courses because those courses have higher enrollments. This allocation is inappropriate because the number of classrooms, not the number of students, drives the amount of rental cost. Since both courses require the same number of classrooms, the rental cost should be allocated equally between them. Several allocation bases would produce an equal allocation, such as the number of classrooms, the number of courses, or a 50/50 percentage split.

Activity-Based Costing

A company that allocates indirect costs using **activity-based costing (ABC)** follows a two-stage process. In the first stage, costs are assigned to pools based on the activities that cause the costs to be incurred. In the second stage, the costs in the activity cost pools are allocated to products using a variety of cost drivers. The first step in developing an ABC system is to identify essential activities and the costs of performing those activities.

A business undertakes **activities** to accomplish its mission. Typical activities include acquiring raw materials, transforming raw materials into finished products, and delivering products to customers. These broadly defined activities can be divided into subcategories. For example, the activity of acquiring raw materials involves separate subcategory activities such as identifying suppliers, obtaining price quotations, evaluating materials specifications, completing purchase orders, and receiving purchased materials. Each of these subcategories can be subdivided into yet more detailed activities. For instance, identifying suppliers may include such activities as reviewing advertisements, searching Internet sites, and obtaining recommendations from business associates. Further subdivisions are possible. Companies perform thousands of activities.

LO 2

Identify cost centers and cost drivers in an activity-based cost system.

Topic Tackler
PLUS
6-1

Identifying Activity Centers

Maintaining separate cost records for thousands of activities is expensive. To reduce record-keeping costs, companies group related activities into hubs called **activity centers.** The overhead costs of these related activities are combined into a cost pool for each activity center. Because the activities assigned to each center are related, a business can obtain rational cost allocations using a common cost driver for an entire cost pool. Determining the optimal number of activity centers requires *cost/benefit analysis.* Companies will incur the higher record-keeping costs for additional activity centers only to the extent that the additional accuracy improves decision making.

Comparing ABC with Traditional Two-Stage Cost Allocation

How do ABC systems differ from the traditional two-stage allocation systems discussed in the appendix to Chapter 4? Traditional two-stage allocation systems pool costs by departments, then allocate departmental cost pools to cost objects using volume-based cost drivers. In contrast, ABC systems pool costs by activity centers, then allocate activity center cost pools to cost objects using a variety of volume- and activity-based cost drivers. ABC systems use many more activity centers than the number of departments in a traditional two-stage allocation system. As a result, ABC improves cost tracing by using more cause-and-effect relationships in assigning indirect costs to numerous activity centers. Exhibit 6.1 illustrates the primary differences between a traditional two-stage allocation system and an ABC system.

EXHIBIT 6.1

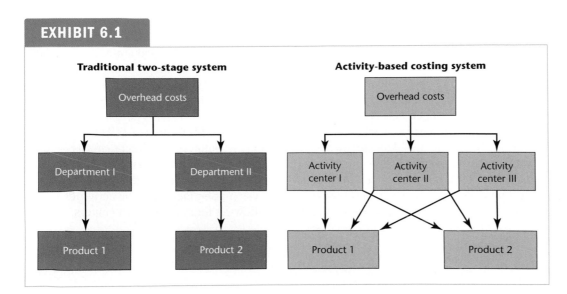

FOCUS ON INTERNATIONAL ISSUES

ELIMINATING NONVALUE-ADDED ACTIVITIES IN A SUSHI BAR

Identifying and eliminating activities that do not add value can lead to increased customer satisfaction and profitability. An emerging trend in Japanese sushi bars validates this point. Sushi delivered via conveyor belt leads to significant cost savings that are passed on to customers. A moving belt, not a waiter, delivers sushi directly to the customers. Chefs fill the merry-go-round conveyor belt, instead of patron orders. The savings associated with the elimination of nonvalue-added activities such as taking orders, delivering food, and avoiding waste have enabled conveyor belt shops to offer customers quality sushi at economy prices—two pieces for $1 vs. $3 to $4 at standard sushi shops. Customers are so wowed by the deal that they are braving waits of up to an hour. Owners are benefiting, too, because diners get their fill and move on faster, thereby increasing turnover and sales volume. The increased volume produced is highly profitable because fixed costs are not affected by the soaring sales. When insights gained through activity-based costing (ABC) lead to changes in the way a business is managed, the process is known as *activity-based management* (ABM).

Source: Miki Tanikawa, "Sushi Bars: What Comes Around," *BusinessWeek*, November 9, 1998, p. 8.

Types of Production Activities

Identify cost centers and cost drivers in an activity-based cost system.

Many companies organize activities into four hierarchical categories to improve cost tracing. These categories are (1) unit-level activities, (2) batch-level activities, (3) product-level activities, and (4) facility-level activities.[1] The overhead costs in each category are pooled and allocated to products based on how the products benefit from the activities. *The primary objective is to trace the cost of performing activities to the products that are causing the activities to be performed.* To illustrate, consider the overhead costs incurred by Unterman Shirt Company.

Unterman has two product lines, dress shirts and casual shirts. The company expects to incur overhead costs of $5,730,000 in the course of producing 680,000 dress shirts and 120,000 casual shirts during 2008. Currently, Unterman assigns an equal amount of overhead to each shirt, simply dividing the total expected overhead cost by the total expected production ($5,730,000 ÷ 800,000 units = $7.16 per shirt, rounded). Each type of shirt requires approximately the same amount of direct materials, $8.20 per shirt, and the same amount of direct labor, $6.80 per shirt. The total cost per shirt is $22.16 ($7.16 + $8.20 + $6.80). Unterman sells shirts for $31 each, yielding a gross margin of $8.84 per shirt ($31 − $22.16).

Bob Unterman, president and owner of the company, believes the direct materials and direct labor costs are reasonable, but the overhead costs must not be the same for both product lines. Mr. Unterman hired a consultant, Rebecca Lynch, to trace the overhead costs. Ms. Lynch decided to use an *activity-based cost* system. She identified the activities necessary to make shirts and classified them into the following four activity cost centers.

---

[1]The types of costs in each category were discussed in Chapter 5. Review the cost hierarchy before continuing in this chapter.

Unit-Level Activity Center

Unit-level activities occur each time a unit of product is made. For example, for every shirt made, Unterman incurs inspection costs, machine-related utility costs, and costs for production supplies. Total unit-level cost increases with every shirt made and decreases with reductions in production volume. Some costs behave so much like unit-level costs that they may be accounted for as unit-level even though they are not strictly unit-level. For example, suppose Unterman employees lubricate production machinery after every eight hours of continuous operation. Although Unterman does not incur lubrication cost for each shirt produced, the cost behavior pattern is so closely tied to production levels that it may be accounted for as a unit-level cost.

Ms. Lynch identified the following unit-level overhead costs: (1) $300,000 for machine-related utilities, (2) $50,000 for machine maintenance, (3) $450,000 for indirect labor and indirect materials, (4) $200,000 for inspection and quality control, and (5) $296,000 for miscellaneous unit-level costs. She assigned these costs into a single *unit-level activity center* overhead cost pool of $1,296,000. This assignment illustrates the first stage of the two-stage ABC allocation system. Of the total $5,730,000 overhead cost, Ms. Lynch has allocated $1,296,000 to one of the four activity centers. The remaining overhead cost is allocated among the three other activity centers.

The second-stage cost assignment involves allocating the $1,296,000 unit-level cost pool between the two product lines. Because unit-level costs are incurred each time a shirt is produced, they should be allocated using a base correlated to production levels. Ms. Lynch chose direct labor hours as the allocation base. Past performance indicates the dress shirts will require 272,000 direct labor hours and the casual shirts will require 48,000 direct labor hours. Based on this information, Ms. Lynch allocated the unit-level overhead costs and computed the cost per unit as shown in Exhibit 6.2.

EXHIBIT 6.2

Allocation of Unit-Level Overhead Costs

	Product Lines		
	Dress Shirts	Casual Shirts	Total
Number of direct labor hours (a)	272,000	48,000	320,000
Cost per labor hour			
($1,296,000 ÷ 320,000 hours) (b)	$4.05	$4.05	NA
Total allocated overhead cost (c = a × b)	$1,101,600	$194,400	$1,296,000
Number of shirts (d)	680,000	120,000	800,000
Cost per shirt (c ÷ d)	$1.62	$1.62	NA

The unit-level costs exhibit a variable cost behavior pattern. Total cost varies in direct proportion to the number of units produced. Cost per unit is constant. Because production volume does not affect the unit-level overhead cost, the pricing of shirts should not be affected by the fact that the company makes more dress shirts than casual shirts.

Batch-Level Activity Center

Batch-level activities relate to producing groups of products. Batch-level costs are fixed regardless of the number of units produced in a single batch. For example, the costs of setting up machinery to cut fabric for a certain size shirt remain unchanged regardless of the number of shirts cut at that particular machine setting. Similarly, the cost of a first-item batch test is the same whether 200 or 2,000 shirts are made in the batch. Materials handling costs are also commonly classified as batch-level because materials are usually transferred from one department to another in batches. For example, all of the size small casual shirts are cut in the sizing department, then the entire batch of cut fabric is transferred in one operation to the sewing department. The cost of materials handling is the same regardless of whether the batch load is large or small.

Because total batch costs depend on the number of batches produced, more batch costs should be allocated to products that require more batches. Ms. Lynch identified $690,000 of total batch-level overhead costs and assigned this amount to a batch-level cost pool.

For the second-stage allocation, Ms. Lynch determined that the casual-shirt line requires considerably more setups than the dress-shirt line because the casual shirts are subject to frequent style changes. Because customers buy limited amounts of items with short shelf lives, Unterman must produce casual shirts in small batches. Ms. Lynch decided more of the batch-level costs should be allocated to the casual-shirt line than to the dress-shirt line. She chose number of set-ups as the most rational allocation base. Since casual shirts require 1,280 setups and dress shirts require 1,020 setups, Ms. Lynch allocated the batch-level costs as shown in Exhibit 6.3.

EXHIBIT 6.3

Allocation of Batch-Level Overhead Costs

	Product Lines		
	Dress Shirts	Casual Shirts	Total
Number of setups performed (a)	1,020	1,280	2,300
Cost per setup ($690,000 ÷ 2,300 setups) (b)	$300	$300	NA
Total allocated overhead cost (c = a × b)	$306,000	$384,000	$690,000
Number of shirts (d)	680,000	120,000	800,000
Cost per shirt (c ÷ d)	$0.45	$3.20	NA

ABC demonstrates that the per shirt batch-level cost for casual shirts ($3.20 per shirt) is considerably more than for dress shirts ($0.45). One reason is that the casual-shirt line incurs more batch-level costs ($384,000 versus $306,000). The other is that Unterman produces far fewer casual shirts than dress shirts (120,000 units versus 680,000). Because batch-level costs are fixed relative to the number of units in a particular batch, the cost per unit is greater the smaller the batch. For example, if setup costs are $300, the setup cost per unit for a batch of 100 units is $3 ($300 ÷ 100 units). For a batch of only 10 units, however, the setup cost per unit is $30 ($300 ÷ 10 units). When batch-level costs are significant, companies should pursue high-volume products. Low-volume products are more expensive to make because the fixed costs must be spread over fewer units. To the extent that cost affects pricing, Unterman should charge more for casual shirts than dress shirts.

Product-Level Activity Center

Product-level activities support specific products or product lines. Examples include raw materials inventory holding costs; engineering development costs; and legal fees for patents, copyrights, trademarks, and brand names. Unterman Shirt Company positions itself as a fashion leader. It incurs extensive design costs to ensure that it remains a trendsetter. The company also incurs engineering costs to continually improve the quality of materials used in its shirts and legal fees to protect its brand names. After reviewing Unterman's operations, Ms. Lynch concluded she could trace $1,800,000 of the total overhead cost to the product-level activity center.

The second-stage allocation requires dividing these activities between the dress-shirt line and the casual-shirt line. Interviews with fashion design staff disclosed that they spend more time on casual shirts because of the frequent style changes. Similarly, the engineers spend more of their time developing new fabric, buttons, and zippers for casual shirts. The materials used in dress shirts are fairly stable. Although engineers spend some time improving the quality of dress-shirt materials, they devote far more time to the more unusual materials used in the casual shirts. Similarly, the legal department spends more time developing and protecting patents, trademarks, and brand names for the casual-shirt line. Ms. Lynch concluded

EXHIBIT 6.4

Allocation of Product-Level Overhead Costs

| | Product Lines | | |
	Dress Shirts	Casual Shirts	Total
Percent of product-level activity utilization (a)	30%	70%	100%
Total allocated overhead cost			
(b = a × $1,800,000)	$540,000	$1,260,000	$1,800,000
Total units produced (c)	680,000	120,000	800,000
Cost per unit (b ÷ c)	$0.79*	$10.50	NA

*Rounded to the nearest whole cent.

that 70 percent of the product-level cost pool applied to casual shirts and 30 percent to dress shirts. She allocated product-level costs to the two product lines as shown in Exhibit 6.4.

Product-level costs are frequently distributed unevenly among different product lines. Unterman Shirt Company incurs substantially more costs to sustain its casual-shirt line than its dress-shirt line. Using a single companywide overhead rate in such circumstances distorts cost measurements. Distorted product cost measurements can lead to negative consequences such as irrational pricing policies and rewards for inappropriate decisions. Activity-based costing reduces measurement distortions by more accurately tracing costs to the products that cause their incurrence.

Facility-Level Activity Center

Facility-level activities benefit the production process as a whole and are not related to any specific product, batch, or unit of production. For example, insuring the manufacturing facility against fire losses does not benefit any particular product or product line. Facility-level costs include depreciation on the manufacturing plant, security, landscaping, plant maintenance, general utilities, and property taxes. For Unterman Shirt Company, Ms. Lynch identified $1,944,000 of facility-level overhead costs. Because no cause-and-effect relationship exists between these facility-level manufacturing costs and the two product lines, she must allocate these costs arbitrarily. Basing the arbitrary allocation on the total number of units produced, Ms. Lynch allocated 85 percent (680,000 ÷ 800,000) of the facility-level cost pool to the dress-shirt line and 15 percent (120,000 ÷ 800,000) to the casual-shirt line as shown in Exhibit 6.5.

Classification of Activities Not Limited to Four Categories

The number of activity centers a business uses depends on cost/benefit analysis. The four categories illustrated for Unterman Shirt Company represent a useful starting point. Any of

EXHIBIT 6.5

Allocation of Facility-Level Overhead Costs

| | Product Lines | | |
	Dress Shirts	Casual Shirts	Total
Percent of total units (a)	85%	15%	100%
Total allocated overhead cost (b = a × $1,944,000)	$1,652,400	$291,600	$1,944,000
Total units produced (c)	680,000	120,000	800,000
Cost per unit (b ÷ c)	$2.43	$2.43	NA

the four categories could be further subdivided into more detailed activity centers. Unterman could establish an activity cost center for unit-level labor-related activities and a different activity center for unit-level machine-related activities. Identifying all potential activity centers in a real-world company can be daunting. Paulette Bennett describes the process used in the Material Control Department at Compumotor, Inc., as follows:

> Recognizing that ordinarily the two biggest problems with an ABC project are knowing where to start and how deep to go, we began by analyzing the activities that take place in our procurement process. As the old saying goes, to find the biggest alligators you usually have to wade into the weeds; therefore, we started by writing down all the procurement activities. Creating a real world picture of costs by activity was our aim. But had we used our initial list we would have designed a spreadsheet so large that no human could ever have emerged alive at the other end.[2]

Ms. Bennett's abbreviated list still included 83 separate activities. The list represented the activity centers for only one department of a very large company. Although the Unterman example used only four categories, the real-world equivalent is far more complex.

CHECK YOURSELF 6.2

Under what circumstances would the number of units produced be an inappropriate allocation base for batch-level costs?

Answer

Using the number of units produced as the allocation base would allocate more of the batch-level costs to high-volume products and less of the costs to low-volume products. Since batch-level costs are normally related to the number of batches rather than the number of units made in each batch, allocation of batch-level costs based on units produced would result in poor product cost estimates; the costing system would overcost high-volume products and undercost low-volume products. It would be appropriate to use the number of units produced only when each batch consists of the same number of product units. Even under these circumstances, the number of units merely serves as a proxy for the number of batches. It would still be more appropriate to use the number of batches to allocate batch-level costs.

Context-Sensitive Classification of Activities

Particular activities could fall into any of the four hierarchical categories. For example, inspecting each individual item produced is a unit-level activity. Inspecting the first item of each batch to ensure the setup was correct is a batch-level activity. Inspecting a specific product line is a product-level activity. Finally, inspecting the factory building is a facility-level activity. To properly classify activities, you must learn to analyze the context within which they occur.

Selecting Cost Drivers

Activity-based costing uses both *volume-based* cost drivers and *activity-based* cost drivers. Volume-based drivers are appropriate for indirect costs that increase or decrease relative to the volume of activity. Using cost drivers such as units, direct labor hours, or machine hours is appropriate for unit-level activities. The flaw in traditional costing systems is that they use a volume-based measure (usually direct labor hours) to allocate all indirect costs. In contrast, the more sophisticated ABC approach uses activity drivers such as number of setups or percentage of utilization for overhead costs that are not influenced by volume. ABC improves the accuracy of allocations by using a combination of volume- and activity-based cost drivers.

---

[2]Paulette Bennett, "ABM and the Procurement Cost Model," *Management Accounting,* March 1996, pp. 28–32.

Using ABC Information to Trace Costs to Product Lines

Exhibit 6.6 summarizes the ABC allocations Ms. Lynch prepared. Mr. Unterman was shocked to learn that overhead costs for casual shirts are virtually three times those for dress shirts. Exhibit 6.7 compares the per unit gross margins for the two product lines using the traditional cost system and using the ABC system. Recall that direct materials and direct labor costs for dress and casual shirts are $8.20 and $6.80, respectively. The difference in the margins is attributable to the overhead allocation. Using a traditional companywide overhead rate allocates an equal amount of overhead to each shirt ($5,730,000 ÷ 800,000 units = $7.16 per shirt). In contrast, the ABC approach assigns $5.29 to each dress shirt and $17.75 to each casual shirt. Total overhead cost is $5,730,000 under both approaches. It is the *allocation* of rather than the *amount* of the overhead cost that differs. ABC shows that making a casual shirt costs more than making a dress shirt. After reviewing the data in Exhibit 6.7, Mr. Unterman realized the company was incurring losses on the casual-shirt line. What options does he have?

Use activity-based costing to calculate costs of products and services.

6-2

Under- and Overcosting

In using the single companywide overhead rate, Unterman Shirt Company has undercosted its casual line and priced the shirts below cost. The obvious response to the ABC gross margin data in Exhibit 6.7 is to raise the price of casual shirts. Unfortunately, the market may not cooperate. If other companies are selling casual shirts at prices near $31, customers may buy

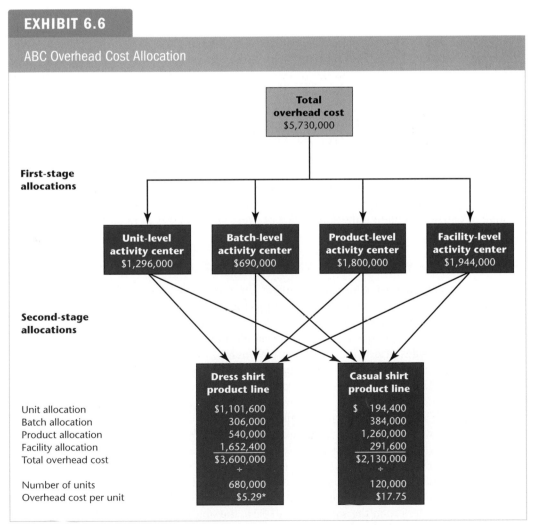

EXHIBIT 6.6

ABC Overhead Cost Allocation

*Rounded to the nearest whole cent.

EXHIBIT 6.7

Gross Margins Using Traditional Versus ABC Costing

	Gross Margins Traditional System		Gross Margins ABC Costing	
	Dress Shirts	Casual Shirts	Dress Shirts	Casual Shirts
Sales price	$31.00	$31.00	$31.00	$31.00
Cost of goods sold				
Materials cost	(8.20)	(8.20)	(8.20)	(8.20)
Labor cost	(6.80)	(6.80)	(6.80)	(6.80)
Overhead	(7.16)	(7.16)	(5.29)	(17.75)
Gross margin	$ 8.84	$ 8.84	$10.71	$ (1.75)

from Unterman's competitors instead of paying a higher price for Unterman's shirts. In a market-driven economy, raising prices may not be a viable option. Unterman may have to adopt a target-pricing strategy.

Target pricing starts with determining the price customers are willing to pay. The company then attempts to produce the product at a low enough cost to sell it at the price customers demand. Exhibits 6.3 and 6.4 indicate that batch-level and product-level costs are significantly higher for casual shirts than for dress shirts. Unterman may be too fashion conscious with respect to casual shirts. Perhaps the company should reduce fashion design costs by focusing on a few traditional styles instead of maintaining a trendsetting position. Also, following established trends is less risky than setting new ones. Retail customers may have more confidence in the marketability of traditional casual shirts, which could lead them to place larger orders, enabling Unterman to reduce its per unit batch costs.

The single companywide overhead rate not only undercosts the casual-shirt line but also overcosts the dress-shirt line. To the extent that the overhead cost affects the selling price, the dress-shirt line is overpriced. Overpricing places the dress shirt business at a competitive disadvantage which can have a snowball effect. If volume declines because of lost market share, sales revenue will decrease and Unterman's fixed costs will be spread over fewer units, resulting in a higher cost per unit. Higher costs encourage price increases, which further aggravate the competitive disadvantage. It is as important for Unterman to consider reducing the sales price of dress shirts as it is to raise the sales price of casual shirts.

Examining the Relevance of Allocated Facility-Level Costs

If Unterman cannot raise the price or lower the cost of its casual shirts, management should consider eliminating the casual-shirt product line. As indicated in Chapter 5, elimination decisions require identifying *relevant revenues and costs*. Relevant revenues and costs are those Unterman can *avoid* by eliminating the casual-shirt line. The relevant revenue is $31, the sales price of a casual shirt. Which of the ABC–allocated overhead costs can Unterman avoid? Companies can usually eliminate or substantially reduce unit-level, batch-level, and product-level costs by eliminating a product line. *Facility-level costs, however, are usually unavoidable; they are not affected by product eliminations.* Unterman will continue to incur such costs as manufacturing depreciation, security, insurance, and property taxes whether or not it makes casual shirts. *Many companies do not allocate facility-level costs to products for decision-making purposes.* For Unterman, the avoidable overhead cost of a casual shirt is $15.32 (unit-level $1.62 + batch-level $3.20 + product-level $10.50). Assuming direct labor and direct materials costs are avoidable, the total avoidable cost is $30.32 ($8.20 materials + $6.80 labor + $15.32 overhead). Because the avoidable cost is less than the sales price of $31, the analysis suggests Unterman should not eliminate the casual-shirt line.

Answers to The Curious Accountant

The USPS commissioned **Coopers & Lybrand (C&L)** (now PricewaterhouseCoopers), a large accounting firm, to conduct activity-based cost (ABC) studies of its key revenue collection processes. C&L developed an ABC model for USPS's existing cash and check revenue collection and a similar ABC model for debit and credit card activities. The ABC model identified costs associated with unit, batch, and product activities. *Unit-level activity* was defined as the acceptance and processing of a payment by item. *Batch-level activities* involved the closeout at the end of the day, consolidation, and supervisory review. *Product-level activities* included maintenance for bank accounts and deposit reconciliation for the cash and checks model and terminal maintenance and training for the credit and debit card system. A comparison of the cost of the two activity models revealed that a significant cost savings could be achieved in the long term by implementing a debit and credit card system. Some examples of expected cost savings included a decrease in the per unit transaction cost due to

the fact that credit card customers tend to spend more per transaction than do cash customers. In addition, the cost of activities associated with the collection of bad debts falls to virtually zero when debit or credit cards are used and the cost of cash management activities declines. Funds are collected earlier (no check collection float occurs), thereby reducing the need for financing and the resultant interest cost. In summary, C&L projected a negative benefit for a debit and credit card system (due largely to high initial implementation costs) through 1997. Projections showed that from 1998 through 2000, the net benefits of card acceptance would be $5.2 million, $15.6 million, and $28.8 million, respectively. So the USPS started accepting plastic because ABC analysis revealed that implementing a debit and credit card program would save money!

Source: Terrel L. Carter, Ali M. Sedghat, and Thomas D. Williams, "How ABC Changed the Post Office," *Management Accounting*, February 1998, pp. 28–36.

Downstream Costs and Upstream Costs

The preceding paragraph analyzed only product costs. Businesses incur **upstream costs** before and **downstream costs** after goods are manufactured. Either upstream or downstream costs may be relevant to product elimination decisions. For example, suppose Unterman pays sales representatives a $2 commission for each shirt sold. Although sales commissions are selling, not product, costs, they are relevant to deciding whether to eliminate the casual-shirt line. Unterman can avoid the commission expense if it sells no casual shirts. Including the sales commission increases the total avoidable cost to $32.32 ($30.32 product costs + $2.00 sales commissions) which is more than the $31 sales price. Unterman would therefore be more profitable if it abandoned the casual-shirt line. Management must also consider upstream costs such as those for research and development. To continue in business, companies must sell products at prices that exceed the *total* cost to develop, make, and sell them.

Employee Attitudes and the Availability of Data

Activity-based costing can lead management to implement cost-cutting measures, including product and product line eliminations, that can result in the loss of jobs. Employees are therefore sometimes uncooperative with management efforts to adopt an ABC system. Companies must help employees recognize that ABC and other **strategic cost management** techniques frequently result in redirecting workers rather than displacing them. Ultimately, jobs depend on the employer's competitive health. The implementation of an ABC system is more likely to succeed when both managers and rank-and-file employees are convinced their own well-being is tied to the company's well-being.

Even when employees cooperate, implementing an ABC system can be difficult. Frequently, the accounting system is not collecting some of the needed data. For example, suppose a manager wants to allocate inspection costs based on the number of hours job inspections take. Inspectors may not record the time spent on individual jobs. Basing the allocation on inspection hours requires inspectors to begin keeping more detailed time records. The accuracy of the allocation then depends on how conscientiously inspectors complete their time reports. Obtaining employee support and accurate data are two of the more challenging obstacles to successfully implementing ABC.

Total Quality Management

Identify the components of quality costs.

Quality is key to a company's ability to obtain and retain customers. What does *quality* mean? It does not always mean the best. A spoon made of silver is of higher quality than a spoon made of plastic, but customers are perfectly willing to use plastic spoons at fast-food restaurants. **Quality** represents the degree to which products or services *conform* to design specifications. The costs companies incur to ensure quality conformance can be classified into four categories: prevention, appraisal, internal failure, and external failure.

Companies incur **prevention costs** to avoid nonconforming products. They incur **appraisal costs** to identify nonconforming products produced in spite of prevention cost expenditures. **Failure costs** result from correcting defects in nonconforming products produced. **Internal failure costs** pertain to correcting defects before goods reach customers; **external failure costs** result from delivering defective goods to customers.

Because prevention and appraisal costs are a function of managerial discretion, they are often called **voluntary costs.** Management chooses how much to spend on these voluntary costs. In contrast, management does not directly control failure costs. The cost of dissatisfied customers may not be measurable, much less controllable. Even though failure costs may not be directly controllable, they are related to voluntary costs. When management spends additional funds on prevention and appraisal controls, failure costs tend to decline. As the level of control increases, quality conformance increases, reducing failure costs. When control activities are reduced, quality conformance decreases and failure cost increases. *Voluntary costs and failure costs move in opposite directions.*

Minimizing Total Quality Cost

Total quality control cost is the sum of voluntary costs plus failure costs. Because voluntary costs and failure costs are negatively correlated, the minimum amount of *total* quality cost is located at the point on a graph where the marginal voluntary expenditures equal the marginal savings on failure cost as shown in Exhibit 6.8.

Exhibit 6.8 indicates that the minimum total quality cost per unit occurs at quality level of less than 100 percent. At very low levels of quality assurance, significant failure costs outweigh any cost savings available by avoiding voluntary costs. In contrast, extremely high levels of quality assurance result in voluntary cost expenditures that are not offset by failure cost savings. Although the goal of zero defects is appealing, it is not a cost-effective strategy. Realistic managers seek to minimize total quality cost rather than to eliminate all defects.

EXHIBIT 6.8

Relationships Among Components of Quality Cost

Cost per Unit

Total quality cost

Voluntary cost (prevention and appraisal)

Failure cost (internal and external)

0   100

Percent of Products without Defects

CHECK YOURSELF 6.3

Is it wiser to spend money on preventing defects or on correcting failures?

Answer

The answer depends on where a company's product falls on the "total quality cost" line (see Exhibit 6.8). If the product falls left of the cost minimization point, spending more on preventing defects would produce proportionately greater failure cost savings. In other words, a company would spend less in total by reducing failure costs through increasing prevention costs. Under these circumstances, it would be wise to incur prevention costs. On the other hand, if the product falls right of the cost minimization point line, the company would spend more to prevent additional defects than it would save by reducing failure costs. Under these circumstances, it makes more sense to pay the failure costs than attempt to avoid them by incurring prevention costs.

Quality Cost Reports

Managing quality costs to achieve the highest level of customer satisfaction is known as **total quality management (TQM).** Accountants support TQM by preparing a **quality cost report,** which typically lists the company's quality costs and analyzes horizontally each item as a percentage of the total cost. Data are normally displayed for two or more accounting periods to disclose the effects of changes over time. Exhibit 6.9 shows a quality cost report for Unterman Shirt Company. The company's accountant prepared the report to assess the effects of a quality control campaign the company recently initiated. Review Exhibit 6.9. What is Unterman's quality control strategy? Is it succeeding?

Prepare and interpret quality cost reports.

Exhibit 6.9 indicates Unterman is seeking to control quality costs by focusing on appraisal activities. The total expenditures for prevention activities remained unchanged, but expenditures for appraisal activities increased significantly. The results of this strategy are apparent in the failure cost data. Internal failure costs increased significantly while external failure costs decreased dramatically. The strategy succeeded in lowering total quality costs. The report suggests, however, that more improvement is possible. Notice that 86.13 percent (appraisal 19.63 percent + internal failure 39.01 percent + external failure 27.49 percent) of total quality costs is spent on finding and correcting mistakes. The adage "an ounce of prevention is worth a pound of cure," applied to Unterman, implies spending more on prevention could perhaps eliminate many of the appraisal and failure costs.

EXHIBIT 6.9

Quality Cost Report for Unterman Shirt Company

	2008		2007	
	Amount	Percentage*	Amount	Percentage*
Prevention costs				
Product design	$ 50,000	6.54%	$ 52,000	6.60%
Preventive equipment (depreciation)	7,000	0.92	7,000	0.89
Training costs	27,000	3.53	25,000	3.17
Promotion and awards	22,000	2.88	22,000	2.79
Total prevention	106,000	13.87	106,000	13.45
Appraisal costs				
Inventory inspection	75,000	9.82	25,000	3.17
Reliability testing	43,000	5.63	15,000	1.90
Testing equipment (depreciation)	20,000	2.62	12,000	1.52
Supplies	12,000	1.57	8,000	1.02
Total appraisal	150,000	19.63	60,000	7.61
Internal failure costs				
Scrap	90,000	11.78	40,000	5.08
Repair and rework	140,000	18.32	110,000	13.96
Downtime	38,000	4.97	20,000	2.54
Reinspection	30,000	3.93	12,000	1.52
Total internal failure	298,000	39.01	182,000	23.10
External failure costs				
Warranty repairs and replacement	120,000	15.71	260,000	32.99
Freight	20,000	2.62	50,000	6.35
Customer relations	40,000	5.24	60,000	7.61
Restocking and packaging	30,000	3.93	70,000	8.88
Total external failure	210,000	27.49	440,000	55.84
Grand total	$764,000	100.00%	$788,000	100.00%

*Percentages do not add exactly because of rounding.

REALITY BYTES

Improving the quality of a product can increase its costs. Are the benefits of the higher quality worth the higher costs? In other words, are companies that spend money to improve the quality of their products rewarded with higher profit margins? This is a difficult question to answer empirically because, among other things, there is not always a definitive, objective measure of the quality of competing products or services.

Nevertheless, we can make some general comparisons based on objective data that are available for automobile manufacturers. Every year **JD Power and Associates** reports on various aspects of quality among auto manufacturers, including the closely watched *initial quality study,* or IQS. The IQS evaluates 135 quality attributes of recently purchased cars and trucks based on surveys of owners. On May 18, the company released its 2005 ISQ, and as in most of the recent years, the **Toyota Motor Corporation** came out on top. Conversely, **Ford Motor Company** received a below average rating. (Some Ford products, notably Jaguar, received very high IQS rankings in 2005.)

What about these companies' comparative profitability? The table below shows the return on assets and return on sales ratios for Ford and Toyota based on data for their 2005 fiscal years. The data on which these ratios are based were prepared in accordance with the GAAP of the United States. However, the computations for Ford are based on unaudited, company-reported information.

Ratio	Ford	Toyota
Return on assets	0.7%	4.8%
Return on sales	1.1	6.3

It would certainly be an oversimplification to attribute all of Toyota's higher profitability to its higher quality evaluations. However, many experts in the automotive business believe Toyota's reputation for building high-quality vehicles is a significant contributor to its success.

<< A Look Back

Many traditional cost systems used direct labor hours as the sole base for allocating overhead costs. Labor hours served as an effective *companywide allocation base* because labor was highly correlated with overhead cost incurrence. It made sense to assign more overhead to cost objects that required more labor. Because direct labor was related to production volume, it was frequently called a *volume-based cost driver.* Other volume-based cost drivers included machine hours, number of units, and labor dollars. Companywide, volume-based cost drivers were never perfect measures of overhead consumption. However, misallocation was not a serious problem because overhead costs were relatively small. If a manager misallocated an insignificant cost, it did not matter.

Automation has changed the nature of the manufacturing process. This change may cause significant distortions in the allocation of overhead costs when the allocation base is a companywide, volume-based cost driver. There are two primary reasons for distortions. First, in an automated environment, the same amount of labor (e.g., flipping a switch) may produce a large or a small volume of products. Under these circumstances, labor use is not related to the incurrence of overhead and is not a rational allocation base. Second, the distortions may be significant because overhead costs are much higher relative to the cost of labor and materials. For example, when robots replace people in the production process, depreciation becomes a larger portion of total product cost and labor becomes a smaller portion of the total.

To improve the accuracy of allocations, managerial accountants began to study the wide array of activities required to make a product. Such activities may include acquiring raw materials, materials handling and storage activities, product design activities, legal activities, and traditional production labor activities. Various measures of these activities can be used as bases for numerous overhead allocations related to determining product cost. Using activity measures to allocate overhead costs has become known as *activity-based costing (ABC).* In an ABC system, costs are allocated in a two-stage process. First, activities are organized into *activity centers* and the related costs of performing these activities are combined into *cost pools.* Second, the pooled costs are allocated to designated cost objects using activity-based cost drivers. Implementing ABC is most likely to succeed when employees understand that it will positively affect their fate and that of the company. Without employee cooperation, collecting data necessary for the system's success may be difficult.

Many ABC systems begin by organizing activities into one of four categories. Total *unit-level activity cost* increases each time a unit of product is made and decreases when production volume declines. Unit-level activity costs can be allocated with a base correlated to the level of production (volume-based cost drivers). *Batch-level activities* are related to producing groups of products. Their costs are fixed regardless of the number of units in a batch. Batch-level costs are assigned so that the products requiring the most batches are assigned the most batch costs. *Product-level activities* support a specific product or product line. Product-level costs are frequently assigned to products based on the product's percentage use of product-level activities. *Facility-level activities* are performed for the benefit of the production process as a whole. The allocation of these costs is often arbitrary.

Accurate allocations prevent the distortions of overcosted or undercosted products. Overcosting can cause a product line to be overpriced. Overpriced products may cause a company to lose market share, and the decline in sales revenue will cause profits to fall. When products are underpriced, revenue is less than it could be, and profitability suffers.

Product costs are frequently distinguished from upstream and downstream costs. *Upstream costs* result from activities that occur *before* goods are manufactured. Examples include research and development, product design, and legal work. *Downstream costs* result from activities that occur *after* goods are manufactured. Examples of downstream costs include selling and administrative expenses. Upstream and downstream costs affect pricing decisions and product elimination decisions.

A Look Forward

The next chapter introduces planning and cost control, including how to prepare budgets and projected (pro forma) financial statements. In addition to quantitative aspects, it illustrates the effect of the budgeting process on human behavior.

 **SELF-STUDY REVIEW PROBLEM**

A step-by-step audio-narrated series of slides is provided on the text website at www.mhhe.com/edmonds2008.

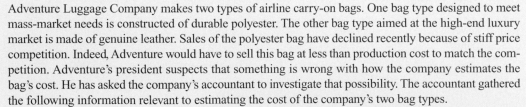

Adventure Luggage Company makes two types of airline carry-on bags. One bag type designed to meet mass-market needs is constructed of durable polyester. The other bag type aimed at the high-end luxury market is made of genuine leather. Sales of the polyester bag have declined recently because of stiff price competition. Indeed, Adventure would have to sell this bag at less than production cost to match the competition. Adventure's president suspects that something is wrong with how the company estimates the bag's cost. He has asked the company's accountant to investigate that possibility. The accountant gathered the following information relevant to estimating the cost of the company's two bag types.

Both bags require the same amount of direct labor. The leather bags have significantly higher materials costs, and they require more inspections and rework because of higher quality standards. Since the leather bags are produced in smaller batches of different colors, they require significantly more setups. Finally, the leather bags generate more legal costs due to patents and more promotion costs because Adventure advertises them more aggressively. Specific cost and activity data follow.

	Polyester Bags	Leather Bags
Per unit direct materials cost	$30	$90
Per unit direct labor cost	2 hours @ $14 per hour	2 hours @ $14 per hour
Annual sales volume	7,000 units	3,000 units

Total annual overhead costs are $872,000. Adventure currently allocates overhead costs using a traditional costing system based on direct labor hours.

To reassess the overhead allocation policy and the resulting product cost estimates, the accountant subdivided the overhead into four categories and gathered information about these cost categories and the activities that caused the company to incur the costs. These data follow.

			Amount of Cost Driver		
Category	Estimated Cost	Cost Driver	Polyester	Leather	Total
Unit level	$480,000	Number of machine hours	20,000	60,000	80,000
Batch level	190,000	Number of machine setups	1,500	3,500	5,000
Product level	152,000	Number of inspections	200	600	800
Facility level	50,000	Equal percentage	50%	50%	100%
Total	$872,000				

Required

a. Determine the total cost and cost per unit for each product line, assuming that Adventure allocates overhead costs to each product line using direct labor hours as a companywide allocation base. Also determine the combined cost of the two product lines.

b. Determine the total cost and cost per unit for each product line, assuming that Adventure allocates overhead costs using an ABC system. Determine the combined cost of the two product lines.

c. Explain why the total combined cost computed in Requirements *a* and *b* is the same. Given that the combined cost is the same using either system, why is an ABC system with many different allocation rates better than a traditional system with a single companywide overhead rate?

Solution to Requirement a

Predetermined Overhead Rate

Polyester		Leather		
2 hr. × 7,000 Units	+	2 hr. × 3,000 Units		
14,000 direct labor hours		6,000 direct labor hours	=	20,000 Hours

Allocation rate = $872,000 ÷ 20,000 hours = $43.60 per direct labor hour

Allocated Overhead Costs

Type of Bag	Allocation Rate	×	Number of Hours	=	Allocated Cost
Polyester	$43.60	×	14,000	=	$610,400
Leather	43.60	×	6,000	=	261,600
Total			20,000		$872,000

Total Cost of Each Product Line and Combined Cost

Type of Bag	Direct Materials*	+	Direct Labor†	+	Allocated Overhead	=	Total
Polyester	$210,000	+	$196,000	+	$610,400	=	$1,016,400
Leather	270,000	+	84,000	+	261,600	=	615,600
Total	$480,000	+	$280,000	+	$872,000	=	$1,632,000

*Direct materials
  Polyester $30 × 7,000 units = $210,000
  Leather   90 × 3,000 units = 270,000
†Direct labor
  Polyester $14 × 14,000 hours = 196,000
  Leather   14 × 6,000 hours = 84,000

Cost per Unit Computations Using Traditional Cost System

Type of Bag	Total Cost	÷	Units	=	Cost per Unit
Polyester	$1,016,400	÷	7,000	=	$145.20
Leather	615,600	÷	3,000	=	205.20
Total	$1,632,000				

Solution to Requirement b

Overhead Cost Allocation Using ABC

	Unit	Batch	Product	Facility	Total
Cost pool	$480,000	$190,000	$152,000	$50,000	$872,000
÷ Cost drivers	Number of machine hours 80,000	Number of setups 5,000	Number of inspections 800	Equally 50%	
= Rate	$6 per machine hour	$38 per setup	$190 per inspection	$25,000	

Overhead Allocation for Polyester Bags

	Unit	Batch	Product	Facility	Total
Weight	20,000	1,500	200	1	
× Rate	$ 6	$ 38	$ 190	$25,000	
Allocation	$120,000	$57,000	$38,000	$25,000	$240,000

Overhead Allocation for Leather Bags

	Unit	Batch	Product	Facility	Total
Weight	60,000	3,500	600	1	
× Rate	$ 6	$ 38	$ 190	$25,000	
Allocation	$360,000	$133,000	$114,000	$25,000	$632,000

Total Cost of Each Product Line and Combined Cost

Type of Bag	Direct Materials	+	Direct Labor	+	Allocated Overhead	=	Total
Polyester	$210,000	+	$196,000	+	$240,000	=	$ 646,000
Leather	270,000	+	84,000	+	632,000	=	986,000
Total	$480,000	+	$280,000	+	$872,000	=	$1,632,000

Cost per Unit Computations Under ABC System

Type of Bag	Total Cost	÷	Units	=	Cost per Unit
Polyester	$ 646,000	÷	7,000	=	$ 92.29
Leather	986,000	÷	3,000	=	328.67
Total	$1,632,000				

Solution to Requirement c

The allocation method (ABC versus traditional costing) does not affect the total amount of cost to be allocated. Therefore, the total cost is the same using either method. However, the allocation method (ABC versus traditional costing) does affect the cost assigned to each product line. Since the ABC system more accurately traces costs to the products that cause the costs to be incurred, it provides a more accurate estimate of the true cost of making the products. The difference in the cost per unit using ABC versus traditional costing is significant. For example, the cost of the polyester bag was determined to be $145.20 using the traditional allocation method and $92.29 using ABC. This difference could have led Adventure to overprice the polyester bag, thereby causing the decline in sales volume. To the extent that ABC is more accurate, using it will improve pricing and other strategic decisions that significantly affect profitability.

KEY TERMS

Activities 249
Activity-based cost drivers 247
Activity-based costing (ABC) 249
Activity centers 249
Appraisal costs 258
Batch-level activities 251

Companywide allocation rate 246
Downstream costs 257
External failure costs 258
Facility-level activities 253
Failure costs 258
Internal failure costs 258
Prevention costs 258

Product-level activities 252
Quality 258
Quality cost report 259
Start-up (setup) costs 247
Strategic cost management 257
Target pricing 256

Total quality management (TQM) 259
Unit-level activities 251
Upstream costs 257
Volume-based cost drivers 247
Voluntary costs 258

QUESTIONS

1. Why did traditional cost systems base allocations on a single companywide cost driver?
2. Why are labor hours ineffective as a companywide allocation base in many industries today?
3. What is the difference between volume-based cost drivers and activity-based cost drivers?
4. Why do activity-based cost drivers provide more accurate allocations of overhead in an automated manufacturing environment?
5. When would it be appropriate to use volume-based cost drivers in an activity-based cost system?
6. Martinez Manufacturing makes two products, one of which is produced at a significantly higher volume than the other. The low-volume product consumes more of the company's engineering resources because it is technologically complex. Even so, the company's cost accountant chose to

allocate engineering department costs based on the number of units produced. How could selecting this allocation base affect a decision about outsourcing engineering services for the low-volume product?

7. Briefly describe the activity-based costing allocation process.

8. Tom Rehr made the following comment: "Facility-level costs should not be allocated to products because they are irrelevant for decision-making purposes." Do you agree or disagree with this statement? Justify your response.

9. To facilitate cost tracing, a company's activities can be subdivided into four hierarchical categories. What are these four categories? Describe them and give at least two examples of each category.

10. Beth Nelson, who owns and runs a small sporting goods store, buys most of her merchandise directly from manufacturers. Ms. Nelson was shocked at the $7.50 charge for a container of three ping-pong balls. She found it hard to believe that it could have cost more than $1.00 to make the balls. When she complained to Jim Wilson, the marketing manager of the manufacturing company, he tried to explain that the cost also included companywide overhead costs. How could companywide overhead affect the cost of ping-pong balls?

11. If each patient in a hospital is considered a cost object, what are examples of unit-, batch-, product- and facility-level costs that would be allocated to this object using an activity-based cost system?

12. Milken Manufacturing has three product lines. The company's new accountant, Marvin LaSance, is responsible for allocating facility-level costs to these product lines. Mr. LaSance is finding the allocation assignment a daunting task. He knows there have been disagreements among the product managers over the allocation of facility costs, and he fears being asked to defend his method of allocation. Why would the allocation of facility-level costs be subject to disagreements?

13. Why would machine hours be an inappropriate allocation base for batch-level costs?

14. Alisa Kamuf's company has reported losses from operations for several years. Industry standards indicate that prices are normally set at 30 percent above manufacturing cost, which Ms. Kamuf has done. Assuming that her other costs are in line with industry norms, how could she continue to lose money while her competitors earn a profit?

15. Issacs Corporation produces two lines of pocket knives. The Arrowsmith product line involves very complex engineering designs; the Starscore product line involves relatively simple designs. Since its introduction, the low-volume Arrowsmith products have gained market share at the expense of the high-volume Starscore products. This pattern of sales has been accompanied by an overall decline in company profits. Why may the existing cost system be inadequate?

16. What is the relationship between activity-based management and just-in-time inventory?

MULTIPLE-CHOICE QUESTIONS

Multiple-choice questions are provided on the text website at www.mhhe.com/edmonds2008.

EXERCISES—SERIES A

All Exercises in Series A are available with McGraw-Hill's Homework Manager®.

Exercise 6-1A   *Classifying the costs of unit-, batch-, product-, or facility-level activities*   **L.O. 3**

Gracestone Manufacturing is developing an activity-based costing system to improve overhead cost allocation. One of the first steps in developing the system is to classify the costs of performing production activities into activity cost pools.

Required

Using your knowledge of the four categories of activities, classify the cost of each activity in the following list into unit-, batch-, product-, or facility-level cost pools.

Cost Activity	Cost Pool
a. Factorywide electricity	
b. Salary of a manager in charge of a product line	
c. Sales commissions	
d. Engineering product design	
e. Supplies	
f. Wages of maintenance staff	
g. Labeling and packaging	
h. Plant security	
i. Ordering materials for a specific type of product	
j. Wages of workers moving units of work between work stations	

L.O. 2

Exercise 6-2A *Identifying appropriate cost drivers*

Required

Provide at least one example of an appropriate cost driver (allocation base) for each of the following activities.
a. Lighting is used for production facilities.
b. Materials are unloaded and stored for production.
c. Maintenance is performed on manufacturing equipment.
d. Sales commissions are paid.
e. Direct labor is used to change machine configurations.
f. Production equipment is set up for new production runs.
g. Engineering drawings are produced for design changes.
h. Purchase orders are issued.
i. Products are labeled, packaged, and shipped.
j. Machinists are trained on new computer-controlled machinery.

L.O. 2, 3

Exercise 6-3A *Classifying costs and identifying the appropriate cost driver*

Lakeshore Manufacturing incurred the following costs during 2007 to produce its high-quality precision instruments. The company used an activity-based costing system and identified the following activities.
1. Materials handling.
2. Inventory storage.
3. Inspection of each batch produced.
4. Salaries of receiving clerks.
5. Setup for each batch produced.
6. Insurance on production facilities.
7. Depreciation on manufacturing equipment.

Required

a. Classify each activity as a unit-level, batch-level, product-level, or facility-level activity.
b. Identify an appropriate cost driver (allocation base) for each activity.

L.O. 3

Exercise 6-4A *Context-sensitive nature of activity classification*

Required

Describe a set of circumstances in which the cost of painting could be classified as a unit-level, a batch-level, a product-level, or a facility-level cost.

Exercise 6-5A   *Context-sensitive nature of activity classification*   L.O. 3

Pinson Company makes two types of circuit boards. One is a high-caliber board designed to accomplish the most demanding tasks; the other is a low-caliber board designed to provide limited service at an affordable price. During its most recent accounting period, Pinson incurred $80,000 of inspection cost. When Pinson recently established an activity-based costing system, its activities were classified into four categories. Categories and appropriate cost drivers follow.

	Direct Labor Hours	Number of Batches	Number of Inspectors	Number of Square Feet
High caliber	4,000	25	3	40,000
Low caliber	16,000	15	2	60,000
Totals	20,000	40	5	100,000

Required

Allocate the inspection cost between the two products assuming that it is driven by (a) unit-level activities, (b) batch-level activities, (c) product-level activities, or (d) facility-level activities.

Exercise 6-6A   *Computing overhead rates based on different cost drivers*   L.O. 2, 3

Obannon Industries produces two electronic decoders, P and Q. Decoder P is more sophisticated and requires more programming and testing than does Decoder Q. Because of these product differences, the company wants to use activity-based costing to allocate overhead costs. It has identified four activity pools. Relevant information follows.

Activity Pools	Cost Pool Total	Cost Driver
Repair and maintenance on assembly machine	$200,000	Number of units produced
Programming cost	420,000	Number of programming hours
Software inspections	30,000	Number of inspections
Product testing	40,000	Number of tests
Total overhead cost	$690,000	

Expected activity for each product follows.

	Number of Units	Number of Programming Hours	Number of Inspections	Number of Tests
Decoder P	20,000	2,000	190	1,400
Decoder Q	30,000	1,500	60	1,100
Totals	50,000	3,500	250	2,500

Required

a. Compute the overhead rate for each activity pool.
b. Determine the overhead cost allocated to each product.

Exercise 6-7A   *Comparing an ABC system with a traditional cost system*   L.O. 1, 3

Use the information in Exercise 6-6A to complete the following requirements. Assume that before shifting to activity-based costing, Obannon Industries allocated all overhead costs based on direct labor hours. Direct labor data pertaining to the two decoders follow.

	Direct Labor Hours
Decoder P	12,000
Decoder Q	18,000
Total	30,000

Required

a. Compute the amount of overhead cost allocated to each type of decoder when using direct labor hours as the allocation base.
b. Determine the cost per unit for overhead when using direct labor hours as the allocation base and when using ABC.
c. Explain why the per unit overhead cost is lower for the high-volume product when using ABC.

L.O. 1, 3

Exercise 6-8A   *Allocating costs with different cost drivers*

Bangkok Company produces commercial gardening equipment. Since production is highly automated, the company allocates its overhead costs to product lines using activity-based costing. The costs and cost drivers associated with the four overhead activity cost pools follow.

	Activities			
	Unit Level	**Batch Level**	**Product Level**	**Facility Level**
Cost	$100,000	$40,000	$20,000	$240,000
Cost driver	2,000 labor hrs.	40 setups	Percentage of use	12,000 units

Production of 800 sets of cutting shears, one of the company's 20 products, took 200 labor hours and 6 setups and consumed 15 percent of the product-sustaining activities.

Required

a. Had the company used labor hours as a companywide allocation base, how much overhead would it have allocated to the cutting shears?
b. How much overhead is allocated to the cutting shears using activity-based costing?
c. Compute the overhead cost per unit for cutting shears using first activity-based costing and then using direct labor hours for allocation if 800 units are produced. If direct product costs are $50 and the product is priced at 30 percent above cost (rounded to the nearest whole dollar), for what price would the product sell under each allocation system?
d. Assuming that activity-based costing provides a more accurate estimate of cost, indicate whether the cutting shears would be over- or underpriced if direct labor hours are used as an allocation base. Explain how over- or undercosting can affect Bangkok's profitability.
e. Comment on the validity of using the allocated facility-level cost in the pricing decision. Should other costs be considered in a cost-plus pricing decision? If so, which ones? What costs would you include if you were trying to decide whether to accept a special order?

L.O. 2, 3

Exercise 6-9A   *Allocating costs with different cost drivers*

Dingle Publishing identified the following overhead activities, their respective costs, and their cost drivers to produce the three types of textbooks the company publishes.

		Type of Textbook		
Activity (Cost)	**Cost Driver**	**Deluxe**	**Moderate**	**Economy**
Machine maintenance ($240,000)	Number of machine hours	250	750	1,000
Setups ($420,000)	Number of setups	30	15	5
Packing ($108,000)	Number of cartons	10	30	50
Photo development ($336,000)	Number of pictures	4,000	2,000	1,000

Deluxe textbooks are made with the finest-quality paper, six-color printing, and many photographs. Moderate texts are made with three colors and a few photographs spread throughout each chapter. Economy books are printed in black and white and include pictures only in chapter openings.

Required

a. Dingle currently allocates all overhead costs based on machine hours. The company produced the following number of books during the prior year.

Deluxe	Moderate	Economy
50,000	150,000	200,000

Determine the overhead cost per book for each book type.

b. Determine the overhead cost per book, assuming that the volume-based allocation system described in Requirement *a* is replaced with an activity-based costing system.

c. Explain why the per unit overhead costs determined in Requirements *a* and *b* differ.

Exercise 6-10A *Computing product cost with given activity allocation rates*

L.O. 3

Paton Manufacturing produces two modems, one for laptop computers and the other for desktop computers. The production process is automated, and the company has found activity-based costing useful in assigning overhead costs to its products. The company has identified five major activities involved in producing the modems.

Activity	Allocation Base	Allocation Rate
Materials receiving & handling	Cost of material	2% of material cost
Production setup	Number of setups	$100.00 per setup
Assembly	Number of parts	$5.00 per part
Quality inspection	Inspection time	$1.50 per minute
Packing and shipping	Number of orders	$10.00 per order

Activity measures for the two kinds of modems follow.

	Labor Cost	Material Cost	Number of Setups	Number of Parts	Inspection Time	Number of Orders
Laptops	$2,500	$10,000	30	42	7,200 min.	65
Desktops	2,100	15,000	12	24	5,100 min.	20

Required

a. Compute the cost per unit of laptop and desktop modems, assuming that Paton made 300 units of each type of modem.

b. Explain why laptop modems cost more to make even though they have less material cost and are smaller than desktop modems.

Exercise 6-11A *Allocating facility-level cost and a product elimination decision*

L.O. 3

Holby Boards produces two kinds of skateboards. Selected unit data for the two boards for the last quarter follow.

	Basco Boards	Shimano Boards
Production costs		
Direct materials	$54	$72
Direct labor	$78	$102
Allocated overhead	$30	$36
Total units produced and sold	4,000	8,000
Total sales revenue	$672,000	$1,776,000

Holby allocates production overhead using activity-based costing. It allocates delivery expense and sales commissions, which amount to $108,000 per quarter, to the two products equally.

Required

a. Compute the net profit for each product.
b. Assuming that the overhead allocation for Basco boards includes $24,000 of facility-level cost, would you advise Holby to eliminate these boards? (*Hint:* Consider the method used to allocate the delivery and selling expense.)

L.O. 4

Exercise 6-12A *Quality cost components and relationships*

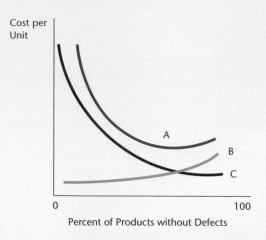

Required

The preceding graph depicts the relationships among the components of total quality cost.
a. Label the lines identified as A, B, and C.
b. Explain the relationships depicted in the graph.

PROBLEMS—SERIES A

L.O. 1, 3

www.mhhe.com/edmonds2008

Problem 6-13A *Comparing an ABC system with a traditional cost system*

Mohnen Electronics produces video games in three market categories, commercial, home, and miniature. Mohnen has traditionally allocated overhead costs to the three products using the companywide allocation base of direct labor hours. The company recently implemented an ABC system when it installed computer-controlled assembly stations that rendered the traditional costing system ineffective. In implementing the ABC system, the company identified the following activity cost pools and cost drivers.

Category	Total Pooled Cost	Types of Costs	Cost Driver
Unit	$720,000	Indirect labor wages, supplies, depreciation, machine maintenance	Machine hours
Batch	388,800	Materials handling, inventory storage, labor for setups, packaging, labeling and shipping, scheduling	Number of production orders
Product	211,200	Research and development	Time spent by research department
Facility	600,000	Rent, utilities, maintenance, admin. salaries, security	Square footage

Additional data for each of the product lines follow.

	Commercial	Home	Miniature	Total
Direct materials cost	$36.00/unit	$24.00/unit	$30.00/unit	–
Direct labor cost	$14.40/hour	$14.40/hour	$18.00/hour	–
Number of labor hours	6,000	12,000	2,000	20,000
Number of machine hours	10,000	45,000	25,000	80,000
Number of production orders	200	2,000	800	3,000
Research and development time	10%	20%	70%	100%
Number of units	15,000	45,000	14,000	74,000
Square footage	20,000	50,000	30,000	100,000

Required

a. Determine the total cost and cost per unit for each product line, assuming that overhead costs are allocated to each product line using direct labor hours as a companywide allocation base. Also determine the combined cost of all three product lines.

b. Determine the total cost and cost per unit for each product line, assuming that an ABC system is used to allocate overhead costs. Determine the combined cost of all three product lines.

c. Explain why the combined total cost computed in Requirements *a* and *b* is the same amount. Given that the combined cost is the same using either allocation method, why is an ABC system with many different allocation rates more accurate than a traditional system with a single companywide overhead rate?

Problem 6-14A *Effect of automation on overhead allocation*

Persian Rug Company makes two types of rugs, seasonal and all-purpose. Both types of rugs are hand-made, but the seasonal rugs require significantly more labor because of their decorative designs. The annual number of rugs made and the labor hours required to make each type of rug follow.

	Seasonal	All-Purpose	Totals
Number of rugs	1,200	2,800	4,000
Number of direct labor hours	120,000	168,000	288,000

Required

a. Assume that annual overhead costs total $144,000. Select the appropriate cost driver and determine the amount of overhead to allocate to each type of rug.

b. Persian automates the seasonal rug line resulting in a dramatic decline in labor usage, to make 1,200 rugs in only 12,000 hours. Persian continues to make the all-purpose rugs the same way as before. The number of rugs made and the labor hours required to make them after automation follow.

	Seasonal	All-Purpose	Totals
Number of rugs	1,200	2,800	4,000
Number of direct labor hours	12,000	168,000	180,000

Overhead costs are expected to increase to $180,000 as a result of the automation. Allocate the increased overhead cost to the two types of rugs using direct labor hours as the allocation base and comment on the appropriateness of the allocation.

Problem 6-15A *Using activity-based costing to improve allocation accuracy*

This problem is an extension of Problem 6-14A, which must be completed first.
Persian's accounting staff has disaggregated the $180,000 of overhead costs into the following items.

(1) Inspection costs	$16,000
(2) Setup costs	10,800
(3) Engineering costs	16,000
(4) Legal costs related to products	6,000
(5) Materials movement cost per batch	2,400
(6) Salaries of production supervisors	40,000
(7) Fringe benefit costs	8,000
(8) Utilities costs	4,000
(9) Plant manager's salary	24,000
(10) Depreciation on production equipment	36,000
(11) Depreciation on building	8,000
(12) Miscellaneous costs	5,000
(13) Indirect materials costs	2,800
(14) Production employee incentive costs	1,000
Total	$180,000

Required

a. Each of Persian's rug lines operates as a department. The all-purpose department occupies 6,000 square feet of floor space, and the seasonal department occupies 12,000 square feet of space. Comment on the validity of allocating the overhead costs by square footage.

b. Assume that the following additional information is available.

   (1) Rugs are individually inspected.

   (2) Persian incurs setup costs each time a new style of seasonal rug is produced. The seasonal rugs were altered nine times during the year. The manual equipment for all-purpose rugs is reset twice each year to ensure accurate weaving. The setup for the technical equipment used to weave seasonal rugs requires more highly skilled workers, but the all-purpose rugs require more manual equipment, thereby resulting in a *per setup* charge that is roughly equal for both types of rugs. Persian undertook 22 setups during the year, 18 of which applied to seasonal rugs and 4 that applied to all-purpose rugs.

   (3) Ninety percent of the product-level costs can be traced to producing seasonal rugs.

   (4) Six supervisors oversee the production of all-purpose rugs. Because seasonal rugs are made in an automated department, only two production supervisors are needed.

   (5) Each rug requires an equal amount of indirect materials.

   (6) Costs associated with production activities are assigned to six activity cost pools: (1) labor-related activities, (2) unit-level activities, (3) batch-level activities, (4) product-level supervisory activities, (5) other product-level activities, and (6) facility-level activities.

Organize the $180,000 of overhead costs into activity center cost pools and allocate the costs to the two types of rugs.

c. Assuming that 90 seasonal and 240 all-purpose rugs were made in January, determine the overhead costs that would be assigned to each of the two rug types for the month of January.

L.O. 1, 3

CHECK FIGURES
a. Cost per student:
  Computer-Assisted:
  $327
  Classroom: $237

Problem 6-16A *Using activity-based costing to improve allocation accuracy*

The Tutor Institute (TTI), is a profit-oriented education business. TTI provides remedial training for high school students who have fallen behind in their classroom studies. It charges its students $300 per course. During the previous year, TTI provided instruction for 1,000 students. The income statement for the company follows.

Revenue	$ 300,000
Cost of instructors	(170,000)
Overhead costs	(85,000)
Net income	$ 45,000

The company president, Sylvia Nieman, indicated in a discussion with the accountant, Jack Ogletree, that she was extremely pleased with the growth in the area of computer-assisted instruction. She observed that this department served 200 students using only two part-time instructors. In contrast, the classroom-based instructional department required 32 instructors to teach 800 students. Ms. Nieman noted that the per student cost of instruction was dramatically lower for the computer-assisted department. She based her conclusion on the following information.

TTI pays its part-time instructors an average of $5,000 per year. The total cost of instruction and the cost per student are computed as follows.

Type of Instruction	Computer-Assisted	Classroom
Number of instructors (a)	2	32
Number of students (b)	200	800
Total cost (c = a × $5,000)	$10,000	$160,000
Cost per student (c ÷ b)	$50	$200

Assuming that overhead costs were distributed equally across the student population, Ms. Nieman concluded that the cost of instructors was the critical variable in the company's capacity to generate profits. Based on her analysis, her strategic plan called for heavily increased use of computer-assisted instruction.

Mr. Ogletree was not so sure that computer-assisted instruction should be stressed. After attending a seminar on activity-based costing (ABC), he believed that the allocation of overhead cost could be more closely traced to the different types of learning activities. To facilitate an activity-based analysis, he developed the following information about the costs associated with computer-assisted versus classroom instructional activities. He identified $48,000 of overhead costs that were directly traceable to computer-assisted activities, including the costs of computer hardware, software, and technical assistance. He believed the remaining $37,000 of overhead costs should be allocated to the two instructional activities based on the number of students enrolled in each program.

Required

a. Based on the preceding information, determine the total cost and the cost per student to provide courses through computer-assisted instruction versus classroom instruction.
b. Comment on the validity of stressing growth in the area of computer-assisted instruction.

Problem 6-17A   *Key activity-based costing concepts*

L.O. 1

Agee Paint Company makes paint in many different colors; it charges the same price for all of its paint regardless of the color. Recently, Agee's chief competitor cut the price of its white paint, which normally outsells any other color by a margin of 4 to 1. Agee's marketing manager requested permission to match the competitor's price. When Gene Taylor, Agee's president, discussed the matter with Kay Spencer, the chief accountant, he was told that the competitor's price was below Agee's cost. Mr. Taylor responded, "If that's the case, then there is something wrong with our accounting system. I know the competition wouldn't sell below cost. Prepare a report showing me how you determine our paint cost and get back to me as soon as possible."

The next day, Ms. Spencer returned to Mr. Taylor's office and began by saying, "Determining the cost per gallon is a pretty simple computation. It includes $1.10 of labor, $3.10 of materials, and $4.00 of overhead for a total cost of $8.20 per gallon. The problem is that the competition is selling the stuff for $7.99 per gallon. They've got to be losing money."

Mr. Taylor then asked Ms. Spencer how she determined the overhead cost. She replied, "We take total overhead cost and divide it by total labor hours and then assign it to the products based on the direct labor hours required to make the paint." Mr. Taylor then asked what kinds of costs are included in the total overhead cost. Ms. Spencer said, "It includes the depreciation on the building and equipment, the cost of utilities, supervisory salaries, interest. Just how detailed do you want me to go with this list?"

Mr. Taylor responded, "Keep going, I'll tell you when I've heard enough."

Ms. Spencer continued, "There is the cost of setups. Every time a color is changed, the machines have to be cleaned, the color release valves reset, a trial batch prepared, and color quality tested. Sometimes mistakes occur and the machines must be reset. In addition, purchasing and handling the color ingredients must be accounted for as well as adjustments in the packaging department to change the paint cans and to mark the boxes to show the color change. Then . . . ."

Mr. Taylor interrupted, "I think I've heard enough. We sell so much white paint that we run it through a separate production process. White paint is produced continuously. There are no shutdowns and setups. White uses no color ingredients. So why are these costs being assigned to our white paint production?"

Ms. Spencer replied, "Well, sir, these costs are just a part of the big total that is allocated to all of the paint, no matter what color it happens to be."

Mr. Taylor looked disgusted and said, "As I told you yesterday, Ms. Spencer, something is wrong with our accounting system!"

Required

a. Explain what the terms *overcost* and *undercost* mean. Is Agee's white paint over- or undercosted?
b. Explain what the term *companywide overhead rate* means. Is Agee using a companywide overhead rate?
c. Explain how Agee could improve the accuracy of its overhead cost allocations.

Problem 6-18A *Pricing decisions made with ABC system cost data*

Conor Sporting Goods Corporation makes two types of racquets, tennis and badminton. The company uses the same facility to make both products even though the processes are quite different. The company has recently converted its cost accounting system to activity-based costing. The following are the cost data that Sue Chapman, the cost accountant, prepared for the third quarter of 2007 (during which Conor made 70,000 tennis racquets and 30,000 badminton racquets):

Direct Cost	Tennis Racquet (TR)	Badminton Racquet (BR)
Direct materials	$14 per unit	$10 per unit
Direct labor	38 per unit	28 per unit

Category	Estimated Cost	Cost Driver	Amount of Cost Driver
Unit level	$ 750,000	Number of inspection hours	TR: 15,000 hours; BR: 10,000 hours
Batch level	250,000	Number of setups	TR: 80 setups; BR: 45 setups
Product level	150,000	Number of TV commercials	TR: 4; BR: 1
Facility level	650,000	Number of machine hours	TR: 30,000 hours; BR: 35,000 hours
Total	$1,800,000		

Inspectors are paid according to the number of actual hours worked, which is determined by the number of racquets inspected. Engineers who set up equipment for both products are paid monthly salaries. TV commercial fees are paid at the beginning of the quarter. Facility-level cost includes depreciation of all production equipment.

Required

a. Compute the cost per unit for each product.
b. If management wants to price badminton racquets 30 percent above cost, what price should the company set?
c. The market price of tennis racquets has declined substantially because of new competitors entering the market. Management asks you to determine the minimum cost of producing tennis racquets in the short term. Provide that information.

L.O. 3

Problem 6-19A *Target pricing and target costing with ABC*

Marsh Cameras, Inc., manufactures two models of cameras. Model ZM has a zoom lens; Model DS has a fixed lens. Marsh uses an activity-based costing system. The following are the relevant cost data for the previous month.

Direct Cost per Unit	Model ZM	Model DS
Direct materials	$30	$15
Direct labor	33	12

Category	Estimated Cost	Cost Driver	Use of Cost Driver
Unit level	$ 27,000	Number of units	ZM: 2,400 units; DS: 9,600 units
Batch level	50,000	Number of setups	ZM: 25 setups; DS: 25 setups
Product level	90,000	Number of TV commercials	ZM: 15; DS: 10
Facility level	300,000	Number of machine hours	ZM: 500 hours; DS: 1,000 hours
Total	$467,000		

Marsh's facility has the capacity to operate 4,500 machine hours per month.

Required

a. Compute the cost per unit for each product.
b. The current market price for products comparable to Model ZM is $146 and for DS is $54. If Marsh sold all of its products at the market prices, what was its profit or loss for the previous month?
c. A market expert believes that Marsh can sell as many cameras as it can produce by pricing Model ZM at $140 and Model DS at $50. Marsh would like to use those estimates as its target prices and have a profit margin of 20 percent of target prices. What is the target cost for each product?
d. Is there any way for the company to reach its target costs?

Problem 6-20A   *Cost management with an ABC system*

Kackle Chairs, Inc., makes two types of chairs. Model Diamond is a high-end product designed for professional offices. Model Gold is an economical product designed for family use. Amy Kackle, the president, is worried about cut-throat price competition in the chairs market. Her company suffered a loss last quarter, an unprecedented event in its history. The company's accountant prepared the following cost data for Ms. Kackle.

Direct Cost per Unit	Model Diamond (D)	Model Gold (G)
Direct materials	$22 per unit	$12 per unit
Direct labor	$24/hour × 2 hours production time	$24/hour × 1 hour production time

Category	Estimated Cost	Cost Driver	Use of Cost Driver
Unit level	$ 300,000	Number of units	D: 15,000 units; G: 35,000 units
Batch level	750,000	Number of setups	D: 104 setups; G: 146 setups
Product level	450,000	Number of TV commercials	D: 5; G: 10
Facility level	500,000	Number of machine hours	D: 1,500 hours; G: 3,500 hours
Total	$2,000,000		

The market price for office chairs comparable to Model Diamond is $114 and to Model Gold is $70.

Required

a. Compute the cost per unit for both products.
b. Sam Maddox, the chief engineer, told Ms. Kackle that the company is currently making 150 units of Model Diamond per batch and 245 units of Model Gold per batch. He suggests doubling the

batch sizes to cut the number of setups in half, thereby reducing the setup cost by 50 percent. Compute the cost per unit for each product if Ms. Kackle adopts his suggestion.

c. Is there any side effect if Ms. Kackle increases the production batch size by 100 percent?

L.O. 4, 5

Problem 6-21A *Assessing a quality control strategy*

The following quality cost report came from the records of Clark Company.

	2007		2006	
	Amount	Percentage	Amount	Percentage
Prevention costs				
Engineering and design	$136,000	13.74%	$ 58,000	3.86%
Training and education	34,000	3.43	12,000	0.80
Depreciation on prevention equipment	58,000	5.86	30,000	1.99
Incentives and awards	88,000	8.89	40,000	2.66
Total prevention	316,000	31.92%	140,000	9.31%
Appraisal costs				
Inventory inspection	50,000	5.05	50,000	3.32
Reliability testing	32,000	3.23	30,000	1.99
Testing equipment (depreciation)	22,000	2.22	24,000	1.60
Supplies	14,000	1.41	16,000	1.06
Total appraisal	118,000	11.92%	120,000	7.98%
Internal failure costs				
Scrap	48,000	4.85	80,000	5.32
Repair and rework	98,000	9.90	220,000	14.63
Downtime	24,000	2.42	40,000	2.66
Reinspection	8,000	0.81	24,000	1.60
Total internal failure	178,000	17.98%	364,000	24.20%
External failure cost				
Warranty repairs and replacement	220,000	22.22	520,000	34.57
Freight	48,000	4.85	100,000	6.65
Customer relations	56,000	5.66	120,000	7.98
Restocking and packaging	54,000	5.45	140,000	9.31
Total external failure	378,000	38.18%	880,000	58.51%
Grand total	$990,000	100.00%	$1,504,000	100.00%

Required

a. Explain the strategy that Clark Company initiated to control its quality costs.
b. Indicate whether the strategy was successful or unsuccessful in reducing quality costs.
c. Explain how the strategy likely affected customer satisfaction.

EXERCISES—SERIES B

L.O. 3

Exercise 6-1B *Classifying the costs of unit-, batch-, product-, or facility-level activities*

Dennis Manufacturing is developing an activity-based costing system to improve overhead cost allocation. One of the first steps in developing the system is to classify the costs of performing production activities into activity cost pools.

Required

Using the four-tier cost hierarchy described in the chapter, classify each of the following costs into unit-level, batch-level, product-level, or facility-level cost pools.

Cost Activity	Cost Pool
a. Factory depreciation	
b. Advertising costs for a particular product	
c. Wages of assembly line workers	
d. Product design costs	
e. Materials requisition costs for a particular work order	
f. Security guard wages	
g. Lubricant for machines	
h. Parts used to make a particular product	
i. Machine setup cost	
j. Salary of the plant manager's secretary	

Exercise 6-2B *Identifying appropriate cost drivers*

L.O. 2

Required

Provide at least one example of an appropriate cost driver (allocation base) for each of the following activities.

a. Workers move materials from the warehouse to the factory floor.
b. Assembly line machines are operated.
c. Workers count completed goods before moving them to a warehouse.
d. A logistics manager runs a computer program to determine the materials release schedule.
e. Janitors clean the factory floor after workers have left.
f. Mechanics apply lubricant to machines.
g. Engineers design a product production layout.
h. Engineers set up machines to produce a product.
i. The production supervisor completes the paperwork initiating a work order.
j. The production manager prepares materials requisition forms.

Exercise 6-3B *Classifying costs and identifying the appropriate cost driver*

L.O. 2, 3

Putin Corporation, a furniture manufacturer, uses an activity-based costing system. It has identified the following selected activities:

1. Incurring property taxes on factory buildings.
2. Incurring paint cost for furniture produced.
3. Setting up machines for a particular batch of production.
4. Inspecting wood prior to using it in production.
5. Packaging completed furniture in boxes for shipment.
6. Inspecting completed furniture for quality control.
7. Purchasing TV time to advertise a particular product.

Required

a. Classify each activity as a unit-level, batch-level, product-level, or facility-level activity.
b. Identify an appropriate cost driver (allocation base) for each of the activities.

Exercise 6-4B *Understanding the context-sensitive nature of classifying activities*

L.O. 3

Required

Describe a set of circumstances in which labor cost could be classified as a unit-level, a batch-level, a product-level, or a facility-level cost.

Exercise 6-5B *Understanding the context-sensitive nature of classifying activities*

L.O. 3

McTyre Company makes two types of cell phones. Handy is a thin, pocket-size cell phone that is easy to carry around. Action is a palm-size phone convenient to hold while the user is talking. During its most recent accounting period, McTyre incurred $150,000 of quality-control costs. Recently McTyre established an activity-based costing system, which involved classifying its activities into four categories. The categories and appropriate cost drivers follow.

	Direct Labor Hours	Number of Batches	Number of Engineers	Number of Square Feet
Handy	26,000	38	10	37,000
Action	24,000	22	5	83,000
Totals	50,000	60	15	120,000

McTyre uses direct labors hours to allocate unit-level activities, number of batches to allocate batch-level activities, number of engineers to allocate product-level activities, and number of square feet to allocate facility-level activities.

Required

Allocate the quality-control cost between the two products, assuming that it is driven by (a) unit-level activities, (b) batch-level activities, (c) product-level activities, and (d) facility-level activities.

L.O. 2, 3

Exercise 6-6B   *Computing overhead rates based on different cost drivers*

Gideon Industries produces two surge protectors: VC620 with six outlets and PH630 with eight outlets and two telephone line connections. Because of these product differences, the company plans to use activity-based costing to allocate overhead costs. The company has identified four activity pools. Relevant information follows.

Activity Pools	Cost Pool Total	Cost Driver
Machine setup	$120,000	Number of setups
Machine operation	300,000	Number of machine hours
Quality control	48,000	Number of inspections
Packaging	32,000	Number of units
Total overhead cost	$500,000	

Expected activity for each product follows.

	Number of Setups	Number of Machine Hours	Number of Inspections	Number of Units
VC620	48	1,400	78	25,000
PH630	72	2,600	172	15,000
Total	120	4,000	250	40,000

Required

a. Compute the overhead rate for each activity pool.
b. Determine the overhead cost allocated to each product.

L.O. 1, 3

Exercise 6-7B   *Comparing an ABC system with a traditional cost system*

Use the information in Exercise 6-6B to complete the following requirements. Assume that before shifting to activity-based costing, Gideon Industries allocated all overhead costs based on direct labor hours. Direct labor data pertaining to the two surge protectors follow.

	Direct Labor Hours
VC620	16,000
PH630	9,000
Total	25,000

Required

a. Compute the amount of overhead cost allocated to each type of surge protector when using direct labor hours as the allocation base.
b. Determine the cost per unit for overhead when using direct labor hours as the allocation base and when using ABC.
c. Explain why the per unit overhead cost is lower for the higher-volume product when using ABC.

Exercise 6-8B   *Allocating costs with different cost drivers*   L.O. 1, 2, 3

Cray Sporting Goods, Inc., produces indoor treadmills. The company allocates its overhead costs using activity-based costing. The costs and cost drivers associated with the four overhead activity cost pools follow.

Activities	Unit Level	Batch Level	Product Level	Facility Level
Cost	$1,000,000	$500,000	$300,000	$900,000
Cost driver	12,500 labor hours	50 setups	Percentage of use	15,000 units

Producing 5,000 units of PFT200, one of the company's five products, took 4,000 labor hours, 25 setups, and consumed 30 percent of the product-sustaining activities.

Required

a. Had the company used labor hours as a companywide allocation base, how much overhead would it have allocated to the 5,000 units of PFT200?
b. How much overhead is allocated to the 5,000 PFT200 units using activity-based costing?
c. Compute the overhead cost per unit for PFT200 using activity-based costing and direct labor hours if 5,000 units are produced. If direct product costs are $337 and PFT200 is priced at 20 percent above cost (rounded to the nearest whole dollar), compute the product's selling price under each allocation system.
d. Assuming that activity-based costing provides a more accurate estimate of cost, indicate whether PFT200 would be over- or underpriced if Cray uses direct labor hours as the allocation base. Explain how over- or undercosting can affect Cray's profitability.
e. Comment on the validity of using the allocated facility-level cost in the pricing decision. Should other costs be considered in a cost-plus pricing decision? If so, which ones? What costs would you include if you were trying to decide whether to accept a special order?

Exercise 6-9B   *Allocating costs with different cost drivers*   L.O. 2, 3

Julian Shoes Corporation produces three brands of shoes, Brisk, Pro, and Runner. Relevant information about Julian's overhead activities, their respective costs, and their cost drivers follows.

Overhead Costs	Cost Driver	Brisk	Pro	Runner
Fringe benefits ($360,000)	Labor hours	10,000	20,000	20,000
Setups ($200,000)	Number of setups	15	25	10
Packing costs ($40,000)	Number of cartons	200	300	300
Quality control ($300,000)	Number of tests	120	200	80

Required

a. Julian currently allocates all overhead costs based on labor hours. The company produced the following numbers of pairs of shoes during the prior year.

Brisk	Pro	Runner
10,000	15,000	20,000

Determine the overhead cost per pair of shoes for each brand.

b. Determine the overhead cost per pair of shoes for each brand, assuming that the volume-based allocation system described in Requirement *a* is replaced with an activity-based costing system.

c. Explain why the per pair overhead costs determined in Requirements *a* and *b* differ.

Exercise 6-10B   *Computing product cost with given activity allocation rates*

Using automated production processes, Raspino Videos produces two kinds of camcorders: N100 is an analog recorder and D200 is a digital recorder. The company has found activity-based costing useful in assigning overhead costs to its products. It has identified the following five major activities involved in producing the camcorders.

Activity	Allocation Base	Allocation Rate
Materials receiving and handling	Cost of materials	3% of materials cost
Production setup	Number of setups	$800 per setup
Assembly	Number of parts	$10 per part
Quality inspection	Inspection time	$25 per minute
Packing and shipping	Number of orders	$80 per order

Activity measures for the two kinds of camcorders follow.

	Labor Cost*	Materials Cost*	Number of Setups	Number of Parts	Inspection Time	Number of Orders
N100	$450,000	$250,000	10	10,000	800 min.	25
D200	300,000	300,000	25	10,000	4,800 min.	50

*Both are direct costs.

Required

a. Compute the cost per unit of N100 and D200, assuming that Raspino made 1,000 units of each type of camcorder.

b. Explain why the D200 digital camcorders cost more to make although their direct costs are less than those for the N100 analog camcorders.

Exercise 6-11B   *Allocating facility-level cost and a product elimination decision*

Kincaid Corporation produces two types of juice that it packages in cases of 24 cans per case. Selected per case data for the two products for the last month follow.

	Orange Juice	Tomato Juice
Production costs		
Direct material	$3	$2
Direct labor	$2	$3
Allocated overhead	$3	$4
Total cases produced and sold	25,000	15,000
Total sales revenue	$280,000	$170,000

Kincaid allocates production overhead using activity-based costing but allocates monthly packaging expense, which amounted to $80,000 last month, to the two products equally.

Required

a. Compute the net profit for each product.

b. Assuming that the overhead allocation for the tomato juice includes $30,000 of facility-level cost, would you advise Kincaid to eliminate this product? (*Hint:* Consider the method used to allocate the monthly packaging expense.)

Exercise 6-12B *Applying concepts of quality cost management*

Rodney Nance, the president of Easeley Industries, Inc., was beaming when he was reviewing the company's quality cost report. After he had implemented a quality-control program for three years, the company's defect rate had declined from 20 percent to 3 percent. Mr. Nance patted Christy Tucker, the production manager, on her back and said: "You have done a great job! I plan to reward you for your hard work. However, I want the defects to disappear completely before I promote you to the position of executive vice president. So, zero-defect is going to be your personal goal for the coming year." Mrs. Tucker responded wearily, "I'm not sure that's really a good idea."

Required

Write a memorandum to the president explaining that zero defect is not a practical policy.

PROBLEMS—SERIES B

Problem 6-13B *Comparing an ABC system with a traditional costing system*

Since its inception, Kenneth Laboratory, has produced a single product, Product S109. With the advent of automation, the company added the technological capability to begin producing a second product, Product N227. Because of the success of Product N227, manufacturing has been shifting toward its production. Sales of Product N227 are now 50 percent of the total annual sales of 20,000 units, and the company is optimistic about the new product's future sales growth. One reason the company is excited about the sales potential of its new product is that the new product's gross profit margin is higher than that of Product S109. Management is thrilled with the new product's initial success but concerned about the company's declining profits since the product's introduction. Suspecting a problem with the company's costing system, management hires you to investigate.

In reviewing the company's records, product specifications, and manufacturing processes, you discover the following information.

1. The company is in an extremely competitive industry in which markups are low and accurate estimates of cost are critical to success.

2. Product N227 has complex parts that require more labor, machine time, setups, and inspections than Product S109.

3. Budgeted costs for direct materials and labor follow.

Direct Cost per Unit	Product S109	Product N227
Direct materials	$24	$24
Direct labor	$15/hour × 2 hours production time	$15/hour × 2.8 hours production time

4. The company presently allocates overhead costs to its products based on direct labor hours. After carefully studying the company's overhead, you identify four different categories of overhead costs. Using your knowledge of this company and similar companies in the same industry, you estimate the total costs for each of these categories and identify the most appropriate cost driver for measuring each product's overhead consumption. Detailed information for each cost category follows.

Category	Estimated Cost	Cost Driver	Use of Cost Driver
Unit level	$ 540,000	Number of machine hours	S109: 20,000 hours; N227: 60,000 hours
Batch level	228,000	Number of machine setups	S109: 1,500; N227: 3,500
Product level	180,000	Number of inspections	S109: 200; N227: 600
Facility level	60,000	Equal percentage for products	S109: 50%; N227: 50%
Total	$1,008,000		

Required

a. Determine the predetermined overhead rate the company is using.

b. Compute the amount of overhead the company assigns to each product using this rate.

c. Determine the cost per unit and total cost of each product when overhead is assigned based on direct labor hours.

d. To remain competitive, the company prices its products at only 20 percent above cost. Compute the price for each product with this markup.

e. Compute the overhead rate for each category of activity.

f. Determine the amount of overhead cost, both in total and per unit, that would be assigned to each product if the company switched to activity-based costing.

g. Assuming that prices are adjusted to reflect activity-based costs, determine the revised price for each product.

h. Based on your results for Requirements f and g, explain why Product N227 costs more to make than previously apparent and why sales prices therefore need to be adjusted.

L.O. 1, 3

Problem 6-14B   *Using activity-based costing to improve allocation accuracy*

Sanchez's Commemoratives makes and sells two types of decorative plates. One plate displays a hand-painted image of Princess Diana; the other plate displays a machine-pressed image of Marilyn Monroe. The Diana plates require 25,000 hours of direct labor to make; the Monroe plates require only 5,000 hours of direct labor. Overhead costs are composed of (1) $140,000 machine-related activity costs including indirect labor, utilities, and depreciation and (2) $100,000 labor-related activity costs including overtime pay, fringe benefits, and payroll taxes.

Required

a. Assuming that Sanchez's uses direct labor hours as the allocation base, determine the amount of the total $240,000 overhead cost that would be allocated to each type of plate.

b. Explain why using direct labor hours may distort the allocation of overhead cost to the two products.

c. Explain how activity-based costing could improve the accuracy of the overhead cost allocation.

L.O. 1, 3

Problem 6-15B   *Using activity-based costing to improve allocation accuracy*

This problem is an extension of Problem 6-14B, which must be completed first.
Assume the same data as in Problem 6-14B with the following additional information. The hours of machine time for processing plates are 1,000 for Diana plates and 2,500 for Monroe plates.

Required

a. Establish two activity centers, one for machine-related activities and the second for labor-related activities. Assign the total overhead costs to the two activity centers.

b. Allocate the machine-related overhead costs to each product based on machine hours.

c. Allocate the labor-related overhead costs to each product based on direct labor hours.

d. Draw a diagram that compares the one-stage allocation method used in Problem 6-14B with the two-stage activity-based costing approach used in this problem.

L.O. 1, 3

Problem 6-16B   *Using activity-based costing to improve business decisions*

Weik CPA and Associates is a local accounting firm specializing in bookkeeping and tax services. The firm has four certified public accountants who supervise 20 clerks. The clerks handle basic bookkeeping jobs and prepare tax return drafts. The CPAs review and approve the bookkeeping jobs and tax returns. Each CPA receives a fixed salary of $8,000 per month; the clerks earn an hourly rate of $18. Because the clerks are paid by the hour and their work hours can be directly traced to individual jobs, their wages are considered direct costs. The CPAs' salaries are not traced to individual jobs and are therefore treated as indirect costs. The firm allocates overhead based on direct labor hours. The following is Weik's income statement for the previous month.

	Bookkeeping	Tax	Total
Revenues	$60,000	$60,000	$120,000
Direct Expenses	(22,500)*	(22,500)*	(45,000)
Indirect Supervisory Expenses	(16,000)	(16,000)	(32,000)
Net Income	$21,500	$21,500	$ 43,000

*1,250 clerical hours were used in each category during the previous month.

Dorothy Weik, CPA and chief executive officer, is not sure that the two operations are equally profitable as the income statement indicates. First, she believes that most of the CPAs' time was spent instructing clerks in tax return preparation. The bookkeeping jobs appear to be routine, and most of the clerks can handle them with little supervision. After attending a recent professional development seminar on activity-based costing (ABC), Ms. Weik believes that the allocation of indirect costs can be more closely traced to different types of services. To facilitate an activity-based analysis, she asked the CPAs to document their work hours on individual jobs for the last week. The results indicate that, on average, 25 percent of the CPAs' hours was spent supervising bookkeeping activities and the remaining 75 percent was spent supervising tax activities.

Required

a. Based on the preceding information, reconstruct the income statement for bookkeeping services, tax services, and the total, assuming that Weik revises its allocation of indirect supervisory costs based on ABC.
b. Comment on the results and recommend a new business strategy.

Problem 6-17B   *Key activity-based costing concepts*

L.O. 1

Wellington Boot and Shoe Company makes hand-sewn boots and shoes. Wellington uses a companywide overhead rate based on direct labor hours to allocate indirect manufacturing costs to its products. Making a pair of boots normally requires 2.4 hours of direct labor, and making a pair of shoes requires 1.8 hours. The company's shoe division, facing increased competition from international companies that have access to cheap labor, has responded by automating its shoe production. The reengineering process was expensive, requiring the purchase of manufacturing equipment and the restructuring of the plant layout. In addition, utility and maintenance costs increased significantly for operating the new equipment. Even so, labor costs decreased significantly. Now making a pair of shoes requires only 18 minutes of direct labor. As predicted, the labor savings more than offset the increase in overhead cost, thereby reducing the total cost to make a pair of shoes. The company experienced an unexpected side effect, however; according to the company's accounting records, the cost to make a pair of boots increased although the manufacturing process in the boot division was not affected by the reengineering of the shoe division. In other words, the cost of boots increased although Wellington did not change anything about the way it makes them.

Required

a. Explain why the accounting records reflected an increase in the cost to make a pair of boots.
b. Explain how the companywide overhead rate could result in the underpricing of shoes.
c. Explain how activity-based costing could improve the accuracy of overhead cost allocations.

Problem 6-18B   *Pricing decisions made with ABC system cost data*

L.O. 3

Schivo Furniture Corporation makes two types of dining tables, Elegance for formal dining and Comfort for casual dining, at its single factory. With the economy beginning to experience a recession, Justin Schivo, the president, is concerned about whether the company can stay in business as market prices fall. At Mr. Schivo's request, Jane Walter, the controller, prepared cost data for analysis.

Inspectors are paid according to the number of actual hours worked, determined by the number of tables inspected. Engineers who set up equipment for both products are paid monthly salaries. TV commercial fees are paid at the beginning of the quarter.

Direct Cost	Elegance (E)	Comfort (C)
Direct materials	$70 per unit	$43 per unit
Direct labor	$36 per hour × 1.5 hours production time	$36 per hour × 1 hour production time

Category	Estimated Cost	Cost Driver	Use of Cost Driver
Product inspection	$120,000	Number of units	E: 2,500 units; C: 7,500 units
Machine setups	75,000	Number of setups	E: 23 setups; C: 27 setups
Product advertising	210,000	Number of TV commercials	E: 5; C: 9
Facility depreciation	405,000	Number of machine hours	E: 5,000 hours; C: 5,000 hours
Total	$810,000		

Required

a. Compute the cost per unit for each product.
b. If management wants to make 30 percent of cost as a profit margin for Elegance, what price should the company set?
c. The market price of tables in the Comfort class has declined because of the recession. Management asks you to determine the minimum cost of producing Comfort tables in the short term. Provide that information.

L.O. 3

Problem 6-19B   *Target pricing and target costing with ABC*

Ingram Corporation manufactures two models of watches. Model Wonder displays cartoon characters and has simple features designed for kids. Model Marvel has sophisticated features such as dual time zones and an attached calculator. Ingram's product design team has worked with a cost accountant to prepare a budget for the two products for the next fiscal year as follows.

Direct Cost	Wonder (W)	Marvel (M)
Direct materials	$8 per unit	$20 per unit
Direct labor	$40/hour × 0.2 hour production time	$40/hour × 0.6 hour production time

Category	Estimated Cost	Cost Driver	Use of Cost Driver
Materials handling	$366,000	Number of parts	W: 700,000; M: 520,000
Machine setups	180,000	Number of setups	W: 50; M: 40
Product testing	28,000	Number of units tested	W: 1,000; M: 400
Facility depreciation	360,000	Number of machine hours	W: 3,200; M: 4,000
Total	$934,000		

Wonder watches have 35 parts, and Marvel watches have 65 parts. The budget calls for producing 20,000 units of Wonder and 8,000 units of Marvel. Ingram tests 5 percent of its products for quality assurance. It sells all its products at market prices.

Required

a. Compute the cost per unit for each product.
b. The current market price for products comparable to Wonder is $36 and for products comparable to Marvel is $110. What will Ingram's profit or loss for the next year be?
c. Ingram likes to have a 25 percent profit margin based on the current market price for each product. What is the target cost for each product? What is the total target profit?
d. The president of Ingram has asked the design team to refine the production design to bring down the product cost. After a series of redesigns, the team recommends a new process that requires purchasing a new machine that costs $400,000 and has five years of useful life and no salvage value. With the new process and the new machine, Ingram can decrease the number of machine setups to four for each product and cut the cost of materials handling in half. The machine hours used will be 4,500 for Wonder and 6,500 for Marvel. Does this new process enable Ingram to achieve its target costs?

L.O. 3

Problem 6-20B   *Cost management with an ABC system*

Kent Corporation manufactures two different coffee makers, Professional for commercial use and Home for family use. Dan Kaiser, the president, recently received complaints from some members of the board of directors about the company's failure to reach the expected profit of $200,000 per month. Mr. Kaiser is, therefore, under great pressure to improve the company's bottom line. Under his direction, Wendy Brown, the controller, prepared the following monthly cost data for Mr. Kaiser.

Direct Cost	Professional (P)	Home (H)
Direct materials	$21 per unit	$7 per unit
Direct labor	$18 per hour × 0.8 hour production time	$18 per hour × 0.3 hour production time

Category	Estimated Cost	Cost Driver	Use of Cost Driver
Product inspection	$ 60,000	Number of units	P: 15,000 units; H: 45,000 units
Machine setups	15,000	Number of setups	P: 30 setups; H: 45 setups
Product promotion	200,000	Number of TV commercials	P: 10; H: 10
Facility depreciation	295,000	Number of machine hours	P: 7,160 hours; H: 4,640 hours
Total	$570,000		

The market price for coffee makers comparable to Professional is $65 and to Home is $22. The company's administrative expenses amount to $195,000.

Required

a. Compute the cost per unit for both products.
b. Determine the company's profit or loss.
c. Tim Sun, the marketing manager, recommends that the company implement a focused marketing strategy. He argues that advertisements in trade journals would be more effective for the commercial market than on TV. In addition, the cost of journal ads would be only $21,000. He also proposes sending discount coupons to targeted households to reach a broad market base. The coupons program would cost $72,000. Compute the new cost of each product, assuming that Mr. Kaiser replaces TV advertising with Mr. Sun's suggestions.
d. Determine the company's profit or loss using the information in Requirement *c*.

Problem 6-21B *Assessing a quality control strategy*

L.O. 4, 5

Bret Eason, the president of Harris Plastic Company, is a famous cost cutter in the plastics industry. Two years ago, he accepted an offer from Harris's board of directors to help the company cut costs quickly. In fact, Mr. Eason's compensation package included a year-end bonus tied to the percentage of cost decrease over the preceding year. On February 12, 2008, Mr. Eason received comparative financial information for the two preceding years. He was especially interested in the results of his cost-cutting measures on quality control. The quality report shown below was extracted from the company's financial information:

Required

a. Explain the strategy that Mr. Eason initiated to control Harris's costs.
b. Indicate whether the strategy was successful or unsuccessful in reducing quality costs.
c. Explain how the strategy will likely affect the company's business in the long term.

	2007		2006	
	Amount	Percentage	Amount	Percentage
Prevention costs				
Engineering and design	$ 65,000	6.57%	$ 69,000	7.39%
Training and education	26,000	2.63	76,000	8.14
Depreciation on prevention equipment	15,000	1.51	15,000	1.60
Incentives and awards	20,000	2.02	20,000	2.14
Total prevention	126,000	12.73%	180,000	19.27%
Appraisal costs				
Product and materials inspection	33,000	3.33	73,000	7.82
Reliability testing	27,000	2.73	67,000	7.17
Testing equipment (depreciation)	38,000	3.83	38,000	4.07
Supplies	10,000	1.01	16,000	1.71
Total appraisal	108,000	10.90%	194,000	20.77%

continued

	2007		2006	
	Amount	Percentage	Amount	Percentage
Internal failure costs				
Scrap	52,000	5.25	120,000	12.85
Repair and rework	46,000	4.65	150,000	16.06
Downtime	64,000	6.46	40,000	4.28
Reinspection	8,000	0.81	24,000	2.57
Total internal failure	170,000	17.17%	334,000	35.76%
External failure cost				
Warranty repairs and replacement	347,000	35.05	125,000	13.38
Freight	75,000	7.58	31,000	3.32
Customer relations	45,000	4.55	28,000	3.00
Restocking and packaging	119,000	12.02	42,000	4.50
Total external failure	586,000	59.20%	226,000	24.20%
Grand total	$990,000	100.00%	$934,000	100.00%

ANALYZE, THINK, COMMUNICATE

ATC 6-1   Business Applications Case   *Using ABC to improve product costing*

Extrusions Unlimited produces metal component parts for companies in the construction supply business. All of the components it produces involve metal extrusion at some stage of the manufacturing process. The company has recently implemented an ABC system for three of its products and is interested in evaluating its effectiveness before converting to an ABC system for all products. To perform this evaluation the company has compiled data for the three products using both the traditional system and the new ABC system. The traditional system used a single driver (direct material costs). The ABC system uses a variety of cost drivers related to the activities used to produce the metal products. The three products involved in the trial run of the ABC system were aluminum door frames, aluminum window frames, and anodized metal lettering and frames used for signs. The following data relate to these products.

Product	Selling Price per Foot	Feet Produced	Total Costs Allocated: Traditional Costing	Cost per Foot: Traditional Costing	Total Cost Allocated: ABC	Costs per Foot: ABC
Door frames	$3.32	275,000	$522,500	$1.90	$508,750	$1.85
Window frames	3.68	160,000	336,000	2.10	329,600	2.06
Metal signs	4.29	20,000	49,000	2.45	69,150	3.46
Totals			907,500		907,500	

Required

a. Determine the gross profit margin for each product produced based on the ABC data [(selling price − ABC cost per foot) × feet produced].
b. Determine the gross profit margin for each product produced based on the traditional costing data [(selling price − traditional cost per foot) × feet produced].
c. Provide an explanation as to why the cost of metal signs may have increased under the ABC system while the cost of door frames decreased.
d. Suggest what action management might take with respect to the discoveries resulting from the ABC versus traditional costing analysis. Assume that Extrusions Unlimited expects to produce a gross profit margin on each product of at least 40 percent of the selling price.

ATC 6-2   Group Assignment   *Using ABC in a service business*

A dialysis clinic provides two types of treatment for its patients. Hemodialysis (HD), an in-house treatment, requires that patients visit the clinic three times each week for dialysis treatments. Peritoneal dialysis (PD) permits patients to self-administer their treatments at home on a daily basis. On average, the clinic serves 102 HD patients and 62 PD patients. A recent development caused clinic administrators to develop a keen interest in cost measurement for the two separate services. Managed care plans such as HMOs began to pay treatment providers a fixed payment per insured participant regardless of the level of services provided by the clinic. With fixed fee revenues, the clinic was forced to control costs to ensure profitability. As a result, knowing the cost to provide HD versus PD services was critically important for the clinic. It needed accurate cost measurements to answer the following questions. Were both services profitable, or was one service carrying the burden of the other service? Should advertising be directed toward acquiring HD or PD patients? Should the clinic eliminate HMO service?

Management suspected the existing cost allocation system was inaccurate in measuring the true cost of providing the respective services; it had been developed in response to Medicare reporting requirements. It allocated costs between HD and PD based on the ratio of cost to charges (RCC). In other words, RCC allocates indirect costs in proportion to revenues. To illustrate, consider the allocation of $883,280 of indirect nursing services costs, which are allocated to the two treatment groups in relation to the revenue generated by each group. Given that the clinic generated total revenue of $3,006,775, an allocation rate of 0.2937633 per revenue dollar was established ($883,280 ÷ $3,006,775). This rate was multiplied by the proportionate share of revenue generated by each service category to produce the following allocation.

Type of Service	Service Revenue	×	Allocation Rate	=	Allocated Cost
HD	$1,860,287	×	0.2937633	=	$546,484
PD	1,146,488	×	0.2937633	=	336,796
Total	$3,006,775	×	0.2937633	=	$883,280

To better assess the cost of providing each type of service, the clinic initiated an activity-based costing (ABC) system. The ABC approach divided the nursing service cost into four separate cost pools. A separate cost driver (allocation base) was identified for each cost pool. The cost pools and their respective cost drivers follow.

	Total	HD	PD
Nursing services cost pool categories			
RNs	$239,120	?	?
LPNs	404,064	?	?
Nursing administration and support staff	115,168	?	?
Dialysis machine operations (tech. salaries)	124,928	?	?
Total	$883,280	?	?

	Total	HD	PD
Activity cost drivers (corresponding to cost pools)			
Number of RNs	7	5	2
Number of LPNs	19	15	4
Number of treatments (nursing administration)	34,967	14,343	20,624
Number of dialyzer treatments (machine operations)	14,343	14,343	0

Data Source: T. D. West and D. A. West, "Applying ABC to Healthcare," *Management Accounting,* February 1999, pp. 22–33.

Required

a. Organize the class into four sections and divide the sections into groups of four or five students each. Assign Task 1 to the first section of groups, Task 2 to the second section, Task 3 to the third section, and Task 4 to the fourth section.

Group Tasks

   (1) Allocate the RN cost pool between the HD and PD service centers.

   (2) Allocate the LPN cost pool between the HD and PD service centers.

   (3) Allocate the nursing administration and support staff cost pool between the HD and PD service centers.

   (4) Allocate the dialysis machine operations cost pool between the HD and PD service centers.

b. Have the class determine the total cost to allocate to the two service centers in the following manner. Select a representative from each section and have the selected person go to the board. Each representative should supply the allocated cost for the cost pool assigned by her respective section. The instructor should total the amounts and compare the ABC cost allocations with those developed through the traditional RCC system.

c. The instructor should lead the class in a discussion that addresses the following questions.

   (1) Assuming that the ABC system provides a more accurate measure of cost, which service center (HD or PD) is overcosted by the traditional allocation system and which is undercosted?

   (2) What is the potential impact on pricing and profitability for both service centers?

   (3) How could management respond to the conditions described in the problem?

ATC 6-3   Research Assignment   *Using Six Sigma to implement TQM at Xerox Corp.*

Six Sigma is one system used in the pursuit of TQM, and the Xerox Corporation is one of many large companies that use it. The article, "How Xerox Got Up to Speed; Learning Fast from GE Capital . . .," which begins on page 103 of the May 3, 2004, issue of *BusinessWeek,* explains what prompted Xerox to adopt Six Sigma. It also discusses some of the benefits Six Sigma has provided the company, and some of the problems the company encountered implementing the system. Read this article and complete the following requirements.

Required

a. How does the article define Six Sigma systems?

b. What caused Xerox to implement the Six Sigma system?

c. According to the article, what financial return did Xerox gain in 2003 from implementing its Six Sigma system, and what amount of investment was necessary to achieve this gain?

d. What did Xerox's CEO identify as the biggest obstacle to implementation of its Six Sigma system?

ATC 6-4   Writing Assignment   *Assessing a strategy to control quality cost*

Lucy Sawyer, who owns and operates Sawyer Toy Company, is a perfectionist. She believes literally in the "zero-defects" approach to quality control. Her favorite saying is, "You can't spend too much on quality." Even so, in 2006 her company experienced an embarrassing breach of quality that required the national recall of a defective product. She vowed never to repeat the experience and instructed her staff to spend whatever it takes to ensure that products are delivered free of defects in 2007. She was somewhat disappointed with the 2007 year-end quality cost report shown here.

	2006	2007
Prevention costs	$120,000	$ 80,000
Appraisal costs	240,000	430,000
Internal failure costs	140,000	560,000
External failure cost	320,000	210,000
Total	$820,000	$1,280,000

Although external failure costs had declined, they remained much higher than expected. The increased inspections had identified defects that were corrected, thereby avoiding another recall; however, the external failure costs were still too high. Ms. Sawyer responded by saying, "We will have to double our efforts." She authorized hiring additional inspectors and instructed her production supervisors to become more vigilant in identifying and correcting errors.

Required

Assume that you are the chief financial officer (CFO) of Sawyer Company. Ms. Sawyer has asked you to review the company's approach to quality control. Prepare a memo to her that evaluates the existing approach, and recommend changes in expenditure patterns that can improve profitability as well as increase the effectiveness of the quality control system.

ATC 6-5   Ethical Dilemma   *Conflicts between controlling cost and providing social responsibility to patients*

This case examines potential ethical issues faced by the dialysis clinic described in ATC 6-2. It is, however, an independent case that students may study in conjunction with or separately from ATC 6-2. The dialysis clinic provides two types of treatment for its patients. Hemodialysis (HD), an in-house treatment, requires patients to visit the clinic three times each week. Peritoneal dialysis (PD) permits patients to self-administer their treatments at home on a daily basis. The clinic serves a number of HMO patients under a contract that limits collections from the HMO insurer to a fixed amount per patient. As a result, the clinic's profitability is directly related to its ability to control costs. To illustrate, assume that the clinic is paid a fixed annual fee of $15,000 per HMO patient served. Also assume that the current cost to provide health care averages $14,000 a year per patient, resulting in an average profitability of $1,000 per patient ($15,000 − $14,000). Because the revenue base is fixed, the only way the clinic can increase profitability is to lower its average cost of providing services. If the clinic fails to control costs and the average cost of patient care increases, profitability will decline. A recent ABC study suggests that the cost to provide HD service exceeds the amount of revenue generated from providing that service. The clinic is profitable because PD services generate enough profit to more than make up for losses on HD services.

Required

Respond to each potential scenario described here. Each scenario is independent of the others.

a. Suppose that as a result of the ABC analysis, the chief accountant, a certified management accountant (CMA), recommends that the clinic discontinue treating HD patients referred by the HMO provider. Based on this assumption, answer the following questions.

   (1) Assume that the clinic is located in a small town. If it discontinues treating the HD patients, they will be forced to drive 50 miles to the nearest alternative treatment center. Does the clinic have a moral obligation to society to continue to provide HD service although it is not profitable to do so?

   (2) The accountant's recommendation places profitability above the needs of HD patients. Does this recommendation violate any of the standards of ethical conduct described in Chapter 1, Exhibit 1.15?

b. Assume that the clinic continues to treat HD patients referred by HMOs. However, to compensate for the loss incurred on these patients, the clinic raises prices charged to non-HMO patients. Is it fair to require non-HMO patients to subsidize services provided to the HMO patients?

c. Suppose that the clinic administrators respond to the ABC data by cutting costs. The clinic overbooks HMO patients to ensure that downtime is avoided when cancellations occur. It reduces the RN nursing staff and assigns some of the technical work to less-qualified assistants. Ultimately, an overworked, underqualified nurse's aide makes a mistake, and a patient dies. Who is at fault—the HMO, the accountant who conducted the ABC analysis, or the clinic administrators who responded to the ABC information?

ATC 6-6   Spreadsheet Assignment   *Using Excel*

Tameron Corporation produces video games in three market categories: commercial, home video, and miniature handheld. Tameron has traditionally allocated overhead costs to the three product categories using the companywide base of direct labor hours. The company recently switched to an ABC system when it installed computer-controlled assembly stations that rendered the traditional costing system ineffective. In implementing the ABC system, the company identified the cost pools and drivers shown in the following spreadsheet. The activity in each of the three product lines appears in rows 3 to 9. The pooled costs are shown in cells E11 to E15.

Required

Construct a spreadsheet like the following one to compute the total cost and cost per unit for each product line. Cells K4 to K9, G12 to I15, E19 to E28, G19 to G28, I19 to I28, and K26 should all be formulas.

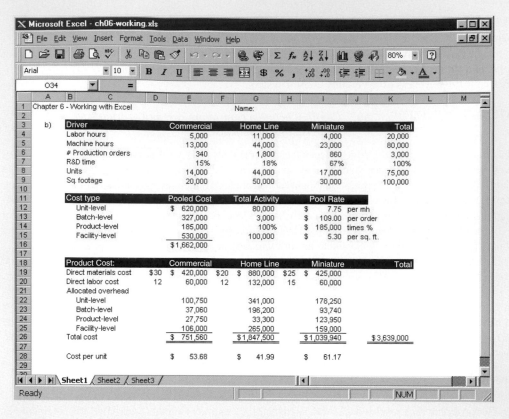

ATC 6-7   Spreadsheet Assignment   *Mastering Excel*

Beasley Company makes three types of exercise machines. Data have been accumulated for four possible overhead drivers. Data for these four possible drivers are shown in rows 3 to 7 of the following spreadsheet.

Required

Construct a spreadsheet that will allocate overhead and calculate unit cost for each of these alternative drivers. A screen capture of the spreadsheet and data follows.

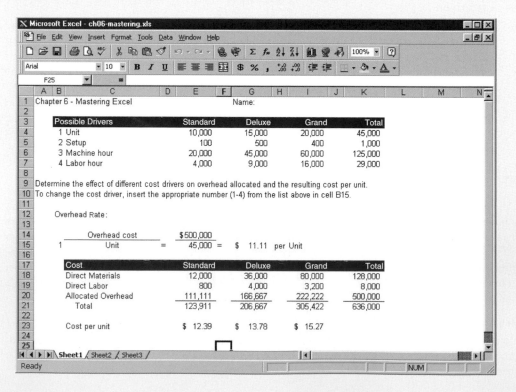

Spreadsheet Tips

1. This spreadsheet uses a function called *vertical lookup*. This function can pull the appropriate values from a table. The form of this function is =VLOOKUP (value, table, column#). In this example, the table is in cells B4 to K7. Three examples of the use of VLOOKUP follow.

2. Cell C15 is =VLOOKUP (B15, B4:K7, 2). This function operates by using the one (1) in cell B15 to look up a value in the table. Notice that the table is defined as B4:K7 and that the function is looking up the value in the second column, which is Unit.

3. Cell E15 is =VLOOKUP (B15, B4:K7, 10). In this case, the function is looking up the value in the tenth column, which is 45,000. Be sure to count empty columns.

4. Cell E20 is =VLOOKUP (B15, B4:K7, 4)*G15. In this case, the function is looking up the value in the fourth column, which is $10,000. Be sure to count empty columns.

5. Cells I15, G20, and I20 also use the VLOOKUP function.

6. After completing the spreadsheet, you can change the value in cell B15 (1-4) to see the effect of choosing a different driver for overhead.

COMPREHENSIVE PROBLEM

To this point we have assumed the Magnificent Modems produced only one type of modem. Suppose instead we assume the company produces several different kinds of modems. The production process differs for each type of product. Some require more setup time than others, they are produced in different batch sizes, and they require different amounts of indirect labor (supervision). Packaging and delivery to customers also differs for each type of modem. Even so, Magnificent Modems uses a single allocation base (number of units) to allocate overhead costs.

Required

Write a brief memo that explains how Magnificent Modems could benefit from an ABC cost system.

CHAPTER 7

Planning for Profit and Cost Control

LEARNING OBJECTIVES

After you have mastered the material in this chapter you will be able to:

1. Describe the budgeting process and the benefits it provides.

2. Explain the relationship between budgeting and human behavior.

3. Prepare a sales budget and related schedule of cash receipts.

4. Prepare an inventory purchases budget and related schedule of cash payments.

5. Prepare a selling and administrative expense budget and related schedule of cash payments.

6. Prepare a cash budget.

7. Prepare a pro forma income statement, balance sheet, and statement of cash flows.

The Curious Accountant

People in television commercials often say they shop at a particular store because, "my family is on a budget." The truth is, most families do not have a formal budget. What these people mean is that they need to be sure their spending does not exceed their available cash.

When a family expects to spend more money in a given year than it will earn, it must plan on borrowing funds needed to make up the difference. However, even if a family's income for a year will exceed its spending, it may still need to borrow money because the timing of its cash inflows may not match the timing of its cash outflows. Whether a budget is being prepared for a family or a business, those preparing the budget must understand the specific issues facing that entity if potential financial problems are to be anticipated. There is no such thing as a "one size fits all" budget.

The **United States Olympic Committee (USOC)**, like all large organizations, devotes considerable effort to budget planning.

Think about the Olympic Games, and how the USOC generates revenues and incurs expenditures. Can you identify any unusual circumstances facing the USOC that complicate its budgeting efforts? (Answer on page 307.)

CHAPTER OPENING

*Planning is crucial to operating a profitable business. Expressing business plans in financial terms is commonly called **budgeting.** The budgeting process involves coordinating the financial plans of all areas of the business. For example, the production department cannot prepare a manufacturing plan until it knows how many units of product to produce. The number of units to produce depends on the marketing department's sales projection. The marketing department cannot project sales volume until it knows what products the* *company will sell. Product information comes from the research and development department. The point should be clear: a company's master budget results from combining numerous specific plans prepared by different departments.*

Master budget preparation is normally supervised by a committee. The budget committee is responsible for settling disputes among various departments over budget matters. The committee also monitors reports on how various segments are progressing toward achieving their budget goals. The budgeting committee is not an accounting committee. It is a high-level committee that normally includes the company president, vice presidents of marketing, purchasing, production, and finance, and the controller. ■

The Planning Process

Describe the budgeting process and the benefits it provides.

7-1

Planning normally addresses short, intermediate, and long-range time horizons. Short-term plans are more specific than long-term plans. Consider, for example, your decision to attend college. Long-term planning requires considering general questions such as:

- Do I want to go to college?
- How do I expect to benefit from the experience?
- Do I want a broad knowledge base, or am I seeking to learn specific job skills?
- In what field do I want to concentrate my studies?

Many students go to college before answering these questions. They discover the disadvantages of poor planning the hard way. While their friends are graduating, they are starting over in a new major.

Intermediate-range planning usually covers three to five years. In this stage, you consider which college to attend, how to support yourself while in school, and whether to live on or off campus.

Short-term planning focuses on the coming year. In this phase you plan specific courses to take, decide which instructors to choose, schedule part-time work, and join a study group. Short-term plans are specific and detailed. Their preparation may seem tedious, but careful planning generally leads to efficient resource use and high levels of productivity.

Three Levels of Planning for Business Activity

Businesses describe the three levels of planning as *strategic planning, capital budgeting,* and *operations budgeting*. **Strategic planning** involves making long-term decisions such as defining the scope of the business, determining which products to develop or discontinue, and identifying the most profitable market niche. Upper-level management is responsible for these decisions. Strategic plans are descriptive rather than quantitative. Objectives such as "to have the largest share of the market" or "to be the best-quality producer" result from strategic planning. Although strategic planning is an integral component of managing a business, an in-depth discussion of it is beyond the scope of this text.

Capital budgeting focuses on intermediate range planning. It involves such decisions as whether to buy or lease equipment, whether to stimulate sales, or whether to increase the company's asset base. Capital budgeting is discussed in detail in a later chapter.

The central focus of this chapter is the *master budget* which describes short-term objectives in specific amounts of sales targets, production goals, and financing plans. The master budget describes how management intends to achieve its objectives and directs the company's short-term activities.

The master budget normally covers one year. It is frequently divided into quarterly projections and often subdivides quarterly data by month. Effective managers cannot wait until year-end to know whether operations conform to budget targets. Monthly data provide feedback to permit making necessary corrections promptly.

Many companies use **perpetual,** or **continuous, budgeting** covering a 12-month reporting period. As the current month draws to a close, an additional month is added at the end of the budget period, resulting in a continuous 12-month budget. A perpetual budget offers the advantage of keeping management constantly focused on thinking ahead to the next 12 months. The more traditional annual approach to budgeting invites a frenzied stop-and-go mentality, with managers preparing the budget in a year-end rush that is soon forgotten. Changing conditions may not be discussed until the next year-end budget is due. A perpetual budget overcomes these disadvantages.

Advantages of Budgeting

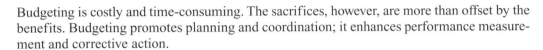

Budgeting is costly and time-consuming. The sacrifices, however, are more than offset by the benefits. Budgeting promotes planning and coordination; it enhances performance measurement and corrective action.

Planning

Almost everyone makes plans. Each morning, most people think about what they will do during the day. Thinking ahead is planning. Most business managers think ahead about how they will direct operations. Unfortunately, planning is frequently as informal as making a few mental notes. Informal planning cannot be effectively communicated. The business manager might know what her objectives are, but neither her superiors nor her subordinates know. Because it serves as a communication tool, budgeting can solve these problems. The budget formalizes and documents managerial plans, clearly communicating objectives to both superiors and subordinates.

Coordination

Sometimes a choice benefits one department at the expense of another. For example, a purchasing agent may order large quantities of raw materials to obtain discounts from suppliers. But excessive quantities of materials pose a storage problem for the inventory supervisor who must manage warehouse costs. The budgeting process forces coordination among departments to promote decisions in the best interests of the company as a whole.

Performance Measurement

Budgets are specific, quantitative representations of management's objectives. Comparing actual results to budget expectations provides a way to evaluate performance. For example, if a company budgets sales of $10 million, it can judge the performance of the sales department against that level. If actual sales exceed $10 million, the company should reward the sales department; if actual sales fall below $10 million, the company should seek an explanation for the shortfall from the sales manager.

Corrective Action

Budgeting provides advance notice of potential shortages, bottlenecks, or other weaknesses in operating plans. For example, a cash budget alerts management to when the company can expect cash shortages during the coming year. The company can make borrowing arrangements well before it needs the money. Without knowing ahead of time, management might be unable to secure necessary financing on short notice, or it may have to pay excessively high interest rates to obtain funds. Budgeting advises managers of potential problems in time for them to carefully devise effective solutions.

Budgeting and Human Behavior

Explain the relationship between budgeting and human behavior.

Effective budgeting requires genuine sensitivity on the part of upper management to the effect on employees of budget expectations. People are often uncomfortable with budgets. Budgets are constraining. They limit individual freedom in favor of an established plan. Many people find evaluation based on budget expectations stressful. Most students experience a similar fear about testing. Like examinations, budgets represent standards by which performance is evaluated. Employees worry about whether their performance will meet expectations.

The attitudes of high-level managers significantly impact budget effectiveness. Subordinates are keenly aware of management's expectations. If upper-level managers degrade, make fun of, or ignore the budget, subordinates will follow suit. If management uses budgets to humiliate, embarrass, or punish subordinates, employees will resent the treatment and the budgeting process. Upper-level managers must demonstrate that they view the budget as a sincere effort to express realistic goals employees are expected to meet. An honest, open, respectful atmosphere is essential to budgeting success.

Participative budgeting has frequently proved successful in creating a healthy atmosphere. This technique invites participation in the budget process by personnel at all levels of the organization, not just upper-level managers. Information flows from the bottom up as well as from the top down during budget preparation. Because they are directly responsible for meeting budget goals, subordinates can offer more realistic targets. Including them in budget preparation fosters development of a team effort. Participation fosters more cooperation and motivation, and less fear. With participative budgeting, subordinates cannot complain that the budget is management's plan. The budget is instead a self-imposed constraint. Employees can hold no one responsible but themselves if they fail to accomplish the budget objectives they established.

Upper management participates in the process to ensure that employee-generated objectives are consistent with company objectives. Furthermore, if subordinates were granted complete freedom to establish budget standards, they might be tempted to adopt lax standards to ensure they will meet them. Both managers and subordinates must cooperate if the participatory process is to produce an effective budget. If developed carefully, budgets can motivate employees to achieve superior performance. Normal human fears must be overcome, and management must create an honest budget atmosphere.

The Master Budget

Describe the budgeting process and the benefits it provides.

Topic Tackler

PLUS

7-2

The **master budget** is a group of detailed budgets and schedules representing the company's operating and financial plans for a future accounting period. The master budget usually includes (1) *operating budgets,* (2) *capital budgets,* and (3) *pro forma financial statements.* The budgeting process normally begins with preparing the **operating budgets,** which focus on detailed operating activities. This chapter illustrates operating budgets for Hampton Hams, a retail sales company that uses (1) a sales budget, (2) an inventory purchases budget, (3) a selling and administrative (S&A) expense budget, and (4) a cash budget.

The sales budget includes a schedule of cash receipts from customers. The inventory purchases and S&A expense budgets include schedules of cash payments for inventory and expenses. Preparing the master budget begins with the sales forecast. Based on the sales forecast, the detailed budgets for inventory purchases and operating expenses are developed. The schedules of cash receipts and cash payments provide the foundation for preparing the cash budget.

The **capital budget** describes the company's intermediate-range plans for investments in facilities, equipment, new products, store outlets, and lines of business. The capital budget affects several operating budgets. For example, equipment acquisitions result in additional depreciation expense on the S&A expense budget. The cash flow effects of capital investments influence the cash budget.

The operating budgets are used to prepare *pro forma statements.* **Pro forma financial statements** are based on projected (budgeted) rather than historical information.

EXHIBIT 7.1

Information Flows in the Master Budget

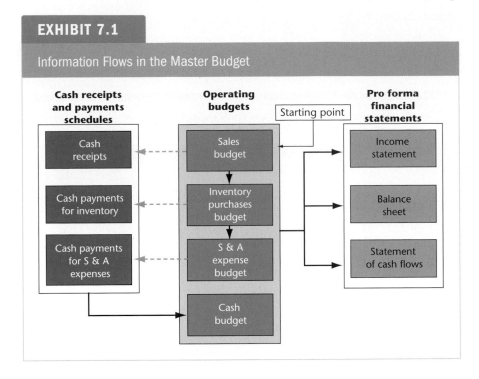

Hampton Hams prepares a pro forma income statement, balance sheet, and statement of cash flows.

Exhibit 7.1 shows how information flows in a master budget.

Hampton Hams Budgeting Illustration

Hampton Hams (HH), a major corporation, sells cured hams nationwide through retail outlets in shopping malls. By focusing on a single product and standardized operations, the company controls costs stringently. As a result, it offers high-quality hams at competitive prices.

Hampton Hams has experienced phenomenal growth during the past five years. It opened two new stores in Indianapolis, Indiana, last month and plans to open a third new store in October. Hampton Hams finances new stores by borrowing on a line of credit arranged with National Bank. National's loan officer has requested monthly budgets for each of the first three months of the new store's operations. The accounting department is preparing the new store's master budget for October, November, and December. The first step is developing a sales budget.

Sales Budget

Preparing the master budget begins with the sales forecast. The accuracy of the sales forecast is critical because all the other budgets are derived from the sales budget. Normally, the marketing department coordinates the development of the sales forecast. Sales estimates frequently flow from the bottom up to the higher management levels. Sales personnel prepare sales projections for their products and territories and pass them up the line where they are combined with the estimates of other sales personnel to develop regional and national estimates. Using various information sources, upper-level sales managers adjust the estimates generated by sales personnel. Adjustment information comes from industry periodicals and trade journals, economic analysis, marketing surveys, historical sales figures, and changes in competition. Companies assimilate this data using sophisticated computer programs, statistical techniques, and quantitative methods, or, simply, professional judgment. Regardless of the technique, the senior vice president of sales ultimately develops a sales forecast for which she is held responsible.

To develop the sales forecast for HH's new store, the sales manager studied the sales history of existing stores operating in similar locations. He then adjusted for start-up conditions.

LO 3

Prepare a sales budget and related schedule of cash receipts.

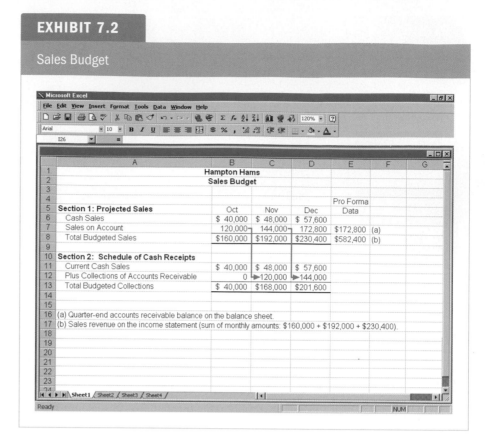

EXHIBIT 7.2

Sales Budget

Hampton Hams
Sales Budget

	Oct	Nov	Dec	Pro Forma Data	
Section 1: Projected Sales					
Cash Sales	$ 40,000	$ 48,000	$ 57,600		
Sales on Account	120,000	144,000	172,800	$172,800	(a)
Total Budgeted Sales	$160,000	$192,000	$230,400	$582,400	(b)
Section 2: Schedule of Cash Receipts					
Current Cash Sales	$ 40,000	$ 48,000	$ 57,600		
Plus Collections of Accounts Receivable	0	120,000	144,000		
Total Budgeted Collections	$ 40,000	$168,000	$201,600		

(a) Quarter-end accounts receivable balance on the balance sheet.
(b) Sales revenue on the income statement (sum of monthly amounts: $160,000 + $192,000 + $230,400).

October is an opportune time to open a new store because customers will learn the store's location before the holiday season. The sales manager expects significant sales growth in November and December as customers choose the company's hams as the centerpiece for many Thanksgiving and winter holiday dinner tables.

The new store's sales are expected to be $160,000 in October ($40,000 in cash and $120,000 on account). Sales are expected to increase 20 percent per month during November and December. Based on these estimates, the sales manager prepared the sales budget in Exhibit 7.2.

Projected Sales

The sales budget has two sections. Section 1 shows the projected sales for each month. The November sales forecast reflects a 20 percent increase over October sales. For example, November *cash sales* are calculated as $48,000 [$40,000 + ($40,000 × 0.20)] and December *cash sales* as $57,600 [$48,000 + ($48,000 × 0.20)]. *Sales on account* are similarly computed.

Schedule of Cash Receipts

Section 2 is a schedule of the cash receipts for the projected sales. This schedule is used later to prepare the cash budget. The accountant has assumed in this schedule that Hampton Hams will collect accounts receivable from credit sales *in full* in the month following the sale. In practice, collections may be spread over several months, and some receivables may become bad debts that are never collected. Regardless of additional complexities, the objective is to estimate the amount and timing of expected cash receipts.

In the HH case, *total cash receipts* are determined by adding the current month's *cash sales* to the cash collected from the previous month's *credit sales* (accounts receivable balance). Cash receipts for each month are determined as follows:

- October receipts are projected to be $40,000. Because the store opens in October, no accounts receivable from September exist to be collected in October. Cash receipts for October equal the amount of October's cash sales.

- November receipts are projected to be $168,000 ($48,000 November cash sales + $120,000 cash collected from October sales on account).

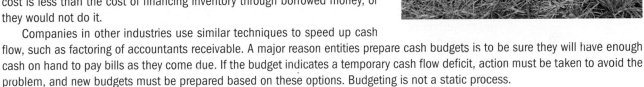

CASH FLOW PLANNING IN BORDEAUX

The year 2005 was considered a great year for wine in the Bordeaux region of France, and the winemakers could look forward to selling their wines for high prices, but there was one catch; these wines would not be released to consumers until late in 2008. The winemakers had incurred most of their costs in 2005 when the vines were being tended and the grapes were being processed into wine. In many industries this would mean the companies would have to finance their inventory for almost four years—not an insignificant cost. The company must finance the inventory by either borrowing the money, which results in out-of-pocket interest expense, or using its own funds. The second option generates an opportunity cost resulting from the interest revenue that could have been earned if these funds were not being used to finance the inventory.

To address this potential cash flow problem, many of the winemakers in Bordeaux offer some of their wines for sale as "futures." That means the wines are purchased and paid for while they are still aging in barrels in France. Selling wine as futures reduces the time inventory must be financed from four years to only one to two years. Of course there are other types of costs in such deals. For one, the wines must be offered at lower prices than they are expected to sell for upon release. The winemakers have obviously decided this cost is less than the cost of financing inventory through borrowed money, or they would not do it.

Companies in other industries use similar techniques to speed up cash flow, such as factoring of accountants receivable. A major reason entities prepare cash budgets is to be sure they will have enough cash on hand to pay bills as they come due. If the budget indicates a temporary cash flow deficit, action must be taken to avoid the problem, and new budgets must be prepared based on these options. Budgeting is not a static process.

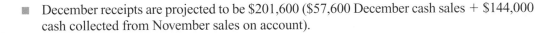

- December receipts are projected to be $201,600 ($57,600 December cash sales + $144,000 cash collected from November sales on account).

Pro Forma Financial Statement Data

The Pro Forma Data column in the sales budget displays two figures HH will report on the quarter-end (December 31) budgeted financial statements. Since HH expects to collect December credit sales in January, the *accounts receivable balance* will be $172,800 on the December 31, 2006, pro forma balance sheet (shown later in Exhibit 7.7).

The $582,400 of *sales revenue* in the Pro Forma Data column will be reported on the budgeted income statement for the quarter (shown later in Exhibit 7.6). The sales revenue represents the sum of October, November, and December sales ($160,000 + $192,000 + $230,400 = $582,400).

Inventory Purchases Budget

The inventory purchases budget shows the amount of inventory HH must purchase each month to satisfy the demand projected in the sales budget. The *total inventory needed* each month equals the amount of inventory HH plans to sell that month plus the amount of inventory HH wants on hand at month-end. To the extent that total inventory needed exceeds the inventory on hand at the beginning of the month, HH will need to purchase additional inventory. The amount of inventory to purchase is computed as follows:

Prepare an inventory purchases budget and related schedule of cash payments.

Cost of Budgeted Sales	XXX
Plus: Desired Ending Inventory	XXX
Total Inventory Needed	XXX
Less: Beginning Inventory	(XXX)
Required Purchases	XXX

It is HH's policy to maintain an ending inventory equal to 25 percent of the next month's *projected cost of goods sold.* HH's cost of goods sold normally equals 70 percent of *sales.* Using this information and the sales budget, the accounting department prepared the inventory purchases budget shown in Exhibit 7.3.

Section 1 of the inventory purchases budget shows required purchases for each month. HH determined *budgeted cost of goods sold* for October by multiplying October *budgeted sales* by 70 percent ($160,000 × 0.70 = $112,000). Budgeted cost of goods sold for November and December were similarly computed. The October *desired ending inventory* was computed by multiplying November *budgeted cost of goods sold* by 25 percent ($134,400 × 0.25 = $33,600). Desired ending inventory for November is $40,320 ($161,280 × .25). Desired ending inventory for December is based on January projected cost of goods sold (not shown in the exhibit). HH expects ham sales to decline after the winter holidays. Because January projected cost of goods sold is only $140,000, the December desired ending inventory falls to $35,000 ($140,000 × .25).

Schedule of Cash Payments for Inventory Purchases

Section 2 is the schedule of cash payments for inventory purchases. HH makes all inventory purchases on account. The supplier requires that HH pay for 60 percent of inventory purchases in the month goods are purchased. HH pays the remaining 40 percent the month after purchase.

EXHIBIT 7.3

Inventory Purchases Budget

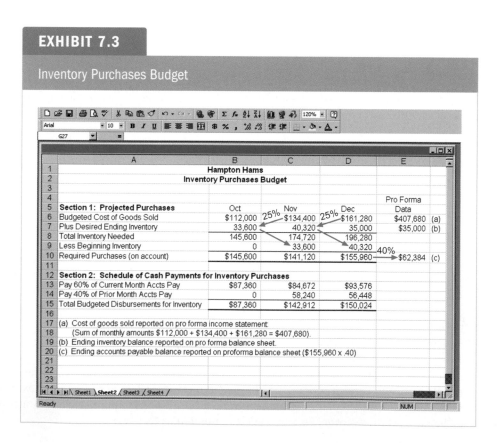

	A	B	C	D	E
1		Hampton Hams			
2		Inventory Purchases Budget			
3					
4					Pro Forma
5	**Section 1: Projected Purchases**	Oct	Nov	Dec	Data
6	Budgeted Cost of Goods Sold	$112,000 25%	$134,400 25%	$161,280	$407,680 (a)
7	Plus Desired Ending Inventory	33,600	40,320	35,000	$35,000 (b)
8	Total Inventory Needed	145,600	174,720	196,280	
9	Less Beginning Inventory	0	33,600	40,320 40%	
10	Required Purchases (on account)	$145,600	$141,120	$155,960	$62,384 (c)
11					
12	**Section 2: Schedule of Cash Payments for Inventory Purchases**				
13	Pay 60% of Current Month Accts Pay	$87,360	$84,672	$93,576	
14	Pay 40% of Prior Month Accts Pay	0	58,240	56,448	
15	Total Budgeted Disbursements for Inventory	$87,360	$142,912	$150,024	
16					
17	(a) Cost of goods sold reported on pro forma income statement.				
18	(Sum of monthly amounts $112,000 + $134,400 + $161,280 = $407,680).				
19	(b) Ending inventory balance reported on pro forma balance sheet.				
20	(c) Ending accounts payable balance reported on proforma balance sheet ($155,960 x .40)				
21					
22					
23					

Cash payments are projected as follows (amounts are rounded to the nearest whole dollar):

■ October cash payments for inventory are $87,360. Because the new store opens in October, no accounts payable balance from September remains to be paid in October. Cash payments for October equal 60 percent of October inventory purchases.

■ November cash payments for inventory are $142,912 (40 percent of October purchases + 60 percent of November purchases).

■ December cash payments for inventory are $150,024 (40 percent of November purchases + 60 percent of December purchases).

Pro Forma Financial Statement Data

The Pro Forma Data column in the inventory purchases budget displays three figures HH will report on the quarter-end budgeted financial statements. The $407,680 *cost of goods sold* reported on the pro forma income statement (shown later in Exhibit 7.6) is the sum of the monthly cost of goods sold amounts ($112,000 + $134,400 + $161,280 = $407,680).

The $35,000 *ending inventory* as of December 31, 2006, is reported on the pro forma balance sheet (shown later in Exhibit 7.7). December 31 is the last day of both the month of December and the three-month quarter represented by October, November, and December.

The $62,384 of *accounts payable* reported on the pro forma balance sheet (shown later in Exhibit 7.7) represents the 40 percent of December inventory purchases HH will pay for in January ($155,960 × .40).

Main Street Sales Company purchased $80,000 of inventory during June. Purchases are expected to increase by 2 percent per month in each of the next three months. Main Street makes all purchases on account. It normally pays cash to settle 70 percent of its accounts payable during the month of purchase and settles the remaining 30 percent in the month following purchase. Based on this information, determine the accounts payable balance Main Street would report on its July 31 balance sheet.

Answer

Purchases for the month of July are expected to be $81,600 ($80,000 × 1.02). Main Street will pay 70 percent of the resulting accounts payable in cash during July. The remaining 30 percent represents the expected balance in accounts payable as of July 31. Therefore, the balance would be $24,480 ($81,600 × 0.3).

CHECK YOURSELF 7.1

Selling and Administrative Expense Budget

Section 1 of Exhibit 7.4 shows the selling and administrative (S&A) expense budget for Hampton Hams' new store. Most of the projected expenses are self-explanatory; depreciation and interest, however, merit comment. The depreciation expense is based on projections in the *capital expenditures budget.* Although not presented in this chapter, the capital budget calls for the cash purchase of $130,000 of store fixtures. The fixtures were purchased on October 1. The supplier allows a thirty-day inspection period. As a result, payment for the fixtures was made at the end of October. The fixtures are expected to have a useful life of 10 years and a $10,000 salvage value. Using the straight-line method, HH estimates annual depreciation expense at $12,000 ([$130,000 − $10,000] ÷ 10). Monthly depreciation expense is $1,000 ($12,000 annual charge ÷ 12 months).

Interest expense is missing from the S&A expense budget. HH cannot estimate interest expense until it completes its borrowing projections. Expected borrowing (financing activities) and related interest expense are shown in the *cash budget.*

LO 5

Prepare a selling and administrative expense budget and related schedule of cash payments.

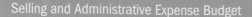

EXHIBIT 7.4

Selling and Administrative Expense Budget

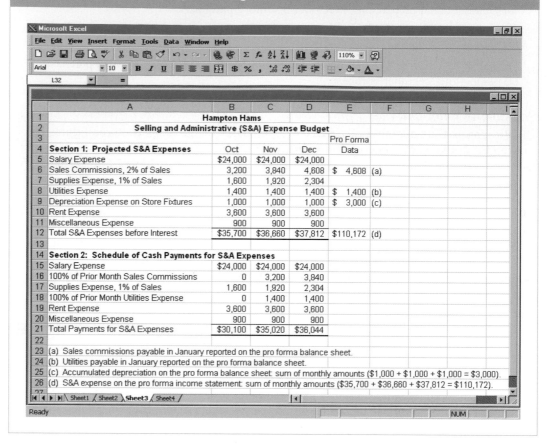

	A	B	C	D	E	F	G	H	I
1	Hampton Hams								
2	Selling and Administrative (S&A) Expense Budget								
3					Pro Forma				
4	**Section 1: Projected S&A Expenses**	Oct	Nov	Dec	Data				
5	Salary Expense	$24,000	$24,000	$24,000					
6	Sales Commissions, 2% of Sales	3,200	3,840	4,608	$ 4,608 (a)				
7	Supplies Expense, 1% of Sales	1,600	1,920	2,304					
8	Utilities Expense	1,400	1,400	1,400	$ 1,400 (b)				
9	Depreciation Expense on Store Fixtures	1,000	1,000	1,000	$ 3,000 (c)				
10	Rent Expense	3,600	3,600	3,600					
11	Miscellaneous Expense	900	900	900					
12	Total S&A Expenses before Interest	$35,700	$36,660	$37,812	$110,172 (d)				
13									
14	**Section 2: Schedule of Cash Payments for S&A Expenses**								
15	Salary Expense	$24,000	$24,000	$24,000					
16	100% of Prior Month Sales Commissions	0	3,200	3,840					
17	Supplies Expense, 1% of Sales	1,600	1,920	2,304					
18	100% of Prior Month Utilities Expense	0	1,400	1,400					
19	Rent Expense	3,600	3,600	3,600					
20	Miscellaneous Expense	900	900	900					
21	Total Payments for S&A Expenses	$30,100	$35,020	$36,044					
22									
23	(a) Sales commissions payable in January reported on the pro forma balance sheet.								
24	(b) Utilities payable in January reported on the pro forma balance sheet.								
25	(c) Accumulated depreciation on the pro forma balance sheet: sum of monthly amounts ($1,000 + $1,000 + $1,000 = $3,000).								
26	(d) S&A expense on the pro forma income statement: sum of monthly amounts ($35,700 + $36,660 + $37,812 = $110,172).								

Schedule of Cash Payments for Selling and Administrative Expenses

Section 2 of the S&A expense budget shows the schedule of cash payments. There are several differences between the S&A expenses recognized on the pro forma income statement and the cash payments for S&A expenses. First, Hampton Hams' pays sales commissions and utilities expense the month following their incurrence. Since the store opens in October there are no payments due from September. Cash payments for sales commissions and utilities in October are zero. In November, HH will pay the October expenses for these items and in December it will pay the November sales commissions and utility expenses. Depreciation expense does not affect the cash payments schedule. The cash outflow for the store fixtures occurs when the assets are purchased, not when they are depreciated. The cost of the investment in store fixtures is in the cash budget, not in the cash outflow for S&A expenses.

Pro Forma Financial Statement Data

The Pro Forma Data column of the S&A expense budget displays four figures HH will report on the quarter-end budgeted financial statements. The first and second figures are the sales commissions payable ($4,608) and utilities payable ($1,400) on the pro forma balance sheet in Exhibit 7.7. Because December sales commissions and utilities expense are not paid until January, these amounts represent liabilities as of December 31. The third figure in the column ($3,000) is the amount of accumulated depreciation on the pro forma balance sheet in Exhibit 7.7. Since depreciation accumulates, the $3,000 balance is the sum of the monthly depreciation amounts ($1,000 + $1,000 + $1,000 = $3,000). The final figure in the Pro Forma Data column ($110,172) is the total S&A expenses reported on the pro forma income statement in Exhibit 7.6. The total S&A expense is the sum of the monthly amounts ($35,700 + $36,660 + 37,812 = $110,172).

Cash Budget

Little is more important to business success than effective cash management. If a company experiences cash shortages, it will be unable to pay its debts and may be forced into bankruptcy. If excess cash accumulates, a business loses the opportunity to earn investment income or reduce interest costs by repaying debt. Preparing a **cash budget** alerts management to anticipated cash shortages or excess cash balances. Management can plan financing activities, making advance arrangements to cover anticipated shortages by borrowing and planning to repay past borrowings and make appropriate investments when excess cash is expected.

Prepare a cash budget.

The cash budget is divided into three major sections: (1) a cash receipts section, (2) a cash payments section, and (3) a financing section. Much of the data needed to prepare the cash budget are included in the cash receipts and payments schedules previously discussed; however, further refinements to project financing needs and interest costs are sometimes necessary. The completed cash budget is shown in Exhibit 7.5.

Cash Receipts Section

The total cash available (Exhibit 7.5, row 7) is determined by adding the beginning cash balance to the cash receipts from customers. There is no beginning cash balance in October because the new store is opening that month. The November beginning cash balance is the October ending cash balance. The December beginning cash balance is the November ending cash balance. Cash receipts from customers comes from the *schedule of cash receipts* in the sales budget (Exhibit 7.2, section 2, row 13).

EXHIBIT 7.5

Cash Budget

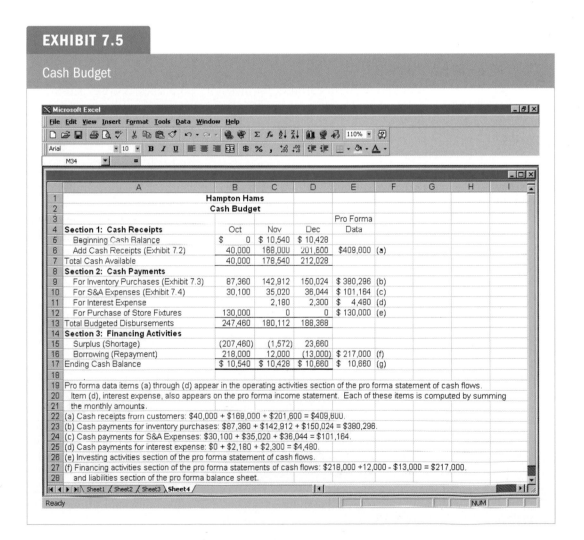

REALITY BYTES

Budgeting in Governmental Entities

This chapter has presented several reasons organizations should prepare budgets, but for governmental entities, budgets are not simply good planning tools—law requires them. If a manager at a commercial enterprise does not accomplish the budget objectives established for his or her part of the business, the manager may receive a poor performance evaluation. At worst, they may be fired. If managers of governmental agencies spend more than their budgets allow, they may have broken the law. In some cases the manager could be required to personally repay the amount by which the budget was exceeded. Since governmental budgets are enacted by the relevant elected bodies, to violate the budget is to break the law.

Because budgets are so important for governments and are not to be exceeded, government accounting practices require that budgeted amounts be formally entered into the bookkeeping system. As you learned in your first course of accounting, companies do not make formal accounting entries when they order goods; they only make an entry when the goods are received. Governmental accounting systems are different. Each time goods or services are ordered by a government, an "encumbrance" is recorded against the budgeted amount so that agencies do not commit to spend more money than their budgets allow.

Cash Payments Section

Cash payments include expected cash outflows for inventory purchases, S&A expenses, interest expense, and investments. The cash payments for inventory purchases comes from the *schedule of cash payments for inventory purchases* (Exhibit 7.3, section 2, row 15). The cash payments for S&A expenses comes from the *schedule of cash payments for S&A expenses* (Exhibit 7.4, section 2, row 21).

HH borrows or repays principal and pays interest on the last day of each month. The cash payments for interest are determined by multiplying the loan balance for the month by the monthly interest rate. Since there is no outstanding debt during October, there is no interest payment at the end of October. HH expects outstanding debt of $218,000 during the month of November. The bank charges interest at the rate of 12% per year, or 1% per month. The November interest expense and cash payment for interest is $2,180 ($218,000 × .01). The outstanding loan balance during December is $230,000. The December interest expense and cash payment for interest is $2,300 ($230,000 × .01). Determining the amount to borrow or repay at the end of each month is discussed in more detail in the next section of the text.

Finally, the cash payment for the store fixtures comes from the *capital expenditures budget* (not shown in this chapter).

Financing Section

HH has a line of credit under which it can borrow or repay principal in increments of $1,000 at the end of each month as needed. HH desires to maintain an ending cash balance of at least $10,000 each month. With the $207,460 projected cash shortage in row 15 of the cash budget ($40,000 cash balance in row 7 less $247,460 budgeted cash payments in row 13), HH must borrow $218,000 on October 31 to maintain an ending cash balance of at least $10,000. This $218,000 balance is outstanding during November. On November 30, HH must borrow an additional $12,000 to cover the November projected cash shortage of $1,572 plus the $10,000 desired ending cash balance. HH projects a surplus of $23,660 for the month of December. This surplus will allow HH to repay $13,000 of debt and still maintain the desired $10,000 cash balance.

Pro Forma Financial Statement Data

Figures in the Pro Forma Data column of the cash budget (Exhibit 7.5) are alphabetically referenced. The cash receipts from customers, item (a), and the cash payment items (b), (c), and (d) are reported in the operating activities section of the pro forma statement of cash flows (Exhibit 7.8). The interest expense, item (d), is also reported on the pro forma income statement (Exhibit 7.6). The figures are determined by summing the monthly amounts. The $130,000 purchase of store fixtures, item (e), is reported in the investing activities section of the pro forma statement of cash flows. The $217,000 net borrowings, item (f), is reported in the financing activities section of the pro forma statement of cash flows (Exhibit 7.8) and also as a liability on the pro forma balance sheet (Exhibit 7.7). The $10,660 ending cash balance, item (g), is reported as the ending balance on the pro forma statement of cash flows and as an asset on the pro forma balance sheet.

CHECK YOURSELF 7.2

Astor Company expects to incur the following operating expenses during September: Salary Expense, $25,000; Utility Expense, $1,200; Depreciation Expense, $5,400; and Selling Expense, $14,000. In general, it pays operating expenses in cash in the month in which it incurs them. Based on this information alone, determine the total amount of cash outflow Astor would report in the Operating Activities section of the pro forma statement of cash flows.

Answer

Depreciation is not included in cash outflows because companies do not pay cash when they recognize depreciation expense. The total cash outflow is $40,200 ($25,000 + $1,200 + $14,000).

Pro Forma Income Statement

Exhibit 7.6 shows the budgeted income statement for Hampton Hams' new store. The figures for this statement come from Exhibits 7.2, 7.3, 7.4, and 7.5. The budgeted income statement provides an advance estimate of the new store's expected profitability. If expected profitability is unsatisfactory, management could decide to abandon the project or modify planned activity. Perhaps HH could lease less costly store space, pay employees a lower rate, or reduce the number of employees hired. The pricing strategy could also be examined for possible changes.

Budgets are usually prepared using spreadsheets or computerized mathematical models that allow managers to easily undertake "what-if" analysis. What if the growth rate differs from expectations? What if interest rates increase or decrease? Exhibits 7.2 through 7.5 in this chapter were prepared using Microsoft Excel. When variables such as growth rate, collection assumptions, or interest rates are changed, the spreadsheet software instantly recalculates the budgets. Although managers remain responsible for data analysis and decision making, computer technology offers powerful tools to assist in those tasks.

Prepare a pro forma income statement, balance sheet, and statement of cash flows.

EXHIBIT 7.6

HAMPTON HAMS
Pro Forma Income Statement
For the Quarter Ended December 31, 2006

		Data Source
Sales Revenue	$582,400	Exhibit 7.2
Cost of Goods Sold	(407,680)	Exhibit 7.3
Gross Margin	174,720	
Selling and Administrative Expenses	(110,172)	Exhibit 7.4
Operating Income	64,548	
Interest Expense	(4,480)	Exhibit 7.5
Net Income	$ 60,068	

Pro Forma Balance Sheet

Most of the figures on the pro forma balance sheet in Exhibit 7.7 have been explained. The new store has no contributed capital because its operations will be financed through debt and retained earnings. The amount of retained earnings equals the amount of net income because no earnings from prior periods exist and no distributions are planned.

EXHIBIT 7.7

HAMPTON HAMS
Pro Forma Balance Sheet
As of the Quarter Ended December 31, 2006

			Data Source
Assets			
Cash		$ 10,660	Exhibit 7.5
Accounts Receivable		172,800	Exhibit 7.2
Inventory		35,000	Exhibit 7.3
Store Fixtures	$130,000		Exhibit 7.4 Discussion
Accumulated Depreciation	(3,000)		Exhibit 7.4 Discussion
Book Value of Store Fixtures		127,000	
Total Assets		$345,460	
Liabilities			
Accounts Payable		$ 62,384	Exhibit 7.3
Sales Commissions Payable		4,608	Exhibit 7.4
Utilities Payable		1,400	Exhibit 7.4
Line of Credit Borrowings		217,000	Exhibit 7.5
Equity			
Retained Earnings		60,068	
Total Liabilities and Equity		$345,460	

Pro Forma Statement of Cash Flows

Exhibit 7.8 shows the pro forma statement of cash flows. All information for this statement comes from the cash budget in Exhibit 7.5.

EXHIBIT 7.8

HAMPTON HAMS
Pro Forma Statement of Cash Flows
For the Quarter Ended December 31, 2006

Cash Flow from Operating Activities		
Cash Receipts from Customers	$409,600	
Cash Payments for Inventory	(380,296)	
Cash Payments for S&A Expenses	(101,164)	
Cash Payments for Interest Expense	(4,480)	
Net Cash Flow for Operating Activities		$ (76,340)
Cash Flow from Investing Activities		
Cash Outflow to Purchase Fixtures		(130,000)
Cash Flow from Financing Activities		
Inflow from Borrowing on Line of Credit		217,000
Net Change in Cash		10,660
Plus Beginning Cash Balance		0
Ending Cash Balance		$ 10,660

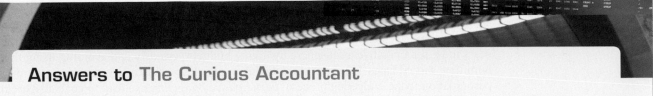

Answers to The Curious Accountant

Budget preparation at the USOC is complicated by the fact that the timing of its revenues does not match the timing of its expenditures. The USOC spends a lot of money helping to train athletes for the United States Olympic team. Training takes place year-round, every year, for many athletes. The USOC's training facilities in Colorado must also be maintained continuously.

Conversely, much of the USOC's revenues are earned in big batches, received every two years. This money comes from fees the USOC receives for the rights to broadcast the Olympic games on television in the United States. Most companies have a one-year budget cycle during which they attempt to anticipate the coming year's revenues and expenses. This model would not work well for the USOC.

Every business, like every family, faces its own set of circumstances. Those individuals responsible for preparing an entity's budget must have a thorough understanding of the environment in which the entity operates. This is the reason the budget process must be participatory if it is to be successful. No one person, or small group, can anticipate all the issues that will face a large organization in the coming budget period; they need input from employees at all levels.

How do pro forma financial statements differ from the financial statements presented in a company's annual report to stockholders?

Answer

Pro forma financial statements are based on estimates and projections about business events that a company expects to occur in the future. The financial statements presented in a company's annual report to stockholders are based on historical events that occurred prior to the preparation of the statements.

CHECK YOURSELF 7.3

A Look Back

The planning of financial matters is called *budgeting.* The degree of detail in a company's budget depends on the budget period. Generally, the shorter the time period, the more specific the plans. *Strategic planning* involves long-term plans, such as the overall objectives of the business. Examples of strategic planning include which products to manufacture and sell and which market niches to pursue. Strategic plans are stated in broad, descriptive terms. Capital budgeting deals with intermediate investment planning. *Operations budgeting* focuses on short-term plans and is used to create the master budget.

A budgeting committee is responsible for consolidating numerous departmental budgets into a master budget for the whole company. The *master budget* has detailed objectives stated in specific amounts; it describes how management intends to achieve its objectives. The master budget usually covers one year. Budgeting supports planning, coordination, performance measurement, and corrective action.

Employees may be uncomfortable with budgets, which can be constraining. Budgets set standards by which performance is evaluated. To establish an effective budget system, management should recognize the effect on human behavior of budgeting. Upper-level management must set a positive atmosphere by taking budgets seriously and avoiding using them to humiliate subordinates. One way to create the proper atmosphere is to encourage subordinates' participation in the budgeting process; *participative budgeting* can lead to goals that are more realistic about what can be accomplished and to establish a team effort in trying to reach those goals.

The primary components of the master budget are the *operating budgets,* the *capital budgets,* and the *pro forma financial statements.* The budgeting process begins with preparing the operating budgets, which consist of detailed schedules and budgets prepared by various company departments. The first operating budget to be prepared is the sales budget. The detailed operating budgets for inventory purchases and S&A expenses are based on the projected sales from the sales budget. The information in the schedules of cash receipts (prepared in conjunction with the sales budget) and cash payments (prepared in conjunction with the inventory purchases and S&A expense budgets) is used in preparing the cash budget. The cash budget subtracts cash payments from cash receipts; the resulting cash surplus or shortage determines the company's financing activities.

The capital budget describes the company's long-term plans regarding investments in facilities, equipment, new products, or other lines of business. The information from the capital budget is used as input to several of the operating budgets.

The pro forma financial statements are prepared from information in the operating budgets. The operating budgets for sales, inventory purchases, and S&A expenses contain information that is used to prepare the income statement and balance sheet. The cash budget includes the amount of interest expense reported on the income statement, the ending cash balance, the capital acquisitions reported on the balance sheet, and most of the information included in the statement of cash flows.

>> A Look Forward

Once a company has completed its budget, it has defined its plans. Then the plans must be followed. The next chapter investigates the techniques used to evaluate performance. You will learn to compare actual results to budgets, to calculate variances, and to identify the parties who are normally accountable for deviations from expectations. Finally, you will learn about the human impact management must consider in taking corrective action when employees fail to accomplish budget goals.

SELF-STUDY REVIEW PROBLEM

A step-by-step audio-narrated series of slides is provided on the text website at www.mhhe.com/edmonds2008.

The Getaway Gift Company operates a chain of small gift shops that are located in prime vacation towns. Getaway is considering opening a new store on January 1, 2007. Getaway's president recently attended a business seminar that explained how formal budgets could be useful in judging the new store's likelihood of succeeding. Assume you are the company's accountant. The president has asked you to explain the budgeting process and to provide sample reports that show the new store's operating expectations for the first three months (January, February, and March). Respond to the following specific requirements:

Required

a. List the operating budgets and schedules included in a master budget.

b. Explain the difference between pro forma financial statements and the financial statements presented in a company's annual reports to shareholders.

c. Prepare a sample sales budget and a schedule of expected cash receipts using the following assumptions. Getaway estimates January sales will be $400,000 of which $100,000 will be cash and $300,000 will be credit. The ratio of cash sales to sales on account is expected to remain constant over the three-month period. The company expects sales to increase 10 percent per month. The company expects to collect 100 percent of the accounts receivable generated by credit sales in the month following the sale. Use this information to determine the amount of accounts receivable that Getaway would report on the March 31 pro forma balance sheet and the amount of sales it would report on the first quarter pro forma income statement.

d. Prepare a sample inventory purchases budget using the following assumptions. Cost of goods sold is 60 percent of sales. The company desires to maintain a minimum ending inventory equal to 25 percent of the following month's cost of goods sold. Getaway makes all inventory purchases on account. The company pays 70 percent of accounts payable in the month of purchase. It pays the remaining 30 percent in the following month. Prepare a schedule of expected cash payments for inventory purchases. Use this information to determine the amount of cost of goods sold Getaway would report on the first quarter pro forma income statement and the amounts of ending inventory and accounts payable it would report on the March 31 pro forma balance sheet.

Solution to Requirement a

A master budget would include (1) a sales budget and schedule of cash receipts, (2) an inventory purchases budget and schedule of cash payments for inventory, (3) a general, selling, and administrative expenses budget and a schedule of cash payments related to these expenses, and (4) a cash budget.

Solution to Requirement b

Pro forma statements result from the operating budgets listed in the response to Requirement *a*. Pro forma statements describe the results of expected future events. In contrast, the financial statements presented in a company's annual report reflect the results of events that have actually occurred in the past.

Solution to Requirement c

General Information				
				Pro Forma
Sales growth rate		10%		**Statement Data**
Sales Budget	January	February	March	
Sales				
Cash sales	$100,000	$110,000	$121,000	
Sales on account	300,000	330,000	363,000	$ 363,000*
Total sales	$400,000	$440,000	$484,000	$1,324,000†
Schedule of Cash Receipts				
Current cash sales	$100,000	$110,000	$121,000	
Plus 100% of previous month's credit sales	0	300,000	330,000	
Total budgeted collections	$100,000	$410,000	$451,000	

*Ending accounts receivable balance reported on March 31 pro forma balance sheet.

†Sales revenue reported on first quarter pro forma income statement (sum of monthly sales).

Solution to Requirement d

General information			
Cost of goods sold percentage	60%		Pro Forma
Desired ending inventory percentage of CGS	25%		Statement Data

Inventory Purchases Budget	January	February	March	
Budgeted cost of goods sold	$240,000	$264,000	$290,400	$794,400*
Plus: Desired ending inventory	66,000	72,600	79,860	79,860†
Inventory needed	306,000	336,600	370,260	
Less: Beginning inventory	0	(66,000)	(72,600)	
Required purchases	$306,000	$270,600	$297,660	89,298‡
Schedule of Cash Payments for Inventory Purchases				
70% of current purchases	$214,200	$189,420	$208,362	
30% of prior month's purchases	0	91,800	81,180	
Total budgeted payments for inventory	$214,200	$281,220	$289,542	

*Cost of goods sold reported on first quarter pro forma income statement (sum of monthly amounts).

†Ending inventory balance reported on March 31 pro forma balance sheet.

‡Ending accounts payable balance reported on pro forma balance sheet ($297,660 × 0.3).

KEY TERMS

Budgeting 293

Capital budget 296

Capital budgeting 294

Cash budget 303

Master budget 296

Operating budgets 296

Participative budgeting 296

Perpetual (continuous)
  budgeting 295

Pro forma financial
  statements 296

Strategic planning 294

QUESTIONS

1. Budgets are useful only for small companies that can estimate sales with accuracy. Do you agree with this statement?

2. Why does preparing the master budget require a committee?

3. What are the three levels of planning? Explain each briefly.

4. What is the primary factor that distinguishes the three different levels of planning from each other?

5. What is the advantage of using a perpetual budget instead of the traditional annual budget?

6. What are the advantages of budgeting?

7. How may budgets be used as a measure of performance?

8. Ken Shilov, manager of the marketing department, tells you that "budgeting simply does not work." He says that he made budgets for his employees and when he reprimanded them for failing to accomplish budget goals, he got unfounded excuses. Suggest how Mr. Shilov could encourage employee cooperation.

9. What is a master budget?

10. What is the normal starting point in developing the master budget?

11. How does the level of inventory affect the production budget? Why is it important to manage the level of inventory?

12. What are the components of the cash budget? Describe each.

13. The primary reason for preparing a cash budget is to determine the amount of cash to include on the budgeted balance sheet. Do you agree or disagree with this statement? Explain.

14. What information does the pro forma income statement provide? How does its preparation depend on the operating budgets?

15. How does the pro forma statement of cash flows differ from the cash budget?

MULTIPLE-CHOICE QUESTIONS

Multiple-choice questions are provided on the text website at www.mhhe.com/edmonds2008.

EXERCISES—SERIES A

All Exercises in Series A are available with McGraw-Hill's Homework Manager®.

Exercise 7-1A   *Budget responsibility*

L.O. 1, 2

Lucy Whitlaw, the accountant, is a perfectionist. No one can do the job as well as she can. Indeed, she has found budget information provided by the various departments to be worthless. She must change everything they give her. She has to admit that her estimates have not always been accurate, but she shudders to think of what would happen if she used the information supplied by the marketing and operating departments. No one seems to care about accuracy. Indeed, some of the marketing staff have even become insulting. When Ms. Whitlaw confronted one of the salesmen with the fact that he was behind in meeting his budgeted sales forecast, he responded by saying, "They're your numbers. Why don't you go out and make the sales? It's a heck of a lot easier to sit there in your office and make up numbers than it is to get out and get the real work done." Ms. Whitlaw reported the incident, but, of course, nothing was done about it.

Required

Write a short report suggesting how the budgeting process could be improved.

Exercise 7-2A   *Preparing the sales budget*

L.O. 3, 7

DigiCam, which expects to start operations on January 1, 2006, will sell digital cameras in shopping malls. DigiCam has budgeted sales as indicated in the following table. The company expects a 10 percent increase in sales per month for February and March. The ratio of cash sales to sales on account will remain stable from January through March.

Sales	January	February	March
Cash sales	$ 40,000	?	?
Sales on account	60,000	?	?
Total budgeted sales	$100,000	?	?

Required

a. Complete the sales budget by filling in the missing amounts.

b. Determine the amount of sales revenue DigiCam will report on its first quarter pro forma income statement.

Exercise 7-3A *Preparing a schedule of cash receipts*

The budget director of Tricia's Florist has prepared the following sales budget. The company had $120,000 in accounts receivable on July 1. Tricia's Florist normally collects 100 percent of accounts receivable in the month following the month of sale.

Sales	July	August	September
Sales Budget			
Cash sales	$ 40,000	$ 44,000	$ 48,400
Sales on account	90,000	99,000	108,900
Total budgeted sales	$130,000	$143,000	$157,300
Schedule of Cash Receipts			
Current cash sales	?	?	?
Plus collections from accounts receivable	?	?	?
Total budgeted collections	$160,000	$134,000	$147,400

Required

a. Complete the schedule of cash receipts by filling in the missing amounts.
b. Determine the amount of accounts receivable the company will report on its third quarter pro forma balance sheet.

Exercise 7-4A *Preparing sales budgets with different assumptions*

Gilbert Corporation, which has three divisions, is preparing its sales budget. Each division expects a different growth rate because economic conditions vary in different regions of the country. The growth expectations per quarter are 2 percent for East Division, 3 percent for West Division, and 5 percent for South Division.

Division	First Quarter	Second Quarter	Third Quarter	Fourth Quarter
East Division	$260,000	?	?	?
West Division	370,000	?	?	?
South Division	170,000	?	?	?

Required

a. Complete the sales budget by filling in the missing amounts. (Round figures to the nearest dollar.)
b. Determine the amount of sales revenue that the company will report on its quarterly pro forma income statements.

Exercise 7-5A *Determining cash receipts from accounts receivable*

Dress Delivery operates a mail-order business that sells clothes designed for frequent travelers. It had sales of $580,000 in December. Because Dress Delivery is in the mail-order business, all sales are made on account. The company expects a 30 percent drop in sales for January. The balance in the Accounts Receivable account on December 31 was $90,400 and is budgeted to be $67,600 as of January 31. Dress Delivery normally collects accounts receivable in the month following the month of sale.

Required

a. Determine the amount of cash Dress Delivery expects to collect from accounts receivable during January.
b. Is it reasonable to assume that sales will decline in January for this type of business? Why or why not?

Exercise 7-6A *Using judgment in making a sales forecast*

Sweet Taste Company operates a candy store located in a large shopping mall.

Required

Write a brief memo describing the sales pattern that you would expect Sweet Taste to experience during the year. In which months will sales likely be high? In which months will sales likely be low? Explain why.

Exercise 7-7A *Preparing an inventory purchases budget*   L.O. 4

Moonlight Company sells lamps and other lighting fixtures. The purchasing department manager prepared the following inventory purchases budget. Moonlight's policy is to maintain an ending inventory balance equal to 10 percent of the following month's cost of goods sold. April's budgeted cost of goods sold is $90,000.

	January	February	March
Budgeted cost of goods sold	$75,000	$80,000	$86,000
Plus: Desired ending inventory	8,000	?	?
Inventory needed	83,000	?	?
Less: Beginning inventory	16,000	?	?
Required purchases (on account)	$67,000	$80,600	$86,400

Required

a. Complete the inventory purchases budget by filling in the missing amounts.
b. Determine the amount of cost of goods sold the company will report on its first quarter pro forma income statement.
c. Determine the amount of ending inventory the company will report on its pro forma balance sheet at the end of the first quarter.

Exercise 7-8A *Preparing a schedule of cash payments for inventory purchases*   L.O. 4

Book Depot buys books and magazines directly from publishers and distributes them to grocery stores. The wholesaler expects to purchase the following inventory.

	April	May	June
Required purchases (on account)	$60,000	$80,000	$100,000

Book Depot's accountant prepared the following schedule of cash payments for inventory purchases. Book Depot's suppliers require that 90 percent of purchases on account be paid in the month of purchase; the remaining 10 percent are paid in the month following the month of purchase.

Schedule of Cash Payments for Inventory Purchases			
	April	May	June
Payment for current accounts payable	$54,000	?	?
Payment for previous accounts payable	4,000	?	?
Total budgeted payments for inventory	$58,000	$78,000	$98,000

Required

a. Complete the schedule of cash payments for inventory purchases by filling in the missing amounts.
b. Determine the amount of accounts payable the company will report on its pro forma balance sheet at the end of the second quarter.

L.O. 4

Exercise 7-9A *Determining the amount of expected inventory purchases and cash payments*

Sharp Company, which sells electric razors, had $356,000 of cost of goods sold during the month of June. The company projects a 5 percent increase in cost of goods sold during July. The inventory balance as of June 30 is $36,800, and the desired ending inventory balance for July is $31,800. Sharp pays cash to settle 80 percent of its purchases on account during the month of purchase and pays the remaining 20 percent in the month following the purchase. The accounts payable balance as of June 30 was $44,000.

Required

a. Determine the amount of purchases budgeted for July.
b. Determine the amount of cash payments budgeted for inventory purchases in July.

L.O. 5

Exercise 7-10A *Preparing a schedule of cash payments for selling and administrative expenses*

The budget director for Vase Window Cleaning Services prepared the following list of expected operating expenses. All expenses requiring cash payments are paid for in the month incurred except salary expense and insurance. Salary is paid in the month following the month in which it is incurred. The insurance premium for six months is paid on October 1. October is the first month of operations; accordingly, there are no beginning account balances.

	October	November	December
Budgeted Operating Expenses			
Equipment lease expense	$ 7,000	$ 7,000	$ 7,000
Salary expense	6,400	6,800	6,900
Cleaning supplies	2,600	2,860	3,146
Insurance expense	1,000	1,000	1,000
Depreciation on computer	1,600	1,600	1,600
Rent	1,800	1,800	1,800
Miscellaneous expenses	600	600	600
Total operating expenses	$21,000	$21,660	$22,046
Schedule of Cash Payments for Operating Expenses			
Equipment lease expense	?	?	?
Prior month's salary expense, 100%	?	?	?
Cleaning supplies	?	?	?
Insurance premium	?	?	?
Depreciation on computer	?	?	?
Rent	?	?	?
Miscellaneous expenses	?	?	?
Total disbursements for operating expenses	$18,000	$18,660	$19,346

Required

a. Complete the schedule of cash payments for operating expenses by filling in the missing amounts.
b. Determine the amount of salaries payable the company will report on its pro forma balance sheet at the end of the fourth quarter.
c. Determine the amount of prepaid insurance the company will report on its pro forma balance sheet at the end of the fourth quarter.

L.O. 4

Exercise 7-11A *Preparing inventory purchases budgets with different assumptions*

Executive officers of Grant Company are wrestling with their budget for the next year. The following are two different sales estimates provided by two difference sources.

Source of Estimate	First Quarter	Second Quarter	Third Quarter	Fourth Quarter
Sales manager	$500,000	$400,000	$360,000	$640,000
Marketing consultant	550,000	480,000	400,000	600,000

Grant's past experience indicates that cost of goods sold is about 70 percent of sales revenue. The company tries to maintain 10 percent of the next quarter's expected cost of goods sold as the current quarter's ending inventory. This year's ending inventory is $30,000. Next year's ending inventory is budgeted to be $32,000.

Required

a. Prepare an inventory purchases budget using the sales manager's estimate.
b. Prepare an inventory purchases budget using the marketing consultant's estimate.

Exercise 7-12A   *Determining the amount of cash payments and pro forma statement data for selling and administrative expenses*   **L.O. 5, 7**

January budgeted selling and administrative expenses for the retail shoe store that June Kesler plans to open on January 1, 2008, are as follows: sales commissions, $20,000; rent, $15,000; utilities, $5,000; depreciation, $4,000; and miscellaneous, $2,000. Utilities are paid in the month following their incursion. Other expenses are expected to be paid in cash in the month in which they are incurred.

Required

a. Determine the amount of budgeted cash payments for January selling and administrative expenses.
b. Determine the amount of utilities payable the store will report on the January 31st pro forma balance sheet.
c. Determine the amount of depreciation expense the store will report on the income statement for the year 2006, assuming that monthly depreciation remains the same for the entire year.

Exercise 7-13A   *Preparing a cash budget*   **L.O. 6, 7**

The accountant for Anne's Dress Shop prepared the following cash budget. Anne's desires to maintain a cash cushion of $14,000 at the end of each month. Funds are assumed to be borrowed and repaid on the last day of each month. Interest is charged at the rate of 2 percent per month.

Cash Budget	July	August	September
Section 1: Cash Receipts			
Beginning cash balance	$ 42,500	$?	$?
Add cash receipts	180,000	200,000	240,600
Total cash available (a)	222,500	?	?
Section 2: Cash Payments			
For inventory purchases	165,526	140,230	174,152
For S&A expenses	54,500	60,560	61,432
For interest expense	0	?	?
Total budgeted disbursements (b)	220,026	?	?
Section 3: Financing Activities			
Surplus (shortage)	2,474	?	?
Borrowing (repayments) (c)	11,526	?	?
Ending Cash Balance (a − b + c)	$ 14,000	$ 14,000	$ 14,000

Required

a. Complete the cash budget by filling in the missing amounts. Round all computations to the nearest whole dollar.
b. Determine the amount of net cash flows from operating activities Anne's will report on the third quarter pro forma statement of cash flows.
c. Determine the amount of net cash flows from financing activities Anne's will report on the third quarter pro forma statement of cash flows.

Exercise 7-14A   *Determining amount to borrow and pro forma statement balances*   **L.O. 6, 7**

Victoria Atwell owns a small restaurant in New York City. Ms. Atwell provided her accountant with the following summary information regarding expectations for the month of June. The balance in accounts receivable as of May 31 is $50,000. Budgeted cash and credit sales for June are $100,000 and $500,000, respectively. Credit sales are made through Visa and MasterCard and are collected rapidly. Ninety percent of credit sales is collected in the month of sale, and the remainder is collected in the following month. Ms. Atwell's suppliers do not extend credit. Consequently, she pays suppliers on the last day of the month. Cash payments for June are expected to be $620,000. Ms. Atwell has a line of credit that enables the restaurant to borrow funds on demand; however, they must be borrowed on the last day of the month. Interest is paid in cash also on the last day of the month. Ms. Atwell desires to maintain a $20,000 cash balance before the interest payment. Her annual interest rate is 9 percent.

Required

a. Compute the amount of funds Ms. Atwell needs to borrow for June.
b. Determine the amount of interest expense the restaurant will report on the June pro forma income statement.
c. What amount will the restaurant report as interest expense on the July pro forma balance sheet?

L.O. 7

Exercise 7-15A   *Preparing pro forma income statements with different assumptions*

Stan Hogan, the controller of Tameron Corporation, is trying to prepare a sales budget for the coming year. The income statements for the last four quarters follow.

	First Quarter	Second Quarter	Third Quarter	Fourth Quarter	Total
Sales revenue	$125,000	$120,000	$132,000	$223,000	$600,000
Cost of goods sold	75,000	72,000	79,200	133,800	360,000
Gross profit	50,000	48,000	52,800	89,200	240,000
Selling & admin. expense	25,000	24,000	26,400	44,600	120,000
Net income	$ 25,000	$ 24,000	$ 26,400	$ 44,600	$120,000

Historically, cost of goods sold is about 60 percent of sales revenue. Selling and administrative expenses are about 20 percent of sales revenue.

Joseph Tameron, the chief executive officer, told Mr. Hogan that he expected sales next year to be 10 percent above last year's level. However, Anita Chance, the vice president of sales, told Mr. Hogan that she believed sales growth would be only 5 percent.

Required

a. Prepare a pro forma income statement including quarterly budgets for the coming year using Mr. Tameron's estimate.
b. Prepare a pro forma income statement including quarterly budgets for the coming year using Ms. Chance's estimate.
c. Explain why two executive officers in the same company could have different estimates of future growth.

PROBLEMS—SERIES A

L.O. 3

eXcel

www.mhhe.com/edmonds2008

CHECK FIGURES
c. Feb: $96,000
   March $115,600

Problem 7-16A   *Preparing a sales budget and schedule of cash receipts*

Melburn Pointers Corporation expects to begin operations on January 1, 2008; it will operate as a specialty sales company that sells laser pointers over the Internet. Melburn expects sales in January 2008 to total $100,000 and to increase 10 percent per month in February and March. All sales are on account. Melburn expects to collect 60 percent of accounts receivable in the month of sale, 30 percent in the month following the sale, and 10 percent in the second month following the sale.

Required

a. Prepare a sales budget for the first quarter of 2008.
b. Determine the amount of sales revenue Melburn will report on the first 2008 quarterly pro forma income statement.
c. Prepare a cash receipts schedule for the first quarter of 2008.
d. Determine the amount of accounts receivable as of March 31, 2008.

Problem 7-17A *Preparing the inventory purchases budget and schedule of cash payments*

Rutledge, Inc., sells fireworks. The company's marketing director developed the following cost of goods sold budget for April, May, and June.

L.O. 4, 7

CHECK FIGURES
a. May: $53,000
c. June: $69,560

	April	May	June	July
Budgeted cost of goods sold	$40,000	$50,000	$80,000	$86,000

Rutledge had a beginning inventory balance of $3,600 on April 1 and a beginning balance in accounts payable of $14,800. The company desires to maintain an ending inventory balance equal to 10 percent of the next period's cost of goods sold. Rutledge makes all purchases on account. The company pays 60 percent of accounts payable in the month of purchase and the remaining 40 percent in the month following purchase.

Required

a. Prepare an inventory purchases budget for April, May, and June.
b. Determine the amount of ending inventory Rutledge will report on the end-of-quarter pro forma balance sheet.
c. Prepare a schedule of cash payments for inventory for April, May, and June.
d. Determine the balance in accounts payable Rutledge will report on the end-of-quarter pro forma balance sheet.

Problem 7-18A *Preparing pro forma income statements with different assumptions*

Top executive officers of Sakrow Company, a merchandising firm, are preparing the next year's budget. The controller has provided everyone with the current year's projected income statement.

L.O. 7

CHECK FIGURE
a. 12.75%

	Current Year
Sales Revenue	$2,000,000
Cost of Goods Sold	1,400,000
Gross Profit	600,000
Selling & Admin. Expenses	260,000
Net Income	$ 340,000

Cost of goods sold is usually 70 percent of sales revenue, and selling and administrative expenses are usually 10 percent of sales plus a fixed cost of $60,000. The president has announced that the company's goal is to increase net income by 15 percent.

Required

The following items are independent of each other.

a. What percentage increase in sales would enable the company to reach its goal? Support your answer with a pro forma income statement.
b. The market may become stagnant next year, and the company does not expect an increase in sales revenue. The production manager believes that an improved production procedure can cut cost of goods sold by 2 percent. What else can the company do to reach its goal? Prepare a pro forma income statement illustrating your proposal.

c. The company decides to escalate its advertising campaign to boost consumer recognition, which will increase selling and administrative expenses to $340,000. With the increased advertising, the company expects sales revenue to increase by 15 percent. Assume that cost of goods sold remains a constant proportion of sales. Can the company reach its goal?

L.O. 5, 6

Problem 7-19A   *Preparing a schedule of cash payments for selling and administrative expenses*

Larsen is a retail company specializing in men's hats. Its budget director prepared the list of expected operating expenses that follows. All items are paid when incurred except sales commissions and utilities, which are paid in the month following their incursion. July is the first month of operations, so there are no beginning account balances.

	July	August	September
Salary expense	$10,000	$10,000	$10,000
Sales commissions (4 percent of sales)	1,440	1,600	1,760
Supplies expense	360	400	440
Utilities	1,200	1,200	1,200
Depreciation on store equipment	2,600	2,600	2,600
Rent	6,600	6,600	6,600
Miscellaneous	720	720	720
Total S&A expenses before interest	$22,920	$23,120	$23,320

Required

a. Prepare a schedule of cash payments for selling and administrative expenses.
b. Determine the amount of utilities payable as of September 30.
c. Determine the amount of sales commissions payable as of September 30.

L.O. 6

Problem 7-20A   *Preparing a cash budget*

Guldry Medical Clinic has budgeted the following cash flows.

	January	February	March
Cash receipts	$100,000	$106,000	$126,000
Cash payments			
For inventory purchases	90,000	72,000	85,000
For S&A expenses	31,000	32,000	27,000

Guldry Medical had a cash balance of $8,000 on January 1. The company desires to maintain a cash cushion of $5,000. Funds are assumed to be borrowed, in increments of $1,000, and repaid on the last day of each month; the interest rate is 1 percent per month. Repayments may be made in any amount available. Guldry pays its vendors on the last day of the month also. The company had a $40,000 beginning balance in its line of credit liability account.

Required

Prepare a cash budget. (Round all computations to the nearest whole dollar.)

L.O. 3, 4, 5

Problem 7-21A   *Preparing budgets with multiple products*

Season Fruits Corporation wholesales peaches and oranges. Maria Deeter is working with the company's accountant to prepare next year's budget. Ms. Deeter estimates that sales will increase 5 percent annually for peaches and 10 percent for oranges. The current year's sales revenue data follow.

	First Quarter	Second Quarter	Third Quarter	Fourth Quarter	Total
Peaches	$240,000	$250,000	$300,000	$250,000	$1,040,000
Oranges	400,000	450,000	570,000	380,000	1,800,000
Total	$640,000	$700,000	$870,000	$630,000	$2,840,000

Based on the company's past experience, cost of goods sold is usually 60 percent of sales revenue. Company policy is to keep 20 percent of the next period's estimated cost of goods sold as the current period's ending inventory. (*Hint:* Use the cost of goods sold for the first quarter to determine the beginning inventory for the first quarter.)

Required

a. Prepare the company's sales budget for the next year for each quarter by individual product.
b. If the selling and administrative expenses are estimated to be $700,000, prepare the company's budgeted annual income statement.
c. Ms. Deeter estimates next year's ending inventory will be $34,000 for peaches and $56,000 for oranges. Prepare the company's inventory purchases budgets for the next year showing quarterly figures by product.

Problem 7-22A *Preparing a master budget for retail company with no beginning account balances*

Thigpen Company is a retail company that specializes in selling outdoor camping equipment. The company is considering opening a new store on October 1, 2007. The company president formed a planning committee to prepare a master budget for the first three months of operation. As budget coordinator, you have been assigned the following tasks.

Required

a. October sales are estimated to be $120,000 of which 40 percent will be cash and 60 percent will be credit. The company expects sales to increase at the rate of 25 percent per month. Prepare a sales budget.
b. The company expects to collect 100 percent of the accounts receivable generated by credit sales in the month following the sale. Prepare a schedule of cash receipts.
c. The cost of goods sold is 60 percent of sales. The company desires to maintain a minimum ending inventory equal to 10 percent of the next month's cost of goods sold. Ending inventory of December is expected to be $12,000. Assume that all purchases are made on account. Prepare an inventory purchases budget.
d. The company pays 70 percent of accounts payable in the month of purchase and the remaining 30 percent in the following month. Prepare a cash payments budget for inventory purchases.
e. Budgeted selling and administrative expenses per month follow.

Salary expense (fixed)	$18,000
Sales commissions	5 percent of Sales
Supplies expense	2 percent of Sales
Utilities (fixed)	$1,400
Depreciation on store equipment (fixed)*	$4,000
Rent (fixed)	$4,800
Miscellaneous (fixed)	$1,200

*The capital expenditures budget indicates that Thigpen will spend $164,000 on October 1 for store fixtures, which are expected to have a $20,000 salvage value and a three-year (36-month) useful life.

Use this information to prepare a selling and administrative expenses budget.
f. Utilities and sales commissions are paid the month after they are incurred; all other expenses are paid in the month in which they are incurred. Prepare a cash payments budget for selling and administrative expenses.

g. Thigpen borrows funds, in increments of $1,000, and repays them on the last day of the month. Repayments may be made in any amount available. The company also pays its vendors on the last day of the month. It pays interest of 1 percent per month in cash on the last day of the month. To be prudent, the company desires to maintain a $12,000 cash cushion. Prepare a cash budget.

h. Prepare a pro forma income statement for the quarter.

i. Prepare a pro forma balance sheet at the end of the quarter.

j. Prepare a pro forma statement of cash flows for the quarter.

L.O. 2

Problem 7-23A   *Behavioral impact of budgeting*

Cooney Corporation has three divisions, each operating as a responsibility center. To provide an incentive for divisional executive officers, the company gives divisional management a bonus equal to 20 percent of the excess of actual net income over budgeted net income. The following is Walker Division's current year's performance.

	Current Year
Sales revenue	$3,600,000
Cost of goods sold	2,160,000
Gross profit	1,440,000
Selling & admin. expenses	720,000
Net income	$ 720,000

The president has just received next year's budget proposal from the vice president in charge of Walker Division. The proposal budgets a 5 percent increase in sales revenue with an extensive explanation about stiff market competition. The president is puzzled. Walker has enjoyed revenue growth of around 10 percent for each of the past five years. The president had consistently approved the division's budget proposals based on 5 percent growth in the past. This time, the president wants to show that he is not a fool. "I will impose a 15 percent revenue increase to teach them a lesson!" the president says to himself smugly.

Assume that cost of goods sold and selling and administrative expenses remain stable in proportion to sales.

Required

a. Prepare the budgeted income statement based on Walker Division's proposal of a 5 percent increase.

b. If growth is actually 10 percent as usual, how much bonus would Walker Division's executive officers receive if the president had approved the division's proposal?

c. Prepare the budgeted income statement based on the 15 percent increase the president imposed.

d. If the actual results turn out to be a 10 percent increase as usual, how much bonus would Walker Division's executive officers receive since the president imposed a 15 percent increase?

e. Propose a better budgeting procedure for Cooney.

EXERCISES—SERIES B

L.O. 1, 2

Exercise 7-1B   *Budget responsibility*

Wes Snowden, the controller of Howard Industries, is very popular. He is easygoing and does not offend anybody. To develop the company's most recent budget, Mr. Snowden first asked all department managers to prepare their own budgets. He then added together the totals from the department budgets to produce the company budget. When Emily Pruett, Howard's president, reviewed the company budget, she sighed and asked, "Is our company a charitable organization?"

Required

Write a brief memo describing deficiencies in the budgeting process and suggesting improvements.

Exercise 7-2B   *Preparing a sales budget*   L.O. 3, 7

Addison Restaurant is opening for business in a new shopping center. Mathew Hill, the owner, is preparing a sales budget for the next three months. After consulting friends in the same business, Mr. Hill estimated July revenues as shown in the following table. He expects revenues to increase 5 percent per month in August and September.

Revenues Budget	July	August	September
Food sales	$20,000	?	?
Beverage and liquor sales	12,000	?	?
Total budgeted revenues	$32,000	?	?

Required

a. Complete the sales budget by filling in the missing amounts.
b. Determine the total amount of revenue Addison Restaurant will report on its quarterly pro forma income statement.

Exercise 7-3B   *Preparing a schedule of cash receipts*   L.O. 3, 7

Blair Imports, Inc., sells goods imported from the Far East. Using the second quarter's sales budget, Steve Lang is trying to complete the schedule of cash receipts for the quarter. The company had accounts receivable of $430,000 on April 1. Blair Imports normally collects 100 percent of accounts receivable in the month following the month of sale.

Sales	April	May	June
Sales Budget			
Cash sales	$120,000	$132,000	$124,000
Sales on account	480,000	568,000	500,000
Total budgeted sales	$600,000	$700,000	$624,000
Schedule of Cash Receipts			
Current cash sales	?	?	?
Plus: Collections from accounts receivable	?	?	?
Total budgeted collections	$550,000	$612,000	$692,000

Required

a. Help Mr. Lang complete the schedule of cash receipts by filling in the missing amounts.
b. Determine the amount of accounts receivable the company will report on the quarterly pro forma balance sheet.

Exercise 7-4B   *Preparing sales budgets with different assumptions*   L.O. 3

Raine International Company has three subsidiaries, Falcon Trading Company, Ammons Medical Supplies Company, and Ocean Shipping Company. Because the subsidiaries operate in different industries, Raine's corporate budget for the coming year must reflect the different growth potentials of the individual industries. The growth expectations per quarter for the subsidiaries are 4 percent for Falcon, 1 percent for Ammons, and 3 percent for Ocean.

Subsidiary	Current Quarter Sales	First Quarter	Second Quarter	Third Quarter	Fourth Quarter
Falcon	$250,000	?	?	?	?
Ammons	350,000	?	?	?	?
Ocean	450,000	?	?	?	?

Required

a. Complete the sales budget by filling in the missing amounts. (Round the figures to the nearest dollar.)
b. Determine the amount of sales revenue Raine will report on the quarterly pro forma income statements.

L.O. 3   **Exercise 7-5B**   *Determining cash receipts from accounts receivable*

Wasson Corporation is about to start a business as an agricultural products distributor. Because its customers will all be retailers, Wasson will sell its products solely on account. The company expects to collect 50 percent of accounts receivable in the month of sale and the remaining 50 percent in the following month. Wasson expects sales revenues of $100,000 in July, the first month of operation, and $120,000 in August.

Required

a. Determine the amount of cash Wasson expects to collect in July.
b. Determine the amount of cash Wasson expects to collect in August.

L.O. 3   **Exercise 7-6B**   *Using judgment in making a sales forecast*

Love Greetings Corporation sells greeting cards for various occasions.

Required

Write a brief memo describing the sales pattern that you would expect Love Greetings to experience during the year. In which months will sales likely be high? Explain why.

L.O.4   **Exercise 7-7B**   *Preparing an inventory purchases budget*

Kain Drugstores, Inc., sells prescription drugs, over-the-counter drugs, and some groceries. The purchasing manager prepared the following inventory purchases budget. Kain desires to maintain an ending inventory balance equal to 20 percent of the following month's cost of goods sold. April's budgeted cost of goods sold amounts to $50,000.

Inventory Purchases Budget	January	February	March
Budgeted cost of goods sold	$40,000	$35,000	$48,000
Plus: Desired ending inventory	7,000	?	?
Inventory needed	47,000	?	?
Less: Beginning inventory	8,000	?	?
Required purchases (on account)	$39,000	?	?

Required

a. Complete the inventory purchases budget by filling in the missing amounts.
b. Determine the amount of cost of goods sold the company will report on the first quarter pro forma income statement.
c. Determine the amount of ending inventory the company will report on the first quarter pro forma balance sheet.

L.O. 4   **Exercise 7-8B**   *Preparing a schedule of cash payments for inventory purchases*

Major Grocery buys and sells groceries in a community far from any major city. Tim Major, the owner, budgeted the store's purchases as follows:

	October	November	December
Required purchases (on account)	$25,000	$24,000	$31,000

Major's suppliers require that 70 percent of accounts payable be paid in the month of purchase. The remaining 30 percent is paid in the month following the month of purchase.

Schedule of Cash Payments for Inventory Purchases			
	October	November	December
Payment for current accounts payable	$17,500	?	?
Payment for previous accounts payable	6,000	?	?
Total budgeted payments for inventory	$23,500	?	?

Required

a. Complete the schedule of cash payments for inventory purchases by filling in the missing amounts.

b. Determine the amount of accounts payable Major will report on the store's quarterly pro forma balance sheet.

Exercise 7-9B   *Determining the amount of inventory purchases and cash payments*   **L.O. 4**

Hart Oil Corporation, which distributes gasoline products to independent gasoline stations, had $400,000 of cost of goods sold in January. The company expects a 2.5 percent increase in cost of goods sold during February. The ending inventory balance for January is $22,000, and the desired ending inventory for February is $25,000. Hart pays cash to settle 60 percent of its purchases on account during the month of purchase and pays the remaining 40 percent in the month following the purchase. The accounts payable balance as of January 31 was $30,000.

Required

a. Determine the amount of purchases budgeted for February.

b. Determine the amount of cash payments budgeted for inventory purchases in February.

Exercise 7-10B   *Preparing a schedule of cash payments for selling and administrative expenses*   **L.O. 5**

The controller for White Laundry Services prepared the following list of expected operating expenses. All expenses requiring cash payments except salary expense and insurance are paid for in the month incurred. Salary is paid in the month following its incursion. The annual insurance premium is paid in advance on January 1. January is the first month of operations. Accordingly, there are no beginning account balances.

	January	February	March
Budgeted Selling and Administrative Expenses			
Equipment depreciation	$ 6,000	$ 6,000	$ 6,000
Salary expense	2,900	2,700	3,050
Cleaning supplies	1,000	940	1,100
Insurance expense	600	600	600
Equipment maintenance expense	500	500	500
Leases expense	1,600	1,600	1,600
Miscellaneous expenses	400	400	400
Total S&A expenses	$13,000	$12,740	$13,250
Schedule of Cash Payments for Selling and Administrative Expenses			
Equipment depreciation	?	?	?
Prior month's salary expense, 100%	?	?	?
Cleaning supplies	?	?	?
Insurance premium	?	?	?
Equipment maintenance expense	?	?	?
Leases expense	?	?	?
Miscellaneous expenses	?	?	?
Total payments for S&A expenses	$10,700	$ 6,340	$ 6,300

Required

a. Complete the schedule of cash payments for selling and administrative expenses by filling in the missing amounts.

b. Determine the amount of salaries payable the company will report on its quarterly pro forma balance sheet.

c. Determine the amount of prepaid insurance the company will report on its quarterly pro forma balance sheet.

L.O. 4   **Exercise 7-11B** *Preparing inventory purchases budgets with different assumptions*

Jenny Neal has been at odds with her brother and business partner, Haley, since childhood. The sibling rivalry is not all bad, however; their garden shop, Neal Gardens and Gifts, has been very successful. When the partners met to prepare the coming year's budget, their forecasts were different, naturally. Their sales revenue estimates follow.

Source of Estimate	First Quarter	Second Quarter	Third Quarter	Fourth Quarter
Jenny	$320,000	$400,000	$280,000	$360,000
Haley	280,000	300,000	320,000	400,000

Past experience indicates that cost of goods sold is about 60 percent of sales revenue. The company tries to maintain 15 percent of the next quarter's expected cost of goods sold as the current quarter's ending inventory. The ending inventory this year is $25,000. Next year's ending inventory is budgeted to be $35,000.

Required

a. Prepare an inventory purchases budget using Jenny's estimate.

b. Prepare an inventory purchases budget using Haley's estimate.

L.O. 5, 7   **Exercise 7-12B** *Determining the amount of cash payments for selling and administrative expenses*

Victor Conway, managing partner of Conway Business Consulting, is preparing a budget for January 2008, the first month of business operations. Victor estimates the following monthly selling and administrative expenses: office lease, $5,000; utilities, $1,600; office supplies, $2,400; depreciation, $12,000; referral fees, $5,000; and miscellaneous, $1,000. Referral fees will be paid in the month following the month they are incurred. Other expenses will be paid in the month in which they are incurred.

Required

a. Determine the amount of budgeted cash payments for January selling and administrative expenses.

b. Determine the amount of referral fees payable the firm will report on the January 31 pro forma balance sheet.

c. Determine the amount of office lease expense the company will report on its 2008 pro forma income statement, assuming that the monthly lease expense remains the same throughout the whole year.

L.O. 6, 7   **Exercise 7-13B** *Preparing a cash budget*

Peter Latta, the accounting manager of Jordan Antique Company, is preparing his company's cash budget for the next quarter. Jordan desires to maintain a cash cushion of $4,000 at the end of each month. As cash flows fluctuate, the company either borrows or repays funds at the end of a month. It pays interest on borrowed funds at the rate of 1 percent per month.

Cash Budget	July	August	September
Section 1: Cash Receipts			
Beginning cash balance	$ 16,000	$?	$?
Add cash receipts	180,000	192,000	208,000
Total cash available (a)	196,000	?	?

continued

Cash Budget	July	August	September
Section 2: Cash Payments			
For inventory purchases	158,000	153,000	171,000
For S&A expenses	37,000	36,000	39,000
For interest expense	0	?	?
Total budgeted disbursements (b)	195,000	?	?
Section 3: Financing Activities			
Surplus (shortage)	1,000	?	?
Borrowing (repayments) (c)	3,000	?	?
Ending Cash Balance (a − b + c)	$ 4,000	$ 4,000	$ 4,000

Required

a. Complete the cash budget by filling in the missing amounts. Round all computations to the nearest whole dollar.

b. Determine the amount of net cash flows from operating activities Jordan will report on its quarterly pro forma statement of cash flows.

c. Determine the amount of net cash flows from financing activities Jordan will report on its quarterly pro forma statement of cash flows.

Exercise 7-14B *Determining amount to borrow and pro forma statement balances*   **L.O. 6, 7**

Vladmir Yushanko, the president of Yuri Corporation, has been working with his controller to manage the company's cash position. The controller provided Vladmir the following data.

Balance of accounts receivable, June 30	$ 40,000
Balance of line of credit, June 30	0
Budgeted cash sales for July	74,000
Budgeted credit sales for July	320,000
Budgeted cash payments for July	400,000

The company typically collects 75 percent of credit sales in the month of sale and the remainder in the month following the sale. Yuri's line of credit enables the company to borrow funds readily, with the stipulation that any borrowing must take place on the last day of the month. The company pays its vendors on the last day of the month also. Mr. Yushanko likes to maintain a $15,000 cash balance before any interest payments. The annual interest rate is 12 percent.

Required

a. Compute the amount of funds Mr. Yushanko needs to borrow on July 31.

b. Determine the amount of interest expense the company will report on the July pro forma income statement.

c. Determine the amount of interest expense the company will report on the August pro forma income statement.

Exercise 7-15B *Preparing pro forma income statements with different assumptions*   **L.O. 7**

Burch Corporation's budget planning meeting is like a zoo. Brian Stull, the credit manager, is naturally conservative and May Simpson, the marketing manager, is the opposite. They have argued back and forth about the effect of various factors that influence the sales growth rate, such as credit policies and market potential. Based on the following current year data provided by Andrea Martinez, the controller, Brian expects Burch's revenues to grow 5 percent each quarter above last year's level; May insists the growth rate will be 8 percent per quarter.

Current Year	First Quarter	Second Quarter	Third Quarter	Fourth Quarter	Total
Sales revenue	$240,000	$200,000	$216,000	$314,000	$970,000
Cost of goods sold	122,000	101,000	106,000	156,000	485,000
Gross margin	118,000	99,000	110,000	158,000	485,000
Selling & admin. expenses	32,000	26,000	26,400	40,600	125,000
Net income	$ 86,000	$ 73,000	$ 83,600	$117,400	$360,000

Historically, cost of goods sold has been about 50 percent of sales revenue. Selling and administrative expenses have been about 12.5 percent of sales revenue.

Required

a. Prepare a pro forma income statement for the coming year using the credit manager's growth estimate.
b. Prepare a pro forma income statement for the coming year using the marketing manager's growth estimate.
c. Explain why two executives in the same company could have different estimates of future growth.

PROBLEMS—SERIES B

L.O. 3

Problem 7-16B   *Preparing a sales budget and schedule of cash receipts*

Larimer Corporation sells mail-order computers. In December 2006, it has generated $700,000 of sales revenue; the company expects a 20 percent increase in sales in January and 10 percent in February. All sales are on account. Larimer normally collects 80 percent of accounts receivable in the month of sale and 20 percent in the next month.

Required

a. Prepare a sales budget for January and February 2007.
b. Determine the amount of sales revenue Larimer would report on the bimonthly pro forma income statement for January and February 2007.
c. Prepare a cash receipts schedule for January and February 2007.
d. Determine the amount of accounts receivable as of February 28, 2007.

L.O. 4, 7

Problem 7-17B   *Preparing the inventory purchases budget and schedule of cash payments*

Hoskin Company's purchasing manager, Scott Medina, is preparing a purchases budget for the next quarter. At his request, Larry Franklin, the manager of the sales department, forwarded him the following preliminary sales budget.

	October	November	December	January
Budgeted sales	$640,000	$768,000	$960,000	$800,000

For budgeting purposes, Hoskin estimates that cost of goods sold is 75 percent of sales. The company desires to maintain an ending inventory balance equal to 20 percent of the next period's cost of goods sold. The September ending inventory is $90,000. Hoskin makes all purchases on account and pays 70 percent of accounts payable in the month of purchase and the remaining 30 percent in the following month. The balance of accounts payable at the end of September is $90,000.

Required

a. Prepare an inventory purchases budget for October, November, and December.
b. Determine the amount of ending inventory Hoskin will report on the end-of-quarter pro forma balance sheet.

c. Prepare a schedule of cash payments for inventory for October, November, and December.

d. Determine the balance in accounts payable Hoskin will report on the end-of-quarter pro forma balance sheet.

Problem 7-18B   *Preparing pro forma income statements with different assumptions*   L.O. 7

Kent Lowery, a successful entrepreneur, is reviewing the results of his first year in business. His accountant delivered the following income statement just five minutes ago.

	Current Year
Sales Revenue	$500,000
Cost of Goods Sold	350,000
Gross Profit	150,000
Selling & Admin. Expenses	90,000
Net Income	$ 60,000

Mr. Lowery would like net income to increase 20 percent in the next year. This first year, selling and administrative expenses were 10 percent of sales revenue plus $40,000 of fixed expenses.

Required

The following questions are independent of each other.

a. Mr. Lowery expects that cost of goods sold and variable selling and administrative expenses will remain stable in proportion to sales next year. The fixed selling and administrative expenses will increase to $68,000. What percentage increase in sales would enable the company to reach Mr. Lowery's goal? Prepare a pro forma income statement to illustrate.

b. Market competition may become serious next year, and Mr. Lowery does not expect an increase in sales revenue. However, he has developed a good relationship with his supplier, who is willing to give him a volume discount that will decrease cost of goods sold by 3 percent. What else can the company do to reach Mr. Lowery's goal? Prepare a pro forma income statement illustrating your proposal.

c. If the company escalates its advertising campaign to boost consumer recognition, the selling and administrative expenses will increase to $150,000. With the increased advertising, the company expects sales revenue to increase by 25 percent. Assume that cost of goods sold remains constant in proportion to sales. Can the company reach Mr. Lowery's goal?

Problem 7-19B   *Preparing a schedule of cash payments for selling and administrative expenses*   L.O. 5

Antoin's Travel Services has prepared its selling and administrative expenses budget for the next quarter. It pays all expenses when they are incurred except sales commissions, advertising expense, and telephone expense. These three items are paid in the month following the one in which they are incurred. January is the first month of operations, so there are no beginning account balances.

	January	February	March
Salary expense	$8,000	$8,000	$8,000
Sales commissions	600	640	800
Advertising expense	500	500	600
Telephone expense	1,000	1,080	1,100
Depreciation on store equipment	4,000	4,000	4,000
Rent	10,000	10,000	10,000
Miscellaneous	800	800	800
Total S&A expenses before interest	$24,900	$25,020	$25,300

Required

a. Prepare a schedule of cash payments for selling and administrative expenses.

b. Determine the amount of telephone payable as of March 31.

c. Determine the amount of sales commissions payable as of February 28.

L.O. 6

Problem 7-20B *Preparing a cash budget*

Pope Company has budgeted the following cash flows:

	April	May	June
Cash receipts	$320,000	$470,000	$624,000
Cash payments			
For inventory purchases	410,000	420,000	464,000
For S&A expenses	80,000	106,000	132,000

Pope had a $36,000 cash balance on April 1. The company desires to maintain a $60,000 cash cushion before paying interest. Funds are assumed to be borrowed, in increments of $1,000, and repaid on the last day of each month; the interest rate is 1.50 percent per month. Pope pays its vendors on the last day of the month also.

Required

Prepare a cash budget.

L.O. 3, 4, 5

Problem 7-21B *Preparing budgets with multiple products*

Silva Enterprises, Inc., has two products, palm-size computers and programmable calculators. Jean Zeigler, the chief executive officer, is working with her staff to prepare next year's budget. Ms. Zeigler estimates that sales will increase at an annual rate of 10 percent for palm-size computers and 4 percent for programmable calculators. The current year sales revenue data follow.

	First Quarter	Second Quarter	Third Quarter	Fourth Quarter	Total
Palm-size computers	$500,000	$550,000	$620,000	$ 730,000	$2,400,000
Programmable calculators	250,000	275,000	290,000	325,000	1,140,000
Total	$750,000	$825,000	$910,000	$1,055,000	$3,540,000

Based on the company's past experience, cost of goods sold is usually 75 percent of sales revenue. Company policy is to keep 10 percent of the next period's estimated cost of goods sold as the current period ending inventory.

Required

a. Prepare the company's sales budget for the next year for each quarter by individual products.
b. If the selling and administrative expenses are estimated to be $500,000, prepare the company's budgeted annual income statement for the next year.
c. Ms. Zeigler estimates the current year's ending inventory will be $78,000 for computers and $32,000 for calculators and the ending inventory next year will be $88,000 for computers and $42,000 for calculators. Prepare the company's inventory purchases budget for the next year showing quarterly figures by product.

L.O. 3, 4, 5

Problem 7-22B *Preparing a master budget for retail company with no beginning account balances*

World Gifts Corporation begins business today, December 31, 2007. Geraldine Lear, the president, is trying to prepare the company's master budget for the first three months (January, February, and March) of 2008. Since you are her good friend and an accounting student, Ms. Lear asks you to prepare the budget based on the following specifications.

Required

a. January sales are estimated to be $250,000 of which 30 percent will be cash and 70 percent will be credit. The company expects sales to increase at the rate of 10 percent per month. Prepare a sales budget.

b. The company expects to collect 100 percent of the accounts receivable generated by credit sales in the month following the sale. Prepare a schedule of cash receipts.

c. The cost of goods sold is 50 percent of sales. The company desires to maintain a minimum ending inventory equal to 20 percent of the next month's cost of goods sold. The ending inventory of March is expected to be $33,000. Assume that all purchases are made on account. Prepare an inventory purchases budget.

d. The company pays 60 percent of accounts payable in the month of purchase and the remaining 40 percent in the following month. Prepare a cash payments budget for inventory purchases.

e. Budgeted selling and administrative expenses per month follow.

Salary expense (fixed)	$25,000
Sales commissions	8 percent of Sales
Supplies expense	4 percent of Sales
Utilities (fixed)	$1,800
Depreciation on store equipment (fixed)*	$5,000
Rent (fixed)	$7,200
Miscellaneous (fixed)	$2,000

*The capital expenditures budget indicates that World will spend $350,000 on January 1 for store fixtures. The fixtures are expected to have a $50,000 salvage value and a five-year (60-month) useful life.

Use this information to prepare a selling and administrative expenses budget.

f. Utilities and sales commissions are paid the month after they are incurred; all other expenses are paid in the month in which they are incurred. Prepare a cash payments budget for selling and administrative expenses.

g. The company borrows funds, in increments of $1,000, and repays them in any amount available on the last day of the month. It pays interest of 1.5 percent per month in cash on the last day of the month. For safety, the company desires to maintain a $50,000 cash cushion. The company pays its vendors on the last day of the month. Prepare a cash budget.

h. Prepare a pro forma income statement for the quarter.

i. Prepare a pro forma balance sheet at the end of the quarter.

j. Prepare a pro forma statement of cash flows for the quarter.

Problem 7-23B   *Behavioral impact of budgeting*

L.O. 2

Bianca Pender, the director of Hume Corporation's Mail-Order Division, is preparing the division's budget proposal for next year. The company's president will review the proposal for approval. Ms. Pender estimates the current year final operating results will be as follows.

	Current Year
Sales revenue	$9,600,000
Cost of goods sold	5,280,000
Gross profit	4,320,000
Selling & admin. expenses	1,920,000
Net income	$2,400,000

Ms. Pender believes that the cost of goods sold as well as selling and administrative expenses will continue to be stable in proportion to sales revenue.

Hume has an incentive policy to reward division managers whose performance exceeds their budget. Division directors receive a 10 percent bonus based on the excess of actual net income over the division's budget. For the last two years, Ms. Pender has proposed a 4 percent rate of increase, which proved accurate. However, her honesty and accuracy in forecasting caused her to receive no year-end bonus at all. She is pondering whether she should do something differently this time. If she continues to be honest, she should propose an 8 percent growth rate because of robust market demand. Alternatively, she can propose a 4 percent growth rate as usual and thereby expect to receive some bonus at year-end.

Required

a. Prepare a pro forma income statement, assuming a 4 percent estimated increase.

b. Prepare a pro forma income statement, assuming an 8 percent increase.

c. Assume the president eventually approves the division's proposal with the 4 percent growth rate. If growth actually is 8 percent, how much bonus would Ms. Pender receive?

d. Propose a better budgeting procedure for Hume Corporation.

ANALYZE, THINK, COMMUNICATE

ATC 7-1   Business Applications Case   *Preparing and using pro forma statements*

Nancy Chen and Tim Hoffer recently graduated from the same university. After graduation they decided not to seek jobs with established organizations but, rather, to start their own small business. They hoped this would provide more flexibility in their personal lives for a few years. Since both of them enjoyed cooking, they decided on a business selling vegetarian wraps and fruit juices from a street cart near their alma mater.

They bought a small enclosed cart for $4,000 that was set up for selling food. This cost, along with the cost for supplies to get started, a business license, and street vendor license, brought their initial expenditures to $5,200. They used $700 of their personal savings, and they borrowed $4,500 from Nancy's parents. They agreed to pay interest on the outstanding loan balance each month based on an annual rate of 6 percent. They will repay the principal over the next two years as cash becomes available.

After two months in business, September and October, they had average monthly revenues of $6,400 and out-of-pocket costs of $3,900 for ingredients, paper supplies, and so on, but not interest. Tim thinks they should repay some of the money they borrowed, but Nancy thinks they should prepare a set of forecasted financial statements for their first year in business before deciding whether or not to repay any principal on the loan. She remembers a bit about budgeting from a survey of accounting course she took and thinks the results from their first two months in business can be extended over the next 10 months to prepare the budget they need. They estimate the cart will last at least three years, after which they expect to sell it for $500 and move on to something else in their lives. Nancy agrees to prepare a forecasted (pro forma) income statement, balance sheet, and statement of cash flows for their first year in business, which includes the two months already passed.

Required

a. Prepare the annual pro forma financial statements that you would expect Nancy to prepare based on her comments about her expectations for the business. Assume no principal will be repaid on the loan.

b. Review the statements you prepared for the first requirement and prepare a list of reasons why Tim and Nancy's business probably will not match their budgeted statements.

ATC 7-2   Group Assignment   *Master budget and pro forma statements*

The following trial balance was drawn from the records of Havel Company as of October 1, 2007.

Cash	$ 16,000	
Accounts receivable	60,000	
Inventory	40,000	
Store equipment	200,000	
Accumulated depreciation		$ 76,800
Accounts payable		72,000
Line of credit loan		100,000
Common stock		50,000
Retained earnings		17,200
Totals	$316,000	$316,000

Required

a. Divide the class into groups, each with 4 or 5 students. Organize the groups into three sections. Assign Task 1 to the first section, Task 2 to the second section, and Task 3 to the third section.

Group Tasks

(1) Based on the following information, prepare a sales budget and a schedule of cash receipts for October, November, and December. Sales for October are expected to be $180,000, consisting of $40,000 in cash and $140,000 on credit. The company expects sales to increase at the rate of 10 percent per month. All accounts receivable are collected in the month following the sale.

(2) Based on the following information, prepare a purchases budget and a schedule of cash payments for inventory purchases for October, November, and December. The inventory balance as of October 1 was $40,000. Cost of goods sold for October is expected to be $72,000. Cost of goods sold is expected to increase by 10 percent per month. The company desires to maintain a minimum ending inventory equal to 20 percent of the current month cost of goods sold. Seventy-five percent of accounts payable is paid in the month that the purchase occurs; the remaining 25 percent is paid in the following month.

(3) Based on the following selling and administrative expenses budgeted for October, prepare a selling and administrative expenses budget for October, November, and December.

Sales commissions (10% increase per month)	$ 7,200
Supplies expense (10% increase per month)	1,800
Utilities (fixed)	2,200
Depreciation on store equipment (fixed)	1,600
Salary expense (fixed)	34,000
Rent (fixed)	6,000
Miscellaneous (fixed)	1,000

Cash payments for sales commissions and utilities are made in the month following the one in which the expense is incurred. Supplies and other operating expenses are paid in cash in the month in which they are incurred.

b. Select a representative from each section. Have the representatives supply the missing information in the following pro forma income statement and balance sheet for the fourth quarter of 2007. The statements are prepared as of December 31, 2007.

Income Statement	
Sales Revenue	$?
Cost of Goods Sold	?
Gross Margin	357,480
Operating Expenses	?
Operating Income	193,290
Interest Expense	(2,530)
Net Income	$190,760

Balance Sheet		
Assets		
Cash		$ 9,760
Accounts Receivable		?
Inventory		?
Store Equipment	$200,000	
Accumulated Depreciation Store Equipment	?	
Book Value of Equipment		118,400
Total Assets		$314,984
Liabilities		
Accounts Payable		?
Utilities Payable		?
Sales Commissions Payable		?
Line of Credit		23,936

continued

Equity	
Common Stock	50,000
Retained Earnings	?
Total Liabilities and Equity	$314,984

c. Indicate whether Havel will need to borrow money during October.

ATC 7-3 Research Assignment *Simplifying the budget process*

By their nature, large entities often generate big, complex budgets. There is a danger, however, that budgets can become so detailed and complex that they do not get used after being prepared. In the article, "Streamline Budgeting in the new Millennium: Concentrate on Simplicity and Usefulness, Not Unrealistic Numbers," *Strategic Finance,* December 2001, pp. 45–50, Bruce Neumann provides suggestions for improving the budgeting process. Read this article and complete the following requirements.

Required

a. What are the five steps of budgeting that the author identifies?
b. Briefly explain what the article means by "the Three C's" of motivation for those preparing a budget.
c. The article describes "activity budgeting" as one method for streamlining an entity's budget. Explain the basic concept of activity budgeting.
d. The article describes "global budgeting" as one method for streamlining an entity's budget. Explain the basic concept of global budgeting.
e. Does the author suggest that more budget categories be devoted to fixed-cost categories or variable-cost categories?

ATC 7-4 Writing Assignment *Continuous budgeting*

HON Company is the largest maker of mid-priced office furniture in the United States and Canada. Its management has expressed dissatisfaction with its *annual* budget system. Fierce competition requires businesses to be flexible and innovative. Unfortunately, building the effects of innovation into an annual budget is difficult because actions and outcomes often are evolutionary. Innovation unfolds as the year progresses. Consequently, HON's management team reached the conclusion that "when production processes undergo continuous change, standards developed annually for static conditions no longer offer meaningful targets for gauging their success."

Required

Assume that you are HON Company's budget director. Write a memo to the management team explaining how the practice of continuous budgeting could overcome the shortcomings of an annual budget process. (For insight, read the article "Continuous Budgeting at the HON Company," *Management Accounting,* January 1996. This article describes HON's real-world experience with a continuous budget system.)

ATC 7-5 Ethical Dilemma *Bad budget system or unethical behavior?*

Clarence Cleaver is the budget director for the Harris County School District. Mr. Cleaver recently sent an urgent E-mail message to Sally Simmons, principal of West Harris County High. The message severely reprimanded Ms. Simmons for failing to spend the funds allocated to her to purchase computer equipment. Ms. Simmons responded that her school already has a sufficient supply of computers; indeed, the computer lab is never filled to capacity and usually is less than half filled. Ms. Simmons suggested that she would rather use the funds for teacher training. She argued that the reason the existing computers are not fully utilized is that the teachers lack sufficient computer literacy necessary to make assignments for their students.

Mr. Cleaver responded that it is not Ms. Simmons's job to decide how the money is to be spent; that is the school board's job. It is the principal's job to spend the money as the board directed. He informed Ms. Simmons that if the money is not spent by the fiscal closing date, the school board would likely reduce next year's budget allotment. To avoid a potential budget cut, Mr. Cleaver reallocated Ms. Simmons's computer funds to Jules Carrington, principal of East Harris County High. Mr. Carrington knows how to buy computers regardless of whether they are needed. Mr. Cleaver's final words were, "Don't blame me if parents of West High students complain that East High has more equipment. If anybody comes to me, I'm telling them that you turned down the money."

Required

a. Do Mr. Cleaver's actions violate the standards of ethical conduct shown in Exhibit 1.15 of Chapter 1?

b. Does the Sarbanes-Oxley Act apply to this case? Explain your answer.

c. Explain how participative budgeting could improve the allocation of resources for the Harris County School District.

ATC 7-6   Spreadsheet Assignment   *Using Excel*

The accountant for Nelly's Dress Shop prepared the fourth quarter 2007 cash budget that appears on the following spreadsheet. Nelly's has a policy to maintain a minimum cash balance of $14,000 before the interest payment at the end of each month. The shop borrows and repays funds on the first day of the month. The interest rate is 2 percent per month.

Required

a. Construct a spreadsheet to model the cash budget as in the following screen capture. Be sure to use formulas where possible so that any changes to the estimates will be automatically reflected in the spreadsheet.

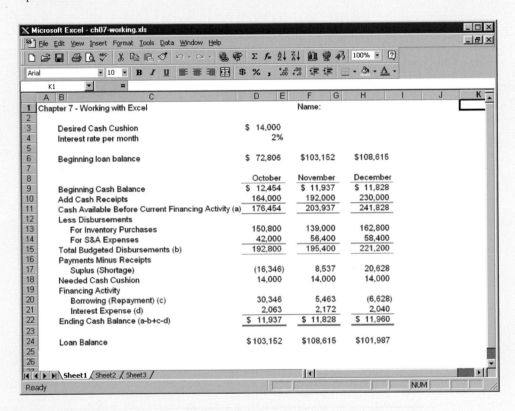

Spreadsheet Tips

(1) Rows 11, 15, 17, 18, 20 to 22, and 24 should be based on formulas.

(2) Cells F6, H6, F9, and H9 should be based on formulas also. For example, cell F6 should be = D24.

ATC 7-7   Spreadsheet Assignment   *Mastering Excel*

Spitzer Company has collected sales forecasts for next year from three people.

Sources of Sales Estimate	First Quarter	Second Quarter	Third Quarter	Fourth Quarter
a. Sales manager	$520,000	$410,000	$370,000	$610,000
b. Marketing consultant	540,000	480,000	400,000	630,000
c. Production manager	460,000	360,000	350,000	580,000

They have estimated that the cost of goods sold is 70 percent of sales. The company tries to maintain 10 percent of next quarter's expected cost of goods sold as the current quarter's ending inventory. The ending inventory of this year is $25,000. For budgeting, the ending inventory of the next year is expected to be $28,000.

Required

a. Construct a spreadsheet that allows the inventory purchases budget to be prepared for each of the preceding estimates.

Spreadsheet Tip

The VLOOKUP function can be used to choose one line of the preceding estimates. See the spreadsheet tips in Chapter 6 for an explanation of VLOOKUP.

COMPREHENSIVE PROBLEM

The management team of Magnificent Modems, Inc. (MMI), wants to investigate the effect of several different growth rates on sales and cash receipts. Cash sales for the month of January are expected to be $10,000. Credit sales for January are expected to be $50,000. MMI collects 100 percent of credit sales in the month following the month of sale. Assume a beginning balance in accounts receivable of $48,000.

Required

Calculate the amount of sales and cash receipts for the months of February and March assuming a growth rate of 1 percent, 2 percent, and 4 percent.

The results at a growth rate of 1 percent are shown as an example.

Sales Budget			
Sales	Jan	Feb	Mar
Cash Sales	$10,000	$10,100	$10,201
Sales on Account	50,000	50,500	51,005
Total Budgeted Sales	$60,000	$60,600	$61,206

Schedule of Cash Receipts			
Current Cash Sales	$10,000	$10,100	$10,201
Plus Collections from Accts. Rec.	48,000	50,000	50,500
Total Budgeted Collections	$58,000	$60,100	$60,701

Use the following forms, assuming a growth rate of 2 percent.

Sales Budget			
Sales	Jan	Feb	Mar
Cash Sales	$10,000		
Sales on Account	50,000		
Total Budgeted Sales	$60,000		

Schedule of Cash Receipts			
Current Cash Sales	$10,000		
Plus Collections from Accts. Rec.	48,000		
Total Budgeted Collections	$58,000		

Use the following forms, assuming a growth rate of 4 percent.

Sales Budget			
Sales	**Jan**	**Feb**	**Mar**
Cash Sales	$10,000		
Sales on Account	50,000	____	____
Total Budgeted Sales	$60,000	____	____
Schedule of Cash Receipts			
Current Cash Sales	$10,000		
Plus Collections from Accts. Rec.	48,000	____	____
Total Budgeted Collections	$58,000	____	____

CHAPTER 8

Performance Evaluation

LEARNING OBJECTIVES

After you have mastered the material in this chapter you will be able to:

1. Describe flexible and static budgets.

2. Classify variances as being favorable or unfavorable.

3. Compute and interpret sales volume variances.

4. Compute and interpret flexible budget variances.

5. Explain standard cost systems.

6. Calculate price and usage variances.

The Curious Accountant

Gourmet Pizzas is located in an affluent section of a major metropolitan area. Its owner worked at a national-chain pizza restaurant while in college. He knew that even though the national pizza chains had a lot of stores, (in 2004 **Domino's**, **Pizza Hut**, and **Papa John's** had approximately 15,000 stores in the United States), more than half of the country's pizzas were sold by other, mostly independently owned, restaurants. Knowing he could not beat the big guys on price, Gourmet Pizzas focuses on quality. Its pizza dough is made from scratch on the premises from organically grown flour, and it offers a wide variety of unusual toppings, such as smoked salmon.

In order to determine a proper selling price of his pies, the owner estimated the cost of making the crusts, among other things. Knowing how much flour, yeast, and so on was needed to make the dough for one pizza and estimating the cost of these ingredients, he determined that the materials for the dough for each pizza should cost him 25 cents. However, after six months in business, he had spent $5,040 on materials needed for making his dough, and had sold 16,250 pizzas. This resulted in an actual price per pizza of 31 cents.

What are two general reasons that may explain why the materials cost for pizza dough was higher than Gourmet Pizzas' owner estimated? (Answer on page 347.)

CHAPTER OPENING

Suppose you are a carpenter who builds picnic tables. You normally build 200 tables each year (the planned volume of activity), but because of unexpected customer demand, you are asked to build 225 tables (the actual volume of activity). You work hard and build the tables. Should management chastise you for using more materials, labor, or overhead than you normally use? Should management criticize the sales staff for selling more tables than expected? Of course not. Management must evaluate performance based on the actual volume of activity, not the planned volume of activity. To help management plan and evaluate performance, managerial accountants frequently prepare flexible budgets based on different levels of volume. Flexible budgets flex, or change, when the volume of activity changes. ■

Preparing Flexible Budgets

Topic Tackler

PLUS

8-1

Describe flexible and static budgets.

A **flexible budget** is an extension of the *master budget* discussed in Chapter 7. The master budget is based solely on the planned volume of activity. The master budget is frequently called a **static budget** because it remains unchanged even if the actual volume of activity differs from the planned volume. Flexible budgets differ from static budgets in that they show expected revenues and costs at a *variety* of volume levels.

To illustrate the differences between static and flexible budgets, consider Melrose Manufacturing Company, a producer of small, high-quality trophies used in award ceremonies. Melrose plans to make and sell 18,000 trophies during 2006. Management's best estimates of the expected sales price and per unit costs for the trophies are called *standard* prices and costs. The standard price and costs for the 18,000 trophies follow.

Per unit sales price and variable costs	
Expected sales price	$80.00
Standard materials cost	12.00
Standard labor cost	16.80
Standard overhead cost	5.60
Standard general, selling, and administrative cost	15.00
Fixed costs	
Manufacturing cost	$201,600
General, selling, and administrative cost	90,000

Static and flexible budgets use the same per unit *standard* amounts and the same fixed costs. Exhibit 8.1 shows Melrose Manufacturing's static budget in column D of the Excel spreadsheet. The amounts of sales revenue and variable costs in column D come from multiplying the per unit standards in column C by the number of units in cell D4 (planned volume). For example, the sales revenue in cell D7 comes from multiplying the per unit sales price in cell C7 by the

EXHIBIT 8.1

Static and Flexible Budgets in Excel Spreadsheet

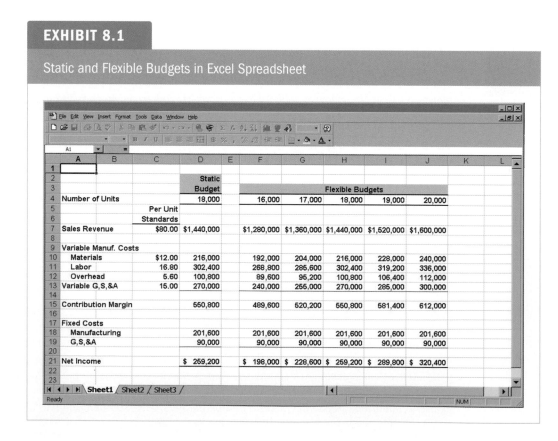

number of units in cell D4 ($80 × 18,000 units = $1,440,000). The variable costs are similarly computed; the cost per unit amount in column C is multiplied by the planned volume in cell D4.

What if management wants to know the amount net income would be if volume were 16,000, 17,000, 18,000, 19,000, or 20,000 units? Management needs a series of *flexible budgets*. With little effort, an accountant can provide *what-if* information on the Excel spreadsheet. By copying to columns F through J the formulas used to determine the static budget amounts in column D, then changing the volume variables in row 4 to the desired levels, the spreadsheet instantly calculates the alternative flexible budgets in columns F through J.

Management can use the flexible budgets for both planning and performance evaluation. For example, managers may assess whether the company's cash position is adequate by assuming different levels of volume. They may judge if the number of employees, amounts of materials, and equipment and storage facilities are appropriate for a variety of different potential levels of volume. In addition to helping plan, flexible budgets are critical to implementing an effective performance evaluation system.

Determining Variances for Performance Evaluation

One means of evaluating managerial performance is to compare *standard* amounts with *actual* results. The differences between the standard and actual amounts are called **variances;** variances can be either **favorable** or **unfavorable.** When actual sales revenue is greater than expected (planned) revenue, a company has a favorable sales variance because maximizing revenue is desirable. When actual sales are less than expected, an unfavorable sales variance exists. Because managers try to minimize costs, favorable cost variances exist when actual costs are *less* than standard costs. Unfavorable cost variances exist when actual costs are *more* than standard costs. These relationships are summarized below.

LO 2

Classify variances as being favorable or unfavorable.

- When actual sales exceed expected sales, variances are favorable.
- When actual sales are less than expected sales, variances are unfavorable.
- When actual costs exceed standard costs, variances are unfavorable.
- When actual costs are less than standard costs, variances are favorable.

Sales Volume Variances

The amount of a **sales volume variance** is the difference between the static budget (which is based on planned volume) and a flexible budget based on actual volume. This variance measures management effectiveness in attaining the planned volume of activity. To illustrate, assume Melrose Manufacturing Company actually makes and sells 19,000 trophies during 2006. The planned volume of activity was 18,000 trophies. Exhibit 8.2 shows Melrose's static budget, flexible budget, and volume variances.

LO 3

Compute and interpret sales volume variances.

EXHIBIT 8.2

Melrose Manufacturing Company's Volume Variances

	Static Budget	Flexible Budget	Volume Variances	
Number of units	18,000	19,000	1,000	Favorable
Sales revenue	$1,440,000	$1,520,000	$80,000	Favorable
Variable manufacturing costs				
Materials	216,000	228,000	12,000	Unfavorable
Labor	302,400	319,200	16,800	Unfavorable
Overhead	100,800	106,400	5,600	Unfavorable
Variable G, S, & A	270,000	285,000	15,000	Unfavorable
Contribution margin	550,800	581,400	30,600	Favorable
Fixed costs				
Manufacturing	201,600	201,600	0	
G, S, & A	90,000	90,000	0	
Net income	$ 259,200	$ 289,800	$30,600	Favorable

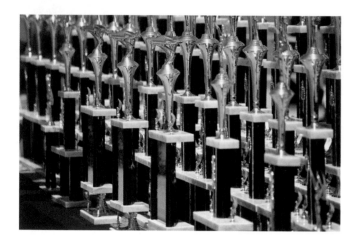

Interpreting the Sales and Variable Cost Volume Variances

Because the static and flexible budgets are based on the same standard sales price and per unit variable costs, the variances are solely attributable to the difference between the planned and actual volume of activity. Marketing managers are usually responsible for the volume variance. Because the sales volume drives production levels, production managers have little control over volume. Exceptions occur; for example, if poor production quality control leads to inferior goods that are difficult to sell, the production manager is responsible. The production manager is responsible for production delays that affect product availability, which may restrict sales volume. Under normal circumstances, however, the marketing campaign determines the volume of sales. Upper-level marketing managers develop the promotional program and create the sales plan; they are in the best position to explain why sales goals are or are not met. When marketing managers refer to **making the numbers,** they usually mean reaching the sales volume in the static (master) budget.

In the case of Melrose Manufacturing Company, the marketing manager not only achieved but also exceeded by 1,000 units the planned volume of sales. Exhibit 8.2 shows the activity variances resulting from the extra volume. At the standard price, the additional volume produces a favorable revenue variance of $80,000 (1,000 units × $80 per unit). The increase in volume also produces unfavorable variable cost variances. The net effect of producing and selling the additional 1,000 units is an increase of $30,600 in the contribution margin, a positive result. These preliminary results suggest that the marketing manager is to be commended. The analysis, however, is incomplete. For example, examining market share could reveal whether the manager won customers from competitors or whether the manager simply reaped the benefit of an unexpected industrywide increase in demand. The increase in sales volume could have been attained by reducing the sales price; the success of that strategy will be analyzed further in a later section of this chapter.

The unfavorable variable cost variances in Exhibit 8.2 are somewhat misleading because variable costs are, by definition, expected to increase as volume increases. In this case the unfavorable cost variances are more than offset by the favorable revenue variance, resulting in a higher contribution margin. The variable cost volume variances could be more appropriately labeled "expected" rather than unfavorable. However, the cost volume variances are described as unfavorable because actual cost is greater than planned cost.

Fixed Cost Considerations

The fixed costs are the same in both the static and flexible budgets. By definition, the budgeted amount of fixed costs remains unchanged regardless of the volume of activity. What insights can management gain by analyzing costs that don't change? Consider the *operating leverage* fixed costs provide. A small increase in sales volume can have a dramatic impact on profitability. Although the 1,000 unit volume variance represents only a 5.6 percent increase in revenue ($80,000 variance ÷ $1,440,000 static budget sales base), it produces an 11.8 percent increase in profitability ($30,600 variance ÷ $259,200 static budget net income base). To understand why profitability increased so dramatically, management should analyze the effect of fixed costs on the higher than expected sales volume.

Companies using a cost-plus pricing strategy must be concerned with differences between the planned and actual volume of activity. Because actual volume is unknown until the end of the year, selling prices must be based on planned volume. At the *planned volume* of activity of 18,000 units, Melrose's fixed cost per unit is expected to be as follows:

Fixed manufacturing cost	$201,600	
Fixed G, S, & A cost	90,000	
Total fixed cost	$291,600 ÷ 18,000 units = $16.20 per trophy	

Based on the *actual volume* of 19,000 units, the fixed cost per unit is actually $15.35 per trophy ($291,600 ÷ 19,000 units). Because Melrose's prices were established using the $16.20 budgeted cost rather than the $15.35 actual cost, the trophies were overpriced, giving competitors a price advantage. Although Melrose sold more trophies than expected, sales volume might have been even greater if the trophies had been competitively priced.

Underpricing (not encountered by Melrose in this example) can also be detrimental. If planned volume is overstated, the estimated fixed cost per unit will be understated and prices will be set too low. When the higher amount of actual costs is subtracted from revenues, actual profits will be lower than expected. To avoid these negative consequences, companies that consider unit cost in pricing decisions must monitor volume variances closely.

The volume variance is *unfavorable* if actual volume is less than planned because cost per unit is higher than expected. Conversely, if actual volume is greater than planned, cost per unit is less than expected, resulting in a *favorable* variance. Both favorable and unfavorable variances can have negative consequences. Managers should strive for the greatest possible degree of accuracy.

Flexible Budget Variances

For performance evaluation, management compares actual results to a flexible budget based on the *actual* volume of activity. Because the actual results and the flexible budget reflect the same volume of activity, any variances result from differences between standard and actual per unit amounts. To illustrate computing and analyzing flexible budget variances, we assume that Melrose's *actual* per unit amounts during 2006 were those shown in the following table. The 2006 per unit *standard* amounts are repeated here for your convenience.

LO 4

Compute and interpret flexible budget variances.

	Standard	Actual
Sales price	$80.00	$78.00
Variable materials cost	12.00	11.78
Variable labor cost	16.80	17.25
Variable overhead cost	5.60	5.75

Actual and budgeted fixed costs are shown in Exhibit 8.3.

Exhibit 8.3 shows Melrose's 2006 flexible budget, actual results, and flexible budget variances. The flexible budget is the same one compared to the static budget in Exhibit 8.2. Recall the flexible budget amounts come from multiplying the standard per unit amounts by the actual volume of production. For example, the sales revenue in the flexible budget comes

EXHIBIT 8.3

Flexible Budget Variances for Melrose Manufacturing Company

	Flexible Budget	Actual Results	Flexible Budget Variances	
Number of units	19,000	19,000	0	
Sales revenue	$1,520,000	$1,482,000	$38,000	Unfavorable
Variable manufacturing costs				
Materials	228,000	223,820	4,180	Favorable
Labor	319,200	327,750	8,550	Unfavorable
Overhead	106,400	109,250	2,850	Unfavorable
Variable G, S, & A	285,000	283,100	1,900	Favorable
Contribution margin	581,400	538,080	43,320	Unfavorable
Fixed costs				
Manufacturing	201,600	210,000	8,400	Unfavorable
G, S, & A	90,000	85,000	5,000	Favorable
Net income	$ 289,800	$ 243,080	$46,720	Unfavorable

from multiplying the standard sales price by the actual volume ($80 × 19,000). The variable costs are similarly computed. The *actual results* are calculated by multiplying the actual per unit sales price and cost figures from the preceding table by the actual volume of activity. For example, the sales revenue in the Actual Results column comes from multiplying the actual sales price by the actual volume ($78 × 19,000 = $1,482,000). The actual cost figures are similarly computed. The differences between the flexible budget figures and the actual results are the **flexible budget variances.**

Calculating the Sales Price Variance

Because both the flexible budget and actual results are based on the actual volume of activity, the flexible budget variance is attributable to sales price, not sales volume. In this case, the actual sales price of $78 per unit is less than the standard price of $80 per unit. Because Melrose sold its product for less than the standard sales price, the **sales price variance** is *unfavorable.* Even though the price variance is unfavorable, however, sales volume was 1,000 units more than expected. It is possible the marketing manager generated the additional volume by reducing the sales price. Whether the combination of lower sales price and higher sales volume is favorable or unfavorable depends on the amount of the unfavorable sales price variance versus the amount of the favorable sales volume variance. The *total* sales variance (price and volume) follows:

Actual sales (19,000 units × $78 per unit)	$1,482,000	
Expected sales (18,000 units × $80 per unit)	1,440,000	
Total sales variance	$ 42,000	Favorable

Alternatively,

Activity variance (i.e., sales volume)	$ 80,000	Favorable
Sales price variance	(38,000)	Unfavorable
Total sales variance	$ 42,000	Favorable

This analysis indicates that reducing the sales price had a favorable impact on *total* contribution margin. Use caution when interpreting variances as good or bad; in this instance, the unfavorable sales price variance was more than offset by the favorable volume variance. All unfavorable variances are not bad; all favorable variances are not good. Variances signal the need to investigate.

CHECK YOURSELF 8.2

Scott Company's master budget called for a planned sales volume of 30,000 units. Budgeted direct materials cost was $4 per unit. Scott actually produced and sold 32,000 units with an actual materials cost of $131,000. Determine the materials volume variance and identify the organizational unit most likely responsible for this variance. Determine the flexible budget variance and identify the organizational unit most likely responsible for this variance.

Answer

The volume (activity) variance is the difference between the expected materials usage at the planned volume of activity and the expected materials usage at the actual volume of activity [($4 $\times$ 30,000 units) − ($4 $\times$ 32,000) = $8,000]. The variance is unfavorable because expected direct materials cost at actual volume was higher than budgeted direct materials cost at planned volume. The unfavorable variance might not be a bad thing. The variance is due to increased volume, which could be a good thing. The organizational unit most likely responsible for the activity variance is the marketing department.

The flexible budget variance is the difference between the expected materials cost at the actual volume ($4 $\times$ 32,000 units = $128,000) and the actual materials cost of $131,000. The $3,000 ($128,000 − $131,000) variance is unfavorable because it cost more than expected to make the 32,000 units. Either the production department or the purchasing department is most likely responsible for this variance.

The Human Element Associated with Flexible Budget Variances

The flexible budget cost variances offer insight into management efficiency. For example, Melrose Manufacturing Company's favorable materials variance could mean purchasing agents were shrewd in negotiating price concessions, discounts, or delivery terms and therefore reduced the price the company paid for materials. Similarly, production employees may have used materials efficiently, using less than expected. The unfavorable labor variance could mean managers failed to control employee wages or motivate employees to work hard. As with sales variances, cost variances require careful analysis. A favorable variance may, in fact, mask unfavorable conditions. For example, the favorable materials variance might have been caused by paying low prices for inferior goods. Using substandard materials could have required additional labor in the production process, which would explain the unfavorable labor variance. Again, we caution that variances, whether favorable or unfavorable, alert management to investigate further.

Standard Cost Systems

LO 5

Explain standard cost systems.

Standard cost systems help managers plan and also establish benchmarks against which actual performance can be judged. By highlighting differences between standard (expected) and actual performance, standard costing focuses management attention on the areas of greatest need. Because management talent is a valuable and expensive resource, businesses cannot afford to have managers spend large amounts of time on operations that are functioning normally. Instead, managers should concentrate on areas not performing as expected. In other words, management should attend to the exceptions; this management philosophy is known as **management by exception.**

Standard costing fosters using the management by exception principle. By reviewing performance reports that show differences between actual and standard costs, management can

focus its attention on the items that show significant variances. Areas with only minor variances need little or no review.

Establishing Standards

Establishing standards is probably the most difficult part of using a standard cost system. A **standard** represents the amount a price, cost, or quantity *should be* based on certain anticipated circumstances. Consider the complexity of establishing the standard cost to produce a pair of blue jeans. Among other things, managers need to know where they can get the best price for materials, who will pay transportation costs, if cash or volume discounts are available, whether the suppliers with the lowest price can reliably supply the quantities needed on a timely basis, how the material should be cut to conserve time and labor, in what order to sew pieces of material together, the wage rates of the relevant production employees, whether overtime will be needed, and how many pairs of jeans will be produced. Obtaining this information requires the combined experience, judgment, and forecasting ability of all personnel who have responsibility for price and usage decisions. Even when a multitalented group of experienced persons is involved in standard setting, the process involves much trial and error. Revising standards is common even with established systems.

Historical data provide a good starting point for establishing standards. These data must be updated for changes in technology, plant layout, new methods of production, and worker

productivity. Frequently, changes of this nature result from initiating a standard cost system. Remember that a *standard* represents what *should be* rather than what *is* or *was*. Engineers often help establish standards, recommending the most efficient way to perform required tasks. The engineers undertake time and motion studies and review material utilization in the process of developing standards. Established practices and policies are frequently changed in response to engineers' reports.

Management must consider behavioral implications when developing standards. Managers, supervisors, purchasing agents, and other affected employees should be consulted for two reasons: (1) their experience and expertise provide invaluable input to standard development and (2) persons who are involved in standard setting are more likely to accept and be motivated to reach the resulting standards. Management should also consider how difficult it should be to achieve standard performance. Difficulty levels can be described as follows: (1) ideal standards, (2) practical standards, and (3) lax standards.

Ideal standards represent flawless performance; they represent what costs should be under the best possible circumstances. They do not allow for normal materials waste and spoilage or ordinary labor inefficiencies caused by machine downtime, cleanups, breaks, or personal needs. Meeting ideal standards is beyond the capabilities of most, if not all, employees. Ideal standards may motivate some individuals to constantly strive for improvement, but unattainable standards discourage most people. When people consistently fail, they become demotivated and stop trying to succeed. In addition, variances associated with ideal standards lose significance. They reflect deviations that are largely beyond employees' control, and they mask true measures of superior or inferior performance, considerably reducing their usefulness.

Practical standards represent reasonable effort; they are attainable for most employees. Practical standards allow for normal levels of inefficiency in materials and labor usage. An average worker performing diligently would be able to achieve standard performance. Practical standards motivate most employees; the feeling of accomplishment attained through earnest effort encourages employees to do their best. Practical standards also produce meaningful variances. Deviations from practical standards usually result from factors employees control. Positive variances normally represent superior performance, and negative variances indicate inferior performance.

Lax standards represent easily attainable goals. Employees can achieve standard performance with minimal effort. Lax standards do not motivate most people; continual success with minimal effort leads to boredom and lackluster performance. In addition, variances lose meaning. Deviations caused by superior or inferior performance are obscured by the built-in slack.

Management must consider employee ability levels when establishing standards. Standards that seasoned workers can attain may represent ideal standards to inexperienced workers. Management should routinely monitor standards and adjust them when it is appropriate to do so.

Selecting Variances to Investigate

Managerial judgment, developed through experience, plays a significant role in deciding which variances to investigate. Managers consider the *materiality* of a variance, the *frequency* with which it occurs, their *capacity to control* the variance, and the *characteristics* of the items behind the variance.

Standard costs are estimates. They cannot perfectly predict actual costs. Most business experience minor variances as part of normal operations. Investigating minor variances is not likely to produce useful information. Many companies therefore establish *materiality* guidelines for selecting variances to analyze. They set dollar or percentage thresholds and ignore variances that fall below these limits, investigating material variances only. A **material variance** is one that could influence management decisions. Material variances should be investigated whether they are favorable or unfavorable. As mentioned earlier, a favorable price variance can result from purchasing substandard materials; the quality of the company's products, however, will suffer from the inferior materials and sales will fall.

How *frequently* a variance occurs impacts materiality. A variance of $20,000 may be immaterial in a single month, but if the same variance occurs repeatedly throughout the year, it can become a material $240,000 variance. Variance reports should highlight frequent as well as large variations.

Capacity to control refers to whether management action can influence the variance. If utility rates cause differences between actual and standard overhead costs, management has little control over the resulting variances. Conversely, if actual labor costs exceed standard costs because a supervisor fails to motivate employees, management can take some action. To maximize their value to the firm, managers should concentrate on controllable variances.

The *characteristics* of the items behind the variance may invite management abuse. For example, managers can reduce actual costs in the short term by delaying expenditures for maintenance, research and development, and advertising. Although cost reductions in these areas may produce favorable variances in the current period, they will have a long-term detrimental impact on profitability. Managers under stress may be tempted to focus on short-term benefits. Variances associated with these critical items should be closely analyzed.

The primary advantage of a standard cost system is efficient use of management talent to control costs. Secondary benefits include the following.

1. Standard cost systems quickly alert management to trouble spots. For example, a standard amount of materials may be issued for a particular job. If requisitions of additional materials require supervisory approval, each time a supervisor must grant such approval, she is immediately aware that excess materials are being used and can act before excessive material usage becomes unmanageable.

2. If established and maintained properly, standard cost systems can boost morale and motivate employees. Reward systems can be linked to accomplishments that exceed the established performance standards. Under such circumstances, employees become extremely conscious of the time and materials they use, minimizing waste and reducing costs.

3. Standard cost systems encourage good planning. The failure to plan well leads to overbuying, excessive inventory, wasted time, and so on. A standard cost system forces managers to plan, resulting in more effective operations with less waste.

Avoiding Gamesmanship

In general, variances should not be used to praise or punish managers. The purpose of identifying variances is to help management improve efficiency and productivity. If variances are used to assign rewards and blame, managers are likely to respond by withholding or manipulating information. For example, a manager might manipulate the cost standard for a job by deliberately overstating the amount of materials or labor needed to complete it. The manager's performance will later appear positive when the actual cost of materials or labor is less than the inflated standard. This practice is so common it has a name: **budget slack** is the difference between inflated and realistic standards. Sales staff may play a game called *lowballing* in which they deliberately underestimate the amount of expected sales, anticipating a reward when actual sales subsequently exceed the budget.

Gamesmanship can be reduced if superiors and subordinates participate sincerely in setting mutually agreeable, attainable standards. Once standards are established, the evaluation system that uses them must promote long-term respect among superiors and their subordinates. If standards are used solely for punitive purposes, gamesmanship will rapidly degrade the standard costing system.

Flexible Budget Manufacturing Cost Variances

LO 4

Compute and interpret flexible budget variances

The *manufacturing costs* incurred by Melrose Manufacturing Company in 2006 are summarized here:

	Standard	Actual
Variable materials cost per unit of product	$ 12.00	$ 11.78
Variable labor cost per unit of product	16.80	17.25
Variable overhead cost per unit of product	5.60	5.75
Total per unit variable manufacturing cost (a)	$ 34.40	$ 34.78
Total units produced (b)	19,000	19,000
Total variable manufacturing cost (a × b)	$653,600	$660,820
Fixed manufacturing cost	201,600	210,000
Total manufacturing cost	$855,200	$870,820

The total flexible budget manufacturing cost variance is $15,620 ($870,820 − $855,200). Because Melrose actually incurred more cost than expected, this variance is unfavorable. The

Answers to The Curious Accountant

As this chapter demonstrates, there are two primary reasons a company spends more or less to produce a product than it estimated it would. First, the company may have paid more or less to purchase the inputs needed to produce the product than it estimated. Second, the company used a greater or lesser quantity of these inputs than expected. In the case of Gourmet Pizzas, it may have had to pay more for flour, yeast, sugar, and so on than the owner estimated. Or, it may have used more of these ingredients than expected. For example, if pizza dough sits around too long before being used, it may have to be thrown out. This waste was not anticipated when computing the cost to make only one pizza. Of course, the higher than expected cost could have been a combination of price and quantity factors.

Gourmet Pizza needs to determine if the difference between its expected costs and actual costs was because the estimates were faulty, or because the production process was inefficient. If the estimates were to blame, the owner would need to revise them so he can charge the proper price to his customers. If the production process is inefficient, he needs to correct it if he is to earn an acceptable level of profit.

sum of the individual flexible budget variances for manufacturing costs shown in Exhibit 8.3 equals this variance:

Variable manufacturing cost variances:		
Materials	$ 4,180	Favorable
Labor	8,550	Unfavorable
Overhead	2,850	Unfavorable
Total variable manufacturing cost variances	7,220	Unfavorable
Fixed manufacturing cost variance	8,400	Unfavorable
Total	$15,620	Unfavorable

Exhibit 8.4 shows how to algebraically compute the flexible budget variable manufacturing cost variances.

EXHIBIT 8.4

Flexible Budget Variances Calculated Algebraically

Variable Mfg. Costs	Actual Cost Per Unit of Product	−	Standard Cost Per Unit of Product	×	Actual Units	=	Flexible Budget Variance
Materials	| $11.78	−	$12.00 |	×	19,000	=	$4,180 Favorable
Labor	| 17.25	−	16.80 |	×	19,000	=	8,550 Unfavorable
Overhead	| 5.75	−	5.60 |	×	19,000	=	2,850 Unfavorable

Note that the difference between the actual and standard cost is expressed as an absolute value. This mathematical notation suggests that the mathematical sign is not useful in interpreting the condition of the variance. To assess the condition of a variance, you must consider the type of variance being analyzed. With respect to cost variances, managers seek to attain actual prices that are lower than standard prices. In this case, the actual price of materials is less than the standard price, so the materials variance is favorable. Since the actual prices for labor and overhead are higher than the standard prices, those variances are unfavorable.

Calculate price and usage
variances.

Topic Tackler

PLUS

8-2

Price and Usage Variances[1]

For insight into what caused the flexible budget variances, management can analyze them in more detail. Consider the $4,180 favorable flexible budget materials cost variance. This variance indicates that Melrose spent less than expected on materials to make 19,000 trophies. Why? The price per unit of material may have been less than expected (price variance), or the company may have used less material than expected (usage variance). To determine what caused the total favorable variance, Melrose must separate the cost per unit of product into two parts, price per unit of material and quantity of material used.

Calculating Materials Price and Usage Variances

Melrose's accounting records indicate the materials cost per unit of product (trophy) is as follows:

	Actual Data	Standard Data
Price **per pound** of material	$ 1.90	$ 2.00
Quantity of materials per unit of product	× 6.2 pounds	× 6.0 pounds
Cost **per unit** of product	$11.78	$12.00

Based on this detail, the total quantity of materials is:

	Actual Data	Standard Data
Actual production volume	19,000 Units	19,000 Units
Quantity of materials per unit of product	× 6.2 Pounds	× 6.0 Pounds
Total quantity of materials	117,800 Pounds	114,000 Pounds

Confirm the price and usage components that make up the total flexible budget materials variance, as follows:

Actual Cost		Standard Cost	
Actual quantity used	117,800	Standard quantity	114,000
×	×	×	×
Actual price per pound	$1.90	Standard price per pound	$2.00
	$223,820		$228,000

Total variance: $4,180 Favorable

To isolate the price and usage variances, insert a Variance Dividing column between the Actual Cost and Standard Cost columns. The Variance Dividing column combines standard and actual data, showing the *standard cost* multiplied by the *actual quantity* of materials purchased and used.[2] Exhibit 8.5 shows the result.

---

[1]Businesses use various names for price and usage variances. For example, materials price and usage variances are frequently called **materials price** and **quantity variances;** labor price and usage variances are frequently called **labor rate** and **efficiency variances.** Regardless of the names, the underlying concepts and computations are the same for all variable price and usage variances.

[2]In practice, raw materials are frequently stored in inventory prior to use. Differences may exist between the amount of materials purchased and the amount of materials used. In such cases, the price variance is based on the quantity of materials *purchased,* and the usage variance is based on the quantity of materials *used.* This text makes the simplifying assumption that the amount of materials purchased equals the amount of materials used during the period.

EXHIBIT 8.5

Materials Price and Usage Variances

Actual Cost		Variance Dividing Data		Standard Cost	
Actual quantity used	117,800	Actual quantity used	117,800	Standard quantity	114,000
×	×	×	×	×	×
Actual price per pound	$1.90	Standard price per pound	$2.00	Standard price per pound	$2.00
	$223,820		$235,600		$228,000

Materials price variance
$11,780 Favorable

Materials usage variance
$7,600 Unfavorable

Total variance: $4,180 Favorable

Algebraic solution. The materials price variance (difference between the Actual Cost column and the Variance Dividing column) can be computed algebraically as follows:

$$\text{Price variance} = |\text{Actual price} - \text{Standard price}| \times \text{Actual quantity}$$
$$= |\$1.90 - \$2.00| \times 117,800$$
$$= \$0.10 \times 117,800$$
$$= \$11,780 \text{ Favorable}$$

Since the actual price ($1.90) is less than the standard price ($2.00), the materials price variance is favorable.

The materials usage variance (difference between the Variance Dividing column and the Standard Cost column) also can be determined algebraically, as follows:

$$\text{Usage variance} = |\text{Actual quantity} - \text{Standard quantity}| \times \text{Standard price}$$
$$= |117,800 - 114,000| \times \$2.00$$
$$= 3,800 \times \$2.00$$
$$= \$7,600 \text{ Unfavorable}$$

Responsibility for materials variances. A purchasing agent is normally responsible for the *favorable price variance.* Management establishes the standard materials cost based on a particular grade of material and assumptions about purchasing terms including volume discounts, cash discounts, transportation costs, and supplier services. A diligent purchasing agent places orders that take advantage of positive trading terms. In such circumstances, the company pays less than standard costs, resulting in a favorable price variance. Investigating the favorable price variance could result in identifying purchasing strategies to share with other purchasing agents. Analyzing favorable as well as unfavorable variances can result in efficiencies that benefit the entire production process.

In spite of a purchasing agent's diligence, unfavorable price variances may still occur. Suppliers may raise prices, poor scheduling by the production department may require more costly rush orders, or a truckers' strike may force the company to use a more expensive delivery system. These conditions are beyond a purchasing agent's control. Management must be careful to identify the real causes of unfavorable variances. False accusations and overreactions lead to resentment that will undermine the productive potential of the standard costing system.

The nature of the *materials usage variance* is readily apparent from the quantity data. Because the actual quantity used was more than the standard quantity, the variance is unfavorable. If management seeks to minimize cost, using more materials than expected is unfavorable. The materials usage variance is largely controlled by the production department. Materials waste caused by inexperienced workers, faulty machinery, negligent processing, or poor planning results in unfavorable usage variances. Unfavorable variances may also be caused by factors beyond the control of the production department. If the purchasing

REALITY BYTES

Most airlines will allow passengers to book a flight almost a year in advance at a price set on the day the reservation is made. Since the airline does not know what it will actually cost to operate a particular flight a year in advance, the price of the ticket will be based on its estimated costs. This could present a problem if costs rise significantly before the flight occurs.

Imagine that on December 14, 2004, Janice Brown booked a flight from Boston to Seattle for September 17, 2005, and that the ticket price was $288. Between December 2004 and September 2005 many of the airline's costs would not change unexpectedly; for example, the airplane had already been purchased and the salaries of the flight crew had been set. However, approximately 20 percent of the operating cost of an airline is for fuel. In December 2004 the spot price for jet fuel was $1.27 per gallon. The spot price of a commodity is the price it would sell for on a given day to someone who had not placed an advance order at a set price. By September 2005 the spot price for jet fuel had risen to $2.36 per gallon, due in part to a series of hurricanes that hit the Gulf of Mexico. In standard costing terminology, this would result in an unfavorable price variance.

How can companies avoid some of the problem of having to set the prices they charge before they know what it will cost them to deliver the promised goods or services? Sometimes they cannot, but jet fuel prices can be hedged. That is, a company can commit to buy fuel at an agreed-upon price at a future date. In 2005 Southwest Airlines hedged 85 percent of its fuel costs. As a result Southwest was not hurt as severely by the rising fuel prices as were other companies. Continental and Delta, by contrast, did not hedge any of their fuel costs in 2005.

Hedging has its own risks. Had fuel prices dropped during 2005 Southwest would still have had to honor its commitments to buy some of its fuel at a price higher than the spot price.

Sources: Federal government data, company reports, and *Travel Weekly,* "Fuel Prices Have Most Airlines over a Barrel," September 19, 2005, p. 12.

agent buys substandard materials the inferior materials may lead to more scrap (waste) during production, which would be reflected in unfavorable usage variances.

Calculating Labor Variances

Labor variances are calculated using the same general formulas as those used to compute materials price and usage variances. To illustrate, assume the labor cost per unit of product (trophy) for Melrose Manufacturing is as follows:

	Actual Data	Standard Data
Price **per hour**	$11.50	$12.00
Quantity of labor per unit of product	× 1.5 hours	× 1.4 hours
Cost **per unit** of product	$17.25	$16.80

Based on this detail, the total quantity of labor is:

	Actual Data	Standard Data
Actual production volume	19,000 Units	19,000 Units
Quantity of labor per unit of product	× 1.5 Hours	× 1.4 Hours
Total quantity of labor	28,500 Hours	26,600 Hours

Using this cost and quantity information, the labor price and usage variances are computed in Exhibit 8.6.

EXHIBIT 8.6

Labor Price and Usage Variances

Actual Cost		Variance Dividing Data		Standard Cost	
Actual hours used	28,500	Actual hours used (AHrs)	28,500	Standard hours (SHrs)	26,600
×	×	×	×	×	×
Actual price per labor hour (AP)	$11.50	Standard price per labor hour (SP)	$12.00	Standard price per labor hour	$12.00
	$327,750		$342,000		$319,200

Labor price variance
$14,250 Favorable

Labor usage variance
$22,800 Unfavorable

Algebraic solution: |AP − SP| × AHrs
|$11.50 − $12.00| × 28,500 = $14,250

Algebraic solution: |AHrs − SHrs| × SP
|28,500 − 26,600| × $12.00 = $22,800

Total variance: $8,550 Unfavorable

Responsibility for labor variances.   The *labor price variance* is favorable because the actual rate paid for labor is less than the standard rate. The production supervisor is usually responsible for the labor price variance because price variances normally result from labor assignments rather than underpayment or overpayment of the hourly rate. Because labor costs are usually fixed by contracts, paying more or less than established rates is not likely. However, using semiskilled labor to perform highly skilled tasks or vice versa will produce price variances. Similarly, using unanticipated overtime will cause unfavorable variances. Production department supervisors control which workers are assigned to which tasks and are therefore accountable for the resulting labor price variances.

Labor usage variances measure the productivity of the labor force. Because Melrose used more labor than expected, the labor usage variance is unfavorable. Unsatisfactory labor performance has many causes; low morale or poor supervision are possibilities. Furthermore, machine breakdowns, inferior materials, and poor planning can waste workers' time and reduce productivity. Production department supervisors generally control and are responsible for labor usage variances.

Price and usage variances may be interrelated. Using less-skilled employees who earned less but took longer to do the work could have caused both the favorable labor price variance and the unfavorable labor usage variance. As mentioned earlier, management must exercise diligence in determining causes of variances before concluding who should be held responsible for them.

DogHouse, Inc., expected to build 200 doghouses during July. Each doghouse was expected to require 2 hours of direct labor. Labor cost was expected to be $10 per hour. The company actually built 220 doghouses using an average of 2.1 labor hours per doghouse at an actual labor rate averaging $9.80 per hour. Determine the labor rate and usage variances.

Answer

Labor rate variance = |Actual rate − Standard rate| × Actual quantity

Labor rate variance = |$9.80 − $10.00| × (220 units × 2.1 hours) = $92.40 Favorable

Labor usage variance = |Actual quantity − Standard quantity| × Standard rate

Labor usage variance = |[220 × 2.1] − [220 × 2.0]| × $10 = $220.00 Unfavorable

CHECK YOURSELF 8.3

Variable Overhead Variances

Variable overhead variances are based on the same general formulas used to compute the materials and labor price and usage variances. Unique characteristics of variable overhead costs, however, require special attention. First, variable overhead represents many inputs such as supplies, utilities, and indirect labor. The variable overhead cost pool is normally assigned to products based on a predetermined variable overhead allocation rate. Using a single rate to assign a mixture of different costs complicates variance interpretation. Suppose the actual variable overhead rate is higher than the predetermined rate. Did the company pay more than expected for supplies, utilities, maintenance, or some other input variable? The cost of some variable overhead items may have been higher than expected while others were lower than expected. Similarly, a variable overhead usage variance provides no clue about which overhead inputs were over- or underused. Because meaningful interpretation of the results is difficult, many companies do not calculate price and usage variances for variable overhead costs. We therefore limit coverage of this subject to the total flexible budget variances shown in Exhibit 8.3.

Fixed Overhead Variances

Variable costs can have both price and usage variances. *Fixed overhead costs* can also have price variances. Remember that a *fixed* cost remains the same relative to changes in production *volume;* it does not necessarily remain the same as *expected.* Companies may certainly pay more or less than expected for a fixed cost. For example, a supervisor may receive an unplanned raise, causing actual salary costs to be more than expected. Similarly, a manager may negotiate a reduced rental cost for manufacturing equipment, causing actual rental costs to be less than expected. The difference between the *actual fixed overhead costs* and the *budgeted fixed overhead costs* is the **spending variance.** The spending variance is favorable if the company spent less than expected (actual cost is less than budgeted cost). The variance is unfavorable if the company spent more than expected (actual is more than budget).

Analyzing fixed overhead costs differs from analyzing variable costs because there is no potential usage variance. If Melrose pays $25,000 to rent its manufacturing facility, the company cannot use more or less of this rent no matter how many units of product it makes. Because the rent cost is fixed, however, the *cost per unit* will differ depending on the number of units of product made. The more units Melrose produces, the lower the fixed overhead cost per unit and vice versa. Because the volume of activity affects the cost per unit, companies commonly calculate a volume variance for fixed overhead costs. The **volume variance** is the difference between the *budgeted fixed cost* and the *amount of fixed costs allocated to production.* The amount of fixed costs allocated to production is frequently called *applied fixed cost.*

To illustrate the fixed overhead variances, return to the overhead spending variance for Melrose Manufacturing Company shown in Exhibit 8.3. The spending variance is the difference between the budgeted fixed overhead and the actual fixed overhead (|$201,600 budgeted − $210,000 actual| = $8,400 spending variance). The variance is unfavorable because Melrose actually spent more than expected for fixed overhead costs. Recall there is no fixed overhead usage variance.

To calculate the overhead volume variance, first calculate the predetermined fixed cost overhead rate: divide budgeted fixed costs of $201,600 by planned volume of 18,000 trophies. The predetermined fixed overhead rate is $11.20 per trophy ($201,600 ÷ 18,000 trophies). Since Melrose actually produced 19,000 trophies, it applied (allocated) $212,800 ($11.20 × 19,000 units) of fixed overhead costs to production. The difference between the budgeted fixed overhead and the applied fixed overhead produces a volume variance of $11,200 (|$201,600 budgeted − $212,800 applied| = $11,200 variance). Exhibit 8.7 shows a summary of the fixed overhead variances.

Responsibility for Fixed Overhead Price Variances

There is no way to know who is responsible for the unfavorable fixed overhead spending variance because all of the fixed overhead costs have been pooled together. To improve accountability, significant controllable fixed overhead costs such as supervisory salaries should be tagged for individual analysis. Fixed overhead costs that are not controllable may nevertheless

EXHIBIT 8.7

Fixed Overhead Spending and Volume Variances for Melrose Manufacturing Company

Actual Fixed Overhead Cost		Variance Dividing Data		Standard Fixed Overhead Cost	
Actual fixed cost	$210,000	Budgeted fixed cost	$201,600	Applied fixed cost	$212,800
		Overhead spending variance		Overhead volume variance	
		$8,400 Unfavorable		$11,200 Favorable	

be reported for management oversight. Even if not controllable in the short term, management should stay abreast of fixed costs because they may be controllable in the long term.

The fixed overhead volume variance is favorable because the actual volume of production was greater than the planned volume, resulting in a decreased cost per unit of product. The lower cost per unit does *not* result from reduced spending. Melrose actually spent more than expected on fixed overhead costs. The volume variance is caused by greater utilization of the company's manufacturing facilities. Melrose has benefited from *economies of scale*. As a rule, a company with high fixed costs should produce as high a volume as possible, thereby lowering its cost per unit of production. Of course, this rule assumes products produced can be sold at prevailing prices. An *unfavorable* volume variance alerts management to the underutilization of manufacturing facilities. In summary, a volume, variance indicates over- or underutilization of facilities, not over- or underspending.

As previously discussed, production managers are not usually responsible for volume variances. The level of production is normally based on sales volume, which is under the control of upper-level marketing managers. Although the volume variance measures the effectiveness of facilities use, the marketing department should be held accountable for volume variances because it is primarily responsible for establishing the volume of activity.

Summary of Manufacturing Cost Variances

To summarize, the total flexible budget variable manufacturing cost variance can be subdivided into materials, labor, and variable overhead variances. These variances can be further subdivided into price and usage variances. Manufacturing fixed cost can be subdivided into spending and volume variances. The *volume variance* is not a cost variance; it shows how volume affects fixed cost *per unit,* but it does not reflect a difference between the *total* amount of actual and expected costs. Exhibit 8.8 summarizes the relationships among the cost variances for Melrose Manufacturing Company. Exhibit 8.9 summarizes the algebraic formulas for the variable and fixed manufacturing cost variances discussed.

General, Selling, and Administrative Cost Variances

Variable general, selling, and administrative (GS&A) costs can have *price and usage* variances. For example, suppose Melrose decides to attach a promotional advertising brochure to each trophy it sells. Melrose may pay more or less than expected for each brochure (a price variance). Melrose also could use more or fewer of the brochures than expected (a usage variance). Businesses frequently compute variances for GS&A costs such as sales commissions, food and entertainment, postage, and supplies. The same algebraic formulas used to compute variances for variable manufacturing costs apply to computing variable GS&A cost variances.

Fixed GS&A costs are also subject to variance analysis. As shown in Exhibit 8.3, Melrose Manufacturing incurred a favorable $5,000 GS&A fixed cost *spending variance*. This means Melrose actually incurred less fixed GS&A cost than expected. A fixed cost *volume variance* could also be computed. Changes in sales volume affect the per unit amounts of fixed GS&A costs.

EXHIBIT 8.8

Relationships among Manufacturing Cost Variances for Melrose Manufacturing Company

Total flexible budget manufacturing cost variances
Total variable cost variance
|Actual cost − Standard cost| × Actual units
|$34.78 − $34.40| × 19,000 = $ 7,220 U

Total variable cost variance	7,220 U
Fixed cost variance	8,400 U
Total manufacturing cost variance	$15,620 U

Total flexible budget materials cost variance
|Actual cost − Standard cost| × Actual units
|$11.78 − $12.00| × 19,000 = → $ 4,180 F

Total flexible budget labor cost variance
|Actual cost − Standard cost| × Actual units
|$17.25 − $16.80| × 19,000 = → 8,550 U

Total flexible budget variable overhead cost variance
|Actual cost − Standard cost| × Actual units
|$5.75 − $5.60| × 19,000 = → 2,850 U

Total variable cost variance	7,220 U
Fixed cost variance	8,400 U
Total manufacturing cost variance	$15,620 U

Materials price variance
|Actual price − Standard price| × Actual quantity
|$1.90 − $2.00| × 117,800 = $11,780 F

Materials usage variance
|Actual quantity − Standard quantity| × Standard price
|117,800 − 114,000| × $2.00 = 7,600 U

Labor price variance
|Actual price − Standard price| × Actual hours
|$11.50 − $12.00| × 28,500 = 14,250 F

Labor usage variance
|Actual hours − Standard hours| × Standard price
|28,500 − 26,600| × $12.00 = 22,800 U

Variable overhead variance	2,850 U
Total variable cost variance	7,220 U
Fixed cost variance	8,400 U
Total manufacturing cost variance	$15,620 U

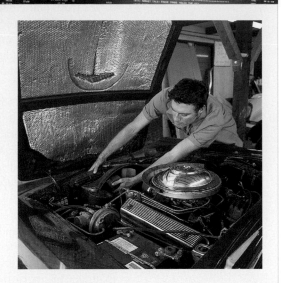

REALITY BYTES

Does standard costing apply to service companies as well as manufacturers? Absolutely! If you take your car into an auto dealership to be repaired and the service invoice shows that the repair took one hour to perform, you should not assume that was the actual time the repair required. The time for which you were charged was probably based on the standard time a repair of that type should have taken. The mechanic may have gotten this standard time from a reference manual such as the *Chilton Labor Guide* or the *Real-Time Labor Guide,* which are available in either print or CD versions. Some repair jobs can be completed in less time than the guides suggest, and some jobs will take longer. But since customers are charged based on a standard time allowed, two customers having the same repair performed will be charged the same price.

EXHIBIT 8.9

Algebraic Formulas for Variances

1. Variable cost variances (materials, labor, and overhead)
   a. Price variance

      |Actual price − Standard price| × Actual quantity
   b. Usage variance

      |Actual quantity − Standard quantity| × Standard price
2. Fixed overhead variances
   a. Fixed overhead spending variance

      |Actual fixed overhead costs − Budgeted fixed overhead costs|
   b. Fixed overhead volume variance

      |Applied fixed overhead costs − Budgeted fixed overhead costs|

Many different individuals are responsible for GS&A cost variances. For example, lower-level sales personnel are responsible for controlling the price and usage of promotional items. In contrast, upper-level administrative officers are responsible for fixed salary expenses. A full discussion of GS&A cost variances is beyond the scope of this text.

A Look Back

The essential topics of this chapter are the master budget, flexible budgets, and variance analysis. The *master budget* is determined by multiplying the standard sales price and per unit variable costs by the planned volume of activity. The master budget is prepared at the beginning of the accounting period for planning purposes. It is not adjusted to reflect differences between the planned and actual volume of activity. Since this budget remains unchanged regardless of actual volume, it is also called a *static budget*. *Flexible budgets* differ from static budgets in that they show the estimated amount of revenue and costs expected at different levels of volume. Both static and flexible budgets are based on the same per unit standard amounts and the same fixed costs. The total amounts of revenue and costs in a static budget differ from those in a flexible budget because they are based on different levels of volume. Flexible budgets are used for planning, cost control, and performance evaluation.

The differences between standard (sometimes called *expected* or *estimated*) and actual amounts are called *variances*. Variances are used to evaluate managerial performance and can be either favorable or unfavorable. *Favorable sales variances* occur when actual sales are greater than expected sales. *Unfavorable sales variances* occur when actual sales are less than expected sales. *Favorable cost variances* occur when actual costs are less than expected costs. *Unfavorable cost variances* occur when actual costs are more than expected costs.

Volume variances are caused by the difference between the static and flexible budgets. Since both static and flexible budgets are based on the same standard sales price and costs per unit, the volume variances are attributable solely to differences between the planned and the actual volume of activity. Favorable sales volume variances suggest that the marketing manager has performed well by selling more than was expected. Unfavorable sales volume variances suggest the inverse. Favorable or unfavorable variable cost volume variances are not meaningful for performance evaluation because variable costs are expected to change in proportion to changes in the volume of activity.

Flexible budget variances are computed by taking the difference between the amounts of revenue and variable costs that are expected at the actual volume of activity and the actual amounts of revenue and variable costs incurred at the actual volume of activity. Since the volume of activity is the same for the flexible budget and the actual results, variances are caused by the differences between the standard and actual sales price and per unit costs. Flexible budget variances are used for cost control and performance evaluation.

Flexible budget variances can be subdivided into *price and usage variances*. Price and usage variances for materials and labor can be computed with the following formulas. Variable overhead variances are calculated with the same general formulas; interpreting the results is difficult, however, because of the variety of inputs combined in variable overhead.

$$\text{Price variance} = |\text{Actual price} - \text{Standard price}| \times \text{Actual quantity}$$

$$\text{Usage variance} = |\text{Actual quantity} - \text{Standard quantity}| \times \text{Standard price}$$

The purchasing agent is normally accountable for the material price variance. The production department supervisor is usually responsible for the materials usage variance and the labor price and usage variances.

The fixed overhead cost variance consists of a spending variance and a volume variance computed as follows:

$$\text{Spending OH variance} = \text{Actual fixed OH costs} - \text{Budgeted fixed OH costs}$$

$$\text{OH volume variance} = \text{Budgeted fixed cost} - \text{Applied (allocated) fixed costs}$$

The overhead spending variance is similar to a price variance. Although fixed costs do not change relative to changes in production volume, they may be more or less than expected. For example, a production supervisor's salary will remain unchanged regardless of the volume of activity, but the supervisor may receive a raise resulting in higher than expected fixed costs. The fixed overhead volume variance is favorable if the actual volume of production is greater than the expected volume. A higher volume of production results in a lower fixed cost per unit. The volume variance measures how effectively production facilities are being used.

Management must interpret variances with care. For example, a purchasing agent may produce a favorable price variance by buying inferior materials at a low cost. However, an unfavorable labor usage variance may result because employees have difficulty using the substandard materials. The production supervisor is faced with an unfavorable usage variance for which she is not responsible. In addition, the purchasing agent's undesirable choice produced a favorable price variance. Favorable variances do not necessarily reflect good performance and unfavorable variances do not always suggest poor performance. The underlying causes of variances must be investigated before assigning responsibility for them.

A Look Forward

Chapter 9 introduces other techniques for evaluating managerial performance. The concept of decentralization and its relationship to responsibility accounting will be covered. You will learn how to calculate and interpret return on investment and residual income. Finally, you will study approaches used to establish the price of products that are transferred between divisions of the same company.

SELF-STUDY REVIEW PROBLEM

A step-by-step audio-narrated series of slides is provided on the text website at www.mhhe.com/edmonds2008.

Bugout Pesticides, Inc., established the following standard price and costs for a termite control product that it sells to exterminators.

Variable price and cost data (per unit)	Standard	Actual
Sales price	$52.00	$49.00
Materials cost	10.00	10.66
Labor cost	12.00	11.90
Overhead cost	7.00	7.05
General, selling, and administrative (GS&A) cost	8.00	7.92
Expected fixed costs (in total)		
Manufacturing	$150,000	$140,000
General, selling, and administrative	60,000	64,000

The 2007 master budget was established at an expected volume of 25,000 units. Actual production and sales volume for the year was 26,000 units.

Required

a. Prepare the pro forma income statement for Bugout's 2007 master budget.
b. Prepare a flexible budget income statement at the actual volume.
c. Determine the sales activity (volume) variances and indicate whether they are favorable or unfavorable. Comment on how Bugout would use the variances to evaluate performance.
d. Determine the flexible budget variances and indicate whether they are favorable or unfavorable.
e. Identify the two variances Bugout is most likely to analyze further. Explain why you chose these two variances. Who is normally responsible for the variances you chose to investigate?
f. Each unit of product was expected to require 4 pounds of material, which has a standard price of $2.50 per pound. Actual materials usage was 4.1 pounds per unit at an actual price of $2.60 per pound. Determine the materials price and usage variances.

Solution to Requirements a, b, and c

Number of units		25,000	26,000	
	Per Unit Standards	Master Budget	Flexible Budget	Activity Variances
Sales revenue	$52	$1,300,000	$1,352,000	$52,000 F
Variable manufacturing costs				
Materials	10	(250,000)	(260,000)	10,000 U
Labor	12	(300,000)	(312,000)	12,000 U
Overhead	7	(175,000)	(182,000)	7,000 U
Variable GS&A	8	(200,000)	(208,000)	8,000 U
Contribution margin		375,000	390,000	15,000 F
Fixed costs				
Manufacturing		(150,000)	(150,000)	0
GS&A		(60,000)	(60,000)	0
Net income		$ 165,000	$ 180,000	$15,000 F

The sales activity variances are useful in determining how changes in sales volume affect revenues and costs. Since the flexible budget is based on standard prices and costs, the variances do not provide insight into differences between standard prices and costs versus actual prices and costs.

Solution to Requirement d

Number of units		26,000	26,000	
	Actual Unit Price/Cost	Flexible Budget*	Actual Results	Variances
Sales revenue	$49.00	$1,352,000	$1,274,000	$78,000 U
Variable manufacturing costs				
Materials	10.66	(260,000)	(277,160)	17,160 U
Labor	11.90	(312,000)	(309,400)	2,600 F
Overhead	7.05	(182,000)	(183,300)	1,300 U
Variable GS&A	7.92	(208,000)	(205,920)	2,080 F
Contribution margin		390,000	298,220	91,780 U
Fixed costs				
Manufacturing		(150,000)	(140,000)	10,000 F
GS&A		(60,000)	(64,000)	4,000 U
Net income		$ 180,000	$ 94,220	$85,780 U

*The price and cost data for the flexible budget come from the previous table.

Solution to Requirement e

The management by exception doctrine focuses attention on the sales price variance and the materials variance. The two variances are material in size and are generally under the control of management. Upper-level marketing managers are responsible for the sales price variance. These managers are normally responsible for establishing the sales price. In this case, the actual sales price is less than the planned sales price, resulting in an unfavorable flexible budget variance. Mid-level production supervisors and purchasing agents are normally responsible for the materials cost variance. This variance could have been caused by waste or by paying more for materials than the standard price. Further analysis of the materials cost variance follows in Requirement f.

Solution to Requirement f

(Actual price − Standard price) ×   Actual quantity   = Price variance
($2.60 − $2.50)   × (4.1 pounds × 26,000 units) = $10,660 U

(Actual quantity − Standard quantity) × Standard price = Usage variance
|(4.1 × 26,000) − (4.0 × 26,000)|× $2.50   = $6,500 U

The total of the price and usage variances [($10,660 + $6,500) = $17,160] equals the total materials flexible budget variance computed in Requirement *d*.

KEY TERMS

Budget slack 346	Labor rate variance 348	Materials price variance 348	Spending variance 352
Favorable variance 339	Lax standard 345	Materials quantity	Standard 344
Flexible budget 338	Making the numbers 340	variance 348	Static budget 338
Flexible budget variance 342	Management by	Practical standard 345	Unfavorable variance 339
Ideal standard 345	exception 343	Sales price variance 342	Variances 339
Labor efficiency variance 348	Material variance 345	Sales volume variance 339	Volume variance 352

QUESTIONS

1. What is the difference between a static budget and a flexible budget? When is each used?

2. When the operating costs for Bill Smith's production department were released, he was sure that he would be getting a raise. His costs were $20,000 less than the planned cost in the master budget. His supervisor informed him that the results look good but that a more in-depth analysis is necessary before raises can be assigned. What other considerations could Mr. Smith's supervisor be interested in before she rates his performance?

3. When are sales and cost variances favorable and unfavorable?

4. Joan Mason, the marketing manager for a large manufacturing company, believes her unfavorable sales volume variance is the responsibility of the production department. What production circumstances that she does not control could have been responsible for her poor performance?

5. When would variable cost volume variances be expected to be unfavorable? How should unfavorable variable cost volume variances be interpreted?

6. What factors could lead to an increase in sales revenues that would not merit congratulations to the marketing manager?

7. With respect to fixed costs, what are the consequences of the actual volume of activity exceeding the planned volume?

8. How are flexible budget variances determined? What causes these variances?

9. Minnie Divers, the manager of the marketing department for one of the industry's leading retail businesses, has been notified by the accounting department that her department experienced an unfavorable sales volume variance in the preceding period but a favorable sales price variance. Based on these contradictory results, how would you interpret her overall performance as suggested by her variances?

10. What three attributes are necessary for establishing the best standards? What information and considerations should be taken into account when establishing standards?

11. What are the three ranges of difficulty in standard setting? What level of difficulty normally results in superior employee motivation?

12. "So many variances," exclaimed Carl, a production manager with Bonnyville Manufacturing. "How do I determine the variances that need investigation? I can't possibly investigate all of them." Which variances will lead to useful information?

13. What is the primary benefit associated with using a standard cost system?

14. A processing department of Carmine Corporation experienced a high unfavorable materials quantity variance. The plant manager initially commented, "The best way to solve this problem is to fire the supervisor of the processing department." Do you agree? Explain.

15. Sara Anderson says that she is a busy woman with no time to look at favorable variances. Instead, she concentrates solely on the unfavorable ones. She says that favorable variances imply that employees are doing better than expected and need only quick congratulations. In contrast, unfavorable variances indicate that change is needed to get the substandard performance up to par. Do you agree? Explain.

16. What two factors affect the total materials and labor variances?

17. Who is normally responsible for a materials price variance? Identify two factors that may be beyond this individual's control that could cause an unfavorable price variance.

18. John Jamail says that he doesn't understand why companies have labor price variances because most union contracts or other binding agreements set wage rates that do not normally change in the short term. How could rate variances occur even when binding commitments hold the dollar per hour rate constant?

19. Which individuals are normally held responsible for labor usage variances?

20. What is the primary cause of an unfavorable overhead volume variance?

21. What is the primary cause of a favorable overhead spending variance?

MULTIPLE-CHOICE QUESTIONS

Multiple-choice questions are provided on the text website at www.mhhe.com/edmonds2008.

EXERCISES—SERIES A

All Exercises in Series A are available with McGraw-Hill's Homework Manager®.

L.O. 2

Exercise 8-1A   *Classifying variances as favorable or unfavorable*

Required

Indicate whether each of the following variances is favorable or unfavorable. The first one has been done as an example.

Item to Classify	Standard	Actual	Type of Variance
Sales volume	40,000 units	42,000 units	Favorable
Sales price	$3.60 per unit	$3.63 per unit	
Materials cost	$2.90 per pound	$3.00 per pound	
Materials usage	91,000 pounds	90,000 pounds	
Labor cost	$10.00 per hour	$9.60 per hour	
Labor usage	61,000 hours	61,800 hours	
Fixed cost spending	$400,000	$390,000	
Fixed cost per unit (volume)	$3.20 per unit	$3.16 per unit	

L.O. 2

Exercise 8-2A   *Determining amount and type (favorable vs. unfavorable) of variance*

Required

Compute variances for the following items and indicate whether each variance is favorable (F) or unfavorable (U).

Item	Budget	Actual	Variance	F or U
Sales revenue	$490,000	$506,000		
Cost of goods sold	$385,000	$360,000		
Material purchases at 5,000 pounds	$275,000	$280,000		
Materials usage	$180,000	$178,000		
Sales price	$500	$489		
Production volume	950 units	900 units		
Wages at 4,000 hours	$60,000	$58,700		
Labor usage at $16 per hour	$96,000	$97,000		
Research and development expense	$22,000	$25,000		
Selling and administrative expenses	$49,000	$40,000		

Exercise 8-3A   *Preparing master and flexible budgets*   L.O. 1

Trent Manufacturing Company established the following standard price and cost data.

Sales price	$ 10 per unit
Variable manufacturing cost	4 per unit
Fixed manufacturing cost	4,000 total
Fixed selling and administrative cost	1,600 total

Trent planned to produce and sell 1,100 units. Actual production and sales amounted to 1,200 units.

Required

a. Prepare the pro forma income statement in contribution format that would appear in a master budget.
b. Prepare the pro forma income statement in contribution format that would appear in a flexible budget.

Exercise 8-4A   *Determining sales volume variances*   L.O. 3

Required

Use the information provided in Exercise 8-3A.

a. Determine the volume variances.
b. Classify the variances as favorable (F) or unfavorable (U).
c. Comment on the usefulness of the variances with respect to performance evaluation and identify the member of the management team most likely to be responsible for these variances.
d. Explain why the fixed cost variances are zero.
e. Determine the fixed cost per unit based on planned activity and the fixed cost per unit based on actual activity. Assuming Trent uses information in the master budget to price the company's product, comment on how the volume variance could affect the company's profitability.

Exercise 8-5A   *Determining flexible budget variances*   L.O. 4

Use the standard price and cost data provided in Exercise 8-3A. Assume that the actual sales price is $9.60 per unit and that the actual variable cost is $4.10 per unit. The actual fixed manufacturing cost is $3,800, and the actual selling and administrative expenses are $1,700.

Required

a. Determine the flexible budget variances.
b. Classify the variances as favorable (F) or unfavorable (U).
c. Comment on the usefulness of the variances with respect to performance evaluation and identify the member(s) of the management team who is (are) most likely to be responsible for these variances.

Exercise 8-6A   *Using a flexible budget to accommodate market uncertainty*   L.O. 4

According to its original plan, Graham Consulting Services Company would charge its customers for service at $200 per hour in 2006. The company president expects consulting services provided to customers to reach 40,000 hours at that rate. The marketing manager, however, argues that actual results may range from 35,000 hours to 45,000 hours because of market uncertainty. Graham's standard variable cost is $90 per hour, and its standard fixed cost is $3,000,000.

Required

Develop flexible budgets based on the assumptions of service levels at 35,000 hours, 40,000 hours, and 45,000 hours.

L.O. 3, 4

Exercise 8-7A   *Evaluating a decision to increase sales volume by lowering sales price*

Camden Educational Services had budgeted its training service charge at $100 per hour. The company planned to provide 40,000 hours of training services during 2009. By lowering the service charge to $90 per hour, the company was able to increase the actual number of hours to 42,000.

Required

a. Determine the sales volume variance, and indicate whether it is favorable (F) or unfavorable (U).
b. Determine the flexible budget variance, and indicate whether it is favorable (F) or unfavorable (U).
c. Did lowering the price of training services increase revenue? Explain.

L.O. 3

Exercise 8-8A   *Responsibility for sales volume variance*

Boyd Company expected to sell 400,000 of its pagers during 2006. It set the standard sales price for the pager at $30 each. During June, it became obvious that the company would be unable to attain the expected volume of sales. Boyd's chief competitor, Lyon Corporation, had lowered prices and was pulling market share from Boyd. To be competitive, Boyd matched Lyon's price, lowering its sales price to $28 per pager. Lyon responded by lowering its price even further to $24 per pager. In an emergency meeting of key personnel, Boyd's accountant, Misty Wayne, stated, "Our cost structure simply won't support a sales price in the $24 range." The production manager, James Coburn, said, "I don't understand why I'm here. The only unfavorable variance on my report is a fixed cost volume variance and that one is not my fault. We shouldn't be making the product if the marketing department isn't selling it."

Required

a. Describe a scenario in which the production manager is responsible for the fixed cost volume variance.
b. Describe a scenario in which the marketing manager is responsible for the fixed cost volume variance.
c. Explain how a decline in sales volume would affect Boyd's ability to lower its sales price.

L.O. 4

Exercise 8-9A   *Responsibility for variable manufacturing cost variance*

Meyer Manufacturing Company set its standard variable manufacturing cost at $24 per unit of product. The company planned to make and sell 4,000 units of product during 2008. More specifically, the master budget called for total variable manufacturing cost to be $96,000. Actual production during 2008 was 4,200 units, and actual variable manufacturing costs amounted to $101,640. The production supervisor was asked to explain the variance between budgeted and actual cost ($101,640 − $96,000 = $5,640). The supervisor responded that she was not responsible for the variance that was caused solely by the increase in sales volume controlled by the marketing department.

Required

Do you agree with the production supervisor? Explain.

L.O. 6

Exercise 8-10A   *Calculating the materials usage variance*

Katherin Justice is the manager of the Lakeshore Bagel Shop. The corporate office had budgeted her store to sell 4,000 ham sandwiches during the week beginning July 17. Each sandwich was expected to contain 6 ounces of ham. During the week of July 17, the store actually sold 4,500 sandwiches and used 27,450 ounces of ham. The standard cost of ham is $0.25 per ounce. The variance report from company headquarters showed an unfavorable materials usage variance of $650. Ms. Justice thought the variance was too high, but she had no accounting background and did not know how to register a proper objection.

Required

a. Is the variance calculated properly? If not, recalculate it.
b. Provide three independent explanations as to what could have caused the materials price variance that you determined in Requirement *a*.

Exercise 8-11A   *Determining materials price and usage variances*

L.O. 6

Nellie's Florals produced a special Mother's Day arrangement that included six roses. The standard and actual costs of the roses used in each arrangement follow.

	Standard	Actual
Average number of roses per arrangement	6.0	6.1
Price per rose	× $0.32	× $0.30
Cost of roses per arrangement	$1.92	$1.83

Nellie's Florals planned to make 760 arrangements but actually made 800.

Required

a. Determine the total flexible budget materials variance and indicate whether it is favorable (F) or unfavorable (U).
b. Determine the materials price variance and indicate whether it is favorable (F) or unfavorable (U).
c. Determine the materials usage variance and indicate whether it is favorable (F) or unfavorable (U).
d. Confirm the accuracy of Requirements *a, b,* and *c* by showing that the sum of the price and usage variances equals the total variance.

Exercise 8-12A   *Responsibility for materials usage variance*

L.O. 6

Meadow Fruit Basket Company makes baskets of assorted fruit. The standard and actual costs of oranges used in each basket of fruit follow.

	Standard	Actual
Average number of oranges per basket	4.00	4.80
Price per orange	× $0.30	× $0.25
Cost of oranges per basket	$1.20	$1.20

Meadow actually produced 25,000 baskets.

Required

a. Determine the materials price variance and indicate whether it is favorable (F) or unfavorable (U).
b. Determine the materials usage variance and indicate whether it is favorable (F) or unfavorable. (U)
c. Explain why the purchasing agent may have been responsible for the usage variance.

Exercise 8-13A   *Responsibility for labor price and usage variances*

L.O. 6

Duffey Manufacturing Company incurred a favorable labor price variance and an unfavorable labor usage variance.

Required

a. Describe a scenario in which the personnel manager is responsible for the unfavorable usage variance.
b. Describe a scenario in which the production manager is responsible for the unfavorable usage variance.

Exercise 8-14A   *Calculating and explaining labor price and usage variances*

L.O. 6

Lowell and Sons, a CPA firm, established the following standard labor cost data for completing what the firm referred to as a Class 2 tax return. Lowell expected each Class 2 return to require 4.0 hours of labor at a cost of $50 per hour. The firm actually completed 600 returns. Actual labor hours averaged 4.4 hours per return and actual labor cost amounted to $46 per hour.

Required

a. Determine the total labor variance and indicate whether it is favorable (F) or unfavorable (U).
b. Determine the labor price variance and indicate whether it is favorable (F) or unfavorable (U).

c. Determine the labor usage variance and indicate whether it is favorable (F) or unfavorable (U).

d. Explain what could have caused these variances.

L.O. 6

Exercise 8-15A   *Determining the standard labor price*

Sullivan Car Wash, Inc., expected to wash 900 cars during the month of August. Washing each car was expected to require 0.25 hours of labor. The company actually used 252 hours of labor to wash 840 cars. The labor usage variance was $336 unfavorable.

Required

a. Determine the standard labor price.

b. If the actual labor rate is $7.50, indicate whether the labor price variance would be favorable (F) or unfavorable (U).

L.O. 5, 6

Exercise 8-16A   *Calculating the variable overhead variance*

Crumbley Company established a predetermined variable overhead cost rate at $10.00 per direct labor hour. The actual variable overhead cost rate was $9.60 per hour. The planned level of labor activity was 75,000 hours of labor. The company actually used 77,000 hours of labor.

Required

a. Determine the total flexible budget variable overhead cost variance.

b. Like many companies, Crumbley has decided not to separate the total variable overhead cost variance into price and usage components. Explain why Crumbley made this choice.

L.O. 6

Exercise 8-17A   *Determining and interpreting fixed overhead variances*

Stanley Company established a predetermined fixed overhead cost rate of $24 per unit of product. The company planned to make 9,000 units of product but actually produced only 8,000 units. Actual fixed overhead costs were $228,000.

Required

a. Determine the fixed overhead cost spending variance and indicate whether it is favorable or unfavorable. Explain what this variance means. Identify the manager(s) who is (are) responsible for the variance.

b. Determine the fixed overhead cost volume variance and indicate whether it is favorable or unfavorable. Explain why this variance is important. Identify the manager(s) who is (are) responsible for the variance.

PROBLEMS—SERIES A

All Problems in Series A are available with McGraw-Hill's Homework Manager®.

L.O. 1, 3

CHECK FIGURES
a. NI = $81,000
b. NI at 29,000 units:
   $72,000

Problem 8-18A   *Determining sales volume variances*

Humphrey Publications established the following standard price and costs for a hardcover picture book that the company produces.

Standard price and variable costs	
Sales price	$36.00
Materials cost	9.00
Labor cost	4.50
Overhead cost	6.30
General, selling, and administrative costs	7.20
Planned fixed costs	
Manufacturing	$135,000
General, selling, and administrative	54,000

Humphrey planned to make and sell 30,000 copies of the book.

Required

a. Prepare the pro forma income statement that would appear in the master budget.
b. Prepare flexible budget income statements, assuming production volumes of 29,000 and 31,000 units.
c. Determine the sales volume variances, assuming production and sales volume are actually 31,000 units.
d. Indicate whether the variances are favorable (F) or unfavorable (U).
e. Comment on how Humphrey could use the variances to evaluate performance.

Problem 8-19A *Determining and interpreting flexible budget variances*

Use the standard price and cost data supplied in Problem 8-18A. Assume that Humphrey actually produced and sold 31,000 books. The actual sales price and costs incurred follow.

Actual price and variable costs	
Sales price	$35.00
Materials cost	9.20
Labor cost	4.40
Overhead cost	6.35
General, selling, and administrative costs	7.00
Actual fixed costs	
Manufacturing	$120,000
General, selling, and administrative	60,000

L.O. 4

CHECK FIGURE
Flexible budget variance of NI: $20,450 U

Required

a. Determine the flexible budget variances.
b. Indicate whether each variance is favorable (F) or unfavorable (U).
c. Identify the management position responsible for each variance. Explain what could have caused the variance.

Problem 8-20A *Flexible budget planning*

Clyde Chen, the president of Creek Computer Services, needs your help. He wonders about the potential effects on the firm's net income if he changes the service rate that the firm charges its customers. The following basic data pertain to fiscal year 2008.

Standard rate and variable costs	
Service rate per hour	$80.00
Labor cost	40.00
Overhead cost	7.20
General, selling, and administrative cost	4.30
Expected fixed costs	
Facility repair	$525,000
General, selling, and administrative	150,000

L.O. 1

www.mhhe.com/edmonds2008

CHECK FIGURES
a. NI = $180,000
c. NI = $162,500

Required

a. Prepare the pro forma income statement that would appear in the master budget if the firm expects to provide 30,000 hours of services in 2008.
b. A marketing consultant suggests to Mr. Chen that the service rate may affect the number of service hours that the firm can achieve. According to the consultant's analysis, if Creek charges customers $75 per hour, the firm can achieve 38,000 hours of services. Prepare a flexible budget using the consultant's assumption.
c. The same consultant also suggests that if the firm raises its rate to $85 per hour, the number of service hours will decline to 25,000. Prepare a flexible budget using the new assumption.
d. Evaluate the three possible outcomes you determined in Requirements *a, b,* and *c* and recommend a pricing strategy.

Problem 8-21A   *Determining materials price and usage variances*

Hancock Fruit Drink Company planned to make 400,000 containers of apple juice. It expected to use two cups of frozen apple concentrate to make each container of juice, thus using 800,000 cups (400,000 containers × 2 cups) of frozen concentrate. The standard price of one cup of apple concentrate is $0.25. Hancock actually paid $220,336.20 to purchase 816,060 cups of concentrate, which was used to make 402,000 containers of apple juice.

Required

a. Are flexible budget materials variances based on the planned volume of activity (400,000 containers) or actual volume of activity (402,000 containers)?
b. Compute the actual price per cup of concentrate.
c. Compute the standard quantity (number of cups of concentrate) required to produce the containers.
d. Compute the materials price variance and indicate whether it is favorable (F) or unfavorable (U).
e. Compute the materials usage variance and indicate whether it is favorable (F) or unfavorable (U).

Problem 8-22A   *Determining labor price and usage variances*

Valarie's Doll Company produces handmade dolls. The standard amount of time spent on each doll is 1.5 hours. The standard cost of labor is $8 per hour. The company planned to make 10,000 dolls during the year but actually used 15,400 hours of labor to make 11,000 dolls. The payroll amounted to $123,816.

Required

a. Should labor variances be based on the planned volume of 10,000 dolls or the actual volume of 11,000 dolls?
b. Prepare a table that shows the standard labor price, the actual labor price, the standard labor hours, and the actual labor hours.
c. Compute the labor price variance and indicate whether it is favorable (F) or unfavorable (U).
d. Compute the labor usage variance and indicate whether it is favorable (F) or unfavorable (U).

Problem 8-23A   *Computing fixed overhead variances*

In addition to other costs, Gulfsouth Telephone Company planned to incur $425,000 of fixed manufacturing overhead in making 340,000 telephones. Gulfsouth actually produced 348,000 telephones, incurring actual overhead costs of $427,000. Gulfsouth establishes its predetermined overhead rate based on the planned volume of production (expected number of telephones).

Required

a. Calculate the predetermined overhead rate.
b. Determine the overhead spending variance and indicate whether it is favorable (F) or unfavorable (U).
c. Determine the overhead volume variance and indicate whether it is favorable (F) or unfavorable (U).

Problem 8-24A   *Computing materials, labor, and overhead variances*

The following data were drawn from the records of Cowley Corporation.

Planned volume for year (static budget)	4,000 units
Standard direct materials cost per unit	3 lbs. @ $2.00 per pound
Standard direct labor cost per unit	2 hours @ $4.00 per hour
Total expected fixed overhead costs	$18,000
Actual volume for the year (flexible budget)	4,200 units
Actual direct materials cost per unit	2.9 lbs. @ $2.10 per pound
Actual direct labor cost per unit	2.2 hrs. @ $3.80 per hour
Total actual fixed overhead costs	$17,600

Required

a. Prepare a materials variance information table showing the standard price, the actual price, the standard quantity, and the actual quantity.

b. Calculate the materials price and usage variances. Indicate whether the variances are favorable (F) or unfavorable (U).

c. Prepare a labor variance information table showing the standard rate, the actual rate, the standard hours, and the actual hours.

d. Calculate the labor price and usage variances. Indicate whether the variances are favorable (F) or unfavorable (U).

e. Calculate the predetermined overhead rate, assuming that Cowley uses the number of units as the allocation base.

f. Calculate the overhead spending variance. Indicate whether the variance is favorable (F) or unfavorable (U).

g. Calculate the overhead volume variance. Indicate whether the variance is favorable (F) or unfavorable (U).

Problem 8-25A   *Computing materials, labor, and overhead variances*

L.O. 6

Garland Manufacturing Company produces a component part of a top secret military communication device. Standard production and cost data for the part, Product X, follow.

CHECK FIGURES
b. Usage variance:
   $3,708 U
d. Price variance:
   $11,948 U

Planned production	40,000 units
Per unit direct materials	2 lbs. @ $1.80 per lb.
Per unit direct labor	3 hrs. @ $8.00 per hr.
Total estimated fixed overhead costs	$936,000

Garland purchased and used 84,460 pounds of material at an average cost of $1.85 per pound. Labor usage amounted to 119,480 hours at an average of $8.10 per hour. Actual production amounted to 41,200 units. Actual fixed overhead costs amounted to $984,000. The company completed and sold all inventory for $2,400,000.

Required

a. Prepare a materials variance information table showing the standard price, the actual price, the standard quantity, and the actual quantity.

b. Calculate the materials price and usage variances. Indicate whether the variances are favorable (F) or unfavorable (U).

c. Prepare a labor variance information table showing the standard price, the actual price, the standard hours, and the actual hours.

d. Calculate the labor price and usage variances. Indicate whether the variances are favorable (F) or unfavorable (U).

e. Calculate the predetermined overhead rate, assuming that Garland uses the number of units as the allocation base.

f. Calculate the overhead spending and volume variances and indicate whether they are favorable (F) or unfavorable (U).

g. Determine the amount of gross margin Garland would report on the year-end income statement.

Problem 8-26A   *Computing variances*

L.O. 6

Jett Manufacturing Company produces a single product. The following data apply to the standard cost of materials and labor associated with making the product.

CHECK FIGURES
a. 1,760 lbs
d. $8.60

Materials quantity per unit	1 pound
Materials price	$5.00 per pound
Labor quantity per unit	2 hours
Labor price	$9.00 per hour

During the year, the company made 1,800 units of product. At the end of the year, the variance accounts had the following balances.

Materials Usage Variance account	$200 Favorable
Materials Price Variance account	$176 Unfavorable
Labor Usage Variance account	$900 Unfavorable
Labor Price Variance account	$1,480 Favorable

Required

a. Determine the actual amount of materials used.
b. Determine the actual price paid per pound for materials.
c. Determine the actual labor hours used.
d. Determine the actual labor price per hour.

Problem 8-27A *Computing standard cost and analyzing variances*

Gate Company manufactures molded candles that are finished by hand. The company developed the following standards for a new line of drip candles.

Amount of direct materials per candle	1.6 pounds
Price of direct materials per pound	$0.75
Quantity of labor per unit	2 hours
Price of direct labor per hour	$6.00/hour
Total budgeted fixed overhead	$126,000

During 2007, Gate planned to produce 30,000 drip candles. Production lagged behind expectations, and it actually produced only 24,000 drip candles. At year-end, direct materials purchased and used amounted to 37,000 pounds at a unit price of $0.60 per pound. Direct labor costs were actually $5.75 per hour and 46,000 actual hours were worked to produce the drip candles. Overhead for the year actually amounted to $130,000. Overhead is applied to products using a predetermined overhead rate based on estimated units.

Required

(Round all computations to two decimal places.)

a. Compute the standard cost per candle for direct materials, direct labor, and overhead.
b. Determine the total standard cost for one drip candle.
c. Compute the actual cost per candle for direct materials, direct labor, and overhead.
d. Compute the total actual cost per candle.
e. Compute the price and usage variances for direct materials and direct labor. Identify any variances that Gate should investigate. Offer possible cause(s) for the variances.
f. Compute the fixed overhead spending and volume variances. Explain your findings.
g. Although the individual variances (price, usage, and overhead) were large, the standard cost per unit and the actual cost per unit differed by only a few cents. Explain why.

Problem 8-28A *Analyzing not-for-profit entity variances*

The North Accounting Association held its annual public relations luncheon in April 2008. Based on the previous year's results, the organization allocated $21,210 of its operating budget to cover the cost of the luncheon. To ensure that costs would be appropriately controlled, Sherry McDougal, the treasurer, prepared the following budget for the 2008 luncheon.

The budget for the luncheon was based on the following expectations.

1. The meal cost per person was expected to be $11.80. The cost driver for meals was attendance, which was expected to be 1,400 individuals.
2. Postage was based on $0.39 per invitation and 3,000 invitations were expected to be mailed. The cost driver for postage was number of invitations mailed.
3. The facility charge is $1,000 for a room that will accommodate up to 1,600 people; the charge for one to hold more than 1,600 people is $1,500.
4. A fixed amount was designated for printing, decorations, the speaker's gift, and publicity.

NORTH ACCOUNTING ASSOCIATION
Public Relations Luncheon Budget
April 2008

Operating funds allocated	$21,210
Expenses	
Variable costs	
Meals (1,400 × $11.80)	16,520
Postage (3,000 × 0.39)	1,170
Fixed costs	
Facility	1,000
Printing	950
Decorations	840
Speaker's gift	130
Publicity	600
Total expenses	21,210
Budget surplus (deficit)	$ 0

Actual results for the luncheon follow.

NORTH ACCOUNTING ASSOCIATION
Actual Results for Public Relations Luncheon
April 2008

Operating funds allocated	$21,210
Expenses	
Variable costs	
Meals (1,620 × $12.50)	20,250
Postage (4,000 × 0.39)	1,560
Fixed costs	
Facility	1,500
Printing	950
Decorations	840
Speaker's gift	130
Publicity	600
Total expenses	25,830
Budget deficit	$(4,620)

Reasons for the differences between the budgeted and actual data follow.

1. The president of the organization, Grace Smith, increased the invitation list to include 1,000 former members. As a result, 4,000 invitations were mailed.
2. Attendance was 1,620 individuals. Because of higher-than-expected attendance, the luncheon was moved to a larger room, thereby increasing the facility charge to $1,500.
3. At the last minute, Ms. McDougal decided to add a dessert to the menu, which increased the meal cost to $12.50 per person.
4. Printing, decorations, the speaker's gift, and publicity costs were as budgeted.

Required

a. Prepare a flexible budget and compute the activity variances based on a comparison between the master budget and the flexible budget.
b. Compute flexible budget variances by comparing the flexible budget with the actual results.

c. Ms. Smith was extremely upset with the budget deficit. She immediately called Ms. McDougal to complain about the budget variance for the meal cost. She told Ms. McDougal that the added dessert caused the meal cost to be $3,730 ($20,250 − $16,520) over budget. She added, "I could expect a couple hundred dollars one way or the other, but a couple thousand is totally unacceptable. At the next meeting of the budget committee, I want you to explain what happened." Assume that you are Ms. McDougal. What would you tell the members of the budget committee?

d. Since this is a not-for-profit organization, why should anyone be concerned with meeting the budget?

EXERCISES—SERIES B

L.O. 2

Exercise 8-1B *Classifying variances as favorable or unfavorable*

Required

Indicate whether each of the following variances is favorable (F) or unfavorable (U). The first one has been done as an example.

Item to Classify	Standard	Actual	Type of Variance
Sales volume	38,000 units	36,750 units	Unfavorable
Sales price	$6.90 per unit	$6.78 per unit	
Materials cost	$2.10 per pound	$2.30 per pound	
Materials usage	102,400 pounds	103,700 pounds	
Labor cost	$8.25 per hour	$8.80 per hour	
Labor usage	56,980 hours	55,790 hours	
Fixed cost spending	$249,000	$244,000	
Fixed cost per unit (volume)	$2.51 per unit	$3.22 per unit	

L.O. 2

Exercise 8-2B *Recognizing favorable vs. unfavorable variances*

Compute variances for the following items and indicate whether each variance is favorable (F) or unfavorable (U).

Item	Budget	Actual	Variance	F or U
Sales revenue	$620,000	$650,000		
Cost of goods sold	$450,000	$400,000		
Materials purchases at 10,000 pounds	$260,000	$290,000		
Materials usage	$270,000	$260,000		
Sales price	$550	$560		
Production volume	890 units	900 units		
Wages at 7,600 hours	$91,200	$90,800		
Labor usage	7,600 hours	8,000 hours		
Research and development expense	$81,000	$90,000		
Selling and administrative expenses	$75,000	$71,000		

L.O. 1

Exercise 8-3B *Preparing master and flexible budgets*

Irvin Manufacturing Company established the following standard price and cost data.

Sales price	$12 per unit
Variable manufacturing cost	8 per unit
Fixed manufacturing cost	20,000 total
Fixed selling and administrative cost	18,000 total

Irvin planned to produce and sell 18,000 units. It actually produced and sold 19,000 units.

Required

a. Prepare the pro forma income statement that would appear in a master budget. Use the contribution margin format.
b. Prepare the pro forma income statement that would appear in a flexible budget. Use the contribution margin format.

Exercise 8-4B   *Determining sales activity (volume) variances*

L.O. 3

Required

Use the information provided in Exercise 8-3B.

a. Determine the volume variances.
b. Classify the variances as favorable or unfavorable.
c. Comment on the usefulness of the variances with respect to performance evaluation and identify the member of the management team most likely to be responsible for these variances.
d. Explain why the fixed cost variances are zero.
e. Determine the fixed cost per unit based on planned activity and the fixed cost per unit based on actual activity. Assuming Irvin uses information in the master budget to price its product, explain how the volume variance could affect the company's profitability.

Exercise 8-5B   *Determining flexible budget variances*

L.O. 4

Use the standard price and cost data provided in Exercise 8-3B. Assume the actual sales price was $11.90 per unit and the actual variable cost was $7.95 per unit. The actual fixed manufacturing cost was $21,000, and the actual selling and administrative expenses were $17,300.

Required

a. Determine the flexible budget variances.
b. Classify the variances as favorable or unfavorable.
c. Comment on the usefulness of the variances with respect to performance evaluation and identify the member(s) of the management team that is (are) most likely to be responsible for these variances.

Exercise 8-6B   *Using a flexible budget to accommodate market uncertainty*

L.O. 4

Escott Cable Installation Services, Inc., is planning to open a new regional office. Based on a market survey Escott commissioned, the company expects services demand for the new office to be between 30,000 and 40,000 hours annually. The firm normally charges customers $40 per hour for its installation services. Escott expects the new office to have a standard variable cost of $25 per hour and standard fixed cost of $550,000 per year.

Required

a. Develop flexible budgets based on 30,000 hours, 35,000 hours, and 40,000 hours of services.
b. Based on the results for Requirement *a,* comment on the likely success of Escott's new office.

Exercise 8-7B   *Evaluating a decision to increase sales volume by reducing sales price*

L.O. 3, 4

At the beginning of its most recent accounting period, Coleman Roof had planned to clean 400 house roofs at an average price of $420 per roof. By reducing the service charge to $390 per roof, the company was able to increase the actual number of roofs cleaned to 450.

Required

a. Determine the sales volume variance and indicate whether it is favorable (F) or unfavorable (U).
b. Determine the flexible budget variance and indicate whether it is favorable (F) or unfavorable (U).
c. Did reducing the price charged for cleaning roofs increase revenue? Explain.

Exercise 8-8B   *Responsibility for sales volume (activity) variance*

L.O. 3

Vincent Manufacturing Company had an excellent year. The company hired a new marketing director in January. The new director's great motivational appeal inspired the sales staff, and, as a result, sales were 20 percent higher than expected. In a recent management meeting, the company president, Carl Nolan, congratulated the marketing director and then criticized Mark Piedra, the company's production manager, because of an unfavorable fixed cost spending variance. Mr. Piedra countered that the favorable fixed cost volume variance more than offset the unfavorable fixed cost spending variance. He argued that Mr. Nolan should evaluate the two variances in total and that he should be rewarded rather than criticized.

Required

Do you agree with Mr. Piedra's defense of the unfavorable fixed cost spending variance? Explain.

L.O. 4

Exercise 8-9B   *Assessing responsibility for a labor cost variance*

Gilliam Technologies Company's 2008 master budget called for using 60,000 hours of labor to produce 180,000 units of software. The standard labor rate for the company's employees is $19 per direct labor hour. Demand exceeded expectations, resulting in production and sales of 210,000 software units. Actual direct labor costs were $1,323,000. The year-end variance report showed a total unfavorable labor variance of $183,000.

Required

Assume you are the vice president of manufacturing. Should you criticize or praise the production supervisor's performance? Explain.

L.O. 6

Exercise 8-10B   *Calculating the materials usage variance*

Natalie Ketali manages the Sweet Candy Shop, which was expected to sell 4,000 servings of its trademark candy during July. Each serving was expected to contain 6 ounces of candy. The standard cost of the candy was $0.20 per ounce. The shop actually sold 3,800 servings and actually used 22,100 ounces of candy.

Required

a. Compute the materials usage variance.
b. Explain what could have caused the variance that you computed in Requirement *a.*

L.O. 6

Exercise 8-11B   *Determining materials price and usage variances*

Safilo Company makes paint that it sells in 1-gallon containers to retail home improvement stores. During 2007, the company planned to make 190,000 gallons of paint. It actually produced 198,000 gallons. The standard and actual quantity and cost of the color pigment for 1 gallon of paint follow.

	Standard	Actual
Quantity of materials per gallon	2.4 ounces	2.5 ounces
Price per ounce	× $0.30	× $0.32
Cost per gallon	$0.72	$0.80

Required

a. Determine the total flexible budget materials variance for pigment. Indicate whether the variance is favorable or unfavorable.
b. Determine the materials price variance and indicate whether the variance is favorable (F) or unfavorable (U).
c. Determine the materials usage variance and indicate whether the variance is favorable (F) or unfavorable (U).
d. Confirm your answers to Requirements *a, b,* and *c* by showing that the sum of the price and usage variances equals the total variance.

L.O. 6

Exercise 8-12B   *Responsibility for materials price variance*

Cream Delight, Inc., makes ice cream that it sells in 5-gallon containers to retail ice cream parlors. During 2008, the company planned to make 100,000 containers of ice cream. It actually produced 97,000 containers. The actual and standard quantity and cost of sugar per container follow.

	Standard	Actual
Quantity of materials per container	2 pounds	2.1 pounds
Price per pound	× $0.39	× $0.40
Cost per container	$0.78	$0.84

Required

a. Determine the materials price variance and indicate whether the variance is favorable (F) or unfavorable (U).

b. Determine the materials usage variance and indicate whether the variance is favorable (F) or unfavorable (U).

c. Explain how the production manager could have been responsible for the price variance.

Exercise 8-13B *Responsibility for labor rate and usage variance*

L.O. 6

Adams Manufacturing Company incurred an unfavorable labor rate variance.

Required

a. Describe a scenario in which the personnel manager is responsible for the unfavorable rate variance.

b. Describe a scenario in which the production manager is responsible for the unfavorable rate variance.

Exercise 8-14B *Calculating and explaining labor price and usage variances*

L.O. 6

Perez Landscaping Company established the following standard labor cost data to provide complete lawn care service (cutting, edging, trimming, and blowing) for a small lawn. Perez planned each lawn to require 2 hours of labor at a cost of $12 per hour. The company actually serviced 500 lawns using an average of 1.75 labor hours per lawn. Actual labor costs were $14 per hour.

Required

a. Determine the total labor variance and indicate whether the variance is favorable (F) or unfavorable (U).

b. Determine the labor price variance and indicate whether the variance is favorable (F) or unfavorable (U).

c. Determine the labor usage variance and indicate whether the variance is favorable (F) or unfavorable (U).

d. Explain what could have caused the variances computed in Requirements *b* and *c*.

Exercise 8-15B *Determining standard labor hours*

L.O. 6

Hair Fashion is a hair salon. It planned to provide 120 hair color treatments during December. Each treatment was planned to require 0.5 hours of labor at the standard labor price of $15 per hour. The salon actually provided 125 treatments. The actual labor price averaged $14.80. The labor price variance was $15 favorable.

Required

a. Determine the actual number of labor hours used per treatment.

b. Indicate whether the labor usage variance would be favorable (F) or unfavorable (U).

Exercise 8-16B *Calculating a variable overhead variance*

L.O. 6

Hughes Manufacturing Company established a predetermined variable overhead cost rate of $10 per direct labor hour. The actual variable overhead cost rate was $9.50 per direct labor hour. Hughes planned to use 150,000 hours of direct labor. It actually used 152,000 hours of direct labor.

Required

a. Determine the total flexible budget variable overhead cost variance.

b. Many companies do not subdivide the total variable overhead cost variance into price and usage components. Under what circumstances would it be appropriate to distinguish between the price and usage components of a variable overhead cost variance? What would be required to accomplish this type of analysis?

L.O. 6

Exercise 8-17B   *Determining and interpreting fixed overhead variances*

Clayton Manufacturing Company established a predetermined fixed overhead cost rate of $135 per unit of product. The company planned to make 19,000 units of product but actually produced 20,000 units. Actual fixed overhead costs were $2,750,000.

Required

a. Determine the fixed overhead cost spending variance. Indicate whether the variance is favorable (F) or unfavorable (U). Explain what this variance means. Identify the manager(s) who is (are) responsible for the variance.

b. Determine the fixed overhead cost volume variance. Indicate whether the variance is favorable (F) or unfavorable (U). Explain what the designations *favorable* and *unfavorable* mean with respect to the fixed overhead volume variance.

PROBLEMS—SERIES B

L.O. 1, 3

Problem 8-18B   *Determining sales volume variances*

Jones Food Corporation developed the following standard price and costs for a refrigerated TV dinner that the company produces.

Standard price and variable costs	
Sales price	$25.96
Materials cost	9.00
Labor cost	2.60
Overhead cost	0.56
General, selling, and administrative costs	4.20
Planned fixed costs	
Manufacturing cost	$500,000
General, selling, and administrative costs	360,000

Jones plans to make and sell 200,000 TV dinners.

Required

a. Prepare the pro forma income statement that would appear in the master budget.

b. Prepare flexible budget income statements, assuming production and sales volumes of 180,000 and 220,000 units.

c. Determine the sales volume variances, assuming production and sales volume are actually 190,000 units.

d. Indicate whether the variances are favorable (F) or unfavorable (U).

e. Comment on how Jones could use the variances to evaluate performance.

L.O. 4

Problem 8-19B   *Determining and interpreting flexible budget variances*

Use the standard price and cost data supplied in Problem 8-18B. Assume that Jones actually produced and sold 216,000 units. The actual sales price and costs incurred follow.

Actual price and variable costs	
Sales price	$25.80
Materials cost	8.80
Labor cost	2.68
Overhead cost	0.56
General, selling, and administrative costs	4.40
Actual fixed costs	
Manufacturing cost	$512,000
General, selling, and administrative costs	356,000

Required

a. Determine the flexible budget variances.
b. Indicate whether each variance is favorable (F) or unfavorable (U).
c. Identify the management position responsible for each variance. Explain what could have caused the variance.

Problem 8-20B   *Flexible budget planning*   L.O. 1

Executive officers of Gulf Seafood Processing Company are holding a planning session for fiscal year 2008. They have already established the following standard price and costs for their canned seafood product.

Standard price and variable costs	
Price per can	$3.00
Materials cost	1.05
Labor cost	0.64
Overhead cost	0.10
General, selling, and administrative costs	0.25
Expected fixed costs	
Production facility costs	$215,000
General, selling, and administrative costs	180,000

Required

a. Prepare the pro forma income statement that would appear in the master budget if the company expects to produce 600,000 cans of seafood in 2008.
b. A marketing consultant suggests to Gulf's president that the product's price may affect the number of cans the company can sell. According to the consultant's analysis, if the firm sets its price at $2.70, it could sell 810,000 cans of seafood. Prepare a flexible budget based on the consultant's suggestion.
c. The same consultant also suggests that if the company raises its price to $3.25 per can, the volume of sales would decline to 400,000. Prepare a flexible budget based on this suggestion.
d. Evaluate the three possible outcomes developed in Requirements *a, b,* and *c* and recommend a pricing strategy.

Problem 8-21B   *Determining materials price and usage variances*   L.O. 6

Sabrina Swimsuit Specialties, Inc., makes fashionable women's swimsuits. Its most popular swimsuit, with the Sarong trade name, uses a standard fabric amount of 6 yards of raw material with a standard price of $2.50 per yard. The company planned to produce 100,000 Sarong swimsuits in 2008. At the end of 2008, the company's cost accountant reported that Sabrina had used 636,000 yards of fabric to make 102,000 swimsuits. Actual cost for the raw material was $1,653,600.

Required

a. Are flexible budget material variances based on the planned volume of 100,000 swimsuits or on actual volume of 102,000 swimsuits?
b. Compute the actual price per yard of fabric.
c. Compute the standard quantity (yards of fabric) required to produce the swimsuits.
d. Compute the materials price variance and indicate whether it is favorable (F) or unfavorable (U).
e. Compute the materials usage variance and indicate whether it is favorable (F) or unfavorable (U).

Problem 8-22B   *Determining labor price and usage variances*   L.O. 6

As noted in Problem 8-21B, Sabrina Swimsuit makes swimsuits. In 2008, Sabrina produced its most popular swimsuit, the Sarong, for a standard labor price of $15 per hour. The standard amount of labor was 1.0 hour per swimsuit. The company had planned to produce 100,000 Sarong swimsuits. At the end of 2008, the company's cost accountant reported that Sabrina had used 107,000 hours of labor to make 102,000 swimsuits. The total labor cost was $1,647,800.

Required

a. Should the labor variances be based on the planned volume of 100,000 swimsuits or on the actual volume of 102,000 swimsuits?

b. Prepare a table that shows the standard labor price, the actual labor price, the standard labor hours, and the actual labor hours.

c. Compute the labor price variance and indicate whether it is favorable (F) or unfavorable (U).

d. Compute the labor usage variance and indicate whether it is favorable (F) or unfavorable (U).

L.O. 6

Problem 8-23B   *Computing fixed overhead variances*

Gallo Sporting Goods Co. manufactures baseballs. According to Gallo's 2007 budget, the company planned to incur $600,000 of fixed manufacturing overhead costs to make 200,000 baseballs. Gallo actually produced 187,000 balls, incurring $592,000 of actual fixed manufacturing overhead costs. Gallo establishes its predetermined overhead rate on the basis of the planned volume of production (expected number of baseballs).

Required

a. Calculate the predetermined overhead rate.

b. Determine the overhead spending variance and indicate whether it is favorable (F) or unfavorable (U).

c. Determine the overhead volume variance and indicate whether it is favorable (F) or unfavorable (U).

L.O. 6

Problem 8-24B   *Computing materials, labor, and overhead variances*

Sean Ferlitto was a new cost accountant at Chapman Plastics Corporation. He was assigned to analyze the following data that his predecessor left him.

Planned volume for year (static budget)	10,000 units
Standard direct materials cost per unit	2 lbs. @ $1.50 per pound
Standard direct labor cost per unit	0.5 hours @ $10.00 per hour
Total planned fixed overhead costs	$12,000
Actual volume for the year (flexible budget)	10,800 units
Actual direct materials cost per unit	1.9 lbs. @ $1.60 per pound
Actual direct labor cost per unit	0.6 hrs. @ $8.00 per hour
Total actual fixed overhead costs	$12,400

Required

a. Prepare a materials variance information table showing the standard price, the actual price, the standard quantity, and the actual quantity.

b. Calculate the materials price and usage variances and indicate whether they are favorable (F) or unfavorable (U).

c. Prepare a labor variance information table showing the standard price, the actual price, the standard hours, and the actual hours.

d. Calculate the labor price and usage variances and indicate whether they are favorable (F) or unfavorable (U).

e. Calculate the predetermined overhead rate, assuming that Chapman Plastics uses the number of units as the allocation base.

f. Calculate the overhead spending variance and indicate whether it is favorable (F) or unfavorable (U).

g. Calculate the overhead volume variance and indicate whether it is favorable (F) or unfavorable (U).

L.O. 6

Problem 8-25B   *Computing materials, labor, and overhead variances*

Burch Corporation makes mouse pads for computer users. After the first year of operation, Angie Burch, the president and chief executive officer, was eager to determine the efficiency of the company's operation. In her analysis, she used the following standards provided by her assistant.

Units of planned production	200,000
Per unit direct materials	1 square foot @ $0.25 per square foot
Per unit direct labor	0.2 hrs. @ $7.00 per hr.
Total estimated fixed overhead costs	$100,000

Burch purchased and used 230,000 square feet of material at an average cost of $0.24 per square foot. Labor usage amounted to 39,600 hours at an average of $6.90 per hour. Actual production amounted to 208,000 units. Actual fixed overhead costs amounted to $102,000. The company completed and sold all inventory for $707,200.

Required

a. Prepare a materials variance information table showing the standard price, the actual price, the standard quantity, and the actual quantity.

b. Calculate the materials price and usage variances and indicate whether they are favorable (F) or unfavorable (U).

c. Prepare a labor variance information table showing the standard price, the actual price, the standard hours, and the actual hours.

d. Calculate the labor price and usage variances and indicate whether they are favorable (F) or unfavorable (U).

e. Calculate the predetermined overhead rate, assuming that Burch uses the number of units as the allocation base.

f. Calculate the overhead spending and volume variances and indicate whether they are favorable (F) or unfavorable (U).

g. Determine the amount of gross margin Burch would report on the year-end income statement.

Problem 8-26B   *Computing variances*

L.O. 6

A fire destroyed most of Sherif Products Corporation's records. Clara Thornton, the company's accountant, is trying to piece together the company's operating results from salvaged documents. She discovered the following data.

Standard materials quantity per unit	2.5 pounds
Standard materials price	$2 per pound
Standard labor quantity per unit	0.6 hour
Standard labor price	$12 per hour
Actual number of products produced	8,000 units
Materials price variance	$792 Favorable
Materials quantity variance	$400 Favorable
Labor price variance	$1,952 Unfavorable
Labor usage variance	$960 Unfavorable

Required

a. Determine the actual amount of materials used.

b. Determine the actual price per pound paid for materials.

c. Determine the actual labor hours used.

d. Determine the actual labor price per hour.

Problem 8-27B   *Computing standard cost and analyzing variances*

L.O. 6

Porzio Manufacturing Company, which makes aluminum alloy wheels for automobiles, recently introduced a new luxury wheel that fits small sports cars. The company developed the following standards for its new product.

Amount of direct materials per wheel	2 pounds
Price of direct materials per pound	$5.50
Quantity of labor per wheel	2.50 hours
Price of direct labor per hour	$8.00/hour
Total budgeted fixed overhead	$168,000

In its first year of operation, Porzio planned to produce 3,000 sets of wheels (four wheels per set). Because of unexpected demand, it actually produced 3,600 sets of wheels. By year-end direct materials purchased and used amounted to 30,000 pounds of aluminum at a cost of $175,500. Direct labor costs were actually $8.40 per hour. Actual hours worked were 2.2 hours per wheel. Overhead for the year actually amounted to $180,000. Overhead is applied to products using a predetermined overhead rate based on the total estimated number of wheels to be produced.

Required

(Round all computations to two decimal places.)

a. Compute the standard cost per wheel for direct materials, direct labor, and overhead.
b. Determine the total standard cost per wheel.
c. Compute the actual cost per wheel for direct materials, direct labor, and overhead.
d. Compute the actual cost per wheel.
e. Compute the price and usage variances for direct materials and direct labor. Identify any variances that Porzio should investigate. Based on your results, offer a possible explanation for the labor usage variance.
f. Compute the fixed overhead spending and volume variances. Explain your findings.

L.O. 2, 3, 4

Problem 8-28B *Analyzing not-for-profit organization variances*

The Marketing Department of Sexton State University planned to hold its annual distinguished visiting lecturer (DVL) presentation in October 2008. The secretary of the department prepared the following budget based on costs that had been incurred in the past for the DVL presentation.

MARKETING DEPARTMENT Distinguished Visiting Lecturer Budget October 2008	
Variable costs	
Beverages at break	$ 375
Postage	312
Step costs*	
Printing	500
Facility	250
Fixed costs	
Dinner	200
Speaker's gift	100
Publicity	50
Total costs	$1,787

*Step costs are costs that change abruptly after a defined range of volume (attendance). They do not change proportionately with unit volume increases (i.e., the cost is fixed within a range of activity but changes to a different fixed cost when the volume changes to a new range). For instance, the facility charge is $250 for from 1 to 400 attendees. From 401 to 500 attendees, the next larger room is needed, and the charge is $350. If more than 500 attended, the room size and cost would increase again.

The budget for the presentation was based on the following expectations:

1. Attendance was estimated at 50 faculty from Sexton State and neighboring schools, 125 invited guests from the business community, and 200 students. Beverage charge per attendee would be $1.00. The cost driver for beverages is the number of attendees.

2. Postage was based on $0.39 per invitation; 800 invitations were expected to be mailed to faculty and finance business executives. The cost driver for postage is the number of invitations mailed.

3. Printing cost was expected to be $500 for 800 invitations and envelopes. Additional invitations and envelopes could be purchased in batches of 100 units with each batch costing $50.

4. The DVL presentation was scheduled at a downtown convention center. The facility charge was $250 for a room that has a capacity of 400 persons; the charge for one to hold more than 400 people was $350. The convention center provided refreshments at break except beverages.

5. After the presentation, three Sexton State faculty members planned to take the speaker to dinner. The dinner had been prearranged at a local restaurant for $200 for a three-course dinner.

6. A gift for the speaker was budgeted at $100.

7. Publicity would consist of flyers and posters placed at strategic locations around campus and business offices, articles in the business section of the local newspapers, and announcements made in business classes and school newspapers. Printing for the posters and flyers had been prearranged for $50.

8. The speaker lives in the adjoining state and had agreed to drive to the presentation at his own expense.

The actual results of the presentation follow.

1. Attendance consisted of 450 faculty, business executives, and students.

2. An additional 100 invitations were printed and mailed when the Marketing Department decided that selected alumni should also be invited.

3. Based on RSVP responses, the department rented the next size larger room at a cost of $350 for the presentation.

4. The speaker's gift cost was as budgeted.

5. The department chairperson decided to have a four-course dinner, which cost $230.

6. Because of poor planning, the posters and flyers were not distributed as widely as expected. It was decided at the last minute to hire a temporary assistant to make phone calls to alumni. The actual publicity cost was $75.

Required

a. Prepare a flexible budget and compute activity variances based on a comparison between the master budget and the flexible budget. Briefly explain the meaning of the activity variances.

b. Compute flexible budget variances by comparing the flexible budget with the actual results. Briefly explain the meaning of the variable cost flexible budget variances. Discuss the fixed cost variances.

c. Calculate the expected and actual fixed cost per attendee. Discuss the significance of the difference in these amounts.

d. Since the department is a not-for-profit entity, why is it important for it to control the cost of sponsoring the distinguished visiting lecturer presentation?

ANALYZE, THINK, COMMUNICATE

ATC 8-1   Business Applications Case   *Static versus flexible budget variances*

Kevin Delo is the manufacturing production supervisor for Value-Tech Headset Company. Trying to explain why he did not get the year-end bonus that he had expected, he told his wife, "This is the dumbest place I ever worked. Last year the company set up this budget assuming it would sell 250,000 headsets. Well, it sold only 240,000. The company lost money and gave me a bonus for not using as much materials and labor as was called for in the budget. This year, the company has the same 250,000 goal and it sells 260,000. The company's making all kinds of money. You'd think I'd get this big fat bonus. Instead, management tells me I used more materials and labor than was budgeted. They say the company would have made a lot more money if I'd stayed within my budget. I guess I gotta wait for another bad year before I get a bonus. Like I said, this is the dumbest place I ever worked."

Value-Tech Company's master budget and the actual results for the most recent year of operating activity follow.

	Master Budget	Actual Results	Variances	F or U
Number of units	250,000	260,000	10,000	
Sales revenue	$3,750,000	$3,950,000	$200,000	F
Variable manufacturing costs				
Materials	(600,000)	(622,200)	22,200	U
Labor	(312,500)	(321,000)	8,500	U
Overhead	(337,500)	(354,700)	17,200	U
Variable general, selling, and admin. costs	(475,000)	(501,300)	26,300	U
Contribution margin	2,025,000	2,150,800	125,800	F
Fixed costs				
Manufacturing overhead	(1,275,000)	(1,273,100)	1,900	F
General, selling, and admin. costs	(470,000)	(479,300)	9,300	U
Net income	$ 280,000	$ 398,400	$118,400	F

Required

a. Did Value-Tech increase unit sales by cutting prices or by using some other strategy?

b. Is Mr. Delo correct in his conclusion that something is wrong with the company's performance evaluation process? If so, what do you suggest be done to improve the system?

c. Prepare a flexible budget and recompute the budget variances.

d. Explain what might have caused the fixed costs to be different from the amount budgeted.

e. Assume that the company's material price variance was favorable and its material usage variance was unfavorable. Explain why Mr. Delo may not be responsible for these variances. Now, explain why he may have been responsible for the material usage variance.

f. Assume the labor price variance is unfavorable. Was the labor usage variance favorable or unfavorable?

g. Is the fixed overhead volume variance favorable or unfavorable? Explain the effect of this variance on the cost of each set of headsets.

ATC 8-2   Group Assignment   *Variable price and usage variances and fixed cost variances*

Kemp Tables, Inc. (KTI), makes picnic tables of 2 × 4 planks of treated pine. It sells the tables to large retail discount stores such as Wal-Mart. After reviewing the following data generated by KTI's chief accountant, the company president, Arianne Darwin, expressed concern that the total manufacturing cost was more than $0.5 million above budget ($7,084,800 − $6,520,000 = $564,800).

	Actual Results	Master Budget
Cost of planks per table	$ 44.10	$ 40.00
Cost of labor per table	26.10	25.50
Total variable manufacturing cost per table (a)	$ 70.20	$ 65.50
Total number of tables produced (b)	82,000	80,000
Total variable manufacturing cost (a × b)	$5,756,400	$5,240,000
Total fixed manufacturing cost	1,328,400	1,280,000
Total manufacturing cost	$7,084,800	$6,520,000

Ms. Darwin asked Conrad Pearson, KTI's chief accountant, to explain what caused the increase in cost. Mr. Pearson responded that things were not as bad as they seemed. He noted that part of the cost variance resulted from making and selling more tables than had been expected. Making more tables naturally causes the cost of materials and labor to be higher. He explained that the flexible budget cost variance was less than $0.5 million. Specifically, he provided the following comparison.

	Actual Results	Flexible Budget
Cost of planks per table	$ 44.10	$ 40.00
Cost of labor per table	26.10	25.50
Total variable manufacturing cost per table (a)	$ 70.20	$ 65.50
Total number of tables produced (b)	82,000	82,000
Total variable manufacturing cost (a × b)	$5,756,400	$5,371,000
Total fixed manufacturing cost	1,328,400	1,280,000
Total manufacturing cost	$7,084,800	$6,651,000

Based on this information, he argued that the relevant variance for performance evaluation was only $433,800 ($7,084,800 − $6,651,000). Ms. Darwin responded, "*Only* $433,800! I consider that a very significant number. By the end of the day, I want a full explanation as to what is causing our costs to increase."

Required

a. Divide the class into groups of four or five students and divide the groups into three sections. Assign Task 1 to the first section, Task 2 to the second section, and Task 3 to the third section.

Group Tasks

(1) Based on the following information, determine the total materials cost variance and the price and usage variances. Assuming that the variances are an appropriate indicator of cause, explain what could have caused the variances. Identify the management position responsible.

	Actual Data	Standard Data
Number of planks per table	21	20
Price per plank	× $2.10	× $2.00
Material cost per table	$44.10	$40.00

(2) Based on the following information, determine the total labor cost variance and the price and usage variances. Assuming that the variances are an appropriate indicator of cause, explain what could have caused each variance. Identify the management position responsible.

	Actual Data	Standard Data
Number of hours per table	2.9	3.0
Price per hour	× $9.00	× $8.50
Labor cost per table	$26.10	$25.50

(3) Determine the amount of the fixed cost spending and volume variances. Explain what could have caused these variances. Based on the volume variance, indicate whether the actual fixed cost per unit would be higher or lower than the budgeted fixed cost per unit.

b. Select a spokesperson from each section to report the amount of the variances computed by the group. Reconcile any differences in the variances reported by the sections. Reconcile the individual variances with the total variance. Specifically, show that the total of the materials, labor, and overhead variances equals the total flexible budget variance ($433,800).

c. Discuss how Ms. Darwin should react to the variance information.

ATC 8-3   Research Assignment   *Nonfinancial performance measures*

The article "He Wrote the Book on Debugging" (*BusinessWeek,* May 9, 2005) by Otis Port is based on an interview of Watts Humphrey, an expert on reducing the number of errors that occur in software programs. Read this article and complete the following requirements.

Required

a. What measurement is used to assess the accuracy of computer software code?
b. The article identifies two tools used to reduce software coding errors, CMM and TSP. In addition to creating more accurate programs, what other benefits are cited as reasons to use the CMM and TSP techniques?
c. The CMM and TSP tools were developed by the Software Engineering Institute at Carnegie Mellon, and companies located in the United States are their most frequent users. List other countries identified in the article whose programmers are using CMM and TSP.
d. According to the article, what are the average error rates for programs written with and without using TSP?

ATC 8-4   Writing Assignment   *Standard costing—The human factor*

Kemp Corporation makes a protein supplement called Power Punch™. Its principal competitor for Power Punch is the protein supplement Superior Strength™, made by Jim Adams Company (JAC). Mr. Adams, a world-renowned weight-lifting champion, founded JAC. The primary market for both products is athletes. Kemp sells Power Punch to wellness stores, which sell it, other supplements, and health foods to the public. In contrast, Superior Strength is advertised in sports magazines and sold through orders generated by the ads.

Mr. Adams's fame is an essential factor in his company's advertising program. He is a dynamic character whose personality motivates people to strive for superior achievement. His demeanor not only stimulates sales but also provides a strong inspirational force for company employees. He is a kind, understanding individual with high expectations who is fond of saying that "mistakes are just opportunities for improvement." Mr. Adams is a strong believer in total quality management.

Mr. Quayle, president of Kemp Corporation, is a stern disciplinarian who believes in teamwork. He takes pride in his company's standard costing system. Managers work as a team to establish standards and then are held accountable for meeting them. Managers who fail to meet expectations are severely chastised, and continued failure leads to dismissal. After several years of rigorous enforcement, managers have fallen in line. Indeed, during the last two years, all managers have met their budget goals.

Even so, costs have risen steadily. These cost increases have been passed on to customers through higher prices. As a result, Power Punch is now priced significantly higher than Superior Strength. In fact, Superior Strength is selling directly to the public at a price that is below the wholesale price that Kemp is charging the wellness stores. The situation has reached a critical juncture. Sales of Power Punch are falling while Superior Strength is experiencing significant growth. Given that industry sales have remained relatively stable, it is obvious that customers are shifting from Power Punch to Superior Strength. Mr. Quayle is perplexed. He wonders how a company with direct market expenses can price its products so low.

Required

a. Explain why JAC has been able to gain a pricing advantage over Kemp.
b. Assume that you are a consultant whom Kemp's board of directors has asked to recommend how to halt the decline in sales of Power Punch. Provide appropriate recommendations.

ATC 8-5   Ethical Dilemma   *Budget games*

Melody Lovelady is the most highly rewarded sales representative at Swift Corporation. Her secret to success is always to understate your abilities. Ms. Lovelady is assigned to a territory in which her customer base is increasing at approximately 25 percent per year. Each year she estimates that her budgeted sales will be 10 percent higher than her previous year's sales. With little effort, she is able to double her budgeted sales growth. At Swift's annual sales meeting, she receives an award and a large bonus. Of course, Ms. Lovelady does not disclose her secret to her colleagues. Indeed, she always talks about how hard it is to continue to top her previous performance. She tells herself if they are dumb enough to fall for this rubbish, I'll milk it for all it's worth.

Required

a. What is the name commonly given to the budget game Ms. Lovelady is playing?
b. Does Ms. Lovelady's behavior violate any of the standards of ethical conduct shown in Exhibit 1.15 of Chapter 1?
c. Recommend how Ms. Lovelady's budget game could be stopped.

ATC 8-6   Spreadsheet Assignment   *Using Excel*

Irvine Publications established the following standard price and costs for a hardcover picture book that the company produces.

Standard price and variable costs	
Sales price	$48.00
Materials cost	12.00
Labor cost	6.00
Overhead cost	8.40
General, selling, and administrative costs	9.60
Expected fixed costs	
Manufacturing	$180,000
General, selling, and administrative	72,000

Irvine planned to make and sell 30,000 copies of the book.

Required

Construct a spreadsheet like the one shown in Exhibit 8.1 to illustrate a static budget and a flexible budget for production volumes of 28,000, 29,000, 30,000, 31,000, and 32,000.

ATC 8-7   Spreadsheet Assignment   *Mastering Excel*

Wilkin Fruit Drink Company planned to make 400,000 containers of apple juice. It expected to use two cups of frozen apple concentrate to make each container of juice, thus using 800,000 cups (400,000 containers × 2 cups) of frozen concentrate. The standard price of one cup of apple concentrate is $0.25. Actually, Wilkin produced 404,000 containers of apple juice and purchased and used 820,000 cups of concentrate at $0.26 per cup.

Required

a. Construct a spreadsheet template that could be used to calculate price and usage variances. The template should be constructed so that it could be used for any problem in the chapter that refers to price and usage variances by changing the data in the spreadsheet. The screen capture on page 384 represents a template for price and usage variances.

Spreadsheet Tip

(1) The shaded cells can be changed according to the data in each problem. All other cells are formulas based on the numbers in the shaded cells.

(2) The cells that label the variances as F or U (favorable (F) or unfavorable (U)) are based on a function called IF. The IF function is needed because the variance can be either favorable or unfavorable. The formula must determine whether actual expenditures exceed budgeted expenditures to determine whether the variance is unfavorable or favorable. As an example, the formula in cell D13 is =IF(B11>E11,'U','F'). The formula evaluates the expression B11>E11. If this expression is true (B11 is greater than E11), the text U is inserted in cell D13. The IF function can also be used to place formulas or numbers in a cell based on whether an expression is true or false. For example, the formula =IF(B11>E11,B11−E11,E11−B11) would calculate the amount of the variance as a positive number regardless of which amount is larger.

(3) An easier way to make the variance a positive number regardless of whether it is favorable or unfavorable is to use the absolute value function. The format of the formula in cells C13 and F13 would be =ABS(left number − right number).

(4) The lines around the variances are produced by using the borders in Excel (Format, Cells, Border).

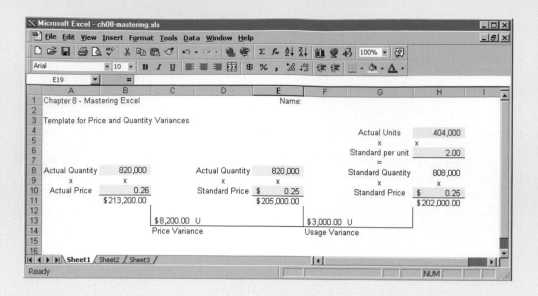

COMPREHENSIVE PROBLEM

The management of Magnificent Modems, Inc. (MMI), is uncertain as to the volume of sales that will exist in 2006. The president of the company asked the chief accountant to prepare flexible budget income statements assuming that sales activity amounts to 3,000 and 6,000 units. The static budget is shown in the following form.

Required

a. Complete the following worksheet to prepare the appropriate flexible budgets.
b. Calculate and show the flexible budget variances for the static budget versus the flexible budget at 6,000 units.
c. Indicate whether each variance is favorable or unfavorable.

Flexible Budget Income Statements

	Cost per Unit	Static Budget	Flexible Budget	Flexible Budget
Number of Units		5,000	3,000	6,000
Sales Revenue	$120.00	$600,000		
Variable Manuf. Costs				
Materials	40.00	200,000		
Labor	25.00	125,000		
Overhead	4.00	20,000		
Variable G, S, & A	6.00	30,000		
Contribution Margin		225,000		
Fixed Costs				
Manufacturing Rent		50,000		
Dep. on Manu. Equip.		60,000		
G, S, & A Expenses		71,950		
Dep. On Admin. Equip.		12,000		
Net Income (Loss)		$ 31,050	$(58,950)	$76,050

CHAPTER 9

Responsibility Accounting

LEARNING OBJECTIVES

After you have mastered the material in this chapter you will be able to:

1. Describe the concept of decentralization.

2. Describe the differences among cost, profit, and investment centers.

3. Prepare and use responsibility reports.

4. Relate management by exception to responsibility reports.

5. Evaluate investment opportunities using return on investment.

6. Identify factors that affect return on investment.

7. Evaluate investment opportunities using residual income.

8. Describe how transfer prices may be established (Appendix).

The Curious Accountant

In 1978 Bernie Marcus and Arthur Blank founded **The Home Depot, Inc.**, and their first store opened in 1979. One year later they had four stores, 300 employees, and sales of $22 million. By 2000 there were 1,123 Home Depot stores with 226,000 employees and annual sales of $45.7 billion. Mr. Marcus was the company's CEO during these 20 years of tremendous growth, and he ran the company with a decentralized management style. He wanted store managers to operate individual stores as if they were their owners. Using this strategy, he saw the company's stock price rise from less than $1 per share to over $45 per share (when adjusted for stock splits). In December 2000, Mr. Marcus stepped down as Home Depot's CEO and an outsider, Bob Nardelli, was appointed as his replacement.

Two significant things happened during the first two years of Mr. Nardelli's tenure. First, he began implementing a much more centralized management system, and second, the stock price fell by 51 percent. A few examples of his management changes are: he required stores to hire more part-time employees and fewer full-time employees whether the local manager wanted to or not; he implemented a centralized purchasing system; he required local stores to carry new product lines, such as small appliances, even if the store manager objected. As a result of the change in management style, several long-time store managers left the company, and others complained. Despite these problems, Mr. Marcus, who still yielded considerable influence as a major stockholder and member of the board of directors, stood behind Mr. Nardelli and the changes he was implementing.

What could explain why a company that had enjoyed so much success under a decentralized management system would switch to a more centralized system? Why would the architect of the decentralized system that had been so successful support the man who replaced his system? (Answers on page 392.)

CHAPTER OPENING

Walter Keller, a production manager, complained to the accountant, Kelly Oberson, that the budget system failed to control his department's labor cost. Ms. Oberson responded, "people, not budgets, control costs." Budgeting is one of many tools management uses to control business operations. Managers are responsible for using control tools effectively. **Responsibility accounting** *focuses on evaluating the performance of individual managers. For example, expenses controlled by a production department manager are presented in one report and expenses controlled by a marketing department manager are presented in a different report. This chapter discusses the development and use of a responsibility accounting system.* ■

Decentralization Concept

LO 1

Describe the concept of decentralization.

Effective responsibility accounting requires clear lines of authority and responsibility. Divisions of authority and responsibility normally occur as a natural consequence of managing business operations. In a small business, one person can control everything: marketing, production, management, accounting. In contrast, large companies are so complex that authority and control must be divided among many people.

Consider the hiring of employees. A small business usually operates in a limited geographic area. The owner works directly with employees. She knows the job requirements, local wage rates, and the available labor pool. She is in a position to make informed hiring decisions. In contrast, a major corporation may employ thousands of employees throughout the world. The employees may speak different languages and have different social customs. Their jobs may require many different skills and pay a vast array of wage rates. The president of the corporation cannot make informed hiring decisions for the entire company. Instead, he delegates *authority* to a professional personnel manager and holds that manager *responsible* for hiring practices.

Decision-making authority is similarly delegated to individuals responsible for managing specific organization functions such as production, marketing, and accounting. Delegating authority and responsibility is referred to as **decentralization.** Decentralization offers advantages like the following.

1. *Encourages upper-level management to concentrate on strategic decisions.* Because local management makes routine decisions, upper-level management can concentrate on long-term planning, goal setting, and performance evaluation.

2. *Improves the quality of decisions by delegating authority down a chain of command.* Local managers are better informed about local concerns. Furthermore, their proximity to local events allows them to react quickly to changes in local conditions. As a result, local managers can generally make better decisions.

3. *Motivates managers to improve productivity.* The freedom to act coupled with responsibility for the results creates an environment that encourages most individuals to perform at high levels.

4. *Trains lower-level managers for increased responsibilities.* Decision making is a skill. Managers accustomed to making decisions about local issues are generally able to apply their decision-making skills to broader issues when they are promoted to upper management positions.

5. *Improves performance evaluation.* When lines of authority and responsibility are clear, credit or blame can be more accurately assigned.

Organization Chart

Exhibit 9.1 displays a partial organization chart for Panther Holding Company, a decentralized business. The chart shows five levels of authority and responsibility arranged in a hierarchical order from the top down. Other companies may have more or less complex organizational charts, depending on their decentralization needs and philosophy.

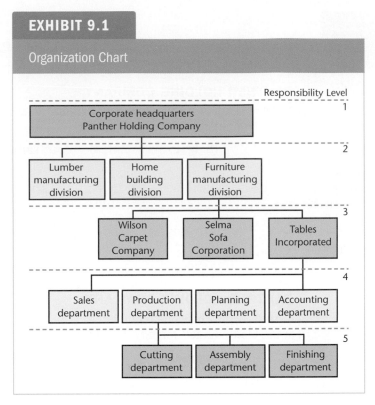

EXHIBIT 9.1

Organization Chart

Responsibility Level

1 — Corporate headquarters Panther Holding Company

2 — Lumber manufacturing division | Home building division | Furniture manufacturing division

3 — Wilson Carpet Company | Selma Sofa Corporation | Tables Incorporated

4 — Sales department | Production department | Planning department | Accounting department

5 — Cutting department | Assembly department | Finishing department

Responsibility Centers

Decentralized businesses are usually subdivided into distinct reporting units called responsibility centers. A **responsibility center** is an organizational unit that controls identifiable revenue or expense items. The unit may be a division, a department, a subdepartment, or even a single machine. For example, a transportation company may identify a semitrailer truck as a responsibility center. The company holds the truck driver responsible for the revenues and expenses associated with operating the truck. Responsibility centers may be divided into three categories: cost, profit, and investment.

LO 2

Describe the differences among cost, profit, and investment centers.

A **cost center** is an organizational unit that incurs expenses but does not generate revenue. In the Panther organization chart (Exhibit 9.1), the finishing department and the production department are cost centers. Cost centers normally fall on the lower levels of an organization chart. The manager of a cost center is judged on his ability to keep costs within budget parameters.

A **profit center** differs from a cost center in that it not only incurs costs but also generates revenue. In the Panther organization chart, the companies at the third level (Wilson Carpet Company, Selma Sofa Corporation, and Tables Incorporated) are considered profit centers. The manager of a profit center is judged on his ability to produce revenue in excess of expenses.

Investment center managers are responsible for revenues, expenses, and the investment of capital. Investment centers normally appear at the upper levels of an organization chart. The second-level division managers (managers of the lumber, home, and furniture divisions) in the Panther organization are responsible for investment centers. Managers of investment centers are accountable for assets and liabilities as well as earnings.

Responsibility Reports

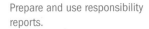

A **responsibility report** is prepared for each manager who controls a responsibility center. The report compares the expectations for the manager's responsibility center with the center's actual performance. A typical report lists the items under the manager's control, both the budgeted amount and the actual amount spent for each item, and the differences between budgeted and actual amounts (variances).

LO 3

Prepare and use responsibility reports.

EXHIBIT 9.2

Responsibility Reports

PANTHER HOLDING COMPANY
Second Level: Furniture Manufacturing Division
For the Month Ended January 31, 2007

	Budget	Actual	Variance
Controllable expenses			
Administrative division expense	$ 20,400	$ 31,100	$(10,700) U
Company president's salary	9,600	9,200	400 F
Wilson Carpet Company	82,100	78,400	3,700 F
Selma Sofa Corporation	87,200	116,700	(29,500) U
Tables Incorporated	48,600	51,250	(2,650) U
Total	$247,900	$286,650	$(38,750) U

PANTHER HOLDING COMPANY
Third Level: Tables Incorporated
For the Month Ended January 31, 2007

	Budget	Actual	Variance
Controllable expenses			
Administrative division expense	$ 3,000	$ 2,800	$ 200 F
Department managers' salaries	10,000	11,200	(1,200) U
Sales department costs	9,100	8,600	500 F
Production department costs	13,500	13,750	(250) U
Planning department costs	4,800	7,000	(2,200) U
Accounting department costs	8,200	7,900	300 F
Total	$ 48,600	$ 51,250	$ (2,650) U

PANTHER HOLDING COMPANY
Fourth Level: Production Department
For the Month Ended January 31, 2007

	Budget	Actual	Variance
Controllable expenses			
Administrative staff expense	$ 900	$ 1,100	$ (200) U
Supervisory salaries	2,800	2,800	0
Cutting department costs	1,400	1,200	200 F
Assembly department costs	2,800	2,900	(100) U
Finishing department costs	5,600	5,750	(150) U
Total	$ 13,500	$ 13,750	$ (250) U

PANTHER HOLDING COMPANY
Fifth Level: Finishing Department
For the Month Ended January 31, 2007

	Budget	Actual	Variance
Controllable expenses			
Wages expense	$ 3,200	$ 3,000	$ 200 F
Direct materials	1,100	1,400	(300) U
Supplies	400	500	(100) U
Small tools	600	650	(50) U
Other expenses	300	200	100 F
Total	$ 5,600	$ 5,750	$ (150) U

Management by Exception

Responsibility reports are arranged to support using the **management by exception** doctrine. Exhibit 9.2 illustrates a partial set of responsibility reports for Panther Holding Company. From the lower level upward, each successive report includes summary data from the preceding report. For example, the detailed information about the finishing department (a level five responsibility center) is summarized as a single line item ($150 unfavorable variance) in the report for the production department (a level four responsibility center).

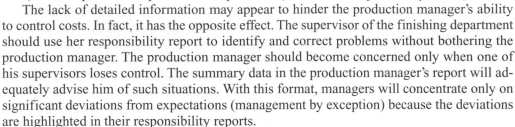

LO 4

Relate management by exception to responsibility reports.

The lack of detailed information may appear to hinder the production manager's ability to control costs. In fact, it has the opposite effect. The supervisor of the finishing department should use her responsibility report to identify and correct problems without bothering the production manager. The production manager should become concerned only when one of his supervisors loses control. The summary data in the production manager's report will adequately advise him of such situations. With this format, managers will concentrate only on significant deviations from expectations (management by exception) because the deviations are highlighted in their responsibility reports.

Applying the management by exception doctrine to the variances in her responsibility report, the division manager of the Furniture Manufacturing Division (second level responsibility center) should concentrate her efforts on two areas. First, the $29,500 unfavorable variance for Selma Sofa Corporation indicates Selma's expenditures are out of line. Second, the $10,700 unfavorable variance for the division manager's own administrative expenses indicates those costs are significantly above budget expectations. The division manager should request detailed reports for these two areas. Other responsibility centers seem to be operating within reason and can be left to their respective managers. This reporting format focuses management's attention on the areas where it is most needed.

The complete responsibility accounting report would also include the first responsibility level, corporate headquarters. At the corporate level, responsibility reports normally include year-to-date income statements to inform management of the company's overall performance. To facilitate decision making, these income statements are normally prepared using the contribution margin format. Exhibit 9.3 shows the January 2007 income statement for Panther Holding Company.

EXHIBIT 9.3

Panther Income Statement (Contribution Margin Format)

PANTHER HOLDING COMPANY
Income Statement for Internal Use
For the Month Ended January 31, 2007

	Budget	Actual	Variance
Sales	$984,300	$962,300	$22,000 U
Variable expenses			
Variable product costs	343,100	352,250	9,150 U
Variable selling expenses	105,000	98,000	7,000 F
Other variable expenses	42,200	51,100	8,900 U
Total variable expenses	490,300	501,350	11,050 U
Contribution margin	494,000	460,950	33,050 U
Fixed expenses			
Fixed product cost	54,100	62,050	7,950 U
Fixed selling expense	148,000	146,100	1,900 F
Other fixed expenses	23,000	25,250	2,250 U
Total fixed expenses	225,100	233,400	8,300 U
Net income	$268,900	$227,550	$41,350 U

Answers to The Curious Accountant

The management at **The Home Depot**, along with former CEO Bernie Marcus, understands that the environment in which a business operates changes and successful companies are willing to alter the way they do business to keep up with those changes. For example, in 2000, Home Depot had nine regional purchasing offices that operated independently. Mr. Nardelli consolidated these into one central office. This reduced the cost of ordering inventory—one purchase order is cheaper to process than nine—and it gave the company more power to negotiate lower prices from its suppliers.

One of Mr. Nardelli's changes was to implement a more detailed performance measurement system for each store. Among other things, this system allowed the company to reduce the amount of inventory it carries, thus saving the company the cost of financing that inventory.

The new CEO was willing to admit if a change did not work and to quickly make another change. His requirement to use more part-time employees led to some customer dissatisfaction, so it was revised.

To be fair, the drop in Home Depot's stock price had many causes. The stock price had grown rapidly over the years because the company had grown rapidly. However, the larger a company becomes, the harder it is to maintain a given growth rate. For example, if a company has only ten stores, it can open one new one and realize a ten percent growth rate. If the company has 1,000 stores, it must open 100 new stores to realize a ten percent growth rate. Furthermore, the economy in general was much weaker during 2001 and 2002 than it had been during the 1990s.

Even though Home Depot's stock price fell during Mr. Nardelli's first two years as CEO, its profit margins were up and its cash balance was up. Also, its sales increased by 27 percent from 2000 to 2002, and its earnings were up 42 percent.

Sources: Company disclosures, stock market data, and Dan Morse, "A Hardware Chain Struggles to Adjust to a New Blueprint," *The Wall Street Journal*, January 17, 2003, pp. A-1 and A-6.

Controllability Concept

The **controllability concept** is crucial to an effective responsibility accounting system. Managers should only be evaluated based on revenues or costs they control. Holding individuals responsible for things they cannot control is demotivating. Isolating control, however, may be difficult, as illustrated in the following case.

Dorothy Pasewark, a buyer for a large department store chain, was criticized when stores could not resell the merchandise she bought at the expected price. Ms. Pasewark countered that the sales staff caused the sluggish sales by not displaying the merchandise properly. The sales staff charged that the merchandise had too little sales potential to justify setting up more enticing displays. The division of influence between the buyer and the sales staff clouds the assignment of responsibility.

Since the exercise of control may be clouded, managers are usually held responsible for items over which they have *predominant* rather than *absolute* control. At times responsibility accounting may be imperfect. Management must strive to ensure that praise or criticism is administered as fairly as possible.

Qualitative Reporting Features

Responsibility reports should be expressed in simple terms. If they are too complex, managers will ignore them. The reports should include only the budgeted and actual amounts of *controllable* revenues and expenses, with variances highlighted to promote management by exception. Report preparers and report users should communicate regularly to ensure the reports provide relevant information. Furthermore, reports must be timely. A report that presents yesterday's problem is not nearly as useful as one that presents today's problem.

Topic Tackler
PLUS

9-1

Managerial Performance Measurement

A primary reason for a responsibility accounting system is to evaluate managerial performance. Managers are assigned responsibility for certain cost, profit, or investment centers. They are then evaluated based on how their centers perform relative to specific goals and objectives. The measurement techniques (standard costs and contribution margin format income reporting) used for cost and profit centers have been discussed in previous chapters. The remainder of this chapter discusses performance measures for investment centers.

Return on Investment

Society confers wealth, prestige, and power upon those who have control of assets. Unsurprisingly, managers are motivated to increase the amount of assets employed by the investment centers they control. When companies have additional assets available to invest, how do upper-level managers decide which centers should get them? The additional assets are frequently allotted to the managers who demonstrate the greatest potential for increasing the company's wealth. Companies often assess managerial potential by comparing the return on investment ratios of various investment centers. The **return on investment (ROI)** is the ratio of wealth generated (operating income) to the amount invested (operating assets) to generate the wealth. ROI is commonly expressed with the following equation.

LO 5

Evaluate investment opportunities using return on investment.

$$\text{ROI} = \frac{\text{Operating income}}{\text{Operating assets}}$$

To illustrate using ROI for comparative evaluations, assume Panther Holding Company's corporate (first level) chief financial officer (CFO) determined the ROIs for the company's three divisions (second level investment centers). The CFO used the following accounting data from the records of each division:

	Lumber Manufacturing Division	Home Building Division	Furniture Manufacturing Division
Operating income	$ 60,000	$ 46,080	$ 81,940
Operating assets	300,000	256,000	482,000

The ROI for each division is:

Lumber manufacturing: $\dfrac{\text{Operating income}}{\text{Operating assets}} = \$60,000 \div \$300,000 = 20\%$

Home building: $\dfrac{\text{Operating income}}{\text{Operating assets}} = \$46,080 \div \$256,000 = 18\%$

Furniture manufacturing: $\dfrac{\text{Operating income}}{\text{Operating assets}} = \$81,940 \div \$482,000 = 17\%$

All other things being equal, higher ROIs indicate better performance. In this case the Lumber Manufacturing Division manager is the best performer. Assume Panther obtains additional funding for expanding the company's operations. Which investment center is most likely to receive the additional funds?

If the manager of the Lumber Manufacturing Division convinces the upper-level management team that his division would continue to outperform the other two divisions, the Lumber Manufacturing Division would most likely get the additional funding. The manager of the lumber division would then invest the funds in additional operating assets, which would in turn increase the division's operating income. As the division prospers, Panther would reward the manager for exceptional performance. Rewarding the manager of the lumber division would likely motivate the other managers to improve their divisional ROIs. Internal competition would improve the performance of the company as a whole.

Green View is a lawn services company whose operations are divided into two districts. The District 1 manager controls $12,600,000 of operating assets. District 1 produced $1,512,000 of operating income during the year. The District 2 manager controls $14,200,000 of operating assets. District 2 reported $1,988,000 of operating income for the same period. Use return on investment to determine which manager is performing better.

Answer

District 1

$$\text{ROI} = \text{Operating income} \div \text{Operating assets} = \$1,512,000 \div \$12,600,000 = 12\%$$

District 2

$$\text{ROI} = \text{Operating income} \div \text{Operating assets} = \$1,988,000 \div \$14,200,000 = 14\%$$

Because the higher ROI indicates the better performance, the District 2 manager is the superior performer. This conclusion is based solely on quantitative results. In real-world practice, companies also consider qualitative factors.

Qualitative Considerations

Why do companies compute ROI using operating income and operating assets instead of using net income and total assets? Suppose Panther's corporate headquarters closes a furniture manufacturing plant because an economic downturn temporarily reduces the demand for furniture. It would be inappropriate to include these nonoperating plant assets in the denominator of the ROI computation. Similarly, if Panther sells the furniture plant and realizes a large gain on the sale, including the gain in the numerator of the ROI formula would distort the result. Since the manager of the Furniture Manufacturing Division does not control closing the plant or selling it, it is unreasonable to include the effects of these decisions in computing the ROI. These items would, however, be included in computing net income and total assets. Most companies use operating income and operating assets to compute ROI because those variables measure performance more accurately.

Measuring Operating Assets

The meaning of ROI results is further complicated by the question of how to *value* operating assets. Suppose Echoles Rental Company's two divisions, Northern and Southern, each rent to customers a vending machine that originally cost $5,000. The vending machines have five-year useful lives and no salvage value. The Northern Division purchased its machine one year ago; the Southern Division purchased its machine three years ago. At the end of the current year, the book values of the two machines are as follows:

	Northern Division's Vending Machine	Southern Division's Vending Machine
Original cost	$5,000	$5,000
Less accumulated depreciation	(1,000)	(3,000)
Book value	$4,000	$2,000

Each machine generates operating income averaging $800 per year. The ROI for each machine this year is as follows:

$$\text{Northern Division:} \quad \frac{\text{Operating income}}{\text{Operating assets}} = \$800 \div \$4,000 = 20\%$$

$$\text{Southern Division:} \quad \frac{\text{Operating income}}{\text{Operating assets}} = \$800 \div \$2,000 = 40\%$$

Is the manager of the Southern Division outperforming the manager of the Northern Division? No. The only difference between the two divisions is that Southern is using an older asset than Northern. Using book value as the valuation base can distort the ROI and cause severe motivational problems. Managers will consider comparisons between different investment centers unfair because the ROIs do not accurately reflect performance. Furthermore, managers may avoid replacing obsolete equipment because purchasing new equipment would increase the dollar amount of operating assets, reducing the ROI.

Companies may minimize these problems by using original cost instead of book value in the denominator of the ROI formula. In the vending machine example, using original cost produces an ROI of 16 percent ($800 ÷ $5,000). Using original cost, however, may not entirely solve the valuation problem. As a result of inflation and technological advances, comparable equipment purchased at different times will have different costs. Some accountants advocate using *replacement cost* rather than *historical cost* as the valuation base. This solution is seldom used because determining the amount it would cost to replace particular assets is difficult. For example, imagine trying to determine the replacement cost of all the assets in a steel mill that has been operating for years.

Selecting the asset valuation base is a complex matter. In spite of its shortcomings, most companies use book value as the valuation base. Management must consider those shortcomings when using ROI to evaluate performance.

Factors Affecting Return on Investment

Management can gain insight into performance by dividing the ROI formula into two separate ratios as follows:

$$\text{ROI} = \frac{\text{Operating income}}{\text{Sales}} \times \frac{\text{Sales}}{\text{Operating assets}}$$

LO 6

Identify factors that affect return on investment.

The first ratio on the right side of the equation is called the margin. The **margin** is a measure of management's ability to control operating expenses relative to the level of sales. In general, high margins indicate superior performance. Management can increase the margin by reducing the level of operating expenses necessary to generate sales. Decreasing operating expenses increases profitability.

The second ratio in the expanded ROI formula is called turnover. **Turnover** is a measure of the amount of operating assets employed to support the achieved level of sales. Operating assets are scarce resources. To maximize profitability, they must be used wisely. Just as excessive expenses decrease profitability, excessive investments in operating assets also limit profitability.

Both the short and expanded versions of the ROI formula produce the same end result. To illustrate, we will use the ROI for the Lumber Manufacturing Division of Panther Holding Company. Recall that the division employed $300,000 of operating assets to produce $60,000 of operating income, resulting in the following ROI:

$$\text{ROI} = \frac{\text{Operating income}}{\text{Operating assets}} = \frac{\$60,000}{\$300,000} = 20\%$$

Further analysis of the accounting records indicates the Lumber Manufacturing Division had sales of $600,000. The following computation demonstrates that the expanded ROI formula produces the same result as the short formula:

$$\text{ROI} = \text{Margin} \times \text{Turnover}$$

$$= \frac{\text{Operating income}}{\text{Sales}} \times \frac{\text{Sales}}{\text{Operating assets}}$$

$$= \frac{\$60,000}{\$600,000} \times \frac{\$600,000}{\$300,000}$$

$$= .10 \times 2$$

$$= 20\%$$

The expanded formula may seem more complicated. It is generally more useful, however, because it helps managers see a variety of strategies to improve ROI. The expanded formula shows that profitability and ROI can be improved in three ways: *by increasing sales, by reducing expenses,* or *by reducing the investment base.* Each of these possibilities is demonstrated using the Lumber Manufacturing Division (LMD) of Panther Holding Company.

1. *Increase ROI by increasing sales.* Because some expenses are fixed, sales can be increased while those expenses are constant. Managers may even be able to reduce variable expenses by increasing productivity as sales increase. As a result, managers can increase their ROIs by increasing sales while limiting growth in expenses. To illustrate, assume the manager of LMD is able to increase sales from $600,000 to $660,000 while controlling expense growth so that net income increases from $60,000 to $72,600. Assuming investment in operating assets remains constant at $300,000, ROI becomes:

$$\text{ROI} = \text{Margin} \times \text{Turnover}$$

$$= \frac{\text{Operating income}}{\text{Sales}} \times \frac{\text{Sales}}{\text{Operating assets}}$$

$$= \frac{\$72,600}{\$660,000} \times \frac{\$660,000}{\$300,000}$$

$$= .11 \times 2.2$$

$$= 24.2\%$$

2. *Increase ROI by reducing expenses.* Suppose the manager of LMD takes a different approach. He decides to eliminate waste. By analyzing spending, he is able to cut expenses without affecting sales or the investment in operating assets. As a result of controlling expenses, operating income increases from $60,000 to $72,000. Assume the other variables remain the same as in the original example. ROI becomes:

$$\text{ROI} = \text{Margin} \times \text{Turnover}$$

$$= \frac{\text{Operating income}}{\text{Sales}} \times \frac{\text{Sales}}{\text{Operating assets}}$$

$$= \frac{\$72,000}{\$600,000} \times \frac{\$600,000}{\$300,000}$$

$$= .12 \times 2$$

$$= 24\%$$

3. *Increase ROI by reducing the investment base.* Managers who focus too narrowly on income frequently overlook this possibility. Reducing the amount of funds invested in operating assets such as inventory or accounts receivable can increase profitability because the funds released can be invested in other, more productive assets. This effect is reflected in the ROI computation. For example, assume the manager of LMD launches a *just-in-time* inventory system that allows the division to reduce the amount of inventory it carries. The manager also initiates an aggressive campaign to collect receivables which significantly reduces the outstanding receivables balance. As a result of these two initiatives, the assets employed to operate LMD fall from $300,000 to $240,000. All other variables remain the same as in the original example. ROI becomes:

$$\text{ROI} = \text{Margin} \times \text{Turnover}$$

$$= \frac{\text{Operating income}}{\text{Sales}} \times \frac{\text{Sales}}{\text{Operating assets}}$$

$$= \frac{\$60,000}{\$600,000} \times \frac{\$600,000}{\$240,000}$$

$$= .10 \times 2.5$$

$$= 25\%$$

The $60,000 of funds released by reducing the operating assets can be returned to headquarters or be reinvested by LMD depending on the opportunities available.

The benefits of increasing the *margin* by increasing sales or reducing expenses are intuitive. They are so obvious that, in their zeal to increase margins, managers for many years overlooked the effect of *turnover.* Growing use of the ROI ratio has alerted managers to the benefits of controlling operating assets as well as expenses. Because ROI blends many aspects of managerial performance into a single ratio that enables comparisons between companies, comparisons between investment centers within companies, and comparisons between different investment opportunities within an investment center, ROI has gained widespread acceptance as a performance measure.

CHECK YOURSELF 9.2

What three actions can a manager take to improve ROI?

Answer

1. Increase sales
2. Reduce expenses
3. Reduce the investment base

Residual Income

Suppose Panther Holding Company evaluates the manager of the Lumber Manufacturing Division (LMD) based on his ability to maximize ROI. The corporation's overall ROI is approximately 18 percent. LMD, however, has consistently outperformed the other investment centers. Its ROI is currently 20 percent. Now suppose the manager has an opportunity to invest additional funds in a project likely to earn a 19 percent ROI. Would the manager accept the investment opportunity?

These circumstances place the manager in an awkward position. The corporation would benefit from the project because the expected ROI of 19 percent is higher than the corporate average ROI of 18 percent. Personally, however, the manager would suffer from accepting the project because it would reduce the division ROI to less than the current 20 percent. The manager is forced to choose between his personal best interests and the best interests of the corporation. When faced with decisions such as these, many managers choose to benefit themselves at the expense of their corporations, a condition described as **suboptimization.**

To avoid *suboptimization,* many businesses base managerial evaluation on **residual income.** This approach measures a manager's ability to maximize earnings above some targeted level. The targeted level of earnings is based on a minimum desired ROI. Residual income is calculated as follows:

$$\text{Residual income} = \text{Operating income} - (\text{Operating assets} \times \text{Desired ROI})$$

LO 7

Evaluate investment opportunities using residual income.

Topic Tackler

PLUS

9-2

FOCUS ON INTERNATIONAL ISSUES

DO MANAGERS IN DIFFERENT COMPANIES STRESS THE SAME PERFORMANCE MEASURES?

About the only ratio companies are required to disclose in their annual reports to stockholders is the earnings per share ratio. Nevertheless, many companies choose to show their performance as measured by other ratios, as well as providing nonratio data not required by GAAP. The types of ratio data companies choose to include in their annual reports provides a sense of what performance measure they consider most important.

A review of several publicly traded companies from the United Kingdom, Japan, and the United States will show that the most common ratios presented are variations of the return on sales percentage and the return on investment percentage, although they may be called by different names. The country in which the company is located does not seem to determine which ratio it will emphasize.

One nonratio performance measure that is popular with companies in all three countries is free cash flow, and it is usually reported in total pounds, yen, or dollars. Be sure to exercise caution before comparing one company's free cash flow, return on sales, or return on investment to those of other companies. There are no official rules governing how these data are calculated, and different companies make different interpretations about how to compute these measurements.

To illustrate, recall that LMD currently earns $60,000 of operating income with the $300,000 of operating assets it controls. ROI is 20 percent ($60,000 ÷ $300,000). Assume Panther's desired ROI is 18 percent. LMD's residual income is therefore:

$$\text{Residual income} = \text{Operating income} - (\text{Operating assets} \times \text{Desired ROI})$$

$$= \$60,000 - (\$300,000 \times .18)$$

$$= \$60,000 - \$54,000$$

$$= \$6,000$$

Now assume that Panther Holding Company has $50,000 of additional funds available to invest. Because LMD consistently performs at a high level, Panther's corporate management team offers the funds to the LMD manager. The manager believes he could invest the additional $50,000 at a 19 percent rate of return.

If the LMD manager's evaluation is based solely on ROI, he is likely to reject the additional funding because investing the funds at 19 percent would lower his overall ROI. If the LMD manager's evaluation is based on residual income, however, he is likely to accept the funds because an additional investment at 19 percent would increase his residual income as follows:

$$\text{Operating income} = \$50,000 \times .19$$

$$= \$9,500$$

$$\text{Residual income} = \text{Operating income} - (\text{Operating assets} \times \text{Desired ROI})$$

$$= \$9,500 - (\$50,000 \times .18)$$

$$= \$9,500 - \$9,000$$

$$= \$500$$

Accepting the new project would add $500 to LMD's residual income. If the manager of LMD is evaluated based on his ability to maximize residual income, he would benefit by

REALITY BYTES

In recent years the residual income approach has been refined to produce a new technique called **economic value added (EVA®).** EVA was developed and trademarked by the consulting firm Stern Stewart & Co. EVA uses the basic formula behind residual income [Operating income − (Operating assets × Desired ROI)]. EVA, however, uses different definitions of operating income and operating assets. For example, research and development (R&D) costs are classified as operating assets under EVA. In contrast, R&D costs are classified as expenses under traditional accounting. As a result, operating assets and operating income are higher under EVA than they are under the residual income approach. There are more than 100 such differences between EVA and residual income. However, most companies make only a few adjustments when converting from the residual income approach to EVA. Even so, these refinements seem to have had significant benefits. In a recent article in *Fortune* magazine, Shawn Tully concluded "Managers who run their businesses according to the precepts of EVA have hugely increased the value of their companies. Investors who know about EVA, and know which companies are employing it, have grown rich."

investing in any project that returns an ROI in excess of the desired 18 percent. The reduction in LMD's overall ROI does not enter into the decision. The residual income approach solves the problem of suboptimization.

The primary disadvantage of the residual income approach is that it measures performance in absolute dollars. As a result, a manager's residual income may be larger simply because her investment base is larger rather than because her performance is superior.

To illustrate, return to the example where Panther Holding Company has $50,000 of additional funds to invest. Assume the manager of the Lumber Manufacturing Division (LMD) and the manager of the Furniture Manufacturing Division (FMD) each have investment opportunities expected to earn a 19 percent return. Recall that Panther's desired ROI is 18 percent. If corporate headquarters allots $40,000 of the funds to the manager of LMD and $10,000 to the manager of FMD, the increase in residual income earned by each division is as follows:

$$\text{LMD's Residual income} = (\$40,000 \times .19) - (\$40,000 \times .18) = \$400$$

$$\text{FMD's Residual income} = (\$10,000 \times .19) - (\$10,000 \times .18) = \$100$$

Does LMD's higher residual income mean LMD's manager is outperforming FMD's manager? No. It means LMD's manager received more operating assets than FMD's manager received.

Calculating Multiple ROIs and/or RIs for the Same Company

You may be asked to calculate different ROI and RI measures for the same company. For example, ROI and/or RI may be calculated for the company as a whole, for segments of the company, for specific investment opportunities, and for individual managers. An example is shown in Check Yourself 9.3.

Responsibility Accounting and the Balanced Scorecard

Throughout the text we have discussed many financial measures companies use to evaluate managerial performance. Examples include standard cost systems to evaluate cost center managers; the contribution margin income statement to evaluate profit center managers; and

CHECK YOURSELF 9.3

Tambor Incorporated (TI) earned operating income of $4,730,400 on operating assets of $26,280,000 during 2009. The Western Division earned $748,000 on operating assets of $3,400,000. TI has offered the Western Division $1,100,000 of additional operating assets. The manager of the Western Division believes he could use the additional assets to generate operating income amounting to $220,000. TI has a desired return on investment (ROI) of 17 percent. Determine the ROI and RI for TI, the Western Division, and the additional investment opportunity.

Answer

Return on investment (ROI) = Operating income ÷ Operating assets
ROI for TI = $4,730,400 ÷ $26,280,000 = 18%
ROI for Western Division = $748,000 ÷ $3,400,000 = 22%
ROI for Investment Opportunity = $220,000 ÷ $1,100,000 = 20%

Residual income (RI) = Operating income − (Operating assets × Desired ROI)
RI for TI = $4,730,000 − ($26,280,000 × .17) = $262,400
RI for Western Division = $748,000 − ($3,400,000 × .17) = $170,000
RI for Investment Opportunity = $220,000 − ($1,100,000 × .17) = $33,000

ROI / residual income to evaluate the performance of investment center managers. Many companies may have goals and objectives such as "satisfaction guaranteed" or "we try harder" that are more suitably evaluated using nonfinancial measures. To assess how well they accomplish the full range of their missions, many companies use a *balanced scorecard.*

A **balanced scorecard** includes financial and nonfinancial performance measures. Standard costs, income measures, ROI, and residual income are common financial measures used in a balanced score card. Nonfinancial measures include defect rates, cycle time, on-time deliveries, number of new products or innovations, safety measures, and customer satisfaction surveys. Many companies compose their scorecards to highlight leading versus lagging measures. For example, customer satisfaction survey data is a leading indicator of the sales growth which is a lagging measure. The balanced scorecard is a holistic approach to evaluating managerial performance. It is gaining widespread acceptance among world-class companies.

◀◀ A Look Back

The practice of delegating authority and responsibility is referred to as *decentralization.* Clear lines of authority and responsibility are essential in establishing a responsibility accounting system. In a responsibility accounting system, segment managers are held accountable for profits based on the amount of control they have over the profits in their segment.

Responsibility reports are used to compare actual results with budgets. The reports should be simple with variances highlighted to promote the *management by exception* doctrine. Individual managers should be held responsible only for those revenues or costs they control. Each manager should receive only summary information about the performance of the responsibility centers under her supervision.

A *responsibility center* is the point in an organization where control over revenue or expense is located. *Cost centers* are segments that incur costs but do not generate revenues. *Profit centers* incur costs and also generate revenues, producing a measurable profit. *Investment centers* incur costs, generate revenues, and use identifiable capital investments.

One of the primary purposes of responsibility accounting is to evaluate managerial performance. Comparing actual results with standards and budgets and calculating *return on investment* are used for this purpose. Because return on investment uses revenues, expenses, and investment, problems with measuring these parameters must be considered. The return on investment can be analyzed in terms of the margin earned on sales as well as the turnover (asset utilization) during the period. The *residual income approach* is sometimes used to avoid *suboptimization,* which occurs when managers choose to reject investment projects that would benefit their company's ROI but would reduce their investment center's ROI. The residual income approach evaluates managers based on their ability to generate earnings above some targeted level of earnings.

A Look Forward >>

The next chapter expands on the concepts you learned in this chapter. You will see how managers select investment opportunities that will affect their future ROIs. You will learn to use present value techniques that consider the time value of money; specifically, you will learn to compute the net present value and the internal rate of return for potential investment opportunities. You will also learn to use less sophisticated analytical techniques such as payback and the unadjusted rate of return.

APPENDIX

Transfer Pricing

In vertically integrated companies, one division commonly sells goods or services to another division. For example, in the case of Panther Holding Company (Exhibit 9.1), the Lumber Manufacturing Division may sell lumber to the Home Building and Furniture Manufacturing Divisions. When such intercompany sales occur, the price to charge is likely to become a heated issue.

Describe how transfer prices may be established.

In a decentralized organization, each division is likely to be defined as an investment center. Division managers are held responsible for profitability. When goods are transferred internally, the sales price charged by the selling division becomes a cost to the buying division. The amount of profit included in the **transfer price** will increase the selling division's earnings and decrease the purchasing division's earnings (via increased expenses). The selling division benefits from getting the highest possible price; the purchasing division seeks the lowest possible price. When managers are competitively evaluated based on profitability measures, the transfer price is the subject of considerable controversy.

Companies use three common approaches to establish transfer prices: (1) price based on market forces; (2) price based on negotiation; and (3) price based on cost. Exhibit 9.4 shows some specific measures and the frequency of their use.

Market-Based Transfer Prices

The preferred method for establishing transfer prices is to base them on some form of competitive market price. Ideally, selling divisions should be authorized to sell merchandise to outsiders as well as, or in preference to, other divisions. Similarly, purchasing divisions should have the option to buy goods from outsiders if they are able to obtain favorable prices. However, both selling and purchasing divisions would be motivated to deal with each other because of savings in selling, administrative, and transportation costs that arise as a natural result of internal transactions.

Market-based transfer prices are preferable because they promote efficiency and fairness. Market forces coupled with the responsibility for profitability motivate managers to use their resources effectively. For example, Jerry Lowe, the manager of the lumber division, may stop producing the high-quality boards the furniture division uses if he finds it is more profitable to produce low-quality lumber.

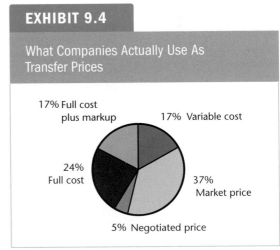

EXHIBIT 9.4

What Companies Actually Use As Transfer Prices

17% Full cost plus markup

17% Variable cost

24% Full cost

37% Market price

5% Negotiated price

Source: R. Tang, "Transfer Pricing in the 1990s," *Management Accounting,* pp. 22–26.

REALITY BYTES

The issue of transfer pricing is mostly relevant to performance evaluation of investment centers and their managers if a company does business in only one country. Transfer prices do not affect the overall profit of the company, because the cost that will be recorded as an expense for the company as a whole is the actual cost incurred to produce it, not its transfer price. However, the situation can be different if the producing division is in one country and the acquiring division is in another. This difference occurs because income tax rates are not the same in all countries.

Assume the Global Tool Company manufactures a product in South Korea for the equivalent of $10. The product is transferred to another segment that operates in the United States where it is ultimately sold for $18. Now, assume the income tax rate is 40 percent in South Korea and 30 percent in the United States. Ignoring all other costs, what amount of taxes will the company pay if the transfer price is set at $10? What amount of taxes will the company pay if the transfer price is set at $18?

If a $10 transfer price is used, then all of the company's $8 per unit profit ($18 − $10) will be recognized in the Unites States. Since the item is assumed to have been "sold" in Korea at an amount equal to its production cost, there will be no profit for the Korean division of the company ($10 − $10 = $0). The United States division will pay $2.40 in taxes ($8 × .30 = $2.40). Conversely, if the transfer price is $18, then all of the profit will be reported in Korea, and $3.20 per unit of taxes will be paid ($8 × .40 = $3.20).

The Internal Revenue Service has rules to prevent companies from setting transfer prices simply for the purpose of reducing taxes, but various companies have been accused of such practices over the years. Remember, it is often impossible to prove exactly what the best transfer price should be. Even though the company in our hypothetical example could not get away with such extreme transfer prices as $10 or $18, it might try to set the price a bit lower than it should be in order to shift more profit to the segment in the United States where the assumed tax rate was lower. Regarding the use of transfer prices to reduce taxes, an article in *BusinessWeek* noted, "Last year, a General Accounting Office study reported that, from 1989 to 1995, an outright majority of corporations, both U.S. and foreign-controlled, paid zero U.S. income taxes."*

*"The Creative Economy," *BusinessWeek,* August 28, 2000, p. 76.

The furniture division can buy its needed material from outside companies that have chosen to operate in the less-profitable, high-quality market sector. The company as a whole benefits from Mr. Lowe's insight. An additional advantage of using market prices is the sense of fairness associated with them. It is difficult for a manager to complain that the price she is being charged is too high when she has the opportunity to seek a lower price elsewhere. The natural justice of the competitive marketplace is firmly implanted in the psyche of most modern managers.

Negotiated Transfer Prices

In many instances, a necessary product is not available from outside companies or the market price may not be in the best interest of the company as a whole. Sometimes a division makes a unique product that is used only by one of its company's other divisions; no external market price is available to use as a base for determining the transfer price. Other times, market-based transfer prices may lead to suboptimization, discussed earlier.

Consider the case of Garms Industries. It operates several relatively autonomous divisions. One division, TrueTrust Motors, Inc., makes small electric motors for use in appliances such as refrigerators, washing machines, and fans. Another Garms division, CleanCo, makes and sells approximately 30,000 vacuum cleaners per year. CleanCo currently purchases the motors used in its vacuums from a company that is not part of Garms Industries. The president of Garms asked the TrueTrust division manager to establish a price at which it could make and sell motors to CleanCo. The manager submitted the following cost and price data.

Variable (unit-level) costs	$45
Per unit fixed cost at a volume of 30,000 units	15
Allocated corporate level facility-sustaining costs	20
Total cost	$80

TrueTrust has enough excess capacity that its existing business will not be affected by a decision to make motors for CleanCo. However, TrueTrust would be required to buy additional equipment and hire a supervisor to make the motors that CleanCo requires.

The TrueTrust manager added a profit margin of $10 per unit and offered to provide motors to CleanCo at a price of $90 per unit. When the offer was presented to the CleanCo division manager, she rejected it. Her division was currently buying motors in the open market for $70 each. Competitive pressures in the vacuum cleaner market would not permit an increase in the sales price of her product. Accepting TrueTrust's offer would significantly increase CleanCo's costs and reduce the division's profitability.

After studying the cost data, Garms's president concluded the company as a whole would suffer from suboptimization if CleanCo were to continue purchasing motors from a third-party vendor. He noted that the allocated corporate level facility-sustaining costs were not relevant to the transfer pricing decision because they would be incurred regardless of whether TrueTrust made the motors for CleanCo. He recognized that both the variable and fixed costs were relevant because they could be avoided if TrueTrust did not make the motors. Since TrueTrust's avoidable cost of $60 ($45 variable cost + $15 fixed cost) per unit was below the $70 price per unit that CleanCo was currently paying, Garms would save $10 per motor, thereby increasing overall company profitability by $300,000 ($10 cost savings per unit × 30,000 units). The president established a reasonable range for a negotiated transfer price.

If the market price were less than the avoidable cost of production, the supplying division (TrueTrust) and the company as a whole (Garms) would be better off to buy the product than to make it. It would therefore be unreasonable to expect TrueTrust to sell a product for less than its avoidable cost of production, thereby establishing the avoidable cost as the bottom point of the reasonable range for the transfer price. On the other hand, it would be unreasonable to expect an acquiring division (CleanCo) to pay more than the price it is currently paying for motors. As a result, the market price becomes the top point of the reasonable range for the transfer price. The reasonable transfer price range can be expressed as follows:

$$\text{Market price} \geq \text{Reasonable transfer price} \geq \text{Avoidable product cost}$$

In the case of Garms Industries, the reasonable range of the transfer price for vacuum cleaner motors is between the market price of $70 per unit and the avoidable production cost of $60.[1] Any transfer price within this range would benefit both divisions and the company as a whole. Garms's president encouraged the two division managers to negotiate a transfer price within the reasonable range that would satisfy both parties.

Under the right set of circumstances, a **negotiated transfer price** can be more beneficial than a market-based transfer price. Allowing the managers involved to agree to a negotiated price preserves the notion of fairness. The element of profit remains intact and the evaluation concepts discussed in this chapter can be applied. Negotiated prices may offer many of the same advantages as market prices. They should be the first alternative when a company is unable to use market-based transfer prices.

Suppose the two division managers cannot agree on a negotiated transfer price. Should the president of Garms Industries establish a reasonable price and force the managers to accept it? There is no definitive answer to this question. However, most senior-level executives recognize the motivational importance of maintaining autonomy in a decentralized organization. So long as the negative consequences are not disastrous, division managers are usually permitted to exercise their own judgment. In other words, the long-term benefits derived from autonomous management outweigh the short-term disadvantages of suboptimization.

---

[1]This discussion assumes the supplying division (TrueTrust) has excess capacity. When the supplying division is operating at full capacity and has external buyers, the minimum price for the reasonable transfer price range would include not only the avoidable cost but also an opportunity cost. An opportunity cost exists when the supplying division must forgo the opportunity to profit from sales it could otherwise make to external buyers. On the other hand, if the supplying division has enough capacity to fill both existing orders and the additional orders on which the transfer price is negotiated, the opportunity cost is zero. In other words, the supplying division does not have to give up anything to accept an order from another division. A full discussion of opportunity cost is complex. It is covered in more advanced courses.

Cost-Based Transfer Prices

The least desirable transfer price option is a **cost-based transfer price.** To use cost, it must first be determined. Some companies base the transfer price on *variable cost* (a proxy for avoidable cost). Other companies use *full cost* (variable cost plus an allocated portion of fixed cost) as the transfer price. In either case, basing transfer prices on cost removes the profit motive. Without profitability as a goal, the incentive to control cost is diminished. One department's inefficiency is simply passed on to the next department. The result is low companywide profitability. Despite this potential detrimental effect, many companies base transfer prices on cost because cost represents an objective number that is available. When a company uses cost-based transfer prices, *it should use standard rather than actual costs.* Departments will therefore at least be responsible for the variances they generate which will encourage some degree of cost control.

SELF-STUDY REVIEW PROBLEM

www.mhhe.com/edmonds2008

A step-by-step audio-narrated series of slides is provided on the text website at www.mhhe.com/edmonds2008.

The following financial statements apply to Hola Division, one of three investment centers operated by Costa Corporation. Costa Corporation has a desired rate of return of 15%. Costa Corporation headquarters has $80,000 of additional operating assets to assign to the investment centers.

HOLA DIVISION
Income Statement
For the Year Ended December 31, 2006

Sales Revenue	$78,695
Cost of Goods Sold	(50,810)
Gross Margin	27,885
Operating Expenses	
Selling Expenses	(1,200)
Depreciation Expense	(1,125)
Operating Income	25,560
Non-Operating Expense	
Loss on Sale of Land	(3,200)
Net Income	$22,360

HOLA DIVISION
Balance Sheet
As of December 31, 2006

Assets	
Cash	$ 8,089
Accounts Receivable	22,870
Merchandise Inventory	33,460
Equipment Less Acc. Dep.	77,581
Non-Operating Assets	8,250
Total Assets	$150,250
Liabilities	
Accounts Payable	$ 5,000
Notes Payable	58,000
Stockholders' Equity	
Common Stock	55,000
Retained Earnings	32,250
Total Liab. and Stk. Equity	$150,250

Required

a. Should Costa use operating income or net income to determine the rate of return (ROI) for the Hola investment center? Explain.

b. Should Costa use operating assets or total assets to determine the ROI for the Hola investment center? Explain.

c. Calculate the ROI for Hola.

d. The manager of the Hola division has an opportunity to invest the funds at an ROI of 17 percent. The other two divisions have investment opportunities that yield only 16 percent. The manager of Hola rejects the additional funding. Why would the manager of Hola reject the funds under these circumstances?

e. Calculate the residual income from the investment opportunity available to Hola and explain how residual income could be used to encourage the manager to accept the additional funds.

Solution to Requirement a

Costa should use operating income because net income frequently includes items over which management has no control, such as the loss on sale of land.

Solution to Requirement b

Costa should use operating assets because total assets frequently includes items over which management has no control, such as assets not currently in use.

Solution to Requirement c

ROI = Operating Income / Operating Assets = $25,560 / $142,000 = 18%

Solution to Requirement d

Since the rate of return on the investment opportunity (17 percent) is below Hola's current ROI (18 percent), accepting the opportunity would decrease Hola's average ROI, which would have a negative effect on the manager's performance evaluation. While it is to the advantage of the company as a whole for Hola to accept the investment opportunity, it will reflect negatively on the manager to do so. This phenomenon is called *suboptimization*.

Solution to Requirement e

Operating income from the investment opportunity is $13,600 ($80,000 × .17)

Residual income = Operating income − (Operating assets × Desired ROI)

Residual income = $13,600 − ($80,000 × .15)

Residual income = $13,600 − $12,000

Residual income = $1,600

Since the investment opportunity would increase Hola's residual income, the acceptance of the opportunity would improve the manager's performance evaluation, thereby motivating the manager to accept it.

KEY TERMS

Balanced scorecard 400
Controllability concept 392
Cost-based transfer price 404
Cost center 389
Decentralization 388
Economic value added 399

Investment center 389
Management by
  exception 391
Margin 395
Market-based transfer
  price 401

Negotiated transfer price 403
Profit center 389
Residual income 397
Responsibility
  accounting 388
Responsibility center 389

Responsibility reports 389
Return on investment 393
Suboptimization 397
Transfer price 401
Turnover 395

QUESTIONS

1. Pam Kelly says she has no faith in budgets. Her company, Kelly Manufacturing Corporation, spent thousands of dollars to install a sophisticated budget system. One year later the company's expenses are still out of control. She believes budgets simply do not work. How would you respond to Ms. Kelly's beliefs?

2. All travel expenses incurred by Pure Water Pump Corporation are reported only to John Daniels, the company president. Pure Water is a multinational company with five divisions. Are travel expenses reported following the responsibility accounting concept? Explain.

3. What are five potential advantages of decentralization?

4. Who receives responsibility reports? What do the reports include?

5. How does the concept of predominant as opposed to that of absolute control apply to responsibility accounting?

6. How do responsibility reports promote the management by exception doctrine?

7. What is a responsibility center?

8. What are the three types of responsibility centers? Explain how each differs from the others.

9. Carmen Douglas claims that her company's performance evaluation system is unfair. Her company uses return on investment (ROI) to evaluate performance. Ms. Douglas says that even though her ROI is lower than another manager's, her performance is far superior. Is it possible that Ms. Douglas is correct? Explain your position.

10. What two factors affect the computation of return on investment?

11. What three ways can a manager increase the return on investment?

12. How can a residual income approach to performance evaluation reduce the likelihood of suboptimization?

13. Is it true that the manager with the highest residual income is always the best performer?

14. Why are transfer prices important to managers who are evaluated based on profitability criteria?

15. What are three approaches to establishing transfer prices? List the most desirable approach first and the least desirable last.

16. If cost is the basis for transfer pricing, should actual or standard cost be used? Why?

MULTIPLE-CHOICE QUESTIONS

Multiple-choice questions are provided on the text website at www.mhhe.com/edmonds2008.

EXERCISES—SERIES A

All Exercises in Series A are available with McGraw-Hill's Homework Manager®.

L.O. 1

Exercise 9-1A *Organization chart and responsibilities*

The production manager is responsible for the assembly, cleaning, and finishing departments. The executive vice president reports directly to the president but is responsible for the activities of the production department, the finance department, and the sales department. The sales manager is responsible for the advertising department.

Required

Arrange this information into an organization chart and indicate the responsibility levels involved.

L.O. 4

Exercise 9-2A *Responsibility report*

Bonn Department Store is divided into three major departments: Men's Clothing, Women's Clothing, and Home Furnishings. Each of these three departments is supervised by a manager who reports to the general manager. The departments are subdivided into different sections managed by floor supervisors. The Home Furnishings Department has three floor supervisors, one for furniture, one for lamps, and one for housewares. The following items were included in the company's most recent responsibility report.

Travel expenses for the housewares buyer
Seasonal decorations for the furniture section

Revenues for the Home Furnishings Department
Administrative expenses for the Men's Clothing Department
Utility cost allocated to the Home Furnishings Department
Cost of part-time Christmas help for the Women's Department
Delivery expenses for furniture purchases
Salaries for the sales staff in the lamp section
Storewide revenues
Salary of the general manager
Salary of the Men's Clothing Department manager
Allocated companywide advertising expense
Depreciation on the facility

Required

Which items are likely to be the responsibility of the Home Furnishings Department manager?

Exercise 9-3A *Organization chart and controllable costs*

L.O. 1, 4

Jenkins Company has employees with the following job titles.

President of the company
Vice president of marketing
Product manager
Controller
Vice president of manufacturing
Treasurer
Regional sales manager
Personnel manager
Cashier
Vice president of finance
Fringe benefits manager
Board of directors
Production supervisors
Vice president of administration
Sales office manager

Required

a. Design an organization chart using these job titles.
b. Identify some possible controllable costs for the person holding each job title.

Exercise 9-4A *Income statement for internal use*

L.O. 1, 3

Cummings Company has provided the following 2006 data.

Budget	
Sales	$408,000
Variable product costs	164,000
Variable selling expense	48,000
Other variable expenses	4,000
Fixed product costs	16,800
Fixed selling expense	25,200
Other fixed expenses	2,400
Interest expense	900
Variances	
Sales	8,800 U
Variable product costs	4,000 F
Variable selling expense	2,400 U
Other variable expenses	1,200 U
Fixed product costs	240 F
Fixed selling expense	400 F
Other fixed expenses	160 U
Interest expense	100 F

Required

Prepare in good form a budgeted and actual income statement for internal use. Separate operating income from net income in the statements.

L.O. 1, 3

Exercise 9-5A *Evaluating a cost center including flexible budgeting concepts*

Pittman Medical Equipment Company makes a blood pressure measuring kit. Jay Thrasher is the production manager. The production department's static budget and actual results for 2007 follow.

	Static Budget	Actual Results
	20,000 kits	*21,000 kits*
Direct materials	$ 300,000	$ 323,400
Direct labor	270,000	277,200
Variable manufacturing overhead	70,000	89,200
Total variable costs	640,000	689,800
Fixed manufacturing cost	360,000	356,000
Total manufacturing cost	$1,000,000	$1,045,800

Required

a. Convert the static budget into a flexible budget.
b. Use the flexible budget to evaluate Mr. Thrasher's performance.
c. Explain why Mr. Thrasher's performance evaluation does not include sales revenue and net income.

L.O. 2, 3

Exercise 9-6A *Evaluating a profit center*

Janet Handley, the president of Washington Toys Corporation, is trying to determine this year's pay raises for the store managers. Washington Toys has seven stores in the southwestern United States. Corporate headquarters purchases all toys from different manufacturers globally and distributes them to individual stores. Additionally, headquarters makes decisions regarding location and size of stores. These practices allow Washington Toys to receive volume discounts from vendors and to implement coherent marketing strategies. Within a set of general guidelines, store managers have the flexibility to adjust product prices and hire local employees. Ms. Handley is considering three possible performance measures for evaluating the individual stores: cost of goods sold, return on sales (net income divided by sales), and return on investment.

Required

a. Using the concept of controllability, advise Ms. Handley about the best performance measure.
b. Explain how a balanced scorecard can be used to help Ms. Handley.

L.O. 5

Exercise 9-7A *Return on investment*

An investment center of Garmon Corporation shows an operating income of $3,600 on total operating assets of $15,000.

Required

Compute the return on investment.

L.O. 5, 6

Exercise 9-8A *Return on investment*

Carson Company calculated its return on investment as 15 percent. Sales are now $180,000, and the amount of total operating assets is $300,000.

Required

a. If expenses are reduced by $18,000 and sales remain unchanged, what return on investment will result?
b. If both sales and expenses cannot be changed, what change in the amount of operating assets is required to achieve the same result?

Exercise 9-9A   *Residual income*

Gary Corporation has a desired rate of return of 10 percent. Rick Wayne is in charge of one of Gary's three investment centers. His center controlled operating assets of $9,000,000 that were used to earn $1,170,000 of operating income.

Required

Compute Mr. Wayne's residual income.

Exercise 9-10A   *Residual income*

Hollis Cough Drops operates two divisions. The following information pertains to each division for 2005.

	Division A	Division B
Sales	$180,000	$60,000
Operating income	$ 18,000	$ 9,600
Average operating assets	$ 72,000	$48,000
Company's desired rate of return	20%	20%

Required

a. Compute each division's residual income.
b. Which division increased the company's profitability more?

Exercise 9-11A   *Return on investment and residual income*

Required

Supply the missing information in the following table for McDow Company.

Sales	$600,000
ROI	?
Operating assets	?
Operating income	?
Turnover	2
Residual income	?
Margin	0.10
Desired rate of return	18%

Exercise 9-12A   *Comparing return on investment with residual income*

The Milwee Division of Sanford Corporation has a current ROI of 20 percent. The company target ROI is 15 percent. The Milwee Division has an opportunity to invest $4,000,000 at 18 percent but is reluctant to do so because its ROI will fall to 19.2 percent. The present investment base for the division is $6,000,000.

Required

Demonstrate how Sanford can motivate the Milwee Division to make the investment by using the residual income method.

Exercise 9-13A   *Return on investment and residual income*

American Home Maintenance Company (AHMC) earned operating income of $9,460,800 on operating assets of $52,560,000 during 2008. The Tree Cutting Division earned $1,496,000 on operating assets of $6,800,000. AHMC has offered the Tree Cutting Division $2,200,000 of additional operating assets. The manager of the Tree Cutting Division believes he could use the additional assets to generate operating income amounting to $440,000. AHMC has a desired return on investment (ROI) of 17 percent.

Required

a. Calculate the return on investment (ROI) for AHMC, the Tree Cutting Division, and the additional investment opportunity.
b. Calculate the residual income (RI) for AHMC, the Tree Cutting Division, and the additional investment opportunity.

Appendix

L.O. 8

Exercise 9-14A   *Transfer pricing*

Gibson Company has two divisions, A and B. Division A manufactures 6,000 units of product per month. The cost per unit is calculated as follows.

Variable costs	$ 6
Fixed costs	20
Total cost	$26

Division B uses the product created by Division A. No outside market for Division A's product exists. The fixed costs incurred by Division A are allocated headquarters-level facility-sustaining costs. The manager of Division A suggests that the product be transferred to Division B at a price of at least $26 per unit. The manager of Division B argues that the same product can be purchased from another company for $16 per unit and requests permission to do so.

Required

a. Should Gibson allow the manager of Division B to purchase the product from the outside company for $16 per unit? Explain.
b. Assume you are the president of the company. Write a brief paragraph recommending a resolution of the conflict between the two divisional managers.

L.O. 8

Exercise 9-15A   *Transfer pricing and fixed cost per unit*

The Potomac Parts Division of East Company plans to set up a facility with the capacity to make 5,000 units annually of an electronic computer part. The avoidable cost of making the part is as follows.

Costs	Total	Cost per Unit
Variable cost	$300,000	$60
Fixed cost	80,000	16 (at capacity)

Required

a. Assume that East's Nolen Division is currently purchasing 3,000 of the electronic parts each year from an outside supplier at a market price of $100. What would be the financial consequence to East if the Potomac Parts Division makes the part and sells it to the Nolen Division? What range of transfer prices would increase the financial performance of both divisions?
b. Suppose that the Nolen Division increases production so that it could use 5,000 units of the part made by the Potomac Parts Division. How would the change in volume affect the range of transfer prices that would financially benefit both divisions?

PROBLEMS—SERIES A

All Problems in Series A are available with McGraw-Hill's Homework Manager®.

L.O. 4

Problem 9-16A   *Determining controllable costs*

Steve Reitz is the manager of the production department of Faraino Corporation. Faraino incurred the following costs during 2007.

Production department supplies	$ 8,000
Administrative salaries	300,000
Production wages	652,000
Materials used	529,200
Depreciation on manufacturing equipment	361,600
Corporate-level rental expense	240,000
Property taxes	68,600
Sales salaries	286,800

Required

Prepare a list of expenditures that Mr. Reitz controls.

Problem 9-17A   *Controllability, responsibility, and balanced scorecard*

L.O. 3, 4

Tracie Buckley manages the production division of Yates Corporation. Ms. Buckley's responsibility report for the month of August follows.

	Budget	Actual	Variance	
Controllable costs				
Raw materials	$30,000	$37,500	$ 7,500	U
Labor	15,000	20,700	5,700	U
Maintenance	3,000	3,600	600	U
Supplies	2,550	1,800	750	F
Total	$50,550	$63,600	$13,050	U

The budget had called for 7,500 pounds of raw materials at $4 per pound, and 7,500 pounds were used during August; however, the purchasing department paid $5 per pound for the materials. The wage rate used to establish the budget was $15 per hour. On August 1, however, it increased to $18 as the result of an inflation index provision in the union contract. Furthermore, the purchasing department did not provide the materials needed in accordance with the production schedule, which forced Ms. Buckley to use 100 hours of overtime at a $27 rate. The projected 1,000 hours of labor in the budget would have been sufficient had it not been for the 100 hours of overtime. In other words, 1,100 hours of labor were used in August.

Required

a. When confronted with the unfavorable variances in her responsibility report, Ms. Buckley argued that the report was unfair because it held her accountable for materials and labor variances that she did *not* control. Is she correct? Comment specifically on the materials and labor variances.

b. Prepare a responsibility report that reflects the cost items that Ms. Buckley controlled during August.

c. Will the changes in the revised responsibility report require corresponding changes in the financial statements? Explain.

d. Explain how a balanced scorecard may be used to improve the performance evaluation.

Problem 9-18A   *Performance reports and evaluation*

L.O. 3, 4

www.mhhe.com/edmonds2008

Duvall Corporation has four divisions: the assembly division, the processing division, the machining division, and the packing division. All four divisions are under the control of the vice president of manufacturing. Each division has a manager and several departments that are directed by supervisors. The chain of command runs downward from vice president to division manager to supervisor. The processing division is composed of the paint and finishing departments. The May responsibility reports for the supervisors of these departments follow.

	Budgeted*	Actual	Variance	
Paint Department				
Controllable costs				
Raw materials	$28,800	$ 30,000	$1,200	U
Labor	60,000	66,000	6,000	U
Repairs	4,800	3,840	960	F
Maintenance	2,400	2,280	120	F
Total	$96,000	$102,120	$6,120	U
Finishing Department				
Controllable costs				
Raw materials	$22,800	$ 22,560	$ 240	F
Labor	43,200	39,600	3,600	F
Repairs	2,880	3,240	360	U
Maintenance	1,680	2,040	360	U
Total	$70,560	$ 67,440	$3,120	F

*Duvall uses flexible budgets for performance evaluation.

Other pertinent cost data for May follow.

	Budgeted*	Actual
Cost data of other divisions		
Assembly	$324,000	$318,240
Machining	282,000	288,480
Packing	421,440	412,920
Other costs associated with		
Processing division manager	240,000	237,600
Vice president of manufacturing	132,000	137,040

*Duvall uses flexible budgets for performance evaluation.

Required

a. Prepare a responsibility report for the manager of the processing division.
b. Prepare a responsibility report for the vice president of manufacturing.
c. Explain where the $6,000 unfavorable labor variance in the paint department supervisor's report is included in the vice president's report.
d. Based on the responsibility report prepared in Requirement *a,* explain where the processing division manager should concentrate his attention.

L.O. 2

Problem 9-19A   *Different types of responsibility centers*

Western Bank is a large municipal bank with several branch offices. The bank's computer department handles all data processing for bank operations. In addition, the bank sells the computer department's expertise in systems development and excess machine time to several small business firms, serving them as a service bureau.

The bank currently treats the computer department as a cost center. The manager of the computer department prepares a cost budget annually for senior bank officials to approve. Monthly operating reports compare actual and budgeted expenses. Revenues from the department's service bureau activities are treated as other income by the bank and are not reflected on the computer department's operating reports. The costs of serving these clients are included in the computer department reports, however.

The manager of the computer department has proposed that bank management convert the computer department to a profit or investment center.

Required

a. Describe the characteristics that differentiate a cost center, a profit center, and an investment center from each other.

b. Would the manager of the computer department be likely to conduct the operations of the department differently if the department were classified as a profit center or an investment center rather than as a cost center? Explain.

Problem 9-20A *Comparing return on investment and residual income*

L.O. 5, 7

Slatten Corporation operates three investment centers. The following financial statements apply to the investment center named Kent Division.

CHECK FIGURE
c. 16.60%

KENT DIVISION
Income Statement
For the Year Ended December 31, 2006

Sales Revenue	$ 91,285
Cost of Goods Sold	(59,620)
Gross Margin	31,665
Operating Expenses	
Selling Expenses	(1,445)
Depreciation Expense	(1,200)
Operating Income	29,020
Non-Operating Expense	
Gain of Sale of Land	(4,180)
Net Income	$ 33,200

KENT DIVISION
Balance Sheet
As of December 31, 2006

Assets	
Cash	$ 19,103
Accounts Receivable	37,432
Merchandise Inventory	38,255
Equipment Less Accum. Dep.	80,000
Non-Operating Assets	9,000
Total Assets	$183,790
Liabilities	
Accounts Payable	$ 7,000
Notes Payable	65,700
Stockholders' Equity	
Common Stock	70,000
Retained Earnings	41,000
Total Liab. and Stk. Equity	$183,790

Required

a. Should operating income or net income be used to determine the rate of return (ROI) for the Kent investment center? Explain your answer.

b. Should operating assets or total assets be used to determine the ROI for the Kent investment center? Explain your answer.

c. Calculate the ROI for Kent.

d. Slatten has a desired ROI of 12 percent. Headquarters has $100,000 of funds to assign its investment centers. The manager of the Kent Division has an opportunity to invest the funds at an ROI of 15 percent. The other two divisions have investment opportunities that yield only 14 percent. Even so, the manager of Kent rejects the additional funding. Explain why the manager of Kent would reject the funds under these circumstances.

e. Explain how residual income could be used to encourage the manager to accept the additional funds.

Problem 9-21A *Return on investment*

Albano Corporation's balance sheet indicates that the company has $400,000 invested in operating assets. During 2006, Albano earned operating income of $60,000 on $800,000 of sales.

Required

a. Compute Albano's margin for 2006.
b. Compute Albano's turnover for 2006.
c. Compute Albano's return on investment for 2006.
d. Recompute Albano's ROI under each of the following independent assumptions.

(1) Sales increase from $800,000 to $1,000,000, thereby resulting in an increase in operating income from $60,000 to $80,000.

(2) Sales remain constant, but Albano reduces expenses, resulting in an increase in operating income from $60,000 to $64,000.

(3) Albano is able to reduce its invested capital from $400,000 to $320,000 without affecting operating income.

Problem 9-22A *Return on investment and residual income*

Quest Company has operating assets of $20,000,000. The company's operating income for the most recent accounting period was $2,500,000. The Western Division of Quest controls $8 million of the company's assets and earned $1,120,000 of its operating income. Quest's desired ROI is 12 percent. Quest has $1 million of additional funds to invest. The manager of the Western division believes that his division could earn $135,000 on the additional funds. The highest investment opportunity to any of the company's other divisions is 13 percent.

Required

a. If ROI is used as the sole performance measure, would the manager of the Western Division be likely to accept or reject the additional funding? Why or why not?

b. Would Quest Company benefit if the manager of the Western Division accepted the additional funds. Why or why not?

c. If residual income is used as the sole performance measure would the manager of the Western Division be likely to accept or reject the additional funding? Why or why not?

Problem 9-23A *Return on investment and residual income*

Beacon Technologies, Inc. (BTI), has three divisions. BTI has a desired rate of return of 13 percent. The operating assets and income for each division are as follows:

Divisions	Operating Assets	Operating Income
Printer	$ 500,000	$ 80,000
Copier	800,000	88,000
Fax	300,000	42,000
Total	$1,600,000	$210,000

BTI headquarters has $100,000 of additional cash to invest in one of its divisions. The division managers have identified investment opportunities that are expected to yield the following ROIs:

Divisions	Expected ROIs for Additional Investments
Printer	15.5%
Copier	13.5%
Fax	12.0%

Required

a. Which division manager is currently producing the highest ROI?

b. Based on ROI, which division manager would be most eager to accept the $100,000 of investment funds?

c. Based on ROI, which division manager would be least likely to accept the $100,000 of investment funds?

d. Which division offers the best investment opportunity for BTI?

e. What is the term used to describe the apparent conflict between Requirements *b* and *d*?

f. Explain how the residual income performance measure could be used to motivate the managers to act in the best interest of the company.

g. Calculate the residual income:

   (1) at the corporate (headquarters) level.

   (2) at the division level.

   (3) at the investment level.

   (4) at the division level after the additional investment.

h. Based on residual income, which division manager would be most eager to accept the $100,000 investment opportunity.

Appendix

Problem 9-24A *Transfer pricing*

L.O. 8

CHECK FIGURE
a. The maximum price should be $28.

Chappel Radio Corporation is a subsidiary of Franklin Companies. Chappel makes car radios that it sells to retail outlets. It purchases speakers for the radios from outside suppliers for $28 each. Recently, Franklin acquired the Duke Speaker Corporation, which makes car radio speakers that it sells to manufacturers. Duke produces and sells approximately 200,000 speakers per year, which represents 70 percent of its operating capacity. At the present volume of activity, each speaker costs $24 to produce. This cost consists of a $16 variable cost component and an $8 fixed cost component. Duke sells the speakers for $30 each. The managers of Chappel and Duke have been asked to consider using Duke's excess capacity to supply Chappel with some of the speakers that it currently purchases from unrelated companies. Both managers are evaluated based on return on investment. Duke's manager suggests that the speakers be supplied at a transfer price of $30 each (the current selling price). On the other hand, Chappel's manager suggests a $28 transfer price, noting that this amount covers total cost and provides Duke a healthy contribution margin.

Required

a. What transfer price would you recommend?

b. Discuss the effect of the intercompany sales on each manager's return on investment.

c. Should Duke be required to use more than excess capacity to provide speakers to Chappel? In other words, should it sell to Chappel some of the 200,000 units that it is currently selling to unrelated companies? Why or why not?

EXERCISES—SERIES B

Exercise 9-1B *Organizational chart and responsibilities*

L.O. 1

Yesterday, Connally Corporation's board of directors appointed Paulette Gaiter as the new president and chief executive officer. This morning, Ms. Gaiter presented to the board a list of her management team members. The vice presidents are Arthur Brown, regional operations; Mark Dailey, research and development; and Pearl Quinn, chief financial officer. Reporting to Mr. Brown are the directors of American, European, and Asian operations. Reporting to Mr. Dailey are the directors of the Tempe, Orlando, and Chicago laboratories. Reporting to Ms. Quinn are the controller and the treasurer.

Required

Arrange the preceding information into an organization chart and indicate the responsibility levels involved.

Exercise 9-2B *Responsibility report*

L.O. 4

Connally Corporation divides its operations into three regions: American, European, and Asian. The following items appear in the company's responsibility report.

European director's salary
Revenues of the French branch

Office expenses of the Japanese branch
Corporation president's salary
Asian director's salary
Revenues of the Taiwanese branch
Revenues of the British branch
Office expenses of the French branch
Revenues of the U.S. branch
Administrative expenses of the corporate headquarters
Office expenses of the Taiwanese branch
Office expenses of the Canadian branch
Revenues of the Japanese branch
Revenues of the Canadian branch
Office expenses of the British branch
Office expenses of the U.S. branch
American director's salary

Required

Which items should Connally include in the responsibility report for the director of Asian operations?

L.O. 1, 4   **Exercise 9-3B**   *Organizational chart and controllable cost*

Mark Dailey, Connally Corporation vice president of research and development, has overall responsibility for employees with the following positions:

Directors of the Tempe, Orlando, and Chicago laboratories
Senior researchers reporting to laboratory directors
A personnel manager in each laboratory
An accounting manager in each laboratory
Research assistants working for senior researchers
Recruiters reporting to a personnel manager
Bookkeepers reporting to an accounting manager

Required

a. Design an organization chart using these job positions.
b. Identify some possible controllable costs for persons holding each of the job positions.

L.O. 1, 3   **Exercise 9-4B**   *Income statement for internal use*

Kahil Company has provided the following data for 2007:

Budget	
Sales	$400,000
Variable product costs	120,000
Variable selling expense	39,000
Other variable expenses	8,000
Fixed product costs	56,000
Fixed selling expense	21,000
Other fixed expenses	2,000
Interest expense	1,000
Actual results	
Sales	$414,000
Variable product costs	122,000
Variable selling expense	42,000
Other variable expenses	7,000
Fixed product costs	60,000
Fixed selling expense	19,200
Other fixed expenses	10,000
Interest expense	1,050

Required

a. Prepare in good form a budgeted and actual income statement for internal use. Separate operating income from net income in the statements.
b. Calculate variances and identify them as favorable (F) or unfavorable (U).

Exercise 9-5B   *Evaluating a cost center (including flexible budgeting concepts)*   L.O. 1

Glen Howell, president of Howell Door Products Company, is evaluating the performance of Keith Ireland, the plant manager, for the last fiscal year. Mr. Howell is concerned that production costs exceeded budget by nearly $21,000. He has available the 2007 static budget for the production plant, as well as the actual results, both of which follow:

	Static Budget	Actual Results
	5,000 Doors	5,250 Doors
Direct materials	$225,000	$231,000
Direct labor	110,000	126,000
Variable manufacturing overhead	60,000	60,900
Total variable costs	395,000	417,900
Fixed manufacturing overhead	205,000	203,000
Total manufacturing cost	$600,000	$620,900

Required

a. Convert the static budget into a flexible budget.
b. Use the flexible budget to evaluate Mr. Ireland's performance.
c. Explain why Mr. Ireland's performance evaluation doesn't include sales revenue and net income.

Exercise 9-6B   *Evaluating a profit center*   L.O. 2, 4

Roberta Juliano, president of World Travel Company, a travel agency, is seeking a method of evaluating her seven branches. Each branch vice president is authorized to hire employees and devise competitive strategies for the branch territory. Ms. Juliano wonders which of the following three different measures would be most suitable: return on investment, operating income, or return on sales (operating income divided by sales).

Required

a. Using the concept of controllability, advise Ms. Juliano about the best performance measure.
b. Explain how a balanced scorecard can be used for Ms. Juliano.

Exercise 9-7B   *Computing return on investment*   L.O. 7

A Hopkins Corporation investment center shows an operating income of $60,000 and an investment in operating assets of $480,000.

Required

Compute the return on investment.

Exercise 9-8B   *Return on investment*   L.O. 5, 6

With annual sales of $5,000,000 and operating assets of $2,500,000, Calder Company achieved a 10 percent ROI.

Required

a. If Calder reduces expenses by $50,000 and sales remain unchanged, what ROI will result?
b. If Calder cannot change either sales or expenses, what change in the investment base is required to achieve the same result you calculated for Requirement *a*?

L.O. 7

Exercise 9-9B   *Computing residual income*

Berry Corporation's desired rate of return is 15 percent. North Division, one of Berry's five investment centers, earned an operating income of $3,600,000 last year. The division controlled $20,000,000 of operational assets.

Required

Compute North Division's residual income.

L.O. 7

Exercise 9-10B   *Computing residual income*

Standard Oil Change operates two divisions. The following pertains to each division for 2007:

	Houston Division	Dallas Division
Sales	$800,000	$600,000
Operating income	$ 60,000	$ 40,000
Average operating assets	$250,000	$200,000
Company's desired rate of return	15%	15%

Required

a. Compute each division's residual income.
b. Which division increased the company's profitability more?

L.O. 5, 7

Exercise 9-11B   *Supply missing information regarding return on investment and residual income*

Required

Supply the missing information in the following table for Ashton Company.

Sales	?
ROI	12%
Investment in operating assets	$600,000
Operating income	?
Turnover	?
Residual income	?
Margin	0.08
Desired rate of return	11%

L.O. 5, 7

Exercise 9-12B   *Contrasting return on investment with residual income*

The St. Louis Division of Missouri Garage Doors, Inc., is currently achieving a 16 percent ROI. The company's target ROI is 10 percent. The division has an opportunity to invest in operating assets an additional $600,000 at 13 percent but is reluctant to do so because its ROI will fall to 15.5 percent. The division's present investment in operating assets is $3,000,000.

Required

Explain how management can use the residual income method to motivate the St. Louis Division to make the investment.

L.O. 5, 6, 7

Exercise 9-13B   *Return on investment and residual income*

Evergreen Insurance Company (EIC) earned operating income of $58,712,000 on operating assets of $372,690,000 during 2007. The Automobile Insurance Division earned $12,520,000 on operating assets of $66,488,000. EIC has offered the Automobile Division $7,250,000 of additional operating assets. The manager of the Automobile Insurance Division believes she could use the additional assets to generate operating income amounting to $1,160,000. EIC has a desired return on investment (ROI) of 14 percent.

Required

a. Calculate the return on investment (ROI) for EIC, the Automobile Insurance Division, and the additional investment opportunity.

b. Calculate the residual income (RI) for EIC, the Automobile Insurance Division, and the additional investment opportunity.

Appendix

Exercise 9-14B   *Transfer pricing*

L.O. 7

Boone Company makes household water filtration equipment. The Aquafresh Division manufactures filters. The Sweet Water Division then uses the filters as a component of the final product Boone sells to consumers. The Aquafresh Division has the capacity to produce 8,000 filters per month at the following cost per unit:

Variable costs	$12
Division fixed costs	10
Allocated corporate-level facility-sustaining costs	8
Total cost per filter	$30

Sweet Water currently uses 6,000 Aquafresh filters per month. Jim Sanders, Sweet Water's manager, is not happy with the $30 transfer price charged by Aquafresh. He points out that Sweet Water could purchase the same filters from outside vendors for a market price of only $24. Amy Mead, Aquafresh's manager, refuses to sell the filters to Sweet Water below cost. Mr. Sanders counters that he would be happy to purchase the filters elsewhere. Because Aquafresh does not have other customers for its filters, Ms. Mead appeals to Frank Pell, the president of Boone, for arbitration.

Required

a. Should the president of Boone allow Mr. Sanders to purchase filters from outside vendors for $24 per unit? Explain.

b. Write a brief paragraph describing what Mr. Pell should do to resolve the conflict between the two division managers.

Exercise 9-15B   *Transfer pricing and fixed cost per unit*

L.O. 8

The Murdock Division of Yesso Company currently produces electric fans that desktop computer manufacturers use as cooling components. The Hart Division, which makes laptop computers, has asked the Murdock Division to design and supply 20,000 fans per year for its laptop computers. Hart currently purchases laptop fans from an outside vendor at the price of $18 each. However, Hart is not happy with the vendor's unstable delivery pattern. To accept Hart's order, Murdock would have to purchase additional equipment and modify its plant layout. The additional equipment would enable the company to add 35,000 laptop fans to its annual production. Murdock's avoidable cost of making 20,000 laptop fans follows:

Costs	Total	Per Unit
Variable costs	$120,000	$6
Fixed cost	$140,000	7

Required

a. What would be the financial consequence to Yesso Company if the Murdock Division makes the laptop fans and sells them to the Hart Division? What range of transfer prices would increase the financial performance of both divisions?

b. Suppose the Hart Division increases production so that it could use 35,000 Murdock Division laptop fans. How would the change in volume affect the range of transfer prices that would financially benefit both divisions?

L.O. 4

Problem 9-16B *Determining controllable costs*

At a professional conference just a few days ago, Jason Callie, the president of Morrow Corporation, learned how the concept of controllability relates to performance evaluation. In preparing to put this new knowledge into practice, he reviewed the financial data of the company's sales department.

Salaries of salespeople	$ 560,000
Cost of goods sold	45,000,000
Facility-level corporate costs	820,000
Travel expenses	64,000
Depreciation on equipment	200,000
Salary of the sales manager	120,000
Property taxes	8,000
Telephone expenses	78,000

Required

Help Mr. Callie prepare a list of expenditures that the sales manager controls.

L.O. 3

Problem 9-17B *Controllability, responsibility, and balanced scorecard*

Gerald Neumeier, president of Friedman Corporation, evaluated the performance report of the company's production department. Mr. Neumeier was confused by some arguments presented by Elaine Grayson, the production manager. Some relevant data follow.

Variances	Amount	
Materials usage variance	$400,000	U
Materials price variance	240,000	F
Labor price variance	76,000	F
Labor usage variance	276,000	U
Volume variance	600,000	U

Ms. Grayson argues that she had done a great job, noting the favorable materials price variance and labor price variance. She argued that she had had no control over factors causing the unfavorable variances. For example, she argued that the unfavorable materials usage variance was caused by the purchasing department's decision to buy substandard materials that resulted in a substantial amount of spoilage. Moreover, she argued that the unfavorable labor usage variance resulted from the substantial materials spoilage which in turn wasted many labor hours, as did the hiring of underqualified workers by the manager of the personnel department. Finally, she said that the sales department's failure to obtain a sufficient number of customer orders really caused the unfavorable volume variance.

Required

a. What would you do first if you were Gerald Neumeier?
b. Did Ms. Grayson deserve the credit she claimed for the favorable variances? Explain.
c. Was Ms. Grayson responsible for the unfavorable variances? Explain.
d. Explain how a balanced scorecard can be used to improve performance evaluation.

L.O. 3, 4

Problem 9-18B *Performance reports and evaluation*

The mortgage division of Mohen Financial Services, Inc., is managed by a vice president who supervises three regional operations. Each regional operation has a general manager and several branches directed by branch managers.

The Coleman region has two branches, Cahaba and Garner. The March responsibility reports for the managers of these branches follow.

	Budgeted*	Actual	Variance	
Cahaba Branch				
Controllable costs				
Employee compensation	$288,000	$300,800	$12,800	U
Office supplies	72,000	70,000	2,000	F
Promotions	152,000	128,000	24,000	F
Maintenance	16,000	21,200	5,200	U
Total	$528,000	$520,000	$ 8,000	F
Garner Branch				
Controllable costs				
Employee compensation	$260,000	$250,000	$10,000	F
Office supplies	76,000	84,000	8,000	U
Promotions	144,000	150,000	6,000	U
Maintenance	20,000	19,200	800	F
Total	$500,000	$503,200	$ 3,200	U

*Mohen uses flexible budgets for performance evaluation.

Other pertinent cost data for March follow.

	Budgeted*	Actual
Cost data of other regions		
Helena	$1,400,000	$1,452,000
Alabaster	1,720,000	1,688,000
Other costs controllable by		
Coleman region general manager	280,000	292,000
Vice president of mortgage	384,000	392,000

*Mohen uses flexible budgets for performance evaluation.

Required

a. Prepare a responsibility report for the general manager of the Coleman region.
b. Prepare a responsibility report for the vice president of the mortgage division.
c. Explain where the $24,000 favorable promotions variance in the Cahaba branch manager's report is included in the vice president's report.
d. Based on the responsibility report prepared in Requirement *a,* explain where the Coleman region's general manager should concentrate her attention.

Problem 9-19B *Different types of responsibility center*

L.O. 2

Seaborn Industries, Inc., has five different divisions; each is responsible for producing and marketing a particular product line. The electronic division makes cellular telephones, pagers, and modems. The division also buys and sells other electronic products made by outside companies. Each division maintains sufficient working capital for its own operations. The corporate headquarters, however, makes decisions about long-term capital investments.

Required

a. For purposes of performance evaluation, should Seaborn classify its electronic division as a cost center, a profit center, or an investment center? Why?
b. Would the manager of the electronic division be likely to conduct the operations of the division differently if the division were classified as a different type of responsibility center than the one you designated in Requirement *a*? Explain.

Problem 9-20B *Comparing return on investment and residual income*

L.O. 5, 7

Taite Corporation operates three investment centers. The following financial statements apply to the investment center named Issac Division.

ISSAC DIVISION
Income Statement
For the Year Ended December 31, 2006

Sales Revenue	$250,975
Cost of Goods Sold	(128,635)
Gross Margin	122,340
Operating Expenses	
Selling Expenses	(13,200)
Administrative Expense	(2,400)
Operating Income	106,740
Non-Operating Expense	
Interest Expense	(6,800)
Net Income	$ 99,940

ISSAC DIVISION
Balance Sheet
As of December 31, 2006

Assets	
Cash	$ 68,360
Accounts Receivable	380,290
Merchandise Inventory	53,750
Equipment Less Accum. Dep.	428,600
Non-Operating Assets	48,000
Total Assets	$979,000
Liabilities	
Accounts Payable	$115,000
Notes Payable	100,000
Stockholders' Equity	
Common Stock	520,000
Retained Earnings	244,000
Total Liab. and Stk. Equity	$979,000

Required

a. Should operating income or net income be used to determine the rate of return (ROI) for the Issac investment center? Explain your answer.

b. Should operating assets or total assets be used to determine the ROI for the Issac investment center? Explain your answer.

c. Calculate the ROI for Issac.

d. Taite has a desired ROI of 8 percent. Headquarters has $300,000 of funds to assign its investment centers. The manager of the Issac Division has an opportunity to invest the funds at an ROI of 10 percent. The other two divisions have investment opportunities that yield only 9 percent. Even so, the manager of Issac rejects the additional funding. Explain why the manager of Issac would reject the funds under these circumstances.

e. Explain how residual income could be used to encourage the manager to accept the additional funds.

L.O. 5, 6   **Problem 9-21B**   *Return on investment*

Loftin Corporation's balance sheet indicates that the company has $600,000 invested in operating assets. During 2007, Loftin earned $96,000 of operating income on $1,920,000 of sales.

Required

a. Compute Loftin's margin for 2007.

b. Compute Loftin's turnover for 2007.

c. Compute Loftin's return on investment for 2007.

d. Recompute Loftin's ROI under each of the following independent assumptions.

(1) Sales increase from $1,920,000 to $2,160,000, thereby resulting in an increase in operating income from $96,000 to $113,400.

(2) Sales remain constant, but Loftin reduces expenses, thereby resulting in an increase in income from $96,000 to $100,800.

(3) Loftin is able to reduce its operating assets from $600,000 to $576,000 without affecting income.

Problem 9-22B *Return on investment and residual income*   L.O. 5, 6, 7

Perryman Company has operating assets of $36,000,000. The company's operating income for the most recent accounting period was $4,070,000. The Denton Division of Perryman controls $12,000,000 of the company's assets and earned $1,750,000 of its operating income. Perryman's desired ROI is 10 percent. Perryman has $3,000,000 of additional funds to invest. The manager of the Denton Division believes that his division could earn $360,000 on the additional funds. The highest investment opportunity to any of the company's other divisions is 11 percent.

Required

a. If ROI is used as the sole performance measure, would the manager of the Denton Division be likely to accept or reject the additional funding? Why or why not?

b. Would Perryman Company benefit if the manager of the Denton Division accepted the additional funds? Why or why not?

c. If residual income is used as the sole performance measure, would the manager of the Denton Division be likely to accept or reject the additional funding? Why or why not?

Problem 9-23B *Return on investment and residual income*   L.O. 5, 6, 7

Tiger Trading Company (TTC) has three divisions. TTC has a desired rate of return of 14%. The operating assets and income for each division are as follows:

Divisions	Operating Assets	Operating Income
Americas	$38,400,000	$ 6,900,000
Asia	19,300,000	3,208,000
Europe	24,300,000	3,300,000
Total	$82,000,000	$13,408,000

TTC headquarters has $600,000 of additional cash to invest in one of its divisions. The division managers have identified investment opportunities that are expected to yield the following ROIs.

Divisions	Expected ROIs for Additional Investments
Americas	16%
Asia	12
Europe	15

Required

a. Which division manager is currently producing the highest ROI?

b. Based on ROI, which division manager would be most eager to accept the $600,000 of investment funds?

c. Based on ROI, which division manager would be least likely to accept the $600,000 of investment funds?

d. Which division offers the best investment opportunity for TTC?

e. What is the term used to describe the apparent conflict between Requirements *b* and *d*?

f. Explain how the residual income performance measure could be used to motivate the managers to act in the best interest of the company.

g. Calculate the residual income:

    (1) At the corporate (headquarters) level.

    (2) At the division level.

    (3) At the investment level.

    (4) At the division level after the additional investment.

h. Based on residual income, which division manager would be most eager to accept the $600,000 investment opportunity?

Appendix

L.O. 8

Problem 9-24B   *Transfer pricing*

ChengKung Electronics Corporation makes a modem that it sells to retail stores for $150 each. The variable cost to produce a modem is $70 each; the total fixed cost is $10,000,000. ChengKung is operating at 80 percent of capacity and is producing 200,000 modems annually. ChengKung's parent company, Wang Corporation, notified ChengKung's president that another subsidiary company, Denton Technologies, has begun making computers and can use ChengKung's modem as a part. Denton needs 40,000 modems annually and is able to acquire similar modems in the market for $144 each.

Under instruction from the parent company, the presidents of ChengKung and Denton meet to negotiate a price for the modem. ChengKung insists that its market price is $150 each and will stand firm on that price. Denton, on the other hand, wonders why it should even talk to ChengKung when Denton can get modems at a lower price.

Required

a. What transfer price would you recommend?

b. Discuss the effect of the intercompany sales on each president's return on investment.

c. Should ChengKung be required to use more than excess capacity to provide modems to Denton if Denton's demand increases to 60,000 modems? In other words, should it sell some of the 200,000 modems that it currently sells to unrelated companies to Denton instead? Why or why not?

ANALYZE, THINK, COMMUNICATE

ATC 9-1   Business Applications Case   *Analyzing segments at Coca-Cola*

The following excerpt is from Coca-Cola Company's 2004 annual report filed with the SEC.

Management evaluates the performance of its operating segments separately to individually monitor the different factors affecting financial performance. Segment profit or loss includes substantially all the segment's costs of production, distribution, and administration. Our Company typically manages and evaluates equity investments and related income on a segment level. However, we manage certain significant investments, such as our equity interests in CCE [Coca-Cola Enterprises], at the Corporate segment. Our Company manages income taxes on a global basis. We manage financial costs, such as interest income and expense, on a global basis at the Corporate segment. Thus, we evaluate segment performance based on profit or loss before income taxes and cumulative effect of accounting change.

Below are selected segment data for Coca-Cola Company for the 2004 and 2003 fiscal years.

	North America	Africa	Europe, Eurasia & Middle East	Latin America	Asia
2004 Fiscal Year					
Net operating revenues	$6,643	$1,067	$7,195	$2,123	$4,691
Segment income before taxes and					
effect of accounting change	1,629	337	1,916	1,270	1,841
Identifiable operating assets	4,731	789	5,373	1,405	1,722
2003 Fiscal Year					
Net operating revenues	$6,344	$827	$6,556	$2,042	$5,052
Segment income before taxes and					
effect of accounting change	1,326	249	1,921	975	1,740
Identifiable operating assets	4,953	721	5,222	1,440	1,923

Required

a. Compute the ROI for each of Coke's geographical segments for each fiscal year. Which segment appears to have the best performance during 2004 based on their ROIs? Which segment showed the most improvement from 2003 to 2004?

b. Assuming Coke's management expects a minimum return of 20 percent, calculate the residual income for each segment for each fiscal year. Which segment appears to have the best performance based on their residual incomes? Which segment showed the most improvement from 2003 to 2004?

c. Your computations for Requirements *a* and *b* above should reveal that for both years the African segment had a higher ROI than the North American segment, yet its residual incomes were lower. Explain how this occurred.

d. Assume the management of Coke is considering a major expansion effort for the next five years. On which geographic segment would you recommend Coke focus its expansion efforts? Explain the rationale for your answer.

ATC 9-2 Group Assignment *Return on investment versus residual income*

Bellco, a division of Becker International Corporation, is operated under the direction of Antoin Sedatt. Bellco is an independent investment center with approximately $72,000,000 of assets that generate approximately $8,640,000 in annual net income. Becker International has additional investment capital of $12,000,000 that is available for the division managers to invest. Mr. Sedatt is aware of an investment opportunity that will provide an 11 percent annual net return. Becker International's desired rate of return is 10 percent.

Required

Divide the class into groups of four or five students and then organize the groups into two sections. Assign Task 1 to the first section and Task 2 to the second section.

Group Tasks

1. Assume that Mr. Sedatt's performance is evaluated based on his ability to maximize return on investment (ROI). Compute ROI using the following two assumptions: Bellco retains its current asset size and Bellco accepts and invests the additional $12,000,000 of assets. Determine whether Mr. Sedatt should accept the opportunity to invest additional funds. Select a spokesperson to present the decision made by the group.

2. Assume that Mr. Sedatt's performance is evaluated based on his ability to maximize residual income. Compute residual income using the following two assumptions: Bellco retains its current asset base and Bellco accepts and invests the additional $12,000,000 of assets. Determine whether Mr. Sedatt should accept the opportunity to invest additional funds. Select a spokesperson to present the decision made by the group.

3. Have a spokesperson from one of the groups in the first section report the two ROIs and the group's recommendation for Mr. Sedatt. Have the groups in this section reach consensus on the ROI and the recommendation.

4. Have a spokesperson from the second section report the two amounts of residual income and disclose the group's recommendation for Mr. Sedatt. Have this section reach consensus on amounts of residual income.

5. Which technique (ROI or residual income) is more likely to result in suboptimization?

ATC 9-3   Research Assignment   *Centralized or decentralized management*

The Curious Accountant story in this chapter related how one company, The Home Depot, grew from a small business into a large business in about 20 years. Another company that has experienced explosive growth since its founding in 1971 is Bed Bath & Beyond, Inc. Read the article "What's Beyond for Bed Bath & Beyond?" by Nanette Byrnes that appears on pages 46 and 50 of the January 19, 2004, issue of *BusinessWeek* and answer the following questions.

Required

a. Does the management at Bed Bath & Beyond operate using a centralized or decentralized organizational style?

b. Give specific examples from the article to support your conclusion in Requirement *a*.

c. Some analysts think Bed Bath & Beyond may not be able to maintain its historic growth rate into the future. What are some of their concerns, and how might a centralized or decentralized management style affect these issues?

d. Based on the related article, "Like Father Like Son," that appears next to the Bed Bath & Beyond story, what role do the children of the founders of Bed Bath & Beyond play at the company, and what are the reasons for this?

ATC 9-4   Writing Assignment   *Transfer pricing*

Green Lawn Mower, Inc., recently acquired Hallit Engines, a small engine manufacturing company. Green's president believes in decentralization and intends to permit Hallit to continue to operate as an independent entity. However, she has instructed the manager of Green's lawn mower assembly division to investigate the possibility of purchasing engines from Hallit instead of using the current third-party supplier. Hallit has excess capacity. The current full cost to produce each engine is $96. The avoidable cost of making engines is $78 per unit. The assembly division, which currently pays the third-party supplier $90 per engine, offers to purchase engines from Hallit at the $90 price. Hallit's president refuses the offer, stating that his company's engines are superior to those the third-party supplier provides. Hallit's president believes that the transfer price should be based on the market price for independent customers, which is $132 per engine. The manager of the assembly division agrees that Hallit's engines are higher quality than those currently being used but notes that Green's customer base is in the low-end, discount market. Putting more expensive engines on Green mowers would raise the price above the competition and would hurt sales. Green's president tries to negotiate a settlement between the assembly manager and Hallit's president, but the parties are unable to agree on a transfer price.

Required

a. Assuming that Green makes and sells 40,000 lawn mowers per year, what is the cost of suboptimization resulting from the failure to establish a transfer price?

b. Assume that you are a consultant asked by the president of Green to recommend whether a transfer price should be arbitrarily imposed. Write a brief memo that includes your recommendation and your justification for making it.

ATC 9-5   Ethical Dilemma   *Manipulating return on investment and residual income*

The October 5, 1998, issue of *Business Week* includes the article "Who Can You Trust?" authored by Sarah Bartlett. Among other dubious accounting practices, the article describes a trick known as the "big bath," which occurs when a company makes huge unwarranted asset write-offs that drastically overstate expenses. Outside auditors (CPAs) permit companies to engage in the practice because the assets being written off are of questionable value. Because the true value of the assets cannot be validated, auditors have little recourse but to accept the valuations suggested by management. Recent examples of questionable write-offs include Motorola's $1.8 billion restructuring charge and the multibillion-dollar write-offs for "in-process" research taken by high-tech companies such as Compaq Computer Corp. and WorldCom, Inc.

Required

a. Why would managers want their companies to take a big bath? (*Hint:* Consider how a big bath affects return on investment and residual income in the years following the write-off.)

b. Annual reports are financial reports issued to the public. The reports are the responsibility of auditors who are CPAs who operate under the ethical standards promulgated by the American Institute of Certified Public Accountants. As a result, attempts to manipulate annual report data are not restricted by the Institute of Management Accountants Standards of Ethical Conduct shown in Exhibit 1.15 of Chapter 1. Do you agree or disagree with these statements? Explain your position.

ATC 9-6   Spreadsheet Assignment   *Using Excel*

Waldon Corporation's balance sheet shows that the company has $600,000 invested in operating assets. During 2006, Waldon earned $120,000 on $960,000 of sales. The company's desired return on investment (ROI) is 12 percent.

Required

a. Construct a spreadsheet to calculate ROI and residual income using these data. Build the spreadsheet using formulas so that the spreadsheet could be used as a template for any ROI or residual income problem. The following screen capture shows how to construct the template.

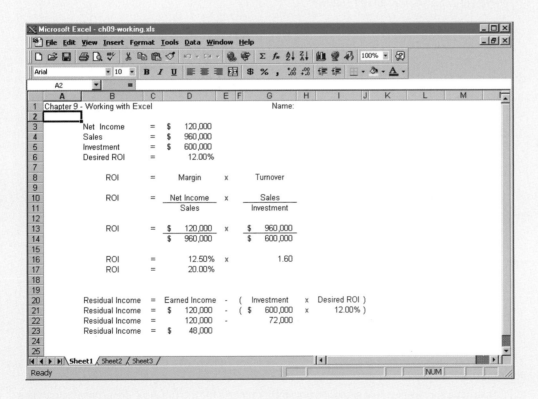

Spreadsheet Tips

(1) The cells below row 12 that show numbers should all be based on formulas. This allows the results to be automatically recalculated based on changes in the data rows 3 to 6.

(2) The parentheses in columns F and J have been entered as text in columns that have a column width of 1.

ATC 9-7   Spreadsheet Assignment   *Mastering Excel*

The Pillar Manufacturing Company has three identified levels of authority and responsibility. The organization chart as of December 31, 2007, appears as follows:

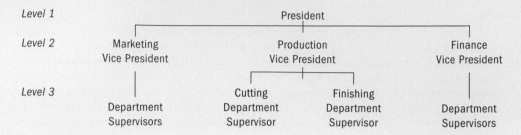

Level 1		President		
Level 2	Marketing Vice President	Production Vice President		Finance Vice President
Level 3	Department Supervisors	Cutting Department Supervisor	Finishing Department Supervisor	Department Supervisors

Pertinent expenses for Level 3 follow:

	Budget	Actual
Finishing Department		
Wages expense	$6,240	$6,000
Direct materials	2,300	2,400
Supplies	840	980
Small tools	1,300	1,140
Other	700	820

Pertinent expenses for Level 2 follow:

	Budget	Actual
Production Department		
Administrative expenses	$ 1,200	$ 1,400
Supervisory salaries	5,800	5,200
Cutting Department	6,800	6,420
Finishing Department	11,380	11,340

Pertinent expenses for Level 1 follow:

	Budget	Actual
President's Office Expense		
Supervisory salaries	$ 4,900	$ 5,100
Clerical staff	800	400
Other expenses	600	700
Production Department	25,180	24,360
Marketing Department	8,850	8,300
Finance Department	5,900	6,220

Required

a. Construct a spreadsheet that shows responsibility reports for the finishing department supervisor, the production vice president, and the president.

b. Include formulas in the responsibility reports that illustrate the interrelationships between these reports. For example, changes in the finishing department report should be automatically reflected in the production department report.

Spreadsheet Tip

(1) Use the absolute value function [=ABS(value)] in the formulas that calculate the variances.

Assume Magnificent Modems (MM) is a division of Gilmore Business Products (GBP). GBP uses ROI as the primary measure of managerial performance. GBP has a desired return on investment (ROI) of 3 percent. The company has $100,000 of investment funds to be assigned to its divisions. The president of MM is aware of an investment opportunity for these funds that is expected to yield an ROI of 3.5 percent.

Required

a. Explain why you believe the president of MM will accept or reject the $100,000 investment opportunity. Support your answer by calculating MM's existing ROI. Base your computation on the information contained in the income statement and balance sheet that you prepared in Chapter 1 (page 52).

b. Name the term used to describe the condition that exists in Requirement *a*. Provide a brief definition of this term.

c. If GBP changes its performance measurement criteria from ROI to residual income (RI), will the new evaluation approach affect the President's decision to accept or reject the $100,000 investment opportunity? Support your answer by calculating MM's residual income for the investment opportunity.

GLOSSARY

absolute amounts   Dollar totals reported on financial statements; using them in financial analysis comparisons can be misleading because they do not reflect materiality levels of the underlying companies. *p. 573*

absorption (full) costing   Reporting method in which all product costs, including fixed manufacturing costs, are initially capitalized in inventory and then expensed when goods are sold. (Contrast with *variable costing.*) *p. 486*

accounts receivable turnover   Financial ratio that measures how quickly accounts receivable are converted to cash; computed by dividing net credit sales by average net accounts receivable. *p. 579*

accrual accounting   Accounting system that recognizes revenues when earned and expenses when incurred regardless of when the related cash is exchanged. *pp. 435, 624*

accumulated conversion factor   Factor used to convert a series of future cash flows into their present value equivalent when applied to cash flows of equal amounts spread over equal interval time periods; this factor can be computed by adding the individual single factors applicable to each period. *p. 435*

acid-test ratio   See *quick ratio.*

activities   Measures an organization undertakes to accomplish its mission. *pp. 25, 249*

activity base   Factor that causes changes in total variable cost; usually some measure of volume when used to explain cost behavior. *p. 64*

activity-based cost drivers   Measures of activities that cause costs to be incurred, such as number of setups, percentage of use, and pounds of material delivered; using such measures as allocation bases can improve the accuracy of cost allocations in business environments where overhead costs are not driven by volume. *p. 247*

activity-based costing (ABC)   A two-stage cost allocation process. First, costs associated with specific business activities are allocated or assigned to activity cost pools. Second, these pooled costs are allocated to designated cost objects by using a variety of appropriate cost drivers. The cost drivers chosen for each cost pool are those that most accurately reflect the demand placed on that cost pool by the cost object. *p. 249*

activity-based management (ABM)   Managing organization activities to add the greatest value by developing products that satisfy the needs of the organization's customers. *p. 25*

activity centers   Cost centers composed of operating activities with similar characteristics; pooling indirect costs into activity centers reduces record-keeping costs by allowing allocations based on a common cost driver for each center. *p. 249*

allocation   Process of dividing a total cost into parts and assigning the parts to the relevant cost objects. *p. 148*

allocation base   The factor used as the base for cost allocation; when possible, a driver of the allocated cost. *p. 148*

allocation rate   The mathematical factor used to allocate or assign costs to a cost object, determined by dividing the total cost to be allocated by the appropriate cost driver or allocation base. *p. 148*

annuity   Series of equal cash flows received or paid over equal time intervals at a constant rate of return. *p. 435*

applied overhead   Amount of overhead costs assigned during the period to work in process using a predetermined overhead rate. *p. 477*

appraisal costs   Costs of identifying nonconforming products produced regardless of prevention cost expenditures. *p. 258*

asset turnover ratio   A measure of revenue dollars generated by the assets invested; calculated as net sales divided by average total assets. *p. 583*

average cost   (per unit) The total cost of making products divided by the total number of products made. *p. 6*

average days to collect receivables (average collection period)   Measure of how quickly, on average, a business collects its accounts receivable; calculated as 365 divided by the accounts receivable turnover. *p. 579*

average days to sell inventory (average days in inventory)   Measure of how quickly, on average, a business sells its inventory; calculated as 365 divided by the inventory turnover ratio. *p. 580*

avoidable costs   Potential future costs an organization can circumvent by choosing a particular course of action. To be avoidable, costs must differ among decision alternatives. For example, if materials cost for two different products is the same for each product, materials cost could not be avoided by choosing to produce one product instead of the other. The materials cost would therefore not be an avoidable cost. *p. 197*

balanced scorecard   A management evaluation tool that uses both financial and nonfinancial measures to assess how well an organization is meeting its objectives. *p. 400*

batch-level activities   Actions taken (e.g., materials handling, production setups) to produce groups of products, the cost of which is fixed regardless of the number of units produced in a batch. *p. 251*

batch-level costs   The costs associated with producing a batch of products, most accurately allocated using cost drivers that measure activity levels. For example, the cost of setting up a press to print 500 copies of an engraved invitation is a batch-level cost. Classifying costs as batch-level is context sensitive. The postage to mail a single product would be classified as a unit-level cost. In contrast, the postage to mail a large number of products in a single shipment would be classified as a batch-level cost. *p. 198*

benchmarking   Identifying best practices used by world-class competitors in a given industry. *p. 25*

best practices   Identifiable procedures used by world-class companies. *p. 25*

book value per share   An accounting measure of a share of common stock, computed by dividing total stockholders' equity less preferred rights by the number of common shares outstanding. *p. 586*

bottleneck   A constraint that limits a company's capacity to produce or sell its products, such as a piece of equipment that cannot produce enough component parts to fully occupy employees in the assembly department. *p. 211*

break-even point   Sales volume at which total revenue equals total cost; can be expressed in units or sales dollars. *p. 106*

budgeting   Form of planning that formalizes a company's goals and objectives in financial terms. *p. 293*

budget slack   Difference between inflated and realistic standards. *p. 346*

by-products   Products that share common inputs with other joint products but have insignificant market values relative to the other joint products.

capital budget   Budget detailing the company's plans to invest in operational assets, new products, or lines of business for the coming year; influences many of the operating budgets and is a formal part of the master budget. *p. 296*

capital budgeting   Financial planning for the intermediate time range involving decisions such as whether to buy or lease equipment, purchase additional assets, or increase operating expenses to stimulate sales. *p. 294*

capital investments   Purchases of operational assets involving a long-term commitment of funds that can be critically important to the company's ultimate success; costs normally recovered through using the assets. *p. 432*

cash budget   A budget detailing expected future cash receipts and payments. *p. 303*

cash inflows   Sources of cash. *p. 621*

cash outflows   Uses of cash. *p. 621*

certified suppliers   Suppliers who have demonstrated reliability by providing the buyer with quality goods and services at desirable prices, usually in accord with strict delivery specifications; frequently offer the buyer preferred customer status in exchange for guaranteed purchase quantities and prompt payment schedules. *p. 202*

companywide allocation rate   Factor based on a single measure of volume, such as direct labor-hours, used to allocate all overhead cost to the company's products or other cost objects. *p. 246*

constraints   Conditions that limit a business's ability to satisfy the demand for its products. *p. 210*

continuous improvement   An ongoing process through which employees learn to eliminate waste, reduce response time, minimize defects, and simplify the design and delivery of products and services to customers; a feature of total quality management (TQM). *p. 25*

contribution margin   The difference between sales revenue and variable cost; the amount available to pay for fixed cost and thereafter to provide a profit. *p. 61*

contribution margin per unit   The sales price per unit minus the variable cost per unit. *p. 106*

contribution margin ratio   The contribution margin per unit divided by the sales price per unit; can be used in cost-volume-profit analysis to calculate in dollars the break-even sales volume or the level of sales required to attain a desired profit. *p. 117*

controllability concept   Evaluating managerial performance based only on revenue and costs under the manager's direct control. *p. 392*

cost   Measure of resources used to acquire an asset or to produce revenue.

cost accumulation   Measuring the cost of a particular object by combining many individual costs into a single total cost. *p. 146*

cost allocation   Process of dividing a total cost into parts and assigning the parts to relevant objects. *pp. 12, 147*

cost averaging   Measuring the cost per unit of a product or service by dividing the total production cost by the total activity base to which the cost pertains; average cost is often more relevant to pricing, performance evaluation, and control than actual cost. *p. 65*

cost-based transfer price   Transfer price based on the historical or standard cost incurred by the supplying segment. *p. 404*

cost behavior   How a cost changes (increase, decrease, remain constant) relative to changes in some measure of activity (e.g., the behavior of raw materials cost is to increase as the number of units of product made increases). *p. 56*

cost center   A responsibility center that incurs costs but does not generate revenue. *p. 389*

cost driver   Any factor, usually a volume measure, that causes cost to be incurred; sometimes described as *activity base* or *allocation base*. Changes in cost drivers, such as labor-hours or machine-hours, cause corresponding changes in cost. *p. 146*

cost objects   Items for which managers need to measure cost; can be products, processes, departments, services, activities, and so on. *p. 145*

cost of capital   Return paid to investors and creditors for supplying assets (capital); usually represents a company's minimum rate of return. *p. 433*

cost per equivalent unit   Unit cost of product determined by dividing total production costs by the number of equivalent whole units; used to allocate product costs between processing departments (amount of ending inventory and amount of costs transferred to the subsequent department). *p. 536*

cost per unit of input   Cost of material, labor, or overhead for one unit; determined by multiplying the price paid for one unit of material, labor, or overhead input by the usage of that input for one unit of product or service.

cost-plus pricing   Strategy that sets the selling price at cost plus a markup equal to a percentage of the cost. *pp. 5, 108*

cost pool   An accumulation of many individual costs into a single total for allocation purposes.

cost structure   The relative proportion of a company's variable and fixed costs to total cost. The percentage change in net income a company experiences for a given percentage change in sales volume is directly related to the company's cost structure. The greater a company's percentage of fixed to total costs, the more its net income will fluctuate with changes in sales. *p. 59*

cost tracing   Assigning specific costs to the objects that cause their incurrence. *p. 147*

cost-volume-profit (CVP) analysis   Management tool that reflects the interrelationships among sales prices, volume, fixed costs, and variable costs; used in determining the break-even point or the most profitable combination of these variables. *p. 105*

current ratio (working capital ratio)   Measure of liquidity; calculated by dividing current assets by current liabilities. *p. 578*

decentralization   Delegating authority and responsibility for business segment operation to lower-level managers. *p. 388*

deferral transactions   Accounting transactions in which cash payments or receipts occur before the related expense or revenue is recognized. *p. 627*

differential costs   Costs that differ among alternative business opportunities; usually relevant for decision making. Some differential costs, however, are not relevant. For example, although depreciation may differ between the alternatives, it is an unavoidable sunk cost and is therefore not relevant for decision making.

direct cost   Cost that is easily traceable to a cost object and for which it is economically feasible to do so. *p. 147*

direct labor   Wages paid to production workers whose efforts can be easily and conveniently traced to products. *p. 10*

direct method   (1) Allocation method that allocates service center costs directly to operating department cost pools; does not account for any relationships among service centers. (2) Method of reporting cash flows from operating activities on the statement of cash flows that shows individual categories of cash receipts from and cash payments for major activities (collections from customers, payments to suppliers, etc.). *pp. 163, 636*

direct raw materials   Costs of raw materials used to make products that can be easily and conveniently traced to those products. *p. 9*

dividend yield   Ratio for comparing stock dividends paid relative to the market price; calculated as dividends per share divided by market price per share. *p. 587*

downstream costs   Costs incurred after the manufacturing process is complete, such as delivery costs and sales commissions. *pp. 14, 257*

earnings per share   Measure of the value of a share of common stock based on company earnings; calculated as net income available to common stockholders divided by the average number of outstanding common shares. *p. 585*

economies of scale   Reducing the unit cost of production by increasing an operation's size. Increasing size usually increases the volume of activity, reducing the per unit fixed cost and resulting in a lower total production cost.

efficient market hypothesis   The proposition that creditors and investors evaluate the underlying substance of business events regardless of how those events are reported in financial reports.

equation method   Cost-volume-profit analysis technique that uses the algebraic relationship among sales, variable costs, fixed costs, and desired net income before taxes to solve for required sales volume. *p. 118*

equipment replacement decisions   Deciding whether to replace existing equipment with newer equipment based on comparing the avoidable costs of keeping the old or purchasing new equipment to determine which choice is more profitable. *p. 207*

equivalent whole units   A quantity of partially completed goods expressed as an equivalent number of fully completed goods. *p. 535*

expense transactions   Business events that decrease assets or increase liabilities in order to produce revenue in the course of operating a business. *pp. 624, 627*

external failure costs   Costs resulting from delivering defective goods to customers. *p. 258*

facility-level activities   Actions taken (e.g., insuring the facility, providing plant maintenance, employing a company president) that benefit the production process as a whole. *p. 253*

facility-level costs   Costs incurred to support the whole company or a segment thereof, not related to any specific product, batch, or unit of production or service and unavoidable unless the entire company or segment is eliminated; they are so indirect that any allocation of facility-level costs is necessarily arbitrary. *p. 198*

failure costs   Costs resulting from producing or providing nonconforming products or services. *p. 258*

favorable variance   Variance indicating that actual costs are less than standard costs or actual sales exceed budgeted sales. *p. 339*

financial accounting   Branch of accounting focused on the business information needs of external users (creditors, investors, governmental agencies, financial analysts, etc.); its objective is to classify and record business events and transactions to produce external financial reports (income statement, balance sheet, statement of cash flows, and statement of changes in equity). *p. 4*

Financial Accounting Standards Board (FASB)   Private, independent standard-setting body established by the accounting profession that has been delegated the authority by the SEC to establish most of the accounting rules and regulations for public financial reporting. *p. 4*

financing activities   Cash inflows and outflows from transactions with investors and creditors (except interest), including cash receipts from issuing stock, borrowing activities, and cash disbursements to pay dividends. *pp. 24, 622*

finished goods   Completed products resulting from the manufacturing process; measured by the accumulated cost of raw materials, labor, and overhead. *p. 6*

Finished Goods Inventory   Asset account used to accumulate the product costs (direct materials, direct labor, and overhead) associated with completed products that have not yet been sold. *p. 472*

first-in, first-out (FIFO) method   Means of computing equivalent units in a process cost system that accounts for the degree of completion of both beginning and ending inventories; more complex than the weighted average method, and used when greater accuracy is desired. *p. 536*

fixed cost   Cost that remains constant in total regardless of changes in the volume of activity; per unit amount varies inversely with changes in the volume of activity. *p. 56*

flexible budgets   Budgets that show expected revenues and costs at a variety of different activity levels. *p. 338*

flexible budget variances   Differences between budgets based on standard amounts at the actual level of activity and actual results; caused by differences between standard unit cost and actual unit cost at the volume of activity achieved. *p. 342*

full costing   See *absorption costing.*

general, selling, and administrative costs   All costs not associated with obtaining or manufacturing a product; sometimes called *period costs* because they are normally expensed in the period in which the economic sacrifice is incurred. *p. 11*

generally accepted accounting principles (GAAP)   Rules and practices that accountants agree to follow in financial reports prepared for public distribution. *p. 4*

high-low method   Method of estimating the fixed and variable components of a mixed cost; the variable cost per unit is the difference between the total cost at the high- and low-volume points divided by the difference between the corresponding high and low volumes. The fixed cost component is determined by subtracting the variable cost from the total cost at either the high- or low-volume level. *p. 67*

horizontal analysis   Financial analysis technique of comparing amounts of the same item over several time periods. *p. 573*

hybrid cost systems   Cost systems that blend some features of a job-order cost system with some features of a process cost system. *p. 523*

ideal standard A measure of the highest level of efficiency attainable; assumes all input factors interact perfectly under ideal or optimum conditions. *p. 345*

incremental revenue Additional cash inflows from operating activities generated by using an additional capital asset. *p. 439*

indirect cost Cost that either cannot be easily traced to a cost object or for which it is not economically feasible to do so. See also *overhead. pp. 12, 147*

indirect method Method of reporting cash flows from operating activities on the statement of cash flows that starts with the net income from the income statement, followed by adjustments necessary to convert accrual-based net income to a cash-basis equivalent. *p. 636*

information overload Condition where so much information is presented that it confuses the user of the information. *p. 572*

interdepartmental service Service performed by one service department for the benefit of another service department. *p. 165*

internal failure costs Costs incurred to correct defects before goods reach the customer. *p. 258*

internal rate of return Rate at which the present value of an investment's future cash inflows equals the cash outflows required to acquire the investment; the rate that produces a net present value of zero. *p. 438*

inventory holding costs Costs associated with acquiring and retaining inventory including cost of storage space; lost, stolen, or damaged merchandise; insurance; personnel and management costs; and interest. *p. 15*

inventory turnover A measure of sales volume relative to inventory levels; calculated as the cost of goods sold divided by average inventory. *p. 580*

investing activities Cash inflows and outflows associated with buying or selling long-term assets and cash inflows and outflows associated with lending activities (loans to others—cash outflows; collecting loans to others—cash inflows). *pp. 24, 622*

investment center Type of responsibility center for which revenue, expense, and capital investments can be measured. *p. 389*

job cost sheet Record used in a job-order cost system to accumulate the materials, labor, and overhead costs of a job during production; at job completion, it summarizes all costs that were incurred to complete that job; also known as a *job-order cost sheet* or *job record. p. 524*

job-order cost system System in which costs are traced to products that are produced individually (e.g., custom-designed building) or in batches (e.g., an order for 100 wedding invitations); used to determine the costs of distinct, one-of-a-kind products. *p. 522*

joint costs Common costs incurred in the process of making two or more products. *p. 158*

joint products Separate products derived from common inputs. *p. 158*

just in time (JIT) Inventory management system that minimizes the amount of inventory on hand by avoiding inventory acquisition until products are demanded by customers, therefore eliminating the need to store inventory. The system reduces inventory holding costs including financing, warehouse storage, supervision, theft, damage, and obsolescence. It can also eliminate opportunity costs such as lost revenue due to the lack of availability of inventory. *p. 15*

labor efficiency variance Standard cost variance that indicates how the actual amount of direct labor used differs from the standard amount required. *p. 348*

labor rate variance Standard cost variance that indicates how the actual pay rate for direct labor differs from the standard pay rate. *p. 348*

lax standards Easily attainable goals that can be reached with minimal effort. *p. 345*

least-squares regression A technique used to draw a line through a data set by minimizing the sum of the squared deviations between the line and the points in the data set. *p. 70*

liquidity ratios Measures of a company's capacity to pay short-term debt. *p. 577*

low-ball pricing Supplier practice of pricing a product below competitors' prices to attract customers and then raising the price once customers depend on the supplier for the product. *p. 202*

making the numbers Expression that indicates marketing managers attained the planned master budget sales volume. *p. 340*

management by exception The philosophy of focusing management attention and resources only on those operations where performance deviates significantly from expectations. *pp. 343, 391*

managerial accounting Branch of accounting focused on the information needs of managers and others working within the business. Its objective is to gather and report information that adds value to the business. Managerial accounting information is not regulated or reported to the public. *p. 4*

manufacturing overhead Production costs that cannot be easily or economically traced directly to products. *p. 12*

Manufacturing Overhead account Temporary account used during an accounting period to accumulate the actual overhead costs incurred and the amount of overhead applied to production. A debit balance in the account at the end of the period means overhead has been underapplied and a credit balance means overhead has been overapplied. The account is closed at year-end in an adjusting entry to the Work in Process and Finished Goods Inventory accounts and the Cost of Goods Sold account. If the balance is insignificant, it is closed only to Cost of Goods Sold. *p. 477*

margin Ratio that measures control of operating expenses relative to sales; computed as operating income divided by sales. Along with *turnover*, a component of return on investment. *p. 395*

margin of safety Difference between break-even sales and budgeted sales expressed in units, dollars, or as a percentage; the amount by which actual sales can fall below budgeted sales before incurring losses. *p. 113*

market-based transfer price Transfer price based on the external market price less any cost savings; it offers the closest approximation to an arm's-length price possible for intersegment transactions. *p. 401*

master budget The combination of the numerous separate but interdependent departmental budgets that detail a wide range of operating and financing plans including sales, production, manufacturing expenses, and administrative expenses. See also *static budget. p. 296*

material variance A variance sufficiently significant that its investigation could influence decision making. *p. 345*

materiality   The point at which knowledge of information would influence a user's decision; can be measured in absolute, percentage, quantitative, or qualitative terms. *p. 573*

materials price variance   Standard cost variance that indicates how the actual price paid for raw materials differs from the standard price for the materials. *p. 348*

materials quantity variance   Standard cost variance that indicates the actual amount of raw materials used to make products differs from the standard amount required. *p. 348*

materials requisition form   A form, either paper or electronic, used to request the materials needed for a specified job. The accounting department summarizes all materials requisitioned for a job on a job cost sheet. *p. 524*

minimum rate of return   Minimum rate of profitability required for a company to accept an investment opportunity; also called *desired rate of return, required rate of return, hurdle rate, cutoff rate,* and *discount rate. p. 433*

mixed costs (semivariable costs)   Costs that have both fixed and variable components. *p. 67*

negotiated transfer price   Transfer price established through mutual agreement of the selling and buying segments. *p. 403*

net margin   Profitability ratio that measures the percentage of sales dollars resulting in profit; calculated as net income divided by net sales. *p. 583*

net present value   Capital budgeting evaluation technique in which future cash flows are discounted, using a desired rate of return, to their present value equivalents and then the cost of the investment is subtracted from the present value equivalents to determine the net present value. A zero or positive net present value (present value of cash inflows equals or exceeds the present value of cash outflows) means the investment opportunity provides an acceptable rate of return. *p. 437*

noncash investing and financing activities   Certain business transactions, usually long-term, that do not involve cash, such as exchanging stock for land or purchasing property by using debt; reported separately on the statement of cash flows. *p. 622*

nonvalue-added activities   Tasks undertaken that do not contribute to a product's ability to satisfy customer needs. *p. 25*

operating activities   Cash inflows from and outflows for routine, everyday business operations, normally resulting from revenue and expense transactions including interest. *pp. 24, 622*

operating budgets   Departmental budgets that become a part of the company's master budget; typically include a sales budget, an inventory purchases budget, a selling and administrative expense budget, and a cash budget. *p. 296*

operating departments   Departments that perform tasks directly related to accomplishing the organization's objectives. (Contrast with *service departments.) p. 163*

operating leverage   Cost structure condition that produces a proportionately larger percentage change in net income for a given percentage change in revenue; measured by dividing the contribution margin by net income. The higher the proportion of fixed cost to total costs, the greater the operating leverage. *p. 56*

opportunity cost   Cost of lost opportunities such as revenue forgone because of insufficient inventory. *pp. 16, 195*

ordinary annuity   Annuity in which cash flows occur at the end of each accounting period. *pp. 436*

outsourcing   Buying goods and services from an outside company rather than producing them internally. *p. 201*

overapplied or underapplied overhead   The difference between the amount of overhead costs actually incurred and the amount of overhead costs allocated to work in process. *p. 477*

overhead   Costs associated with producing products or providing services that cannot be traced directly to those products or services in a cost-effective manner; includes indirect costs such as indirect materials, indirect labor, utilities, rent, depreciation on manufacturing facilities and equipment, and planning, design, and setup costs related to the product or service. *p. 6*

overhead costs   Indirect costs of operating a business that cannot be directly traced to a product, department, process, or service, such as depreciation. *p. 147*

participative budgeting   Technique in which upper-level managers involve subordinates in setting budget objectives, thereby encouraging employee cooperation and support in attaining the company's goals. *p. 296*

payback method   Capital budgeting evaluation technique in which the length of time necessary to recover the initial net investment through incremental revenue or cost savings is determined; the shorter the period, the better the investment opportunity. *p. 446*

percentage analysis   Financial analysis technique of comparing numerical relationships between two different financial statement items to draw conclusions; circumvents difficulties caused by differing materiality levels. *p. 574*

period costs   General, selling, and administrative costs that are expensed in the period in which the economic sacrifice is incurred. (Contrast with *product costs.) p. 11*

perpetual (continuous) budgeting   Maintaining a budget that always reflects plans for the coming 12 months by adding a new monthly budget to the end as the current month's expires; keeps management constantly involved in the budget process to allow timely recognition of changing conditions. *p. 295*

postaudit   After-the-fact evaluation of an investment project; the capital budgeting techniques employed in originally deciding to accept the project are used to calculate the results of the project using actual data; provides feedback regarding whether the expected results were actually achieved. *p. 449*

practical standard   A measure of efficiency in which the ideal standard has been modified to allow for normal tolerable inefficiencies. *p. 345*

predetermined overhead rate   Allocation rate calculated before actual costs or activity are known; determined by dividing the estimated overhead costs for the coming period by some measure of estimated total production activity for the period, such as the number of labor-hours or machine-hours. The base should relate rationally to overhead use. The rate is used throughout the accounting period to allocate overhead costs to work in process inventory based on actual production activity. *pp. 158, 477*

present value index   Present value of cash inflows divided by the present value of cash outflows. Higher index numbers indicate higher rates of return. *p. 442*

present value table Matrix of factors to use in converting future values into their present value equivalents; composed of columns that represent alternative rates of return and rows that represent alternative time periods. *p. 434*

prestige pricing Strategy that sets the selling price at a premium (more than average markup above cost) under the assumption that customers will pay more for the product because of its prestigious brand name, media attention, or some other reason that has piqued the interest of the public. *p. 108*

prevention costs Costs incurred to avoid making nonconforming products. *p. 258*

price-earnings ratio Measure that reflects the values of different stocks in terms of earnings; calculated as market price per share divided by earnings (net income) per share. *p. 586*

pro forma financial statements Budgeted financial statements that reflect the master budget plans. *p. 296*

process cost system System in which costs are distributed evenly across total production of homogeneous products, such as chemicals, foods, or paints; the average cost per unit is determined by dividing the total product costs of each production department by the number of units of product made in that department during the accounting period. The total costs in the last production department include all costs incurred in preceding departments so that the unit cost determined for the last department reflects the final unit cost of the product. *p. 522*

product costs All costs related to obtaining or manufacturing a product intended for sale to customers; accumulated in inventory accounts and expensed as cost of goods sold at the point of sale. For a manufacturing company, product costs are direct materials, direct labor, and manufacturing overhead. (Contrast with *period costs*.) *p. 5*

product costing Classifying and accumulating the costs of individual inputs (materials, labor, and overhead) to determine the cost of making a product or providing a service. *p. 5*

product-level activities Actions taken (e.g., holding inventory, developmental engineering) that support a specific product or product line. *p. 252*

product-level costs Costs incurred to support specific products or services; allocated based on the extent to which they sustain the product or service, and avoidable by eliminating the product line or type of service. *p. 198*

productive assets Assets used to operate the business. May also be called *long-term assets*. *p. 24*

profit center Responsibility center for which both revenues and costs can be identified. *p. 389*

profitability ratios Measures of a company's capacity to generate earnings. *p. 583*

qualitative characteristics Features of information such as company reputation, employee welfare, and customer satisfaction that cannot be quantified but may be relevant to decision making. *p. 197*

quality The degree to which products or services conform to their design specifications. *p. 258*

quality cost report Accounting report that typically lists the company's quality costs both in absolute dollars and as a percentage of total quality cost. *p. 259*

quantitative characteristics Features of information that can be mathematically measured, such as the dollar amounts of revenues and expenses, often relevant to decision making. *p. 197*

quick ratio (acid-test ratio) Measure of immediate debt-paying ability; calculated by dividing highly liquid assets (cash, receivables, and marketable securities) by current liabilities. *p. 578*

ratio analysis Same as *percentage analysis*. *p. 577*

raw materials Physical commodities (e.g., wood, metal, paint) transformed into products through the manufacturing process. *p. 9*

Raw Materials Inventory Asset account used to accumulate the costs of materials (such as lumber, metals, paints, chemicals) that will be used to make the company's products. *p. 472*

reciprocal method Allocation method that uses simultaneous linear equations to account for two-way relationships among service centers (service centers both provide services to and receive services from other service centers); the resultant cost distributions are difficult to interpret. *p. 167*

reciprocal relationships Two-way relationships in which departments provide services to and receive services from one another. *p. 167*

recovery of investment Recovery of the funds used to acquire the original investment. *p. 447*

reengineering Business practices companies design to improve competitiveness in world markets by eliminating or minimizing waste, errors, and costs in production and delivery systems. *p. 25*

regression analysis See *least-squares regression*.

relaxing the constraints Opening bottlenecks that limit the profitable operations of a business. *p. 211*

relevant costs Future-oriented costs that differ among alternative business decisions; also known as *avoidable costs*. *p. 195*

relevant information Decision-making information about costs, cost savings, or revenues that: (1) is future-oriented and (2) differs among the available alternatives; decision specific (information relevant to one decision may not be relevant to another decision). *Relevant costs* are also called *avoidable* or *incremental* costs and *relevant revenues* are also called *differential* or *incremental* revenues. *p. 194*

relevant range Range of activity over which the definitions of fixed and variable costs are valid. *p. 64*

residual income Performance measure that evaluates managers based on how well they maximize the dollar value of earnings above some targeted level of earnings. *p. 397*

responsibility accounting Performance evaluation system in which accountability for results is assigned to a segment manager of the business based on the amount of control or influence the manager has over those results. *p. 388*

responsibility center Identifiable part of an organization where control over revenues or expenses can be assigned. *p. 389*

responsibility reports Performance reports for the various company responsibility centers that highlight controllable items; show variances between budgeted and actual controllable items. *p. 389*

retained earnings Portion of stockholders' equity that represents the amount of net income kept in the business since inception (revenues minus expenses and distributions for all accounting periods).

return on assets The ratio of net income divided by average total assets. See also *return on investment*. *p. 584*

return on equity Profitability measure based on earnings a company generates relative to its stockholders' equity; calculated as net income divided by average stockholders' equity. *p. 584*

return on investment Profitability measure based on earnings a company generates relative to its asset base; calculated as net income divided by average total assets. ROI can be viewed as the product of net margin and asset turnover. Also called *return on assets* or *earning power*. *pp. 393, 584*

revenue transactions Business events that increase assets or decrease liabilities by providing services or products to customers in the course of operating a business. *pp. 624, 627*

sales price variance Variance attributable to the actual sales price differing from the standard sales price; calculated as the difference between actual sales revenue and flexible budget sales revenue (the standard sales price per unit times the actual number of units sold). *p. 339*

sales volume variance Variance attributable to the actual volume of sales differing from the budgeted volume of sales; calculated as the difference between the static budget (standard sales price times standard level of activity) and the flexible budget (standard sales price times actual level of activity). *p. 339*

Sarbanes-Oxley Act of 2002 A federal law that regulates corporate governance. *p. 22*

scattergraph Method of estimating the variable and fixed components of a mixed cost by plotting cost data on a graph and visually drawing a regression line through the data points so that the total distance between the points and the line is minimized. *p. 68*

schedule of cost of goods manufactured and sold Internal accounting report that summarizes the manufacturing product costs for the period; its result, cost of goods sold, is reported as a single line item on the company's income statement. *p. 484*

Securities and Exchange Commission (SEC) Government agency authorized by Congress to regulate financial reporting practices of public companies; requires companies that issue securities to the public to file audited financial statements with the government annually. *p. 4*

segment Component part of an organization that is designated as a reporting entity. *p. 204*

semivariable costs See *mixed costs*.

sensitivity analysis Spreadsheet tool used to answer "what-if " questions to assess the sensitivity of profits to simultaneous changes in fixed cost, variable cost, and sales volume. *p. 116*

service departments Departments such as quality control, repair and maintenance, personnel, and accounting that provide support to other departments. (Contrast with *operating departments*.) *p. 163*

single-payment (lump-sum) A one-time future cash flow that can be converted to its present value using a conversion factor. *p. 434*

solvency ratios Measures of a company's capacity to pay long-term debt. *p. 580*

special order decisions Deciding whether to accept orders from customers who offer to buy goods or services at prices significantly below selling prices regular customers pay. If the order's differential revenues exceed its avoidable costs, the order should be accepted unless qualitative factors, such as the order's effect on the existing customer base, could lead to unfavorable consequences. *p. 199*

spending variance Difference between actual fixed overhead costs incurred and budgeted fixed overhead costs. *p. 352*

split-off point Stage in the production process where products made from common inputs become separate and identifiable. *p. 158*

standards Budgeted per unit selling prices or costs that are based on anticipated circumstances; multiplying the per unit standards for cost and quantity produces the per unit standard cost. *p. 344*

start-up (setup) costs Costs of activities performed to prepare to make a different product or batch of products, such as resetting machinery, changing the production configuration, and conducting inspection. *p. 247*

statement of cash flows The financial statement that classifies and reports a company's sources and uses of cash during an accounting period. *p. 24*

static budget A budget based solely on the planned level of activity, such as the master budget; not adjusted for changes in activity volume. *p. 338*

step method Two-step allocation method that accounts for one-way interdepartmental service center relationships by allocating costs from service centers to service centers as well as from service centers to operating departments; does not account for reciprocal relationships between service centers. *p. 165*

strategic cost management Newer techniques managers can use to more accurately measure and control costs; implemented as a response to the complex modern automated business environment. These strategies include eliminating nonvalue-added activities, designing more efficient manufacturing processes, and developing more effective ways, like activity-based costing, to trace overhead costs to cost objects. *p. 257*

strategic planning Long-range planning activities such as defining the scope of the business, determining which products to develop, deciding whether to discontinue a business segment, and determining which market niche would be most profitable. *p. 294*

suboptimization Condition in which the best interests of the organization as a whole are in conflict with managers' own self-interests. *p. 397*

sunk costs Costs that have been previously incurred; not relevant for decision making. For example, in an equipment replacement decision, the cost paid for the existing machine presently in use is a nonavoidable sunk cost because it has already been incurred. *p. 194*

T-account method Technique for determining the cash inflows and outflows for the period by analyzing changes in balance sheet accounts from the beginning to the end of the period; infers the period's transactions from income statement and other data. *p. 624*

target pricing (target costing) Strategy that sets the selling price by determining the price at which a product that will satisfy market demands will sell and then developing that product at a cost that results in a profit. *pp. 108, 256*

theory of constraints (TOC) A management practice used to increase profitability by identifying bottlenecks or resource limitations that restrict operations and then removing them by relaxing the constraints. *p. 211*

time value of money The concept that the present value of one dollar to be exchanged in the future is less than one dollar because of interest, risk, and inflation factors. *p. 432*

times interest earned   Ratio that measures a company's ability to make its interest payments; calculated by dividing the amount of earnings available for interest payments (net income before interest and income taxes) by the amount of the interest payments. *p. 673*

total quality management (TQM)   Management strategy that focuses on (1) continuous systematic problem-solving by personnel at all levels of the organization to eliminate waste, defects, and nonvalue-added activities; and (2) managing quality costs in a manner that leads to the highest level of customer satisfaction. *pp. 25, 259*

transferred-in costs   Costs transferred from one department to the next; combined with the materials, labor, and overhead costs incurred in the subsequent department so that when goods are complete, the total product cost of all departments is transferred to the Finished Goods Inventory account. *p. 523*

transfer price   Price at which products or services are transferred between divisions or other segments of an organization. *p. 401*

trend analysis   Study of business performance over a period of time. *p. 573*

turnover   Measure of sales in relation to operating assets; calculated as sales divided by operating assets. Along with *margin*, a component of return on investment. *p. 395*

turnover of assets ratio   See *asset turnover ratio*.

unadjusted rate of return (simple rate of return)   Measure of profitability computed by dividing the average incremental increase in annual net income by the average cost of the original investment (original cost divided by 2); does not account for the *time value of money*. *p. 447*

unfavorable variance   Variance indicating that actual costs exceed standard costs or actual sales are less than budgeted sales. *p. 339*

unit-level activities   Actions taken (e.g., using direct materials or direct labor) each time a unit of product is produced. *p. 251*

unit-level costs   Costs incurred with each unit of product made or single service performed; exhibit variable cost behavior; avoidable by not producing the unit of product or providing the service. Similarly, unit-level costs increase with each additional product produced or service provided. *p. 198*

upstream costs   Costs incurred before beginning the manufacturing process, such as research and development costs. *pp. 13, 257*

value-added activity   Any part of business operations that contributes to a product's ability to satisfy customer needs. *p. 25*

value-added principle   The benefits attained (value added) from a process should exceed the cost of the process. *p. 5*

value chain   Linked sequence of activities that create value for the customer. *p. 25*

variable cost   Cost that in total changes in direct proportion to changes in volume of activity; remains constant per unit regardless of changes in activity volume. *p. 55*

variable costing   Costing method in which only variable manufacturing costs are capitalized in inventory; all fixed costs, including fixed manufacturing overhead, are expensed in the period incurred. On a variable costing income statement, all variable costs are subtracted from revenue to determine contribution margin, then all fixed costs are subtracted from the contribution margin to determine net income. Under variable costing, production volume has no effect on the amount of net income. (Contrast with *absorption costing*.) *p. 487*

variances   Differences between standard (budgeted) and actual amounts. *p. 339*

vertical analysis   Financial analysis technique of comparing items within financial statements to significant totals. *p. 575*

vertical integration   Maintaining control over the entire continuum of business activity from production to selling, such as a company owning both a grocery store and a farm. *p. 202*

visual fit line   Line drawn by visual inspection on a scattergraph of data points to minimize the total distance between the data points and the line; used to estimate fixed and variable cost. *p. 68*

volume-based cost drivers   Measures of volume such as labor-hours, machine-hours, or quantities of materials that are highly correlated with unit-level overhead cost; serve as appropriate bases for allocating unit-level overhead costs. *p. 247*

volume variance   Standard cost variance that indicates how actual production levels differed from budgeted production levels; measured as the difference between budgeted fixed cost and the amount of fixed cost allocated to production. *p. 352*

voluntary costs   Discretionary quality costs incurred for prevention and appraisal activities. *p. 258*

weighted average method   Means of computing equivalent units in a process cost system that accounts for the degree of completion of ending inventory only; ignores the state of completion of items in beginning inventory, accounting for them as if complete. *p. 536*

working capital   A measure of the adequacy of short-term assets; computed as current assets minus current liabilities. *pp. 439, 577*

working capital ratio   See *current ratio*. *p. 578*

Work in Process Inventory   Asset account used to accumulate the product costs (direct materials, direct labor, and overhead) associated with incomplete products that have been started but are not yet completed. *p. 472*

work ticket   Mechanism (paper or electronic) used to accumulate the time spent on a job by each employee; sometimes called a *time card*. It is sent to the accounting department where wage rates are recorded and labor costs determined. The amount of labor costs for each ticket is summarized on the appropriate job-order cost sheet. *p. 524*

PHOTO CREDITS

Chapter 1
p. 3 © Krista Kennell/ZUMA/Corbis, p. 4 Image reprinted with permission from Sears Roebuck and Co., p. 15 Courtesy of Ford Motor Company, p. 20 © Win McNamee/Reuters/Landov, p. 22 © Royalty-Free/CORBIS

Chapter 2
p. 55 © PETER MORGAN/Reuters/Corbis, p. 57 © Cer/Corbis Sygma, p. 66 Costco Wholesale, p. 69 © Corbis

Chapter 3
p. 105 © Royalty Free/Corbis, p. 110 Courtesy of SAP, p. 113 © Jeff Haynes/AFP/Getty Images, p. 120 © John A. Rizzo/Getty Images

Chapter 4
p. 145 © Royalty-Free/CORBIS, p. 146 © Cele Seldon, p. 149 Courtesy of Southwest Airlines, p. 156 © Royalty-Free/CORBIS

Chapter 5
p. 193 © Photodisc/Getty Images, p. 194 © Royalty-Free/CORBIS, p. 196 © Janice Christie/Getty Images, p. 198 © Stephen Mallon/Getty Images, p. 203 © John Crall/Transtock Inc./Alamy

Chapter 6
p. 245 © David Young-Wolf/PhotoEdit, p. 246 © Royalty-Free/CORBIS, p. 250 © Royalty-Free/CORBIS, p. 260 Courtesy of J. D. Power and Associates

Chapter 7
p. 293 © Karl Mathis/EPA/Landov, p. 295 © Kim Steele/Photodisc/Getty Images, p. 299 © PhotoLink/Getty Images, p. 304 © Peter Gridley/Getty

Chapter 8
p. 337 © Kevin Sanchez/Cole Group/Getty Images, p. 340 © Royalty-Free/CORBIS, p. 344 © The McGraw-Hill Companies, Inc./Christopher Kerrigan, photographer, p. 350 © Don Tremain/Getty Images, p. 355 © Royalty-Free/CORBIS

Chapter 9
p. 387 Courtesy of Home Depot, p. 389 © Royalty-Free/CORBIS, p. 398 © Royalty-Free/CORBIS, p. 399 © Kim Steele/Photodisc/Getty Images, p. 402 © Steve Allen/Getty Images

Chapter 10
p. 431 © Tim Boyle/Getty Images, p. 432 © Photodisc, p. 439 © Dynamic Graphics/Jupiter Images, p. 443 © Creatas/PunchStock

Chapter 11
p. 471 Courtesy of Stickley Furniture, p. 473 © Royalty-Free/CORBIS, p. 476 © Allan H. Shoemaker/Taxi/Getty

Chapter 12
p. 521 © F. Schussler/PhotoLink/Getty Images, p. 522 Everett Collection, p. 525 © David Buffington/Getty Images, p. 544 © Royalty-Free/CORBIS

Chapter 13
p. 571 © Mark Lennihan/AP Photo, p. 572 AP Photo, p. 583 © STAN HONDA/AFP/Getty Images, p. 589 Securities and Exchange Commission

Chapter 14
p. 621 © Nick Koudis/Getty Images, p. 628 © Royalty-Free/CORBIS, p. 632 © Steve Cole/Getty Images, p. 634 © Royalty-Free/Corbis, p. 635 © Royalty-Free/CORBIS

Page numbers followed by n indicate notes.